100 YEARS
SIMON & SCHUSTER

A HISTORY OF

GEORGE JONES AND TAMMY WYNETTE

TYLER MAHAN COE

ILLUSTRATIONS BY WAYNE WHITE

SIMON & SCHUSTER

NEW YORK LONDON TORONTO SYDNEY NEW DELHI

1230 Avenue of the Americas
New York, NY 10020

First Simon & Schuster hardcover edition September 2024

SIMON & SCHUSTER and colophon are registered trademarks of Simon & Schuster, LLC

Simon & Schuster: Celebrating 100 Years of Publishing in 2024

For information about special discounts for bulk purchases,
please contact Simon & Schuster Special Sales at 1-866-506-1949 or business@simonandschuster.com.

The Simon & Schuster Speakers Bureau can bring authors to your live event.
For more information or to book an event, contact the Simon & Schuster Speakers Bureau
at 1-866-248-3049 or visit our website at www.simonspeakers.com.

Interior design by Ruth Lee-Mui

Manufactured in the United States of America

1   3   5   7   9   10   8   6   4   2

Library of Congress Cataloging-in-Publication Data has been applied for.

ISBN 978-1-6680-1518-6
ISBN 978-1-6680-1520-9 (ebook)

For Eli and Bill

CONTENTS

Preface x

✧ ✧ ✧

One: The Starday Machine 1

Two: Outlawed Tradition 31

Three: "White Lightnin" 43

Four: Nashville Sound 55

Five: Run, Bull, Run 89

Six: Red Flags 99

Seven: Blood and Sand 115

Eight: All to Pieces 123

Nine: Fit to Kill 147

Ten: Ol' Pappy 153

Eleven: Little Wars 165

Twelve: Daddy's Girl 175

Thirteen: Strongly Worded Letters 199

Fourteen: Stand By Your Man 207

Fifteen: Thrones 227

Sixteen: Country Royalty 235

Seventeen: Prized Beauty 257

Eighteen: Unhappy Homes 263

Nineteen: Selling Soap 285

Twenty: Divorce/Death 297

Twenty-One: Dangerous Threads 317

Twenty-Two: Pulling Strings 327

Twenty-Three: Cocaine Blues 351

Twenty-Four: The Dark 361

Twenty-Five: Living Legends 381

Twenty-Six: Living Lies 389

Twenty-Seven: Stoned Singers 417

Twenty-Eight: Back to Life 429

Twenty-Nine: For the Roses 453

Thirty: Baby Boy 463

✧ ✧ ✧

Acknowledgments 477

A Note on Sources 479

Index 481

COCAINE & RHINESTONES

PREFACE

This book is adapted from the second season of *Cocaine & Rhinestones*, a podcast about the history of twentieth-century country music. The most common misconception regarding this genre is that it was created a long time ago by people in the middle of nowhere with very little exposure to modern civilization or mainstream culture and certainly no interest in pop music. As you'll see, these are ridiculous notions which need to be corrected. Therefore, to serve as remedy, a true history of country music must present relevant information from the histories of modern civilization, mainstream culture and pop music. The inclusion of these topics in a book about country music may be unexpected but it is necessary in order to form a comprehensive appreciation of the genre. Strictly speaking, it's not necessary to cover such wide-ranging territory through abrupt twists and turns while largely leaving the reader to connect the dots for themselves . . . But that is what I've chosen to do because it's a lot more fun. There's a difference between handing someone a twenty dollar bill and handing them a treasure map.

As with any treasure map the full value of this book can only be unlocked by the reader willing to act on their own behalf. Every song and album mentioned by name is at least as significant as any other fact presented throughout the text. Those who fail to investigate the particulars of these musical recordings—lyrical content, vocal performances, emotional tone, degree of effort, etc.— are guaranteed to miss the point of entire chapters. Fortunately we live in an era of technology the previous generation of music aficionado would regard as nothing short of miraculous. Where years were once spent in search of a physical copy merely to discover what some rare country record actually sounds like, today the quest is as simple as running a search on YouTube. (And, yes, when it comes to older country music you will frequently find the goods uploaded to YouTube rather than standard streaming services, which are often stocked with nothing but the type of rerecordings discussed at length in chapter 10.)

Finally, this is a book about George Jones and Tammy Wynette. To those who know nothing of their real lives and/or have only been exposed to near-fictional portrayals of this as a comedy or fairy-tale romance, the only decent thing to do is offer a warning: there is much more pain and heartache ahead than there is happiness. Some of the things that happened here are horrifying. I have tried to make sure you will never, ever forget them.

—TMC

THE STARDAY MACHINE

⬦ Gambling Games ⬦ Jukeboxes in Texas ⬦ An Independent Country Operation ⬦
Introducing George Jones ⬦ Cover Songs vs. Soundalikes ⬦ Rock & Roll's War on Country
⬦ Taking the Fight to Nashville ⬦ Bluegrass Boom ⬦ Truckin' Hits ⬦

Nearly everybody's confused by their first interaction with a pinball machine. Hang around a busy pinball bar for longer than an hour and you'll see several newcomers believe the first game they've chosen to play is broken because they don't know to press the START button after inserting a coin. However long it takes them to get the game going, the ball then launches out onto the playfield and rushes down the angled surface toward this rookie, who maybe bats the ball upward with a flipper once or twice before draining, which brings the whole thing to an end only seconds after it began. And why would anybody spend money on that experience? Even if you get good enough at using the flippers to gain control of the ball, sending it up ramps, through spinners and into flashing targets for big points, pinball is not a game you win. Sure, multiple players can compete to see who gets the highest score before they lose. Should any of you rack up a high enough score, the machine may even offer the reward of a free credit to play again. But you're going to lose the free game, too. No matter how good you get, every game of pinball ends with the ball going down the drain. This is not a game you win. It's a game you try to play for as long as you can before losing. In other words, if you're the kind of person who knows you could do better if given another chance, pinball is inherently addictive . . . which may have been the only argument American politicians needed in order to successfully outlaw the game across much of the nation for roughly thirty years. However, there were additional concerns, such as the fact these addictive machines were being used in illegal gambling operations across the United States.

But why would anyone gamble on a game nobody can win? How would that even work? Well, it all comes down to the flippers. The flipper setup on modern pinball machines is the only thing that allows a player to temporarily control the ball in order to aim shots. No game had such flippers until the second half of the twentieth century. Prior to then, a playfield may have had a flipper here or there, but you'd have been lucky to use it more than once to affect the ball's path of travel. These early machines somewhat resembled Japan's pachinko, only kicking one larger ball at a time out onto a mostly horizontal playfield of pins and pockets rather than dumping a bunch of tiny balls at once down a vertical wall of pins and pockets. On most early pinball machines the player's only hope of directing a ball was by using their hands, hips or knees to nudge and bump the entire machine in a grinding sort of dance. (At least, that's what it looked like to country artist Red Foley, who sang about this technique in 1954's "Pin Ball Boogie.") Hit a machine too hard, though, and your game would instantly end, thanks to the tilt mechanism designed to keep unscrupulous players from lifting the table off the ground at an angle to cheat the ball around. With such limitations on one's ability to significantly alter the trajectory of a ball, early pinball was nearly entirely a game of chance, not skill, and therefore suitable for gambling purposes, which is what country artist Hank Locklin was singing about on 1950's "Pinball Millionaire."

When Fiorello La Guardia became mayor of New York City in 1934, he immediately made good on campaign promises to take down the mafia, particularly mob boss Frank Costello's illegal citywide slot machine operation. La Guardia ordered a couple thousand of Costello's slots confiscated and destroyed. Those slots were then quickly replaced with pin games and the illegal gambling continued while politicians argued over whether pre-flipper pinball was truly a game of skill or chance. In 1942, after nearly a decade of back and forth on the topic, La Guardia armed the NYPD with sledgehammers and gave them a mandate to smash pinball machines on sight. Some ten thousand tables were destroyed in New York City while he served as mayor—many were dumped into the Hudson. Because who cares about pollution as long as nobody's gambling, right? (Plus, it made for a nice photo op in the newspapers.)

Even after modern flipper mechanisms hit the market in 1950, avid gamblers kept pre-flipper machines in high demand. One extremely popular gambling pin was only introduced after the invention of flippers in 1951 with artwork and a layout themed upon bingo cards. The playfield featured square grids of numbered pockets that corresponded to bingo cards on the backlit display box above the game. Successfully landing five balls into numbers lining up a bingo won free credits, which you could use to keep playing . . . Or, if you were somewhere without much concern for what was and wasn't legal, those credits could be cashed in with the house for real money. Without flippers, it wasn't easy to win but these bingo pins were popular enough to remain in production well into the 1980s. When you hear stories about outlaw country artists Waylon Jennings and Tompall Glaser being addicted to pinball in the '60s and '70s, they weren't gamers; they were gambling addicts, pumping bingo pins full of money with no regard for the laws in any given state. Waylon used to drive all night after playing a concert just to get back to his favorite pins in Nashville. Tompall put so much cash into pin games, the second time he went back to a new spot with a machine he liked the owner had installed six more.

The aggressive laws, policies and positions against the original form of pinball were not rewritten when flippers came along in 1950, which meant modern pinball—a game of skill—was illegal before it even existed. In fact, it took several decades for most people to realize the invention of flippers had changed the whole nature of the game. For much of its existence, "pinball" was one word we used to refer to two very different things. This is why movies and TV shows set in the 1980s or prior will often feature a modern (and possibly illegal) pinball machine in the backgrounds of bars and hangouts we're meant to read as sketchy or rough. This is why rebellious and/or dangerous characters from the same era love to play modern pinball. Because of its hazy legality and conflation with the game's previous incarnation, pinball became a signifier of people with ambiguous morals who were willing to break the law if the reward was having a good time. In the mid-1950s Elvis Presley was known to play pinball while in Shreveport to appear on the *Louisiana Hayride* radio show, despite all pinball being illegal in Shreveport until 1970, when a 10-to-8 vote barely overturned the ban. Laws against pinball stayed on the books in New York City until 1976, when Roger Sharpe took a couple of modern machines into a courtroom and saved the future of the game by demonstrating how many things he could do on purpose . . . before losing. In Tennessee there was a law against kids under the age of eighteen playing pinball unsupervised until the year 2000, so we'll charitably assume Bobby Bare, Jr., was never left alone with the three machines his father kept in an office on Nashville's Music Row during Bobby's childhood.

The confusion surrounding pinball from its start is perhaps fitting, as the very first coin-operated pin game to become popular was named Baffle Ball. Baffle Ball sold fifty thousand units in 1931. The manufacturer produced four hundred machines a day and still could not keep up with demand, which one distributor recognized as an opportunity to launch a rival game. In 1932, that distributor sold close to fifty thousand units of a pin named Ballyhoo, thereby founding the company many readers may recognize from casinos and jukeboxes bearing the name Bally. Keep in mind, this was only a few years into the Great Depression. The entire economy had gone to hell and two separate entrepreneurs struck it rich on a product that didn't even exist when the market crashed in '29. By the way, these first breakout pins lacked the replay mechanisms needed for gambling. They merely provided a few moments of addictive distraction at the cost of a penny. Again, given the financial circumstances of the era, this was probably the only ammunition needed by the nation's Fiorello La Guardias to brand a game immoral, parasitic, a blight upon all citizens, etc.

Perhaps you would even have agreed at the time. But the fact remains: pinball is directly responsible for some of the greatest country music ever made.

◇ ◇ ◇

In 1931, a twenty-nine-year-old accountant at the Southern Pacific Railroad Company in Houston, Texas, decided to stop waiting for his turn to be laid off during Depression-era downsizing and investigate whether people truly do continue spending money on entertainment during a recession. That accountant's name was Harold Daily. In fewer than five years his South Coast Amusement Company became the largest coin-operated amusement machine business in the state of Texas and secured exclusive local distribution of a new form of music jukebox manufactured by Bally. Daily made his money by both selling and operating coin-op machines. Selling a machine was simple enough: the customer bought it, it belonged to them and they did whatever they wanted with it. If that customer owned a bar or soda shop, though, things may not be so simple. For them, coin-op machines were just a way to get more people in the door, make 'em hang out a little longer and buy more food and drinks at the counter, which is where the business made all its money. This type of customer didn't want to waste their own time fixing broken pinball games or keeping a jukebox stocked with the latest records patrons want to hear. So they'd probably work out a deal with Daily for him to park one or two of his machines on the premises and take care of all the upkeep himself (a.k.a. "operating" the units) in exchange for a percentage of the money earned by the machines. By the early 1940s Harold Daily sold and operated more pin games and jukeboxes than anyone else in Texas. Then World War II rations halted the manufacture of most nonmilitary machinery within the United States. Without a supply of new pin games and jukeboxes to sell, Daily's primary focus became running those he already had in operation.

Billboard magazine had launched back in 1894, intending to publish news related to the advertisement industry. Around the turn of the century, they pivoted to covering the entire entertainment industry, which included coin-operated amusement machines. By the mid-1930s, in addition to reporting sales figures of various pin games, *Billboard* had begun using data from jukebox play counters to chart the most-played records in major American markets, thereby informing operators around the nation which popular songs they should consider stocking in machines to maximize transactions. In the mid-1940s, when these piles of coins suddenly became his only revenue stream, Harold Daily found himself paying a lot of attention to those *Billboard* charts. In 1946, the year after World War II's end, Daily opened a record store in Houston, Texas. Operating more jukeboxes than anyone else in the state meant owning the most data on the regional market and Daily was able to stock the shelves of his record store accordingly. His business flourished to the degree that other store owners within driving distance started paying Daily to also place orders for them whenever he called record labels to buy new stock.

Pretty soon Daily began to think of himself as having a good enough ear to predict which new records were likely to become hits and turned his ear toward discovering local talent. When you own a record store, wannabe singers and musicians tend to hang around the place, especially after word gets out you're helping the best of them sign record deals with the California-based label 4 Star. The list of future country icons who released their first notable recordings on 4 Star after being sent there by Daily includes Webb Pierce and Hank Locklin. Summing up the role Daily played in launching the careers of so many artists, Locklin saddled him with a nickname he'd carry the rest of his life: Pappy. And, yeah, we could spend all day debating the ethics of Pappy Daily using his army of jukeboxes and the power of being a trusted buyer for so many record stores to potentially influence which songs and artists became local hits. But the fact is this system worked so well for everyone involved nobody ever questioned it. In 1950, MGM Records made him their exclusive distributor in southern Texas.

◇   ◇   ◇

Also in 1950, a young country singer named Lefty Frizzell played a show in Beaumont, Texas, at a honky-tonk named Neva's for owner Neva Starnes. After Neva's husband, Jack, found out Lefty Frizzell's management kept two-thirds of all Lefty's income, Jack decided to become Lefty's new manager. He dropped everything else to spend a week on tour with Lefty, going above and beyond to solve every little problem, even dipping into his own pocket to cover expenses, knowing he'd be more than reimbursed later if he nailed this audition. And it worked. Lefty ditched his original management and signed a two-year contract that gave Jack Starnes exclusive control over his concert schedule for a slightly less-parasitic 50 percent cut.

But Jack knew he only received that 50 percent during the term of the contract, so he began working Lefty as hard as possible. By the end of 1951, Lefty was a superstar, having appeared on the *Louisiana Hayride* and the *Grand Ole Opry*, toured with Hank Williams and released four #1 singles, including his landmark hit and signature song, "If You've Got the Money, I've Got the Time." Lefty made so much money he could afford to buy a tour bus and his own private airplane to keep up with Jack's nonstop concert schedule. But he was also flat worn out by this blitzkrieg approach. On one particularly exhausting trip Lefty called home to have his wife check the contract and see just how long it would be until he could take some time off, which is when she found the clause giving Jack Starnes an option to renew the whole deal for an additional two years. This being an option Starnes would unquestionably choose to exercise, Lefty flipped out. He threatened to quit right then, to hell with the contract, he was going home. When Jack in turn threatened to have him thrown in prison, Lefty said he'd finish out the original two-year term but after that he was going home, which is what he did, prompting a lawsuit from Jack. Lefty filed a countersuit and, when all was said and done, Lefty wound up settling out of court in June of 1952 for twenty-five thousand dollars, which was an incredible amount of money in 1952. Jack basically took Lefty for everything he had, even his backing band, who'd signed a separate contract with Neva Starnes to tour under the name Blackie Crawford & The Western Cherokees.

Jack and Neva put Lefty's old band behind whichever local singers were good enough to send on tour. Working with non-superstars, it didn't take Jack very long to figure out they could book better shows for an act who had a new single out, especially one receiving a lot of plays on juke-boxes and radio in the region. But why should Jack give a record label a piece of the action when he had the money and a backing band to make records on his own? After looking around for someone else in the area who could benefit from the ability to press their own records, Starnes landed on Pappy Daily as a potential business partner. By this time Pappy had years of experience scouting Texas talent and helping them cut singles in order to profit from the local sales and jukebox plays. (He'd also recently realized how much 4 Star in California was screwing him in the deal, but we'll come back to that in a second.) And so it was a June 1953 issue of *Billboard* came to run a small blurb on the formation of a new independent record label based out of Beaumont, Texas: Starday Records. ("Star" from "Starnes," "day" from "Daily.") As planned, Starday's first releases were from artists managed by Jack and Neva Starnes. Pappy distributed the records to store shelves and juke-boxes, which helped Jack and Neva book artists on bigger and better shows, where larger audiences were exposed to music they could then go find in stores and on jukeboxes in Texas. It was a solid system. The fourth single they worked this way became a nationwide hit and an instant standard of country music.

For the rest of his life Arlie Duff told the story as if he'd merely been a schoolteacher on a long drive toward somewhere else when he got hungry and pulled into Neva's for a bite to eat. Upon hearing a band playing in a back room, Arlie accidentally stumbled into country music history by making up a song on the spot that knocked everyone out. He must have thought that sounded cooler than the truth, which is he'd written the song maybe six months earlier and it was burning a hole in his pocket as he walked into Neva's, knowing precisely what he was there to do. See, word traveled fast after touring acts began driving away from some random honky-tonk gig in Beaumont with record deals, management contracts and promises of fame and fortune. Just like wannabes hung around Pappy's record store to see if he thought they had what it took to make a hit record, they came out of the woodwork to visit Neva's and see if Jack thought they could become the next Lefty Frizzell. The day it was Arlie Duff's turn, he left Beaumont with a recording contract. Starday's first major local hit was Arlie's "You All Come," an upbeat tune extending an open invitation for family and friends to come visit him out in the sticks. The single came out in fall of 1953, which is when Jack and Pappy realized that in order to break records outside of Texas, in order to turn a local hit into a national hit, they were going to need to . . . Well, they didn't actually know what they needed to do.

◇   ◇   ◇

Don Pierce learned the record business as an employee and part owner of 4 Star Records in Los Angeles, California. And he loved the record business, right up until a guy named Bill McCall bought a majority stake in the company and became Don's new boss. Don thought his new boss was an asshole and did not agree with the way he conducted business. For example, McCall had this guy out in Texas who wasn't even an employee of the label fronting his own money to send in tapes of the best local singers he could find. Whenever this guy sent in the tapes he also ordered a sufficient quantity of records to cover 4 Star's manufacturing costs, then put his own network of jukeboxes and record stores behind promoting the new product he'd effectively gifted to 4 Star. For several years, Pappy Daily functioned as a one-man, self-funded and uncredited subsidiary label who sent free money to 4 Star. This is only one example of Bill McCall's many questionable practices. After a great deal of hassle Don Pierce was eventually able to sell his shares in 4 Star and break free of McCall. But then he couldn't find any other country music business in L.A. and turned to industry trades looking for new opportunities. Some time around September 1953, he noticed a new record label on the Texas country music charts. After discovering Pappy Daily was part of the new venture, Don figured it was worth a phone call to see if Starday needed any help. Turns out, they needed a lot of help.

When Pappy received Don's call, "You All Come" was already a huge hit in the Houston area and Starday simply had no idea how to take the single to the next level. Pappy's background was essentially that of an A&R man and local distributor, who curated and recorded talent, then made it possible for customers in the area to spend money on the product. The Starnes couple were venue owners, booking agents and tour managers. This collective skill set was not enough to run a record label. For one fairly important thing, none of them knew how to get a record played on the radio or stocked in stores at a national level. Don Pierce knew how to do those things, so Pappy brought him in. They launched a new publishing company attached to Starday and split everything in three equal shares between Jack, Pappy and Don. Don was to be the only partner who worked full-time at the label and publishing company. In November 1953, Starday placed a full-page ad in *Billboard* to promote the Arlie Duff record, now being pressed and shipped with the shorter title "Y'all Come." The following month, the single hit Top 10 in the nation and Don Pierce called record stores all over the country to pitch them on stocking not only "Y'all Come" but also Starday's future releases. At some point Don gave a copy of the record to Bing Crosby's bandleader, who played it for his boss. Crosby's subsequent recording of "Y'all Come" sold half a million units and turned the song into a standard, a song everyone and their uncle felt the need to record at once. BMI named it the Most Popular Song of 1953. Starday Records had existed for fewer than six months.

◇   ◇   ◇

January 1954: Starday brings George Jones into the studio for the first time. To be clear, Starday's "studio" is Jack Starnes' living room, where he records artists on the cheap. And Jack's nineteen-year-old son, Bill, is the engineer, which means he's stashed away in some other room of the house with all of the recording gear and a switch to control the living room light. Between takes, all the musicians stand in the dark, still and silent, waiting for the living room light to come on to let them know the tape is rolling. They do have to stand still, too, since they've been carefully positioned around the only microphone in the room. There is no possibility of overdubbing anything or fixing any mistake on the tape. If someone messes up or a loud vehicle drives by in the middle of a take, they have to fully reset and start the song over. But this is about as good as it gets for home studios in 1954. Besides, it's not like they're recording the greatest country singer ever. This George Jones kid is just some Marine with enough of a reputation for being a good singer that Starnes had sent him a letter saying to stop by Starday whenever he came home to Texas. Being a devout Lefty Frizzell fan it's likely George was marginally aware of Starnes' connection to the supernova phenomenon that was Lefty Frizzell's early career, if not the full particulars of how all that worked out for Lefty. So, when George got out of the service and returned to Beaumont in November of 1953, just as Starday's "Y'all Come" was becoming the biggest song in the country, he certainly wasted little time before swinging by the label. Now he's here, standing in the dark, waiting for the light to come on and let him know it's time to start singing . . .

And he just can't help himself. Every show he plays, no matter what, he always covers a few Lefty Frizzell songs. His Lefty impersonation is so dead-on the crowds always go nuts for it, especially on the ballads, those slow songs with enough space to twist the words all into knots, rolling up and down through the notes exactly the way Lefty does. Sometimes audience members say he sounds just as good as Lefty. When this light comes on in Jack Starnes' living room, George will be singing with Lefty Frizzell's actual band and there'll be a recording he can listen to later. Needing to know what his Lefty impersonation really sounds like, he lays right into it on both of the session's mid-tempo, begging-for-love ballads, "For Sale or For Lease" and "If You Were Mine." After that, George kicks over to an equally popular impersonation of his personal favorite singer, putting more than a little Hank Williams in the next couple of songs. Due to the slangy title, journalists who don't waste time listening to music before writing about it often erroneously refer to "Play It Cool Man—Play It Cool" as a rock or rockabilly song. In truth, it is straight-up honky-tonk country, as is the session's other Hank Williams knockoff, "You're in My Heart." Both songs provide plenty of chances for George to lean all the way in to his version of Hank's full-throated high holler. Of everything recorded in this living room session, George Jones' first single sounds the least like a tribute to any one other singer and the most like a different genre of music. For the rollicking tongue twister "No Money in This Deal," George switches between both his Hank Williams and Lefty Frizzell impersonations for a near-rockabilly update of Lefty's "If You've Got the Money, I've Got the Time." When the record comes out in February, George drives copies around to local radio stations and asks them all to play it. Some do but not enough to make much of a splash. Failing to become a star right away, George picks up some session work playing flat-picked acoustic guitar on Arlie Duff's "Let Me Be Your Salty Dog" and "Back to the Country."

The next month, Starday launches the *Houston Hometown Jamboree*, a country music concert broadcast live on radio, featuring a core lineup of artists from the Starday roster, plus a few guest singers each week. George Jones is on the first broadcast, along with Starday's two main money-makers, Arlie Duff and Sonny Burns. Arlie brings in more money because he's got the bigger record but Sonny Burns is an extremely popular live act in the Houston area. Sonny also happens to think George Jones is a great singing (and drinking) partner. *Jamboree* crowds love it when Sonny and Jones sing duets, which makes the pair a bigger draw and worth more money if booked together on road gigs. They end up spending a lot of time traveling, singing and partying together. Due to their immediate live popularity Starday tries recording some duets in Starnes' living room about a month after the first *Jamboree*. But their most significant recording session together happens another month later in a much better studio.

Bill Quinn's Gold Star Studios in Houston was not a state-of-the-art studio like those then being built by Owen Bradley in Nashville. It was, however, a far sight fancier than Jack Starnes' living room. Sonny Burns and George Jones recorded the downtrodden "Heartbroken Me" at Gold Star. Presumably because he was the bigger star and therefore positioned closer to the microphone, Sonny's straightforward vocal is more upfront in the mix but Jones' backwoods warble makes much more sense over the sound of the clumsy and often off-pitch studio musicians. Though the single wasn't a hit, the song worked well in concert and, soon after the recording session, their growing esteem as live performers found Sonny Burns, George Jones and Arlie Duff all added to a *Grand Ole Opry* package tour featuring Ray Price and Marty Robbins at the top of the bill.

Pappy Daily had, by this time, begun to take a special interest in young George. Anyone could hear the boy sang his ass off and concert audiences seemed to adore him, so Pappy made a habit of being in the studio whenever George recorded, just in case there was anything he could do on the front-end to help the kid get a hit. It took about another year from the *Opry* tour for anything special to happen on tape. In that interim Starday lost one of its founding partners and released one of the best country songs of all time.

◇ ◇ ◇

According to "Big Red" Hayes, he grew up with pretty philosophical parents. Most of the ideas in his song's lyrics came from things his mother said over the years, while the title came from the time his father said to guess who was the richest man in the world. Hayes threw out a few names of famous rich men but to each one his father said no before stating something to the effect of "the wealthiest person is a pauper at times compared to the man with a satisfied mind." Jean Shepard, Red Foley and Porter Wagoner were all in Springfield, Missouri, to perform on the *Ozark Jubilee* the first time they heard Hayes sing "A Satisfied Mind." All three artists knew it was a hit and wanted the song for themselves, so they made a deal for everyone to cut it and release their singles simultaneously, giving each of them a fair chance at having the hit. They all had the hit. Shepard and Foley both went Top 5 while Porter took it all the way to #1. The list of artists who've recorded the song since is impossibly long. Within two years of launching a little country music label and publishing company Starday was cashing checks for two of the biggest hits of the decade, songs still being performed and recorded today.

And that's when Jack Starnes took the opportunity to cash out his shares then walk, which may seem like a pretty stupid thing to do—because it was—but Jack only ever viewed Starday as a tool in service of his booking and management business. Should he find himself on the phone trying to book some premium gig and the jerk on the other end of the line asks if Jack's artist had a new single out, what's the point of owning a record label if Starnes couldn't lie, say yes, and throw something together real fast to land the check for the concert? Well, ask Don Pierce and he'd have told you the primary point of owning a record label was to also own a publishing company and stay in business long enough to build a catalog of earning copyrights, a.k.a. hit songs that you own and are paid for whenever other artists record those songs. Abandoning studio schedules or promotion-and-release strategies in order to suit the immediate needs of a part owner's booking agency wasn't even a way to stay in business long enough to become a profitable label. However many times Don needed to say all of this to Starnes, Jack finally understood Starday would not drop everything else to meet his demands, at which point he got mad and sold his end to Pappy Daily. Once Jack was out, Pappy turned around and sold half of Jack's shares to Don so the partnership remained equal. Then they got some interesting tape on the Jones kid.

According to Pappy, the extent of his involvement "producing" these early George Jones sessions was limited to allowing the studio musicians complete creative control while occasionally telling George to stop impersonating other singers. Pappy would wait until the end of a take and say it was the best damned mockingbird act he ever heard but could George now, please, sing one like George Jones so they might sell some records? The man had a point. Those honky-tonk crowds may have loved a good impersonation but, when it came to buying singles, they already had Hank Williams and Lefty Frizzell records at home. George hadn't yet learned that the tricks he relied on for cheers in a barroom were worth very little in a recording studio. Run through his early sessions and you can hear the layers of paint being sanded away until the natural grain of his own voice starts to show through.

March 1955: George cuts "What's Wrong with You." It sounds like someone overdubbed honky-tonk piano and vocals onto a slowed-down and warbled tape of Hank Williams. In other words it sounds more than a little bit like Roy Acuff. On "Painless Heart," George takes another step toward singing like Roy Acuff. There's no telling whether it's on purpose or not. For nearly his entire adult life, it would be an understatement to call George Jones a bundle of nerves and this would be a stressful situation for anyone. He's in his fifth recording session ever and one of the owners of his record label is in the studio saying to stop singing like Hank and do something different. Consciously or not, George reaches deeper into his bag of voices and pulls out whatever's there. Roy Acuff would certainly have been deeper in that bag. For nearly a decade prior to Hank's first single, Roy was George's favorite country singer.

In July of 1955, Pappy managed to get George to sound mostly like himself on "What Am I Worth," though pay close attention to the way he sings the word "kid" and you'll hear just a second of Ernest Tubb's influence. As Jones worked backward through his earliest influences, cherry-picking keepsakes on the way to discovering his own voice, country music fans began paying attention. "What Am I Worth" came out as a single in January 1956 and hit the Top 10 Country Records . . . as the follow-up to a Top 5 single already released from the same session.

Believe whichever version of the story you like best. Maybe Sonny Burns was supposed to record a duet with George but Sonny got too drunk or felt he had something better to do—who knows what happened—he failed to show up. Whether any of that's true or not, whether the song was planned as a duet or not, George Jones did show up for a session at Gold Star, where they did have the equipment for him to overdub a second vocal and turn "Why Baby Why" into a duet with himself. His is the only voice on the original recording of this song, which George wrote with a childhood neighbor named Darrell Edwards, who began bringing around hit songs when he found out the kid next door had grown up to become a Starday recording artist. (George probably wound up with co-writing credit on many songs he did not actually help Darrell Edwards write, but his credit on "Why Baby Why" was earned. Darrell was off in the Coast Guard when it came time to record this unfinished earworm, so George wrote the rest himself.) Don Pierce later claimed he always knew "Why Baby Why" was a hit but conceded to Pappy Daily, who favored a different song from the session. This was possibly an untrue cover story to save face for the fact that George Jones' first hit was released as the B-side of a record. If so, the excuse was unnecessary. Anyone else in the 1950s who didn't own a magic crystal ball would put a spliced-together fake duet on the B-side of a record, especially when the A-side held the timeless ballad "Seasons of My Heart," another fantastic Darrell Edwards song. Although clearly sung by an enormous Hank Williams fan, Pappy Daily must have heard enough George Jones in "Seasons of My Heart" to believe it was the moneymaker. When the single shipped in fall of 1955, radio DJs who flipped it and played the B-side found "Why Baby Why" a bigger favorite with listeners. After Starday heard about this, they quickly changed their promo campaign to push the B-side and "Why Baby Why" soon went #4 Country. (For what it's worth, Pappy wasn't necessarily wrong about the hit potential of "Seasons of My Heart." Jimmy C. Newman took it to the Top 10 the following year and so did Johnny Cash when he cut it five years later.)

As soon as George Jones began releasing Top 10 records, he received a crash course in the then-standard industry practice of major labels covering the latest hit records of newer artists. From the perspective of a major label, the strategy is a no-brainer. You take a song starting to do well for some lesser-known act and put your comparatively massive resources behind it. Simple. You've got a bigger budget for everything from recording to promotion, much wider distribution and a far more famous artist who already has a huge audience. Prior to national radio conglomerates and the Internet, when many separate regional markets still existed, this used to be nearly un-fuck-up-able. However, from the perspective of an independent label, a major label doing this to your latest would-be hit could kill your record. In fact, that's why it's called "covering" a song. The idea was for the major label record to blanket the national market, "covering" the original regional hit from sight. And this was what caused Pappy Daily a great deal of concern when superstar country singer Webb Pierce covered "Why Baby Why" as an actual duet with Red Sovine.

Webb Pierce was still working a day job as a shoe salesman at Sears while scrounging around for country singer gigs at night when Pappy Daily discovered him. Not much happened with the Webb Pierce recordings Pappy sent to 4 Star but, after Webb signed to Decca, he first hit #1 Country in 1951 and had yet to miss the Top 10 with any new single when he covered "Why Baby Why." It was guaranteed to be a smash for Decca and guaranteed to smother Starday's George Jones record. So Pappy cashed in the favor. He called Webb and convinced him to have Decca pull their single from the market in order to give George's record enough room to breathe. Decca acquiesced and the Jones record eventually peaked at #4. A month later, Decca rereleased the Webb Pierce and Red Sovine cover. Sure enough, it hit #1 and became one of the ten Best-Selling Country Singles of 1956.

This was a monumental favor Webb Pierce did for Pappy Daily. Anyone who researches the history of the record industry will almost never come across someone going to such lengths, certainly delaying and potentially greatly diminishing huge profits on a sure thing #1 single only in order to repay a personal debt. This is just as much a testament to Pappy's support of young and unknown artists as it is a testament to Webb's sense of loyalty. It cannot have been easy for Webb to convince a major label or Red Sovine to pull what everyone knew was a hit single. Note that the B-side on Decca's original release of "Why Baby Why" featured Red Sovine's solo cover of "Sixteen Tons," the Merle Travis song Tennessee Ernie Ford had burning up the charts. When Decca later rereleased "Why Baby Why," it went #1 with a different Red Sovine recording swapped out on the B-side, a song Sovine wrote himself. The extra royalties he stood to receive as the songwriter likely incentivized Sovine to go along with Webb's request. As for how Webb was able to talk Decca into this whole rigamarole, it's anyone's guess.

By the time Webb and Red reached #1 with their cut of "Why Baby Why," George Jones had ridden his lesser hit to an appearance on the *Louisiana Hayride*, followed by more hit records and bigger package tours with country stars like Johnny Cash, Ray Price and Carl Smith. These tours took him all over North America, even Canada. In early 1956, he played the *Grand Ole Opry* for the first time and in August of the same year they made him a member. Various magazines voted him Best New Country this and that, and the upward trajectory of his career soon led Starday into a merger with Mercury Records.

◇   ◇   ◇

But let's circle back to cover songs for a minute because that phenomenon illustrates how radically different the recording industry was when regional markets existed. If the tale of "Why Baby Why" inspires feelings of pity for those little indie artists getting their records covered by the big, bad majors, you should know the street ran both ways. Thanks to regional markets it was entirely possible for an indie label artist to outperform the major label artists on a local level. Such was the power of a big fish in a small pond. For example, a February 1956 issue of *Billboard* lists the Best-Selling and Most-Played Country Singles in the United States but also contains lists of which records were performing best in various regions of the nation. In this issue, Decca's "Why Baby Why" by Webb Pierce and Red Sovine is the third Best-Selling Country Single in the nation, down from #2 the previous week. Starday's "Why Baby Why" by George Jones is only the twelfth Best-Selling Country Single in the nation, down from #7. Flip over to the local charts and it's mostly the same story in every region, the newer major label record outperforming the indie artist they covered . . . except in Houston, New Orleans and St. Louis, three major markets in the path of George Jones' regular touring circuit. In those cities, George is kicking Decca's ass with his follow-up single, "What Am

I Worth." In Houston, not so small a pond, it's the #1 Best-Selling Single. Thanks to regional markets, it was even possible to take a local artist and successfully cover a national hit before it reached your turf. If you did it correctly, the record-buying audience in your area may never care as much about the original major label record whenever they eventually heard it.

Then, in the mid-1950s, everything began to change. Each year's advancements in telecommunications technology made it more difficult for independent labels to beat the majors in regional markets. Through nationally syndicated radio, then variety shows on national television, music fans were increasingly likely to learn about the exact same songs and artists at the exact same time as the rest of the country. Subsequent exposure to any similar-sounding local artists, even if they provided the inspiration (or direct source material) for major label artists, made the locals appear unoriginal and uncool in comparison, like the cheap and generic imitation of a popular cereal brand. However, there's always a customer for the cheap, generic imitation of anything and music is no exception. As covering national hits with regional artists became a completely untenable strategy, indie labels leaned in to the practice of creating "soundalikes," which were basically audio forgeries of popular recordings, not exactly bootlegs but more like a cheaper alternative version of major label hits, often produced and packaged in such a way as to allow unsuspecting buyers to believe they may have simply found a great deal on the actual popular recordings. Because of the obvious potential for negative fallout from doing this, steps were taken to protect the identities and legitimate careers of artists who recorded soundalikes. Singers hired to impersonate famous artists all worked under pseudonyms, while producers traded soundalike recordings with indie labels in other regions of the nation to put distance between locally famous voices and the fans who could recognize them.

Studying industry trends during this period of such rapid change, Starday's Don Pierce reached two conclusions. One, most country music was purchased by adults rather than children or teens. Two, adults preferred buying the new EP and LP formats rather than the two-song singles purchased by younger audiences. In response to these findings, Starday launched the Dixie Records subsidiary to release EP compilations of soundalikes without compromising the main label's integrity. By cramming three songs on each side of three 45 rpm records then packaging them as one unit, Dixie could fit eighteen songs in a set of EPs. One side of each record typically contained the actual original recording of at least one legitimate hit—either a past hit from Starday's catalog or one licensed in trade from another label running the same racket—and these tracks were always clearly specified on the label as "The Original Hit Recording." Surrounding those genuine hits, though, were soundalikes of other hit popular titles. At bargain prices, the Dixie EP collections flew off store shelves.

Don's forays into market research also influenced Starday's less dubious business strategies. In October of 1956, the label released their first LP, *Country Song Hits*, by "Grand Ole Opry's New Star" George Jones. Nearly every song on the album had already been released on one side or the other of an earlier single, but George's fans still bought it. Maybe they didn't want to get off the couch every three minutes to change a record after every song? Maybe their old singles were worn out, scratched or stolen? Three of the fourteen songs had been Top 10 hits, so maybe fans decided to save shelf space by replacing multiple records with one LP? In any case, Starday's eventual business model was set in wax with this first LP and the Dixie EPs: allow the potential buyer to see a few familiar hits on an album's packaging and that buyer will likely suspect the rest of the product is of similar quality, which gets you most of the way toward making a sale.

The other major paradigm shift during the mid-1950s was rock & roll, practically a political movement in the existential threat it posed to country music. At the beginning of 1956, Elvis Presley's cut of "Heartbreak Hotel" was the biggest song in the United States and his second not-country-in-any-way single to go #1 on the Country charts. Just imagine what it's like to be in the business of trying to put records as close as you can to the top of Country charts when along comes some kid who starts tossing hits up there like it's nothing, without even bothering to make sure he's in the right genre. Even if you're working with your own young country singer who recently began hitting the Top 10, playing all the radio shows and package tours every artist plays on their way to becoming The Next Big Thing in country music . . . Maybe it starts to look like The Next Big Thing in country music isn't going to be A Thing at all. Maybe it starts to look like the party's over. George Jones once described this era to Nick Tosches by saying, ". . . with rock-and-roll getting as strong as it was at that time, it seemed like country music was really a losin' battle except for the three or four major artists that had it made at that time, like Lefty Frizzell, Ernest Tubb, Roy Acuff, some of those people . . ." This explains why most country artists who were active during the 1950s spoke of rock & roll like they thought it sounded as bad as wet garbage smells in 100 degree weather. They said they were confused as to why anyone would want to listen to some teenager have a fake conniption fit into a microphone while a backing band played their instruments poorly, either on purpose or because they just weren't very good musicians. Plus, this new noise appeared almost sentient in its mission to conquer and replace country music. Rather than build new platforms from the ground up, rock & roll acts went where the stages and audiences already were, invading the many barn dances and radio shows dedicated to country music. As the tropes of this new genre crystallized with its growing popularity, hordes of screaming teenagers drove away and replaced the audience who'd previously filled country music venues. Just as rock & roll invaded country's markets, stages and radio stations, so did the first hit rock & roll records invade Country charts, with trend-driven sales towering above even the best-selling artists still using a country music sound. Some country acts recognized the money to be made in rock & roll and tried adopting the new sound. Others viewed that as tantamount to switching sides in what they and many fans felt had become an us-versus-them battle. In particular, singers—the people whose names and faces appeared on album covers—were hesitant to risk their reputations with country fans by trying to court a rock audience. But country music was technically much more difficult to play than rock & roll, so country singers and instrumentalists all knew they could perform rock without even trying. And if a country singer who was already doing soundalike work did decide to earn a few bucks off of rock & roll, well, everyone in the industry already knew how to keep their identity a secret . . .

All of which explains how an indie country label like Starday could take their most promising singer (who they'd repeatedly begged to stop singing like other artists) and send him into a studio in March of 1956, mere weeks after charting his second Top 10 Country hit, to record an entire session of soundalikes, including Elvis Presley's "Heartbreak Hotel." The recording was not credited to George Jones. Rather, it was released under the pseudonym "Hank Smith" after being traded to the Tops label in Los Angeles. In George's next session they had him record even more rock material which was released under the alias "Thumper Jones." These are not important singles by any measure. But the fact that they exist is interesting because, for the rest of his career, any time someone asked, George dismissed these records with negative comments and attempted to distance himself from this thing nobody was ever supposed to know he'd done. Even more interesting: when George hit #1 Country for the first time, only a few years after these soundalike recordings that so embarrassed him, it was with a song he continued to perform for the rest of his career, a song he never bad-mouthed in any way and a song that was undeniably more rock than country.

Perhaps most country artists of the era really did believe rock & roll sounded like wet, hot trash. It's a fact that many were told by their labels to ditch the fiddles and steel guitars if they wanted to keep their record deals, which is certainly the kind of thing that can inform what a person feels and says about a style of music. But, given the auditory evidence, it's just as likely some of those remarks in liner notes and interviews were nothing more than the result of PR-minded record execs instructing artists to give good copy by throwing strong opinions into a divisive cultural argument. The truth is that country music was one of the foundational genres necessary for rock & roll to come into existence. On a purely sonic level the dividing lines between a lot of early rock music and hardcore honky-tonk were impossibly blurry. For instance, Glenn Barber's "Ice Water." Despite the jazzy slang sprinkled throughout the lyrics for anyone hip enough to spot it ("I can't sleep if I'm a real cool cat," "if I don't jump when the band gets hotter," etc.), there's no question this single sounded like a straight-up steel-guitar-drenched country barn burner to most anyone who happened to hear it at the time. "Ice Water" was released on Starday in 1954 after being cut in the same living room as George Jones' first Starday sessions. Glenn Barber later played guitar on "Why Baby Why." Starday's flirtation with rock & roll went much deeper than secret pseudonym sound-alikes and treating steel guitar like country music camouflage. By 1956, Glenn Barber had moved on to cutting undisguised rock & roll material, complete with saxophone, like "Shadow My Baby." Sonny Fisher was another Starday country act who began unapologetically recording rockabilly music, like "Pink and Black," in the mid-1950s. Despite the fact that all of these songs are amazing, not many people have ever heard of Sonny Fisher or Glenn Barber, probably because one of Starday's owners legitimately hated rock & roll. After decades of referring to the label's rockabilly sessions as a failed experiment, Don Pierce finally admitted he never even really tried to promote these rock records because he didn't have the first clue where to start.

But Don staying in his lane is what kept Starday releasing country hits in an era when the rest of the country industry was taking huge swerves to try to figure out where they were on the map. Just take a look at Ray Price's activity in this period. His iconic country shuffle "Crazy Arms" may have spent more weeks at #1 Country than any other individual song in 1956 but Ray Price only had the one #1 Country record in 1956, a year when Elvis Presley released four. Elvis held the top spot for more weeks than any other artist that year. The following year, hoping to get back above rock songs from Elvis, Jerry Lee Lewis and the Everly Brothers, Ray Price jumped all the way into the Nashville Sound on the silky smooth ballad "I'll Be There (When You Get Lonely)." Since everyone already owned records by pop artist Johnnie Ray, Price's single didn't even crack the Country Top 10, which prompted an immediate return to his country shuffle on "My Shoes Keep Walking Back to You," the record that walked Ray Price back up to #1 Country. Then, in 1958, Price charted at #1 for three months by blending his old sound with the Nashville Sound on "City Lights." None of his 1960s singles hit #1 but continuing to straddle the sonic line dividing Texas from Nashville did keep him near the top of the chart for much of the decade. Conversely, there was Starday, whose first LP release—the collection of George Jones' singles in late 1956—made a big splash in the market only a month after the release of a new single not included on the LP, the barroom ballad "Just One More." Fans who bought the George Jones LP also bought enough copies of "Just One More" as a single to send it Top 10 Country—just as they did with Benny Barnes' Starday debut, the stone country anthem "Poor Man's Riches"—all while Elvis sat at #1 Country with the not-country-at-all "Don't Be Cruel." This was more than surviving during a confusing and career-ending time in a genre. This was an independent label routinely outperforming the majors by sticking to what they knew best and dealing almost exclusively in country music. Most other indies who released notable country records in this period needed to branch out and work multiple other genres to stay alive. None of the exclusively country operations were anywhere near as successful as Starday, which is why Mercury Records chose Starday to pitch a new country music venture.

◇   ◇   ◇

The head of Mercury's country division knew they were headed into 1957 with a barely there roster of The Stanley Brothers, Jimmie Skinner and Carl Story, so he quit the label to go take a job at the *Grand Ole Opry*. When Mercury decided it would really only be worth the trouble to hire a new head of country operations if they actually had country operations, they looked around at who was doing well in the genre and hit on Starday. In November 1956, Mercury co-founder Art Talmadge met Pappy Daily at a radio DJ convention in Nashville and proposed placing Mercury's vast resources behind Starday's laser-focused approach to running a country label. This deal went into effect on January 1, 1957, and the new business was called Mercury-Starday. Since Don Pierce was still the only partner working full-time at Starday, this merger affected his day-to-day operations more than anyone else's. After he relocated to a new office building in Nashville, it soon became clear that Mercury didn't only want Don to promote Mercury-Starday product; they wanted him to promote the entire Mercury catalog, every genre, in addition to everything else Don was already doing. So he needed to hire another person whose only job would be record promotion. Enter Shelby Singleton, an industrial engineer from the Shreveport area who, in the process of helping his wife, Margie, pursue a career as a singer, had befriended Pappy Daily when Margie Singleton and George Jones were both performers on the *Louisiana Hayride*. Pappy signed Margie to Starday and she released a few singles, like "One Step Nearer to You" and "Teddy." These singles were good but they didn't do much, probably because Don Pierce absolutely hated Margie's high-pitched voice and her rockabilly-tinged sound. Still, when Don needed help with his new workload, he hired Shelby Singleton to become Mercury's new Southern Promotions Manager. (That basically meant Shelby drove boxes of records around to industry tastemakers—radio programmers, DJs, distributors, etc.—and got drunk with them for two or three days at a time so they would get the records stocked in stores and played on radio.)

Only a year and a half into Mercury-Starday's five-year contract, Mercury terminated the deal early. Decades later, Don Pierce would grudgingly admit Mercury had a valid complaint, which was that the vast majority of singles released on Mercury-Starday came from Starday's publishing company and that factor seemed to be of much higher priority to Don than whether or not the songs were any good. Don's views on the matter (and this is a direct quote), "Why would we go to a publisher who 'lets' us be privileged enough to use their song and then put all of our money into promoting their stuff? Fuck that." If more of those songs from Starday's catalog happened to become hits, Mercury likely wouldn't have cared where they came from. But they weren't hits and

Mercury-Starday had also failed to produce any new moneymaking artists like George Jones, so Mercury wanted out of the entire arrangement and wanted to keep the few artists who did sell records. Pappy Daily told Don it wouldn't even be worth fighting because Mercury had too much money and big-time lawyers who would just find some way to wrestle out of the contract. When Pappy then mentioned he and Shelby Singleton would be staying at Mercury along with George Jones, Don saw the whole picture.

And right here's where everyone else learned the value in Don Pierce's perspective on owning a record label and publishing company. He and Pappy agreed to split the Starday catalog by tossing a coin to determine who got first pick, then taking turns calling out a letter of the alphabet to secure all the song titles beginning with that letter. So, when Don won the coin toss and called out "S" as his first pick, he walked away with the label's biggest earner, "A Satisfied Mind," and all the other songs starting with "S." On Don's next turns he picked "Y" for "Y'all Come," then "W" for "Why Baby Why," and so on. Meanwhile, Pappy Daily used his first three turns to pick songs he personally thought were good with no consideration of any given title's proven or potential monetary value. Then Pappy received his first post-split royalty check, which was nowhere near what he knew 50 percent of the Starday catalog to be worth and he slapped Don with a lawsuit. A mutual friend eventually locked them in a hotel room together during a business conference to force them to work out a more equitable deal. When all was said and done, Starday (a.k.a. Don) walked away with roughly half the label's publishing catalog but also 50 percent of the publisher's share on George Jones compositions for the following eighteen months and Mercury-Starday's new office building in Nashville.

Though Don Pierce would later say the move to Nashville is what opened the door for Starday to become "a force" in country music, he'd deliberately chosen a location for Mercury-Starday that stood at a significant remove from the rest of the Nashville industry, all of whom he regarded as competition. Starday inherited this building ten miles away from Music Row and set up shop as the leading alternative to Nashville's mainstream brand. Downtown, major labels created so-called country records with the Nashville Sound to fish for attention from pop and rock audiences. Outside of town, hardcore country lived on in Starday's Anti-Nashville Sound. The majors dumped money into promoting hot new singles on the radio to court a younger audience. Don knew he didn't need to go through radio to sell product to those children's parents, most of whom didn't like the new music they heard on the radio anyway. All Don needed to do was package a few hits along with some filler on an LP, then use all twelve inches of the cover to sell it from the shelf. To this day, vintage Starday product practically jumps out of a stack of country albums. The loud jackets featured color photographs, gaudy fonts and, usually, some type of genre manifesto disguised as liner notes. You'll see the word "country" a lot and it'll be next to words like "real" and "authentic" and "true." If you take a drink for every cowboy hat you see on a Starday album while browsing the country section in a record store, you will die. Photos on Starday albums show artists proudly holding the old-timey instruments supposedly feared by Nashville producers like Chet Atkins and Owen Bradley. Or, you know, holding a rooster, maybe while standing near a horse or sitting on a horse, near a fence, near a barn, in a field, by a creek. Starday used album jackets to tell anyone who may care to know that their label was still making country music the way it was made in the good old days before rock & roll. And they had the sound to back it up.

It doesn't get any more direct than Wayne Raney's "We Need a Whole Lot More of Jesus (And a Lot Less Rock and Roll)." Wayne was a songwriter and harmonica player who hosted a Cincinnati radio show on which Don Pierce bought advertising, which meant whenever Raney played a song from Starday he'd be sure to tell listeners they could buy it directly from the label and plugged the mail-order catalog Don sent free of charge to any distributor, retailer or individual customer who requested it. When the Nashville labels and metropolitan country radio stations began catering to younger rock and pop audiences, older country music fans felt forgotten. Starday's direct-to-consumer sales helped reinforce the label's identity as the Anti-Nashville. It not only sent the message "We haven't forgotten you or your kind of country" but went the further step of saying "And we'll ship it right to your doorstep." Hell, if you wanted to make your own country records, Starday would do that, too. All you needed to do was send in a tape of an original song along with a little more than one hundred dollars and Starday would send back three hundred copies of your brand-new single, one hundred of which were pressed on higher quality vinyl, then packaged and pre-addressed to the one hundred nearest radio stations most likely to play it. There was the small matter of signing a release form that assigned the song's publishing rights to Don Pierce, in case he ever wanted to release it on Starday proper, but whenever this happened clients were paid a standard royalty rate. If by some small chance a custom press client happened to become any kind of hit, the release form also gave Starday the option to retain their services as a recording artist, making it essentially a probationary contract with the artist covering their own studio costs and promotional legwork while the label sat back and waited to see if there was anything worth pursuing. A whole lot of wannabes and a few gonna-bes tried to get their start in the business through Starday's custom press program. In 1957, Willie Nelson sent in his very first single to be pressed by Starday. "No Place for Me" did not instantly turn Willie into a star but at that time he was working as a DJ and used his radio show to promote the initial run, which sold out so he ordered another batch and kept selling them.

Starday's custom press operation was one of the most reliable in the nation, but they were not the first or only label to do that. Don Pierce oversaw a nearly identical service all the way back at 4 Star in California. While Don was there, another country music DJ named Slim Willet sold out his initial order of "Don't Let the Stars Get in Your Eyes" quickly enough to warrant immediately ordering another five thousand units, at which point Don figured they ought to go ahead and release it on 4 Star. The single went #1 Country in 1952. Perry Como covered it the same year and took it to #1 on the Pop charts. In 1953, following Kitty Wells' controversial "It Wasn't God Who Made Honky Tonk Angels" (an answer song to Hank Thompson's "The Wild Side of Life" and the first record by a woman solo artist to go #1 Country), Goldie Hill became the second woman solo artist to go #1 Country, also with an answer song, called "I Let the Stars Get in My Eyes." Goldie's lyrics were adapted from the original by her brother, Tommy Hill, who also wrote the hit song "Slowly" for Webb Pierce around this same time. Decca signed both Goldie and Tommy Hill to artist contracts, but Tommy didn't chart a #1 single right away like his sister, so the label dropped him. After several years without his career gaining much traction, Tommy began playing in the backup bands of other singers while trying to find another record deal for himself, which is what he was still doing when he met Don Pierce in Nashville near the end of 1958, just after the Mercury-Starday split. Don needed another pair of hands to pack and ship records at the Starday warehouse, so he offered Tommy the job and an opportunity to make more recordings. Tommy did cut some singles and compilation filler (like the woefully underrated "Oil on My Land"), but the most important role he played in Starday's history was behind the scenes as an employee. After hanging around long enough to get a feel for Don's approach to business, Tommy pointed out how much money Starday could save if they built their own recording studio. He then went and found the label's first post-Mercury hit to help cover the cost of construction.

Frankie Miller was another of those singers Pappy Daily sent to 4 Star before co-founding Starday. Don Pierce later remembered Frankie's early stuff being quite good, too. But Frankie got drafted to serve in Korea in 1952. When he came back in 1954 and signed with Columbia Records, the deal went away after only a couple of years. See, in those days Frankie Miller was practically a Hank Williams impersonator and, what with rock & roll taking over, the Hank Williams way of doing things was out of fashion. A few years spent plugging away on the live circuit and fronting his own money to record here and there brought Frankie to Starday in early 1959. Anyone who needs more evidence of the industry's general wariness toward hardcore country music at the time need look no further than Frankie's "Black Land Farmer." He had recorded it a full two years earlier at Gold Star Studios in Houston—that's Glenn Barber on guitar again—and spent those two years pitching the song to everyone he could reach through his many connections. No label wanted it. Then Tommy Hill heard "Black Land Farmer" and knew it was just the kind of thing Don Pierce would want for Starday, a solid and simple rhythm beneath a catchy honky-tonk vocal about a farmer living a plain but satisfying life. After releasing the single in March 1959, it went #5 Country and the money allowed Starday to break ground on their own studio. When construction was completed in May of the following year and the labels on Starday releases began to read "A Tommy Hill Starday Studios Production," it was because Don put Tommy in charge of operating the studio he'd conceptualized and helped fund. Some of Tommy's go-to session players were Pete Drake on pedal steel, Hank Garland on guitar, Junior Huskey on bass and Willie Ackerman on drums. In other words, the Anti-Nashville Sound record label used several of the same musicians who had helped create and continued to cut the Nashville Sound ten miles away.

It wasn't only Frankie Miller and other unsigned artists in this period who struggled to sell the major labels on hard country. The artists they'd actually signed couldn't do it, either. With few exceptions, acts who insisted on showing up to the studio with undiluted twang after it started being outsold by rock & roll were told to stop showing up at all. Don Pierce found room at Starday for the major label castoffs who wanted to continue making country music. His label went from branding itself as the little guy still making country music the way Nashville did back in the good old days to literally making country music the way Nashville did back in the good old days, putting the exact same people to work in a different building just down the road. It's worth noting the handful of country artists Mercury originally brought to the Mercury-Starday merger—Jimmie Skinner, Carl Story, The Stanley Brothers—all later wound up on Starday. Some other acts Don picked up from various labels were Red Sovine, Justin Tubb, Lonzo & Oscar, Cowboy Copas, Archie Campbell, Johnny Bond, Floyd Tillman, Pee Wee King, the Blue Sky Boys and T. Texas Tyler. According to Don, "If they were an established act, I wasn't interested in putting out singles because I couldn't get them on jukeboxes. But if they'd played twenty years on the *Opry* I knew they could sell albums." Starday also began releasing material from artists you could call "legacy acts" or "musicians' musicians," like Minnie Pearl, Texas Ruby, Harry Choates, Stringbean Akeman, Shot Jackson, Buddy Emmons, Moon Mullican and members of Roy Acuff's band, the Smokey Mountain Boys. As far as Don was concerned, the more twang, the easier he could sell it. And there aren't many twangier sounds than the style of music which by the late 1950s had come to be known as "bluegrass."

◇　　◇　　◇

In 1958, the Kingston Trio hit big on the Pop charts with a version of the traditional folk murder ballad "Tom Dooley." The trio's lackluster arrangement accompanying the violent lyrics is unintentionally hilarious, doubly so in contrast to the earliest known recording of the song from three decades prior, the unruly cut by Grayson and Whitter. But the Kingston Trio's single made millions of dollars, so, naturally, a bunch of musicians launched pop-folk acts, signed record deals and began releasing their own huge hits, same as any other craze in the music business. Only, this particular craze happened to pull from folk music, which happened to lead a certain percentage of curious listeners to the source material. It's likely these music fans first discovered the Kingston Trio's immediate predecessors—artists like Woody Guthrie, Pete Seeger & The Weavers or The Clancy Brothers with Tommy Makem—before working their way further back to earlier recordings of the same songs, which nearly always sounded a hell of a lot livelier than the near-comatose pop-folk versions all over the radio. As musicians caught a taste for this vintage musical form, they typically wound up creating local folk scenes or migrating to a place that already had one, resulting in little pockets of folkies who were dedicated to getting as near as possible to "the real thing," whatever they believed that meant. The most famous of these pockets was the Greenwich Village scene of the early 1960s, which gave us Bob Dylan. You've probably heard more than a little bit about that. What everyone alive at the time heard was a metric shit-ton of banjo, at every level of the folk explosion, from the Kingston Trio down to the Village, down to college campuses and bus stations; banjos all the way down. The banjo being an integral element of bluegrass music quickly caused bluegrass to be swept up in this folk craze shortly after Starday Records established itself as the de facto home of bluegrass. Don didn't have the guys who sold enough units to keep their major label deals—Bill Monroe, Flatt & Scruggs, Jimmy Martin—but he'd signed damn near everyone else dropped by Music Row and some of the all-time great bluegrass recordings came out on Starday: "Rank Stranger" by the Stanley Brothers, Bill Clifton and His Dixie Mountain Boys' *Code of the Mountains*, Charlie Monroe's *Tally Ho!*, "Lonesome Wind" by Buzz Busby, Bashful Brother Oswald's "Black Smoke." Starday's bluegrass catalog combined with Don's tried-and-true compilation LP strategy brought in money hand over fist . . . right up until 1965, when the whole thing died on its feet.

Don tried to say Starday's bluegrass sales dropped off due to the genre's association with all those folkie scenes and their predominately leftist politics. You know, a bunch of dope-smoking pinkos kept showing up to Vietnam War protests playing folk songs on banjos and it just didn't sit right with rural country people, so they stopped buying banjo music. That's pretty much what Don wrote in a letter to *Bluegrass Unlimited* magazine in 1967, saying it's what he'd been told by Starday's mail-order clientele. The only problem with that theory is leftist politics and protest songs were a highly visible part of folk scenes from the start, long before the Kingston Trio crossed over to pop stardom. That probably did bother a lot of people, but it's not at all likely they were the same people responsible for bluegrass music suddenly crossing over to pop sales figures. A much more likely explanation is that Bob Dylan giveth and Bob Dylan taketh away. This is more or less what bluegrass expert Neil Rosenberg says happened to bluegrass in his 1985 genre bible, *Bluegrass: A*

History, in which Rosenberg draws attention to Dylan going electric at the Newport Folk Festival in 1965. After shocking his audience's sensibilities with this stunt, Dylan spent the following two years tugging them over to the electric rock side of popular music and that's where they went. Rosenberg was there and watched this happen. He also responded to Don Pierce's letter by writing *Bluegrass Unlimited* to suggest Starday would probably sell more albums if Don prioritized releasing new material instead of constantly repackaging the same well-known titles in Starday's endless compilation LPs until they became indistinguishable from one another save for a shuffled tracklist and new cover art. Pierce didn't even bother denying it. All he did was send in another letter to explain Rosenberg's proposed business model would involve much greater risk, what with the higher costs of sourcing, recording, distributing, and promoting new and unproven material. Unlike major labels, Don could not afford to bankroll all of the misses in between the hits. This was true but it didn't make Rosenberg any less correct, Dylan any less electric or bluegrass any more profitable.

Roughly a year after that little back-and-forth in the bluegrass press, Don Pierce began looking for a way out of the record business. And if it really was because "hippies invaded bluegrass," then Don could have simply just gone back to selling country music, especially since the number of U.S. radio stations dedicated to country programming had grown from about eighty in the year 1961 to more than six hundred by 1970, the year Don retired. It wasn't the longhairs and it wasn't that Don somehow stopped being good at his job right as the country music market became bigger than ever before. If anything, Don was too good at his job and that was the whole problem. The exponential rise in country radio stations can be largely attributed to the Country Music Association educating the radio industry on how much money adult fans of country music spend buying records and may be willing to spend buying the products of radio sponsors. Don Pierce was a founding member of the CMA in 1958 and served on the board for years, regularly firing off motivational rants to industry trades on topics like how and why Nashville should convince radio stations around the nation to launch country music programs, how and why Nashville should prioritize overseas distribution of country records, how and why Nashville should position itself as the capital of music publishing in all genres, etc. In 1959, *Billboard*'s Country and Western Man of the Year was Don Pierce. It is no exaggeration to say he played a pivotal role in helping the genre become too profitable for his independent label to survive. Where Starday couldn't risk the financial investment required to promote new material to six hundred country radio stations, the major labels could well afford to do so while eating the costs of whichever records didn't hit. Don's strategy had always been to fill the gaps left open in the country market whenever major labels pursued a larger audience. When they sold 45s, he sold LPs. When their country artists went pop or rock, his stayed hard core. When they dropped country artists, he picked them up. But by the mid-1960s, country music was so profitable the majors had enough money to circle back and fill the gaps themselves. All they had to do was keep one hardcore country singer like Merle Haggard or Loretta Lynn for every five pop country Patsy Clines or Glen Campbells and the majors were making more money on both sides of the fence than Starday had ever seen, leaving a smaller and smaller corner of the market for Don.

Johnny Bond signed with Starday sometime around 1962. Years later, Johnny told the Country Music Hall of Fame he chose Starday because Don Pierce wanted to make a full LP with him, not just a single or two. In 1965, Johnny had the biggest hit of his entire career on a rerecording of a spoken word novelty number he'd released to little fanfare more than a decade earlier on Columbia. The thing about the remake of "Ten Little Bottles," though, is it was recorded during the 1964 DJ Convention in front of a live audience of country music DJs, which is who you hear laughing in the background as Johnny seems to get progressively drunker while telling a story about getting progressively drunker. When those DJs went home and received Starday's recorded souvenir of their business trip/party time, they played it so much on the radio that the single sold nearly a million units, stayed at #2 Country for a whole month and nearly broke into the Top 40 Pop records. (Please tell this story to anyone who doubts the impact of payola and/or airplay on the written history of music.) But "Ten Little Bottles" was a gimmick with a corny product and even Don Pierce admitted he thought the record was horrible. That was not a trick they could repeat often, if ever. As for Johnny Bond's LP hopes, by this time the majors were promoting LPs just as hard as singles, shoving Don out of territory he'd called his own for years. He could no longer compete. He tried everything, even the unthinkable.

Following the British Invasion, when major labels started dropping American pop acts, Starday tried signing a few, like Guy Mitchell, who originally broke through on Columbia Records in 1950 with the Top 5 Pop hits "My Heart Cries for You" and "The Roving Kind." Guy kept his career going long enough to hit #1 Pop in 1956 with a corny version of Melvin Endsley's "Singing the Blues," just after Marty Robbins had the country hit. In 1959, Guy scrounged up another #1 Pop hit by sucking the life out of Harlan Howard's "Heartaches by the Number," just after Ray Price had the country hit. By 1967, Guy Mitchell couldn't get a hit if he ran out into the middle of the interstate, so Starday figured it'd be worth signing him to see what happened. Maybe recording what seems to be a ripoff of Roger Miller's "Engine Engine No. 9" just a couple years after it was a huge hit seemed like a good idea at the time but "Traveling Shoes" didn't get much attention and neither did Starday's rerecordings of Guy's two #1 Pop hits from the previous decade. The other legacy pop acts Don signed were similarly unsuccessful.

In February 1968, Glen Campbell won four Grammy Awards, two in Pop categories and two in

Country categories. So he was already a pretty big deal when someone called Starday's office to say they were in possession of some unreleased Glen Campbell recordings they were willing to sell for ten thousand dollars. Don bit, paying ten grand for what wound up being a bunch of low-quality demo recordings from a decade earlier. Don knew Glen Campbell would sue if the demo recordings were released but he did it anyway, figuring Starday could sell enough copies to settle the lawsuit and still turn a profit. That's exactly what happened. Even though Campbell did sue, Starday came out the other side ahead on the investment.

Don Pierce was great at his job and exploited every opportunity for maximum return. There just didn't seem to be any more opportunities left to exploit. Gimmicks, flukes, unreleased demos from the early careers of now-major stars, these were not replicable strategies an indie label could adopt as a business model. Nearing the end of the '60s, Don knew he needed an exit and, in 1968, arranged for Starday to purchase another independent label, King, in order for both labels (along with subsidiaries and publishing catalogs) to be sold as Starday-King for a little over five million dollars. Starday-King then consistently lost money for about a year and a half until the new owners decided to take a hit and sell at a loss, which is the same thing it took the next buyers a couple of years to do, and the whole thing eventually wound up back in the hands of . . . Tommy Hill. Prior to the initial Starday-King sale, Tommy saw where things were headed and left to take a job at MGM Records. Then, in 1972, Tommy launched his own label, named Gusto, which he quickly turned around and sold ownership of so he could focus on producing records for the label. In 1975, Gusto purchased Starday-King for a mere $375,000. Gusto went on to similarly acquire many other indie labels, like Little Darlin, Chart and Musicor. The label still exists but as something of an aggregate for all these catalogs, working reissues and licensing deals for the many hit recordings they own. Typically, soon after being purchased by Gusto the individual labels ceased to exist as standalone, functional entities. One interesting thing about Starday, though: they managed to release their biggest-selling single ever after folding into Gusto.

◇   ◇   ◇

Back in 1959, a truck driver named Lonnie Irving began sending tapes into Starday's custom press service. Lonnie said his songs were about the people he met and the things he saw while on the road. Hopefully he was at least partly lying. If he wasn't, then "Pinball Machine" is about a trucker he met who was so desperately addicted to gambling on bingo pins that his family couldn't afford food or heat, his children died and his wife killed herself. When Lonnie sings "bet all I ever made in a pinball machine, I'd get four catty-corners then I'd miss the 16," he's talking about failing to finish a winning pattern on a bingo pin. The toughest shot to hit was the pocket in the center of a grid, often numbered 16. (Those familiar with Americanized versions of European folk songs, may recognize the melody of "Pinball Machine" as "Rye Whiskey," "Jack o' Diamonds" or "Way Up on Clinch Mountain.") As a result of nothing more than Lonnie Irving using the preassembled promo kits from Starday to mail his record to various radio stations, "Pinball Machine" became an instant hit. The song landed at a very appropriate #13 on the Country chart and BMI gave Lonnie an award in 1960.

Lonnie's was not the first hit on a truckin' song but it was the first on Starday, so Don Pierce told his other artists to consider recording similar material. In 1961, Starday released Jimmy Simpson's jaunty "The Alcan Run." In 1962, they put out Tom O'Neal's recording of "Sleeper Cab Blues" featuring a recitation from Johnny Bond and a persistent three-note bass line that just about had to be written by someone on methamphetamines. Neither single was a hit. Then—in 1963, not on Starday—Dave Dudley dropped "Six Days on the Road." It hit #2 Country, went Top 40 Pop and set a pace for truckin' songs in the 1960s to make the slow climb toward long-haul truck drivers somehow landing at the direct center of American pop culture in the following decade. For whatever reason, Hollywood storytellers in the 1970s decided truckers were the ideal protagonists for blue-collar fantasies and Starday once more found itself in a position to capitalize on the foresight of Don Pierce. A month after Dave Dudley released "Six Days on the Road," Bobby Sykes was in Starday Studios cutting the perennially sinister "Diesel Smoke, Dangerous Curves," a song originally done by Doye O'Dell in 1952, followed by Sons of the Pioneers (whose manic version features a jaw-dropping steel solo from Speedy West), then a serviceable pop adaptation by Burl Ives. Nobody touched it again until Don Pierce needed filler for a truckin' song compilation. Sykes' cut of "Diesel Smoke, Dangerous Curves" wound up as the title track of Starday's first trucker comp. Following Don's go-to playbook, the LP cover is a full-frame color photo of a leggy truck stop waitress whose next customer can be seen through the diner window climbing down off a big rig in the parking lot. It sold about ten thousand copies per year for at least the first five years of its existence. Small potatoes compared to major label sales figures but more than enough to put Starday in the business of truckin' songs for quite some time.

In 1964, the Willis Brothers went Top 10 with the comedic "Give Me Forty Acres (To Turn This Rig Around)." Starday threw it on the hit pile for future compilations, scheduled more pretty lady photo shoots and kept right on truckin'. In this particular subgenre, the label's experience with flashy album covers gave them a pretty huge advantage and high curb appeal. As for the music itself, Don Pierce had long ago given Tommy Hill his most important requirement from a Starday recording session: "I want to hear the melody. I don't want no hot licks in there." Unless it was an instrumental recording, Don considered Starday's product to be the singers and the songs they were singing. No session musician, no matter how good they were, ever needed to put an instrument in the way of that product. As such, records cut in Starday's studio tend to feature a clear vocal all the way at the front of the mix, which makes the singer easier to hear and the lyrics easier to understand in noisy environments, like a crowded bar or the cab of a truck running a diesel engine.

Webb Pierce's old duet partner Red Sovine released his first #1 as a solo artist in 1965. "Giddy-up Go" was a sappy recitation about a long-lost father and son who reconnect when they run across each other on the road while both working as truck drivers. It being the final record Starday put at #1 while Don Pierce ran the show, it's fair to assume this was around the time he began wondering if the best he could do was no longer good enough to justify staying in the game. Red Sovine's next major hit was a story even more outlandish than "Giddyup Go," called "Phantom 309." Another trucking recitation, this time about a hitchhiker who gets picked up by a ghost truck driver in a ghost semi truck or something. By the time "Phantom 309" went Top 10 in late 1967, Don had already made up his mind to quit the business. After the sale (and subsequent resales) of the label, after it ended up back with Tommy Hill at Gusto, Red Sovine released Starday's final #1 Country record. Sandwiched between C.W. McCall's late-1975 #1 Pop hit "Convoy" and the commercial peak of truckin' culture in 1977 with *Smokey and the Bandit*, Red Sovine took a truck driver recitation all the way to Top 40 radio in 1976. For anyone who's ever actually listened to CB radio for longer than thirty minutes, "Teddy Bear" is one of the most implausible tales of all time. Perhaps CB still being fairly new in 1976 helped Sovine and his co-writers get away with this emotionally manipulative yarn about a disabled boy with a dead dad using a CB radio to convince a bunch of truck drivers to abandon their routes and line up on his street, taking turns giving the boy truck rides before leaving his mother with a bunch of money. Gusto threw it on the hit pile for their next compilation.

TWO

OUTLAWED TRADITION

◇ Moonshine: How and Why ◇ A Whiskey Rebellion ◇
The Temperance Movement ◇ Wayne Wheeler's Anti-Saloon League
◇ Prohibition Goes Wrong ◇ Outrunning the Law ◇

Hypothetically, here's one way a person could make moonshine. It all starts with malt, which is a mixture of grains—usually some combination of corn, barley and/or rye—sprouted in water and then laid out to dry, halting germination at a point where enough of the grains' starches have converted to the sugar necessary for fermentation to take place. Then you need a lot of water. The foremost authority on this method of cooking liquor was Popcorn Sutton, who always said you can't make good moonshine using chemical-filled city water at any stage of the process. But nearly anyone who's ever made moonshine in the United States spent at least a week breaking the law in a fairly conspicuous way to do it, so let's assume you're off in the hills, somewhere far away from modern civilization, near a natural source of pure spring water. If you manage to pull a few runs in one spot without any strangers wandering by or trouble from government agents, perhaps you'll set up a more permanent operation. Until then, all you're looking for is a decent-sized mound of earth where you can dig a hole into one side and, using clay, pack in a big metal trash can to serve as a furnace. Level off the earth on top of the mound like a stovetop, then build a fire in the trash can. This furnace will heat the water you place above it in a big pot. When you see the water just start thinking about boiling remove the pot of steaming water and stir in your malt. Once that mixture of hot water and malt has cooled down, pour it into however many barrels it fills and leave it to ferment (or "work off") into a mash. Depending on the season and ambient temperature, working off a mash may take as long as a month, but you'll want to start checking it after about a week to ensure the taste is bitter, which is an early indicator of good moonshine.

However long the mash takes to get funky, use that time to build a still. That's "still" as in "distilled spirits," which is what you want to make and how you want to make it. Picture a chemistry lab and the distillation apparatus is the one where a scientist lady with half her face covered by goggles slides a lit Bunsen burner beneath a big glass container of colored liquid. Some of that heated liquid evaporates into steam, which travels through coiled tubes, more glass containers and more tubes until a few tiny drops of clear liquid come out of a spout at the end of the chain. Those few drops of clear liquid are the distilled and concentrated extract of whichever elements in the original container of colored liquid have a lower boiling point than everything else, the first ingredients to cook off into vapor and race toward condensation at the end of all those tubes and containers. You don't have a chemistry lab and you're trying to produce a lot more booze than just a few drops, so you need to build a still. The first container in the chain, sometimes called a "boiler," is essentially a giant stockpot placed above your version of a Bunsen burner, the furnace you dug into the ground. Even if you owned giant pieces of lab-grade glassware it wouldn't be easy hauling them out to the hills, so to make the boiler you'll probably need to weld together a huge vat made of copper or, if strictly adhering to Popcorn Sutton's method, stainless steel. Once you're ready to cook, the mash will go in the boiler over the furnace. When the mash is hot enough to begin steaming, you are officially making liquor, so seal the top of the boiler with a lid in order to send that vapor through a pipe to the next container. Now, here's the kicker: ethanol doesn't have the lowest or highest boiling point of all the stuff in that mash. Throughout the rest of this process, you'll want to keep the fire in the furnace at a consistent level to distill as much ethanol alcohol as possible from the middle of the mash. Toward the same end the next container in the chain is a "thump keg," often an actual keg or barrel meant to trap most but not all of the heat piped in with the steam from the boiler. As this vapor swirls around inside the thump keg, it loses some heat and the elements with higher boiling points fall out of the steam cloud into liquid at the bottom of the keg, leaving ethanol and the other elements above their vapor points to travel onward through the next pipe. At this stage of a still many moonshiners include a second thump keg to further refine the product through a third distillation, creating a purer concentration of ethanol alcohol. (The XXX on jugs of hooch in cartoons was supposedly used by real-life moonshiners to indicate triple-distilled liquor.) The pipe leaving a second thump keg travels not to the next container but through it. This final keg—called the "cooling drum" or condenser—is full of cool, running mountain water, constantly supplied by the totally separate aqueduct system you built off a nearby stream while waiting for the mash to work off. The section of pipe running through a condenser is called the "refrigeratory" (this is the source of the word "refrigerator") or, more simply, the "worm." The worm is shaped into a tight coil within the condenser keg so as to maximize the hot steam's exposure to cooler temperatures provided by the fresh spring water, which speeds the vapor's condensation into the liquid dispensed from the bottom of the worm.

Conventional moonshiner wisdom states the first portion of liquid produced in a run (called the "foreshot") is straight-up poison, containing all kinds of junk with a low boiling point that nobody would drink if they knew it was in their liquor: methanol, acetone, a few aldehydes, real nasty shit. The liquid just after the foreshot (called the "heads") still contains enough of that junk to make it undesirable for drinking but also holds enough ethanol to make it worth saving to throw back in the boiler with your next batch of mash. Same thing goes for the last liquid produced in a run, called the "backins" or "tails." Somewhere in the middle, though, between the heads and the tails, about one-third of the liquid extracted from a properly cooked batch of mash will be the "hearts," good moonshine whiskey that is smooth with a slightly sweet taste.

The more success you have finding, applying and maintaining the target temperature to vaporize ethanol and little else, the purer your whiskey will be. One common method to gauge the potency of moonshine is the bubble test. You pour some young whiskey into a mason jar, screw on a lid, shake the jar and inspect the bubbles. Small bubbles that linger are supposed to indicate a mistake somewhere in the run, whereas large bubbles that pop quickly are thought to suggest strong liquor, possibly upwards of 180 proof. But remember, this brief crash course is all hypothetical and comes nowhere near covering the many complications one must consider in order to avoid causing serious injury or death to themselves and others while attempting to make or procure moonshine. For example, unscrupulous bootleggers who don't care to secure repeat business by keeping their customers alive may add various adulterants to junk whiskey in order to fake the bubble test. Even well-intentioned moonshiners have made the tragic mistake of using old automobile radiators for condensers, causing themselves and other drinkers to go blind and/or die from unknowingly consuming lead and/or antifreeze. Here, too, we find a commonly used safety measure, which is the bottle cap test. Pour a little young whiskey into a bottle cap or sewing thimble and light it on fire. Ethanol is known to burn blue while lead, in theory, should burn red. (Hence the easily remembered saying, "If it's blue, you're true; if it's red, you're dead.") The problem, of course, is that not all clear liquids which happen to be dangerous or fatal to humans will produce a red flame when they burn. Speaking of fire, the bottle cap test is only possible because of how extremely flammable concentrated ethanol is in both liquid and vapor form. Any mistake in sealing the entire vapor path of an indoor still will almost certainly result in a gas leak which will almost certainly cause an explosive fire. Same thing should any sort of clog create a buildup of pressure at any point in the still. These risks present further reasons why it would be a good idea to cook liquor outdoors in a remote location even if making moonshine were legal, which it inherently is not.

◇   ◇   ◇

American adults who'd like to distill and sell their own whiskey without breaking the law can totally do it. All you need is a federal permit from the ATF and probably a distiller's license from your state government. Then you just have to pay all the associated taxes and fees, abide by a whole slew of regulations, submit to safety inspections and, hey, you're good to go. The main argument for cooking moonshine instead is "fuck all that," which is precisely what makes it moonshine. Even though nobody's certain about the origin of the word, "moonshine" really only makes sense as a reference to cooking untaxed whiskey outdoors by the light of the moon so government agents won't see the smoke from a still's furnace. This practice began in the early eighteenth century in Europe. Soon after Scotland and England joined to become Great Britain, their government came up with some brand-new taxes to generate funds for the brand-new nation. Two years after the U.S. Constitution went into effect in 1789, the first Secretary of the Treasury, Alexander Hamilton, suggested the exact same solution to repay national debts incurred during the American Revolution.

Hamilton's proposed tax on distilled liquor instantly became known as the "whiskey tax" because everyone knew what he was really trying to do. In those days, the middle and upper classes drank rum, which was regarded as more upscale. Whiskey, on the other hand, was consumed by physical laborers and the poor in such great quantities it had become a wholly separate economy, especially in communities on the geographic fringe of modern civilization, slowly pressing into (and serving as a nice human shield against) the wilderness to the west. To those rural folk, homemade whiskey was a currency. Since farmers already grew the ingredients needed to make whiskey and whiskey was far more valuable than those ingredients, they made a lot of whiskey. If a farmer didn't own a still, someone else in the area surely did and they'd probably let him use it for no greater fee than a few jugs of the whiskey produced in the run. Once that farmer made his whiskey it could be stored in barrels to sell or to offer as payment to hired farm laborers or even traded for goods at a store in town. Most working-class people without a moral aversion to alcohol used bottles and barrels of whiskey in the barter system of colonial America, the same system which treated fur and tobacco like currencies at remote trading posts. So Alexander Hamilton wasn't merely trying to tax the manufacture and sale of distilled spirits. He was trying to give the brand-new government a cut of the liquid money used by the lower classes. The reason he did this was not to create new social programs for the greater good, not to improve infrastructure, not to improve the lives of average American citizens in any way. Rather, Hamilton's proposed whiskey tax was intended to help the United States pay back loans from the kind of people who had enough money to lend an upstart nation the millions of dollars required to fight and win a revolutionary war, a.k.a. the wealthiest people on the planet, for whom the rate of Hamilton's whiskey tax was lower and for whom such taxes demanded a much smaller percentage of income. In other words, Hamilton wanted to tax the poor to pay the rich.

After the federal government put the whiskey tax into effect, they easily collected the money from major commercial distilleries, who were also taxed at a lower rate in return for their ability to pay a lump sum in advance. Wealthy private citizens also paid the new tax without any trouble. But the poor sons of bitches Uncle Sam sent to collect taxes from rural communities, who'd literally just fought an entire war in order to not have to put up with this specific variety of bullshit, those officials were told to take a hike. The ones who didn't listen got hurt—beaten, tarred and feathered, the usual mob justice. Any other government agents (a.k.a. G-men) or tax collectors (a.k.a. T-men) who came around asking questions about what happened to those first guys could expect to receive the same treatment. When Alexander Hamilton asked President George Washington to treat such violent defiance of the law as an act of war against the nation and respond accordingly with military force, Washington refused . . . until a couple years later, when he deployed the U.S. military against its own citizens in order to prevent the all-out class warfare brewing in what is now known as the Whiskey Rebellion.

In 1794, a U.S. Marshal went to tell at least sixty Pennsylvania moonshiners about their federal court dates back in Philadelphia for not paying whiskey taxes. After residents of the Pittsburgh area—then a small but growing town which served as the last real stop for anyone headed further west, out into the middle of nowhere—learned a marshal had come their way with subpoenas, a mob of approximately thirty people headed down to the local tax collector's home ready to run that marshal out of town. As it happens, the marshal wasn't inside the house but the local taxman was and he was armed, so he shot and killed a member of the mob, causing everyone else to run away. The mob returned the next day, having added more than five hundred residents of the area to their number. This being what the T-man assumed would happen, the night before he'd sent for the cavalry and there were now ten U.S. Army soldiers in the house with him. When the inevitable gunfight broke out, those soldiers shot and killed the mob's tactical leader, so someone set fire to the T-man's house, giving everyone inside no choice but to surrender. Fast forward a couple weeks. The mob is now a full-blown militia of roughly seven thousand disaffected poor Americans, calling themselves the Whiskey Rebels, who've gathered in a field outside Pittsburgh to decide what they will do next. Suggestions range from a simple demonstration march through town all the way up to dragging landowners out of their homes and showing them what a guillotine does. Residents of Pittsburgh catch wind of this and send a messenger to communicate they are very much on the side of the Whiskey Rebels and would sincerely prefer the demonstration march over the guillotine. Since a lot of the people gathered in that field were the actual feet on the ground during the

American Revolution, nobody has any reason to doubt the Whiskey Rebels are prepared to fight another revolution for themselves. When George Washington finally does as Alexander Hamilton requested years earlier and orders thirteen thousand U.S. soldiers to assemble for battle and march on the field outside Pittsburgh, he simultaneously sends "negotiators" ahead of the Army, probably not so much to negotiate anything as to make sure the Whiskey Rebels understand they're about to be slaughtered by a military close to twice their number. By the time those soldiers arrive in Pittsburgh, there is no longer a Whiskey Rebellion. But G-men and T-men are ultimately never successful in collecting whiskey taxes from rural areas, where much moonshine continues to be made.

◇ ◇ ◇

About a hundred years after the Whiskey Rebellion, the entire nation had a temperance tantrum. A society that uses bottles of homemade liquor as currency to the extent government officials get dollar signs in their eyes over the idea of taxing it, one would be within their rights to wonder if such a society maybe had a bit of a drinking problem. Colonial America unquestionably had a drinking problem and the Revolutionary War unquestionably made it worse. (Delving into the overwhelming and detailed evidence of this would be extremely depressing, but it's worth noting a primary source for modern concepts of alcoholism came from this precise point in space and time: a Pennsylvania doctor named Benjamin Rush, published in 1784.) Throw in a Civil War and, by the early 1900s, just about every American who wasn't drunk all the time was ready to pass some kind of law to prevent other Americans from getting so drunk all the time. Many concerned citizens joined one anti-alcohol group or another to push a range of potential solutions, from zero-tolerance "Ban All Alcohol" programs to more moderate variations on "Hey, adults should be able to have a casual beer or two, but everyone needs to admit the current situation is wildly out of control." Though this wide ideological spectrum appealed to just as wide a variety of people, they were all viewed as belonging to one political movement, called temperance. To some, the temperance movement meant they didn't want a saloon and/or liquor store in their city, county or state because they didn't want to live with an abusive alcoholic or worry about him spending all the family's grocery money on booze. To many religious denominations, temperance meant crime and poverty would disappear and society would thrive once rid of the sinful moral weakness of drunkenness. To the ruling class, who knew any new laws wouldn't apply to them anyway, temperance meant a more efficient workforce clocking in without hangovers and no more drinking on the job. Most individuals within the temperance movement did not campaign, march and vote for what became the Eighteenth Amendment in hopes of entirely outlawing alcohol. But there was one individual who did.

Wayne Wheeler had a cool name but he was not a cool guy. He's one of those villains with an origin story that usually inspires some degree of empathy. As a child Wheeler was injured in a

pitchfork accident caused by a farmhand showing up drunk to work, which was surely a traumatiz-
ing experience. But that little kid grew up to be an authoritarian, extremist, mass-murdering zealot
who bent a nation to his will through the Anti-Saloon League (ASL), no mere group beneath the
umbrella of temperance but the most effective of them all. After taking over the ASL in the first
decade of the twentieth century, Wheeler used his background as a lawyer and his understanding
of the machinations of American politics to coordinate local ASL chapters around the country
and ally with any federal or state politicians running on platforms anywhere near the temperance
agenda. Wheeler then presented himself to Washington, D.C., as the head of a major grassroots
movement prepared to steamroll any elected official who wouldn't get with the program. As far as
D.C. could tell, it looked like this guy really did front such a crusade because he'd managed to co-
opt about a century's worth of political activism.

Following the American Revolution, when that Pennsylvania doctor published his report on
alcoholism, one of the things he suggested was it may be more treatable if regarded as a disease
rather than a lack of moral fiber or willpower. This idea proved quite influential and concerned
citizens soon began forming activist groups to dissuade family, friends and neighbors from exposing themselves to alcohol. Over the next hundred years, these temperance groups campaigned and
voted to enact varying degrees of Prohibition laws in certain towns, counties, even whole states,
where saloons and/or sales of hard liquor were limited or banned. Their mission was greatly helped
along by natural alliances with other groups fighting for like-minded causes. For example, anything resembling a women's rights group was all but guaranteed to support temperance. There
were many reasons for this but two main ones were that women couldn't vote at the time and—by
custom, often by law—nearly all saloons served an exclusively male clientele. As such, women (and
their children) were largely relegated to the role of horrified witnesses and abused victims in this
culture of rampant alcoholism. Consider a woman named Carrie Nation. Widowed after her husband drank himself to death, Carrie dedicated the rest of her life to waging war against alcohol.
She first made a name for herself by breaking custom to enter saloons and sing church hymns at
the men drinking inside, then graduated to breaking laws by bringing a hatchet with her to destroy
alcohol supplies. Arrested for such behavior at least thirty times, Carrie was given many opportunities to explain her actions in front of courtrooms and reporters, thus spreading her message that
saloons and liquor were an active enemy of American families, contributing to all manner of sin
and vice in men, the worst of whom were as likely to drunkenly beat their wives as hear any criticism on the subject. Carrie Nation also believed women should be allowed to vote. Most notable
suffragists of the time (Susan B. Anthony, Fredrick Douglass, etc.) similarly supported temperance.
In fact, one of the main anti-suffragist arguments in the United States was that women shouldn't

be allowed to vote because the first thing they'd vote for was a national imposition of total Prohibition. But it wound up happening the other way around.

When federal Prohibition passed in 1919, the year before women (or, at least, white women) got the vote, it was largely due to Wayne Wheeler's talent for harnessing the momentum of various other causes and exploiting them in service of the Anti-Saloon League, even when those causes would seem to be at odds with one another. For instance, the temperance movement aligned with the ideology of suffragists like Carrie Nation but also that of innumerable religious organizations, most of whom—yes, even the women—were staunchly against giving women the right to vote. Wheeler was able to get such varied groups to gloss over these differences and work together in a single-issue campaign with the ability to attack alcohol from any and every possible angle. The religious temperance groups, in particular, had already set a precedent for shaming would-be upright citizens of a community into taking pledges of moderation or total abstinence from alcohol. Wheeler used this strategy to gain political power by having Anti-Saloon League activists hound candidates in local and federal elections until all were forced to take a hard stance one way or the other on Prohibition. Nearly every politician running on a promise to improve the world in any way had to at least pretend to support Prohibition and, once they did, Wheeler had them in his grip. Should any elected official who'd so much as muttered slight approval of temperance fail to follow through with significant action, Wheeler turned on a negative PR campaign like the flick of a light switch: "Look at the hypocrite, the flip-flopper, the bribe-taker, the do-nothing defender of the status quo," etc. Should that fail to bring someone back in line, Wheeler progressed to extortion and violence. It's not a coincidence that Prohibition only became federal law after Wheeler formed an alliance with the second incarnation of the Ku Klux Klan, a terrorist hate group whose own temperance was rooted in their white Protestant identity and disgust for what they viewed as the Roman Catholic drinking culture of Irish and Italian immigrants.

With KKK strong-arm tactics, widows, preachers and so many other winds in his sail, Wheeler was able to bring the Eighteenth Amendment to fruition, outlawing the "manufacture, sale or transportation of intoxicating liquors." This language did not ban possession or personal use of alcohol. The precise meaning of "intoxicating liquors" was also left undefined, a matter for some further piece of legislation. And guess who secured the job of writing that further piece of legislation? In a bill called the Volstead Act, Wayne Wheeler made it a federal crime to "manufacture, sell, barter, transport, import, export, deliver, furnish or possess any intoxicating liquor," which he defined as any liquid over 0.5 percent alcohol by volume. In a development nearly nobody had requested or anticipated, any alcoholic beverage stronger than kombucha became entirely illegal in the United States. President Woodrow Wilson promptly vetoed the Volstead Act but was overridden by politicians of the Senate and House, who voted to uphold "the will of the people," even though it was truly the will of only an extremist minority. The vast majority of "the people" had no clue what was about to be brought down upon them.

Regardless of the fact that not even a majority of Prohibitionists were teetotalers and almost everyone in America differentiated hard liquor from wine or beer, Wheeler's dream of absolute Prohibition came true. In 1920, the U.S. government began enforcing his law. Well, kind of. Prohibition made exceptions for "medicinal" alcohol prescribed by doctors and purchased from pharmacies, so booze remained legal for anyone who could afford the higher price of a longer supply chain. There are not many examples of wealthy families being brought up on charges for having a wine cellar or serving booze at a party, with or without a doctor's prescription. But everyone else who wanted to take a drink had to break the law, which is what they started doing. Not only did criminalizing alcohol fail to bring about the promised improvement of the nation's moral character, it also thoroughly undermined respect for all branches of government, especially the justice system, as most American adults chose to openly participate in illegal activities. Winemakers began shipping bricks of grape juice concentrate to market with labels giving detailed instructions for how to avoid accidentally breaking the law by accidentally allowing the grape juice to ferment into accidental wine. Only slightly outdone by ski masks, semi trucks and subprime loans, Prohibition was one of the best things to ever happen to organized crime in the United States. American men and women drank together as never before, gathering in unprecedented numbers in illegal speakeasies, which were quite often operated by or affiliated with a mob outfit. As for trouble from the law, even if cops, their bosses and their wives weren't speakeasy patrons themselves (which they very likely were), bribes and threats typically kept the local government looking the other way.

Wayne Wheeler responded to all of this by getting the federal government to hand him a special unit of what eventually became the IRS, along with a sizable budget to hire the additional agents needed to enforce his Volstead Act. As there were no real qualifications necessary to become an agent of Wheeler's new unit, it was quickly staffed with anyone who wanted the job and these assholes were soon crawling all over the place with no idea what they were doing, most of them even more crooked than the cops. Wheeler's men took the same bribes as local police to ignore the major crime outfits but still had to keep up appearances, which meant heading out of the cities to go after speakeasies and country moonshiners unaffiliated with mob bootlegging operations. In other words, the U.S. government funded and authorized a bunch of thugs to enforce organized crime's monopoly on illegal alcohol distribution in most major markets of the nation. This is how Chicago came under the thumb of Al Capone. Sure, Capone was eventually targeted by Eliot Ness and the Untouchables but that unit of police officers were only called "untouchable" because of their surprising ability to resist the near-universal corruption laid bare by Prohibition. It must have driven Wayne Wheeler nuts to witness his dream come true only to fall apart in front of him, his own agents helping to undermine the righteous plan. But there is no justifying what he did next.

Along with the exception for medicinal alcohol, the law also exempted industrial manufacture of alcohol for use in cleaning agents, fuels, paints and various other products, which usually contained ingredients a person wouldn't want to drink but so does a mash and we all know how to take care of that, right? As a result, much of the hooch sold in bottom-end speakeasies "fell off the back of a truck" on the way to some janitor supply company, then went through some sort of distillation or filtering process before being served in cocktails with strongly flavored mixers to mask the alcohol's poor quality. The solution the Prohibition Bureau rolled out in 1926 could not have been any simpler: murder. Wayne Wheeler forced manufacturers of industrial liquids to add formaldehyde and other inextricable poisons to products containing ethanol alcohol, for no reason other than to make ingestion fatal. Critics of this plan suggested humans could be prevented from drinking these liquids by adding revolting and nonconcealable flavoring agents, but Wheeler refused to consider such alternatives. Only fatal levels of poison would suit his agenda. Some estimates of the number of U.S. citizens he murdered are as low as ten thousand, others as high as fifty thousand. Obviously this would have been a difficult statistic to track. When Americans wanted to know why their family and friends were now dead, Wheeler basically said it was suicide. According to him, all those people knew they were breaking the law and the federal government was not in the business of keeping outlaws safe from harm. While the backlash was enough to entirely discredit Wheeler and end his career, federal Prohibition was not repealed until 1933. A few states with laws predating the Eighteenth Amendment stayed dry for several more years. The last to go wet was Mississippi, which held out until 1966.

While his impact on American legislation was slow to fade away, Wayne Wheeler's impact on American culture may have been permanent. Prohibition could hardly have been more successful in revealing the government's vulnerability to corruption or the justice system's preferential treatment toward upper-class citizens. In truth, the United States never banned alcohol. Prohibition changed approximately nothing for the ruling class, slightly inconvenienced the white-collar crowd and helped federal law enforcement side with big-city crime bosses to wage war against everyone too poor or remote to take part in the newly sanctioned ecosystem of alcohol consumption. The best argument to be made for Prohibition's egalitarianism would be Wayne Wheeler's wholesale poisoning of industrial alcohols, except there aren't many examples of senators who died as a result. In 1930, a bootlegger named George Cassiday was arrested and admitted to having spent the previous ten years selling illegal liquor to roughly four out of every five members of the U.S.

Senate. He told the whole story in a series of articles for the *Washington Post* but not one senator was ever named or arrested in connection with the case, even though the Senate gave Cassiday offices in government buildings to make it easier for politicians to illegally purchase liquor. There were countless speakeasy busts all over the nation in which local mayors, councilmen, judges and police officers were rounded up and hauled away with all the other criminal drinkers, and those were only the ones who were too drunk or too stupid to pretend they'd been working undercover as part of the sting. No adult could fail to observe the absurd hypocrisy of it all.

And, yeah, the good ole boys cooking moonshine up in the hills resisted arrest because they resisted everything about this. Going out there on a still hunt was a great way to get shot and it really didn't matter if you were wearing a badge given to you by some murderer in Washington, D.C. Trying to catch a moonshiner in the act of transporting goods wasn't likely to be a car ride through the park, either, since most rural operations large enough to be chased by the feds were making more than enough cash to soup up car engines toward the end of outrunning the law. Drivers who could avoid getting caught were paid well for it and had plenty of time to stand around bragging about their talent behind the wheel. Pretty soon these guys were racing their hot rods against each other and, as Prohibition phased out, stock car racing caught on with noncriminals around the country, moving from the straightaways and back roads on to tracks built for race cars. By the time race promoter Bill France, Sr., managed to get everyone on the same page with rules and regulations by forming NASCAR in 1948, many of the younger drivers had never even worked as bootleggers. However, both Wendell Scott and Junior Johnson, two early heroes of NASCAR, were known to have history running moonshine. Wendell was once caught in the act and given three years' probation. Junior did a year in prison after feds busted him with a working still but he was never chased down on a run.

◇   ◇   ◇

In 2008, notorious moonshiner Popcorn Sutton was busted with more than five hundred gallons of untaxed liquor on his property. In 2009, rather than serve a year and half in prison for offering to sell nearly one thousand gallons of moonshine to an undercover government agent, Popcorn chose to take his own life. He was sixty-two years old.

THREE

"WHITE LIGHTNIN"

◇ George Jones' First #1 Record ◇ Rock or Country? ◇
The Big Bopper ◇ Nashville Forms a Country Music Association
◇ The Greatest Country Singer Ever ◇ Did Johnny PayCheck Do It First? ◇

The song "White Lightning" isn't exactly about outrunning the law with a trunk full of moonshine but it sure sounds that way. The whole thing starts with Buddy Killen's standup bass turning over like a car engine and all the sudden you're chugging down a mountain, Pig Robbins' piano tinkling around somewhere in the back with all the glass jars, Floyd Robinson's guitar lines whipping by faster than passing tree trunks outside the windows. Then everything drops out when the air goes sideways in a hairpin curve, George Jones wheezes out the words "white lightnin'" and puts the pedal to the metal again. But that's just the way it sounds. There is no car chase in the lyrics. The protagonist of the story is a moonshiner named Pappy, the narrator's father, who brews such "powerful stuff" customers come to him in Popcorn Sutton's home state of North Carolina, which went dry in 1908—more than a decade before federal Prohibition—and stayed dry until 1937. It's moonshine country and Pappy's supplying the whole area. Even city slickers travel out to the boonies to wet their whistles. G-men, T-men and revenuers are all trying to shut down the party but none of those squares can find Pappy's still.

"White Lightning" was George Jones' first #1 Country single and his first to cross over to the Pop charts, climbing about a quarter of the way up the Hot 100 to #73, the best Pop chart performance of his entire career. Though Jones is now held up as the very definition of country music, back in the days when many fans of the genre regarded anything with drums on it as pop country, the instrumentation and arrangement of "White Lightning" went far beyond, as deep into rock & roll territory as material Jones previously used a fake name and put-on voice to record. He cut the song near the end of 1958, the same year Jerry Lee Lewis hit #1 Country and #2 Pop with "Great

Balls of Fire," inarguably a rock & roll song. "White Lightning" sounds like a triple-distilled version of Jerry Lee's hit, which probably wasn't an accident, considering Jones had already released a clone of Jerry Lee's first hit, "Whole Lotta Shakin' Goin' On." Recorded in 1957 with Grady Martin and Hank Garland on guitars and Floyd Cramer on piano, "Maybe Little Baby" rocks harder than anything released under the name Thumper Jones and was an obvious attempt to piggyback on Jerry Lee Lewis' debut smash from earlier in the year. If we time-traveled back to 1957 with the intent of building a case against rock & roll's corrupting influence on the youth of America, "Maybe Little Baby" could go near the top of the stack of records played in the courtroom. There's no mistaking the George Jones of this song is hornier than a cartoon wolf because it's the only thing the song is about. His unrestrained moaning and howling at a girl make him sound like a guy who pops Viagra just to go walking around in public wearing tight pants. "Maybe Little Baby" was recorded for Mercury-Starday but not released as a single, probably because all Don Pierce heard was a rock song, which he hated and had no idea how to sell, so he didn't even try. At least Jerry Lee Lewis yelled about having chickens in the barn so executives at his record label could pretend "Whole Lotta Shakin' Goin' On" was a) country and b) also about a party, not just sex. By the time George Jones and Pappy Daily finally figured out the trick of placing lyrics set in the country on top of rock music and then shipping it to country radio, Mercury-Starday had dissolved and Don Pierce was no longer tasked with pushing George's singles. Mercury's promo team had an easier time selling "White Lightning" to country stations because Jones kept his voice and accent on the country side of the fence instead of hiding behind a put-on voice, fake hiccups or any of the other rock & roll clichés he'd used in the past. Strip those vocals from the track, though, and you're left with a rock song, written by none other than J. P. Richardson, a.k.a. the Big Bopper.

A few months before Jones cut "White Lightning," the Big Bopper released "Chantilly Lace," a dirty-talk-phone-call novelty song originally cut for Pappy Daily's small D Records label, then sent up to Mercury once it began selling in big numbers, eventually hitting the Pop Top 10. The timing could not have been better for Pappy. Just as Mercury was deciding to end their relationship with Starday, here came a huge hit record from Pappy's little farm club label in Texas. On the off-chance his business relationship with George Jones wasn't enough to keep Pappy around, the success of "Chantilly Lace" certainly secured his future with Mercury. One year prior, J. P. Richardson had just been some Beaumont, Texas, DJ using the Big Bopper as an on-air persona. When he decided to try for his own music career, Richardson signed with Pappy Daily as an artist and a writer, which was the best way for someone to get George Jones to record their songs. The first Richardson composition Jones cut was "Rain, Rain" in late 1957. This was the same Mercury-Starday session as "Maybe Little Baby," which means Grady Martin and Hank Garland are on guitars here, too, and we probably have

Garland's background in jazz to thank for the smooth, cocktail-lounge samba vibe hanging over the song like curtains, occasionally parting to reveal glimpses of an entirely separate hardcore country number. "Rain, Rain" surely perplexed Don Pierce just as much as "Maybe Little Baby" and was similarly held back from release until years later.

The first Richardson song to actually see light of day as a George Jones single was "Treasure of Love," recorded the same night as "White Lightning" in late '58. This happens to be one of the most legendary recording sessions in country music history. Most of the stories focus on Jones showing up to work that night half drunk and getting the rest of the way there in between songs. But that in itself is entirely unremarkable, being true of most Jones sessions. The only reason people care how drunk Jones was this night is because he also managed to lay down four incredible performances in one session. Three of those four songs were written by J. P. Richardson, which was partly an attempt to see if the guy who just wrote a huge hit for himself could write one for Pappy Daily's biggest artist but also a result of Richardson's willingness to list George Jones as a co-writer on two of the songs. One of those songs was "Treasure of Love," a no-frills honky-tonk number kicked off by Dale Potter's fiddle clearing a path for steel guitar, half-sloppy bass and a backbeat that sounds like it was played on an aluminum trash can. Jones' drunken rhythm guitar is off time for nearly the entire song. It's one of his greatest recordings. There's no chance Pappy Daily missed the similarities between Richardson's lyrics and "A Satisfied Mind," Starday's biggest earner, which Don Pierce recently chose first when splitting the label's catalog. "Treasure of Love" was also George Jones' most unique vocal take to date, a showcase for the techniques he'd developed while searching for his own voice. Since this was the way Pappy had always asked him to sing, "Treasure of Love" was selected as the first single to be released from the session. It charted at #6 Country, a big enough hit for the B-side to get plenty of airplay, too. Another Richardson-Jones composition, the title of "If I Don't Love You (Grits Ain't Groceries)" came from a line in Titus Turner's "All Around the World," a Top 5 R&B hit for Little Willie John in 1955. That one reference aside, though, the Jones song is an entirely separate work, a goofy ditty tailor-made for his humorous side. Once "Treasure of Love" b/w "Grits Ain't Groceries" finally began sliding down the charts, it was time to release another single and they only had one more Richardson song in the can.

After you know to listen for it you can hear mistakes caused by Jones' drunkenness on everything from the whole session. But "White Lightning" was the biggest pain in the ass to record, so it's the song everyone talks about in all the stories. Jones just couldn't get it right, false start after false start. Buddy Killen played the bass intro eleven times until his fingers blistered. He played the bass intro forty times until his fingers bled. He played the bass intro eighty times until his hand fell off. It all depends on who you ask. They did manage a few complete takes but never one without Jones mangling at least a word or two, so everyone finally just gave up, deciding whichever take contained the fewest mistakes would have to be good enough. Most country fans over the years have noticed how Jones gets hung up on the word "slug" in the released single but, just after that, right after all the instruments hit a stop, listen closely and you'll hear Pig Robbins hit a bum note when he brings back the piano in between Jones singing the lines "mighty mighty pleasin'" and "yer pappy's corn squeezins." Make no mistake, Pig Robbins was one of the greatest piano players in country music history. When you hear piano on a George Jones song anywhere between this session and the year 2000, odds are you're listening to Pig Robbins. But "White Lightning" was the first major session Pig ever worked. So when Jones screwed up before all the players hit a stop, Pig probably assumed they'd kill the take right there and start over, as they'd already done countless times that night. Then everyone kept going and Pig rushed back into place, leaving only the slightest of errors on the recording. Of course, everyone else in the room had the advantage of being able to see what the other musicians were doing. Pig Robbins lost his eyesight in an accident at the age of three. He was trying to climb up into a chair while holding on to a half-open pocketknife he'd found in a pair of his father's pants when he fell and stabbed himself in one eye. By the time his parents weighed conflicting medical advice and decided to have the sightless eye removed, what's known as a sympathetic infection caused Pig to also lose vision in his other eye. His own take on it was, "My music teacher used to say you shouldn't look at the keys anyway."

Small mistakes and all, "White Lightning" was sent to press. J. P. Richardson gave the single some advance promotion by writing letters of recommendation to his former colleagues in radio. Written on official Big Bopper stationery and dated January 31, 1959, the typed letter opened with thanks to DJs and programmers for playing "Treasure of Love" (a subtle reminder of how well George Jones' previous record performed at their stations), then made sure they were aware he'd also written Jones' upcoming single. He said he'd appreciate any "help" in "getting it out there." These letters were almost certainly written, signed and mailed (with J. P.'s consent, of course) by someone on staff at Mercury because, on the given date of January 31, Richardson himself happened to be dealing with the flu while on a Buddy Holly tour in the middle of nowhere. Three days later—Tuesday, February 3—every DJ and programmer who received one of those letters woke up to the news that Ritchie Valens, Buddy Holly and the Big Bopper had all died in a plane crash the previous night. "White Lightning" came out six days later. And maybe this rock & roll record would have gone #1 Country without all those DJs and programmers honoring J. P.'s final, direct request of them. It's a great song and surely would have been a significant hit no matter what. But facts are facts. It's a fact Pappy Daily and Mercury chose "Treasure of Love" over "White Lightning" when selecting the first single from the session. This decision wasn't any kind of bunt strategy to load the bases before bringing out a home run hitter. In late '50s major label country, you came out swinging for the fences on every A-side or you got sent back to the minors. The suits had every reason to believe "Treasure of Love" would be the biggest hit. In addition to those already given, the recording session took place four days after the Country Music Association was formed with the singular purpose of wrestling country music platforms back from rock & roll. Something like the CMA doesn't appear one day out of nowhere. It comes into existence as a result of people who work in the same industry having the same worried conversation every day, over and over, until some of them finally decide to do something about it. True, Pappy hedged his bet by also getting Jones to record a rock song in the session, but if he believed the CMA—a.k.a. all his friends, coworkers and competition in the Nashville country music industry—had any chance of succeeding in the one goal they all agreed to work toward together, then "Treasure of Love" was the clear choice for a single. Besides, if that song didn't hit on anything calling itself country radio then probably he and George ought to just go back home to Texas and jukeboxes.

It's also a fact that "White Lightning" turned out to be the very last of the blatant first-wave rock & roll songs to go #1 Country. Jerry Lee Lewis and Elvis Presley put a couple more rock records in the Country Top 5 over the next year or so, but the CMA did manage to reclaim country music platforms, thereby forcing rock & roll to establish its own identity and its own industry as a popular genre. From here through most of the 1960s, country radio stations only allowed rock artists to cross over if they sounded sufficiently country. Country radio in this period played the Nashville Sound style of country, pop country and pop-masquerading-as-country mixed in with some twang-heavy Bakersfield Sound and a twist of Johnny Cash's one-flat-tire post-rockabilly. Country charts of the era reflect this shift, listing artists with a hard country approach—like Porter Wagoner, Buck Owens and Loretta Lynn—alongside the Jim Reeves-in-a-tuxedo brand of pop country artist. These were the glory days of Nashville Sound producers Owen Bradley and Chet Atkins. While George Jones never worked with either man, his uncredited producers in Owen Bradley–built studios over the next ten years were all co-authors of the Nashville Sound, A-Team musicians like Buddy Killen, Bob Moore and Tommy Jackson. As such (and despite his reputation among fans for being an outsider to the entire Nashville system), every second of music recorded by Jones in Nashville from the 1950s forward owes a profound debt to Owen Bradley. George's entire subsequent discography can be viewed as a living document of evolving definitions for the Nashville Sound. There's no exaggeration in saying it was the Nashville studio system running on autopilot behind George Jones, The Greatest Country Singer Ever.

◇   ◇   ◇

As for when George Jones became The Greatest Country Singer Ever, it's difficult to say. At some point in the mid-to-late 1950s, singer and songwriter Joe Carson is supposed to've gotten drunk and confronted Ray Price with the news that Jones had become better than Price, therefore the best country singer alive. This may be the earliest documented instance of anyone with any authority to speak on the matter heaping such a superlative on George Jones. The list of similar statements made since is endless. His earliest major influence as a vocalist, Roy Acuff, once said he'd give anything to be able to sing like George Jones. Buddy Killen, who in his lifetime worked with nearly every notable Nashville artist of the twentieth century: "I can say, without hesitation, that George Jones is the greatest country music singer who has ever lived." Buddy also said, "I've never known another singer who has the phenomenal respect as a singer by his peers as George Jones has." One of those peers would be Dolly Parton, who said, "Anyone who knows or cares anything about real country music will agree that George Jones is the voice of it." When asked who his favorite country singer was, Johnny Cash would often reply, "You mean, besides George Jones?" Tom T. Hall once said, "I've never talked to a country music person whose favorite singer wasn't George Jones." On his 1980 album *Music Man*, Waylon Jennings wrote a song, called "It's Alright," with these lyrics in a verse: "George might show up flyin' high, if George shows up at all / But he can be, unconsciously, the greatest of 'em all / From the Beatles and me in Nashville, to the 'billies and the Rolling Stones / if we could all sing like we wanted to, we'd all sound like George Jones." This opinion is not exclusive to the Nashville country music industry. In 1988, Buck Owens said, "I thought George was the greatest thing since sliced bread." Elsewhere, Buck described his own early records by saying, "you're sure gonna hear George Jones because he was a big influence on me as far as the singers go." Emmylou Harris said, "When you hear George Jones sing you are hearing a man who takes a song and makes it a work of art—always. He has a remarkable voice that flows out of him effortlessly and quietly but with an edge that comes from the stormy part of the heart. In the South we call it 'high lonesome.' I think it is popularly called 'soul.'" Merle Haggard famously impersonated other country singers as part of his act from the very beginning of his career. Once, after doing some impersonations on TNN's *Prime Time Country* talk show, Merle was asked by host Gary Chapman why he never impersonated George Jones, to which Merle responded, "Y'know, some people . . . I like to do George's songs. I do Jimmie Rodgers songs. Some people it's beyond that." When Jones died, Merle Haggard eulogized him in *Rolling Stone* magazine by writing, "His voice was like a Stradivarius violin: one of the greatest instruments ever made. He could interpret any given set of words better than anybody I've ever heard. You'd have to go back to Hank Williams or Ernest Tubb to compare, and he may have outdone them both." In 1980, Johnny PayCheck was interviewed on television by Tom Snyder, who asked PayCheck to name some of his influences. The first name out of PayCheck's mouth was George Jones, who he then called "the all-time best." The Haggard and PayCheck endorsements are perhaps the most important, as these are two of the most commonly suggested names put forth by country music fans as challengers for the throne of Greatest Country Singer Ever.

This is a subject of intense debate for many people and emotions can run high, so we must lay out precise terms with care. The suggested honorific is Greatest Country Singer Ever. It's nothing to do with anything other than the vocal performances on the recordings, so forget about who wrote the songs, played the instruments, produced the sessions, etc. It's nothing to do with commercial success, so forget about George Jones having more entries on the Country singles chart and more Top 40 Country singles than any other artist in the twentieth century; forget about Eddy Arnold and George Strait—two artists no sane person would claim were better singers than Jones—being the only individuals to chart more Top 10 Country singles in the twentieth century. It's nothing to do with career longevity, so forget about Jones being the only person in history to appear on the Country Top 40 in seven different decades. It's nothing to do with who had the most hits or sales and nobody's talking about money or fame. If it helps, think of the title as Greatest Country Vocalist Ever. Nobody's saying he has to be your favorite country singer. His doesn't have to be the voice you find most pleasing or most enjoy hearing. The only thing that matters is how many things he could do that other singers can't. It's just as much about athleticism as it is about art. George Jones' athletic ability as a country singer was partly determined at birth and partly a result of dedicating his entire life to the genre. Anatomy, dexterity, skill and experience were the physical palette from which his creative intelligence painted a body of vocal work no other human could reproduce.

One of the most common arguments against classifying Jones as The Greatest Country Singer Ever hinges on the erroneous theory that he stole it all (or some significant percentage) from Johnny PayCheck after PayCheck was hired to sing background vocals for Jones. Fans who believe this theory are under the impression Jones heard PayCheck sing, decided to copy his style, then reaped fame and fortune. Anyone who investigates all of the available evidence will find this theory has no basis in reality. For starters, George Jones had absolutely developed his own identity as a singer before he first heard PayCheck sing. You can hear Jones begin to peek out from behind the Hank Williams imitation all the way back in 1955 on "Why Baby Why." His biggest hit of the following year, "Just One More," goes even further in an original direction, still displaying a lot of Hank in the bleating moments and more than a little Ernest Tubb in the verses but neither Hank nor Ernest could ever have put over that chorus the way Jones does. By 1957, some of his sessions were held in Nashville's superior studios, where the better equipment brought a huge boost in quality and clarity across the board, particularly in the vocal tracks. According to Jones, "When I went to Mercury I got my first halfway decent sounds. 'Window [Up Above]' and 'Color of the Blues' didn't sell that big, but they got me a lot of radio play." This is where we and probably even Jones himself start to hear what he could actually do. The second time he walked into Owen Bradley's Quonset Hut, in the fall of 1957, Jones recorded the Top 10 ballad "Color of the Blues." That vocal sounds more like George Jones than it does any other singer in the world. About a year later, going by the name Donny Young at the time, Johnny PayCheck walked into the very same room for his first session as a recording artist. He'd been signed to Decca Records by Owen Bradley, who became Donny's producer. On all three songs from this first session, it is extraordinary how much of the Johnny PayCheck style was already in his voice at twenty years old. He wrote his own first single, "It's Been a Long, Long Time for Me." If you listen, you'll definitely hear some Hank Williams in there, along with a hint of Donny's friend Roger Miller (who sang harmony on the record's B-side), but mostly he just sounds like a young Johnny PayCheck. Close your eyes and you can imagine his lower jaw jutting forward on the low moans and kicking over to the side for the yelps, just the way it did the rest of his life. On the day of Donny's first session, they also captured "I Guess I Had It Coming," another great performance of another song he wrote for himself. On the day after Donny's first session, George Jones used the same studio to record "White Lightning" and "Treasure of Love" while drunk off his ass. It's not surprising we can hear many of the same traits in the style of these two singers when the lists of their influences were practically identical. The only major difference is that George Jones was a huge influence on Donny Young for several years before Jones could possibly have known that Donny existed, let alone heard him sing, let alone spent such time listening to him as would be required to clone his style.

When Jones did a fan Q&A session for CMT.com in 2005, someone point-blank asked him if Johnny PayCheck influenced his singing. Jones said, "Johnny didn't have any influence on my vocal style [. . .] I would imagine I had some influence on his style." While it's true Donny Young arrived in Nashville in the late 1950s and was hired as one of several backup singers on some George Jones sessions, there is no argument to be made that any studio backup singer had a significant impact on Jones' singing style at this or any other point in his career. The very first George Jones session Donny Young worked, Jones walked in the room and sang a song called "Mr. Fool." If you ever want to make a major label country singer nervous, play that recording for them and say their contract depends on whether or not they can sing it exactly the way Jones does. Throughout "Mr. Fool" he routinely tumbles between eight precisely placed pitches in the sonic space where most other vocalists would only be able to hit three, then belts out a sound that can only be compared to a tornado siren. Even if we had reason to believe Jones and PayCheck met at any point prior to this session, which we don't, Donny Young was not doing shit like that in 1959. Nobody was doing shit like that in 1959. Donny's next recording session for Decca took place about nine months later, after he spent the entirety of 1959 singing harmony on every George Jones session except for one.

The single chosen from Donny's session doesn't just sound like Jones, it was written by Jones and there's a pretty solid chance Jones taught him how to sing it. Donny's recording of "Shakin' the Blues" is practically a George Jones impersonation. Any striking similarities between PayCheck and Jones were always a product of PayCheck aping Jones, not the other way around. PayCheck's voice was deeper and huskier, which is perhaps why many country fans retroactively credit him for the way Jones began to sound when his voice dropped with age many years later. But there is simply no chance Donny Young could have arrived in Nashville singing the way he did without first studying George Jones' Starday and Mercury-Starday output. When he then got hired to sing backup on Jones' Mercury sessions, Donny continued studying Jones in person, absorbing everything he could. The proof is right there on the tapes and the recording dates are well-documented. Run through everything Jones cut in this period and you will not find one instance of him changing the way he sings in order to sound like any of his background singers. In September 1959, Jones did nothing he hadn't been doing for years on "The Last Town I Painted." Same thing in the following day's session for "Revenooer Man," a rewrite of "White Lightning" by Donny Young. (Swinging for the fences every time in late '50s country music meant taking whatever kind of sequel hit you could get after a #1 record. "Revenooer Man" is what happens when that sequel hit is successful enough to try again a third time. Donny Young wasn't around when Jones recorded the first sequel, "Who Shot Sam," about a liquor party with a twist of manslaughter. But that one hit #7 so Donny closed out the Moonshine Trilogy by writing "Revenooer Man," which is basically "White Lightning" from the government's perspective.) Even though "Revenooer Man" was written by Donny and presumably pitched to Jones in person by Donny, thereby providing every opportunity and motive for Jones to adopt some of Donny's vocal mannerisms, even if only as some kind of an inside joke, nothing about the performance sounds like anyone other than George Jones. On January 8, 1960, Jones cut "Out of Control," "Glad to Let Her Go" and "You're Still on My Mind." None of these songs find Jones doing anything he wasn't doing on record three years earlier, much less some radical shift in the wake of Donny Young's arrival on the scene. A year later, in Donny Young's first session of 1961, he cut a version of "Window Up Above," George Jones' recent #2 hit. Compare these recordings back-to-back and it's clear which singer had a greater influence on the other. Donny's "Window Up Above" has a faster tempo, and he certainly cannot hit all the same notes, but he otherwise mimics the Jones recording to such a degree that they traded and licensed the tape to various indie labels for use as a soundalike.

While impossible to definitively state Johnny PayCheck had no influence whatsoever on George Jones as a singer, it's nothing more than ignorant to argue PayCheck walked away from some bit harmony work on some recording sessions having left a discernible mark on Jones' singing style, especially when every piece of evidence suggests the influence flowed in the other direction. Jones was a successful recording artist with several major hits to his name and voice. Donny's records all flopped miserably. One man had a reason to keep borrowing from other singers while trying to find a commercial voice of his own, the other man didn't. When Decca dropped Donny from his contract, Jones—now a friend and supporter—helped him get a deal at Mercury with Shelby Singleton, who'd by this time taken over producing Jones' sessions. At Mercury, Donny cut "One Day a Week," another example of how many Johnny PayCheck tropes were firmly in place from the start of his career. For example, the way he delivers the word "walk" belongs 100 percent to him. Still, this is yet another vocal performance heavily indebted to George Jones and for very good reason: only months earlier, Shelby Singleton had produced two huge hits for Jones, "Tender Years" and "Aching, Breaking Heart." Both are hall-of-fame worthy vocal takes. "Aching, Breaking Heart" hit #5 and "Tender Years" became Jones' second #1 record. Around the time Pappy Daily took Jones away from Mercury in 1962, a still-unsuccessful Donny Young was again dropped from his record deal. Skip ahead a couple more years, late 1964 at the earliest, and Jones hired Donny to play bass and sing harmony in his backing band on tour. It's here, singing together night after night for perhaps a year in the mid-1960s, when it is theoretically possible PayCheck had some small influence on Jones' phrasing, though never to a degree which would justify the notion that Jones somehow owed his success to PayCheck's style of singing.

◇   ◇   ◇

Truthfully, there are two other artists, both aggressively idiosyncratic singers, who also worked with George Jones in the mid-'60s and would make much more sense to argue were unsung influences upon him: Melba Montgomery and Gene Pitney. Yet even here the word "influence" should not be taken to mean some direct transfer or carbon copy of vocal technique. Rather, these were all marvelous singers who each brought such a wondrously unique sound to their side of the table it could not help but inspire the others to push themselves toward great heights. In these recording sessions everyone with a microphone in their face brought their best game because they didn't want to be left in the dust. They were all making huge choices, practically daring each other to extremes. The music will be examined in greater detail later but Melba Montgomery enters this story in 1963, after Jones asks Pappy Daily to give her a record deal because of how much he actively wishes to sing with her. They cut several duet albums and tour together for many more years than Jones ever spent with PayCheck. During that time, Jones falls in love with Melba. If anyone's going to influence the way a person sings, how could it not be a longtime duet partner, especially one they were in love with? Just listen to the way Melba and Jones urge each other on through "We Must Have Been Out of Our Minds." Then there's Gene Pitney, the pop singer who broke in 1961 on "Town Without Pity," followed in 1962 by two major hits ("The Man Who Shot Liberty Valance" and "Only Love Can Break a Heart"), then another smash in 1963 with "24 Hours from Tulsa." After the British Invasion happened, American kids stopped buying American accents, so Gene Pitney's label decided to try selling him to adults. George Jones sold to adults, he was signed to the same label and that was all it took for duet sessions with Pitney to be scheduled. When Pitney met Jones in a hotel room to sing with him for the first time and practice for their recordings, he said he could tell from the start that Jones had no intention of changing anything about his phrasing or the way he sang on these duets. Pitney realized he would need to be the one to adapt his style if they were ever going to get anywhere, which is the same decision made by everyone who was ever any good at singing with George Jones.

◇   ◇   ◇

In the fall of 1965, Johnny PayCheck (now going by that name) had his first minor success with the song "A-11." Since he was still on tour playing bass in George Jones' band when the record hit, Jones would introduce PayCheck in the middle of his concerts and hand over the stage for Pay-Check to perform "A-11." With Jones' blessing, PayCheck soon quit the bass player gig to follow his own career. Take a listen to the next #1 George Jones single, "Walk Through This World with Me." How much Johnny PayCheck do you hear? How much Melba Montgomery or Gene Pitney? Trace amounts, perhaps, but it's a high concentrate of Jones.

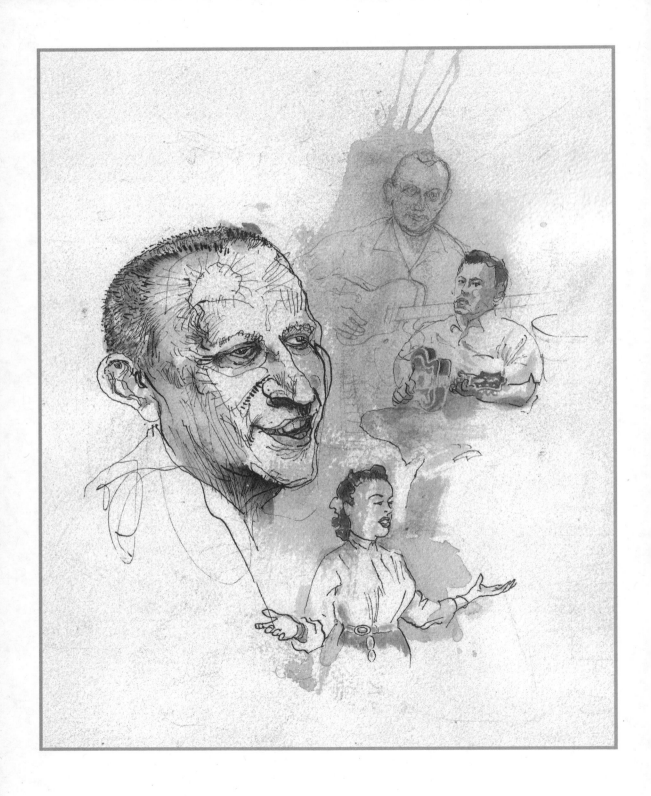

FOUR

NASHVILLE SOUND

◇ Ice Cold Industry ◇ When Nashville Hated Country Music ◇
Owen Bradley Takes Charge ◇ No, It Was Not Chet Atkins ◇ A New Kind of Studio
◇ Pop or Country? ◇ The A-Team's Instrumental Influence ◇

Music Business magazine released a full issue dedicated to the city of Nashville in 1964. In one of the articles, producer Owen Bradley says, "You know, music could be compared to ice cream. When we were kids there were only about three ice creams—vanilla, chocolate and strawberry—and only about two music styles, slow and fast. The other day I went into a Dipper Dan parlor and they had forty-eight different flavors, including licorice. And, today, there are many, many flavors of music. I suppose you call them 'trends' but they go down in history and frequently are revived."

◇   ◇   ◇

The year is 1955. Little Richard releases a song named "Tutti-Frutti." Most listeners assume he's singing about ice cream or, at least, comparing the girls he dates to flavors of ice cream. And he kind of is, since tutti-frutti is a minced fruit ice cream that has been served in Europe since at least the mid-1800s. But there's a bit more to the story. Richard Penniman, a self-described "omnisexual" and ex–drag queen, began his music career during the 1940s in gay nightclubs, hammering on piano keys while screaming out songs like "Tutti-Frutti," which his producer and several band members recall originally contained the chorus "Tutti-Frutti! Good booty!" The verses were mostly improvised, typically riffing on the theme of why and how members of the audience should have anal sex. Years later, during a short break from an unproductive recording session in which Richard is struggling to cut loose the way he does in concert, he goes over to a piano and launches into the old vulgar standby. His producer knows at once it's a certain hit . . . and that everyone involved will be thrown in jail if the lyrics aren't changed. So, he calls on a wannabe songwriter named Dorothy LaBostrie to clean up the language. Dorothy will later claim Little Richard wrote none of "Tutti-Frutti." According to her, she carried that title in her head ever since seeing the flavor in an ice cream shop some years earlier. When asked to write new words for Richard's song, she's the one who came up with the title and scribbled out lyrics in fifteen minutes with no input from anyone else. Cute story and it could be true, if told twenty years earlier by Slim Gaillard or Slam Stewart, writers and performers of "Tutti-Frutti," a song unquestionably about ice cream and a #3 Pop hit from 1938, when Little Richard was an impressionable five-year-old child. Given the all-but-identical chorus, Richard's song very likely began as a crass parody of a familiar hit, not an idle thought in the mind of a lady in line for a waffle cone. But music really can be compared to ice cream . . .

◇   ◇   ◇

It's easy to forget how much modern refrigeration changed the world, how fast that happened and how recently it was. Before refrigerators became a commonplace household appliance, not many people were excited about dinner every night. The ruling class has always eaten comparatively well, so, naturally, none of this applies to them. It's also true working-class families have always celebrated special occasions with food worth bragging about to the other kids at school. If a family was wealthy enough to send someone to the market every few days, dinner could even be pretty great several nights a week. But when we watch 1940s or 1950s movies and television shows about a group of children with blue-collar parents and there's one kid who always rushes home to see what Mom made for dinner, every night, even though it's just a Tuesday, no special occasion? The reason that character began showing up in that era is because it's when his family got a fridge (and/or when a TV show's station picked up a name brand appliance sponsor). Prior to the 1940s, the closest thing to a fridge found in most homes was an icebox: a small, cabinet-like box with an ice compartment to keep the contents cool but not refrigerated. An icebox was basically a shitty vertical cooler with shelves. The reason Irma Rombauer's landmark cookbook, *The Joy of Cooking*, placed such priority on reusing leftovers, including a dish unappetizingly named Eggplant Filled with Leftover Food, is because it came out in 1931, when leftovers had much shorter shelf lives. Perishable food not eaten or hidden in another recipe would soon spoil in an icebox, leaving little room for surprise or wonder over what would be served for dinner on any given night.

Just as coolers need a steady supply of fresh ice to keep cool, so it was with an icebox. Since ice produced by mechanical means didn't become standard until around the year 1900, for most of humanity's existence we relied on natural sources of ice. People have lived near mountaintops and in Arctic regions for millennia and used the readily available ice in various ways according to the tools and knowledge of their time. But just about every major city in history with any potential access to a natural source of ice was home to a ruling class who wanted ice, even if only to serve cool drinks or slushy desserts at a party. This ice could be harvested by sawing bricks out of frozen lakes, as was done in China at least as early as 11 BC; freezing shallow sheets of water by manipulating cold air in the desert at night, as was done in Persia at least as early as 5 BC; or sending a team of people a hundred miles away to climb a mountain and bring back some ice without letting it melt. Of course, anyone who could fund such labor-intensive enterprises could also afford to build an icehouse: a small, specially insulated structure on one's property that was used to store large pieces of ice, from which smaller pieces would be chipped as needed. Some enterprising mind eventually thought to build commercial-sized icehouses to store huge amounts of ice and supply owners of personal icehouses in the area. Thus, the ice trade was born. As the only practical way to obtain and transport commercial amounts of ice was the big-blocks-sawed-from-frozen-lakes method, ice distributors either hired a supplier or traveled to source the product themselves, then forwarded costs along to the customer, which caused ice to remain an expensive luxury commodity in most of the world for most of history. Accordingly, when a dessert we'd recognize as ice cream showed up it was a dish for the privileged few. While the French certainly discovered some form of ice cream prior to the 1500s (when Catherine de Médici is wrongly believed to have imported it from Italy), no reasonably affordable café in Paris offered ice cream until the late seventeenth century.

It wasn't until the early 1800s that Frederic Tudor worked out a method to ship unprecedented volumes of ice blocks from New England to icehouse depots in the Caribbean, then onward to the southern United States, launching an Industrial Era upgrade of the ice trade. This natural resource being far more plentiful than, say, gold, Tudor's business model immediately attracted heavy competition, which drove down the price of ice around the world. Things then progressed rapidly. Within ten years of the horse-drawn ice cutter's invention in 1825, ice became affordable to pretty much everyone. Within another ten years the patent was filed for a hand-cranked ice cream churn, which led to a greater number of ice cream parlors and mobile vendors around the world. At roughly the same time, the food industry began shipping commercial quantities of perishables long distance alongside huge blocks of ice packed inside insulated compartments on ships and railroad cars. The rollout of reliable ice manufacturing technology and industrial freezers in the early 1900s saw another increase in ice cream parlors and mobile vendors, followed by another when federal Prohibition hit in the 1920s and adults craved alternative indulgences, like sugary frozen desserts and malted milkshakes from a soda shop counter. Speaking of drinks, iced tea wasn't even invented until the 1860s, soon after the insulated railway car, and most people didn't learn of the new beverage until the same 1904 World's Fair in St. Louis that popularized ice cream served in a waffle cone. The waffle cone had been done before but, for whatever reason, the one ice cream vendor serving waffle cones at this World's Fair began outselling all the other vendors, so everyone switched to waffle cones and established a trend.

Even at that point in history ice cream remained a dessert for special occasions. One could even call it a "destination dessert," typically requiring at least a trip into town and far likelier to present itself at events or locations already deemed special, like theme parks or beach towns or a World's Fair. Those willing to go through the trouble did have the option of making ice cream themselves. According to a 1943 *New York Times* article, pilots in World War II tied five-gallon buckets of ice-cream mixture to the outside of their planes before flying on missions so that when (or if) they landed, it was with a bucket of ice cream, thoroughly frozen from the extremely cold temperature of flying at high speed and great altitude. Most people just used the hand-cranked churn. However you got your hands on some ice cream, though, the only thing you could do with it was eat it before it melted. Then World War II ended in the fall of 1945 and factories commissioned to manufacture war supplies returned to making domestic products, allowing the freezer to become a common household appliance within the United States. The option to take ice cream home and keep it frozen revolutionized the industry and resulted in a smorgasbord of new flavors. Gourmet vendors in major cities were able to offer greater variety and the menu at Howard Johnson's restaurants eventually grew to feature twenty-eight flavors. However, Owen Bradley was not exaggerating when he said vanilla, chocolate and strawberry were all he knew as a child. The original Howard Johnson's location opened with only those three flavors in 1925, when Owen Bradley was ten years old. By the time Baskin-Robbins hit thirty-one flavors in 1953, Owen was just one year away from opening the first modern recording studio in Nashville, where he continued to manufacture the take-home containers of sound he'd been producing since the 1940s.

◇   ◇   ◇

The story of how Nashville became the capital of country music begins in the middle of the 1920s with the launch of the WSM radio show that would become called the *Grand Ole Opry*. But that's only the beginning. There remained a possibility of several other Southern cities assuming the title "Country Music USA" all the way up until the 1940s, when the *Opry* moved into the Ryman Auditorium, finally gaining a reliable venue after twenty years of location changes caused by local complaints over the noise and traffic from out-of-towners attending the big country music show every weekend. Nobody wanted to live next to that circus. Even wealthy residents whose neighborhoods were never directly inconvenienced still worried over the reputation WSM's hoedown may give to the city as a whole. They didn't want the rest of the world to believe Nashville was populated with low-class hillbillies playing a lower class of music. Indeed, anyone with this impression of the city would have been mistaken. Though there were some honky-tonks, they were no more prevalent, popular or accepted than in any other city of the South. "Disreputable" is a word frequently used by country musicians of that time to describe the way they were viewed and treated when trying to eat at restaurants or check into hotel rooms in Nashville. If you took a drive around town looking for live music, the nicer evening spots were more Cab Calloway than cowboy, same as any other metropolis in the 1920s and 1930s, the era of big band and swing jazz. That may have come as a shock to some early *Opry* listeners who made the pilgrimage to attend a broadcast, expecting to find a city built of hay bales and chicken wire. But that didn't stop them from coming back, more each year and from farther away as WSM expanded its reach.

In 1939, WSM partnered with NBC's affiliate network and the *Opry* gained a nationwide audience. This deal went through the year after Roy Acuff joined the show's lineup and he was instantly transformed from the hot new thing in country music to a full-fledged star across the nation. In 1940, Roy took his band, the Smokey Mountain Boys, to Los Angeles and played "Wabash Cannonball" in the movie *Grand Ole Opry*, which (not counting Hollywood singing cowboys) made him the most famous country singer on the planet. In 1942, he co-founded the Nashville publishing company Acuff-Rose. The idea was to own his publishing himself and employ fairer business practices toward country writers who, like himself, were tired of being treated like dumb hillbillies or novelty acts easily screwed over by big-city publishers and their go-betweens. From then on, guest artists in Nashville to perform on the *Grand Ole Opry* could expect to be pitched the latest songs in the Acuff-Rose catalog and many of those artists wound up signing to Acuff-Rose as writers themselves.

When the biggest hoedown on American radio then found a real home at the Ryman, it signaled a point of no return to the country music industry. Artists invited to join the *Opry* lineup moved to Nashville without a second thought and the city quickly became the national epicenter of country talent, touring and songwriting. But there were still no modern recording studios, so artists traveled to New York City or L.A. or Chicago to make records in cities where their labels already had studios, offices and publishing company "relationships." As more and more, then most, of the country songs in those big-city sessions began coming from the Acuff-Rose catalog, the rest of the industry realized they needed feet on the ground in Nashville to stay competitive within the genre. Then World War II ended in the fall of 1945, lifting wartime rations which limited access to materials needed for making records. It took Nashville less than a year to start pumping out product. By the time Ernest Tubb opened a record shop in Nashville in 1947 and advertised on the *Opry* that his store would ship country music anywhere in the nation, there was no denying the genre had a new headquarters.

◇   ◇   ◇

Back in the 1930s, Owen Bradley was in his late teens/early twenties, arranging music and playing piano as a frontman for a big band orchestra in Nashville. Prior to banks of prerecorded audio, stations needed live musicians to play the music listeners heard between or behind announcements, commercials and DJ segments, so in 1940—soon after the affiliate deal with NBC's national network—WSM hired Owen Bradley's orchestra as their house band. "WSM" stood for "We Shield Millions," motto of the National Life & Accident Insurance Company, who'd launched the radio station to promote insurance policies. In order to maximize sales, WSM attempted to secure as wide a listenership as possible, which is why they programmed nearly nothing but the most popular genres of music in their first few decades on the air. Serious efforts to support the *Grand Ole Opry* with a handful of other country music shows did begin later in the 1940s but WSM was not a country station and never switched to an all-country format until the year 1980. Prior to then, WSM largely stuck to the middle of the road by playing whatever most listeners wanted to hear. You know, boring stuff. (The biggest record of 1940 was Tommy Dorsey and His Orchestra with Frank Sinatra singing "I'll Never Smile Again.") If "big band orchestra" didn't already spell it out, the kind of music Owen Bradley's band played was rarely even a little bit country. What WSM wanted from him nearly entirely fell on the "classically influenced" or "easy listening" side of big band jazz, which came easy to Owen because he grew up loving both classical music and jazz.

When he was a kid, after his family inherited some money and bought a piano, Owen quickly learned to play it, then learned everything he could about the sounds he heard in commercial music. This was because he hoped to one day earn a living as a musician, not because of his personal taste. Despite the widespread mischaracterization, Owen Bradley grew up loving country music just as much as any other kid born in middle Tennessee in 1915. Before his family could afford a piano, the first instrument Owen learned was guitar, playing country music with his younger brother, Harold, plucking along on a banjo. But working musicians must play what the crowd wants to hear or they starve. Aside from the *Grand Ole Opry*, there weren't many paying gigs for country musicians in Nashville because the genre was still commonly regarded as a joke. After Owen switched to playing his family's new piano, he gave the guitar to Harold and said to learn it. He told Harold that guitar, not banjo, would be the sound of the future. Again, this was purely a career-minded statement, not a value judgment. Recently invented electric guitars and amplifiers had made it possible for guitarists to play lead lines over big band instrumentation in a fashion previously impossible with feedback-prone acoustic guitars. Owen correctly predicted the effect this would have on the popularity of guitars.

Even after Owen began working primarily in big band jazz, he took country gigs whenever they were offered. Anyone investigating his country music pedigree need look no further than the fact he's a co-writer on Roy Acuff's 1942 hit, "Night Train to Memphis." After Owen established a reputation as the leader of a sophisticated musical outfit, though, he often did country work under a pseudonym, similar to the way country artists a decade later would use fake names to cut rock records. In 1946, the first single released on the Bullet label was credited to Brad Brady and His Tennesseans. Although other musicians—starting with DeFord Bailey in the 1920s—had already recorded in Nashville using portable units, "Zeb's Mountain Boogie" is typically considered the birth of what became the Nashville recording industry; not because it was cut at WSM's facilities, as several major label singles had already been, but because Bullet was the first record label based in Nashville and this first single's success inspired many more labels to set up shop in town, thereby creating a greater need for local recording studios. As for the music itself, "Zeb's Mountain Boogie" probably sounds to modern ears more like jazz than country but what you're hearing is essentially 1940s pop country: Zeb Turner's version of a country guitar boogie taking a joyride up a mountain with Owen Bradley's jazz orchestra in the back of the truck. Once orders began pouring in, Owen told Bullet they could put his real name on the record instead of "Brad Brady." The B-side was a cover of Elton Britt's #3 Country hit, the staid "Wave to Me, My Lady," not exactly a foot stomper. These were the sounds of the time.

After Bullet's big hit cut a trail for others to follow, a few WSM engineers decided to get serious about using the station's facilities during off-hours to meet Nashville's sudden demand for studio space. They named the enterprise Castle Recording Laboratories (a.k.a. Castle Studios), after WSM's nickname "Air Castle of the South." This is where Hank Williams' first professional recording session—including "Never Again (Will I Knock at Your Door)"—took place in 1946. Since there wasn't enough room at WSM for Castle's massive recording machine, they housed the unit in another building and forwarded the audio signal to it through a phone line. This was how they cut the first song recorded in Nashville to go #1 Pop.

Before pivoting to a career as a radio DJ, Francis Craig had been a bandleader at WSM and "Near You" was intended as a final farewell to his life as a musician. But then the single—with an intro of Francis shredding on piano for a full minute before singing anything—came out in 1947, hit the top of the Pop charts and brought the Castle team far too much business to handle during late nights at WSM. They found a run-down banquet room at the Tulane Hotel, converted it to a studio and Nashville finally had its first commercial recording space. Over the next seven years, Castle's hotel studio housed sessions for most major label artists who recorded in the city, including Ernest Tubb, Burl Ives, Red Foley, the Stanley Brothers, Ray Price, Bill Monroe, Webb Pierce and Kitty Wells.

Artists who didn't arrive at Castle with a full band were typically backed by Owen Bradley and whichever supplemental musicians he chose to hire for the session. When you hear piano or organ on those recordings, there's a good chance you're listening to Owen. He played on Kitty Wells' "It

Wasn't God Who Made Honky Tonk Angels" and he played on many of Hank Williams' Nashville sessions, which followed Castle from WSM to the hotel in 1947 and stayed there for the rest of Hank's life. Whenever you hear Ernest Tubb calling out for "Half-Moon" to take a piano lead on a record, like "The Lovebug Itch" with Red Foley and Minnie Pearl, he's poking fun at Owen Bradley, telling him to go ahead and chop out a piece half as good as virtuoso honky-tonk pianist Moon Mullican. The skill set Owen acquired in his years as a bandleader translated well to the studio. He knew how to scout, schedule and direct musicians. He was able to quickly arrange a song, show everyone what he wanted them to play on it, then lead the session on piano. Producers who held sessions at Castle increasingly relied upon him until what began with Owen hiring and leading the musicians turned into Owen doing nearly all the work credited to those producers. This was most notably the case with Paul Cohen of Decca Records. Paul lived in New York City and previously brought country artists to record in studios located there or Chicago. Then Castle opened and Decca's biggest country acts, like Ernest Tubb and Red Foley, wanted to work near home with musicians they knew rather than travel to other cities to work with strangers who may not know or care about country music at all. So, Paul started going to Nashville for two or three weeks at a time to oversee recording sessions. For that to work he needed a local liaison, some musician known and respected by the other musicians in the room but who was also able to view and direct operations from Paul's business-minded perspective. Less than a year after Castle moved into the Tulane Hotel, Paul created an Assistant Producer position at Decca for Owen Bradley. It's important to note this was a job title at Decca, not a credit given to Owen on the labels of records. Paul continued to receive sole credit as the producer of these sessions, which begs the question: was Paul Cohen a producer or not? By modern definitions of the term, no, not really. But neither were the vast majority of the era's "producers," nearly none of whom did most of the work we now associate with that job title.

Nearly all the first record producers were nothing more than A&R executives. That's "A&R" for Artists and Repertoire, as in these were the guys (yes, almost exclusively guys) who scouted the artists to sign to labels and therefore had a vested interest in quality control over said artists' repertoires. They chose or approved songs for their artists and supervised production of the product they brought to the label. When early producers went in the studio with an artist it was mostly to make sure everything went down the way it was supposed to go down. Paul Cohen wasn't there to select the key of each song, arrange and assign parts or give any technical input to the musicians other than "that's good" or "that's bad." He was there to keep artists from making last-minute decisions to cut songs he hadn't approved. He was there to make sure some bass player didn't waste costly studio time trying to change the rhythm of a waltz to a rumba. If one of the musicians showed up too drunk to play or had an out-of-tune instrument, Paul needed to find out about that during the session while there was still time to fix it, not after it was already committed to an expensive-but-worthless tape. In today's language, "presented by Paul Cohen" would make more sense as a label credit. The same is true for nearly every one of his peers and predecessors. According to Gordon Stoker of the Jordanaires, Elvis Presley was the real producer on every Elvis session Gordon ever worked, regardless of whether Chet Atkins or Steve Sholes received credit on the label. Anyone ever "produced" by Pappy Daily will tell you Pappy was mainly there to look at his watch while the session leader did all the actual work. If we're talking production in the modern sense, a person who wields the greatest control over the sound and music of multiple artists' records, Owen Bradley was probably the first producer in Nashville—he was certainly the most influential. No matter what the credits on the label say, Owen made most of the important technical and creative decisions, arranging all the pieces and players into the music we hear on records "produced" by Paul Cohen and several other executives.

In Michael Kosser's *How Nashville Became Music City USA*, Muscle Shoals studio bassist Norbert Putnam gives an account of Owen Bradley's audition process. Norbert was hired to play a show at a dinner club without any rehearsal and no foreknowledge of the set list. When Norbert discovered the band would be himself on bass, Owen on piano and a drummer performing light jazz standards as a trio, he wondered if Owen was aware the Muscle Shoals scene Norbert came from mostly featured R&B music. But Owen was only interested in learning how well Norbert could handle unfamiliar material, how quickly he could figure out what to do on bass by following Owen's left hand on piano, all while under the pressure of being watched by a live audience. Well, at the end of the night, Norbert was told he'd be Owen's new third-call bassist, meaning if neither Bob Moore nor Junior Huskey could make a session, then Owen would call Norbert. He was then given a stack of records and told to go home and work on his Bob Moore and Junior Huskey impersonations because that's all he was ever, ever going to be asked to do in the studio. The most important, unbreakable rule: never play something fancy over one of Owen's singers. Norbert did receive enough of those third-on-the-list phone calls to get a feel for how Owen Bradley ran a recording session, too. After later becoming a producer himself, Norbert called Owen's way the "correct" way to run a session. Owen's Way: walk in the studio, call everyone over to the piano and play through a song one time while instructing each musician and singer what to do during each segment of the song. If anyone has a question, this is the time to ask, because after the rundown everyone goes to their places and plays through the complete song once, giving engineers enough time to make sure all the mics and cables are working while Owen listens to the performance and makes sure everyone understood his instructions. After that, the engineers press record and everyone performs the song again. And you have to play for keeps on this second performance because it sometimes ends up being the record. More often, though, it's a reference take for all the musicians to join Owen in the control room and listen to playback of what they've just done. The tape is played at a loud enough volume for Owen to walk throughout the room and quietly give comments to each musician without allowing anyone else to hear if it's praise or further instruction. Everyone then goes back in the live room and makes a record, usually in one or two additional takes. This is the method Owen developed all those years back at Castle and it's what Paul Cohen hired him to do at Decca in 1947.

Before we get all the way into this, it's worth pointing out as a frame of reference the guys most rock history books credit with pioneering the art of record production—Phil Spector, Joe Meek, George Martin, etc.—none of them did anything that matters to the history of record production until the late 1950s. When Paul Cohen left Decca in 1958, Owen Bradley stepped up to become the head of the Nashville division and finally began receiving production credit after more than a decade of uncredited work. After all these years, it is now time to also give him credit for the Nashville Sound.

◇   ◇   ◇

In order to answer one simple question—what is the Nashville Sound?—it is necessary to correct decades of misinformation and confusion caused by fundamental mistakes in the most well-respected and commonly cited books on country music history. Let us begin by asking if we can identify the first record that represents the Nashville Sound. Nearly every attempt to answer this question presents a list of singles from the year 1957, featuring songs like Ferlin Husky's "Gone," Jim Reeves' "Four Walls" or Jimmy C. Newman's "A Fallen Star." None of those singles are the first Nashville Sound record and neither is any other from the year 1957. Neither is "Young Love" by Sonny James, but it is one of many earlier records which debunk the idea that the Nashville Sound began in 1957. The only way anyone could listen to "Young Love" and then argue it is not an example of the Nashville Sound would be if they believe the things they read in a book more than they trust their own ears and judgment. "Young Love" was produced by Ken Nelson in late 1956 the first time Sonny James recorded at a studio built by Owen Bradley two years earlier. The following month, Ferlin Husky recorded "Gone" in Owen Bradley's studio. The first time Jimmy C. Newman used Owen Bradley's studio, he recorded "A Fallen Star."

Owen's reasons for building a studio link back to one of the biggest controversies in the country music industry. A WSM employee named Jim Denny was in charge of booking musical acts on the station and on the *Grand Ole Opry*. About a decade after the founding of Acuff-Rose, Denny and Webb Pierce launched the competing Cedarwood Publishing and soon there were a lot of Acuff-Rose artists complaining about how they no longer received good time slots on the *Opry*. This led to an internal power struggle at WSM in 1953 which caused all WSM employees to enter 1954 with reasonable certainty the station would soon declare any outside gigs in the music industry a conflict of interest. When the WSM engineers running Castle then learned the Tulane Hotel was scheduled for demolition, rather than look for a new studio space they decided to shut down the operation and keep their day jobs in radio. But Nashville still lacked a modern recording studio. Sure, there were other rooms being used to make records but none were designed and built specifically for studio use, none were of any higher quality than Castle's repurposed hotel banquet room. One day Paul Cohen told Owen Bradley he was thinking of moving Decca's whole country music operation down to Texas after Castle closed and Owen suggested an alternative plan: the two of them could go in fifty-fifty to build a new studio in Nashville themselves. Though Paul agreed, he never actually put up his end of the money and Owen moved forward on his own, taking out a loan to purchase a house at 804 16th Avenue South. The reputation Owen and his team of musicians already had for making hit records was almost entirely why the rest of the Nashville recording industry soon followed him to the same neighborhood. Today it is known as Music Row.

Of the above singles most commonly listed as the first Nashville Sound records, the only one not cut at Owen Bradley's new studio was "Four Walls" by Jim Reeves, so let's take a look at why it has no business being a part of this conversation. In 1954, RCA Records started renting a big, unused meeting room in a building owned by a Methodist church organization. This was a very similar setup to Castle, a repurposed room not built for audio but decent enough to serve as RCA's Nashville studio for the next several years. That is where Jim Reeves recorded "Four Walls" in 1957 in a session produced by Chet Atkins. As such, people who mistakenly believe this to be the first Nashville Sound record also mistakenly believe Chet Atkins created the Nashville Sound. The lists of singles from 1957 and attribution of credit to Chet Atkins are always presented as de facto matters of historical record. They are never backed up by supporting evidence or informed context because the fact is they can't be. And there really are millions of folks who'll believe and repeat something they saw in a documentary or read in a book more than they'll trust what they can hear with their own ears. In 1968, Bill C. Malone published *Country Music USA*, the first serious scholarly work on the genre, in which he wrote of the way Chet Atkins moved to town and "immediately began to shape and direct the style of music heard in Nashville." The only problem is that's not remotely close to what actually happened. *Country Music USA* goes on to greatly overstate Chet Atkins' role compared to Owen Bradley's in creating and reinventing the sound of Nashville recording sessions. While *Country Music USA* returns to Chet over a dozen times, Owen receives only two passing mentions in the book. This oversight has proven disastrously influential amongst country music historians. As one would expect from the title, Paul Hemphill's *The Nashville Sound* has been the first and only source consulted and cited on this topic by most interested parties ever since it was published in 1970. Following set precedent, *The Nashville Sound* tells readers that if one man can be credited with creating the Nashville Sound, then that man is Chet Atkins. This is objectively untrue. In his own autobiography, Chet Atkins remembered the first Nashville session he ever worked as a musician being produced by (you guessed it) Owen Bradley in 1946, the year before Chet signed an artist contract with RCA. Rather than moving to town and immediately beginning to shape and direct its style of music, as Bill Malone claimed, the fact is Chet's early RCA records failed to sell well enough to justify remaining in Nashville, so he left. While Owen had already spent years establishing what would become the Nashville methods of recording, arrangement and production, Chet was of such little importance he was unable to afford rent in the city. Chet Atkins did not move back to Nashville until 1950. When he did, it was only because the Carter Sisters and Mother Maybelle joined the *Grand Ole Opry* and Chet was their guitar player. By that time, Owen Bradley was indisputably the most important producer in Nashville. (A lone example would be his incredible production on Red Foley's "Chattanoogie Shoeshine Boy," the #1 Country song in the nation for three months in 1950.) Even after Chet's return, he spent several more years working as a session guitarist before reaching any significant level of influence as a musician, let alone session leader, let alone producer or label executive. In fact, he was still being hired to play guitar on Owen's sessions at least as late as 1953, when Webb Pierce cut "There Stands the Glass" and "Slowly" and Hank Locklin cut "Let Me Be the One," all produced by Owen Bradley, all including unremarkable guitar parts from Chet Atkins. According to Chet himself, he spent every session studying Owen's approach to production. By the time he started leading sessions at RCA, Chet and everyone else in Nashville were simply doing things the way Owen had taught them. These two careers did follow a similar path—from studio musician to session leader to producer to powerful label executive—but Chet Atkins would be the first to tell you he was always following in Owen Bradley's footsteps, never actually innovated much of anything and worked with at least three employees who deserved more credit than he ever did for the sound of his sessions. Nashville A-Team musicians used to joke with each other about how it was impossible to make a mistake bad enough for Chet to say another take was necessary. This in contrast to Owen, who heard every wrong note and accepted nothing less than what he walked in the room knowing he wanted on the record. When RCA finally built a modern studio in Nashville and put Chet Atkins in charge, there was a sound engineer he never got along with, so Chet had the guy transferred somewhere else and advertised the open position. In 1959, Bill Porter got the job. Whatever sound fans, critics and historians attributed to RCA's studio, Chet always credited to Bill Porter. This was backed up by studio bassist and producer Bob Moore, who said, "Bill Porter changed the sound of the room when he got there in 1959." Conversely, every account of Owen Bradley building his studio five years before Bill Porter showed up at RCA involves Owen personally tinkering with every minor detail to control sound waves in the rooms where he produced records.

When Owen bought 804 16th Avenue, he and his brother, Harold, entirely gutted the home and took out most of the ground level's floor in order to turn the basement into a live room with a two-story tall ceiling. Owen also bought a kit for a seventy-five-foot-long by thirty-five-foot-wide and -high Quonset hut made of corrugated sheet metal, which he put in the backyard. The idea was to record music in the house and use the hut to film visual content, like all the great Al Gannaway footage currently available to watch on YouTube. Harold Bradley said it may have been producer Don Law who first booked the bigger studio out back to record music. If Harold's memory was correct, this would have been the April 1957 Mel Tillis session featuring "Juke Box Man," which doesn't sound too bad for a record cut in a big, metal garage. Since that was around the time the record industry began to standardize stereo technology, creating more sonic space to fill with bigger arrangements, which required more musicians and singers, it's likely Don Law asked for the larger building out back so they had more room for everyone to spread out. As more and more producers kept asking to book the bigger building to make records, Owen decided to convert the video studio to an audio studio. This would not have been an easy thing to do with a curved, metal building but (two years before Bill Porter showed up and gave RCA's studio its "sound"), Owen went in his Quonset hut and turned it into The Quonset Hut, a state-of-the-art facility including makeshift versions of modern studio implements like baffles, isolation booths and various other devices to control sound waves. Some improvements came by happy accident, like the time a Gannaway video shoot called for a section of wooden flooring to be built over the hut's tile floor and it fixed a weird sound nobody had been able to track down, so they kept the wood there. Other solutions were based on the decade of trial-and-error experience Owen had under his belt. Curved metal ceilings not being ideal for sound, they built a giant, rectangular window shutter–looking thing out of wood, suspended it above the live room, then piled old curtains on top to absorb errant sound waves. This is how invested Owen Bradley was in the sound of his rooms, thus impacting not only his own work but that of anyone else who worked there, which is why it's significant that nearly all of the so-called "first Nashville Sound" records were made there.

Sometimes it seems like almost nobody has given serious consideration to whatever they believe they're talking about when they use the term "Nashville Sound." Most modern fans of classic country music use "Nashville Sound" as derogatory shorthand to refer to 1950s pop country or pop masquerading as country with string sections and/or background singers in place of fiddle and steel guitar. This is more than a little strange because that sound existed decades earlier and

Nashville had exactly nothing to do with it. The source of that music was soundtracks of Hollywood Western movies from the 1930s and 1940s. When Ernest Tubb spoke about being one of the first country artists in Nashville to use a string section and vocal chorus in 1951, six years prior to the supposed invention of the Nashville Sound, he called it a "novelty." What he meant was those strings and the vocal chorus made him sound like a Hollywood cowboy, far more "western" than "country," and the most mainstream pop culture version of western, at that. Many fans believe the "& Western" part of the genre Country & Western is a reference to western swing. It's not. It's a reference to western music, or at least Hollywood's version of western music, performed by singing actors in Western movies, a.k.a. "horse operas," the biggest of which were given exponentially larger marketing budgets than the entire country music division of any record label at the time. That is precisely how and why the same sounds later wound up on major label country music recorded in Nashville during the 1950s. Note the vocal arrangement on Sons of the Pioneers' 1941 Decca recording of "Cool Water." Sons of the Pioneers sang the song again in the 1945 movie *Along the Navajo Trail* (starring Roy Rogers) and rerecorded it several times in the course of their career, including a 1948 big band jazz version with Vaughn Monroe that became a Top 10 Pop hit. One year later, Vaughn Monroe released the most well-known recording of "Ghost Riders in the Sky," hitting #1 Pop with a song Gene Autry sang the same year in a movie titled *Riders in the Sky*. In 1942's *The Forest Ranger*, Dick Thomas sang "(I've Got Spurs That) Jingle Jangle Jingle," written by *Guys and Dolls*' Frank Loesser. Later in the year, Kay Kyser's big band cover stayed at #1 Pop for two months. Gene Autry's version went #14 Pop and sold more than a million copies. Another Broadway musical guy, Cole Porter, wrote "Don't Fence Me In," first sung by Roy Rogers in 1944's *Hollywood Canteen*, then again a year later in the movie *Don't Fence Me In*. Bing Crosby's version went #1 Pop and Gene Autry's hit #4 Country.

What we're looking at here is the same thing major label record executives saw at the time: millions of people watching blockbuster movies about singing cowboys then going to stores and buying records of the songs from those movies. In 1949, following years of indecision over what to call their "poor Black people music" chart and "poor white people music" chart, *Billboard* replaced their "Race Records" chart with the Rhythm & Blues chart and the "Folk Records" chart became the Country & Western chart. To be clear, this was the leading music industry trade broadcasting an intention to chart the commercial success of Western movie soundtracks and their ilk alongside all other country-adjacent records, as if these products were all created and promoted with comparable resources and for one single to outperform another was merely an indicator of superior quality. They did this two years after Owen Bradley was hired to manufacture commercial product for Decca. His bosses wanted to open *Billboard* and see Owen's records taking a significant share of the market. They wanted Owen's artists to win industry awards in categories that would be named after these charts. They wanted Owen's records to move units in stores that would organize inventory based on these charts. Once Owen's direct competition became Hollywood Western soundtracks with massive marketing budgets and silver screens around the nation promoting their product, he had no other choice than to try beating them with their own sonic tropes. If he didn't do it, his bosses would have just hired someone else to do it.

However, there were some huge differences between Hollywood Western soundtracks and Owen Bradley's Nashville Sound. Composers for 1930s and 1940s Hollywood Westerns had the same goal as all other popular music forms of the era, which was to treat as many customers as possible to the familiar experience they expected to have. They were not writing scores with the intention of deviating from the standard formula in any way that would challenge audiences with revolutionary sounds. (That didn't happen until the rise of composers like Ennio Morricone in the 1960s.) Let's go back to Sons of the Pioneers for a second. One of their most popular songs was "Tumbling Tumbleweeds," made famous by Gene Autry in the 1935 movie *Tumbling Tumbleweeds*. But listen to the recording Sons of the Pioneers made themselves on Decca the prior year. Then listen to a song from a few years later named "If I Didn't Care" by the Ink Spots, an immensely successful vocal group also signed to Decca. "If I Didn't Care" is one of the best-selling and most popular singles of all time and there's no denying the arrangement sounds a lot like Sons of the Pioneers' 1934 recording of "Tumbling Tumbleweeds." There are differences between the songs—they have different melodies, the Ink Spots record has a lead singer, the Sons of the Pioneers record has a faster tempo—but the only difference in instrumentation is that one record has a fiddle where the other has a piano. Either group could easily provide the other's vocal harmonies. None of this was by accident. These were commercial products created by the same record label, then sold to as many customers as possible via separate divisions of the label telling fans of separate genres the product was made for them when, in reality, both songs were pop music with one or two small concessions—the clothing worn by the artists, the thematic content of the lyrics, the presence of a certain instrument—suggesting the record belonged in the genre it was marketed as. This is the way it's always worked. It's the reason we can say a song sounds like it was made in the 1950s or 1980s and everyone gets the reference. It's not a simple matter of the technology available in those decades; it's a matter of industry professionals all using it the same way, trying to create and sell the most profitable iteration of approximately the same popular product.

Now imagine you're Marty Robbins in 1955 and you record "Singing the Blues" in Owen Bradley's pre–Quonset Hut basement studio. (Don Law gets credit for producing the session but Owen's there on piano, so you do the math. Or take it from country singer Johnny Bush, who wrote in his autobiography that the best thing about A&R men like Don Law is "they kept their fucking mouths shut and they left the musicians to work it out and let the artists be artists.") "Singing the Blues" comes out in 1956, goes #1 Country and even makes the Top 20 Pop songs. If you're Marty Robbins, this is great, right? But then Guy Mitchell puts out a cover that sounds like he's got a Yankee Doodle feather up his ass the whole time he's singing, and it goes #1 Pop, selling three to five times as many copies, a difference of millions of records and millions of dollars. Does Guy Mitchell deserve those sales just because his product has a bigger marketing budget and his genre receives more attention from the media? How many times do you have to hear his record all over the radio before saying, "Well, if more people want to buy it that way, I can make it that way"?

In January of 1957, Marty Robbins went to New York City to record in the same studio as Guy Mitchell, with Guy Mitchell's arranger and session leader, Ray Coniff. Marty walked out of the session with "A White Sport Coat (And a Pink Carnation)," which hit #2 Pop and would remain the biggest hit of his entire career had he not gone full Hollywood cowboy on "El Paso" two years later. It's important to note the instrumentation on "A White Sport Coat" is identical to other 1957 singles commonly cited as early examples of the Nashville Sound. Country fans who thoughtlessly use the term as shorthand for "pop country with strings and/or a vocal chorus" probably do place this record in that category but those interested in a practical definition of the Nashville Sound should spend time comparing it to the records coming out of Owen Bradley's studio the same year. The differences you'll notice lie in a collection of recording techniques and production practices standardized by Owen Bradley and his favorite Nashville studio musicians during the 1950s and 1960s. That is the only sensible definition of the "Nashville Sound." One reason it's important to adopt this definition is it does not limit itself to pop country, since the Nashville Sound was never limited to any one genre or subgenre of music.

As the Nashville Sound took hold in the mid-to-late 1950s, coinciding with rock & roll's shake up of the country music industry, Webb Pierce began to experiment with recording both rock and country material. It seems he was acutely aware of the potential for controversy, since all his singles from this period that feature fiddle or steel guitar do not feature a string section or vocal chorus and vice versa. Webb's 1956 recording of "Any Old Time" kicks off with Dale Potter and Tommy Jackson screaming their fiddles at each other over a chugging honky-tonk rhythm like two freight trains racing toward a cliff, so that's obviously a country song. Two months later, Webb's first stab at rock music, "Teenage Boogie" (later seemingly ripped off by Marc Bolan for T-Rex's "I Love to Boogie"), features the Jordanaires on background vocals—no steel guitar, no fiddle—so that's obviously a rock song. Every other song on the session (like "We'll Find a Way," recorded only a matter of minutes from "Teenage Boogie") was country, complete with fiddle and/or steel. This rule of instrumentation held hard and fast for Webb Pierce. Despite the title of "Honky Tonk Song" and the fact that the Jordanaires were there to sing the words "honky tonk" a hundred times in the background, the presence of a vocal chorus forbade use of fiddle or steel, making it a rock song about honky-tonks. Though fiddle players and vocal choruses were booked to work on the same sessions, they were never used on the same single. So either "the Nashville Sound" was a switch in the studio they flicked on and off between takes depending on the genre or all of these recordings are examples of the Nashville Sound.

Let's play a guessing game. Everyone is familiar with Bobby Helms' recording of "Jingle Bell Rock." Listen to it again while considering what genre you'd call it if the lyrics were about any topic other than Christmas. Perhaps it's too difficult to separate the song from a lifetime of associating it with a holiday. Try the same exercise with Bobby's previous single, "My Special Angel." It was recorded by the same musicians in the same room as "Jingle Bell Rock." What genre would you call that one? Here's a hint: both singles came out in 1957 . . . after being recorded in Owen Bradley's studio . . . That's right, "My Special Angel" and "Jingle Bell Rock" are both country songs! Or, at least, Paul Cohen at Decca decided to pretend they were. These and many other Nashville Sound records were promoted and sold as country product, even though they were intentionally created to appeal to pop music consumers. That is why you can put "My Special Angel" on a playlist of 1950s pop music, play it at a crowded party and not one person will ask why you tried to sneak a lone country song on to the playlist, which is exactly what would happen if you tried doing the same thing with "Just a Little Lonesome" from Bobby Helms' previous session. "Just a Little Lonesome" is an unmistakable country song, complete with steel guitar and honky-tonk piano. Even though it doesn't have a string section or background singers, it's also an example of the Nashville Sound, if we use the definition that applies to all of Webb Pierce's mid-to-late '50s singles, the definition that explains the difference between Marty Robbins recording in New York City and Marty Robbins recording in Nashville: it's an example of the collection of recording techniques and production practices standardized by Owen Bradley and his favorite Nashville studio musicians during the 1950s and 1960s.

Even those who refuse to let go of ahistorical and uninformed concepts of the Nashville Sound have no choice but to acknowledge Owen Bradley as its primary catalyst. Remember when Ernest Tubb talked about using strings and a vocal chorus as "a novelty" in 1951, two years after *Billboard* created the Country & Western chart? Owen Bradley played organ and produced the session at Castle. The strings went on a version of "Kentucky Waltz" for the record's A-side, and the B-side was "Strange Little Girl" featuring the Anita Kerr Singers, who Owen signed to Decca around this time, five years before the Jordanaires ever sang with Elvis Presley. Novel though it may have been, relegated to the B-side as it was, "Strange Little Girl" became a Top 10 Country & Western hit, making it the first successful example of "1950s pop country from Nashville with strings or a vocal chorus." Using a sensible definition of the Nashville Sound, no recording from Castle qualifies because they didn't yet have the rooms or equipment necessary to create and record its complex dynamics.

◇   ◇   ◇

The dynamic range of an instrument comprises the span from quietest to loudest tones it can produce. If you tap a snare drum head with a drumstick as lightly as possible, then hit it as hard as you can, the extreme difference in resulting loudness is the snare drum's dynamic range. Prior to the invention of the piano, sometime around the year 1700, keyboard instruments built for concert performance were limited to pipe organs and variations on the harpsichord. Neither instrument offers much dynamic range, meaning any individual tone sounded on a pipe organ or harpsichord will be roughly equivalent in loudness, regardless of how much force is or isn't applied by the musician. There's nothing stopping anyone from playing the beginning of "Moonlight Sonata" on a pipe organ but, it being the loudest instrument on the planet, it would sound ridiculous and convey none of the subtlety intended by the composer. Similarly, Keith Jarrett's pulsating *Köln Concert* would not be one of the best-selling jazz albums ever had he chosen to play a harpsichord rather than a piano, which was deliberately invented to introduce dynamic range to keyboard instruments. "Harpsichord with soft and loud" is the literal English translation of Bartolomeo Cristofori's initial design, soon abbreviated to *pianoforte*, meaning "soft loud." (Because of how quickly his creation evolved, we now refer to the original design as *fortepiano* to distinguish it from modern pianos.) Pressing a key on Cristofori's piano caused a small hammer to strike a string inside the instrument with a variable level of force, determined by the force of the key press. This required intricate construction, which set a high price tag on early pianos, and they were affordable only to the ruling class, like Cristofori's benefactors, the rich and powerful Médici family. For nearly the first hundred years of its existence, piano belonged exclusively to society's financial elite and musicians they funded or favored. Then came the Industrial Revolution, which made pianos easier and less expensive to manufacture, even with updates widening the design to eighty-eight keys, thus providing the full range of a standard orchestra, from the lowest note on a contrabassoon to the highest note on a piccolo. And what composer wouldn't kill to have a miniature orchestra on call 24/7 to try out every idea that comes up in the process of writing a symphony? Increased access to this dynamic instrument, able to roar out chords and sing single-note phrases (even simultaneously, if you like), coincides with the beginning of classical music's Romantic era as composers became more adventurous and their music more complicated, more personal, more emotional.

Of course, once pianos became affordable to the general public in the 1800s, they were also used to play other kinds of music. Country singer Loretta Lynn once summed up the difference between fiddle and violin by saying "a fiddle is a fiddle but a whole buncha fiddles is a violin." Well, in much the same way, "pie-ann-uh" became something very different to poor individuals in the United States who didn't have "a whole buncha fiddles" at their beck and call. Following several centuries of classist and racist exclusion, the expressive power of an orchestra was handed over to the people. Within a hundred years, calloused fingers created completely new genres, like ragtime and vaudeville, both major influences heard in pop, rock, jazz and country music to this day. Any musician with access to a piano gained the ability to compose and arrange for a full band on an instrument that could be used to show each band member their part without requiring anyone involved to be able to read sheet music. So, pianos showed up in country music as soon as they showed up in the country. Nobody's entirely sure where the term "honky-tonk" came from but it could be a modified form of "honkatonk," which was probably an onomatopoeic reference to piano played with a heavy backbeat, as it had to be played in order to be heard in the loud and lowly drinking establishments everyone eventually started calling honky-tonks, where pianos went long stretches without any tuning whatsoever and generally suffered a level of physical abuse unknown by instruments uptown. Rather than mangle popular melodies attempting single-note runs on an out of pitch instrument, honky-tonk players favored a heavy rhythmic approach with many chords to help disguise or even incorporate the dissonance of any warped individual tones, the way Owen Bradley plays piano on Webb Pierce's "Honky Tonk Song."

If one were to sum up Owen Bradley's whole philosophy of sound in a word, it would be "dynamic." By the time Patsy Cline cut "Walkin' After Midnight" at 804 16th Avenue in late 1956, Owen had begun receiving an Associate Producer label credit for his work in Paul Cohen sessions. "Walkin' After Midnight" was not Patsy Cline's most dynamic hit but it was her first and she had no others until 1961, after she was finally released from a bad contract with 4 Star Records in California and Owen gained full control over Patsy's sessions. As soon as he was free to select her material and record it the way he wanted, Owen produced "I Fall to Pieces." Because it's a shuffle, the bass and drums in "I Fall to Pieces" are fairly static—they begin and end with the song, remaining at the same loudness throughout—while other instruments, such as the piano and steel guitar, find little pockets of space to inject dynamic splashes of sound. The static elements are there to provide a constant frame of reference for the dynamic elements to weave in and out of the recording. When this is done correctly, it holds our attention and keeps us looking forward to whatever may happen next. That fluttery little stumble half the instruments take after Patsy sings the title in every chorus is what Nashville session musicians called a "syncopation." (Note that there are several types of syncopation and many classically trained musicians would dispute the Nashville usage of the term.

Nearly none of the A-Team players were classically trained.) This word shares a Latin root with "swoon" and was initially used to refer to the process of dropping syllables from multiple words in order to form contractions, like how the "o" and "u" are syncopated from "you all" to create "y'all." In musical applications, a syncopated rhythm disrupts or toys with the established rhythm of a song. You could think of the syncopation in "I Fall to Pieces" as grabbing the song and shaking so that everything momentarily . . . falls to pieces. It forces a brief seven-note riff into the song's 4/4 rhythm. This shouldn't work at all, but it becomes the musical hook, a dynamic element keeping us ready and waiting for whatever comes next in the song, even and especially if we've heard it a thousand times. Owen Bradley loved a good syncopation. Really, he'd use any kind of musical cue to play into the theme of a song. He was sometimes as blatant and literal as the song title but could also be more abstract, as in Patsy Cline's following two singles. For "She's Got You," the musical cue is Floyd Cramer's twinkly piano, presumably representative of the love trance some other "she" has placed upon Patsy's bewitched ex-lover. In "Crazy," it's the dizzy, off-kilter way every instrument takes turns falling behind and catching up to the beat; even the drums seem to subtly falter here and there. In both of these songs, you can hear Bob Moore's bass playing a much more dynamic role than in "Walkin' After Midnight."

Those looking for the original line in the sand of the great "does modern country sound too much like popular music?" debate will find it in the beat. Also commonly called "rhythm," as in rhythm & blues, a heavy beat accompanying or, especially, in place of a melody was all-but-guaranteed to piss off country music purists in the first half of the twentieth century. And God forbid you use a backbeat, accenting the 2's and 4's to make the beat stand out even more. This is the rhythmic space between notes of a bass line where upright bassists of pro-backbeat country bands slap the strings and fingerboard like a percussion instrument. Backbeat is one of the specific problems many traditionalists (and racists) had with Bob Wills using drums in the 1930s and 1940s, since drums were then primarily associated with Black musical forms, like popular swing jazz. This is the specific controversy Hank Williams tried to skirt by not having a drummer in the band, instead having a rhythm guitarist relax his grip on a barre chord to deaden the strings and forcefully strum a backbeat on the 2 and 4. You can hear this technique mimicking a brushed snare from Hank's first hit, "Move It On Over" in 1947, all the way through to the last single released during his lifetime. Hank wanted a heavy rhythm but didn't want the grief that came with putting a drummer in a country band. For all the flak he caught over his backbeat anyway, he may as well have hired a drummer. Even into the 1960s, when country fans referred to popular music's "negative" influence on their beloved genre, one of the things they were talking about was any use of backbeat, with or without drums. Prior to Nashville native Buddy Harman becoming the staff drummer on the *Grand Ole Opry* in 1959, there was no staff drummer at the *Grand Old Opry* because drums weren't allowed on the *Opry* stage. (This rule was broken several times by various people before the ban was officially lifted.) By the time Buddy took the *Opry* gig, he'd played on hits for Brenda Lee, the Everly Brothers, Elvis Presley, you name 'em. His first session work was at Castle in 1952, backing Moon Mullican on Boudleaux Bryant's drumming pun, "Sugar Beet." Even after taking the *Opry* gig, Buddy continued working sessions for everyone from major labels down to little indies, like Starday. His instrument being so controversial, it's quite illuminating to observe the various ways he was asked to play by various producers. For example, Buddy's iconic drum part on the Everly Brothers' "Cathy's Clown" was created in 1960 with the help of a cutting-edge tape looping machine on loan from RCA's New York City studio. Bill Porter (the guy credited with giving RCA's Nashville studio its "sound") manually turned the machine on and off while the band played to create a delay effect live-to-tape and make Buddy sound like two drummers doubling a part. Years later, Bill told the Country Music Hall of Fame how Don Everly had always instructed Buddy Harman to "play them drums loud, man, and hard!" RCA sessions under the control of Chet Atkins typically came with different instructions. Chet usually wanted the drums audible and not a bit louder. It's possible—if not probable—Chet is the unnamed producer in a story Buddy used to tell about being asked to play softer and softer until he finally pulled out a handkerchief and started hitting the cymbals with it, asking if that was soft enough.

To some fans, the *Grand Ole Opry* hiring Buddy to play drums in 1959 meant they'd sold out and gone pop country. To everyone else, it just meant country music now had drums in it. In the wake of the *Opry*'s decision, many artists felt more freedom to experiment with drums. But, of course, the decision was only made because of how many artists already had. By 1959, George Jones, Hank Snow and Ray Price were all regularly using flagrant drums on record and had done so for at least a couple of years. Most Ernest Tubb records from 1953 forward have a lone drum, usually either a brushed and barely there snare or a closed hi-hat. Take a song like 1955's "Have You Seen (My Boogie Woogie Baby)." The title probably caused some fans to wonder if Tubb had switched sides in the rock & roll war but whatever the drummer on the session played that day is completely buried in the mix. The drum on Tubb's next session is audible but just barely. On "The Yellow Rose of Texas" it pushes the backbeat only an inch or so further than Hank Williams had done with guitars alone. Ray Price records are perhaps the most interesting case study of drums in 1950s country music. His first singles came out in 1952 with no drums, though the piano player on his cover of "Don't Let the Stars Get in Your Eyes" does slip into a heavy backbeat rhythm with the left hand during a honky-tonk-style solo. Ray had no major singles in 1953. "Much Too Young to Die" from 1954 has exactly three snare hits in it, as a ticking clock special effect beneath the lyric "time is passing, passing, passing us on the fly." (We're not counting the accidental hit you can hear when the drummer mistakenly thinks he's at that same part in the song.) Ray had no major singles in 1955. There is an unmistakable drum played with brushes on his first big hit of 1956, "Run Boy," but the song is also a waltz, in 3/4 time, so there's no backbeat to upset anyone. Then we reach "Crazy Arms," the country shuffle which went #1 for five months and sent a whole section of the genre in a new direction. After analyzing his previous records, straining to hear any hint of percussion, "Crazy Arms" sounds like there's a drum circle on it. Yet there are no drums, not one. What you're hearing is a combination of the old honky-tonk acoustic guitar trick plus an electric guitar clicking around on muted notes adjacent to the bass line, creating something very close to what would soon be called tic-tac bass. Ray's next big hit of the year does the same thing; there are not any drums on "I've Got a New Heartache," just a ton of tick-tick-ticking sounds made by stringed instruments. By 1957, Ray had become the king of dance-hall country and no longer needed to tiptoe around the beat. His big hit of the year was "My Shoes Keep Walking Back to You," another #1 record, this time with Buddy Harman playing the drums loud, man, and hard.

◇   ◇   ◇

Tic-tac bass is not an instrument. It's a sound created by the interplay of two instruments, the big, booming notes of an upright bass doubled by the clicking, palm-muted strings of a baritone electric guitar. (Technically, tic-tac was first played with an electric six-string bass, but Nashville musicians colloquially referred to it as a baritone.) Many books about recording music in the first half of the twentieth century, contain stories about how difficult it was to get a good standup bass sound in the studio. There were several points in the signal chain where they just didn't yet have sufficient technology to create or capture a satisfactory low end, so everyone experimented to find different workarounds. After moving to Nashville from Alabama in 1960, bassist Henry Strzelecki did a few sessions with Owen Bradley and Henry said even at that time Owen was still moving the microphone for the standup bass to different places in the room depending on the key of a song. That's what they had to do to get a good sound and if the weather outside made the air in the studio too humid, the bass was probably going to sound like shit no matter where they put the mic. But by the time Henry came to town, everyone was using tic-tac bass to help mask the problem. Instead of wasting time trying to capture a perfect balance of punchy attack and huge timbre from one instrument, tic-tac allowed the big bass to bring a fat low end and it was fine if the tone got a little muddy because the picked electric provided a defined attack when doubling the notes. If it was humid outside, the electric could pick out additional notes to create a busier sound on top of the standup bass, as heard on "Crazy Arms." Virtually everyone recording upright bass in any genre of music took notice of the Nashville Sound method for creating and capturing low end. These sounds, developed by Nashville musicians while recording country and pop hits, regularly reached Top 40 radio and influenced artists around the world. In 1961, after Owen Bradley gained full control over Patsy Cline's sessions and the tropes of the Nashville Sound were well defined, Owen had Patsy cut a new, poppier version of "Walkin' After Midnight." Note the prominent tic-tac bass, toy organ and background vocal arrangement. A few months later, the Beach Boys recorded their first single. The sound Brian Wilson landed on in just a few short years owes a clear debt to Owen Bradley's work with Patsy Cline, Brenda Lee and other pop or crossover artists.

The intro of Brenda Lee's "Heart in Hand" teases a standard 1950s pop verse before her voice stomps into center stage and it sounds as if she's actually planning to rip out her own heart with her hand. She sings the song like it's trying to kill her and, indeed, the music almost seems to sadistically toy with her, providing a place to stand only to disappear from beneath her feet, occasionally lifting her head but only to force her to look up and take note of how far she's fallen. Near the end, just before Brenda slips into a recitation, the violin takes over her vocal melody as if it knows she can't last much longer. Then the music drops out completely in order to come crashing back with her final note. These are dynamic choices. This is the Nashville Sound, produced by Owen Bradley in 1962. The biggest hits of Brenda's career were all produced by Owen in the early 1960s and there is nothing country about any of them, which is why (following Owen's promotion to head of Decca's Nashville division) the label did not ship the records to country radio, they were not played on country radio nor were they country hits. The genre lines were not even blurry enough to cross over to country radio after becoming major pop hits, as often happened in this era. Yet Brenda Lee's brand of the Nashville Sound was as influential upon the city's production of country music and other genres as everything else Owen Bradley did. Records like "Heart in Hand," "I'm Sorry," "That's All You Gotta Do" and "I Want to Be Wanted" are examples of why the Nashville Sound cannot be summed up as some bland, lifeless era in music, whether country or otherwise. Sure, there were bland and lifeless records created with Nashville Sound techniques, as is true of any new, popular "sound" in the history of the record industry, but its main architect and innovator made vibrant recordings that are still considered dynamic even by modern standards. Owen Bradley and his Nashville Sound cannot be reduced to or blamed for the rest of the industry's commercially motivated attempts to piggyback on his masterpieces.

Compare Owen's work on "Heart in Hand" with what Chet Atkins did the same year on Skeeter Davis' "The End of the World." This is a fair comparison to make. These songs have very similar chord progressions. Both have a bridge and a recitation. They share lyrical themes. Floyd Cramer, Buddy Harman, Bob Moore and the Anita Kerr Singers perform on both records. It's easy to imagine two producers working in the same city at the same time with the same musicians on two very similar songs about the same thing would end up making a somewhat similar product. But the standard 1950s pop intro on "The End of the World" is never subverted or transcended. It never becomes anything else. For a song about someone who's surprised the entire planet hasn't treated her broken heart like a stop sign, "End of the World" is almost military in its steady, rhythmic persistence. (The piano, in particular, is truly relentless. Focusing on that instrument while listening may single-handedly ruin this song for you.) The closest thing to a surprise happens when a pedal steel gently insinuates itself into the mix a couple of times. The closest thing to any kind of tension happens a little over halfway through, when all the instruments (even the piano) pause to give the march a ten-second rest . . . before starting right back up again. Where Brenda Lee sings "Heart in Hand" like she's gonna die because there's an Owen Bradley arrangement behind her, Skeeter Davis sings "End of the World" like she swallowed two Klonopin because there's a Chet Atkins arrangement behind her. When Skeeter delivers the recitation, it sounds like a teacher has asked her to read out loud in front of a classroom. If you stripped the vocal from the record, everything else would be just as suitable for a song about a little kid's pet goldfish swimming around in its bowl. It's all subdued. Buddy Harman is definitely using brushes instead of sticks on his snare and Chet probably would have replaced the drums with a metronome if he thought he could get away with it. "End of the World" is heartache music for people who've either never had their heart broken or can't handle being reminded of it. This safe, commercial product was also a #2 Pop hit. Comparatively, "Heart in Hand" is an emotionally dangerous record, which could easily ambush a person who's had their heart broken and make it impossible for them to leave their house that day. It charted at #14. Since RCA shipped Skeeter Davis' "End of the World" to country radio and promoted it as though it were a country song, it also hit #2 Country. In fact, "End of the World" was such a big hit Owen Bradley had Brenda Lee record a version in 1963. (It's possible this was partly a response to how many people called out the change in Skeeter Davis' sound after Owen had a #1 Pop record in 1960 with Brenda Lee's string-heavy "I'm Sorry" and Skeeter's records were all of a sudden drenched in strings.) Owen made no radical changes to the song structure or instrumentation for Brenda's "End of the World." He even had Buddy Harman use brushes on his drums. But this was no military affair. Owen brought the tempo way down and made all the instruments take turns lagging ever-so-slightly behind the beat. Brenda, in particular, comes in almost aggressively late to deliver most of her lines. The whole song drags, as if the world in which it exists may be slowing as it comes to an end. Pay close attention to the piano part and, unlike the monotonous slog of Chet's record, you'll hear the individual notes played with varying force, like a child still learning to play scales or a record slightly wobbling on a damaged turntable. That is the sound of heartache. The record was not a hit.

Skeeter Davis cut her follow-up single to "End of the World" in the same room with many of the same musicians but one enormous difference: Anita Kerr, who had arranged only the strings for "End of the World," was given full control of the session for "I'm Saving My Love." Anita once told Henry Strzelecki how frustrated she was with the major labels in Nashville. They wanted her vocal group on sessions and wanted her to arrange string parts, but nobody would officially hire her in an A&R position and allow her to become a real producer. They let her run a session every now and then, even gave her label credit sometimes, but nobody would give her the full-time job. A few years after "I'm Saving My Love," she seems to have sued her way out of the Anita Kerr Singers' contract with RCA, broken up the group and moved to Los Angeles to see if it was any better out there. There's no telling why RCA let her produce this session, maybe Chet Atkins called in sick, but the difference between "I'm Saving My Love" and "End of the World" is mind-blowing. And either both records are examples of the Nashville Sound, or the Nashville Sound is just what we call the Skeeter Davis singles we think are boring. The influence of Owen Bradley on the dynamics of "I'm Saving My Love" is undeniable from the moment the song starts. Everything opens with a bolero-influenced drum breakdown, meaning Buddy Harman gets to actually hit his snare a few times before the verse falls into reverie. Floyd Cramer's piano part is lifted directly from what he played two years earlier on Patsy Cline's "She's Got You," so we must have another sort of trance on our hands. Although it's clear from the jumpy beginning Skeeter won't be going on a zombie walk like "End of the World," it does sound like she's out on a bit of a melancholy stroll, dwelling on a past love. The chorus then skips over to an entirely separate melody, strong enough that the record could easily have been taken apart into two different songs. When Skeeter starts singing about time, not that she's waited but how long she's waited, it's almost like she's now singing about a different person, a future person, the soulmate she has awaited. For the first time in the song, another voice joins Skeeter's and it's her own voice, overdubbed, doubling her, mirroring her, beginning to pull her from this sad spell into the future, where the bolero builds . . . She briefly returns to the verse and sings the old words again but now with new meaning, not faith but knowledge of what she's foreseen. Then the bolero pulls her forward in time, toward the second voice, and the song ends as it began, only now Skeeter doesn't have to sing it alone. This is a piece with movement, a journey. The record was produced by Anita Kerr not to play it safe but for maximum dramatic effect in an attempt to craft a record the way Owen Bradley would. It's also a pop record, which RCA shipped and promoted as country. It hit the Country Top 10 and barely missed the Pop Top 40; a decent commercial success but much less of one than "End of the World."

Many of Owen Bradley's first call session musicians, the original Nashville A-Team, regularly "led" countless sessions for other producers in Nashville, doing uncredited production work the way they'd learned from Owen. When Owen first booked guitarists Grady Martin and Hank Garland for a Webb Pierce session at Castle in 1951, they cut Webb Pierce's first #1 Country song, "Wondering." Over the next ten years, either Grady Martin or Hank Garland played lead guitar on close to 100 percent of Webb Pierce's sessions and it's not outrageous to guess they probably played lead on more than 50 percent of all the Top 10 Country hits recorded by everyone in Nashville during the same period. Above any other musicians, these two set the tone for guitar in the Nashville Sound. If Garland's career hadn't been ended by a car accident in 1961, it's likely he would have gone down in history alongside Bob Moore, Grady Martin and Harold Bradley as one of the most recorded musicians and uncredited producers in history. You may know his name as the guitarist on Marty Robbins' "El Paso" but Grady Martin is also one of the most prolific uncredited producers of all time. When you see Grady listed as a guitarist on a session for any producer other than Owen Bradley, chances are very good Grady did a lot more than play guitar. Johnny Horton's first #1 hit, "When It's Springtime in Alaska (It's Forty Below)," would have been cut in waltz time if Grady hadn't changed it to 4/4. Don Law, credited producer of Horton's second #1 hit, "The Battle of New Orleans," was not even on the property the day Grady led that session. Don Law relied on Grady to such a degree he would bring Grady into Columbia Records' office whenever managers, publishers or agents were pitching a potential new artist. They auditioned for Grady, not Don.

Bob Moore was first hired to play bass in an Owen Bradley session in the year 1950 and went on to play nearly every session Patsy Cline ever did. He was also an uncredited producer for dozens, if not hundreds, of other artists. Listen to his work on Roy Orbison's "Running Scared," recorded in 1961. According to Harold Bradley, producer Fred Foster normally only paid attention to Roy Orbison's vocal and left the studio musicians to handle everything else. It seems "Running Scared" did have a bit more involvement from Fred than usual, though, because he had to pull rank and stop Bob from trying to force the song into a steady rhythm rather than the series of crescendos we know from the finished version. The lyrics have Orbison worrying himself into a state of near-panic over his lover's ex showing up on date night to try and get her back. For whatever reason, maybe there's only one place to hang out in this town, he seems certain this confrontation will take place. The problem is he doesn't know what his girlfriend will do. Will she stay with him? Will she return to the ex? This is his swirling and building turmoil throughout the song. From the string arrangement alone, it is obvious Bob Moore had worked thousands of Owen Bradley sessions. Bob's strings lay out for nearly the entire first minute, until Orbison really starts to get himself worked up, then the strings join in with the other instruments to mimic the pulse of his pounding heart, as all his thoughts and feelings circle this one fear, approaching the moment of truth. Suddenly, the song breaks open and the instruments scatter as, there, standing in the cleared space: it's the ex. There are two direct references in the lyrics to this rival's physical presence and each is trailed by high siren calls from the strings, a sonic representation of the all-consuming fear Orbison has anticipated from the beginning of the song. This is identical to the way important characters in an opera may have recurring musical themes or motifs accompanying their presence, especially when in epic conflict with other characters who have their own themes and motifs. This technique was certainly learned from Owen Bradley.

◇   ◇   ◇

In the academic debate over what constitutes pop, country, or pop country music, much has been made of how supposedly impossible it is to define what's called the "twang" element in country music, which is a ridiculous notion. Remember when you were a kid and you put a rubber band around two fingers then plucked it with your other hand? That's twang. The sounds we associate with country music came from poor people working out techniques to produce art using cheap, low-quality, often damaged, sometimes straight-up broken instruments. For many country fans in the mid-twentieth century, major label producers like Chet Atkins, Paul Cohen and Steve Sholes making pop records with finely tuned piano and calling it country music was tantamount to selling out the genre by returning the instrument to how it sounded when the lower classes had no access to it. It came across like some rich assholes believed country music sounded broken and were trying to fix it. But the music wasn't broken. It was bent just the way country fans like it.

Floyd Cramer's first notable job in the music business was playing piano for Webb Pierce when Webb was still on the *Louisiana Hayride*. The first time Floyd went to Nashville was for a Webb Pierce recording session produced by Owen Bradley, which is where Floyd met Chet Atkins, who was also hired to play on the session. Owen's chosen instrument being central to the Nashville Sound for reasons that should by now be self-evident, after Chet began regularly leading sessions for RCA, he needed a piano player in order to keep doing things the way Owen did them. So, in 1955, Chet talked Floyd Cramer into moving to Nashville and becoming a studio musician. This is how Floyd came to play on "Heartbreak Hotel," Elvis Presley's first single for RCA and his first record to sell a million copies. Like Chet himself at the time, Floyd was not an exclusive employee of RCA and other producers in town began to book him. He soon became a favorite of Owen Bradley's and played sessions for Brenda Lee and Patsy Cline. Floyd was another person Chet Atkins frequently credited for much of what people mistakenly believed was Chet's "sound." Chet consistently asked Floyd's input on creative decisions, arrangements, etc. But we must give credit to Chet for handing Floyd a technique he would use for the rest of his life, to great fame and fortune.

Don Robertson, the writer of a song Hank Locklin was scheduled to record, had played piano on the demo tape in an unusual style that Chet wanted on the single, so he gave the tape to Floyd

Cramer and told him to figure out how to replicate it. Floyd listened to the tape, copped Don's basic method and then made significant modifications to clean up and exaggerate the effect. The result came to be called slip-note piano, debuted on Hank Locklin's #1 Country and Top 10 Pop hit, "Please Help Me, I'm Falling." Floyd's playing on this record in 1960 was so influential, listening from this side of history it sounds less like the revelation it was and more like someone merely playing country piano the correct way. What you're hearing is something Floyd always described as "an intentional error." On the way to playing "correct" (or consonant, in-key) notes of a chord, he briefly strikes "wrong" (or dissonant, "blue") notes, typically a full step away from the destination rather than the more common slight slur of a half step. In other words, slip-note is a little touch of wrong on the way to making something sound right. You could think of it as a method to reintroduce some twang to a finely tuned piano. Like exploitation of dynamics, syncopation or allowing tic-tac bass to become slightly out of sync with itself for dramatic effect, slip-note piano is another Nashville Sound trope that playfully toys with our expectations and keeps us anticipating whatever may happen next. After Locklin's record became such a huge hit, Floyd leaned all the way into slip-note and released an instrumental record featuring the method. Written to showcase his new trick, nearly every chord of "Last Date" contains slipped notes. The record barely missed the Country Top 10 but it became a #2 Pop hit and cemented slip-note's place in the Nashville Sound.

A year after hitting big with "Last Date," Floyd was in his first session for Loretta Lynn, which was her first session produced by Owen Bradley. Owen would remain Loretta's producer from 1961 all the way into the 1980s, producing all her greatest hits, including "Coal Miner's Daughter." Everything she recorded with Owen is an example of the Nashville Sound and every second of it is country music, as if anything featuring the twang of Loretta's voice could ever be anything else. In that first session, they cut "Success," on which you can hear Harold Bradley and Bob Moore's tic-tac bass and Floyd Cramer's slip-note piano alongside Cecil Brower and Tommy Jackson on fiddles. When Owen signed Loretta in 1961, he signed a country singer and produced her as such, which is why her Nashville Sound includes traditional country instruments and arrangements where Brenda Lee's Nashville Sound does not.

◇   ◇   ◇

While the presence of a Nashville-style vocal chorus is not the difference between a Nashville Sound record and some other kind, it can be the difference between a great record and an unlistenable one. For example, once you notice what the Jordanaires are doing behind the guitar solos on Elvis Presley's "Hound Dog," well, suffice to say it's not many people's favorite part of the song. However, just like records produced by Chet Atkins, vocal groups cannot be written off completely. When they're great, they're great. But when it's bad, it's the fucking worst. One common criticism applied to both the Jordanaires and the Anita Kerr Singers is they often sound like a bunch of mooing cows, which is not an egregious claim. The problem is background vocal parts live or die by their arrangements and these were typically left unwritten until in a session to record songs the backup singers had never heard. There were a lot of challenges with creating art on a production line and this was arguably the biggest one. When the singers weren't working from a good arrangement, it can be impossible to ignore. For better or worse, these vocal groups were used a lot in the Nashville Sound era. But one of the strangest things about country purists who view this as an invasion of pop music elements is they never seem to ask where pop music got it from . . .

The Jordanaires were a gospel group formed in the late 1940s in Springfield, Missouri. After getting a record deal with Capitol and joining the *Grand Ole Opry* in 1949, they started showing up as background vocalists whenever major country artists like Ernest Tubb or Red Foley wanted to record some gospel music. Elvis Presley, an enormous fan of country and gospel, immediately fell in love with the Jordanaires' sound and swore to use them as his backing singers if he ever got a major record deal, which he did in 1956. The first time he went in the studio for RCA, the day he recorded "Heartbreak Hotel," Elvis asked if he could have the Jordanaires in the following day's session. Well, the Jordanaires were signed to Capitol and Presley's session leader, the musician tasked with hiring the other musicians, just so happened to be Chet Atkins, who just so happened to've recently signed a different gospel group to RCA. Chet was extremely confident that whatever single was released from this session was going to be a massive hit. Elvis was obviously on his way to the top, which is why RCA acquired him from Sun in a bidding war. The huge price RCA paid to acquire Elvis meant they were sure to throw their full promotional weight behind his first single for the label. So, probably figuring Elvis wouldn't even know the difference, Chet hired only Gordon Stoker from the Jordanaires and had him sing alongside Chet's newly hired gospel group, in order to associate the RCA act with Presley's inevitable hit. But Elvis did know the difference and did not appreciate Chet's ruse. Still, he cut a #1 record for his new label. When Chet tried the same trick on Presley's next session a few months later, the results were disastrous. Everyone got stuck doing failed takes of one song over and over and they never even got a complete usable take. Producer Steve Sholes had to manufacture Elvis' second #1 hit by splicing together tape of two different attempts at "I Want You, I Need You, I Love You." Elvis wouldn't even return to Nashville for his next session. To keep him happy, RCA flew all of the Jordanaires to the New York City studio where Elvis cut his next single. Both sides of the record went #1. And the reason the Jordanaires' part on "Don't Be Cruel" is so much better than their part on "Hound Dog" is that the B-side was recorded earlier in the session, prior to the point when one of the other studio musicians had to leave and Gordon Stoker was moved to piano, where he couldn't sing with the rest of his group on the A-side.

Regardless, this was Elvis Presley's best-selling single in the United States ever, so the Jordanaires sang on nearly everything he recorded until 1970. It was largely the gravitational pull of Elvis in all commercial genres of music which caused the Nashville vocal chorus to be branded a "pop" sound when it became a standard feature of Music Row sessions and a trope of the Nashville Sound.

◇   ◇   ◇

There was a big market for what Chet Atkins did with the Nashville Sound, just like there's always a big market for the "safer," watered-down alternative to any trend. RCA and other major labels didn't even have to go out of their way to create this alternative, just like the leading brand of soy sauce doesn't need to build a whole new factory to make lower sodium soy sauce. It's the same exact sauce they're already making with some of the salt taken out and sold in a different color bottle. If that's what some people want, no problem, take out some salt and get it on the shelf. It's not fair to say, as many do, that Chet Atkins hated country music. He made a business decision to provide the low sodium Nashville Sound and he caught so much shit for it he even apologized. In a 1976 issue of *Rolling Stone*, after saying he hoped country music would never lose its whole identity, Chet said, "I apologized for anything I did in taking it too far uptown, which I sometimes did because we were just trying to sell records." Chet does deserve some credit for productions most country fans enjoy, like Hank Locklin's "Please Help Me I'm Falling" and Don Gibson's "Oh, Lonesome Me." When other major label suits in country music were wary of signing a Black man to a record deal, Chet took a chance on Charley Pride, as unadulterated a country voice as you will ever hear. It is absolutely not Chet Atkins' fault so many fans, critics and historians have erroneously given him so much of the credit that should rightly have gone to Owen Bradley. All of that being said, it would take a while to tell the stories of every legendary artist who only found lasting success after struggling against and winning their freedom from Chet's one-size-fits-all production methods. Bobby Bare, Waylon Jennings and Porter Wagoner are only a few. Chet Atkins either didn't hear or didn't care to hear when an individual singer wouldn't fit the mold he had in mind for them. Artists did not have that problem with Owen Bradley. He knew country records and pop records are created in the studio, not later, when the label decides it'd be easier to launch a pop product by following the old rock & roll formula of exploiting country music markets. He understood the sauce should be chosen to complement the singer and the song. There are no one-sauce-fits-all solutions, which is a lesson Owen learned near the beginning of his career as a producer.

In December 1950, Eddy Arnold and his band went into RCA's New York City studio and cut a version of Bill Monroe's "Kentucky Waltz." Bill Monroe was signed to Decca, so when someone at his label (probably Paul Cohen) heard Eddy Arnold had cut a Monroe song in a New York City session, they got the bright idea to beat Eddy to the punch by having Monroe do a new version of

"Kentucky Waltz" with the more modern instrumentation Decca assumed would be on Eddy's record. Monroe went to Castle with his mandolin but without his band to record with Owen Bradley's studio guys. You can tell this wasn't a normal Bill Monroe session because they had Farris Coursey there to play drums and Owen Bradley on organ. The results sound a lot like circus music. The best thing captured that day was probably "The Prisoner's Song," but the fact is Bill Monroe just doesn't fit into the arrangements used on the session. His sound is so unique it's unsettling to hear him attempt anything else. Following this failed experiment, Monroe was allowed to run his own sessions, as you can hear on "Dark as the Night, Blue as the Day," recorded in January of 1959 in the Quonset Hut. Those still seeking (or resisting) a practical definition will note the only morsel of Nashville Sound on this tape is the room where it was made because Owen Bradley believed "producing" Bill Monroe meant leaving him and the Blue Grass Boys to do whatever they wanted to do. But none of his other artists were Bill Monroe, which is why nearly everything else Owen worked on after Castle Studios closed is an example of the Nashville Sound.

Most recording sessions of the era came with a set of questions that needed asked and answering ahead of time, like "Is this a country singer or a pop singer?" and "Is this potentially a country hit or potentially a pop hit?" As we've seen, it was often the case the answers weren't exactly either/or. For example, "Don't Touch Me," written by Hank Cochran in 1966, was obviously a country song, dealing as directly with mature emotional and sexual feelings as Kris Kristofferson's "Help Me Make It Through the Night" would do a few years later. By 1966, Hank Cochran had written country hits for Patsy Cline, Ray Price and Johnny PayCheck. He wrote this song for his girlfriend, Jeannie Seely, and she recorded it in her first session for Monument, produced by Fred Foster with Floyd Cramer on piano, Charlie McCoy on bass and Buddy Harman on drums. Just to recap, this was a producer we already know focused solely on his artist's voice and left the music to the musicians; this was Patsy Cline's piano player, harmonica player and drummer; and this was a song by the author of "She's Got You" and co-author of "I Fall to Pieces." There is no universe where these guys wouldn't try to make "Don't Touch Me" the record they'd have made with Patsy Cline if she didn't die in a plane crash a few years earlier. To be clear, at no point does Jeannie Seely attempt to sing like Patsy. What she does is her own thing and it's great. But the arrangement and production are an undisguised tribute to Owen Bradley's work with Patsy Cline. The prerecording rundown may as well have been a 45 of "I Fall to Pieces" slowed to 33 rpm. As soon as Owen heard Jeannie singing it on the radio, he understood what it was and scheduled a session to cover "Don't Touch Me."

It was obviously a pop song, written by Hank Cochran, who'd by this time written pop hits for Patsy Cline, Eddy Arnold and Burl Ives. The words told of a search for commitment on the dating scene but were phrased simply enough for mass consumption. (For example, the clumsy little lyric "to have you then lose you wouldn't be smart on my part" was probably only there to create a rhyme with the word "sweetheart.") A few years earlier, Owen had signed Wilma Burgess to Decca because he thought her voice possessed a similar quality to Patsy Cline's, in that it wouldn't seem out of place on country or pop radio. Aside from signing to Patsy's record label to work with Patsy's producer, musicians and songwriters, Wilma Burgess had also recently purchased Patsy's old house in Nashville. So, it's safe to assume she didn't miss all of the references to Patsy's sound in the Jeannie Seely record. Now, around the time Owen signed Wilma to Decca, he also sold his studios at 804 16th Avenue to Columbia Records. In 1965, he opened Bradley's Barn, an actual barn converted to a studio on his land outside Nashville. But when he booked the session to cover "Don't Touch Me," even though he had a whole new studio right in his backyard, Owen rented the Quonset Hut from Columbia Records in order to use the same room he'd used with Patsy Cline, in order to make the record he would have made with Patsy if she was still alive to sing the song. It's a testament to the versatility of the Nashville A-Team that several of the same musicians played on both the Jeannie Seely and Wilma Burgess records. Buddy Emmons' pedal steel parts are the most remarkable points of contrast. Behind Jeannie his playing is tasteful but typical, weaving in and out of a slow country song as he'd done on so many others. Behind Wilma, his instrument is barely recognizable. You could easily convince someone they're hearing a theremin or synthesizer, especially since the background vocals sound like they were arranged by Brian Wilson for the *Pet Sounds* sessions. Only this was recorded two months before *Pet Sounds* came out and once we notice the dream sequence rhythm guitars shimmering above the tic-tac bass—tropes used by Owen for a decade at that point—it's maybe time to start asking just how many Owen Bradley–produced records Brian Wilson was listening to in his room. There's honestly no telling what instructions or reference points Owen gave the musicians to get these sounds on "Don't Touch Me." It may have been as simple as telling them to imagine the door to heaven referenced in the lyrics had actually opened up in the middle of the room. Jeannie's country record snuck into the Pop Hot 100 at #85 and went #1 Country everywhere except *Billboard*, where it's possible Wilma's smaller hit cut into Jeannie's action and kept her out of the top position. Wilma's single went #12 Country and did nothing on the Pop chart. Wilma's "Misty Blue," recorded in the same Quonset Hut session as "Don't Touch Me," came out six months later. It was a Top 5 Country song, still nothing on the Pop charts. But the low-sodium version of "Misty Blue" that Chet Atkins produced for Eddy Arnold came out the following year, hit #57 on the Hot 100 and went #3 Country, despite featuring zero sonic elements of country music whatsoever.

It's easy to see how the Nashville Sound and Chet Atkins' role within it came to be so widely misunderstood when Chet's "safer" alternative regularly outsold and out-charted Owen's source material. Like Owen always used to say to Whisperin' Bill Anderson: "Remember, vanilla still outsells all those thirty-one other flavors of ice cream." Chet's commercial success with vanilla, of course, then inspired other producers to create their own iterations, leading to a greater volume of the safer alternative than exists of the original source material. So the takeaway for most casual listeners and critics (and historians who came to town after Owen Bradley left Music Row) wound up as something like "the Nashville Sound is what it was called when record labels tried to sell the most boring version of Frank Sinatra music on country radio," which then led to endless debates over how much pop should be allowed in country, an argument about genre that never had anything at all to do with the production techniques of the Nashville Sound. It's as ignorant as arguing over what genre a guitar is. Genre is determined not by the presence of a guitar but by the way it is used. The Nashville Sound is determined not by the genre of music but by a systematically applied style of record production. It's in the way instruments are arranged, played, mic'd and mixed for a record. These techniques can be and were used for different genres of music. Some producers did use the Nashville Sound to pull country music in a pop direction. But it's just as fair to say Owen Bradley pulled pop music in a country direction both with the far-reaching influence of his work and the work itself.

In the early 1960s, country songwriter Harlan Howard was in a meeting with Owen when Harlan brought up a rock & roll singer he knew who secretly wanted to record country music, only nobody would let him. After listening to a tape, Owen signed Conway Twitty to Decca and became his producer. In 1965, "Together Forever" was released as Conway's first Decca single. You know you're in for undiluted country music when it kicks off pretending to be a cover of Buck Owens' smash hit from the year before, "Together Again." Owen remained Conway's producer until 1979. They recorded more than 30 Top Five Country singles together, twenty of which hit #1. Even as mainstream pop absorbed disco tropes and those influences made their way into the Nashville Sound, many of Conway's hits (like "I See the Want To in Your Eyes") remained unapologetically country. Hell, they were recorded in a Barn. Looking at Owen Bradley's career from beginning to end, we see a journey toward country music, not away from it. Say we're able to forget his co-writing credit on "Night Train to Memphis" and ignore all the early years with Ernest Tubb, Red Foley, Webb Pierce and Hank Williams; pretend he was just cashing paychecks and hated every second of it. Wipe the entire slate clean of everything before he took over at Decca and Owen Bradley still signed a rock singer to help him make country music. He was never interested in trying to force a square peg into a round hole. He was there to serve the artist, the material and the sound. Owen was there to make something iconic and timeless, something cooler than cool.

FIVE

RUN, BULL, RUN

⬦ Hemingway Reports Back from Spain ⬦ Killing Bulls: A Human Tradition ⬦
Sociopolitical Animal Torture on the Iberian Peninsula
⬦ Spain's French Teenager King ⬦ Daredevil Peasants ⬦

Most Americans learn everything they know about bullfighting from Bugs Bunny and Ernest Hemingway. Daffy Duck played at being a matador in the 1947 cartoon *Mexican Joyride* but 1953's *Bully for Bugs* is the one more people remember. It's one of the most-referenced episodes of *Looney Tunes* ever made; the one where Bugs misses the left turn at Albuquerque, says "stop steamin' up my tail!" and "of course, you realize this means war . . ." Allegedly, cartoonist Chuck Jones was drawing a bull for some other clip when Eddie Selzer, head of Warner Brothers Cartoons, walked through the room, noticed what Chuck was drawing and loudly declared he didn't want to see any cartoons about bullfights because bullfights were not funny. Since everyone knew Eddie was always wrong about everything, that was all it took for Chuck and a coworker to book a research trip to Mexico. The cheers and boos of the audience in the finished cartoon were recorded at an actual bullfight but the realism ends there. Not many people would have laughed at a documentary approach. See: Ernest Hemingway.

Every year, a week before Hemingway's birthday in July, the city of Pamplona celebrates San Fermin, a nine-day festival with eight days of bulls. If you've ever seen pictures or video of a "running of the bulls," this is the biggest and most famous one. Most of the people who run with the bulls of San Fermin are tourists. (When Orson Welles said Hemingway ruined Spain by writing about it and sending all those tourists, Orson neglected to point out he was one of them, having first gone to Spain at the age of eighteen after reading Hemingway.) The protagonists of *City Slickers* are introduced as American thrill-seekers when the movie opens on their running with the bulls in Pamplona. After Billy Crystal gets a horn shoved up his ass, the movie follows him and his buddies to a doctor's office. But if the action remained with the run, we'd see the bulls arrive at Pamplona's bullring, where they would be killed in front of an audience later that day. For eight days in a row during San Fermín, there's a running every morning to transport bulls to the stadium for each afternoon's bullfights. A man of Ernest Hemingway's disposition would find pleasure in all of this, as well as other loud and chaotic traditions of the festival, like how Pamplona is swarmed with people who fill the streets at all hours of the day and there are fireworks every night. Each year, one night of San Fermín is randomly selected as the night everyone will go outside and, one minute before midnight, begin making as much noise as they possibly can, which they will continue doing until dawn. From top to bottom, this was Hemingway's kind of party. But the bulls affected him more deeply and powerfully than any party ever could. Reading him on the topic feels like finding the diary of a person who has discovered a new sexual fetish. From his writing it appears he was aware of this and of the fact that his new fetish hinged on torturing an animal for twenty minutes or so before slaughtering it in a needlessly stressful way. Hemingway himself called bullfighting indefensible. Still, he could not stay away. After his first San Fermín (in the summer of 1923, just before he turned twenty-four years old) the bulls brought him back the following year, when he witnessed a human casualty during one morning's run—perhaps the reason Hemingway never chose to run with the bulls. In 1925, he returned to Pamplona for a third consecutive year, by which time these trips had become research for a nonfiction book Hemingway intended to write on Spanish bullfighting. But then his small group of friends and tagalongs created so much drama he decided to instead write a fictionalized account of the trip as a novel.

The Sun Also Rises was an immediate hit upon publication in 1926 and changed American literature forever by stripping the story down to a skeleton of unheroic characters and unexplained events, delivering readers in the United States the effect of fact-based reporting from a distant world, a world that perhaps felt more "honest" or "real" than the inherited culture they were all too familiar with at home. Young Americans began dressing and grooming themselves to resemble their favorite characters from the book, then wore their black berets and red scarves down to local hangouts, where they practiced their new personalities and offered opinions on bullfights and matadors they'd never seen. There were many more such opinions formed in 1932, after Hemingway did publish that nonfiction book on Spanish bullfighting, *Death in the Afternoon*. In 1959, *Life* magazine hired him to write a series of articles on bullfights, which sent him back to Spain, where he found a professional rivalry between two matadors, Luis Miguel Dominguín, the superstar veteran trying to hold on to his torch rather than pass it down to his younger brother-in-law, Antonio Ordóñez, son of the man Hemingway had used as inspiration for the great matador in *The Sun Also Rises*. Hemingway spent weeks watching these two attempt to outdo each other with their performances in the ring and wrote more than ten times the material he was hired to write for the magazine. The series of articles in *Life* wound up being excerpts from a whole other nonfiction book on Spanish bullfighting, *The Dangerous Summer*, eventually published in 1985. Ever since the first edition of *The Sun Also Rises*, Hemingway's most devoted readers made pilgrimages to Spain, to earn the right to complain about Hemingway ruining San Fermin with tourists, to see for themselves the great Spanish tradition of the bullfight.

◇ ◇ ◇

If we widen and backdate the definition of "bull" to include horned and dangerously aggressive males of wild bovine species, such as aurochs and bison, then humans have been fighting bulls for as long as we've been human. Those prehistoric cave paintings in France from the end of the Paleolithic Age, nearly twenty thousand years ago? The largest animals painted there are bulls, probably remnants of a ceremonial act intended as either thanks or summoning, depending upon whether the artists' bellies were full or empty of meat. Throughout history, bulls show up often in the parables, texts, pantheons and even the laws of most major religions. There's no way to know how many billions of bulls our ancestors sacrificed to various gods. There's no way to know how many bulls have been forced to participate in our demonstrations of strength and courage or how many of those acts may have been called "bullfighting" at the time. Some form of wrestling young bulls has surely been an adolescent rite of passage in most societies who've ever kept cattle behind a fence. Humans and bulls were certainly forced to fight each other to the death in the Colosseum of Rome. Versions of these rituals and others span history and the globe. This culture stretches back to the dawn of humanity. For as long as we've had dreams, we've dreamt of public ways to fight and kill bulls for food, fun and worship. While Spanish bullfighting is just another extension of this tradition, it's also a modern invention—hardly any older than the United States—the young child of a marriage between two ancient taurine spectacles.

The "Bull-Leaping Fresco" from approximately 2000 BC seems to depict Greek daredevils using wild bulls in some type of Cirque du Soleil shenanigans but it's difficult to tell what action is actually meant to be taking place in the rudimentary and stylized painting. Could it possibly be a back handspring launched off the spine of a charging bull? To say the least, it looks like a very dangerous combination of rodeo and gymnastics. A couple thousand years later, Julius Caesar, Nero and Claudius all entertained the Roman masses by presenting staged hunts in which bulls were run into a stadium to be chased, attacked and killed by "hunters" on horseback. One way to think of modern Spanish bullfighting is as a combination of the Greeks' artistic displays of fearlessness and the Romans' ritual sacrifice celebrating our place at the top of the food chain. Modern Spanish bullfighting is intended as a microcosmic allegory of the universal life force. However, premodern bullfights on the Iberian Peninsula were nothing more than a scaled-down version of the staged Roman hunt. And even though we call it a "bullfight" in English, the Spanish have never, then or now, considered this activity to be a fight or a sport. The Spanish term is *la corrida de toros*, "the run of the bulls." This is a reference both to what happened once the bulls were sent into the ring to run around and the aforementioned method of getting them there, which was the only way to transport beef cattle on the Iberian Peninsula in the Middle Ages. Before the days of refrigeration, ranch hands would periodically run a few cattle from the fields into corrals near town, where they were butchered for fresh meat to be sold at the local market. Whenever a major holiday or royal celebration, such as the birth of a prince, called for a feast, a much greater number of cattle were run into town, thereby announcing the beginning of festivities with the thunder of their hooves. Brave, foolish or drunken townsfolk who got swept up in the excitement would sometimes run with the herd. There's no telling why people still do this in Pamplona today but, in the Middle Ages, entertainment was scarce, which is also the likeliest explanation for what they started doing to some of those bulls in the fifth century.

Prior to the practice of building arenas specifically to host bullfights, temporary bullrings were thrown together by simply corralling off a town square. Bleachers were put up to seat commoners while property owners with buildings facing the plaza relinquished their balconies to the royal and noble classes. As for the action inside the ring, everyone was there to watch knights on horseback demonstrate riding skills while chasing or being chased by bulls and repeatedly stabbing the bulls with spears. All the while, servants, slaves or employees on foot helped direct the bulls: toward any riders with spears poised to stab, away from any unseated riders whenever their horses were inevitably gored. When an individual bull began to display signs of exhaustion after being run all over the ring and stabbed many times, *el matador*, "the killer," stepped in to execute the animal without delay, flourish or fanfare. For more than one thousand years, matadors were nothing more than another helpful poor person on foot and the bullfight was merely a drawn-out slaughterhouse job presented to the masses as cheap, bloody entertainment.

The aristocracy, who owned these bulls and were killing many more for meat outside the ring, staged a production around the deaths of a few in order to give commoners a little circus with their bread, thus reinforcing the big shots on horses in the ring and watching from balconies above as protective warriors and great providers of the community. In this sense, you could say bullfighting on the Iberian Peninsula was always political. Then, in the eighth century, most of the peninsula was conquered by Arabian warriors, kicking off a period of roughly eight hundred years during which Christianity and Islam fought each other for control of the land. In the beginning, wealthy Christian families of territories conquered by Muslims were allowed to pay a special tax in order to continue living by their own religious beliefs and customs. After a less tolerant and more funda-mentalist strain of Islam came to power, further conflict arose. Since Islam specifically prohibits beating animals or treating them without compassion, there were many attempts to completely ban bullfights, which continued to be held only now as a form of defiant resistance to Muslim rule and, increasingly, as a declaration of Christian identity. Most of the holidays, a.k.a. "holy days," used as an excuse to feast were Catholic in title and intent, so there was already a loose association between Christianity and tons of bulls running into town. During these holy wars between Chris-tianity and Islam, explicitly religious pageantry seeped into the bullfight itself. Catholic Mass was frequently given from inside the ring and the bulls to be slaughtered were regularly dedicated to Christ or the patron saint of a festival. At the end of the fifteenth century, following hundreds of years of war, Christian forces regained power over the peninsula and the medieval bullfight sur-vived into the modern age, more popular and prevalent than ever.

Now that bullfights no longer served the purpose of galvanizing Christians against enemies in a holy war, the Catholic church began to voice concerns over Spanish people treating this brutal act like some kind of Christian ritual, as if animal sacrifices to God had been brought back with a twist of pro wrestling showmanship. After Cortés and Pizarro committed enough murder to establish Spanish culture as the main European export to the Americas, Rome decided they needed to make a move. In 1567, the pope effectively banned Roman Catholics from bullfights, threatening ex-communication to anyone involved in presenting or attending a bullfight and denying a Christian burial to anyone who died in the bullring. Nothing changed. Spanish nobility in the Old World and the New continued holding bullfights despite the risk to their eternal souls. The next pope, looking to save face, lifted the ban but asked everyone to pretty please at least stop treating bullfights like a Roman Catholic ceremony and stop holding them on religious holidays. Catholic priests remained under threat of excommunication for even attending a bullfight, let alone offering Mass in connec-tion with one. Everybody pretty much ignored that pope, too. Bullfights continued unchanged for another century.

◇   ◇   ◇

It's quite a long story how this happened but, in the year 1700, a French teenager became the King of Spain. Philippe V, who hailed from the French House of Bourbon and didn't even speak Span-ish, was only seventeen years old when he ascended to Spain's throne. Though his new subjects expected bullfights as part of any proper royal celebration, young Philippe viewed things through the lens of a different culture. To him, the bullfight was nothing but a barbaric and foolish form of slaughter. It's debatable how successful or disastrous any attempt at an outright ban may have been but Philippe chose a different, smarter tactic. Rather than make bullfighting illegal, he made it uncool. Loudly and often, Philippe told members of his court how ridiculous and undignified it was that Spanish nobility pranced around on horses while stabbing bulls with spears all to provide crude entertainment for commoners. Should it not be the other way around? Shouldn't the commoners provide entertainment for the ruling class? Were royals to be seen as noble princes or savage court jesters? His mockery of the aristocracy's participation in bullfights was merciless. Once Phillipe removed bullfights from nearly every royal celebration and made no secret of his reason for doing so, the practice quickly fell out of fashion with Spanish nobles, who didn't want to be thought of as fools or singled out for ridicule by the new king. But that ruling class also understood the important role such diversions as the bullfight played in keeping their subjects happy, so they decided to allow commoners to perform bullfights instead. Within about two decades, the ritual saw its first significant modifications since the Middle Ages and began to take on characteristics of the modern practice.

The illusion Philippe had shattered was something everyone not watching from a balcony or stabbing a bull from horseback must have seen the entire time, that the rich guys in the ring were never the stars of the show. Sure, they were applauded for presenting and participating in the ritual but, viewing the medieval bullfight as a series of transactions in blood, the noblemen in saddles risked nearly nothing, certainly the least of any beating hearts in the ring. In fact, every beating heart other than the bull's was only in the ring to assist and protect the noblemen in saddles, making it even safer and easier for them to stab bulls from an elevated position before a poor person stepped in to finish the job. You'd think the worst part in a bullfight would go to the bull but horses were always the most tragic role in this play. However many bulls have been killed in this ritual, the number of dead horses is exponentially greater. For nearly two thousand years the horses were not put in armor, allowing them to be gored and mutilated two or three at a time to prove the danger posed by each particular bull, to demonstrate its power, to verify the possibility that men may die in the ring. It was definitely an effective tactic but only the most sick and twisted minority of spectators could ever have been delighted to witness living horses try to understand having their own guts ripped out by the horns of a bull. The fact those horses would not even be in the ring if not for their riders' need to keep a safe, elevated position only drew further attention to the nobility's paltry contribution of risk compared to the attendants, who faced much greater danger on the ground with the bulls, trying to survive using their own bodies as a distraction to protect the lives of the guys with enough money to be sitting on horses. We're literally talking about medieval wealth disparity here, so there were always plenty of incentives to help put on a good show. For a peasant who elevated the role beyond mere survival to a crowd-pleasing performance, especially one that played up the danger to make the big shots on horses look brave for even being in the ring, the benefits could go well beyond money: a better job, a better home, a better life. Most of the guys on foot were just performing a theatrical rendition of their everyday occupations. Bullfighting could only have ever come from a ranching society because it requires a steady supply of bulls. The same industry which provided these bulls on the Iberian Peninsula also provided humans skilled at every step of the beef trade's supply line, from roping and herding to killing and butchering. That was the source material of the play. By the time Philippe V saw them in action, the assistants in a bullfight knew how to heighten the drama. If you want to, it is entirely possible to maintain a safe distance from a bull while successfully distracting it away from an unhorsed rider. Alternately, it's possible to come into unsafe proximity to a bull, provoke it and risk being gored like the horse it just killed to make sure everyone understands the harm which may come to others in the ring if they weren't conveniently using your provided distraction to return to a position of near-absolute safety on top of another horse. If this is starting to sound like show business, well, that's precisely where bullfighting went once Philippe effectively dissolved the Spanish aristocracy's monopoly on what proved to be a very lucrative entertainment when added to the lineup of fairs and carnivals.

Between other bloody events, like bear-beating, and ranching culture diversions, such as roping calves and riding wild horses, the bullfight first attempted to carry on as handed down from the ruling class. But the mythology of the warrior champion on horseback simply could not hold up in the competitive free market. Without wealth, power, title or the supposed preferences of God keeping peasants from upstaging the man on a horse, there wasn't a single good reason for peasants to hold back and watch that guy collect a bigger paycheck. Attendants on the ground began exploiting their greater range of motion and dangerous interactions with the bulls in order to steal the show through flamboyant and acrobatic maneuvers, like using a lance to pole-vault over a charging bull. Those were the death-defying acts audiences wanted to see, not some rich jerk stabbing a bull from on top of a horse. Following that logic, it was only a matter of time before someone decided the person who came closest to being killed by the bull should be the person who kills the bull.

The first matador to become famous for fighting and killing bulls on foot was named Francisco Romero. In the early 1720s, he moved the spotlight away from every other role in the performance to *el matador* by finishing bulls using a method he's said to have invented, *recibiendo*, which is to stand and "receive" a charging bull by waiting until the last second to reach forward and drive a sword down between its shoulder blades while stepping sideways to avoid the horns. This was incredibly difficult and dangerous. Attempts to kill *recibiendo* are rarely seen from today's matadors, who are largely unwilling to risk their performances or lives on the maneuver which gave them their present role in the ring. Before Francisco Romero, a matador's job description had been as basic as the title: kill. If the only aim is to dispatch a spent bull after a man on a horse has tortured it to the point of visible exhaustion, there is no risk or showmanship required. The matador's job used to be as simple as walking up to the side of a bull while it was distracted by someone else and putting a blade into its neck. After Romero started killing *recibiendo* and became a star, his innovation spread, though slowly, because any other matador who decided he could be a star had to prove it by facing a charging bull and killing it with a sword.

Prior to this point, assistants in a bullfight held various types of weapons—spears, whips, wooden clubs, chairs, whatever they preferred or had available. Many went into the ring with nothing but the clothing on their back. Capes, cloaks and other such draping upper-body wear being prevalent in Spanish fashion, chances are very high some bullfighters used similar pieces of fabric before Francisco Romero used a cape. However, he is the matador who standardized use of capes and introduced a smaller red cape, *la muleta*, used exclusively by the matador in the final part of a fight, when everything will get extremely messy and painful if he cannot keep a charging bull running directly toward the sword. (Presenting a smaller target to the bull helps minimize deviations from its course.) Within thirty years of Romero giving himself a special cape in order to kill bulls face-to-face, the matador became the most popular role in a bullfight.

In the 1760s, Joaquín Rodríguez Costillares recognized the full implications of public adoration having shifted from a position previously held by noblemen on horseback over to a matador of common birth. Even though he came to be a matador through working in a slaughterhouse, even though he was merely the son of a man who'd also worked in a slaughterhouse, Costillares began entering the bullring dressed in the formal attire of Spanish royalty.

SIX

RED FLAGS

◇ The Trouble with Jones ◇ Early Lessons in Studio and Stage ◇
A Disappearing Act ◇ Searching for a Ballad ◇ Money Matters ◇

George Jones once told the *Chicago Tribune*, "All my life, I've been runnin' from something. If I knew what it was, I could run in the right direction. I know where I want to go but I always seem to end up goin' the other way. I know there's nothing down that way. I been down there too many times." By the time he gave that interview, in 1981, everyone who knew George Jones' name knew he had problems. That's why he was trying to find a way to describe how profoundly lost and confused he'd felt for as long he could remember, because that part of the story had already begun to cast the shadow which has eclipsed his talent as a vocalist ever since.

Jones often claimed he didn't start drinking alcohol regularly until he joined the Marines in the 1950s. The truth is he began displaying what we'd recognize as early signs of alcoholism in Texas honky-tonks during the 1940s, when he was just a teenage survivor of child abuse, singing country music the way his drunk dad had forced him to under threat of another beating. When Jones came out of the Marines in the 1950s and went straight back to the honky-tonks, he was still drinking, though perhaps not to a degree the crowd around him would find concerning or even remarkable. Taking a few drinks before, during and after some show in some bar was just getting on the same wavelength as everyone else. Then he signed an artist contract with Starday Records and the problem became more noticeable. He consistently flouted expectations of professionalism by pregaming for expensive recording sessions as if they were any other one-night stand on a plywood stage in the middle of nowhere. Many session musicians did verify Jones' claims that he simply sang better with a little buzz. Pig Robbins once said, "When he'd only had a few drinks but before he'd gone too far overboard, he could just moan his ass off and just put a whole lot more feeling into those ballads." But Pig also said, "There was a point when he'd go over the line and get kind of . . . feisty." Though there are similar quotes dating back to his earliest recording sessions in Texas, Jones always claimed his drinking didn't get out of control until the early 1960s. Admittedly, there's no imagining how George Jones personally defined "out of control," especially relative to his cocaine-fueled psychotic break from reality in the late 1970s. However, it is true his alcohol use worsened in the 1960s, by which time he'd also begun taking speed pills while touring and trying and failing to deal with the pressure of having turned himself into a living legend.

Already believed by most people paying attention in the 1950s to be the greatest country singer alive, the records he cut in the 1960s reinforced those opinions. The newspaper headlines generated by his troublemaking behavior only added to the legend. And the legend definitely made everything worse. All the rational explanations he was ever able to give for getting too drunk to perform or skipping out on a concert sound a lot like acute social anxiety disorder mixed with extreme stage fright. In his 1996 autobiography, Jones wrote, "I never wanted to be a star and only occasionally wanted to be a performer. I always wanted to be a singer." So, not only did he not ask to be The Greatest Country Singer Ever, every time someone called him that it made his job harder to do. Sitting backstage before concerts, he'd start thinking about all the people out there waiting to hear him sing, everyone who had bought a ticket to see the guy who was supposed to be the best to ever do it. If he went out there and gave anything less than the actual most impressive performance they've heard in their whole lives, he'd be a disappointment, a letdown, a fraud. Was this an irrational fear for such a freakishly great singer as George Jones? Probably, yeah, unless he chose to silence those thoughts by taking a drink, then another . . . and another . . . until he was so drunk his only options were to run away or, probably even worse, go onstage and do the very thing he was worried about by giving a performance so poor he would know in detail exactly what to fear the next time he found himself sitting backstage before a concert, thinking about taking a drink to calm his nerves . . . While it's safe to assume the few people he grew close to in life always understood the dangers of this tightrope act, the way his actions played out in headlines and self-referential drinking songs for the rest of his career allowed country music audiences with their shared cultural memories of federal Prohibition to cast George Jones as a rebellious good-timer doing whatever it took to keep the party going without giving a fuck about anything else. In reality, it was never much of a party.

There's a story about a nightclub owner who booked Jones to play a week of shows in 1962 during a time when Jones was doing his best to stay completely off booze. But this club owner wanted him to drink. Each night, the guy pestered Jones to have a drink with him because he wanted to be able to say he got drunk with famous party animal George Jones. Well, after the last show of the week, the club owner got what he wanted. Jones took a drink with him, then another . . . and another . . . until the whole bottle was gone, at which point Jones started demolishing the night-club and tried to fistfight the owner. Many people who hear that story laugh and, admittedly, it is pretty funny to imagine that dickhead's face when he realized the consequences of treating another human being's battle with addiction as a form of entertainment. But the reason many people have laughed at this and other stories over the years is because of the romanticized image which largely persists to this day of No-Show Jones being some kind of noble or heroic drunk. As is so often the case, the truth was much more complicated and unsettling. For one thing, "drunk" doesn't begin to cover it. Even broadening the scope to "addict," as if this is simply what extreme addiction looks like, isn't going to get the job done either. Jones' problems didn't all come from a baggie or a bottle. There's no doubt substance abuse made it all far worse, but there's also no telling how much of this story would have happened the same way even if he had never ingested a mind-altering substance in his life. George Jones was a veritable collection of neuroses, rocket-fueled by stress and sub-stance abuse until he eventually reached full-blown, medically diagnosed schizophrenic psychosis. You ever met somebody who just can't handle it when things are going well? The kind of person who's only ever had it all suddenly steer so wrong that they can't trust happiness or security as anything other than a sign they're about to once more be kicked in the face by life? Someone who will sabotage everything themselves just to get it over with and feel like they at least had a fraction of control over the nothing they're left with this time rather than waiting around to see what new torture fate had in store. A true loser, in every sense of the word.

His decision to become a professional recording artist like his hero Hank Williams may be more to blame than anything else for all the wrong turns he took. George Jones effectively inher-ited Hank's audience. "Why Baby Why" hit fewer than two years after Hank's death. How many Hank Williams fans could possibly have heard Jones as anything other than the newer model? How many of those fans had skipped buying a ticket to see Hank because they figured he'd come through town again in the near future rather than wind up dead at the age of twenty-nine? Once Jones gained the reputation of being both a better singer and a worse alcoholic than Hank, no-body wanted to risk missing his concerts, as any one of them could be the last. It's not difficult to imagine those thoughts, too, ran through Jones' mind more than once when he was sitting back-stage trying to not drink before a concert. In late 1964 or early 1965, during Johnny PayCheck's brief tenure in the band, Jones got drunk backstage before a concert and said he wouldn't come out to sing until he was introduced as Hank Williams. Maybe PayCheck thought he was joking, or just didn't want to do it, but as the band launched into the first song, PayCheck introduced him as George Jones and Jones stood off to the side of the stage, refusing to come on until he was introduced as Hank Williams. Eventually PayCheck introduced him as Hank, at which point Jones yelled out a demand to also be introduced as Johnny Horton, the country singer who'd married Hank Williams' widow before also dying young on tour. So PayCheck introduced him as Johnny Horton. Jones walked onstage, grabbed the microphone and sang the first line of the song as he kept walking, right off the stage, right out the door and right off the property, causing a per-plexed and angry audience to riot. We can't know everything going through his mind that night, and it's doubtful Jones himself ever gave a rational explanation. But it's pretty self-evident he was thinking and drinking about how much he didn't want to be there, thinking and drinking about the death of his idol and the death of another man who, in a different way from Jones, had also followed in that same idol's footsteps. At several points in his life, Jones stated he was convinced he'd die like Hank Williams, saturated with pain-numbing chemicals in the back of some vehicle en route to a concert.

Another frequent source of frustration was how he always seemed to end up without any money no matter how many concerts he played. It took until the late 1970s for a doctor to finally suggest, like many adults who were physically abused as children, Jones suffered from an intense self-loathing which made him feel guilty and unworthy over all the adoration and money he earned from singing. This theory was reinforced in the 1980s by Rick Blackburn, an executive at Jones' rec-ord label, who said, "There's something that runs true to entertainers and performers, particularly if an entertainer comes out of a low-income, almost borderline-on-poverty background. As their success comes and their financial means is elevated, it's almost like a guilt trip for them. I've seen it happen to a lot of artists. It's like they feel they don't deserve it. There's a guilt trip that sets in because usually the friends back home, or certainly the family, have not been able to enjoy the kind of [power and money] that comes with [fame and success]." All of which perhaps explains why there are dozens of people with credible claims of witnessing George Jones take fistfuls of hundred dollar bills and flush them down toilets, light them on fire or otherwise destroy perfectly good cash he very much should have kept if he didn't want to spend decades of his life broke.

For these reasons and others, Jones taking a couple drinks to calm his nerves before a show could lead to his total disappearance by set time. He once phoned Don Pierce's Mercury-Starday office after a wild night in Elizabethtown, Kentucky. Hungover, penniless and left behind by the rest of the artists on the tour, Jones asked if anybody could drive up from Nashville to fetch him. Don said to find someone who'd lend him bus fare and take a Greyhound, which set Jones to cuss-ing and yelling. He didn't think *Grand Ole Opry*'s New Star ought to be seen traveling by passenger bus. Another time, Jones went into Starday's office while drunk and demanded money he felt he was owed. When they couldn't get him to leave, someone called the cops to come take him away.

Jones returned sober the next day, as remorseful as could be. Everybody always knew he'd be sorry the next day. Just a few years into his recording career he'd started cutting a decent amount of gospel songs and anyone who checked the label credits saw he was the main writer on most of them, like 1957's "Wandering Soul" written with Bill Dudley. So, whenever fans who were with him from the beginning saw Jones get drunk and mess up—or, later, after he reached such a level of fame his misdeeds were printed in newspapers and magazines—they knew he thought of himself as a sinner like all the rest, trying to work his way back to the straight and narrow. He tried to be good. He wanted to do right.

◇   ◇   ◇

Late in the summer of 1954, about a year after returning to Texas from the Marines, George Jones met a young woman named Shirley, a carhop at the drive-in hamburger joint he frequented when in Houston to perform on the *Hometown Jamboree*. One day, George gifted Shirley with a copy of his first Starday single, released a few months prior. Two weeks later, they were married in a fall wedding and moved in with some of his family around Beaumont. By the end of the year, Shirley was pregnant with their first son. George got a day job as probably the worst DJ ever hired at KTRM, where he met and befriended J. P. Richardson, later known as the Big Bopper. As of this writing, no recordings have surfaced of George's time as a DJ but the same anxiety that made him want to take a few drinks before a show or recording session always made him even more nervous about speaking on the air. *The Complete Starday and Mercury Recordings* box set from Bear Family Records includes some radio promo spots from a couple of years later in which you can hear how much uncertainty and awkwardness remained in his voice even after having several hit records. One way George found to work around his nerves on the radio was by mimicking the voices of people who were already successful. He often spoke in an imitation of Ferlin Husky's Simon Crum character. His Hank Williams impersonation was, of course, always popular with listeners. Though his radio career was brief, George worked at the station long enough for another DJ to saddle him with a nickname he would never shake, "Possum." (Various after-the-fact explanations for the nickname have been given, some by George himself, but the truth is everyone just thought he looked like a possum. Not that he was unattractive or anything, but he really did, what with the way the features of his face seemed to gather in a small cluster at the front of his head, the pointy nose and wide set of teeth behind thin lips, shadows often covering his deep-set eyes.) When his records started selling, George quit the radio station.

As many legends as Don Pierce and Pappy Daily helped get started in the business, as many advantages as they had over the competition in the huge and influential country music market of Texas, it's remarkable George Jones was the only artist who started and stayed hitting at a national level while on Starday. Taking a cynic's perspective on the record industry, between Pappy's jukebox operation and distributorship and Starday's *Hometown Jamboree*—only one step away from the *Louisiana Hayride*, itself only another step away from the *Grand Ole Opry*—these guys should have been printing money. But perhaps we shouldn't take a cynical perspective when it comes to Pappy Daily. Speaking to *Billboard* in 1964 on the topic of gatekeepers in the music business, he said, "The disc jockeys today have set themselves up as experts. I don't believe anybody is qualified to say whether a record is good or bad. In my thirty-some-odd years I have learned that there are no experts. The public decides as to whether or not a record is good or bad—the people that spend the money for the record." Starday did sell records, net many hits and do good business but they never struck upon another fortune like the one that came from plugging George Jones into their system.

Although his first records didn't sell many copies, he was an instant hit on the *Jamboree* and the label expanded his fan base by sending him around to play at every honky-tonk in broadcast range. George bought a used 1951 Packard four-door with a gold paint job and had his name painted down the side in purple script above the words "STARDAY RECORDING ARTIST" with a phone number to call for bookings. There's a black-and-white photo of him leaning up against this car while wearing his stage clothes, a basic Colonel Sanders suit and tie, as he'd not yet earned rhinestones with a #1 hit. While the car is perfectly in focus, George is for some reason slightly blurry. It almost looks like he accidentally tripped and fell a little sideways into the car a split-second before the shutter snapped. His lean is at least as unnatural as his speech on live radio, as is the awkward smile on his face. The midday sun shines down from above leaving two black holes where his eyes should be. He looks like pure abyss wearing a George Jones mask, empty and waiting for the spirits to take control. Stare at the picture long enough and it starts to feel pretty creepy. Even if you manage to convince yourself it's just a not-so-good photograph from a long time ago, it's still a kid in his twenties with no idea he's headed directly toward Hell.

In the beginning, George and early Starday hitmaker Sonny Burns covered most of Texas playing with whatever pickup bands awaited at various destinations, which was fine. As he built a name for himself, though, the bigger package tours dragged him and Sonny all over the continent, teaching George how deeply he hated touring that way. With too many people and instruments crammed into a four-door sedan on overnight drives, there were many times in those habit-forming early days when he got drunk just to pass out and pretend it was sleep. According to Sonny Burns, this was when Jones began drinking heavily. Again, there is no question both men already knew their way through a bottle, but Sonny noticing an uptick marks the beginning of a recurring pattern in which Jones' substance abuse escalated in direct proportion with his fame and success.

When the *Hometown Jamboree* launched, Sonny Burns was the bigger name, so he got paid ten dollars a week more for being on the show. After a few months, Sonny started goading George, saying he'd obviously become just as important to the program and should be paid the same money per week. While drinking about it, the two singers came up with a plan to walk in Pappy's office and demand raises to put them both at twenty-five dollars a week. If Pappy didn't go for it, they'd pretend to quit and then he'd surely come around. Well, the plan worked until they got to the part where Pappy called their bluff, accepted their resignations, said to be careful wherever their little party ended up and not to call unless they landed in jail. The boys stormed out, picked up another bottle and drove a couple hours away to Sonny's mom's house in Nacogdoches, where they kept drinking and pretending to brag over the way they'd just quit Pappy's stupid radio show. Or, at least, that's what Jones did. Sonny wasn't pretending. It's likely this whole stunt came together because he was already looking for an excuse to quit the business, which is what he did, disappearing into a bottle for the next three or four years. But George's career was just getting off the ground. Starday was about to release his next single and he knew Pappy would welcome him back as if nothing had happened, which is what he did.

In August of 1955, George went to a *Louisiana Hayride*-affiliated concert in Conroe, Texas, and talked the emcee into letting him get onstage and play his upcoming Starday single, "Seasons of My Heart." When it came out a month later—around the time Shirley Jones gave birth to their first son—radio DJs found their audiences preferred the B-side of Jones' record and "Why Baby Why" became the first big George Jones hit, prompting his first appearance on the *Louisiana Hayride*. Since Shirley had missed out on most of her husband's early career highlights while pregnant at home, George invited her to leave the baby with family and come along to Shreveport for his debut on the *Hayride*. The lineup at this time featured, among others, Johnny Horton, Jimmy C. Newman, Johnny Cash and Elvis Presley. Now, even if Shirley Jones had heard rock & roll music before and/or had any opinion on it, this would have been the first time she ever saw Elvis Presley perform, as his onstage gyrations had not yet been televised. And it's sometimes difficult to express to modern folks what was so shocking about the way Elvis moved his hips, so just imagine you're at a rock show, all the guys in the band take off their pants, get hard and start hula-hooping with erections while playing a song. That's exactly what Elvis looked like to most adults in the 1950s. Shirley Jones was horrified, terrified, scandalized, the entire bit. Though presumably not as overtly sexual as Elvis, witnesses of early George Jones shows say he was an energetic and high-strung performer who danced and moved all over the stage as he sang. Several sources say that when he shared a bill with Elvis, George was even known to copy some of Presley's moves as a joke. Until this night, Shirley had only ever been supportive of her husband's career. But now that she'd seen Elvis do those wicked things with his pelvis, it cast a whole new light on some things she'd seen George do onstage and she came unglued. She told her husband the things he did onstage were "dirty," that they embarrassed her. *He* embarrassed her. From that moment forward, George Jones went onstage, hit his mark and sang into the microphone. You may catch him swaying side to side, going up on his toes here and there to put an extra dip in a waterfall of notes or kicking one boot out to show everyone he was having a good time but, otherwise, he moved his head to sing, his arms to play guitar and that was it. And if Shirley Jones was so upset about the things her husband did onstage until she put that shame inside him, it's safe to assume she abhorred the relationship George developed with alcohol after becoming a successful entertainer.

It probably took a while for her to realize what was happening. George was always gone on tour. On the rare occasion he came home for more than a few weeks at a time, everything would be fine for a while, perhaps as long as a couple months. But then one day he'd leave home with no warning and stay gone—no phone call, no contact of any kind—for maybe a week or more before showing back up as if nothing out of the ordinary had happened. Maybe the first few times he offered some excuse about picking up a last-minute show out of town or said she must have forgotten about a one-off gig he'd mentioned. But he wasn't always careful to get far enough away from home when he disappeared and soon rumors started drifting back to Shirley about her husband being seen drunk off his ass in a honky-tonk just a few miles down the road, leaving at the end of the night with a woman who certainly wasn't her. That was Jones on his best behavior at home, trying and failing to drop the routine he'd developed while gone for work. Away from home on tour, he was drunk more often than he wasn't.

◇   ◇   ◇

When "What Am I Worth" came out as the follow-up to "Why Baby Why" and hit lower on the charts it was no cause for concern because the record still went Top 10. When the single after that failed to chart at all, George retraced his steps and wrote what was basically a double-time remake of "Why Baby Why," called "You Gotta Be My Baby." The first attempt at recording the song wasted an entire session. It's likely Jones had a few drinks, but he doesn't sound noticeably trashed in the surviving takes. If we want to nitpick, the Texas studio players weren't up to Nashville standards but there are not any glaring errors there, either. Even though at least three of the takes sound totally acceptable, especially by Starday standards, none were issued as a single. The likeliest explanation is Elvis Presley's "Heartbreak Hotel" had hit the month before, making the guitar, bass, piano and fiddle instrumentation on the first session for "You Gotta Be My Baby" sound like a 1930s string band in comparison. The next time George and Pappy Daily went back in the studio to try the song, instead of fiddles they brought two electric guitars and, for the first time ever on a George Jones session, pedal steel. When the record came out in early 1956, that updated sound snagged George another Top 10 Country hit and his first invitation to be a guest on the *Grand Ole Opry*. In his autobiography, George complains the *Opry* really should have had him on as a guest before "You Gotta Be My Baby" and even goes so far as to imply he would've been on the program at some earlier point if only he was willing to go along with whatever system of bribery he alleges was then in place. But "You Gotta Be My Baby" was only his third minor hit on an indie label from Texas and he didn't really have a connection to the Nashville country music industry until the *Opry* gave him one by making him a member later in the year. Around the same time, George wrote a song either for or with Ray Price. It's difficult to tell what truly happened because George put his part of the song in Shirley's name so the officially listed (but maybe not really) cowriter Ray Price could file it with Cedarwood. In any case, when "You Done Me Wrong" came out on the B-side of Ray Price's record-breaking hit "Crazy Arms" while George's own "You Gotta Be My Baby" was still on the charts, it made for some good-sized checks showing up in the Jones family's mailbox.

Three months after George joined the *Opry*, Art Talmadge of Mercury Records initiated the Mercury-Starday merger, bringing George's recording sessions to Nashville. To match the upgrade in quality of his music, George upgraded his management and booking teams to Nashville heavy-weights, then toured the continent with some of the genre's biggest stars, like Johnny Cash, Ray Price, Carl Smith and Faron Young. This new level of success correlates with a new plateau in Drunk George Jones stories, for all the psychological reasons already described but also because his new status as a major artist meant he now spent all his time around other major artists and important industry figures. This is when Jones became so great at his job most of his daily cowork-ers were great enough at their own jobs to also become legends who would someday be interviewed about their own careers. Any conversation about the best and most important work done in coun-try music history is invariably going to find its way around to George Jones, at which point you're invariably going to hear a Drunk George Jones story.

There are maybe five totally separate stories in Jones' autobiography where he gets in some kind of fight and ends up with a broken arm. Stonewall Jackson was one of many artists who toured with Jones at the beginning of their careers and he remembered a whole lot of fighting. The worst one was outside a roadhouse in Texas. All they did was pull into the parking lot to pick up a six pack of beer for the drive but, before they could even get inside the bar, a local group of tough guys started some shit. Jones never worried much about his diminutive stature when it came to a fight, so he swung on the biggest guy, got knocked out, stomped on and left facedown in a mud puddle. The gang kicked the hell out of Stonewall, too, but at least left him conscious enough to drag Jones' head out of the puddle of water so he wouldn't drown. Another time George and Faron Young drove out to some radio station to do interviews and promote a concert. Since the mayor of this town and his wife had come to the radio station to watch the interview, Faron was behaving as properly as he was able when Jones decided to screw with his friend by walking into the studio and yelling a bunch of cuss words in the background. Faron tried to ignore it, but the cussing kept coming until Faron finally rage-quit the interview in order to have a fistfight with George Jones on live radio, in front of the mayor, the mayor's wife and everyone listening at home.

Most country artists who toured extensively in the 1950s could tell some stories about things getting out of control at some point or another. Every artist who toured with George Jones in the 1950s could tell stories about things routinely getting out of control. But they weren't just drinking and fighting. Somehow, they found time to also create legendary music. Stonewall Jackson's first hit record was "Life to Go" in 1958. In every version of the song's origin story, certain details don't add up, and we'll probably never know the whole truth, but both Stonewall and Jones said they were playing a show at a prison and wrote these lyrics based on a prisoner's response when asked how long a sentence he had to serve. Jones and Stonewall came to some sort of agreement whereby Jones wound up with the writing credit and first recording in late 1957 but Mercury-Starday didn't release that until Stonewall's version on Columbia Records hit #2 in *Billboard* and #1 in *Cash Box* nearly a full year later. This relationship between Jones' drinking life and professional life worked both ways, which is to say George Jones often got drunk with his famous coworkers but, in some cases, drinking with Jones presented an opportunity to become one of his famous coworkers. When he first met Roger Miller in early 1957, Roger was pushing luggage carts and operating the elevator as a bellhop at the Andrew Jackson Hotel, one of the places Jones liked to stay in Nashville. (According to Don Pierce, one of Ernest Tubb's daughters also liked to stay there . . . in George's room.) Roger Miller being one of the funniest humans and best songwriters to ever live (and, evidently, more discreet than Don Pierce), he and Jones were fast friends. Within a month of their meeting, George brought Roger to Mercury-Starday and became the first artist to cut "Tall, Tall Trees," a #1 hit for Alan Jackson about forty years later. George was also the first artist to record "That's the Way I Feel," a Top 10 hit for Faron Young the following year. Jones was given half the writing credit on "Tall, Tall Trees" and "That's the Way I Feel," as these songs were supposedly written during the drive from Nashville to Texas so Mercury-Starday could avoid paying Nashville studio rates for a session on an unknown bellhop. Though George and Roger really did take this trip together, it's very likely Roger was the sole composer. His career wouldn't take off until the mid-1960s but his writing style was unmistakable from the beginning and Jones was listed as 50 percent writer on all the Roger Miller songs he was first to record, not just the ones from this trip to Texas. The records Roger cut for Pappy Daily and Don Pierce didn't do anything and his early hits as a writer were few and far between, so Pappy and a few other producers in town put him to work doing soundalikes. Roger was probably who eventually brought in Donny Young to also do soundalike work for Pappy, which was probably how Donny Young got hired to sing background vocals in Jones' recording sessions.

With all the reasons already given for why Starday put "Seasons of My Heart" on the A-side of a record and "Why Baby Why" on the B-side, there's still one more: the industry-wide belief in the career longevity promised to an artist who could hit with a ballad. (Here used in the modern, colloquial sense to mean pretty much any slow song, not necessarily a story song.) It was and still is generally accepted wisdom that any flash-in-the-pan act can hit on a fun, dumb, up-tempo rhythm or two, which audiences may treat as a soundtrack to drinking and dancing before moving on to the next thing and leaving that artist to drift into obscurity. But someone who can make the party crowd stop dancing long enough to listen to the words and become emotionally affected is much more likely to have a career with staying power. Jimmy C. Newman was one example of this. He was a *Grand Ole Opry* member for fifty years, spent about fifteen of those years releasing hit records and most of his early hits were slow songs, beginning with "Cry, Cry Darlin'," the Top 10 Country single that got him added to the *Louisiana Hayride* in 1954, right around the time George Jones came back from the Marines. One of the first gigs George found when he returned to Beaumont was playing guitar for Chuck Guillory and His Rhythm Boys, the band that also gave Jimmy C. Newman one of his first jobs in the business when he was just a teenager. So when Jimmy checked in with his old boss to find a guitar player for a few road dates, Chuck Guillory sent George Jones. When Jones joined the *Louisiana Hayride* a few years later, Jimmy was still on the lineup and the two old acquaintances began traveling together to share the driving on package tours. According to Jimmy, George was completely obsessed with the idea of getting a hit with a ballad. He'd talk about how much success Jimmy had had with slow songs and how badly he wanted the same for himself. Much later in life, George said he always looked at up-tempo songs as something he needed to do every now and then so the crowd would let him sing some more slow songs, which was what he loved most of all. And he still hadn't put a slow song on the charts when he joined the *Grand Ole Opry* in August of 1956, which just so happened to be the same month Jimmy C. Newman joined the *Opry*, placing the two singers right back in a car on tour together, George still going on and on about how much he needed a hit with a ballad . . . having no idea he'd already written and recorded one earlier in the month down at Gold Star in Texas.

"Just One More" was George Jones' first hit on the downtrodden type of drinking song with which his name would eventually become synonymous. Released as his final single for Starday in September of '56, the record peaked at #3 Country. Right as it began to pick up steam but before anyone knew it would be his biggest hit to date, George, Jimmy C. Newman and Jimmy's fiddle player Rufus Thibodeaux followed a performance on the *Opry* by once more loading up in a car for the overnight drive to a show the next day. While everyone else slept, Jimmy took the first shift at the wheel and kept himself awake by creating melodies in his head. After hitting on one he liked, he started working on words to go with it. By the time they stopped for breakfast in the morning, he had a fragment of a chorus called "Don't Stop the Jukebox." George liked the basic idea and pretty soon came back to Jimmy with a finished song, now called "Don't Stop the Music." As this was several years before split-publishing became common and George and Jimmy were signed to different publishing companies, they realized only one of them could take writing credit. Jimmy figured George did most of the work and let him have it. Later, he said, "It was my melody, but he sure wrote the words good." In December, Jones took "Don't Stop the Music" and Rufus Thibodeaux into his first Nashville recording session. It was chosen as the flagship Mercury-Starday single and soon hit the Top 10.

When his little indie record label from Texas merged with a big-time Chicago label and opened an office in Nashville mostly on the strength of George Jones releasing enough hit records to become a member of the *Grand Ole Opry*, he must have thought he'd reached the top of the mountain. In addition to Rufus Thibodeaux, his first session in Nashville featured the legendary Jimmy Day, famous for playing steel guitar on hits by Ray Price, Webb Pierce and Hank Williams. Then, for his next session the following month . . . Mercury-Starday sent him back to Gold Star in Texas, as if Jones hadn't just hit with two ballads in a row, one of them the biggest hit of his young career. The label probably sold this to him as a way to save money recording filler tracks, unlikely to be released as singles or promoted heavily. The cost difference really was significant. To record in Nashville in 1957 you had to pay each musician about $40 a session. In Texas, each player cost $5 a song. At four songs a session, you're talking about spending twice as much money in Nashville and that's just to hire the musicians. But you're also talking about the difference between good musicians and some of the greatest musicians of all time. Hank Garland, Grady Martin, Tommy Jackson and Buddy Emmons are only a few of the legendary names on Jones' Nashville session logs in 1957. There's simply no comparison and, again, that's just the musicians. The difference in quality tracks across the whole process, from the guitar amps and vocal mics to the room sound of the studio and separation in the mix, all of this clearly audible on records. We also have to keep in mind that nobody in the country music industry or audience of this era would have favored "lo-fi" or raw-sounding tape for aesthetic reasons. Rockabilly fans in the 1950s or 1970s may have loved the energy and technical imperfections in a recording like "Take the Devil Out of Me." It's truly an electrifying performance. The only problem is it was written by Jones and recorded at Gold Star for inclusion not on a rock album but a gospel album marketed to country fans. What sounds to us like a starkly powerful old recording just sounded cheap and of poor quality to the intended audience of its time.

Once George heard what his music sounded like in a Nashville studio, going down to Texas must have felt like a huge step backward. What's the point of merging with a big money label if you can't leave the small money mentality behind? If there's such a thing as being a country music star, shouldn't it bring in enough cash to not have to cut corners like this? If George didn't ask himself these questions the very first time they sent him back to Gold Star, he definitely did the second time, taking an unknown Nashville bellhop with him to be recorded in the same fashion Mercury-Starday felt it was appropriate to record a *Grand Ole Opry* star, just like they felt it was fine for that same star to be seen taking a Greyhound bus. Have another listen to "Tall, Tall Trees" or "That's the Way I Feel," the Roger Miller songs Jones cut on that trip. There's a ton of either room noise or tape hiss and the vocal sounds like they put a sock over the microphone. The sound quality is roughly on par with a 1940s recording from Castle, which isn't terrible, but it was a serious retrogression from the few sessions George had already done in Nashville by this time. There's no chance he was happy about making new recordings that sounded at least five years older than stuff he'd cut three months earlier, like his second Mercury-Starday single, "Too Much Water," with Hank Garland on some real snappy electric guitar and—in his first recording session ever— legendary pedal steel guitarist Lloyd Green. The sound quality alone is three times cleaner than anything George ever recorded in Texas, and he wasn't even using Owen Bradley's studio yet. Less than half of George Jones' Mercury-Starday material is of such quality because more than half of his sessions for the label were held at Gold Star. In fact, when he entered the Quonset Hut for the famous "White Lightning" session in September 1958, it was the first time he'd walked into a Nashville studio in nearly a year, as his previous four sessions were all in Texas. But those were his last sessions for Mercury-Starday and, after "White Lightning" hit #1, Mercury let Jones record at the Quonset Hut whenever he wanted.

◇   ◇   ◇

There's a brief period when George appears to've let himself believe the dream really came true. Maybe he thought dropping the Starday connection made all the difference or having a #1 record meant smooth sailing from then on. "White Lightning" earned him his first song suit from the original rhinestone cowboy, Nudie Cohn. As required by custom, the design featured images of moonshine jugs and lightning bolts taken at face value from the lyrics and plastered all over the fabric. The sleeves and legs spelled out the words "White Lightning" in a rhinestone-studded and colorized update of the famous black-and-cream sheet music suit Nudie had made for Hank Williams. In addition to flashier stage outfits, the first big checks from Mercury went toward buying a house. He and Shirley had a second son in 1958 and, for the first time, George was able to move his young family into a home he owned. Soon after, he built a larger ranch house in the Beaumont suburb of Vidor, where he acquired enough land to keep horses and cattle. George then bought another house in the area for his parents. According to Shirley, this was the happiest time in their marriage. They leased a building in town and opened the George Jones Chuck Wagon restaurant, the first of George's many, many attempts to establish a business outside and on the back of his recording career. The restaurant also housed a small museum of George Jones memorabilia.

For a few years, there, it seemed like everything was just great. Shirley managed day-to-day operations at the restaurant and handled the family's finances (or, at least, everything that showed up in their mailbox in the form of a check). Meanwhile, Jones' big hits brought constant touring opportunities and his recording sessions were now held exclusively in Nashville, so he was gone nearly all of the time. But at least that meant he didn't come home long enough for an aura of restlessness to accumulate a little more each day until it needed to be destroyed with a weeklong binge three towns over. As for his relationship with their children, even in this picturesque period, it doesn't sound like George would win any Father of the Year awards. To quote Shirley, "Not that he was mean to 'em, just that he didn't have any time or any love for 'em." Still, given the few years of experience Shirley had with the drunken alternative, Jones' occasional presence and relative sobriety while home were an improvement she should appreciate. She also understood his own childhood hadn't exactly left him with a model of what a good father even was, let alone how to actually be one. George's parents may have still been married and living nearby in the home their son purchased for them, but his father still drank as much as ever and it still scared his mother enough for her to frequently run away to stay with George and Shirley. Much later in life, after long-overdue personal growth and reflection, George would realize he'd never been taught the importance of a man sharing his emotions with loved ones. As far as he knew, feelings were meant to be expressed in music, the place he'd learned to put all of his: "Maybe my singin' might be the cause of a lot of my problems. You might be a bastard in other things you do, you might be a sorry son of a gun, but as long as they relate to you in your songs, it seems to be all right. I don't show a lot of affection. I have probably been a very unliked person among family, like somebody who was heartless. I saved it all for the songs. I didn't know you were supposed to show that love person to person. I guess I always wanted to, but I didn't know how. The only way I could would be to do it in a song."

SEVEN

BLOOD AND SAND

◇ Dressed for Success ◇ Mechanics of Murder ◇
A Suit of Lights ◇ Juan Belmonte: A Revolution in Pain ◇

Fewer than twenty years prior to *The Sun Also Rises* changing American literature forever by stripping a story down to its skeleton, Juan Belmonte did the same thing to bullfighting. Though much gravitas and prestige was introduced to the ritual in the two centuries after Spanish noblemen handed bullfights down to commoners, anyone who believes they know what it looks like when a matador engages a bull—even if your only frame of reference is a Bugs Bunny cartoon—would think you were watching the most nervous bullfighter in history should you witness the work of any matador prior to Juan Belmonte. During the event's carnival sideshow era, as soon as the main character in a bullfight moved from a man on horseback to a man on the ground, a simple philosophy was formed: either you move or the bull moves you. Pull off whatever stunts are necessary to make it appear as though you are the big, brave man who's entirely in control of this situation . . . But when a thousand-pound bull charges with the intent to kill, if you don't want to die, then you need to get out of the way, even if it means turning and running for your life. That is what every matador believed and what every matador did for a period of two hundred years . . . until Juan Belmonte stopped getting out of the way.

◇   ◇   ◇

To fully understand Belmonte's impact, we must take a closer look at the mechanics of Spanish bullfighting before he came along, when most matadors were content to follow in the footsteps of Joaquín Rodríguez Costillares, whose eternal influence cannot be overstated. Having recognized the audience's desire for a game of Kill or Be Killed, Costillares took it upon himself to dress for the occasion of either outcome and began to fight bulls while wearing clothes fit for a king. Earning three times more money than his assistants, Costillares could well afford the cost of the expensive fabrics and lavish embroidery then in style amongst Spanish royalty. When aristocratic fashion abandoned such trends, Costillares did not, thereby establishing the notion a matador and his team of bullfighters should wear a certain kind of costume in the ring. Costillares viewed everything within the ring that he could control as an opportunity to manipulate the experience of spectators. Where previous bullfighters had used a cape as a simple tool to attract and direct a bull's attention, Costillares saw his cape as an instrument of drama and introduced a formalized technique of cape passes involving large, sweeping flourishes. He is the matador said to've invented an early version of the *verónica*. Named for the sainted woman who wiped the bloody face of Jesus as he carried a cross to Calvary (thus reinforcing the bull as avatar of universal life force), a basic *verónica* is the pass a bullfighter initiates by using both hands to hold up a large cape at roughly torso height, as would a devout infantryman raise the banner of his lord's noble house while marching to battle. This posture in itself is nothing more than a visual novelty, a means to no practical end. The true purpose of every functional act in a bullfight is to bring and keep the bull's head low enough to eventually kill it by reaching over the otherwise-deadly horns and stabbing it through the back. Each and every torture suffered by a bull in the ring is meant to damage its extraordinarily strong neck muscles, inflicting enough pain to prevent the bull from raising its head or otherwise engaging these muscles unless it believes there's a chance to kill a bullfighter and stop the hellish experience.

And bulls are not so stupid as we may assume from watching one after another die trying to attack a cape instead of attacking the man who holds the cape. As a charging bull approaches the *verónica* or any derivative pass, the cape comes to occupy more and more of the bull's field of vision until it can see little else. So long as that cape is held right in the bull's face, it obscures the presence of the matador, who waits until the horns have passed or turned away to snatch the cape backward or up toward the sky just before the bull can connect with it. What we're seeing is not the stupidity of a bull but the intelligence of a killer, who knows he cannot let that bull run through or even touch the cape without the bull developing *sentido*, the sudden awareness (or "sense") it has been trying to attack an illusion, at which point it will find something real to attack. Thus, the margin for error in capework is gravely small. A single gust of wind may mean the difference between life or death and the smarter the bull, the fewer mistakes can be made. Even if the matador never slips up once, each bull learns more about its predicament with every pass. That is the entire reason there's a time limit on each fight: most bulls bred for the ring require little more than half an hour to figure out the trick of the cape whether they've made contact with it or not. Any indication of that lightbulb coming on in the mind of a bull means it's time to immediately kill the bull. No matador wants to try reaching over horns informed by *sentido*.

Costillares' introduction of prolonged capework exposed each bull he fought to many more passes, which made Francisco Romero's method of killing *recibiendo* even riskier than it already was, so Costillares invented a new coup de grâce. To kill *volapié*, the matador essentially reverses the action of *recibiendo*. Rather than standing to receive a charging bull, the matador runs his cape toward a standing bull and dives over the horns to deliver a fatal blow into a stationary target. Though this acrobatic maneuver is still very dangerous and the effect is visually sensational, its true purpose was to provide the matador with an easier kill of a smarter bull while satisfying popular demand for death-defying circus acts. Foundational as Costillares was in establishing so many core tenets of modern Spanish bullfighting, what most modern aficionados would call his lasting contributions to the aesthetic of elegance and flair, contemporary detractors saw as flamboyance and femininity. They complained Costillares' flashy new techniques came at the sacrifice of substance; they much preferred the work of his great rival, Pedro Romero, who perfected his grandfather's "manlier" *recibiendo* method and used it to kill more than five thousand bulls in three decades as a matador.

In 1793, three decades into his own career, Costillares petitioned all major bullrings to update their dress codes. At the time, remnants of sumptuary laws intended to prevent commoners dressing above their station allowed only bullfighters on horseback to use silver thread in their costumes. As Francisco Romero had long ago relegated bullfighters on horseback to the role of assistants, Costillares' request was granted and all bullfighters were allowed to wear silver thread. Near the end of the decade, when the great master painter Goya made a portrait of Pedro Romero, the matador's entire torso was wrapped in silver thread. (Though he was never a bullfighter, when Goya painted a self-portrait near the end of the eighteenth century, he depicted himself wearing the outfit of a matador, indicating the eminence and heroism that had become associated with the occupation.) A later update to the dress code granted matadors exclusive use of golden thread in their costumes, reflecting their new role as *maestro* of the bullfight and leaving silver thread to the assistants.

In 1836, matador Francisco Montes Reina, a.k.a. "Paquiro," wrote the book on Spanish bullfighting. *Tauromaquia* ("bull killing") codified the structure of a professional bullfight by officially delineating the separate segments of a fight, specifying the number of bullfighters to a team and so on. Paquiro was said to've counterbalanced Costillares' feminine influence by introducing certain physical postures that communicated an arrogant machismo within the matador persona, a trend which has only escalated in the two centuries since. Paquiro was the matador who began waiting as long as possible before jumping out of the way of a charging bull, exaggerating the suspense and heightening the danger to prove he could remain calm in the face of death. Perhaps to decrease the chances of being caught by a horn while doing this, he was the matador who modified the cuts on his costume so it hugged tighter to the body, which came with the added benefit of bringing a greater range of motion to the arms. Since "bull killing" has always been done in the afternoon sun, Paquiro added reflective sequins to his costume's already outrageous configuration of golden-threaded embroidery, thereby inventing *el traje de luces*, or "suit of lights," which remains visually synonymous with bullfighters to this day. He was the first matador to wear that black hat with two almost–Mickey Mouse ears on it, sunlight sparkling radiantly off his clothing, chin raised high in defiance and shoulders set back as he thrust either chest or hips forward, physically challenging the bull to come do its worst. Paquiro became nothing less than a superstar in Spain with the accompanying wealth, social status and publicized private life to show for it. After him, a famous matador's sexual conquests outside the ring became as much a part of their image as any performance given in the ring.

In the late 1800s, the matador Frascuelo was involved in a bit of a scandal when he entered the bullring wearing his *traje de luces*, which the audience instantly recognized as matching the colors of a dress worn by a woman of Spanish nobility already seated in a place of honor in the stands. Though we can't be certain of her detailed motives for shamelessly broadcasting intimate foreknowledge of Frascuelo's chosen colors for the day, she was obviously either some kind of exhibitionist and/or had a reason to want to piss off her aristocratic family by making sure everyone knew she was fucking a bullfighter. However much old money may look down upon those who achieve wealth through celebrity in the entertainment business, that doesn't stop the poorest members of society from looking up to the most visible representations of former peers who gained freedom from financial worry. While famous matadors predate the existence of famous baseball players (and, again, Spanish bullfighting has never been a sport), celebrity athletes are the closest parallel we have in modern society. As illustrated magazines and large billboards came into existence, marketing agencies increasingly turned to celebrity endorsements and matadors were paid to hawk wines, tobaccos and various other "masculine" products. Children in the Spain of Pablo Picasso's youth hunted packs of cigarettes to collect matador cards rather than baseball cards. And still, every last one of these legendary matadors would be made to look like a day one rookie if he was forced to share the ring with Juan Belmonte.

To be clear, common knowledge of the era held standing still in front of a fighting bull's charging horns to be somewhere in the realm of suicidally insane. In the late nineteenth century, an entirely separate daredevil act developed around this very notion. To perform the *Don Tancredo* any idiot desperate for money, thrills or bragging rights merely needed to stand as still as his nerves would allow upon a stool or some other platform while an angry wild bull was run into the ring to decide whether or not this human statue was worth demolishing. Things often went very poorly for the statue. Since all matadors of the era believed they must move or be moved, they all remained light on their toes whenever close to a bull and did a great deal of running or hopping away from bulls, similar to the physical behavior of a rodeo clown. No matter how cocky these particular rodeo clowns seemed to be about their job or fame or wealth or the way they were dressed, no matter how many arrogant postures and death-defying stunts they pulled to demonstrate a lack of fear, they all remained visibly prepared to cut and run if a bull tried to gore them. One early twentieth-century matador even found a way to spin this necessity by exaggerating his seemingly fearful movements to the point they played as comedy. Rafael Gómez Ortega, a.k.a. *El Gallo* or "The Rooster," would have been a popular guest on the TV show *Jackass*. While regarded as a great matador, *El Gallo* would occasionally give in to "terror" and run away from a bull while high-stepping like a rooster, working the audience for laughs. When *El Gallo* "conquered" his fear to slay the beast with skill, crowds loved him all the more. And he was a rare exception, one of the few matadors able to continue performing his act unchanged for another fifteen years after Juan Belmonte changed everything.

◇   ◇   ◇

As Hemingway wrote in *The Sun Also Rises*, the rapid growth of Belmonte's fame can be partly attributed to the common opinion among fans and other bullfighters that any interested parties should see Belmonte at their earliest opportunity, since he was sure to be a dead man very soon. Where other matadors stayed in near-constant motion while near a bull, half-crouched in case they were forced to jump and run away, Belmonte prepared for a standard pass by shuffling his feet into position, fully planting them on the ground and locking his knees to stand erect as the bull ran by. He then shuffled in pursuit of the bull to stay close enough to do it again . . . and again . . . and again. Few spectators could believe what they were seeing and nearly nobody thought Belmonte even knew what he was doing. Matadors of this era were supposed to project pure alpha energy while performing with as much physical grace as possible. Belmonte's body was weak and frail. His posture was poor and he fought with a visibly obvious absence of any formal training or technique. Yet there he was, working closer to the bull and for longer periods of time than anyone had ever done or thought could be possible. Throughout the first year of Belmonte's career there were various theories put forth attempting to explain his method. Some said a medical condition kept his muscles from developing and/or his legs were damaged in childbirth, therefore Belmonte simply could not run away from the bull like other matadors. Others suspected they were witnessing a man more desperate, deranged or drunk than any they'd seen perform a *Don Tancredo* take a version of the same act to extreme lengths.

It is true Belmonte's preshow ritual was to visualize himself being gored and killed over and over and over with the belief that if he could accept beforehand he was only going out there in order to be gored and killed, then the fear of it happening would never affect his performance. However, the full truth is Juan Belmonte was born into poverty in 1892 and grew up, not anywhere near a ranch or bulls, but in the city streets of Sevilla, the capital of Andalucia. He was the oldest of his father's eleven children and the family never had enough food for those kids to build strong bodies. Juan only went to school from the ages of four to eight, so he could read and write but little more, and he never successfully held down any kind of job before becoming a matador. He and the other poor boys of the alleys in Sevilla all dreamt of growing up to become rich and famous matadors, as did all poor boys in every alley of Spain. Unlike most of those boys, Belmonte and his friends actually tried, walking miles outside of the city to trespass on private property and fight bulls in pastures in the middle of the night. Now, if those had been bulls bred for fighting, then probably nobody would've ever heard the name Juan Belmonte because he'd have been killed in adolescence, either gored by an industrial-strength bull or shot by the vigilant guards hired to prevent dumbasses from doing this and inadvertently teaching *sentido* to wild bulls who would someday be in a bullfight. But bulls of just about any breed can be incited to charge and this was how Belmonte developed the mechanics of his style, using his jacket as a cape while standing inside what little light his friends could provide with two gas lanterns. If the engaged bull moved outside that circle of light, then it would disappear into the surrounding darkness, where it would still be very angry at who was now the single most well-lit being in the entire field. That's why Belmonte learned to get close and stay close, where he discovered for himself how the cape effect could be pushed far beyond its believed limitations. These may not have been fighting bulls, but they still weighed hundreds of pounds and had horns. Belmonte was hurt often during this learning process but it only served to teach him what he could survive, a lesson he learned again and again when gored by fighting bulls in nearly every one of his first real fights during the year 1910. Unhealed injuries sustained in previous fights were another true cause for his sickly appearance and poor posture. But no matter how much blood Belmonte left in the ring, he performed previously unthinkable acts and walked away a killer of bulls. No matter how many people said he was a fluke or anomaly, a lucky idiot who would soon be dead, Belmonte did not die. Instead, he got even better, fighting in the light of the sun and with real capes designed for the purpose. By the third year of his career, many were calling him the greatest matador in history. He became so famous it was necessary to wear a cap low over his face in order to sneak on his first merry-go-round ride, an unfulfilled wish he could never afford in childhood.

Because a typical bullfight features three matadors with teams who each take turns fighting and killing their own bull, then repeat the cycle with a second bull for each team, then a third bull, every matador in a bullfight has to follow every other matador's act. So, if one of those guys walks out there and starts doing some totally crazy shit like standing fairly still while performing capework in sustained proximity to a bull, far beyond what any matador in history previously believed could be done, the other two matadors are going to look like frightened teenagers, hopping around like a couple of bunny rabbits as if a stone-cold murderer wasn't just in that same ring. The longer Belmonte worked without dying, the more other matadors were forced nearer to the bull and for longer periods of time. Matadors unwilling to take greater risks were booed and several left more than blood in the ring trying to please crowds without understanding how Belmonte did what he did.

El Gallo, the "rooster" who ran for laughs, he had a younger brother known by the name of Joselito who was already regarded as a marvelous matador when Belmonte came along. Of Belmonte's ninety fights in the year 1915, sixty-eight were with Joselito. Though aficionados of the time believed them to be bitter rivals, the two young bullfighters in fact became fast friends as they traveled and fought in the same rings together for several seasons. Joselito recognized Belmonte's style as the future of bullfighting and learned what he could, then returned the favor by sharing his own formal training with Belmonte. Each matador so greatly affected the other, it would be accurate to say from this point forward Belmonte fought with a trace of Joselito's technique while Joselito fought with a trace of Belmonte's daring. Or, as Joselito is supposed to've once said to Belmonte, "You can fight a bull better than me, but I am a better bullfighter than you." They became as two sides of the same coin. The true feud was always between their fans, who argued and fought and cheered and booed according to their preferred side of the coin. These years are now regarded by most aficionados to have been a golden age in bullfighting, but contemporary fans of both matadors grew increasingly dissatisfied as this "rivalry" wore on. The problem, essentially, was that Belmonte and Joselito got too good at their jobs. As they became more adept at fighting ever closer to the bull and for longer periods of time, they were gored less often. Even though they were both performing feats considered downright impossible only a few years earlier, continuing to push past even their own limits, they became good enough to make it look easy. Audiences were convinced these famous matadors had grown too rich and comfortable to keep taking great risks. Because if they weren't playing it safe, then why were they not bleeding as much as they used to bleed? Crowds seeing Belmonte for the first time, in particular, could not help but be disappointed after having heard all the stories of this drunk, mangled lunatic with nothing to lose who was sure to be dead any day now. It was bad enough Belmonte continued to live but now he had the audacity to keep his blood inside his body and fans were sure they'd been cheated, convinced he held back a more daring performance out of laziness or complacency. Joselito and Belmonte were booked together for a series of fights in the year 1920. On the first day, the crowd heckled them so savagely Joselito refused to return on the second day. He instead went to fight in another city, where he was fatally gored at the age of twenty-five. Juan Belmonte kept fighting another fifteen years. He was never killed by a bull.

EIGHT

ALL TO PIECES

◇ George Jones, Hit Songwriter ◇ From Mercury to United Artists ◇
"She Thinks I Still Care" ◇ Pining for Melba Montgomery ◇ "The Race Is On"
◇ Gene Pitney Goes Country ◇ A Golden Era at Musicor ◇
"Walk Through This World with Me" ◇ The King of Broken Hearts ◇

There's a myth, believed and repeated by many country music fans, which usually goes something like: "George Jones never wrote a song in his life but he sure could sing one." This is probably due to how many stories exist of George taking partial credit on songs he truly had no hand in writing. But that was a universally standard practice of the industry at the time—it still is, in certain corners—and George doing the same thing as everyone else doesn't mean he never wrote a song. According to Pappy Daily, George could sit down with a guitar and make up songs all day long. The problem was he'd rarely record demos or even write down his compositions. Pappy seemed to think George just didn't give a shit but it's likely the opposite was true. If George held himself to a standard of songwriting that was half as high as the standard he held for his singing, there's no reason to think he'd write down a song unless he believed it was particularly good. We know for a fact he didn't even think all the ones good enough to write down were necessarily good enough to record himself. George never recorded "Shakin' the Blues," the song he wrote and gave to Donny Young. George wrote both sides of Benny Barnes' first Starday single and never cut either song. If the way Benny sang it is any indication, "Once Again" was another early attempt to channel Hank Williams. And Benny's first record may very well have been a hit if Starday had put "No Fault of Mine" on the A-side. (That's George playing lead guitar.) Not everything George Jones ever wrote was a hit but several songs were. He wrote "You Gotta Be My Baby" and "Just One More" entirely on his own; "Life to Go" and "Don't Stop the Music" are known to be legitimate co-writes.

For a singer who rarely gets his due as a writer, "The Window Up Above" is a monster of a song. Examine the writing style of Leonard Cohen, a devout George Jones fan, and ask yourself how many hours Cohen must have spent obsessing over the opening lines: "I've been living a new way / of life that I love so / but I can see the clouds are gathering / and the storm will wreck our home." Since "the storm" is revealed to be marital infidelity, witnessed by a husband from his second-story bedroom window, and George's own marriage began to fall apart within a couple years of this "rare" George Jones composition, many fans have speculated this song was inspired by true events. Because George's favorite songs to sing were the slow and sad ones, if you look at most of what he ever wrote for himself you'll find slow and sad songs, given to themes of failed relationships. Several months prior to "Window Up Above," he recorded another of his own songs, called "Glad to Let Her Go," written on the same theme and using part of the same melody he would later recycle for "Window Up Above." In the lyrics of "Glad to Let Her Go," George has already gone cold on the relationship by the time the wife starts cheating. There is no reason to suspect either of these very similar songs was inspired by the behavior of George's wife, as they were both written near the beginning of the two- or three-year period Shirley Jones herself described as the happiest time in their marriage. George wrote "Window Up Above" one morning at home while Shirley cooked breakfast for the family. Whatever storm clouds he may or may not have foreseen years in the future, they didn't come from Shirley's side of the relationship.

If anything, that storm would have been delayed by "Window Up Above." Released in September of 1960, it stayed on the charts for thirty-four weeks and peaked at #2, a big enough hit to justify another Nudie suit, as literal as any ever made, clouds and windows, straight from the lyrics. The single was all over the airwaves in October, when the Country Music DJ Convention took place at the Hermitage Hotel in Nashville. A young singer named George Riddle, who'd come to Nashville earlier in the year to try breaking into the music business, was wandering the halls of the hotel when he heard what sounded a lot like George Jones singing inside a room, so Riddle just walked inside, where he found George Jones laying on a bed, playing guitar and singing. When Riddle introduced himself as a fan and aspiring country singer, Jones threw out a couple songs to hear the kid sing and then said he'd actually been hoping to hire a harmony vocalist while in Nashville because he had a tour starting the next day. Since Riddle was able to leave town the next day, he became George Jones' first full-time band member, which meant no more relying entirely upon honky-tonk house bands or borrowed players from other acts on a tour. With Riddle (who soon found himself being called "Georgie" what with having the same first name as his boss and all), Jones now had a traveling sidekick who knew all his latest records, sang harmony and kept those pickup bands on track while Jones focused on singing. On most of Jones' television appearances in the early 1960s, it's Riddle you see leaning into frame to sing harmony. George could have hired someone to do all of this stuff at any point after "White Lightning" hit #1 and put him in a higher tax bracket. The sudden need for a touring backup singer stemmed from "Window Up Above" hitting #2 as the first George Jones release to feature a Nashville-style vocal group, the Anita Kerr Singers. Because of those background vocals and previously mentioned misconceptions, this is often incorrectly referred to as Jones' first Nashville Sound recording. Really, that happened when Hank Garland worked the session for "Too Much Water" in 1957. The A-Team players on "Window Up Above"—Garland, Grady Martin, Floyd Cramer, Tommy Jackson, etc.—had all done Jones' Nashville sessions for years by this time. However, this was his highest charting record to date with an actual country song and it was a ballad to boot, so Jones reinforced his position by adding a second vocalist to concerts in order to give fans something a bit closer to what they heard on the record.

Jones didn't need to go back in the studio for another ten months, partly because "Window Up Above" was such a huge hit and partly because Mercury already had a ton of tape in the can. The day before recording "Window Up Above," Jones cut an entire twelve song LP of Hank Williams hits in one marathon session that extended from three o' clock in the afternoon to probably past midnight. As was often the case with Pappy Daily's quantity-over-quality filler sessions, the arrangement of every song is nearly identical, which does make for a monotonous listening experience but it's interesting to hear how secure Jones had grown in his vocal identity, only rarely slipping into what it would be more accurate to call acknowledgments rather than imitations of the voice he once clung to like a security blanket, even on Hank Williams classics like "I Can't Help It (If I'm Still in Love with You)" or "There'll Be No Teardrops Tonight." A couple days prior to the marathon Hank session, Jones pulled another nine hours or so cutting a bunch of covers and rerecordings of his own biggest hits, like "Why Baby Why." All of this material was almost certainly chosen and rush-recorded in such mass quantity in order to compete with the George Jones catalog left behind at Starday, since the sessions roughly coincided with the end of the eighteen-month period during which Don Pierce continued to receive half the publisher's share of George Jones' writing royalties. Those would've been some pretty huge checks to just stop receiving one day and Don Pierce made up for the lost revenue by doing what everyone always knew he was going to do: repackaging the George Jones tapes still owned by Starday and flooding the market with compilation LPs of his earliest hits, soundalikes, even the earliest sessions when Jones still sounded like a Hank Williams impersonator. The best George and Pappy could do was try to compete with newer versions of his old hits, newer versions of Hank covers, etc. After a few decades spent fielding questions on Thumper Jones material and the soundalikes nobody was ever supposed to know he did, George eventually grew to hate this side of the record business. Only a few years after the first time this happened, in the mid-1960s, Starday released another batch of early Jones soundalikes and a collection of early, cheap-sounding Buck Owens demos and soundalikes, which prompted George and Buck to get angry and drive over to Starday together to kick up some dirt about it. According to Buck, they left about a half an hour later with their arms full of rare country albums any fan would love to have and no memory of why they'd been so mad.

By the time Jones finally got back in the studio, on February 8, 1961, Shelby Singleton had become his producer at Mercury. Shelby brought future A-Team guitarist/producer Jerry Kennedy up from Louisiana to lead the sessions, but it sounds like Shelby and Jerry were still hanging back to learn how Nashville musicians did things. The instrumentation was nearly identical to Jones' previous, pre-Shelby session for "Window Up Above." Tommy Jackson returned on fiddle. Buddy Harman was back on drums. Pig Robbins did a spotless Floyd Cramer impersonation on piano. The biggest change came from replacing the Anita Kerr Singers with (for the first time on a George Jones session) the Jordanaires, who brought along Millie Kirkham. Known as the "Nashville soprano," Millie's extra-high-pitched background vocals had already been featured in Elvis Presley's "Blue Christmas" and Ferlin Husky's "Gone." While the instrumentation stayed the same, the arrangement and performance of the first single released from Jones' first session with Shelby was much more dynamic. The Owen Bradley influence on "Tender Years" is there from the opening notes: piano, front and center, accompanied by bass and a brushed snare. Jones' voice slowly makes its way through a verse, three or four words at a time, accompanied by lazy fiddle and fingerpicked acoustic guitar. Where we expect a second verse, the song instead suddenly lifts into a quick chorus with the Jordanaires behind Jones like the soundtrack of a cartoon sunrise. On the second half of the chorus Millie Kirkham soars in to join the vocal interplay before all the background singers drop out to give Jones another verse on his own, pedal steel now replacing the fiddle until the cycle repeats. A/B "Tender Years" against "Window Up Above" and you'll immediately hear which song has the more dynamic arrangement. On the earlier track, any time you hear George Jones, you will also hear the Anita Kerr Singers because they stay right with him the whole song. Conversely, after the piano break on "Tender Years," Pig Robbins stays in the mix, throwing around splashes of high notes à la Floyd Cramer until the song's end. If it were possible to copyright production techniques, Owen Bradley would have made a lot of money on this recording, mostly thanks to two other first-timers in a George Jones session, Walter Haynes (one of Owen's favorite pedal steel guitarists, who would soon play on most of Patsy Cline's greatest hits) and bassist Bob Moore (who by this time had worked with Owen for ten years and would soon become George Jones' uncredited producer through most of the 1960s—while also playing on all those Patsy Cline hits). After "Tenders Years" became Jones' second #1 song, the next single released from the session went #5. "Aching, Breaking Heart" picks up the tempo while keeping the Bradley-esque dynamics in place. Listen to the way all the musicians hit a stop at the end of the verse then jump back in all together once Jones kicks off the chorus. (There's a small piece of trivia attached to this preview of the Owen Bradley impersonation Bob Moore would perform on George Jones records for most of the '60s, itself a preview of the way Billy Sherrill would use Owen's studio and musicians to stretch the limitations of the Nashville Sound on George Jones records in the '70s and '80s. "Aching, Breaking Heart" was written by Rick Hall of FAME Studios in Muscle Shoals, Alabama. But FAME was originally located across the river in Florence until Rick split with one of his founding partners, Billy Sherrill, who moved to Nashville about a year before this session.)

George's second session with Shelby Singleton took place later the same day as the first with one major difference, Shelby, ever the hustler, brought his wife to work. Don Pierce may have hated Margie Singleton's Starday records but if Jones had any problems with her voice he never made a comment about it. For what it's worth, he loved doing duets, especially with women, and it sounds like he was having a good time on these recordings. The lead single, co-written by Margie, naturally, was called "Did I Ever Tell You." A silly, upbeat love song, far more pop than country, it still charted at #15. Their second single sounds as if it may have been the first song George and Margie recorded together, perhaps even the first time they ever sang together at all. Beautifully written by Jack Rhodes, co-writer on "A Satisfied Mind," "The Waltz of the Angels" was first cut by Lefty Frizzell as a B-side in 1956 and has since been recorded by everyone from Kitty Wells to Johnny Pay-Check. Wynn Stewart's version is particularly great. George and Margie's version is not particularly great. Their phrasing is noticeably out of sync for most of the song, probably the result of everyone assuming they didn't need to practice what had become a genre standard over the previous five years. Despite such faults, the song was a pretty sure thing on its own merits, and the record hit #11.

With a handful of duet and solo hits from those two February 8th sessions, George took another seven-month break from recording to focus on more nonstop touring. When he did return to the studio in September of 1961, everyone knew they were cutting his final tape for Mercury. *Billboard* had announced his new deal at United Artists the same month. True to form, Shelby Singleton used his last day working with George Jones to record nothing but duets with Margie, rushing through ten songs in five hours, which gave Mercury enough to press a full duet LP. Due to the purpose of the sessions and the absence of Bob Moore, the results are largely uninteresting with one standout exception. Far and away the most dynamic cut of the bunch, only ever released as a B-side, "When Two Worlds Collide" was one of Roger Miller's sadder compositions. Whether inspired by the singular vibrato of Margie's voice, the appropriately sparse arrangement, or the fact he was leaving the label and truly didn't care how it sold, George made some epic choices on this track. He practically hijacks his own vocal cords, predicting some of the more extreme vocal acrobatics he'd perform years in the future, as well as the aching horniness of Conway Twitty. It sounds like he's trying to see if it's possible to pull a muscle in his throat.

✧　　✧　　✧

The five-year contract Jones originally signed with Mercury-Starday went into effect in January 1957 and was therefore set to expire in January of 1962. But that did not necessarily preordain his exit from Mercury at that time. Once Starday was dropped from the equation, George instantly began charting bigger hits and recording exclusively in a state-of-the-art studio with the best musicians available. Money may not be able to buy happiness but it can buy everything else. It's probably not a coincidence that the period Shirley Jones called the happiest of their marriage roughly coincides with her husband's time as a hit machine for Mercury Records. So why would Pappy Daily not leverage his artist's proven track record to negotiate an even better contract with Mercury? Why leave a label where everything was going so well? When reporters asked George such questions, he said Mercury's interests had turned from country to rock & roll. This was just as true then as it had been several years earlier, when Mercury dropped Starday's country operation while going through great lengths to retain the contract of George Jones, whose sales figures then exponentially increased as he released one Top 5 single after another, including two #1s. There's no question Mercury remained very "interested" in George Jones, regardless of what he said in interviews, probably nothing more than repeating whatever talking points Pappy Daily gave him in case the subject came up.

Pappy insisted there was never a formal management contract between himself and George Jones, which is entirely plausible. But the only reason anyone ever asked that question was because of how much Pappy walked, talked and made deals exactly like he was George Jones' manager, because, contract or not, he effectively always was. Pappy's formal title may have been "producer" but the closest he ever got to production work was in the old school sense of selecting and negotiating terms for the material George recorded. Wielding such control while having George signed to a publishing contract in an era when major artists received partial writing credit as compensation for cutting songs meant Pappy took down a way larger percentage than whatever he'd net from a standard management deal. If we're looking for the actual reason George left Mercury, we're looking for a man by the name of Art Talmadge, one of Mercury's co-founders, the man who (according to Shelby Singleton) was the main mover and shaker at the label during the 1950s. In June of 1960, Talmadge left Mercury, presumably for a greater profit share and near-unilateral control as Vice President of United Artists Records. The same September 1961 issue of *Billboard* that announced George Jones had joined United Artists also announced Pappy Daily as the label's new head of Country & Western A&R. Long story short, Art Talmadge once more went through Pappy Daily to poach George Jones over to another label, similar to the way he'd taken George from Starday to Mercury.

◇   ◇   ◇

Still in the happy era of home life, one way Jones stayed out of trouble was by hanging out with friends in places other than honky-tonks. About fifteen miles down the road from his ranch in

Vidor, Texas, in the town of Beaumont, there was a new studio called Gulf Coast Recording, opened near the end of 1961 by producers Bill Hall—the first person to technically hold the title of George Jones' "manager" back in the mid-1950s, though, again, Pappy always ran the show—and "Cowboy" Jack Clement, who was one of those larger-than-life, infinitely quotable characters. Like every other producer, Cowboy owned a publishing company and two of his writers had come up with a song so perfect for George Jones it probably kept Jack awake at night imagining how good it would sound if George cut it. Every time Jones came by Cowboy picked up a guitar and sang the song, not to him but at him. George wasn't sure about it. He thought the lyrics were too repetitive, what with how every line started with the words "just because" over and over and over. Whenever Cowboy started pitching it again, George would deflect to this little tape recorder unit in the office, asking how much money they'd take for it. After running through that routine a few times, Bill Hall finally said they'd give him the damn tape recorder if Jones just cut the song. In the end Cowboy had to give up 50 percent of the publishing to Pappy Daily but when Jones' contract with Mercury expired he hit the studio right away to cut Cowboy's song in the very first recording session for United Artists.

Dickey Lee and Steve Duffy wrote "She Thinks I Still Care" as something of a pop take on Hank Williams' "I Can't Help It (If I'm Still in Love with You)," admitting to the same pathetic behavior but trying to play it off with wacky sarcasm. (Think Daffy Duck or Jack Lemmon in *Some Like It Hot* delivering lines like "just because I rang her number by mistake today, she thinks I still care.") But Cowboy knew this silly song would play an entirely different way if someone like George Jones sang it as though there was nothing funny about it at all. And he was right. When you hear people compare Jones' voice to a pedal steel guitar, "She Thinks I Still Care" is one of the performances they're referencing. It's in the way Jones glides smoothly between and through the notes. He careens throughout his vocal range, demonstrating unbelievably tight control wherever he goes, veering back and forth like slow-motion footage of a motorcyclist illegally navigating traffic on a four-lane highway. The single came out in February 1962 and spent six weeks at #1, his second #1 in two years, establishing a new standard in the genre and George's eternal status as a superstar, a paragon of country music.

From this moment in time forward, walking into any half-decent honky-tonk in the world and loudly insulting George Jones would be a pretty quick way to get your ass handed to you. Some of his first singles had been covered by other artists but once George began hitting with ballads and showing off everything his voice could do, the contemporary covers pretty much stopped. It took four years for Johnny Cash to record "Just One More" and even then it was a filler track on a whole album of covers. Other than some lowly soundalikes, a Stanley Brothers single that bombed and a few uses as album filler, nobody really touched "Window Up Above" until Mickey Gilley had a hit with it fifteen years after the original. There were zero notable contemporary covers of "Don't

Stop the Music" or "Color of the Blues." Songwriters used to say George Jones cutting one of your songs was a blessing and a curse. On one hand, you got to hear him sing your song and there was a decent chance it'd be a hit. On the other hand, you weren't likely to have many other people record it because nobody wanted their version to be compared to George Jones. Because another thing everyone used to say about George was when he sang a song, it stayed sung. Then, with "She Thinks I Still Care," something changed. The way he sang it made everybody else want to sing it, too. Not because they thought they could also have a hit with it. Not because they thought they could sing it better. Not even because they felt they had something to add. George just sang it so well, they had to sing it, too. Ferlin Husky, Eddy Arnold, the Wilburn Brothers and Faron Young all recorded "She Thinks I Still Care" within a few years of the initial hit record. This was when other artists began doing "a Jones song," either one of his hits adapted to their own style (as Cash did with "Just One More") or adopting key traits of Jones' style in near-impersonation. It was something more than appreciation, appropriation or commentary. It was homage to a living legend. Six months after George's hit, international pop superstar Connie Francis recorded it as "He Thinks I Still Care," which wound up on the B-side of a Top 40 pop hit and was immediately covered by international pop superstar Cher on her first solo album. It's important to note these pop artists did not re-introduce the comedy intended by the songwriters, who originally wrote it as a goofy pop song. Connie Francis made every effort to mimic Jones' apathy, going so far as to record her version at the Quonset Hut in Nashville with the A-Team. Even Cher, with Sonny Bono's cheap imitation of Phil Spector circus music behind her, was unable to put any kind of humor into her performance. That's how sung this song stayed after George Jones was done with it.

The industry dumped a pile of awards on him at the 1962 DJ Convention. *Billboard* and *Cash Box* both named him Male Vocalist of the Year for 1962 and 1963. And even though he continued to steadily release major hits, those were the last major awards he received until the 1970s, probably because everyone in the business was worried if they gave George Jones an award he may show up to accept it. Somewhere in here, as "She Thinks I Still Care" started to become something more than just another #1 record, Jones lost control. Ever since childhood he'd been told how great a singer he was but drunk people in honky-tonks saying you're the best they've ever heard is one thing. This was a totally different thing. Once other major label artists began doing "a Jones song"—not merely covers but tributes to a master stylist—anyone with the idea George Jones may be The Greatest Country Singer Ever was able to sit down with a stack of records and make comparisons between multiple vocalists attacking the exact same song. An overwhelming majority of people who've ever performed this experiment walk away having reached the same conclusion, which may be the worst thing that could've happened to George Jones. This was the point when honky-tonk crowds went from yelling he was their favorite or the best they'd ever heard to yelling he was the best to ever do it, calling out his heroes by name and saying he was better than they'd ever been—better than Roy Acuff, better than Lefty Frizzell, better than Hank Williams. It wasn't just the honky-tonk crowds anymore, either. It was everyone, the magazines, other country stars, even some of those same heroes. This was the point when his stage fright during TV appearances became consistently and visibly apparent. Watching the footage, you can see it in his eyes. It's not anxiety. It's terror. The only times he doesn't look drunk and afraid are the times he looks so cadaverously hungover from the night before he couldn't have felt anything but a splitting headache, which was probably the whole point of getting that drunk. There's a black-and-white video of "She Thinks I Still Care" with Georgie Riddle on the *Grand Ole Opry* from 1962. At the beginning, Jones' voice sounds as scratchy as if he'd been punched in the throat, but he works through the sandpaper and gets where he needs to go. When the camera moves in close, the bags under his eyes are so severe they look like bruises covered with makeup, as if he didn't sleep for two days and then got into a fight, which could very well be what happened.

According to Riddle, Jones managed to get in at least one big fight per tour from the very beginning. That was the baseline, a dependable and evidently acceptable side effect of substance abuse on tour, even in the period when his still-happy home life and not-yet-living-legend level of fame were not gigantic sources of stress. From there Riddle watched it all get worse. Call it Phase II of George Jones' addictions. When Jones later tried to claim his drinking didn't get out of control or become violent until the early 1960s, he was talking about this transition into Phase II—not the beginning of what most people would call problematic intake but the next stage of its evolution. This was when Jones started failing to show up to concerts often enough to build a reputation for it. This was when rumors of his alcoholism became such stuff of legend that one obnoxious night-club owner hounded George to have a drink until George finally did have a drink, then tried to break everything in sight, including that club owner's face.

In 1962, George shared a road manager and did a lot of touring with Johnny Cash. One night they were all in a hotel room when Jones got pissed off for some reason and broke something. Cash, his first #1 record hitting back in 1956, was a few years ahead of Jones and had already been through most of this stuff. He calmly stated the dollar amount the hotel would charge Jones for the item he'd just broken. When Jones responded by breaking something else, Cash again announced how much he'd be billed and it turned into a sort of game for Jones, to see if he could break something Cash hadn't broken before. Turns out, he couldn't. When the bill came Cash's inventory of the charges was almost dead-on. He'd priced everything correctly except two lamps.

Also in 1962, George played two days in a row at the New River Ranch, an outdoor stage in the middle of some woods near the Maryland-Pennsylvania border. He showed up drunk on the first day, cussed out the local backing band in front of an all-ages audience, fired the band onstage in the middle of the show, then left Georgie Riddle to deal with the mess while Jones stomped off in his fancy western suit and cowboy boots a half mile down the road to the nearest telephone, presumably to cuss out an agent or perhaps ask Pappy Daily why in the fuck are he and Georgie Riddle out here in the middle of nowhere playing with some band of strangers who don't even know his records? How was he supposed to put on a good show under these conditions, let alone meet the zealous expectations now placed upon him by everyone hoping to witness The Greatest Country Singer Ever? It goes back to the big Mercury-Starday question: if there's such a thing as being a country music star, shouldn't it pay enough money to not have to cut corners? Never mind that Pappy Daily or whoever else was likely to respond by presenting invoices for trashed hotel rooms or bringing up all the stories they'd heard about their *Grand Ole Opry* star lighting hundred dollar bills on fire and flushing 'em down toilets. Jones was probably under the impression a country music star's income should be sufficient to cover those expenses, too. The second day at New River Ranch he returned wearing hungover embarrassment and the same suit as the day before. Backed by the very same musicians he'd fired onstage, he played the whole show without any problems.

◇   ◇   ◇

When George Jones returned to New River Ranch in 1963, it was in his very first tour bus which also carried the Jones Boys, the band Georgie Riddle had been told to hire soon after the previous year's incident. Georgie stuck around to lead the Jones Boys for about another year, then quit in late 1964 or early 1965, after it had become evident a bus and a band were not going to keep the George Jones show on the road. Also advertised on the poster for George Jones & The Jones Boys' 1963 concert at New River Ranch: Melba Montgomery.

Melba was born in Tennessee in 1938 but raised in Florence, Alabama. Her father sang, played guitar and fiddle and taught music to his children. In 1958, a decade after Melba received her first guitar at the age of ten, she and one of her brothers made it into the final round of an amateur talent contest on WSM, where Roy Acuff was one of the judges. Acuff happened to be looking for someone to replace the "Prettiest Smokey Mountain Boy" June Webb and he was impressed enough by Melba to give her the spot in his band. She sang and toured with the Smokey Mountain Boys for four years, until, with Acuff's blessing, she went solo in 1962. Both of her singles on the indie label Nugget were produced by Shot Jackson and feature his slide resonator guitar along with Buddy Emmons' pedal steel on top of thumping country rhythms, every word of Melba's self-penned lyrics twisted into knots by her deep Alabama accent. When George Jones heard the unfiltered honky-tonk of "Your Picture (Keeps Smiling Back at Me)," he fell in love with Melba's voice before he even knew what she looked like. He wanted to cut some duets with her right away, so he tasked Pappy Daily with tracking her down to set up a meeting . . . having no idea they'd already met.

According to Melba, she was still in Roy Acuff's band when she finished playing the *Opry* one night, went across the alley behind the Ryman into the backroom of Tootsie's and ran into a blacked-out George Jones. Without sharing exactly what he said to her, Melba intimated it was a remark that would have come across as sexually suggestive except even Jones knew he was in no shape to back it up, so it played for a laugh. Then, close to a year later, here comes Pappy Daily offering up a United Artists recording contract, saying George Jones wants to sing with her. George's interest at this time does seem to've been purely in her voice. Later in life, looking back over his career, George would praise the many women he sang duets with before admitting, regardless of which pairing sold the most albums, Melba Montgomery fit his vocal style the best. She's certainly the only singing partner he ever sent a recording contract. Imagine the confirmation he must have felt when Melba responded to being asked if she had any good duet songs by picking up a guitar and singing "We Must Have Been Out of Our Minds." According to Melba, George began harmonizing with her the first time she played it, then claimed he knew it would be a hit. They cut it the following day. Released in March of 1963, the single made a slow climb up to #3 in July, spending a total of twenty-three weeks on the charts. Over the following five years, George Jones and Melba Montgomery charted six more duets and toured together extensively. George had sung with other artists before, but this was his first serious collaborative and commercial partnership, much different from the studio rush job LP with Margie Singleton, the two singles documenting his early party days with Sonny Burns or even his tour-only, never-on-record work with Georgie Riddle. The lone singer who may possibly have had a chance to beat Melba to this territory was Jeanette Hicks, only her career was never given a chance to play out.

Jeanette became the first woman to sing on record with George Jones when they cut a few songs at Houston's Gold Star Studios in the summer of 1956. One of those songs, "Yearning," was included on George Jones' and Starday's first LP, the *Grand Ole Opry's New Star* compilation. There are moments in the chorus where it sounds as if Gold Star's gear can barely withstand such powerful voices singing at the same time. After being released as a single, "Yearning" went Top 10 in January of 1957 and was reissued with greater distribution and promotion on the brand-new Mercury-Starday label. The important thing to note about "Yearning," though, is it was always secretly a Jeanette Hicks record featuring George Jones. You can tell because the B-sides on both the Starday and the Mercury-Starday pressings are solo recordings by Jeanette. In technical terms, "Yearning" isn't even a duet because George never sings by himself. Jeanette takes the verses on her own and he only joins on the chorus. George stated in interviews his preference for the woman's voice to take lead in duets between a man and a woman but that's not what's happening here. This was a rising country star doing a favor for his record label, adding his name and voice to a single in order to give the label's new artist a boost. To return that favor the label got songwriter Eddie Eddings, who'd previously cut "Yearning" without crediting any other writer, to list George as a co-writer on the Jeanette Hicks recording. Financial motivations aside, the product is stellar. After "Yearning" hit Top 10, Mercury-Starday was ready to get all the way behind Jeanette, starting with adding her to all of George Jones' tour dates, which was when Jeanette's husband decided to end her career. Maybe he'd assumed he only needed to pretend to support her dreams for a while before she'd fail and give up. Maybe he'd never given serious consideration to the prospect of his wife leaving their small children at home with him for several weeks at a time while she went on tour with George Jones and a bunch of male musicians. Whatever his reasoning, he absolutely forbade her from going on the tour. When she disregarded his wishes and left anyway, she took the kids, determined to follow through on her hit record even if it meant simultaneously being a single mother while on the road. But the husband tracked her down at the first motel stop, told her to come home, she listened to him and that was that. Jeanette Hicks was never able to capitalize on her one hit or pursue a recording career with Mercury. Years later, on Shelby Singleton's final day of recording George Jones and Margie Singleton, one of the songs they did was "Yearning."

So, prior to anyone else, Melba Montgomery became George's first real singing partner, and he was totally obsessed with her voice. Even though they each possessed a strongly defined and adventurous vocal identity at the time they met, they were still young enough—she in her mid-twenties, he in his early thirties—to be forever influenced by working together. Again, you will not hear any noticeable transfer of mannerisms from one to the other in either direction. As on "We Must Have Been Out of Our Minds," instead of either singer pulling the other toward their own comfort zone, both reached ahead toward something new, moaning and howling into sonic territory they would not have found without each other. To George, working with Melba hardly felt like work at all. Touring was easier knowing she'd be there to sing with him, onstage and off, bonding over shared influences and teaching each other their favorite country songs. There's no telling exactly how soon he fell in love with her, but it happened fast and he began asking her to marry him. Melba did enjoy his company very much and said she felt a lot of love for him. She said George never directed his "bad side" toward her, that he was sweet and shy, treated her with respect. At some point in 1963, Melba's niece racked up an outrageous medical bill, so George held a benefit show and raised money to pay it. Still, no matter the possibility of romantic feelings, Melba did recognize the "bad side" was there and that was only one of several reasons George was undatable. He was an already-married, barely functioning alcoholic with an evidently fundamental misconception of how money even works. One time George bought hundreds of dollars in tackle and bait to go fishing with Melba. They had a great time and everything but after using the gear only once Jones saw no further need of it, so he left it all in Melba's car for her to deal with. In addition to habitually getting blackout drunk and trying to fight people, this was the period when Stonewall Jackson claims to've noticed that Jones stopped arriving anywhere in the same car twice. If he saw another car he liked more than the one he'd driven to wherever he was, right then and there he'd offer to trade pink slips with the other vehicle's owner, regardless of either car's value. That's not the guy you marry. It's his screwup friend who gets too drunk at every party, gives everyone there the wildest story they'll ever tell, then has to hitchhike home.

Melba Montgomery's career, on the other hand, was already hitched to Jones for the foreseeable future. *Cash Box* may have named her 1963's Second-Most Promising Country & Western Female Artist but that was largely on the strength of "We Must Have Been Out of Our Minds" and this award was the biggest accolade she had received at the time. Sales and airplay of her solo records were not comparable to the duets with Jones. In addition to her artist contract at United Artists, Pappy Daily had signed both Melba and her brother to writing contracts at one of his publishing companies, Glad Music. This was not Melba's brother Carl Montgomery, co-writer of Dave Dudley's "Six Days on the Road," but Earl "Peanutt" Montgomery, who began writing songs as a young boy just to prove he was equally worthy of the praise their mother gave to Carl. Peanutt was writing at the Wilburn Brothers' Sure-Fire Music when he stopped by the session for "We Must Have Been Out of Our Minds" and immediately became George Jones' new best drinking buddy, at which point Pappy Daily also hired Peanutt away to write at Glad Music. So, it was in everyone's best interests for George and Melba to continue working together despite any awkwardness stemming from his unrequited love for her. And with unrequited love for his ever-present singing partner tacked on to the list of all the things that made Jones want to take a drink, you'd better believe there was awkwardness. In the studio, on tour and even for television appearances together, he'd come up with any excuse to play Melba's guitar instead of his own, proudly displaying her name on a custom-tooled leather guitar strap for all to see. If he was drunk enough onstage (and in Phase II he often was), he'd interrupt whatever song they were singing in order to propose marriage over the microphone for all the audience to hear. This went on for years.

◇   ◇   ◇

Jones recorded "The Race Is On," in June 1963, in a session where he was allegedly so drunk he needed to be carried to his hotel room thirty minutes after the final take. It seems a likely story. Every witness agreed Jones was shit-faced during the "White Lightning" session and there, same as here, he only botched one word of the lyrics. In "The Race Is On," it's the part in the first verse where he misses the initial "b" in "break right down and bawl," causing most listeners to hear "rake right down," "lay right down" or something similar. This being the only song cut in the session, it's safe to assume there were many more takes with many more mistakes, but the performance chosen for release was otherwise flawless. The single went #3 Country and stayed there for six weeks. The lyrics are such a logistical nightmare it's possible being drunk may have helped get them right. Songwriter Don Rollins spent a day at a horse racing track and got the idea to use all the jargon of horse race betters for another of those "wacky heartache" songs so popular at this time. Almost every single line in the resulting lyrics achieves the seemingly impossible task of using either twice as many or half as many words as it should, thus forcing a vocalist to alternate between cramming syllables together and stretching them out in order to stay approximately on meter by repeatedly pulling ahead of and then falling back behind the beat, like a carousel horse pulling ahead and falling behind the other horses in the same row. It's no easy trick Jones accomplished here. This song is so exhausting to perform that nearly every other person who's ever attempted to record "The Race Is On" needed to alter the lyrics or tempo just to get a version of it down on tape. They changed "cold and deep inside" to "goin' deep inside." "My heart's sprung a big break" usually became "my heart's gonna break." "Break right down and bawl" sometimes morphed into "break right down and cry." The vast majority of vocalists took all manner of shortcuts to make the song easier, which, of course, stripped the risk and excitement from their performances and the end results feel nothing like a horse race at all. For instance, Jack Jones' 1965 cover, which hit #15 on the Pop chart, despite sounding like a room temperature cup of decaf coffee in comparison to the original. Just like how one mistake in "White Lightning" caused it to be the last single released from its session, United Artists held back "The Race Is On" for more than a year before putting it out in September of 1964, by which time Pappy Daily and Art Talmadge were already planning on moving George to yet another record label at the end of the year.

After a guy named Aaron Schroeder was lucky enough to get co-writing credit on some of the biggest Elvis Presley hits, he used the royalty money to partner with Art Talmadge in founding an independent label named Musicor. Talmadge's investment seems to have been personal and unaffiliated with his role as VP of United Artists but United Artists did distribute Musicor's records. As this was all happening, Schroeder discovered a young songwriter barely in his twenties named Gene Pitney, who turned in three songs: "Rubber Ball," recorded by Bobby Vee; "Hello Mary Lou," recorded by Ricky Nelson; and "He's a Rebel," recorded by the Crystals. All three songs were international pop hits. Pitney wanted to be a singer, too, so Schroeder decided to see what would happen if he put out Pitney's records on Musicor. Long story short, Pitney soon began releasing his own international pop hits, like "(The Man Who Shot) Liberty Valence," "Only Love Can Break a Heart" and "24 Hours from Tulsa." So Pitney was in a better position than most young American singers when records by the Beatles hit the States in early 1964 and instantly changed the spending habits of teenagers. Gene Pitney records still sold in other countries, and he leaned into it, cutting Italian and Spanish versions of his singles. But his sales and success in the United States weren't so great anymore, which was probably why Aaron Schroeder agreed when Musicor co-owner (and then President at United Artists) Art Talmadge offered to buy out Schroeder's shares in the label and become sole owner of Pitney's recording contract. By this time, Art Talmadge knew Pappy Daily was not going to build out a major country roster for United Artists. Talmadge would also have been aware of the massive sales figures on George Jones' biggest hits ever since the first time he poached him to a record label in the 1950s. Therefore, it seems likely that Talmadge bought Musicor in 1964 already having every intention of moving Jones to Musicor at the end of the year when his contract at United Artists expired, which was exactly what happened. This was how George Jones and Gene Pitney came to be on the same record label. Or, more accurately, it's how a national country star and an international pop star became a record label. Pappy negotiated for Jones to receive a percentage of ownership in Musicor but this was a guy who lit cash on fire and flushed it down toilets. It's unlikely Jones cared about much other than Melba Montgomery also being moved to the new label, so he could continue his romantic obsession with his singing and touring partner. The only real difference for Jones between United Artists and Musicor was Musicor wanted him to make records with a pop star, which, by the way, was the very first thing they wanted him to do.

Gene Pitney did chart a couple Top 10 records in the United States in the second half of 1964, after Talmadge took over, but such minor success doesn't really matter during a craze like the British Invasion, when the vast majority of sales goes to singles representing the new fad in the Top 5, leaving everyone below to fight over scraps. Pitney went on to have a long career with many huge hits around the world, even a few more Top 40 records in America, but he never hit the Pop Top 10 in the United States again. To the country music industry and its adult consumers, though, the British Invasion meant approximately nothing. (When pedal steel guitarist Pete Drake got the phone call to play on *All Things Must Pass* near the beginning of the '70s, he had no idea who George Harrison was.) When Talmadge and Daily moved George Jones over to Musicor in January of 1965, they had a plan to try selling the vocal stylings of Gene Pitney to Jones' audience of American adults. The first session Jones did for Musicor was that very same month and it was a duet session with Pitney. Nobody involved with this experiment ever said they knew ahead of time it would work, commercially or creatively. Pitney only found out he and Jones sounded good together after they began warming up in the studio and all the musicians stopped what they were doing to listen. As predicted, George changed nothing about his singing style or phrasing in consideration of his new partner's pop background, but you can hear he had fun working with and around such a peculiar and dynamic voice as Gene's. Even though all the songs were covers of old country hits Jones had sung thousands of times, the unique sound and nature of the project kept him engaged. Truth be told, Pitney didn't alter much about his own style, either, though if you pay close attention to their first single, the old Faron Young hit "I've Got Five Dollars and It's Saturday Night," you will notice Pitney change the way he throws around a few vowel sounds in order to hang with Jones. The most noticeable concession made to Pitney's background as a pop artist was the arrangement on some songs being slightly poppier than what would typically be played on a George Jones session. The bass may be a little busier, the beats a little stilted, the fiddles a bit more like violins at times . . . But they also often sound like fiddles and there's plenty of pedal steel guitar. In the truest sense of the term, this was pop country music. Check out their version of the Ray Price hit, "I've Got a New Heartache." Gene and George each take a verse, then pair up on the chorus, where you can hear Gene do the thing he talked about doing, singing around George Jones instead of with him. George begins most of the lines in each chorus on his own, then Gene comes in a little later and a little faster in order to catch up. It's like an audio version of the little kid who has to run in short bursts to keep pace with his big brother's longer walking stride.

The way the new label packaged these duets for release was a pretty clever bit of business. After the duet sessions, Jones spent the next two days recording his first Musicor solo album, which did *not* contain his first Musicor solo single. Instead, since the whole point of this plan was to introduce Gene Pitney to Jones' existent audience of country music fans, who were known to prefer buying LPs over 45s, Jones' first solo single for Musicor was placed on the *George and Gene* duet LP, along with the first George and Gene single. As a result, "I've Got Five Dollars and It's Saturday Night" went #16 on the Country singles chart while the strategically boosted sales sent the LP to #3. Happy with the results of their test, Musicor continued to record Gene Pitney with George Jones.

They also put Gene in the studio with Melba Montgomery to similarly great ends, both sonically and financially. The first Melba and Gene single, Dallas Frazier's "Baby, Ain't That Fine," sold about as well as Pitney's first single with Jones. Their second single did nothing to speak of, which is a shame because it's a wonderful piece of music. Melba Montgomery wrote "Being Together" with her brother, Peanutt. The lyrics are about two platonic friends driven by heartache to pretend to be in a romantic relationship, which then destroys their friendship. It's a heavy story and the vocal performance sells every line. Technically not a duet because they accompany each other the whole time ("being together"), this record is a master class in synchronized phrasing and delivery. The large gaps between each instance of singing present a challenge for two vocalists, who must come in not only at the exact same time as each other but at a matching level of emotional intensity as the song continues to build and build. Even with the drummer providing a helpful metronome on the rim of his snare, nothing about that is easy, jumping back in together with such precision, over and over and over. Gene and Melba absolutely nail it. After a couple years, Musicor ended Gene Pitney's country music experiments, probably deciding his continued international success as a pop star was enough to not need to reconquer America in any genre.

◊   ◊   ◊

The way George Jones later told it, all Musicor did was make him record a ton of songs in marathon sessions produced by someone who wasn't really a producer. It wasn't exactly a lie. Driven by the need to build a catalog to compete with those he'd left at his previous labels, George recorded nearly three hundred songs in the seven years he spent on Musicor. Just in his first five years with the label, Musicor released more than twenty George Jones albums. But if you love great country music, then Pappy Daily bringing Jones and a few hundred songs to the Nashville A-Team in the mid- to late 1960s and getting out of the way was not a bad thing. Because that's when Owen Bradley understudy Bob Moore usually took over to provide much of the same Nashville Sound magic heard on, for example, Patsy Cline and Roy Orbison records. Moore recognized the uniqueness of the instrument that was George Jones' voice and the version of the Nashville Sound he placed around it rarely opts for musical cues or other gimmicks. The adjectives commonly used to describe the arrangements for Jones' Musicor years include words like "elegant," "poised" and "sublime." Restraint and subtlety form small, spotlit stages upon which Jones spills out tragedy.

Here's as good a place as any to acknowledge the inherent sadism of being a George Jones fan. Someone once explained the allure of Jones as knowing, no matter how bad you felt, there was someone out there who felt even worse. Whoever first said that, it's since been repeated ad nauseam and for good reason. George once explained, "I know when I go in to record or I'm onstage singin' each song I sing, I'm actually livin' that two or three minutes. I put my heart and soul in it. I see this person. I see this happening. I live the words, the idea, the story of the song." He also consistently claimed musical performance was the only way he knew how to process his own emotions. When we hear George Jones sound sad, it's because he's drawing on his own misery as a fuel source and he came to Musicor during the most miserable years of his adult life to date. He was in love with Melba Montgomery but she couldn't love him back. After he began making public displays of affection (and marriage proposals) toward Melba in 1963, the "happy times" in George's marriage to Shirley Jones came to an end. Shirley landed in the arms of J.C. Arnold, owner of the building leased for the George Jones Chuck Wagon Restaurant and Museum. George found out about the affair roughly a year into it and things got sloppy. Probably not as sloppy as the persistent rumor that George actually caught J.C. and Shirley in bed together, then put a load of buckshot in J.C.'s ass . . . But whatever did happen wasn't good and nothing about the marriage ever got any better.

George and Shirley grew increasingly spiteful in their behavior toward each other. Sometimes he'd run a Johnny Cash Special on his own home, smashing the place up like it was any old hotel room in the middle of nowhere. One source alleged Jones slapped Shirley when he caught her flirting with some random guy outside of a honky-tonk. She asked for a divorce several times but George always talked her out of it. Maybe because of the kids? The shame? The holy oath? Maybe there were moments when they both legitimately thought he could get better. Jones' first stay in some kind of rehab or psych ward took place during this period, possibly an attempt to save the marriage. But the white walls didn't fix anything. Even though their divorce was still a few years down the road, the irreparable harm had been done. Jones was drinking and taking pills at a higher rate than ever before, leaving his body in no condition to weather all of the mental and emotional stress of life on tour. And, man, you can hear him going through every bit of it on the sad songs. His first Musicor single, "Things Have Gone to Pieces," originally packaged on the LP with Gene Pitney, was literally a man listing all the ways his life has fallen apart. Jones was probably just drunk in the session, but something about how close he gets to butchering the word "faucet" in the intro sounds like he's trying to keep from crying before the song even gets started. He then manages to stutter out a few more syllables before breaking apart with the rest of the song. By the end he's got nothing left but the memories of his broken dreams, a template for the characters he would go on to portray or embody in the most popular and enduring songs of his career. This was how Jones came out of the gate at Musicor. "Things Have Gone to Pieces" went Top 10.

Even though Jones' first solo LP on Musicor was rush-recorded the same week as the Gene Pitney collaborations and contained no singles, *Mr. Country and Western Music* is one of the finest albums he ever made. The cover features an illustration of him dressed more than a little like a matador in a red suit with gold stitching, strumming an acoustic guitar while standing in front of some ranch house in the middle of nowhere. Among the advertised "Twelve Brand New Hit Songs by George Jones" are tracks from such great writers as Hank Cochran, Leon Payne, Eddie Noack, Darrell Edwards and Wayne Walker, as well as Melba, Peanutt and Carl Montgomery. Jones' take on Joe Poovey's "Worst of Luck" is perhaps the best version of one of the best "I'll hate you forever for breaking my heart" songs. There isn't a more perfect example of what hooks Jones fans to the Musicor period than "I Can't Get Used to Being Lonely." Here's everything you need to know: it's George Jones singing a song about being doomed to loneliness because you're in love with someone who doesn't love you back . . . and the song was written by Melba Montgomery. From the sweeping intro, more violin than fiddle, to perhaps the most subtle kick drum in the history of the genre and one of the greatest harmony vocals ever, this is an emotionally dangerous recording. The best/worst part of how miserable Jones sounds on the sad songs in this era is how relaxed he also sounds, as if he's accepted the open wounds will never heal. He knows this is the way things will be for him from now on and if anything about the situation does change it's sure to be a change for the worse.

Not everything was all doom and gloom from here forward. "The Race Is On" was such a huge hit back at United Artists they were still working it hard enough to make it the title track of a new George Jones LP released in April 1965. So, two months later, Pappy Daily had Jones cut "Love Bug," the kind of upbeat, goofy song every artist in Nashville was trying to find after Roger Miller finally broke through in 1964. Few songwriters hit the mark as well as Wayne Kemp on "Love Bug." With a Nashville-does-Bakersfield arrangement, it went Top 10 Country and even gave Jones another rare appearance at the bottom of the Pop Hot 100. But, by his own admission, the happy songs were just something he did so the audience would let him sing more sad ones. For every hit in the 1960s like "Love Bug" or "The Race Is On" there were at least three singles where Jones was trying to tear out your heart, like "Least of All," the Top 20 record sandwiched between those two up-tempo hits. Here, Jones wouldn't wish the pain of his broken heart on anyone, even and especially the woman who broke it. Or listen to how much more tortured he sounds a year later, in May of 1966, on "Don't Keep Me Lonely Too Long," also written by Melba Montgomery. By that time Melba had started dating Jones Boys guitarist Jack Solomon, who she would go on to marry a couple years later. But anyone assuming that relationship put a stop to Jones drunkenly proposing marriage to Melba onstage during concerts would be wrong. And if "Don't Keep Me Lonely Too Long" sounds like he spent years hopelessly pining over the woman who wrote it, that's because he did.

Two nights after recording "Don't Keep Me Lonely Too Long," in his sixth session of the month, Pappy Daily had to get Jones drunk so he'd cut a song he absolutely hated. Since the lyrics of "Walk Through This World with Me" so perfectly describe the way George felt about Melba, it may be more accurate to say he was afraid of it. Because if he was able to get through recording it without crying in the studio . . . and if it became the massive hit Pappy said it would be . . . then Jones was going to have to sing it every night on tour with Melba Montgomery right there in the room. Even though the lyrics are essentially a marriage proposal, Jones sings them like a funeral dirge. When Pappy released the single and, sure enough, the immediate response showed all the indicators of a particularly huge hit, George convinced Pappy to let him record it again. Now that he knew for a fact he was going to have to sing the fucking thing at every concert for the immediate future, George wanted to at least do it faster, in a higher key and try to make it sound like there may be some way to consider it a happy song rather than an audio document of the depths of his own depression. Because "Walk Through This World with Me" was his first and only #1 record while at Musicor, George did have to sing it quite a lot over the next several years. You can find a certain video of him doing it on TV near the beginning of the hit's life cycle. There are two ways you can tell the appearance is from when the song was still fresh and he hadn't yet sung it enough for repetition to numb some of the pain. The first is his flattop Marine haircut, which he got rid of within the next year or so. The second is he barely makes it through the performance. Once you learn to recognize the look in his eyes as terror drowning in alcohol, most clips of George Jones singing on television become difficult to watch. This one is especially bad. He's visibly trashed, which is no surprise during Phase II. But when the camera goes in close on the first line of the song, we can see his eyes are unfocused in a maybe-not-alcohol-induced way as he sways too far back from the microphone and remains there for a little too long. At first, it seems he's on drunken autopilot and spacing out a bit. Then, after flubbing a couple words, he smiles about the mistake and overcorrects into an emotional connection with the lyrics, which it instantly becomes clear is what he was trying to avoid at the beginning for fear of breaking down on television. After that come several visible tics unique to this performance, tics you won't find in clips of him doing the song later, once he gained some distance from it. His eyelids begin to blink more frequently, the way yours sometimes do when you're trying not to cry. His jaw goes a little slack, the way yours sometimes does when you're trying not to cry. His eyes seem to get a bit shinier around the time he finishes the line, "I've looked for you a long, long time." He appears to have great difficulty with the last line of the chorus. In order to deliver the words "come take my hand and walk through this world with me," he has to put on the smile you try to wear while swallowing the lump that forms in your throat when you walk into a party and see the person who broke your heart three days earlier. His reward for making it through the first chorus is the chance to get himself back in focus during the guitar break. But he spends the rest of the song looking like he's playing it at Melba Montgomery's wedding to another man. He stares his dead eyes at the camera, only occasionally remembering to fake another smile. He spends a lot of time glancing down at the floor or up at the ceiling in order to avoid making eye contact with anyone. His most genuine smile comes at the end, when the applause means he's allowed to stop. A little slurred enunciation aside, his singing is flawless. Anyone who witnessed any song do this to him on television or in concert must have known they were looking at a broken person. No matter what his stage clothing looked like, George Jones was no matador. The songs were the matadors. Jones was the bull no matador could kill. But it's not like we're terrible people for witnessing this tragedy, right? There is also sympathetic resonance in being a George Jones fan. If we'd never known pain, we wouldn't recognize what it looks or sounds like. If it were really a bullfight, we'd pardon any bull still standing after such a performance as this. Immediately upon moving to Musicor, George came to embody this love-scarred character to such a degree that even his old record labels updated his persona when repackaging and releasing their back catalogs. In

1965, Mercury released an LP titled *Heartaches and Tears* while United Artists came out with one called *King of Broken Hearts*. That's who George Jones was to fans in this period.

◇   ◇   ◇

If Phase II began somewhere in 1962, then it picked up speed in 1963 and, by 1964, Jones had it running wide open, staying wasted for weeks at a time. He acquired such a reputation for missing and/or bailing on shows, unprincipled concert promoters began advertising and selling tickets to George Jones dates they'd never actually booked. When the scheduled day came around, these scammers would wait until after the whole audience arrived at the venue and had spent several hours buying beer before telling everyone Jones must have gotten too drunk to show up. Even after refunding the price of admission for however many fans chose not to keep their ticket stub as a No Show Jones souvenir, revenue from beer sales made it a profitable scam. That concert where he refused to go onstage until Donny Young introduced him as Hank Williams and Johnny Horton, then caused a riot by letting the audience watch him walk out, happened somewhere in this era.

There must be at least thirty books which partially recount the Madison Square Garden story. In 1964, the Garden scheduled a comprehensive "Who's Who in Country Music" lineup, featuring George Jones, Ernest Tubb, Ray Price, Webb Pierce, Bill Monroe, Dottie West, Buck Owens, Skeeter Davis, Bill Anderson, Stonewall Jackson, Porter Wagoner and several other notable acts. What with having well over fifteen major artists on the bill, each would play only two songs. The promoters were especially concerned with keeping the show on schedule because the whole event would instantly become a loss should they be forced to pay an overtime rate to the many union workers at the Garden. For obvious reasons, everyone behind the scenes saw Jones as the single largest potential threat to financial solvency. The safest move would've been to have him play early so any disasters could be adjusted for well before curfew, but he'd gained such status in recent years they needed to promote and schedule him as a headliner. Still, they put him next-to-last on the lineup, giving themselves a one co-headliner buffer between Jones' set and curfew. Singing at Madison Square Garden in New York City would normally have scared George Jones shitless but nearly every other major country star was there with him and the co-headliner scheduled to close out the night just so happened to be Buck Owens. As mentioned, Buck Owens was a huge fan of George Jones. Buck learned to sing from listening to Jones' records and when Buck needed a pseudonym to secretly cut his own rock records, he went with Corky Jones. However, Buck Owens was also capable of being an unapologetic asshole and had developed a half-friendly rivalry with Jones while spending much of the previous year on tour together. You see, 1963 was the year Buck finally had his first #1 record on "Act Naturally." As far as Buck was concerned, Jones being his musical hero had nothing to do with who should headline a concert, so almost every day of this tour he and Jones would argue with each other and the show promoters to determine who would open for who on each night. Since Buck did presently have a #1 Country record on the charts, he often won the arguments and closed the shows. But Jones rarely let it end there. One night he waited until Buck got into singing a real serious ballad, then snuck up on the stage behind the guitar amps while wearing a pair of khaki shorts. Every time Jones popped up from behind the amps and did a dumb rooster dance with his pasty white legs sticking out of those shorts, the audience fell into hysterics and Jones would duck back down behind the amps before Buck could turn around, all pissed off, trying to see what the hell was so funny. Another time when Jones lost the argument and had to play first, instead of singing his own songs he went out on stage and sang Buck Owens' entire set list. Buck was left with no choice but to walk out there and sing all the songs George Jones had just sung, which is every country singer's actual worst nightmare. So, when Jones showed up to Madison Square Garden in 1964 and found out he was "opening" for Buck Owens once again, stage fright was the last thing on his mind. He had a show to put on. After playing his two songs, he launched into a third and everyone backstage who'd spent the whole day worried this exact thing would happen found a clock or wristwatch to stare at. Ralph Emery, the show's emcee, tried to use another microphone to thank Jones over the PA and usher him off stage but Jones ignored it, played out his third song and rolled right into a fourth with the crowd going crazy. Meanwhile, as the curfew crept closer, the promoters were pulling out their hair. Even if they did get him to stop before the union overtime rate threw the whole event into the red, Buck Owens still needed to play two songs or they'd be dealing with angry audience members demanding refunds. When Jones started a fifth song, Bill Monroe finally went over to Ralph Emery and said he'd take care of it. Monroe and one of the Blue Grass Boys went onstage, lifted Jones by the arms and, as he continued singing, carried him off the stage. Fortunately, Buck Owens & The Buckaroos knew how to play fast. They ripped through two songs at a breakneck tempo and saved everyone's paychecks with only seconds to spare.

Other stories from this era are far less amusing, like the way Jones' already-frivolous attitude toward combining mind-altering substances with automobiles entered new and disturbing territory. He traded and gave away cars to strangers with a frequency that became impossible to track. When he forgot where he parked a car or which one in a parking lot was his, he never bothered to find out and simply bought another. Sometimes friends would find him passed out on the ground with a driver's-side door still hanging open and six-figure sums of cash spilled all over the passenger seat. Where other country artists took speed pills to stay awake on long drives, Jones took speed just in order to stay awake and sit in a chair and drink more booze. Whatever he thought about when he did this, sometimes it made him want to take out a gun and shoot holes in things, so he'd do that, too. One night after a concert, he instructed the tour bus driver to drop off the Jones

Boys at their hotel, then aimlessly spend all night driving Jones around the highways of whatever city they were in. He didn't sit up front to talk with his driver. He sat alone, in the back of the bus, drinking. When Jones loaded up a revolver and began shooting holes in the ceiling, walls and floor of his own tour bus, the driver just kept driving. But he didn't show back up for work the next morning . . . or ever again. For as long as Jones owned that bus the bullet holes stayed, letting in diesel fumes during the summer and biting cold air during the winter.

George Jones and Charley Pride played many shows together in this period and became good friends. One night Charley decided to hang out with Jones at some local DJ's house and take a couple drinks. Jones didn't really like for any of his drinking partners to only have a couple while Jones was trying to take down a whole bottle or two, so he said Charley needed to match him drink for drink. Charley agreed but soon passed out, at which point the DJ and Jones decided, what with Charley Pride being Black and all, it would be funny to go outside and paint "KKK" on Charley's car. Jones then went back inside the house and passed out in the same bed as Charley. When everyone woke up the next morning, that DJ started acting like the Klan had showed up in the middle of the night and told Charley to go look out the window at his car. Charley, dealing with a headsplitting hangover, actually believed the Klan story for a minute before realizing these two idiots thought they were being funny.

◇   ◇   ◇

At some point in 1965, The King of Broken Hearts rushed back to Texas after being informed his father was hospitalized. It wasn't much of a surprise. Two years earlier, the old man was sent to a state mental hospital to dry out. Only, this time the doctors said George's father could be about to die. It seemed the decades of heavy drinking may have finally caught up with the old man for good. One day, waiting at home to see if his father was going to die or not, George walked outside, got behind the wheel of a Cadillac he owned and proceeded to drive the car through a shed, a barn and all the fencing on his ranch, freeing his horses and cattle to roam the countryside and totaling the Cadillac. George's brother-in-law, one of several people who had been more of a father figure to George than his actual father, assumed Jones must be drunk and went looking for him to prevent further catastrophe. When the brother-in-law found George totally sober, he asked why on earth George had caused all this damage to his own property. George couldn't come up with a reason. The only thing he'd say was, "I just done it, is all I know. I just done it." A few days later, having wrecked his own car, George caught a ride with family to go visit his father in the hospital. Someone cracked a joke about it probably being the first time in a long time that George Jones found himself riding in such an old beater of a pickup truck and George started crying. He pleaded with his family to understand he didn't think he was any better than them. The truth is he knew they were better than him.

NINE

FIT TO KILL

◇ Functional Fashion ◇ These Boots Are Made for War ◇ A Taller Cowboy ◇

As frivolous as tropes of western wear may appear to modern observers with no experience or awareness of the cowboy way of life, many individual elements of the fashion arose as practical solutions to serious, potentially life-threatening problems. Most of these problems predate the American West, nearly all of which had been conquered and claimed by Spain by the first half of the sixteenth century. In the early 1800s, after declaring itself independent from Spain, Mexico spent the rest of the century losing huge chunks of territory as various states declared themselves to also be independent republics . . . only to then become part of the United States following a little or a lot of war. So, much of what we think of as western or cowboy culture was well established long before the existence of the American West, then filtered through the indigenous peoples of Mexico and South America after being directly imported from a centuries-old ranching tradition on the Iberian Peninsula.

In Spanish a *rodeo* is what American cowboys would call a roundup of cattle and modern American rodeos evolved from virtually identical competitions dating back to the Iberian Peninsula, where hands from different ranches would pit their work skills against each other. The word "chaps" is short for *chaparreras*, which were chaps worn by *vaqueros* to protect their legs and pants while riding through *chaparral*, dense thickets native to both Mexico and Spain. Cowboy hats are an update of the *sombrero*. A lack of outdoor shade on hot, sunny days is not an occupational hazard exclusive to ranchers, wranglers or cattle drovers but articles of all-purpose outdoor clothing have a tendency to become thought of as western wear after receiving modifications to address the specific needs of cowboys.

The concept of using cheaper, coarser and more durable fabrics for work clothing is as old as the concept of work clothing but denim is named for Nimes, France, where weavers were nearly successful in replicating the cheap fabric used since at least the early 1600s for work clothing made in the Italian Republic of Genoa, which in French sounds a lot like the word "jean." In the early 1930s, a tailor named Rodeo Ben watched a rodeo cowboy get a gap between the buttons of his shirt hung up on a saddle horn, resulting in that cowboy being thrashed all over an arena by a seriously pissed-off bronco. Rodeo Ben immediately stopped using buttons on the shirts and denim jeans that he made for cowboys. For the shirts, he switched to snaps which came undone when physically stressed. Snaps being an impractical and potentially scandal-causing choice for the fly of a cowboy's pants, Ben went with a zipper, essentially inventing Wrangler jeans, though it was another ten years before Wrangler hired him for these designs. Between rodeo events and the occupations upon which they are based, there is no way to know how many lives were saved by these innovations.

Humans have worn boots since before we wore shoes, for the same reason cowboys still prefer boots, to protect the feet and lower legs from hazards while outdoors. For most of history, boots were all-purpose. The pair a person wore to protect their legs (and, once fashion came along, to protect their clothing) were the same pair worn for outdoor labor, recreational activities, even military engagements. Soldiers who wanted extra protection for their legs in battle wore external armor rather than specialized footwear. Since most of the people who actually fight in wars have always been poor, most body armor was usually not made of the expensive plate metal we tend to associate with imagery of knights in battle. The most common means of torso protection was the padded jack, a heavy vest constructed from dozens of layers of various fabrics, then finished on the outside with tough canvas or leather. In the 1600s, around the time military uniforms first appeared in Europe, the concept of the padded jack spread to the feet and legs of heavy cavalry riders in the form of the jackboot. "Heavy cavalry" was always just a nice euphemism for the first people to die in battle and that usually happened right around the time the wearer fell out of a saddle, so these boots were not made for walking. Some versions of the original jackboot had chain mail sewn between the layers of leather and fabric, which made for a very heavy piece of manly footwear. About two hundred years prior, the less utilitarian cavalier boot came into fashion. This was just another all-purpose knee- or thigh-high boot but made from soft leather. Especially in Tudor-era England, the cavalier largely replaced the shoes and soled leggings previously worn by macho noblemen of the European gentry. The German soldiers who fought with the British against the United States in the American Revolution were known as "Hessians," which is also what everyone began calling their new style of boot. The hessian—a cross between the jackboot and the cavalier—was made from sturdy leather and meant to offer some protection to the leg but without the thick layers and weight of armor, allowing greater mobility to soldiers while not seated on a horse. Toward the same end, the hessian featured a rounded toe for easier insertion and removal from stirrups. This being a German military, fashionista concerns were addressed by some trim and a tassel at the top of each boot. In the early nineteenth century, the first Duke of Wellington modified the Hessian design by getting rid of the decorative flair and using softer leather to create a tighter fitting boot, which became known as the Wellington.

Cowboys of North America who could afford a pair of boots wore Hessians or Wellingtons until the second half of the nineteenth century, when the arrival of insulated railway cars and reefer ships allowed fresh beef on ice to be sent hundreds and thousands of miles away without spoiling, thereby bringing an exponential boost in profits to the U.S. cattle industry. Earning more money, a greater number of ranchers and wranglers and cattle drovers were able to afford pairs of custom-made boots. As bootmakers noted the most common requests for practical updates on Wellington or Hessian designs, the cowboy boot was born. One modification cowboys typically asked for was a taller heel because these were not "cow men," which would be the literal translation of the source word *vaqueros*. The Spanish word got downsized in English because cowboying in what was becoming the American West was generally regarded as too remote and dangerous a job for a man with family or other dependents. Ranchers typically hired young teenagers, freed slaves or other people regarded as less valuable to society than adult white men. The tall heels of the first cowboy boots have often been attributed to the vanity of young boys, not yet fully grown, wanting to appear taller. That may have been a factor, but the higher heel certainly made it easier to climb up into the saddle on a horse tall enough to offer a view over a whole herd of cattle. The high heel also put a more pronounced notch on the underside of the boot to catch and hold in place in a stirrup.

While the pointed toe of modern cowboy boots is typically explained as easier to insert and remove from the stirrup, the round toe of Hessians and Wellingtons had already addressed this concern and pointed toes only came about in the mid-twentieth century, purely as a product of fashion trends. But other seemingly superficial aspects of the cowboy boot do exist for practical reasons. The decorative stitching and additional pieces of leather on the uppers (or shafts) of cowboy boots offer reinforcement, keeping the boot stiff and upright near the leg, less susceptible to falling apart on a weeks- or months-long cattle drive. This is also why extra layers of fabric and embroidery were similarly added to western shirts, vests and jackets. Bib front (or cavalry) shirts come with an extra thick rectangle of material buttoned onto the front for warmth, padding and durability, which is the same purpose served by shoulder yokes on western shirts and jackets.

Even the ornamental designs chosen for implementation of these practicalities were far more significant than superficial. Cowboys requested imagery and symbols reflective of their environment, backgrounds, talents, hobbies and reputations. Again, these were not family men. In addition to all the horse heads, rope, and steer skull imagery you'd expect, cowboys rolled into town wearing boots and clothing adorned with snakes, scorpions, guns, dice, knives, cards, women, etc. Star shapes were not introduced to clothing by western wear but they have always been very prevalent in the style. For one thing, in the early nineteenth century, Texas was a sovereign republic, the "lone star" between Mexico and the United States. But even without that, even prior to the visual pollution of electric lighting, cowboys out on the trail have always spent more time than anyone looking up at the most stars.

TEN

OL' PAPPY

◇ Where'd the Money Go? ◇ The Case Against Pappy Daily ◇
Four Songs in Three Hours: The Singles-Oriented Studio System
◇ Filler Sessions and Buried Treasure ◇ Hate the Game ◇

1966: A reporter asks George Jones what advice he'd give to country singers try-ing to become a star like him. Jones' advice is, essentially, don't. He says he knows he would be a happier person if he could make a living doing anything else and gives some reasons why. When you're a country star, everyone wants something more from you, even and especially if you've already given them everything you've got. You'll have very little control over whether you spend the whole day surrounded by strangers who want to talk to you or alone in a hotel room and nobody will care much which one you feel like doing on any given day. Even though you don't like these sudden shifts between pandemonium and isolation, you'll soon acclimate to the point where one doesn't feel right without the other. So, whenever you do take some time off, instead of rest you'll probably just get restless. But you can't just call up some friends to go hang out somewhere or else you're right back to being reminded how much privacy you no longer have.

By 1966, when George gave that interview, he was already more than a country music star; he was a country music superstar, which is to say still hardly a blip on the radar of mainstream pop culture. He'd never been a guest of Ed Sullivan, Johnny Carson, Jack Benny or appeared on any TV show catering to a noncountry audience. Even at such a relatively low level of exposure, he developed a deep distrust of fame along with anyone who tried to exploit his celebrity for their own financial or social gain. When it came to strangers he was almost pathologically charitable. One time Jones and Georgie Riddle drove by a gas station where an attendant was pumping gas in the rain without a raincoat, so Jones went to a store, bought a raincoat, drove back to the gas station and gave the raincoat to the attendant. He was known to hand bags containing thousands of dollars in cash to people who were visibly in need, then walk away. But whenever he handed a bag of cash to a friend for no reason, it wasn't charity. It was a test. If the friend turned down the money, they passed the test. If the friend took it, George knew what kind of person they were. Sometimes failing that test was enough for a friend to be instantly cut out of his life forever.

In 1966, Tammy Wynette's debut single became a minor hit. In 1967, she signed with the booking agency that represented George Jones, which led to George and Tammy spending a lot of time together on tour, then singing together, onstage and off, bonding over their shared influences and sharing their favorite country songs with each other . . . We've seen this movie before, haven't we? Only, this time, Jones got the girl. Loyal subjects who'd spent years watching The King of Broken Hearts eviscerate himself on stages across the land now saw the beginning of what they believed would be his fairy-tale ending, the love story of a couple they soon began calling The King and Queen of Country Music. George and Tammy went public with their relationship the same month Tammy recorded "Stand By Your Man," soon to be one of the most well-known songs in the English language, making her one of the most famous women on the planet. George Jones would have needed a time machine to do a better job documenting the perilousness of this situation in advance. Measured purely by Tammy Wynette's sales figures, every single thing George complained about in that 1966 interview became about a million times worse less than two years later as a direct result of the one personal relationship bringing him more happiness than any other. A couple more years down the road, George went all-in on that relationship, breaking his professional alliance with Pappy Daily to join the same record label as Tammy and marry his career to hers.

Most biographers seem to regard the split from Pappy as inevitable, which is a view almost entirely shaped by accepting George's after-the-fact criticisms, especially those shared in his autobiography, where he begins building a case against Starday Records and Pappy Daily pretty much as soon as those topics are introduced. Some of George's complaints were valid. For example, Pappy was not a real producer and he did care more about quantity than quality in the studio. But those things were true from the beginning of George's career all the way through nearly two decades of working together, during which time George stuck with Pappy through three different record label changes.

George always had a larger public platform than Pappy, so the version of reality he eventually decided on is what became canon. In that reality, Pappy was a greedy parasite who made off with all kinds of money that should rightfully have gone to George. The music industry has always been full of such men but to argue Pappy Daily was one of them is a nonstarter. This was a guy who went into his own pocket to help so many young artists get their first record deals, one of them nicknamed him "Pappy." In the archives of the Country Music Hall of Fame and Museum there's an 8×10 promo picture Melba Montgomery signed, "To Pappy, I owe it all to you. Your Grateful Daughter—Love, Melba." Business-minded? Yes. Budget-conscious? Yes. But we cannot call the man greedy. Pappy also held no delusions regarding who was more important to who: "I've had a lot of people say that I made George Jones. I says, 'No, I didn't make him . . . I just gave him a chance.'" That in itself was a charitable choice of words because Pappy gave George many, many more chances than one. Compare the stress these men caused each other and it's not even close to equal. Were it possible to fashion the experience of being George Jones' manager during Phase II of his addictions into some kind of a pill, doctors would prescribe it to patients with low blood pressure. But George could not have successfully sold his version of the story if there wasn't some truth to it, so what parts are true?

◇   ◇   ◇

It's true Pappy Daily issued many singles from imperfect takes, which George—always his own worst critic—would have found excruciating to hear on the radio, even if nobody else ever noticed. (Anyone susceptible to having enjoyment of your favorite songs ruined by someone pointing out flaws may want to skip the rest of this paragraph . . .) "Window Up Above" was a #2 hit but the quality of the recording makes it sound like something cut in Castle's hotel banquet room ten years earlier. Whether due to a glitch in the mastering process or maybe a mistake caused by mixing Jones with a vocal chorus for the first time—possibly even something as amateur as a dirty audio cable?—listen with a critical ear and there are scratchy artifacts throughout the whole song. But what was Pappy supposed to do? Book another session for a singer who famously never sang a ballad the same way twice, then hope he showed up in a state of sobriety conducive to recreating what Pappy knew was a hit take? Should Pappy have made George take another swing at "She Thinks I Still Care" because of the spit you can hear catch in his throat on the word "idea" at 1:45 and stay there through the end of the song? Perhaps. But what he chose to do was recognize they probably just heard the best vocal take of the decade, which he released as a single and which turned his artist into a living legend.

Piano player Pig Robbins, the musician who said there was a sweet spot with Jones where he'd consumed just enough booze to relax but not so much he got belligerent, also once said, "Pappy always thought he ought to get five or six songs on a session." This statement was made in comparison to the four song per session standard of Music Row. Similar things were said on the subject of Pappy Daily by many session players, none of whom were prepared to waive their studio fees or ever had to cover the costs when Jones arrived too drunk to do anything other than endless takes of the same song, swearing over and over that he'd get the next one right. There's a recording session from May 1959 most everyone agrees probably took place while Jones was drunk because it started at midnight, ran to 3 a.m., there are several technical errors in the recordings and they only cut two gospel songs, "Have Mercy on Me" and "If You Believe," both by Darrell Edwards. "Have Mercy on Me" may be a fascinating recording to modern fans. (Is that Jackie Phelps singing harmony or is it George Jones disguising his voice to overdub his own harmony? Nobody knows.) But the commercial value of this tape at the time was essentially zilch, and it's not like Pappy Daily received any kind of "George was drunk and wanted to sing about Jesus at midnight" discount when the invoice for that session showed up on his desk.

It may be surprising for many fans to learn, according to Pig Robbins' coworker, bassist and uncredited producer Bob Moore, Pappy Daily was usually who broke out the bottle in the studio. Pappy was known to drink a lot himself, occasionally to the point of failing to show up for recording sessions, but establishing the precedent that he would be the one to bring the booze sure sounds like a much-more-subtle-than-has-been-recognized method of controlling what everyone agreed was the most important part of a George Jones session: keeping him in the sweet spot where he sang a little better but wasn't too drunk. The bottle being located in the control room prevented Jones from overserving himself and allowed Pappy to dole out swigs according to both his artist's temperament and whether or not they were cutting important material.

Now, wait . . . Wouldn't a good producer treat everything they recorded as equally important and try to create the best product possible for every track? Looking at it from this side of the LP format's impact on music history, yeah, maybe. However, the only reason a producer would adopt such a philosophy in a singles-oriented market was if they hated money. A label accidentally putting two huge hit songs on one record always made for cool stories and good ad copy but behind closed doors they knew they were bragging about losing money by not releasing the two hits as A-sides of separate records. For one thing, they could have charged the artist's fans full price twice to acquire those songs as separate units rather than selling both as a two-for-one. But even if a label somehow saw into the future and packaged two huge hits as A-sides of separate records, they still wouldn't release both of those records simultaneously. Every hit song has a life cycle and putting out singles one at a time exploits each to its maximum potential, allowing it to do everything it's going to do in the market before introducing the most competitive product possible, another record from the same artist marketed to the same audience. This is how and why the studio system developed a standard of recording four songs in a three-hour session. In the singles-oriented industry, producers only booked studio time when they believed they'd found the right combination of artist and material to cut a hit single or two. Call these songs Maybe Hits. Since you wouldn't want to put a Maybe Hit on the B-side of a record and potentially cannibalize airplay of the Maybe Hit on the A-side, you also brought along a pile of Good Enough songs. The main priority of any session was to capture satisfactory takes of the Maybe Hits, even if that meant spending more time or even the whole session on those songs and never getting around to anything from the Good Enough pile. But studio time, musicians and engineers were expensive, so whenever you successfully cut your Maybe Hits and there were still twenty paid-for minutes on the clock you wouldn't just let everyone go home early. You'd also not try to rush through and potentially waste another Maybe Hit. That's when you reached for a song from the Good Enough pile to give the Maybe Hit a B-side. Sometimes songs from the Good Enough pile wound up sounding more like Maybe Hits after being recorded. Sometimes the label recognized that in advance and promoted such a song to the A-side of its own single. Sometimes songs from the Good Enough pile wound up sounding more like Not Good Enough, even for the B-side of a record, and the label put it on a shelf. Recordings such as these were an unavoidable waste by-product of the four-songs-in-three-hours, singles-oriented studio system. Then along came the LP format, like a big ol' casserole dish just waiting to be filled with every label's leftovers. Scraps previously considered Not Good Enough to be 50 percent of the product on a record suddenly became Good Enough to bury among all the other songs on an LP, thereby creating a return on investment for recordings that otherwise would have been a complete financial loss. While some producers and artists did recognize the artistic possibilities of this new medium and adjust their approach, most of the industry originally reacted to the LP by lowering their standards for Good Enough material. That applied to both what they already had sitting on their shelves and what they took into future sessions to record. In fact, after LPs came along there were entire sessions dedicated to recording as much Good Enough material as could be churned out in a day. These all-filler, no-killer days took place for several reasons. When a label knew their artist was about to jump ship to another label and wanted to make sure they had enough tape to keep repackaging the hits on LPs for years to come? Filler session. When an artist's new label needed to quickly build a catalog to compete with the catalog said artist left at a previous label? Filler session. When a label wanted to fast track an LP packaged around an artist's latest hit(s)? Filler session.

Because of these strategies, the number of times George Jones changed labels and how much more commercially successful he became with each of those label jumps, he is possibly the most over-recorded artist in country music history. There was a consistent uptick in filler sessions during his final year with each label in the '50s and '60s, probably the result of Pappy Daily working out favorable exit terms by agreeing to leave behind plenty of tape on Jones singing popular songs that fans would recognize by name when browsing the racks in a store. Then, as soon as Pappy got Jones over to the next label, they needed to turn right around and do more filler sessions, creating a whole new catalog of product to compete with everything they'd left at previous labels. For example, after leaving Mercury with the Hank Williams tribute LP made to compete with the

Hank Williams soundalikes previously left with Starday, Pappy then had George cut another Hank tribute album at United Artists for the exact same reason. From the early 1960s forward, going to a store to pick up the new George Jones LP could be quite a confusing experience, as shelves were usually full of fresh product from various record labels, all claiming to be the "latest" album or compilation, often featuring many of the same song titles. Heading home with a newly purchased LP, you didn't know whether it would be so good it blew your mind or a compilation of old recordings George would erase from existence if given the chance. For these and other reasons, to be a George Jones fan was to know he could let you down at least as easily as he could achieve greatness.

Since Pappy Daily was certainly why so many label switches took place, it's fair to say he's the reason there is so much filler content in the George Jones discography. But it's not as simple as "singles good, filler bad." There are many, many songs Pappy pulled from the Good Enough pile and never treated as anything more than filler which went on to become all-time favorite recordings of most fans. Take "Lonely Street," credited to Carl Belew and two other writers but probably purchased from the true author, Wynn Stewart, then put at #5 on the Pop charts by Andy Williams and recorded by Ray Price on his landmark *Night Life* LP. Years later, Jones cut a version of this already popular hit that sounds like he was trying to convince Pappy it should be the title track of the next LP . . . but it was only ever used for album filler, never even issued as a B-side. Jones' incomparable take on "Lonely Street" came out a few years before a young Emmylou Harris joined a circle of friends who all swapped homemade mixtapes of their favorite George Jones songs. It is quite unlikely these college-age kids would have cared enough to trade such tapes with each other if they hadn't first spent so much time searching through George's massive catalog to find the gold. There's a difference between handing someone a twenty dollar bill and handing them a treasure map. In 1989, Emmylou Harris recorded "Lonely Street" for her album *Bluebird*.

It's also not as simple as classifying all George's rerecordings of his earlier hits as inferior versions. Most of them? Blatant examples of Jones half-heartedly going through the motions. But there are some iconic exceptions. For whatever reason he was sometimes able to go in the studio and reconnect with a song he'd performed thousands of times as if he'd just fallen in love with it all over again. The day he recorded "She Thinks I Still Care" in that first session for United Artists he also rush-recorded the other eleven songs on his first album for the label, *The New Favorites of George Jones*. "Poor Little Rich Boy," "She Once Lived Here," "Imitation of Love," "Open Pit Mine," "She Thinks I Still Care" and "Sometimes You Just Can't Win" are all phenomenal takes recorded on that one day. "Sometimes You Just Can't Win" wound up charting at #17 as the B-side of "She Thinks I Still Care," which is impressive enough, but Jones cut the song again as an A-side eight years later and it hit the Top 10. There are fans who prefer the relatively understated production on the original and fans who prefer the bombastic arrangement on the remake, but the performances on both are amazing. Neither can be written off as a trifling redundancy.

The same logic applies to the follow-up rewrites of his biggest hits. As a general rule most come nowhere near the greatness of the original song. The vast majority of people who love "White Lightning", do not react as strongly to "Who Shot Sam" or "Revenooer Man" or "Root Beer," the years-too-late postscript on the Moonshine Trilogy, recorded the same day as the rest of George's first United Artists LP for all the reasons mentioned above. It's like listening to Jones rip himself off over and over. But George Jones sometimes accomplished amazing things while ripping himself off. After Cowboy Jack Clement got him to record "She Thinks I Still Care" and it became a huge hit, Cowboy churned out two rewrites, "Not What I Had in Mind" and "A Girl I Used to Know." Listening to all three songs in succession, the motives and intentions of everyone involved couldn't be any clearer. Judged independently of each other, though, these shameless rewrites also happen to be great. Cowboy was a genius songwriter. The musicians, singers and arrangements are all wonderful. George brought some serious singing to both of the rewrites. When issued as A-sides, "Not What I Had in Mind" went to #7 and "A Girl I Used to Know" hit #3. The unsung quality doesn't stop there. Check out the B-side of "Not What I Had in Mind." Cut in the same session, "I Saw Me" is one of George's most impressive vocal performances. From the back side of that record it broke into the Top 40 Country singles.

All of which brings us to the final subset of the quantity-over-quality complaints lodged against Pappy Daily, a lack of good songwriting in much of the filler material he chose for George Jones to record, which is generally assumed to be a result of Pappy's refusal to consider songs from writers outside of the publishing companies he owned. As with virtually every other criticism of Pappy Daily, this would be more aptly applied to the entire recording industry of the time than to him. Remember Don Pierce's statement: "Why would we go to a publisher who lets us be privileged enough to use their song and then put all of our money into promoting their stuff? Fuck that." Such attitudes were not invented by Don or Pappy and, despite near-universal acceptance in the business, Pappy's not even a good example of someone who rigidly stuck to that philosophy. United Artists A&R man Kelso Herston once said Pappy's artists always selected most of the material they recorded: "I never heard the man make a suggestion. He wasn't a producer, even though he got credit for being one." To be clear, Kelso was saying what we already know, Pappy Daily wasn't a producer by modern definitions, but he also meant Pappy wasn't really even a producer in the original A&R sense of the term. The evidence supports that claim. Whenever Jones found a song he wanted to record, Pappy worked out the best deal he could and booked the studio time to record it. When Jones didn't have a song he wanted to record, which was more and more often the case after Phase II began in the 1960s, Pappy defaulted to material from his own publishing companies. Anytime George met some songwriter he enjoyed writing and/or drinking with—like Melba Montgomery's brother Peanutt—Pappy simply signed that writer to one of his publishing companies and sat back to let nature take its course, as it did when Peanutt became one of the main suppliers of George Jones songs. That was going to happen whether Pappy profited from it or not. All he did was find a way to profit from it.

The second time George went in the studio with Melba Montgomery, they were brainstorming last-minute ideas for duets to record and George brought up the Louvin Brothers. He asked Melba if she knew the song "God Bless Her ('Cause She's My Mother)" and, being from Alabama like the Louvins, Melba did know it. They had someone call Acuff-Rose to send over copies of the lyrics, along with lyrics for the Louvin Brothers' song "Alabama," then recorded both songs even though Pappy had no piece of the publishing on either one. But what about songwriters who didn't happen to be personal heroes of George Jones? Was it true Pappy refused to consider their songs unless he got the publishing and George's name was added as a writer? The more accurate thing to say would be that's how Pappy opened negotiations and it would have been ignorant to do anything else in an era when this was such a routine deal most writers agreed without any hesitation. If and when a writer did push back, Pappy's subsequent negotiations were based on the quality of the song. Was it worth recording without the extra royalties from owning the publishing or getting his artist credited as a writer? If not, he'd walk away from the table. If so, could the song's publisher perhaps be talked into splitting the publishing? That's what Pappy did with Cowboy Jack on "She Thinks I Still Care" and the publisher of "The Race Is On" because he felt the hit potential of both songs made that deal worth it. In the rare instance when Pappy couldn't secure any of the above terms but a song was just too damn good to walk away . . . he'd still get George to cut it and still release it as a single, just like he did in 1970 with "A Good Year for the Roses," 100 percent written and published by Jerry Chesnut. Accepted industry practices meant Pappy almost never had to leave that much money on the table but, if that's what it came to, he would and did do that very thing for the sake of a song.

The legends of Pappy's ruthlessness in business dealings were furthered by various songwriters whose meetings with Pappy ended in failure to negotiate a deal. Take a guy named Darrell McCall, one of Donny Young's buddies who also did harmony work on some George Jones sessions. Darrell wrote a song he said Jones really wanted to record but couldn't because Pappy wouldn't allow it after Darrell refused to credit Jones as a writer. Consider the fact that Darrell's song, called "If You Don't Believe I Love You, Just Ask Me," contained the lyrics "I'd even marry your cat just to get in your family." It's obvious we're not talking about "She Thinks I Still Care," here. In fact, the way Darrell told the story makes it sound an awful lot like George probably asked Pappy to be the bad guy and pretend to be the reason they weren't going to cut this stupid song. According to Darrell, the first thing Pappy asked was who had publishing on the song, to which Darrell responded it wasn't yet published so Pappy could have 100 percent of the publishing. These are terms Pappy would normally have found favorable . . . except that's the point in negotiations when Pappy did a hard pivot and began acting like Jones getting 50 percent of the writing credit was the only thing that mattered. Darrell walked away from the deal and spent the rest of his life telling everyone Pappy Daily wouldn't let George Jones record anything unless George's name was added as a writer. Multiply that interaction by however many other songwriters could tell a similar story and it adds up to a solid rumor. (There's a funny postscript on this story, too. In 1975, Darrell McCall recorded his own version of "If You Don't Believe I Love You, Just Ask Me" and his producer, Glenn Sutton, was credited as a co-writer on the song. Turns out Darrell never did manage to find someone who thought the song was worth cutting without that extra writing credit.)

Another young writer who as early as 1958 was already under the impression he probably didn't even want George Jones to record one of his songs was Glenn Douglas Tubb, Ernest Tubb's nephew and co-writer of Henson Cargill's "Skip a Rope." One time Glenn and Jones happened to be at the same party and Jones heard Glenn singing a couple of his own songs. When Jones said he'd like to record them, Glenn said he'd rather that didn't happen, since the songs were already assigned to a different publishing company and everyone knew Pappy Daily had to acquire the publishing in order to release a song as a single or get behind promoting it. George recorded Glenn's songs anyway and, sure enough, they went entirely unreleased for many years, only eventually seeing the light of day as rarities included on compilations. Just as Glenn suspected, right? That's the story he told for decades. Except both of Glenn's songs were amateur at best. "There's Gonna Be One" is a cheeky number about how if there's one woman in the world who'd love the singer, then there's probably another so he may as well go ahead and try to find out how many more "fish" there are in the sea. Holding to that oceanic theme, "Stay on Board" likens a romantic relationship to being the captain of an actual ship and uses all the painfully labored metaphors you would imagine. Since the only other song Jones recorded that day was called "The Likes of You," which also makes reference to "fish in the ocean" and bears a nearly identical arrangement to the other two songs, it's possible all of this material was intended for some sort of concept LP which never came out. "The Likes of You" was easily Jones' best vocal take of the day and Pappy Daily owned the publishing. Yet it, too, was left entirely unreleased until a couple of years after Jones moved to a different record label. Of all the possible explanations for why Glenn's songs were shelved along with the rest of that entire day's work, Pappy's greed cannot be considered one of them.

Pappy's unearned reputation was a product of the music business being far more complex than it appears from the perspective of any single entity within the system. In such a system, rumors can become self-fulfilling prophecy. Because of what many songwriters heard about Pappy, they never even tried pitching songs to him or George Jones, limiting the pool of material available for Jones to consider, at which point it was easier to just keep recording whatever Pappy's own writers had ready to go. Bear in mind, Roger Miller was once one of those writers, as were Leon Payne, Dallas Frazier, Melba Montgomery, Peanutt Montgomery, Eddie Noack, Darrell Edwards and George Jones himself. It's true nearly all of George's singles "produced" by Pappy were supplied by the same stable of hit songwriters . . . because that's the entire point of owning a stable of hit songwriters, all of whom were equally capable of churning out the Good Enough throwaway songs that were viewed as a practical necessity to the singles industry.

Of course, none of that stops the worst filler in George's discography from being downright embarrassing. Hell, George himself was embarrassed by some of it at the time. One of the most infamous examples would be Peanutt Montgomery's "Unwanted Babies," recorded in 1967. It is mind-boggling to consider how many people actively participated in the creation of that record without wondering whether someone was pulling some kind of practical joke on them. There's no telling what kind of social commentary Peanutt believed he was delivering with this sort of folky protest anthem, covering everything from social strife between neighbors to mistreated veterans of war and capping it all off with a vague, unpacked reference to, yes, unwanted babies. For some reason, Pappy chose to release "Unwanted Babies" as a single, but Jones refused to put his name on the label, telling them to use his middle name and his mother's name to place the blame on "Glenn Patterson." Ralph Emery once played "Unwanted Babies" on his radio show while Jones was with him in the studio and Jones supposedly said on air, "It's not me, Ralph!" (It's unclear whether he meant the song didn't represent his own idea of what a George Jones record should be or if he was trying to outright deny the voice on the record came out of his mouth.) But anyone imagining a scenario where all this filler would be of higher quality had Pappy Daily pulled material from more varied sources is dealing in pure fantasy, ignoring the entire history of an industry and hating on one individual player who didn't even play the game as ruthlessly as most others did. If Pappy hadn't been there to steer the course of George's career, somebody else would have taken the wheel and there's no reason to assume they'd have done a better job.

◇　　◇　　◇

George Jones was so uninterested in managing his own life that he kept the flattop haircut given to him by the Marine Corps for more than a decade after being discharged, until the late 1960s, when he began having an affair with a former professional hairstylist we know by the name of Tammy Wynette. It takes a bit more time to make changes bigger than a haircut, but if Tammy hadn't come along it's possible George would have stood by Pappy forever.

ELEVEN

LITTLE WARS

◇ Restless Warriors ◇ The Medieval Tournament ◇ Chivalry and Fantasy ◇
King Henri II's Fatal Joust ◇ Catherine de Médici: From Orphan to Queen
◇ Merry-Go-Round ◇

In the fifth century, after the fall of the Roman Empire, pretty much all of Europe was up for grabs. Entire nations of people immigrated to the continent while other entire nations fled. It was the time of Viking marauders. Anything was yours if you could take it by force, whether your own or that of an alliance held together through any combination of wealth, religion, family or fear. Various territories formed themselves into kingdoms, states and republics with names you weren't taught in school because those territories were soon conquered or allied through new treaties and renamed, again and again and again. As political order began to define itself from within this chaos, the most successful nations turned out to be those with prosperous lands and enough wealth to afford hiring and rewarding the militaries needed to defend and acquire more prosperous lands and wealth. Following great victories, the warriors who'd excelled in battle stood—or kneeled—to receive knighthood, money, advantageous marriage, desirable properties and serfs, all meted out according to (and possibly including a promotion of) rank and title.

In the peacetime between wars, however brief and intermittent, such knights found themselves with too much free time and not enough people to kill. Imagine you're a king or some lesser lord. You don't want this warrior aristocracy sitting around with no reason to keep themselves or their battle skills in shape. Even worse, you don't want them conspiring with each other to find an excuse to use those battle skills, possibly against you in a coup d'état. By the end of the tenth century, entering the High Middle Ages, a solution to the problem was discovered: miniature, pretend wars, called "tournaments." Do not be fooled by the word "miniature." These pretend wars may not have spanned the lands of entire nations but, like a real war, tournaments were scalable. The designated in-bounds area of any given tournament could be an enormous size, as large as all the connecting forests and pastures of the wealthiest participating or sponsoring lords, sometimes several miles of land. Sometimes it was more like acres, sometimes as small as a field or fenced-in enclosure without even enough room to use horses in the fight. Whatever the scale this was different from any earlier combat sport or training exercise. It was medieval warfare with everything but the political grievances and killing . . . or, at least, without as much. Smaller tournaments were often every man fighting for himself but the larger affairs usually involved teams. When teams were chosen it was sometimes arbitrarily, sometimes according to very real and serious sociopolitical divides with participating knights grouped on to opposing sides of personal feuds or governmental conflict. For instance, teams could be split by which of two countries knights were born in or which country they intended to support in a war everyone knew could start any minute, perhaps even during the tournament if someone got too worked up to remember the part about not killing each other in this game.

The idea was to keep tournaments nonlethal but the idea was also to beat the shit out of each other with blunted swords. Larger tournaments typically began with both sides launching a full cavalry charge at each other. Accidents happened. "Accidents" could also very easily be made to happen in such an environment, should personal vendetta or political gain provide sufficient motive. Etymological evidence points to the term "freelance" originating as a noun to describe a knight-for-rent, available to any noble house who may have need of representation in some prestigious tourney. Should said noble house have need for a certain knight to be killed in the tourney, well, it was probably a good idea to send in a freelance rather than a knight officially sworn to their house. Even without contract killing the very nature of medieval warfare made this an extremely lucrative game for mercenaries. In nontournament war real weapons were used to kill people on the other side . . . but not all of the people on the other side. All men were not born equal in the Middle Ages. Infantrymen and commoners died by the thousands in war but if a knight surrendered in battle or you were otherwise able to capture a knight as a prisoner, the smart thing to do was keep him alive. The closer he sat to any throne by blood or marriage, the greater his value as a political bargaining chip. Should the prisoner's family happen to be rich, and there's a solid chance they were, a large ransom could be demanded for his release. The thing about tournaments is that everyone on the other side was a knight. In fact, it was a rule that everyone had to be a knight. In fact, you could say this was the only rule of a tournament, implying all the others with one simple twist on a familiar concept: it's war, except everyone's a knight. Since knights were meant to be captured and not killed in war, everyone may as well use blunted swords and so on. In war—real or pretend—a captured knight owed his captor a ransom of money, weapons, armor, a horse, whatever was deemed valuable enough to grant the knight's release. The particulars of these and other tournament matters were dictated by ever-evolving customs of warfare and a thing called "chivalry."

Like the entire feudalist system, chivalry is a concept that has been defined and redefined to a point of mass confusion and near meaninglessness. Regardless of modern connotations, chivalry began having not much at all to do with ensuring men held doors open for women. The original scope of chivalric concerns was much more to do with warfare, as knights were primarily weapons of war. The word "chivalry" comes from *chevalier*, the French word for "knight," which shares a Latin root with both "cavalry" and *caballero*, the Spanish word for "gentleman." All of these words implied at least ownership of a horse, if not full knighthood. The word "cavalier" comes from the same place and also meant "knight" before it became an adjective used to describe men who walk around with their heads up their own asses, which, as we're about to see, is not a coincidence. Modern misconceptions of chivalry are probably the lasting result of how much fiction written in and about this period leans on romantic plots both to rationalize and soften the violent behavior of knights, the typical male protagonists. How to treat a lady of the court as opposed to a common woman, that was covered by the code of chivalry, sure. But at nowhere near a level of priority as how a knight should conduct himself in pursuit of his military obligations toward God, church, country, honor itself and the various other personal pledges he had likely sworn. Remaining faithful to all these loyalties at once would pose quite a challenge, especially in an era prior to concepts like separation of church and state, a time in which popes selected from noble families chose to assign important government positions to relatives and formed political alliances with kings, who were believed to rule by divine right. Such great potential for internal conflict is exactly what made and continues to make the knight an attractive character for storytellers. The very nature of his existence demands sacrificing one loyalty in aggressively violent defense of another, thus revealing his most deeply held convictions. Within a hundred years or so of pretend war between knights becoming a popular form of entertainment to the ruling class, poems, novels and "history" books written in the twelfth century changed chivalry forever by presenting epic fantasies about legendary characters doing magical things during a golden age of chivalry that supposedly existed hundreds and hundreds of years prior—Saint George killing a dragon, King Arthur and his knights relentlessly questing to become ever more pure while searching for the Holy Grail, etc. Because these stories required glorious acts of violence from knights, such behavior was provoked and motivated through artificially inflated romance and fantasy. These extremely popular texts became the instruction manuals of chivalry, documents of contemporary ideals projected on to heroes in a distant and magical past. It never mattered whether any of it was real or not. People wanted it to be real, so it came true in the way knights of the twelfth century and later were expected to behave at court, on the battlefield and in tournaments. Men can turn anything into a competition, even and especially trying to act like the heroes of popular stories, which is how chivalry became the overwrought pageantry of a knight attempting to perform the righteous and lionhearted role society expected of him because of the fictional books everyone read. You could think of it like playing a character at a renaissance fair except using real swords to kill real people.

This so-called New Age of Chivalry lasted around five hundred years, until the beginning of the seventeenth century, when Miguel de Cervantes—a military veteran who'd been wounded in battle, captured and held prisoner of war for nearly five years—comprehensively mocked the culture to death in *Don Quixote*. Were there knights during the five-hundred-year New Age of Chivalry who shirked trends and ignored the expectations placed on them by society? Probably. There were certainly knights who never cared about fighting in miniature wars. But knights who did enter tournaments cared about chivalry a lot. A knight entering of his own volition (whether motivated by ego, honor or whatever else) would need to be trained and skilled enough in combat to win fights. If he was already doing the hard part, why not lean into the whole chivalry thing and reap all the social benefits? Even a knight with mercenary motives, attracted to the game by money and prizes, would at least need to fake a sense of honor. Any noble family hiring a knight to represent their house would expect displays of chivalry.

All of which goes to explain how, largely based on twelfth-century fairy tales about things that never really happened some thousand years earlier, knights entering tournaments began advertising their "romantic" dispositions—their commitment to chivalry—by wearing a lady's favor. This was some visible token of feminine affection. It could be jewelry, though a more typical favor was a kerchief or similar piece of fabric, sewn and embroidered by a woman or her servant for this explicit purpose because they were trying to play their part and behave like the women characters in popular fairy tales. In those books, the purpose of a lady's favor varied according to plot. Most often it was merely to help a knight carry memories of his beloved on long journeys and dangerous quests or to superstitiously provide God with a nominal excuse to give the knight a safe journey home, so he could "return the favor." Sometimes the lady's favor was meant as a good luck charm or (more commonly, what with the existence of magic in so many of these stories) an enchanted item granting the knight special powers and/or protection. In the books, these types of favors would often be worn under armor to keep them secret and safe. Not so with favors worn in the New Age of Chivalry to broadcast that a knight fought for the love and honor of a lady, especially when fighting as her champion to settle some dispute or perceived insult. This was the favor worn in tournaments and it was to be proudly displayed for all in the audience to see, perhaps even given to the knight in front of the audience should he request the favor from a lady upon entering the field of battle.

As with most acts of chivalry, the entire point was to be noticed, otherwise these knights and ladies could've kept this whole charade to themselves.

About a hundred years after twelfth-century literature married romance to chivalry, the performative aspect of this culture shifted the main attraction at tournaments from epic battles held across miles of woods and pastures back closer to town, to what had before been a side event entered by only the most skilled warriors because it was considered much too dangerous for young princes and royal heirs to compete. The one rule for this side event was exactly the same as the rest of the tournament: it's war, except everyone's a knight. This version of war even began with a cavalry charge. The only difference was it scaled war down to one-on-one combat, in an act known as the joust. Being part of a cavalry charge and being the entire cavalry charge are very different things. Your chances of dying go way up when it's just you and one other guy charging at each other on horses while aiming long, sharp sticks at each other, as you've each practiced doing thousands of times. As if those stakes weren't high enough, the whole thing happened directly in front of an audience. The larger team and free-for-all battles mostly took place out in the fields and spectators who wished to do so were able to observe that action but only from a great distance. Specific details of what happened out there were only learned after the fact, when all the knights came in and told stories of their accomplishments. The joust distilled combat to brute simplicity and gave its audience a front row seat to the action, which was barely safer than one-on-one combat in real war. Should two knights from opposing houses meet in the wild during a real war, again, they'd both endeavor to capture the other one as a prisoner, which could be accomplished by such unchivalrous methods as spearing the other knight's leg or killing his horse to take him down to the ground. These tactics would not do in front of an audience, where knights had to fight by the rules of chivalry. The victor of a tournament joust was usually determined by tallying the points each knight received for shattering a lance upon the shield or in-bounds armor of his opponent. There were, however, other paths to victory. Directly striking an opponent's chest armor or helmet was likely to knock him off his horse and cause him to lose conscious, perhaps even killing him, which would secure a win. Should the unhorsed knight remain conscious and wish to keep fighting, the battle would continue on the ground with blunted swords until one knight or the other surrendered by removing his own helmet. Win or lose, this all happened right in front of a crowd, who watched everything as it took place.

After the joust became the most popular tournament event in the exhibitionist culture of chivalry, it needed to be made safer or else too many princes and kings would die trying to prove they were great and honorable warriors like the heroes of popular stories. In the fourteenth century, to prevent head-on collisions, jousting riders were separated into defined lanes by a short fence or suspended length of rope called a "tilt," likely because it forced lances to impact at an angle, tilted indirectly at the opposing rider rather than thrust straight ahead into his body. From then on "tilting" was another term for the joust. Special tournament lances were fashioned to be lighter and more easily shattered by hollowing out the centers of the shafts. The pointed tips of regular lances were replaced by multipronged or blunt ends to dull and spread impact, theoretically lowering the chances a lance would pierce another knight's armor and kill him. Some unchivalrous knights were said to use trick lances, built with a weak safety tip designed to break off and uncover a sharp, reinforced, armor-piercing shaft. But even with no subterfuge and all manner of precaution in place, there's no way to predict how a lance will shatter . . .

◇　　◇　　◇ ·

The main cause usually given for the joust's gradual fall from popularity in the second half of the sixteenth century is the death of King Henri II of France in 1559. It's definitely the reason knights stopped jousting in France because King Henri's wife, Catherine de Médici, was watching from the stands when sharp pieces of a broken lance flew through the visor of her husband's helmet and impaled his brain. After Henri died, Catherine dressed in black for the rest of her life, adopted the personal emblem of a broken lance and banned jousting in France. All of this despite the fact that Henri had been jousting while wearing the favor and house colors of another woman who he was in love with. In his defense, the marriage to Catherine never had anything to do with love and was arranged when they were both fourteen years old in 1533.

◇　　◇　　◇

The Médicis, one of the wealthiest and most powerful families in all of Europe during the Late Middle Ages, had effectively controlled the Republic of Florence for much of the previous century. There were decades-long periods when the only thing keeping Florence "a republic" was the illusion that most government officials were not bought and/or planted by the Médicis. Just prior to Catherine marrying Henri, the Médicis had done away with the illusion and established a monarchy in Florence, then all of Tuscany, a reign that more or less lasted another two hundred years. Had Catherine's parents not become ill and died immediately after her birth it's a near certainty the family would've chosen her father to rule over Florence. But her parents did die, leaving behind an orphan girl of common birth who would normally never be considered suitable for marriage to a prince, except this particular orphan girl's uncle happened to be the pope. With papal promises of an enormous dowry, Catherine was married to Henri, the second oldest son of the King of France; not next in line to the throne but, still, a prince. Then, right after the wedding, the Médici pope became ill and died. The next pope? Not a Médici. Worse, the new pope said the Church was under no obligation to pay the outrageous sum pledged by his predecessor for Catherine's dowry. So the

King of France came out of the whole deal with none of the money he was promised and no political alliance to the new pope, just an orphan girl of common birth married to one of his sons. The general consensus at his court was a prince's hand in marriage had been entirely wasted.

A year after the wedding, fifteen-year-old Henri took a lover, Diane de Poitiers, a thirty-five-year-old woman who tutored him on French culture. Young Henri needed these lessons because he didn't learn much about France during the four years he spent in a prison cell in Spain, where he'd been sent as collateral to secure his father's release from the same prison after the King of France had been captured in war. Henri remained in love with Diane de Poitiers for the rest of his life. In an age of arranged marriages it was common for men to have a mistress, or many mistresses, and there wasn't much need for secrecy. But by the time Henri's older brother became ill and died, leaving Henri as heir to the throne of France, he'd moved well beyond openly flaunting the relationship with Diane de Poitiers. They went everywhere and did everything together, his wife, Catherine, trailing behind silently, if at all. Henri had Diane's initials embroidered on his clothing. He and Diane created a hybrid signature of their names to sign letters, as if speaking to one was as good as speaking to the other. When his father died and Henri became King of France in 1547, Diane was as involved in his daily political life as any advisor. Catherine was not.

Even though Catherine was now literally Queen of France, she continued playing the part of rescued orphan girl, just grateful to be fed and clothed and protected by royal guard. Anyway, Diane had been one of the few nobles at court who came to Catherine's defense when everyone else said the orphan girl without a dowry should be sent away so a suitable bride could be found for the prince. Diane continued to defend her as the years passed without Catherine becoming pregnant, when many people said the prince should have a bride who could make more princes. Surely anticipating the threat some other woman with more confidence may pose to her relationship with Henri, Diane encouraged him to keep trying to have kids with Catherine. After ten years of marriage, a royal doctor finally noticed a peculiarity of Henri's anatomy and suggested the royal couple try a different position during sex. Soon after this suggestion Catherine did become pregnant and went on to bear Henri many children, including boys, thus securing her place at court. Still, she remained a passive observer in her own marriage, accepting Diane's intrusions and largely avoiding affairs of state . . . right up until the moment King Henri was fatally wounded in a joust. When the pieces of lance went into Henri's head it didn't kill him instantly. Doctors recognized at once his injuries would be mortal but the king lived another ten days. From his deathbed, he asked to see Diane but, after decades of silence, Catherine played her hand. The Queen of France said Diane de Poitiers was not to be permitted an audience with the dying king and Diane knew there was no recourse against the royal command. Further, Diane understood its full implications and quickly fled from Paris, retreating to a beautiful castle Henri had gifted her years earlier, a beautiful castle Catherine had always wanted for herself. After Catherine's husband died and her teenage son became the new king of France, she ordered Diane to vacate the beautiful castle and return it to the royal family.

Over the following thirty years, as one after another of her sons sat upon France's throne, Catherine de Médici sat behind them, pulling strings of European politics and culture. One of her first acts was to ban jousting within France. Tournaments continued but the ever-so-dangerous joust was replaced by an event that all but guaranteed survival to any idiot who could stay on top of a horse. It turned out, as long as all the pomp and chivalry remained in place, audiences were willing, even enthused, to watch knights compete in what had previously been a mere practice exercise: tilting at rings. Rather than get themselves killed trying to learn how to joust by jumping right in and doing it, young noblemen learned accuracy with a lance by riding horses around a course and spearing metal rings suspended from strings. Trainees not yet comfortable holding a lance on a real horse sat atop a wooden horse in a cart and had assistants wheel them past the rings. Alternately, a wooden horse could be attached to one end of a plank suspended at waist height parallel to the ground and then rotated to simulate riding in a circle while tilting at rings.

Since at least the first century, humans had fashioned similar rides by hanging two baskets at each end of a pole but the rise of tournament culture in Europe coincided with a spread of the practice horse version across the continent. After enterprising folk took notice of how many women and children with no hopes of ever becoming knights enjoyed riding around in circles on unused wooden horses, the modern carousel was born by adding more planks to the central axis with a horse at each end of each plank. Operators spent winter months hand-carving new horses for the apparatus they then hauled around from town to town when the weather turned warm, charging mere pennies for a ride on their "flying horses." Later designs hung each horse on a vertical pole suspended from overhead beams, which caused the horses to lift up and away with centrifugal force as the central axis spun, creating a more dynamic and crowd-pleasing ride. Sometime in the 1700s, after platforms started being built under the horses to prevent them from lifting away, competitive operators reintroduced a dynamic element to the ride by attaching the pole of each horse to a simple gear, causing the horse to move in a vertical "o" path and simulate a gallop as the axis spun. By this time carousels had grown in size to include multiple horses per row, each on a pole attached to its own gear, causing the riders in each row to feel like they were galloping independently of each other while moving forward as a pack. It was all great fun but operators kept the galloping mechanism off of the outside horse in every row. This was partly a safety issue, what with the outside of a spinning disc moving faster than the inside, but also a matter of curb appeal, since operators always proudly displayed the best-looking and most intricately designed of their hand-carved horses on the outside of a row to attract customers. Then operators in the late 1800s noticed they were losing money on the outside horses of each row as groups of kids or entire families waited for the next ride to make sure everyone got a galloping horse. So they brought back tilting at the ring. Once a carousel got up to speed, a metal arm would swing into place with a dispenser on the end presenting one ring at a time for riders on the outside horses to reach out and grab. Nearly all of the rings were made of iron or steel and these types of ring were worthless. Still, you had to grab for whatever the dispenser held out, even if only for practice, even if only to make sure your hand knew where it needed to be and what it needed to do if it ever got the chance to grab for a brass ring. Because if you did ever manage to grab one, and there was usually only one, the brass ring was worth another ride. Successfully grabbing a brass ring was so rare that many riders who accomplished the feat chose to keep the ring as a good luck charm, never turning it in to receive the free ride. To this day there are some carousels in Europe where, rather than having riders grab with their hands, they are provided with small sticks to lance the rings. And, of course, the word "carousel" comes from an Italian word meaning "little war."

TWELVE

DADDY'S GIRL

◇ Wynette ◇ The Byrd Brothers ◇ Motherhood ◇
Singing for Tips ◇ Euple Byrd: Villain or Stepping Stone? ◇ The Great Porter Wagoner Lie
◇ Billy Sherrill Creates Tammy Wynette ◇ Hitting #1 with David Houston ◇
The Upgrade to George Jones ◇

In 1942, having suffered migraine headaches his entire adult life, William Pugh checked into a hospital where his skull was cut open and doctors discovered a brain tumor which could not be removed. William was going to die, soon, but first he would go blind. The nurse who cared for him as he recovered from the surgery and diagnosis was named Wynette. (The first syllable rhymes with "win.") She must have been especially great at her job because when William's only child was born five months later he named her Virginia Wynette Pugh. Most of the family addressed the young girl by her middle name, Wynette, or "Nettiebelle."

Prior to receiving his death sentence William Pugh had been a farmer, who lived and worked on the six hundred acres of land owned by his father-in-law on the Mississippi side of the Alabama state border. William and his brothers grew up with fantasies of one day becoming professional musicians. They even played in a little band with a cousin and a couple of friends but, a handful of local gigs aside, all the pickin' they ever did was at family get-togethers. In the nine months he was able to spend with his infant daughter—as William lost more, then most, then all of his sight—he found solace in sitting with the baby on his lap at a piano, pressing her tiny hands onto the keys so she could hear the different tones produced by each touch. Wynette would later say she possessed no memories of her father whatsoever, which may be just as well, since recalling those early piano lessons could've come with the cost of also remembering his screaming fits of rage as the growing tumor dragged him further into darkness. William died at the young age of twenty-six but not before making his wife, Mildred, promise to foster any future interest their daughter showed in music. That promise was kept, though mostly by Mildred's parents, who Wynette addressed as Mama and Daddy for the rest of her life. Mama taught Nettiebelle shape note singing so she could participate in Sacred Harp hymnals at the local Baptist church, but the child preferred their occasional visits to William's old Pentecostal congregation. Guitars were allowed at the Church of God service, so the music over there had a little more fire in it. At the age of eight, Wynette began taking piano lessons but the teacher quit after realizing the student was playing her homework from memory instead of learning to sight read sheet music. Still, she kept at the instrument on her own and it remained her best, even after also picking up guitar, accordion and—for high school band—the flute.

◇   ◇   ◇

The above information is all probably true but any rigorous investigation into the facts of Wynette's life will uncover that she may have been one of the most unreliable narrators in the history of country music. There are many instances where the version of reality she presented cannot be squared with documented and verifiable history, the accounts given by nearly every other first-hand witness or even her own contradictory accounts of the same events given at various other times. For example, Wynette would tell you that growing up on a farm meant she picked cotton from the age of six until she left home at seventeen; if she happened to get more Christmas presents than the other kids in her school, it wasn't because her family had more money but because she was an only child in an area where other families had as many as ten kids; she wasn't particularly popular or considered especially pretty at school and she was always much too fixated on music to be (her term) "boy crazy" like all of her friends. Except in other conversations she'd also tell you she was ten when she accepted Mama's offer of staying in the house to help with the cooking instead of picking cotton. She'd tell you about her aunt Carolyn, who was only five years older and raised like a sister in the same home, where Nettiebelle and Carolyn (and every other member of the immediate family) received a clean fifty dollar bill from Mama and Daddy every Christmas. Fifty dollars at that time was worth more than five hundred dollars in modern currency and that was in addition to all of the other presents. They only received such a lavish bounty every year because, again, Daddy owned six hundred acres of farmland, which was worked by the hired parents of several schoolmates Wynette later tried to claim were her financial equals. It's also difficult to believe Wynette could have been considered unpopular and ugly at school while also being voted prom queen, which she irrefutably was. It doesn't require comparing many sources to spot these inconsistencies. All of this conflicting information came from Wynette herself in a 1977 profile and a 1979 autobiography, both authored by/with a writer named Joan Dew, who later revealed how much truth she knew had been obscured by Wynette's distortions of reality.

◇   ◇   ◇

Those seeking a more accurate source of history would do well to read Jimmy McDonough's fascinating 2010 biography, *Tammy Wynette: Tragic Country Queen*, written from several years of immersive research and dozens of interviews with witnesses from every period of her life. As Jimmy's title suggests, much of what truly did happen to Wynette, from the circumstances of her birth all the way through to the circumstances of her death, was pure tragedy. Some of her fabrications were standard celebrity efforts to sanitize certain aspects of her life which didn't conform to society's expectations of women. However, most of the lies she told were clearly attempts to make her life seem even more tragic than it was, thus presenting herself as deserving of even more sympathy. As with most prolific fabulists, these attempts to cover up and manufacture reality often ultimately achieved the opposite of her intention, revealing much about her true self, true fears and true desires to those capable of reading between the lines of stories she created in response to her inner critical voice, arguing aloud against her own memory's persistent reminders of what really did happen. Several of the true stories she told were equally instructive, especially those she felt compelled to retell over and over throughout her life, like the time she was close to ten years old but hadn't yet made the deal with Mama to cook instead of picking cotton. (It seems pretty likely this story was why Mama's deal got put on the table.) When Wynette said how much she wanted to go to the county fair, she was told to pick a certain amount of cotton by a certain time of day and then she could go. Well, with that deadline fast approaching and her bags not yet heavy enough, Wynette did the single worst thing a cotton picker can do. She put rocks in her sack to make it heavier. Before she even made it off the property on her way to fair, one of the rocks in her bag caused a fire at the communal cotton gin, burning the entire day's haul from multiple farms in the area. Daddy knew right away what had happened and started bringing an ass whipping in her direction, so she ran from it. When she tripped and cut her knee on a rock, her first thought when she saw the blood was, in her words, "Oh, this is great because now he won't whip me." Expecting sympathy for her wound, she received a whipping instead. It would not be the last time.

◇   ◇   ◇

In the house where Wynette grew up Mama and Daddy kept separate bedrooms. Nettiebelle slept in Daddy's bed every night until she was about thirteen years old, when, for obvious reasons, he said she must start sleeping in her own bed. She believed Daddy was punishing her by making her spend nights alone, a thing she couldn't stand to do for the rest of her life. By that time her biological mother, Mildred, had moved back to the farm with a new husband, Foy Lee, and the newlyweds lived in a separate house on the property. So Wynette responded to Daddy's "punishment" by dragging her little bed across a field to move in with Mildred and Foy Lee . . . until she got in trouble for something over there and dragged the bed back across the field to Mama and Daddy's, repeating this show of force pretty much any time she was seriously scolded.

While she claimed to've been too obsessed with music to care about boys or her own unpopularity at school, Wynette's schoolmates (including one of her first singing partners) recalled her being very popular and said neither music nor any other subject stood in the way of her being the most "boy crazy" girl they ever met. The more other witnesses share their memories of Wynette, the more it appears that she consistently introduced certain topics in order to try establishing her own narrative on those topics before anyone else who was there could tell a different story. According to everyone but her, Wynette was considered very pretty by all the boys in school and she found time to spend with most of them, older boys, younger boys, popular boys, loner boys, boys, boys, boys. Her popularity at school meant classmates took an interest in her romantic activities, an interest Wynette eagerly cultivated by involving friends in secret and elaborate plots to help her elope with whichever boy she was seeing at the time. She'd then suddenly drop the plan along with the boy, only to choose a different boy a couple weeks later and repeat the cycle of fantasy, essentially creating a middle-school soap opera with herself as the star. Whether she went all, most or some of the way with any of these boys doesn't really matter, but Wynette did try to impress upon the other kids at school that she had firsthand knowledge of sex, which soon gave her a reputation, one she relished. In response to this, Mildred and Foy Lee took her away to live in Memphis, probably thinking the young girl couldn't get herself into any trouble in a city where she didn't know anybody. Then Wynette began sneaking out at night with Memphis boys to smoke cigarettes and do who knows what else. Worried her daughter would soon end up pregnant, missing or dead, Mildred brought the girl back to the farm.

In her autobiography and several interviews throughout her career Wynette pointed out her astrological sign was Taurus and said telling her no would be like waving a red cape in front of a bull. She also remembered how badly she needed freedom from the farm and from Mildred, freedom to do the things she wanted to do. Like many farm girls with similar feelings in this era she began to view marriage as the only way out. Wynette would later claim to've been on fewer than a dozen dates prior to her first marriage, which would be difficult to believe even if she claimed to have gone on dates with fewer than a dozen individual boys. According to friends, she was known to use all-girl sleepovers as a cover to climb out a window and disappear for a few hours with whoever she was dating. Around the age of sixteen she worked up another plot to elope and this time she meant it. She selected a boy, picked out rings from a mail-order catalog and had them shipped to school so no parents would catch on and foil everything. Despite such precautions Mildred was warned before the scheme could be put into action and she shut it down. Wynette was furious.

Not heartbroken, furious. Once Mildred knew how far her teenage daughter was willing to go to escape, she kept an even tighter leash. Wynette saw no other choice but to knuckle down, finish high school, then make her final getaway. Still settled on marriage as a necessary step in the plan, she continued to hold auditions for a husband, which led to working her way through the Byrd brothers.

◇　◇　◇

The version Wynette settled on later was she briefly dated D.C. Byrd before deciding to instead marry his younger brother, Euple. If you believe nearly everyone else who was there, the truth is Wynette became full-blown obsessed with D.C., who she conveniently forgot to mention was already married at the time. Her "dating" him broke up his marriage but then D.C. crushed her heart by remarrying his ex-wife. So Wynette proceeded to date all three of his younger brothers, one after the other, at least partially and perhaps entirely in order to remain near D.C., who was still her true obsession. Mildred was horrified by all of this, naturally. Her distress was so great she even tried pushing Wynette toward dating a substitute math teacher from school, probably figuring he was at least an unmarried man so there'd be less risk of someone getting shot and killed in the deal. But Wynette carried on with the Byrd brothers, which eventually brought about some kind of physical altercation between her and her mother. Wynette later claimed Mildred attacked her with a belt and the metal buckle caught her in the face but that seems to be a story she only started telling after appropriating it from an acquaintance in the late 1960s. Whatever did happen between her and Mildred, it brought a premature end to Wynette's high school career. In 1959, at the age of seventeen, she left home and married Euple, the Byrd brother who truly did love her, though Wynette admitted she never really loved him back. They spent their wedding night in the Byrd family home, in a bed loud enough for Wynette to become embarrassed over the fact that everyone else in the house could surely hear what they were doing. After her husband fell asleep she lay awake for hours, feeling disappointed with all her new freedom.

When the young married couple found jobs in Tupelo, Mississippi, they moved into a small apartment in town. Six months later, they'd both lost their jobs and Wynette was already pregnant, so they moved back to Daddy's farm, into a dilapidated log cabin built in the 1800s way back in the woods on those six hundred acres. That's where Wynette's first daughter, Gwendolyn Lee Byrd, was born in 1961. Six months later, Wynette was already pregnant again. The log cabin had been wired for electricity but it only worked half the time and the stove was broken anyway, so Wynette did all the family's cooking in a fireplace. Since the cabin did not have indoor plumbing, every drop of drinking, bathing, laundry and cooking water needed to be brought up from a creek about a hundred yards away. If she needed more water when no other adults were around, Wynette, several months pregnant, would lift a leg of the bed to put baby Gwen's dress under it and keep her pinned to one spot while Wynette retrieved buckets of water from the creek. When she entered labor with her second child she walked the half mile from the cabin to Mildred's house with Gwen under one arm and a suitcase needed for the hospital under the other. Jacquelyn Fay Byrd was born in 1962.

Twenty years old with two kids and a husband she claimed couldn't or wouldn't hold down a job, Wynette began borrowing money from Mildred in order to attend beauty school. But then, still according to her, the same good-for-nothing husband got a job in Memphis, so she dropped out of beauty school and the family moved to Memphis. One day, walking down the sidewalk with little Gwen and carrying baby Jackie, Wynette heard honky-tonk piano being played in a bar and stopped outside to listen for a minute. The owner of the bar saw her out there and said they wouldn't be open for a while yet if she'd like to bring in the kids and listen to the music. When the owner then said he was looking for a server to run drinks to tables, Wynette took the job. Soon she was picking up extra tip money by getting onstage to sing one or two songs while the piano player took his breaks.

She always loved music. Some of those elopement fantasies Wynette used to concoct for schoolmates ended with her becoming a famous singer after leaving the farm. As a younger child she and a couple friends started singing gospel songs together and Mildred drove them around to various talent contests in the area. They never won anything but did get the opportunity to sing on a few small radio shows, like *Carmol Taylor and Country Pals* out of Hamilton, Alabama. One time they even got to sing on local TV. In addition to gospel, Wynette enjoyed contemporary R&B music, like the Platters, the Drifters and the Coasters. At the end of the day, though, country music was her favorite. With Hank Williams' unreleased recordings still trickling out a few years after his death, Wynette was about fifteen years old and knew she was hearing a ghost when she became obsessed with his song "No One Will Ever Know." She would listen to the record over and over to hear the dead man sing about living a lie. It's unclear exactly when George Jones became her mother's favorite singer, but his first single was released a few months before Wynette's twelfth birthday, so Mildred was certainly back in her daughter's life by the time she began buying every Jones single and album as soon as they came out. Though mother and daughter butted heads on most other subjects, here they found no quarrel: George Jones was The Greatest Country Singer Ever. By the time Wynette left home at seventeen years old and married Euple Byrd, she knew the lyrics of every Jones release on Starday. However, regardless of these personal interests and childhood fantasies, there is no indication she ever seriously considered or pursued the possibility of a career in music until patrons of a Memphis honky-tonk found out she could sing and began tipping her the first dollars she ever earned with her voice. That's when everything changed.

The exact truth of what took place over the next several years will never be possible to ascertain. Wynette undoubtedly portrayed ordinary individuals as the larger-than-life heroes and villains required by her various narratives. There's a great deal of evidence suggesting she took extreme measures to cover up the terrible actions of one person she needed everyone to believe played the part of her noble rescuer. When there is overwhelming eyewitness testimony she did the inverse, exaggerating or fabricating hostile behavior from those cast as villains in her stories, the only question is whether she resorted to the same extreme measures. It's a question worth raising whenever hers is the only surviving account, as is the case with this period of her life.

According to her, the family moved away from Memphis after learning Jackie had been born diabetic, which made it too stressful to leave the baby home with Euple at night while Wynette did her singing waitress thing at the bar. So 1963 found them living in the back rooms of a Mississippi beauty salon where Wynette resumed work toward her beautician's license while Euple's job on a remote construction crew took him away for two or three weeks at a time. These absences were fine with Wynette because mostly all they did when he came home was argue. She never explicitly stated what it was they argued about but, judging from her own descriptions of these living conditions, it seems they didn't have enough money to afford what she considered basic comforts, like buying a television, paying someone else to watch the kids while she and Euple went out to a movie or, really, did any of the exciting things she'd assumed being a married adult with freedom meant one could do, rather than work all the time in order to raise and provide for two children. Her only form of entertainment was the beauty salon's gossip magazines, which she read to pass the time, keeping up with the latest storylines of various soap operas she didn't have a TV to watch, learning details about rich and famous movie stars with big houses and fancy lives, all glamorous and interesting enough to be reported as if it were real news. One day, she decided to start dying her brown hair a platinum blonde color. While it seems most of the arguments between Wynette and Euple were over her disappointment with the contrast between gossip magazines and real life, the one thing she said they never argued about was sex, even though she found that disappointing, too. The reason they never argued about sex was simple. Her husband wanted it and she believed it was a wife's duty to give it . . . until she got a kidney infection. A doctor took her off birth control and said she shouldn't have sex until the infection was healed but Euple still wanted it, so now they did have to argue about sex before she invariably relented. By this point, Wynette knew she wanted a divorce but was too scared to try getting one. She knew her family would probably disown her and she'd either lose the children to Euple or be left to raise them alone. Then that doctor discovered she'd become pregnant again, meaning she could die if the persistent kidney infection wasn't allowed to heal and she seriously needed to stop having sex with her husband. Once it became a matter of life or death, she went home and told Euple they were getting divorced and that was that. They argued about it all night and, after realizing he wasn't going to leave, she fell into some kind of fit and began (her words) "screaming hysterically." Euple tried to bring her out of it by shaking her, then slapping her face. But she just kept screaming. Even though she was aware of what was happening and wanted to quit screaming, she couldn't quit. By the time Euple got her to a hospital and told the doctors he thought she'd gone crazy, the screaming had finally stopped but Wynette was now nonresponsive. As the doctors asked questions, all she could do was stare blankly or cry. Their solution was to apply twelve electroshock treatments to her brain and send her home, where she calmly informed Euple they were definitely getting a divorce. This time, he believed her and left.

The only source for the events in the above paragraph is Wynette's 1979 autobiography. Since she was known to appropriate stories she felt were effective, it's relevant that elsewhere in the same book she mentions going to see *One Flew Over the Cuckoo's Nest* while it was in theaters in 1975. That movie prominently featured varied states of hysteria and catatonia as well as ECT treatment. It also won five Academy Awards and six Golden Globes in 1976, thus proving the commercial appeal of such storylines immediately prior to Wynette taking the opportunity to present her own version of her life story. In the account Wynette gave Joan Dew at some point prior to Joan's 1977 profile, she simply claimed Euple "deserted" her and their children, which sounds nothing like the narrative she eventually settled on for the autobiography, to which we now return . . .

According to Wynette, after separating from her husband she moved into a new apartment only to return home one night and find all her stuff had been stolen (and presumably sold) by Euple, who then had her arrested for being an unfit mother and tried but failed to have her declared mentally incapable of raising their children. Two weeks later, she went to pick up the kids from daycare and learned they'd already been taken by a man and woman whose descriptions sounded a lot like Euple and Mildred. So Wynette called her mother, who claimed to have no idea what she was talking about. Wynette then spent nearly a week panicked over where her kids may be before deciding to drive out to Mildred's house, where she found the children playing in the front yard. Mildred, believing divorce to be wrong, had conspired with Euple to kidnap the kids. So Wynette retrieved her children and went to live in Birmingham with her father's family, the Pughs. Rather than "desert" her and the kids, Euple tracked Wynette to Alabama and talked his way into her bed for a night, which legally nullified their divorce proceedings and forced her to file all over again. Several weeks later, their third daughter, Tina, was born, at which point Euple talked his way back again, convincing Wynette to move the family into another apartment and give the marriage another chance. When they learned baby Tina had spinal meningitis Wynette stayed in the hospital with her for weeks while Euple stuck around for close to six months, then left.

That's what Wynette's autobiography claimed happened after the alleged ECT treatments. Regardless of how many details are true or not, if you forget about everything in the middle of the story to look only at the beginning and the end, it's her explanation of how she went from earning the first dollar singing ever made her as a waitress in a Memphis barroom to living in Birmingham, where her father's music-loving brothers owned two nearby radio stations and another uncle was the chief engineer at a TV station with the most popular country music show in the area. As for the details of what really did take place between Memphis and Birmingham, once Wynette actually filed for divorce from Euple Byrd other parties became involved, which is where Jimmy McDonough's biography picked up some additional sources of information, sources that create a radically different picture of likely events.

Everyone who knew Euple said he was completely and hopelessly devoted to his wife, despite Wynette's own family members admitting she cheated on him throughout their entire marriage. Multiple witnesses claimed Wynette even kept sneaking off to spend time with D.C. Byrd after marrying his little brother, a man she admitted she didn't love. She once allegedly brought home a sailor from a bar, presumably just to see what Euple would do about it. That daycare kidnapping conspiracy makes Wynette a much more relatable victim than what other witnesses claim was the truth: Euple and Mildred went over to a motel where Wynette was shacked up with some guy and took the children away from what they considered to be an improper environment. Such rampant infidelity would provide some context for a story one of Wynette's friends told about seeing an angry Mildred knock down her pregnant daughter in a driveway. Again and again, Wynette presented scenes of Euple and his family mocking her taste in "hillbilly" music and dumping on her dreams of becoming a singer. But Euple's family couldn't have formed an opinion one way or the other until the job in Memphis gave her those dreams and, according to the Byrds, the reason Wynette and Euple moved so many times after living in Memphis was because he actively supported her attempts to become a professional singer. Where Wynette portrayed Euple as the kind of guy who would steal and sell all her stuff just because he wanted to make her life difficult and/or was unwilling to hold down a job, Euple's sister-in-law said it wasn't possible for him to keep a job when he'd come home from work to find Wynette had sold all of their belongings so they could move to another town where she thought she had a better chance of being discovered as a singing waitress. Euple made all of those moves with her. He drove her around to different honky-tonks so she could talk her way into getting on stage to sing a song or two. The only remotely discouraging thing he ever said was it may be a good idea to wait until the children were a little bit older and could take better care of themselves while both parents worked before Wynette seriously tried to pursue a music career that wasn't bringing in enough money to significantly help support the family. To Wynette's way of thinking that comment alone may have justified her subsequent vilification of Euple Byrd.

According to Wynette's autobiography, Euple left a few months after Tina was born. She hadn't seen him for weeks, maybe months, when he just so happened to drive by the moment she just so happened to be packing a car to make the move from Birmingham to try for the big leagues of country music in Nashville. Euple stopped by long enough to make fun of his wife for still trying to be a hillbilly singer, then drove away. Wynette claimed she didn't see him again until ten years later, when he stood in a line to get her autograph. What a great story, huh? You can just imagine that scene in the movie Wynette would make about her own life. She knew the presence of an unambiguous villain often made the difference between a good story and a great one. She also knew the complete truth about her life wouldn't fit the persona that had been created for her by the time this tale was told. Despite the grief caused to the Byrd family by Wynette's autobiography, there was later a reconciliation that allowed Euple to come visit with his daughters and be part of their lives. After Euple died in 1996, the family found a box full of news clippings he kept from articles about Tammy Wynette, the character the woman he had loved became soon after moving on from Birmingham.

◇   ◇   ◇

In Birmingham, Wynette found a job at another beauty salon, then began walking through all the doors her uncles were able to open for her. These were the uncles who'd played in her father's band before she was born, so they knew how happy William Pugh would be to see his daughter become a singer and they tried to help any way they could. Turns out owning two radio stations and getting her an audition with *The Country Boy Eddie Show* on local TV was plenty of help. The Pughs were able to watch Wynette's children while she got up early enough to go do the TV show, wrap at eight a.m. and drive back to a full day's shift at the beauty salon. She did that five days a week along with whatever radio appearances could be squeezed in. Within a year, that routine took her to Nashville. Her version of how that happened involves another pack of lies, but Wynette's flights of fancy get a lot easier to debunk once they start involving people as famous as Porter Wagoner.

Wynette claimed Porter came through Birmingham in 1965, right after splitting with his pre–Dolly Parton sidekick, Norma Jean. They needed a woman artist to replace Norma on the concert bill, so one of the radio stations suggested Wynette and she was given the spot without even doing an audition. Wynette just knew this was finally her big break. Porter would hear her sing and hire her straightaway to Nashville to become the next costar on his immensely popular TV show. But Porter didn't come out of his dressing room at all during Wynette's set. She was about to head home with all her disappointment when someone from the tour came to ask if she could jump on a few more dates. Wynette agreed, thinking surely Porter would hear her sing at one of these additional shows. But he never paid any attention to her at all. She returned home quite sad, then became quite mad at Porter Wagoner for not caring about her dreams. She decided to go to Nashville, to prove to him and everyone else she had what it takes to make it.

The first problem with that crock of absolute horseshit is Porter Wagoner and Norma Jean had not quit working together in 1965. In fact, 1965 was the year Norma's career entered its peak and she remained on Porter's TV show and tours for at least another two years after Wynette claimed these events took place. The second problem is that anyone looking to "replace" Norma Jean on a Porter Wagoner concert bill would have been looking for a woman to sing with Porter, not play a solo set while Porter stayed in his dressing room. A more likely scenario is what Wynette's second husband said she told him: one time she opened for Porter Wagoner before moving to Nashville, the end.

The truth is her move to Nashville was not inspired by anger at Porter or anyone else. Rather, it was the support of an Alabama disc jockey named Fred Lehner, who fancied himself a songwriter and asked Wynette to sing on his demos. The earliest available tape we have of Wynette Byrd singing anything is one of Fred's songs, called "You Can Steal Me." Just the way a young Johnny PayCheck arrived in Nashville with his trademark vocal style almost completely in place, there is no mistaking the person on that demo tape for anyone other than Tammy Wynette. Where George Jones connected to a song in different ways every time he sang it, if Wynette were to rerecord "You Can Steal Me" twenty years later, you can bet it would sound almost exactly like that demo. Her voice rises and falls and breaks in all the same ways millions of people would come to know from some of the biggest hit records in country music history. George Richey, a man who will eventually play a major role in this story, heard the Wynette Byrd demo of "You Can Steal Me" and assigned it to one of the artists he was then producing, Bonnie Guitar, who had a minor country hit with the song in 1967. Another Fred Lehner song, "The Way Things Were Going," was recorded as a duet by Johnny PayCheck and Micki Evans in 1966, after they heard the Wynette Byrd demo. Wynette's first visit to Nashville took place in 1965, when she accompanied Fred Lehner and his wife to the DJ Convention. While in town the three of them visited all the standard country pilgrimage destinations. The day they went to see the Ryman Auditorium there was a flatbed trailer parked outside with a cover band playing on it and a sign encouraging tourists to hop on the makeshift stage to sing with a real live country band in Nashville. Wynette got up and sang Hank Williams' "Your Cheatin' Heart." If this were the Hollywood movie, it would be the part where a crowd instantly gathers to hear the unknown prodigy who then gets discovered by an industry executive in attendance . . . But even she admitted nobody really paid any attention. Same story when Fred and his wife drove Wynette over to audition for the record labels and publishing companies on Music Row. Nobody thought they were hearing anything special, so the country music hopefuls went home to Birmingham. Only, Wynette now knew it was possible to just go knock on doors to audition for industry gatekeepers, so she began making return trips to Nashville on her own. She claimed someone at Hickory Records said they were looking to sign a female version of Don Gibson, their biggest artist at that time. She said she was given a stack of Gibson's albums to take home and learn his vocal phrasing. That could not possibly have happened, though, because Don Gibson was an RCA artist at the time and for at least five years before and after Wynette first came to town. She said Owen Bradley turned her down at Decca and Owen's old boss, Paul Cohen, would've liked to sign her to Kapp Records but he didn't have a budget to actually do anything with her. Cohen suggested she try some bigger labels, like Columbia or RCA. RCA told her they weren't signing anymore women that year. Whenever Mildred and other family members asked how these trips to Nashville were going, Wynette would make up lies about how many labels were interested in working with her.

In January of 1966, without a single lead on a record deal or even any kind of day job, she moved to Nashville. What she did have was a lead on her next husband and the next villain in what would soon become her very famous backstory. Unlike Euple Byrd, Don Chapel probably did deserve most of the scorn heaped upon him by Wynette. For one thing, it seems he was a world-class liar. Chapel's account of the night they met in 1965 cannot possibly be true because it hinged upon him impressing and seducing Wynette with a publishing deal he didn't have until 1966, a record deal he didn't have until 1967 and taking her to a nightclub George Jones didn't open until 1967. But what Chapel really did have was plenty enough to interest a twenty-two-year-old wannabe singer from Alabama who didn't know one other person in the city. He had a stage name that he took to match the stage name of his fairly successful songwriting sister, Jean Chapel, and Jean and Don were the younger siblings of Martha Carson, writer and singer of the gospel staple "Satisfied." So even though Chapel was only a clerk at the front desk of the first motel where Wynette stayed in Nashville, he was still able to talk a big game about his industry connections and confidently assert a career as a hit songwriter was just around the corner for him. He was also able to save Wynette some money on her return trips to Nashville by sneaking her into his room at the motel, free of charge. If they didn't become romantically involved on her first trip, it happened soon after. Then she moved to Nashville and the two of them combined efforts to break into the business. They'd knock on doors and follow leads, then sing together on any shows either of them was able to secure.

After about six months of this, Chapel got the opportunity to pitch some of his songs to George Jones. Since he knew Wynette kept a notebook in which she'd written all the lyrics to all the songs Jones recorded, Chapel figured he'd impress his girlfriend by bringing her along to meet her favorite singer. They went up to George's hotel room, where they found the country star wearing a bathrobe while drinking and hanging out with several people, including a young woman who sat with Jones on his bed the whole time. Chapel played his songs, George said he liked one, called "From Here to the Door," and his people would be in touch about it. George then went back to talking with his friends. Sensing Wynette's disappointment at being ignored by her hero, Chapel tried to introduce her as a singer and asked who they may be able to talk to at Musicor about getting her an audition . . . but Jones still barely looked in her direction as he said the name of some person who worked at the record label. Wynette sulked for days. Within six months she would have her own record deal but not at Musicor. Even though George Jones had liked one of Chapel's songs enough to record it, which helped Chapel also land a publishing deal with Pappy Daily, Wynette never got to audition for George, Pappy or anyone at Musicor.

A few weeks after that hotel room meeting, Wynette was still knocking on Music Row office building doors when Kelso Herston at United Artists recognized her potential and said he'd sign her on the spot, if only he hadn't just signed Billie Jo Spears. The label wouldn't let him sign another woman because Billie Jo made three women on his roster and he couldn't dump her because he was pretty sure they'd get a hit by marketing her as "the female George Jones." Still trying to get an audition at George's label, Wynette asked if Kelso knew who to talk to at Musicor or how she could get in touch with Pappy Daily. Kelso replied that Pappy and George both lived in Texas, so Wynette's best shot at getting a record deal in Nashville would probably be to go see Billy Sherrill at Epic, a subsidiary of Columbia Records.

◇   ◇   ◇

Now, just about everyone working in this era of country music who ever commented on the first time they heard Tammy Wynette, whether that was on the radio or in person, said some version of the same thing, a thing she also always said about herself: she was technically not a great vocalist, but her singing conveyed a great deal of emotion and she sounded different from anyone who came before her. Jan Howard was once talking to the Country Music Hall of Fame and Museum about iconic singers, those unmistakable voices everyone can identify the second they begin to sing, and she listed Tammy Wynette as an example. Merle Haggard said Tammy stood out from other women in country music because "she had her own style" and wasn't trying to sound like Patsy Cline or Loretta Lynn or anyone else. That's what Kelso Herston recognized in his office and it's what Billy Sherrill heard when Wynette came to see him the following day. She did not have Patsy Cline's range. She did not have Loretta Lynn's attitude. What she had was Something Different. There was a unique pain in her voice and she could take it from quiet to loud and back at the drop of a hat, hurtin' the whole way. Billy Sherrill understood the inherent value of Something Different but nobody in Nashville was writing songs for a voice like hers because there wasn't a voice like hers in Nashville. He told her to come back when she found a hit song. Wynette soon returned with "She Didn't Color Daddy," a Scotty Turner and Ray Warren song from the B-side of a Kay Adams record. Billy took Wynette's phone number and said he'd call when he had time to cut the record, which was industry speak for he didn't give a shit about the song and was never going to call her. If she just went home to wait for the phone to ring, Tammy Wynette would probably have never existed. When she hadn't heard from Billy after about a week, Wynette called to see where they stood. He said to come back to his office, as in: hang up the phone and get over there, right now. He'd found a hit.

Ten years prior, musician and songwriter Bobby Austin moved from the state of Washington down to Los Angeles, ready to see what he could shake out of the city. He found work as a bass player in recording sessions at Capitol Studios, then joined Wynn Stewart's band during the period when Wynn was driving back and forth between gigs in L.A. and Las Vegas. When Merle Haggard became Wynn Stewart's bass player in 1962, he was filling the vacancy left by Bobby Austin, who'd finally secured his own artist contract with Capitol after releasing a handful of singles on various indie labels. But Bobby's Capitol singles all bombed and the label dropped him after a year. In 1966, he put out another record, called "Apartment #9." While you wouldn't know it from the credits on the label, Bobby wrote nearly the whole song by himself. Johnny PayCheck happened to be staying with him in Las Vegas at the time and PayCheck came up with the opening lines of the chorus, so Bobby generously gave him half the song. After splitting the other half with producer Fuzzy Owen, Bobby placed his own share of the credit under his wife's name, Fern Foley. When it came time to make the record, PayCheck sang harmony and Ralph Mooney played pedal steel. Tally, the same tiny Bakersfield label that put out Merle Haggard's first singles in the early '60s, released Bobby Austin's "Apartment #9" in July 1966. One month later, Wynette Byrd walked out of Billy Sherrill's office in Nashville for the final time, having been told he would call her when he found time to cut the song she liked. With Wynette out of his hair Billy got back to doing his actual job, which as far as he was concerned began with finding a hit song and ended with making sure nobody in the studio screwed up the hit song. To Billy's way of thinking if they didn't take at least one hit song into a session, then nothing else mattered, not the artist, the musicians or the producer. So, when he looked at the Top Country Singles chart in a magazine and noticed a record coming in from the bottom on a piddly little label whose name he hadn't seen since they discovered Merle Haggard a few years earlier, Billy sent someone out to buy the single so he could hear it. He liked what he heard well enough to start making phone calls out to California, trying to license the recording in order to reissue it on Epic with real distribution and real marketing to turn it into a real hit. When Tally turned down his offer they did it with a "we don't need your Nashville money" type of attitude, so Billy hung up having formed a new plan. He'd just cover the song and bury their fucking record. That's when his phone rang. Wynette Byrd wanted to know if they were really going to cut the song she'd found or if Billy was just trying to get rid of her and, please, be honest. This was maybe her last shot at a music career and she needed to know whether it was happening or not. He said to get over to his office ASAP. He'd found her first hit single.

With a song, Something Different and something to prove, Billy got to work putting everything together into a complete package. First thing first, the name "Wynette Byrd" had to go or they'd spend three years waiting until every radio DJ and hack record reviewer in the world fell out of love with all their own bird puns and actually listened to the music. Once he thought about it Wynette kind of reminded him of Debbie Reynolds' title character in *Tammy and the Bachelor*, a movie about "an unsophisticated backwoods girl" whose naive approach to life wins the heart of a wealthy bachelor after her guardian figure grandfather is thrown in jail for making moonshine whiskey. Billy said her new name would be Tammy Wynette, gave her a copy of "Apartment #9" and told her to be at the Quonset Hut a week later for her session. The first song they cut was "She Didn't Color Daddy" but, considering it was never released until a comprehensive box set that came out about twenty-five years later, Billy was probably just letting her warm up and get comfortable by pretending the song she'd found mattered enough to record. Then they did the one he wanted for a single.

The most important thing to understand about Billy Sherrill's approach to record production is that he was hands down the biggest Owen Bradley fanboy in history. By the time Columbia hired Billy to run Epic the label had purchased 804 16th Avenue from Owen, so Billy chose a room right upstairs from the Quonset Hut for his own office and recorded in Owen's studio with Owen's musicians, applying the same principles of dynamics as Owen's Nashville Sound. But Billy Sherrill was the next generation. He grew up listening to Owen's use of dynamics and developed a tolerance. He needed a larger dose to scratch the itch. In the same sonic space Owen Bradley would have used to create high drama, Billy condensed the audio equivalent of a hysterical episode. His peaks were higher, the valleys lower and the transitions between covered the full spectrum from subtle insinuation to jarring volatility. Several artists who were objectively better singers than Tammy Wynette cut versions of "Apartment #9." But, just like the best work of Owen Bradley, Tammy's record transcends genre. The beginning is fairly standard country fare, as long as your standards come from Nashville and include Pete Drake's invisible tone bar. Then all of the musicians hit a stop so the voices of two Tammy Wynettes can take the record into outer space. There was nothing new or different about a singer overdubbing their own harmony vocal. By this point in the genre you could even say it was old hat. What's different about Tammy's "Apartment #9" is that it's from the first real recording session of an artist who had never overdubbed her own harmony part and did not know how to do it. While she's able to keep the second vocal track in the harmony lane most of the time, there are a few spots where Tammy, probably from lack of confidence, accidentally drifts over into doubling the lead vocal. Her phrasing is also often slightly out of sync between the two vocal tracks. The result is something like the blood harmony of identical twins who were separated at birth and have never sung together. Tammy's amateur approach combined with the masterful Nashville Sound techniques on display in every other element of the song is nearly psychedelic. Her naive overdubs achieve the same effect all over her first LP. Another notable example is "Send Me No Roses," where the double-tracked vocal part begins with more slightly out-of-sync phrasing, then gives way to two Tammy Wynettes screaming about how she knows roses are red. (Billy would push Tammy even further into this double-tracked screaming approach on the song "It's My Way" from her second album.) To help Tammy stay on time in her first session, Jerry Kennedy played stop-and-start rhythm guitar as cleanly and simply as possible. While she remained in the studio to do those wild overdubs Jerry found a telephone and called indie song publisher Al Gallico to let him know there was a new singer in town who'd just cut something incredible and Gallico should probably try to sign her as a writer, like, immediately.

During playback of the final take on "Apartment #9," Billy Sherrill looked over at Tammy and noticed her sweater had a hole in it, so he arranged for his wife to take the poor girl shopping for some new clothes. She was about to be famous and needed to dress the part. When the record came out in October 1966, it created enough buzz just in time for that year's DJ Convention, where Tammy was taken around with her new clothes and new name to all the best parties and introduced as the Next Big Thing, which she did turn out to be. An issue of *Billboard* said her debut single would likely hit the Country Top 10, but Tally had by this time licensed the Bobby Austin recording to Capitol and those major label resources behind a reissue of the original record had it simultaneously climbing the chart, each version limiting the potential of the other. Bobby's single peaked at #21 and that was the last time most people ever heard his name. Tammy's just missed the Country Top 40 and introduced the world to a legend.

Though it wasn't a major hit Tammy Wynette's debut received enough airplay to put everyone in Nashville on notice: a new voice had come to town. Loretta Lynn and Dolly Parton both said they knew Tammy would be a huge star the first time they heard "Apartment #9." When George Jones came to Nashville for that year's DJ Convention, Pappy Daily booked studio time to cut some filler and one of the songs they chose was "Apartment #9." Tammy happened to stop by Billy's office while that session was taking place and, upon learning George Jones was downstairs doing "Apartment #9," she freaked out, certain George would release it as a single and kill her record. Billy settled her nerves, said George would only use the song for album filler, then took her down to the studio to meet her hero. This was probably their first real conversation, though George's anxiety and lovesick obsession with Melba Montgomery tracked to Tammy as him still being standoffish.

Years later, when someone asked George what he thought the first time he heard Tammy Wynette sing, he said he liked her voice because she didn't sound like other girls.

Radio stations back in Wynette's old Mississippi and Alabama turf placed "Apartment #9" into heavy rotation and DJs boasted on the local girl made good, which she claimed led Euple Byrd to assume she must now be rich and try suing her for his share of the money. Tammy went to Billy Sherrill with the problem and Billy had some of Columbia Records' lawyers explain to Euple how recording contracts work, that the woman who was still legally his wife owed many thousands of dollars to the label and would remain in such debt unless she began selling many more records . . . but if Euple wanted to talk about his own fiscal responsibility in the situation, then they could have that conversation. Euple disappeared again. Whether or not that actually happened, it's true Tammy's first single was a loss on paper. She'd assumed having a record deal meant booking agencies would automatically want to sign her and put her on major tours, but she was wrong. Moeller Talent (formerly the Jim Denny Artist Bureau) passed because they believed it wasn't worth the trouble to sign women artists. Most had husbands and children trying to keep them home all the time and the ones who would actually hit the road for real were eventually going to find themselves in some kind of trouble or other, spending night after night in rooms full of drunk men, etc. That story and others like it were what Tammy heard all over town, so she again went to Billy Sherrill with the problem. He made a few calls and, next thing you know, Hubert Long was ready to give her a shot, booking Tammy into the Playroom in Atlanta for a whole week, doing five sets each night. Since she'd only released the one single, her early concerts were essentially cover sets of contemporary hits, many of which wound up on her first LP. Her gross revenue for the week was five hundred dollars, which is less than half of what a Nashville A-Team session musician would earn for the same hours in the same year. After Tammy gave fifty percent to the house band for backing her up, then covered expenses such as gas, food and a motel room, she made it back home with eighty-two dollars. But it was eighty-two dollars she didn't need to borrow from family or friends and she continued to take whatever gigs came her way. Six months after earning five hundred dollars for that first week of concerts in Atlanta, Tammy Wynette was making five hundred dollars per concert.

Billy Sherrill's policy of never taking artists into the studio without a hit song often came down to a last-minute writing session to create the hit himself, usually with one of his regular cohorts. That's what he and Glenn Sutton did for the title track of Tammy's first album, "Your Good Girl's Gonna Go Bad." One aspect of Billy's genius was his ability to find and/or create songs that reinforced and advanced the public personas of his artists. He encouraged singers to write their own material if they could and he only took professional songwriters seriously to whatever degree they were able to craft narratives his artists could sell as autobiographical to fans, who formed ideas about these artists' identities from album covers, marketing campaigns, interviews, tabloid head-lines and so on. Contrary to oft-repeated mass misunderstanding, Billy did not do this to appeal to traditional country music fans or their supposedly disproportional need for "authenticity." Quite the opposite. The dynamics on Billy Sherrill records may owe strong debts to Owen Bradley, but Billy's philosophies of instrumentation and marketing came directly from Chet Atkins' most bla-tant attempts to capture a pop audience. Pop culture functions like a roving spotlight that lands on some preexisting subculture and turns it into the hot, new trend until that subculture is overrun by uncool commercial interests, at which point the spotlight begins searching for the next cool subculture to repeat the process with something that by comparison feels more organic and "real," until all the money-hungry bandwagon jumpers start to make that feel "fake," too. Therefore, it is often fans, journalists and even artists approaching country music from backgrounds in pop (or rock) music who themselves have this authenticity fetish, which they project onto fans of whatever subculture they've just discovered and hope to join. That is how and why producers like Chet At-kins and Billy Sherrill were able to consciously and deliberately sell the country genre to such fans in a pop crossover package, by taking country singers, giving them compelling personas and plac-ing them within a sonic context that metropolitan listeners found appealing. Billy Sherrill had no interest whatsoever in catering to the ears or wallets of purely traditional country music fans and nothing he ever did was toward that end. Were that the case his name certainly would not invoke such disdain from country fans who believe the genre peaked prior to Billy's rise in the 1960s . . . and Tammy Wynette's second single certainly would not kick off with Henry Strzelecki's electric bass doing its best imitation of a bad boy's motorcycle revving up to take a country girl out on a date in her first black leather jacket. The lyrics of "Your Good Girl's Gonna Go Bad" play to Billy's first draft of the Tammy Wynette persona, a naive backwoods girl who wandered into the city, landed herself a record deal and got her heart broken by those fast, two-timing honky-tonk men. Now she's here, doing a fairly unconvincing job of swearing she'll "go bad," just as soon as she figures out how to drink whiskey and swing. It's anyone's guess how aware Glenn Sutton and Billy Sherrill may have been they were writing a perfect allegory of Billy's genre-bending intentions, with Tammy as country-singer-gone-bad by way of Billy's corrupting pop- and rock-informed sonic influences. The single came out in February 1967, hit #3 Country and every record she released from there until 1975 went at least Top 5. Of the fourteen singles by women solo artists to go #1 Country in the 1960s, six were by Tammy Wynette.

With her first royalty checks Tammy was able to finally get a divorce from Euple Byrd, at which time Don Chapel immediately asked for her hand in marriage. As with Euple, Wynette already knew she did not love Chapel. But they'd been together about a year, both working toward careers in music, which meant they could tour together and she wouldn't have to be alone on the road. She agreed to the proposal and they were married in April of 1967. Between her royalties and touring revenue Tammy was soon able to buy a house in Nashville. Or, really, she bought two houses, one for Mildred and Foy Lee, who she told to retire and move to Nashville, the other for her, her three daughters, Don and Don's three children from a previous marriage. It would have been a real-life *Brady Bunch* situation, except most of the kids were left at home with family or babysitters while Tammy and Don and Don's oldest daughter hit the road. With fourteen-year-old Donna Chapel singing backup, fans of the Tammy Wynette character created by Billy Sherrill arrived at concerts and found much more of a wholesome family band vibe than they'd expected. Their good girl hadn't gone bad at all, she'd gone remarried.

Despite a steadily rising rate of failed marriages and the fact it takes two to tango, divorced women in the late 1960s were still largely viewed and treated as sinners who'd ruined their one chance at a happy life and would never get another. Billy Sherrill recognized the potential for Wynette's divorce to cause a scandal but decided to lean into it as an opportunity to present the rapidly increasing number of American divorcées with an identifiable figure, someone who'd been through a similar experience to their own. For Tammy's third single, Billy and Glenn Sutton wrote a song so successful in blurring the line between the public image and personal life of their artist that she found it difficult to perform for the rest of her career. The title of "I Don't Wanna Play House" is what the narrator overhears her young daughter tell a friend and, knowing her own failed marriage is why the child fears the game, it breaks the narrator's heart. Recorded in June 1967 and released in July, this was Tammy's first #1 Country song as a solo artist. It also won a Grammy Award for Best Female Country Vocal Performance. But "I Don't Wanna Play House" was actually the second #1 record with her name on the label. The previous month Epic had released a duet between Tammy and Billy Sherrill's other major artist, David Houston.

◇   ◇   ◇

Billy made his and David Houston's first #1, "Almost Persuaded," right around the time Wynette was moving to Nashville. When "Apartment #9" came out and Tammy couldn't get signed to a booking agency? The phone call Billy made was to David Houston's manager, Tillman Franks, who told Houston's agent to give the new girl on Epic a chance and then start booking her as a package with Houston if she worked out, which is what happened. After a few months of their artists touring together, Billy Sherrill suggested to Tillman they try cutting some duets between Tammy and Houston. He even had a hit song all ready to go.

Back at this time the publishing company Tree Music dedicated a wall of their Music Row offices to a large map of the United States with markers indicating all the places country music stars came from: Utah, Birmingham, Memphis, Nashville, Nebraska, Alaska, etc. Well, songwriter Curly Putman—who'd already written "Green, Green Grass of Home," one of the most lucrative titles ever filed with Tree—was sitting in that office one day, absentmindedly looking over the big map on the wall when it struck him that each of those markers represented a person who'd uprooted their entire life, often along with the lives of loved ones, just to chase down a dream. This realization turned into the beginning of the song "My Elusive Dreams," which Curly asked Billy Sherrill to help him finish. Tammy Wynette and David Houston recorded and released it in June of 1967. In his tell-all memoir, *I Was There When It Happened*, Houston's manager, Tillman Franks, wrote about purchasing a full-page ad in *Billboard* to promote "My Elusive Dreams." He never explicitly stated this was a form of payola or detailed the unspoken benefits he may have received for that ad buy but, elsewhere in the book, he did disclose how reliably effective he found payola to be as a promotional strategy. In close proximity to such statements, he repeatedly mentioned purchasing full-page ads in *Billboard*, *Cash Box* and other industry trades, so you do the math.

After "My Elusive Dreams" became Houston's third and Tammy's first #1 single, their concert bookings together became much bigger and brought in a lot more money. Tammy being the less-established artist, she always played her set before David, who headlined the shows and finished the night by bringing out Tammy to close with their big hit. Then booking agent Hubert Long got the idea to package Tammy and David together with another major client, George Jones, still riding high (and feeling low) from his latest #1 record, the devastating "Walk Through This World with Me." Hubert booked this lineup on a Canadian tour, then set some warm-up dates in the States. The U.S. shows went off without a hitch; Tammy and Houston kept their act the same, then Jones closed out the bill. The first date in Canada went so poorly it altered the course of country music history.

As is so often the case with stories involving Tammy Wynette, there are multiple versions of how this went down. While her account makes absolutely no sense, it was corroborated by Don Chapel, another documented liar, and repeated in George Jones' autobiography, a book almost entirely composed of other people's memories rather than his own. Since all of that makes Tammy's story the one most people have heard and believe to be true, here's a brief rundown of it. The first night in Canada, Tillman Franks asked Tammy if David Houston could play first because David and Tillman needed to leave early to be somewhere else. This was fine with Tammy until Tillman said she would still need to go out to finish David's opening set with their hit duet. Tammy refused, due to some convoluted logic about how the crowd needed to see both singers separately before seeing them together, which was when Tillman lost his shit, began screaming at her that David

Houston was the bigger star and implied Tammy slept her way to where she was in the business. There are way too many reasons that doesn't add up to cover all of them but, for one thing, this being the first night of a tour in another country makes it very unlikely anyone would request major lineup changes at the last minute. Go ahead and double that improbability factor because Tammy claimed Tillman tried to do the exact same thing again the next night in a different town. She presented it like Tillman was pulling some kind of power move to prove he could get his way on behalf of his artist but, nine times out of ten, any manager trying to make a lineup change to act like a big shot would try to push their artist closer to the headlining spot, not argue for them to be an opener early in the evening before the whole audience even arrived. Then there's the fact these were U.S. artists working in another country, which makes it awfully strange to suggest Tillman and Houston had some vague, unspecified engagement requiring their early departure from both the first and second shows, especially when Houston's band was backing Tammy on the tour. For Tillman and Houston to split early would mean leaving the rest of Houston's band behind. Tammy also claimed there were a bunch of journalists there when Tillman screamed at her, leading her to suspect the whole thing was staged as some kind of publicity stunt, which would be a whole lot easier to believe if any of those alleged journalists ever wrote a single word about any of this. Of course, they did not because this is all probably an overly complicated lie.

Conversely, Tillman Frank's memoir is the definition of a tell-all book. Among other difficult truths, he disclosed the already-mentioned payola tactics, admitted to every instance of a stolen melody in a song he was credited with writing or co-writing and offered a sincere apology to Barbara Mandrell for the trivial crime of once calling her ungrateful. He also detailed his many legal struggles with Johnny Horton's widow following Tillman's survival of the same car wreck that killed Johnny. At no point do any of his stories rely upon the convoluted logic of someone trying to sell a lie. Tillman wrote that he never even spoke with Tammy Wynette on the first night of the Canadian tour. When one of the promoters said Tammy wanted David Houston to sing their hit duet during her set instead of his, Tillman replied David would be happy to do that. After going to tell Tammy her request could be met, the promoter returned and said Tammy decided she would now not sing the duet with Houston at all. According to Tillman, there was never any kind of verbal altercation between Tammy and himself or Tammy and David. He claimed he never said anything negative about Tammy Wynette in any context or setting and, having worked closely with many women in the industry, would never say such an ignorant and vulgar thing as she accused him of saying about the reason for her success. Even while refuting her accusations, Tillman refrained from saying anything insulting about her. The most critical thing he wrote was, "my account of what happened certainly does not jibe with what she wrote." When David Houston and his band went to leave the venue after the show that night, they found someone had put sand in the gas tanks of their vehicles.

Similar to Wynette's journey from Memphis to Birmingham, if you forget the details in the middle of the Canada story, focusing only on the beginning and the end reveals the same outcome: another upgrade for her career. Tammy couldn't have known David Houston only had about five years left before chart placement payola would no longer hide a lack of corresponding sales and he'd wind up playing nursing homes. But she didn't need to know any of that to recognize an opportunity to secure a much better duet partner, who also happened to be her personal hero and The Greatest Country Singer Ever, George Jones. Whether George decided on his own to come to her rescue or Tammy arranged it ahead of time by privately selling him some version of the same power struggle story she later put in print, George called her up to sing with him on the first night of the Canadian tour and every night after.

The Canada incident took place in March of 1968. Tammy had been married to Don Chapel for about a year, during which time he must have noticed how many fans were disappointed each time "Don Chapel's wife" hit the stage instead of Billy Sherrill's good girl gone bad or even the downtrodden divorcée. Concert promoters routinely complained to Hubert Long that audiences had paid to see Tammy Wynette, not the Chapel Family Band Show. But Don was at least as opportunistic as his wife and couldn't help but see her growing fortune and fame in terms of furthering his own ambitions. He thought it was time to quit focusing only on songwriting and start launching his own career as a major recording artist. Chapel pestered Tammy to have Billy Sherrill sign him to Epic and, hell, while she was at it go ahead and get a contract for his daughter Donna, too. Wynette knew her husband's singing would never pass an audition for Billy and was mortified by the thought of asking but Chapel wouldn't stop asking, so Tammy finally set it up. Almost certainly as a favor to Tammy, Billy produced two singles for Don and one for Donna Chapel. Nobody can say Don wasn't given a fair shot at Epic. There are promo copies of an earlier record that was apparently shelved but the first of Don's singles to be released by Epic was the Ray Pennington song "Hurtin' Time." The song is very good and so is the piano lick Billy came up with for the record, but it bombed. Same with Don's second single. Donna's record was never even pressed. When Tammy upgraded from David Houston to George Jones, Don Chapel was initially pleased. He and Tammy were married, so whatever was good for her could only be good for him, right? He thought nothing of it when Tammy began riding from show to show not with the Chapels but with Jones. They were now duet partners, so it made sense to practice singing together while in transit.

Immediately after the Canadian tour was finished, George's wife, Shirley, filed for a long over-due divorce. As he did with every one of his ex-wives, George gave Shirley all she asked for in the separation: three houses, two plots of land, 50 percent of his songwriting royalties, pretty much everything except the other half of his royalties, two cars, a tour bus, some stock in Musicor, a Florida vacation home and some empty land in Texas. Suddenly cash poor, George borrowed a thousand dollars from his brother-in-law and moved from Texas to a hotel room in Nashville. When the divorce paperwork went through and he legally became a single man, the first thing George did was drive over to Tammy's house to tell her the good news.

THIRTEEN

STRONGLY WORDED LETTERS

◇ Martin Luther Picks a Holy Fight ◇
Machiavelli's *The Prince* ◇ Médici Popes
◇ The Valois-Habsburg Conflict ◇

Martin Luther was not the first person of the Modern Age to diagnose or denounce the corruption that had overtaken the (soon to be known as Roman Catholic) Church during the Middle Ages but he was certainly the most effective. While he may have never nailed his *95 Theses* to the front door of a church as some grand, dramatic statement, the persistence and provocative nature of that legend is a testament to the historical impact of one Augustinian friar submitting a point-by-point refutation of incorrect-yet-commonplace beliefs, teachings and practices plaguing Western European Christianity in the year 1517. Luther always claimed he never set out to question the integrity and authority of the pope or other higher clergymen. His intent was to question what he perceived as a bottom-up misunderstanding of fundamental doctrine and remedy it by organizing a scripturally based argument with which he was most confident any honorable pope would agree. Because for the pope to disagree with Luther's scripturally based argument would mean there was not, in fact, a bottom-up misunderstanding. For the pope to disagree with the *95 Theses* would indicate a top-down problem, a product of Church leadership having been infiltrated nearly a thousand years earlier by the noble families of Europe who cynically and godlessly employed the Church's assets and institutions primarily toward amassing more wealth, prestige and political power for themselves rather than administering spiritual and humanitarian aid to the masses. A professor of philosophy, very well-educated for his time, Martin Luther used subtext to convey this message to every informed person able to read between the lines of the *95 Theses*, a comprehensively scathing attack on practices and attitudes surrounding the Church's sale of plenary indulgences.

Two years prior, Pope Leo X found himself deep in debt after burning through every cent in the papal treasury to fund his own extravagant lifestyle and his noble family's various wars. In other words, Pope Leo lived like a king and, like many kings, he went broke doing it. Once he'd borrowed as much money as he could from anyone who would lend it he turned to selling off jewels and furniture from inside the Vatican. When he needed money to continue rebuilding St. Peter's Basilica, what is now the largest church in the world, Leo funded construction by selling indulgences, spiritual VIP passes believed to bring you and yours straight to heaven's gate without having to wait for your souls to be distilled of sin in purgatory. It's worth noting that Leo invented none of these ideas. Concepts of purgatory predate Christianity and the Church had sold various indulgences for hundreds of years prior to this point in history. Leo didn't even create a new indulgence to fund construction at St. Peter's. That indulgence was introduced by his predecessor. All Leo did was bring it back, while also placing an eight-year moratorium on any other indulgence being sold by the Church. So, if you wanted an indulgence, there was only the one available and Pope Leo made it clear to his priests how much he wanted their congregations to buy that indulgence, which led to many sermons resembling sales pitches more than gospel, as if heaven now simply had a cover charge. As wealth and worldly power held priority above, so it became below.

Martin Luther was never really a fan of indulgences. But when he noticed members of his own flock were no longer coming to hear him read from scripture, no longer coming to confess their sins, then found out it was because they'd bought some piece of paper from another priest who told them it was the only one-way ticket to heaven they'd ever need, Luther sat down and began writing. Conveniently, this single issue laid bare what he believed were several major discrepancies between contemporary Christianity and its claimed source material. In the *95 Theses* he asked the Church to please make sure everyone understood official doctrine aligned with scripture on topics like forgiveness of sin being the sole domain of God, not the pope. He asked the Church to make sure everyone understood the removal of souls from purgatory was left to the discretion of God, not the pope. Luther was positive the Church would agree salvation is not earned or purchased from the pope but received from God; the fate of one's eternal soul is determined not by earthly acts of kindness, service and charity—especially any type of financial donation, no matter how large—but solely through repentance and faith in Christ crucified, which would naturally inspire such benevolent acts. This last idea most of all held central to Luther's theology. He believed our souls can never be saved by good behavior, the way we spend our money or the way we behave when others are watching, only by our private relationships with God. In order to drive his point home, Luther ended the *95 Theses* by asking what he was supposed to tell poor members of his congregation when they asked why the pope, a man born into one of the richest families to ever exist, needed money from peasants and the working class to build some big, fancy church when there were so many suffering people in the world who could be clothed, fed and sheltered with that money.

Formatting these allegations as an earnest attempt to clear up popular misunderstanding of official doctrine forced Church superiors to process the document through proper channels, exposing its contents in semipublic theological debates rather than burying the matter by having Luther excommunicated, declared a heretic and burned at the stake, as would have been the immediate response were he to directly state his grievances. A few years later, once the full implications of the *95 Theses* were unpacked in those formal debates (and widely read throughout all of Europe, thanks to the printing press and spread of literacy), Martin Luther was excommunicated, declared a heretic . . . and he would've been burned at the stake except for how many people agreed with what he said and helped keep him alive by sheltering him from the Church. Luther and his followers, called Lutherans, were declared outlaws. His writings and ideas were made illegal in Catholic territories, like France, Spain, most of the Italian peninsula and the Holy Roman Empire, located approximately where Germany is today. Everyone who protested the Church's official response to Luther became known as Protestant, soon the umbrella term for all schismatic groups of Christians who stood in opposition to the Vatican, even when many of those denominations also stood in opposition to each other. If that sounds like the beginning of a war, it was actually the beginning of dozens of wars, as these religious divisions were instantly mapped onto preexisting political conflicts. Noble families tired of watching better jobs, marriages and kingdoms go to houses positioned nearer to the papacy now had an alternative to playing the long game of thrones. Instead of working or buying their way up the ranks of the Vatican, they could become Protestant, fight for the new team and be rewarded with positions of greater power in a wholly separate regime.

◇ ◇ ◇

Prior to separation of Church and State the various noble families of Europe vied for control of the Church in order to wield its power over the people's lives and afterlives as tools of the State, a.k.a. the governments of territories ruled by noble families. In the eighth century, such political maneuvering with Church assets brought into existence the Papal States of Italy, a sovereign governmental entity like any other republic or city-state but ruled by the sitting pope. This is one reason why Niccolò Machiavelli's *The Prince* regards the papacy as if it were simply another throne in Europe. It was.

Because of what his name came to represent, it is important to recognize Machiavelli did not invent the use of duplicitous political strategies in service of tyranny. All he did, intentionally or not, was leak the playbook. *The Prince* was Machiavelli documenting and analyzing what he'd witnessed during a career in government, including the backstabbing and murderous methods of

Cesare Borgia, whose father ruled as Pope Alexander VI during the time Machiavelli was stationed at Cesare Borgia's court, where he observed firsthand the young prince's treacherous dealings. After Pope Alexander died in 1503 and the papacy fell to a rival family, Machiavelli observed as Cesare lost the backing of the Church, then lost his throne, then lost his life.

The ideology within *The Prince* is nearly always reduced to some version of "the end justifies any means." In other words, this isn't pretend time and there are no rules in a fight for one's life. To Machiavelli's intended recipient, a prince (which is to say, any person with any immediate path to any throne), the fight for one's life is synonymous with the fight to maintain one's way of life, the fight to maintain the State and one's power over it, the fight for the throne. That is the end which justifies any means, reflected in the literal translation of Machiavelli's original title, *Of Principalities*, the territories ruled by princes. "The end justifies any means" is a fair interpretation of the ideology within *The Prince* but incomplete without noting the degree to which the strategy's success hinges upon a prince's ability to privately exploit and betray his own public persona, that of an honorable man and chivalrous knight. Indeed, a prince must even be prepared to entirely sacrifice that public reputation should loss of the throne be his only alternative. Machiavelli observed it is best for a prince to be simultaneously loved and feared by the people but, if a choice must be made, it is better to be feared than loved. Reading those words may have caused a few lesser houses to realize they'd been fighting with one chivalrous hand tied behind their backs but, again, Machiavelli birthed none of the centuries-old game theory. All he did was write it down, using the common vernacular rather than Latin to draft an easily understood manuscript which was then immediately copied, circulated throughout Europe and studied by all interested parties beginning in 1513, the year a voting council of high-ranking clergy chose Giovanni de Médici to become Pope Leo X, Bishop of Rome, Sovereign of the Papal States, etc.

One reason Leo burned through the Vatican's massive wealth in only two years—freely spending money on parties and worldly pleasures, funding his family's various wars, doling out cash to friends, charities, artists, pretty much anyone who asked—is because he was more interested in being loved than feared, which was also probably why he tried to clear up Martin Luther's apparent confusion over plenary indulgences instead of immediately having Luther executed before the Protestant Reformation could shuffle the deck of noble house alliances in Europe.

◇   ◇   ◇

As implied by its name, the leaders of the Holy Roman Empire were "elected" by a council of powerful Church officials. In the imperial election of 1519, one of the seven clergymen with a vote was the archbishop to whom Martin Luther had originally sent the *95 Theses*. Though there were other candidates, everyone knew the next Holy Roman Emperor would be either Charles of the House of Habsburg, sitting King of Spain, or François of the House of Valois, sitting King of France. Since Charles had more money to bribe voters and he brought an entire army with him to where the vote was held, he became Holy Roman Emperor Charles V. He also became the brand-new archnemesis for life of François, House of Valois. When Charles was made Holy Roman Emperor it put the House of Habsburg in power over countries bordering France on all sides. François did not consider this a "wait and see what happens" situation. But he did still wish to become Holy Roman Emperor and still considered Pope Leo a friend. So François told the Médici family there were no hard feelings, he'd love to have them on France's side, if possible, but, no matter what, he was going to attack Charles. Regardless of what Pope Leo privately wanted to do, he couldn't possibly ally against Charles without watching the Holy Roman Empire change its name to the Holy Protestant Empire and start marching toward Rome with an army Leo couldn't afford to pay anyone to fight. Leo had no choice but to side with his Holy Roman Emperor when the Valois-Habsburg conflict broke out in 1521.

A few months into the fighting, Leo became ill and died. But not before stacking the Vatican deck to Médici favor, creating dozens of new, top-floor positions and stocking them with loyalists, mostly family, including a cousin of illegitimate birth who required a special papal decree falsely stating the cousin had actually been of legitimate birth the whole time, therefore eligible to become a cardinal. In 1523, two years after Leo died, that cardinal cousin became the next Médici pope, Clement VII. Clement and Leo were technically cousins but had been raised as brothers, so Clement was an active participant and advisor during Leo's entire papacy. He'd also seen enough of the Valois-Habsburg fight play out to believe he needed Charles to lose. If Charles took power in France, then the House of Habsburg would control nearly every major throne in Western Europe except for England and the papacy, Clement's throne. As soon as François won a significant battle against Charles, Clement took the opportunity to formally switch sides, just in time for François to get ass kicked and captured, then thrown in a prison cell in Spain. Clement was forced to turn around and pretend to make up with Charles, then keep that act going for an entire year while François resisted signing a treaty of surrender. When François did finally surrender, the Habsburgs demanded his two oldest sons—then seven and eight years old—take their father's place in the Spanish prison cell, just in case François went back on the treaty. François agreed, sent for his sons, made the exchange and was released from prison. The first chance he got, children in captivity and everything, François went back on the treaty. Pope Clement again betrayed the Holy Roman Emperor to side with the house of Valois in attacking the Habsburgs. So Charles decided to stop screwing around. He assembled a huge army of his own men, augmented it with more than twice as many German Protestant forces and dispatched the whole horde toward Rome. On the way there these troops discovered they'd been sent without money or food, which provided an incentive for what they did upon arrival in Rome. In short, they sacked the city, which means every terrible thing you think it means. Pope Clement allowed the carnage to last for nearly a month while he hid in a castle and resisted surrender. After Clement finally surrendered, Charles made him *stay* in the castle for another six months while Rome continued to be thoroughly decimated. Sometimes you've just gotta prove a point. Clement did eventually manage to escape Rome but the damage was already done. Charles once more stomped all over François and at this point could probably have gotten away with beheading both the pope and the King of France. Instead, he asked if both men were ready to settle down and let the Habsburgs control Europe. Clement and François agreed. For some reason that was enough for Charles, who allowed them to sign yet another treaty and walk away clean.

François did have to pay a large fortune to get his sons back from the Spanish prison but he was allowed to remain King of France. To remind Clement there were benefits of being a friend to the Habsburgs, Charles restored the Médici family to power in Florence by sending an army to lay siege to the city for most of a year, until Florence gave up notions of existing as a republic and submitted to Médici rule. During the nine-month siege mobs of Florentines periodically gathered outside the walls of a convent where they knew the pope's niece, Catherine de Médici, was being raised. The crowd yelled for the nuns inside to send out "the little duchess." Inside the convent the ten-year-old girl listened as they yelled for her by name and detailed all of the unspeakable things they wanted to do to her.

After Charles gave Florence back to the Médicis, Clement spent the remaining four years of his life doing just about everything the Holy Roman Emperor told him to do, which would get into an entirely separate stretch of history regarding how badly Henry VIII of England wanted a divorce but there are already too many Henrys and too many divorces in this story. Most histories of Pope Clement VII treat him as a man who truly did have good intentions, at least more so than his direct predecessors and successors, but who also inherited untenable positions, then died before there were many opportunities for redemption. One of the last things he did was circle back to his old partner-in-crime François to offer France a ton of money in the form of a niece's dowry. François thought the price sounded right for his second-eldest son, Henri.

If this were a chivalric romance novel, Catherine de Médici and Henri of the House of Valois would fall madly in love based on their similarly traumatic childhoods, hers as the most famous and hated orphan in Florence while her uncle lay siege to the city and his as a seven-year-old boy whose father traded him into prison only to recklessly endanger his life through further treacherous acts of war. But this is not a chivalric romance novel.

FOURTEEN

STAND BY YOUR MAN

◇ A Sincere Fuck You to Feminism ◇ Tammy Wynette vs. Women's Liberation ◇
D-I-V-O-R-C-E ◇ Loving George Jones, Leaving Don Chapel
◇ Escape to Florida ◇ Domestic Violence ◇

"Stand By Your Man" was purposefully designed from the ground up to be an anti-feminist anthem, but many journalists, critics and fans are still able to perform the mental gymnastics required to spin the song as some kind of egalitarian, even pro-woman statement. Nearly all of these back handsprings of the brain are launched off the single lyric, "'cuz, after all, he's just a man." There are college professors who deliver this line to rooms full of students as if it's a mic drop on fifty years of "Stand By Your Man" being as misunderstood as Bruce Springsteen's "Born in the USA," as if the lyric was in any way intended as criticism of stereotypically male behavior rather than excusing such men to continue their philandering ways because it's in their nature. Regardless of any notions concerning the subjectivity of art and it all being open to interpretation, this song was deliberately written as a middle finger aimed directly at feminists. Billy Sherrill stopped short of titling it "Stand By Your Man, Not Woman's Lib" but that's exactly what he meant and only a fool or a liar would claim otherwise.

Tammy Wynette always tried to portray "Stand By Your Man" as something she and Billy threw together without much thought in about twenty minutes, then spent the rest of their lives defending. But she also said, "There's no mistakin' that Tammy Wynette is not one for Women's Liberation." Such a statement cannot be ignored. Some of the things Tammy said while criticizing feminism were based in popular misconceptions about feminists being a bunch of bra-burners who hated men, sex, aesthetic beauty and children. She sometimes reduced her problems with feminism to such trivial statements as, "I wouldn't want to lose the little courtesies we've always been extended, like lighting cigarettes and opening doors . . . I guess I just enjoy bein' a woman."

Whether those sentiments were sincere or strategic defense, Tammy Wynette was an adult who understood and fundamentally disagreed with several core tenets of feminism. It's true she supported and exemplified some feminist ideals. She often spoke of how much it bothered her to see women demonized for sexual behavior while men openly bragged of their own. She'd seen girls kicked out of her high school and saddled with the full responsibility of pregnancy while the teenage fathers received no punishment and high fives from their friends. Tammy spoke critically of the hero worship heaped onto male country artists for behaving badly on tour—drinking, missing shows, destroying hotel rooms, sleeping with fans—while women in the industry had to either remain professional or watch their careers end in scandal. There are countless interviews where she gave quotes which can be partially excerpted by fans intent on rewriting the script to paint her as a feminist. For instance, she was always quick to point to herself as an example of a strong-willed woman who was the primary breadwinner of the family for nearly her entire adult life. So how is this person not a feminist? If she so clearly diagnosed such lack of equality in society and her industry, why and where did she place a line between herself and the Women's Liberation movement? Well, the full, unedited interview quotes always include Tammy saying success, fame and financial independence left her miserable when she didn't have a man to share it with and subjugate herself to. She was consistently open about her emotional dependence on men, point-blank stating she didn't think she could be happy without a strong man, or at least the illusion of one, to place above herself in the home. She said, "I was raised to believe in marriage as a woman's greatest fulfillment and I guess deep down that's what I still believe." That is the philosophy of "Stand By Your Man" and anyone hoping to retcon Tammy Wynette as a feminist will find so much more than one song and a pile of quotes standing in their way. Most of her biggest hits reword the same message over and over: a woman is worthless without a man and when (not if) your man cheats on you, then the fault is either yours for not "loving" him enough or the other woman's for tempting him—it's never his fault—so you just have to forgive him and do whatever it takes to get him back home or else you'll go to bed alone at night and/or end up raising a child on your own. This was not an ideology cynically adopted in order to sell records through the persona of Tammy Wynette. It's who Virginia Wynette Pugh was every day of her adult life and accepting that is the only way we can begin to understand her.

What's often called the "second wave" of feminist activism grew out of the Civil Rights Movement of the 1950s and 1960s and, by 1965, had come to dominate enough of the cultural conversation within the United States for Billy Sherrill to decide he ought to write a song for everyone who thought these ladies should shut up and go home. He said, "I wanted it to be a song for the truly liberated woman, one who is secure enough in her identity to enjoy it." Billy claimed his first idea for a title, "I'll Stand By You, Please Stand By Me," was partially lifted from the Ben E. King megahit "Stand By Me." Billy also consistently claimed to've stolen the melody from Johann Strauss II but, strictly speaking, that doesn't seem to be true. He never named an individual composition as his source of inspiration but it seems most likely that he built an original melody by deconstructing a brief moment in one of the crescendos of the "Wine, Women and Song" waltz from 1869. Tammy Wynette may have only spent twenty minutes thinking about the song before cutting it but by the time she first heard it Billy had worked on the song for three years, never finishing it until August of 1968, when one of Tammy's recording sessions committed the ultimate sin of boring him, meaning they didn't have a hit. Billy sent the studio musicians out on a break, took Tammy upstairs to his office and showed her the song. She helped finish it by adding two lines, then they went back downstairs to make a record. It was only after the session that Tammy became concerned about what they'd done, not because of the lyrical content but because she thought the finished product came out sounding more R&B than country, especially after Billy Sherrill removed Pete Drake's pedal steel guitar intro and had Jerry Kennedy play a simple electric guitar line to kick off the song. Tammy also wasn't sure about her high note at the song's climax. It reminded her of a squealing pig. When she played it for George Jones, he wasn't so sure about the song, either. But that's because they were both thinking of it as a country record, not a record that was about to sell more copies than any country single by a woman ever had.

Once sales passed one million units, Epic's marketing copy began referring to Tammy Wynette as The First Lady of Country Music. (Tammy was probably not the first woman in country music to actually sell a million units, just the first to do so after certain sales tracking systems were put in place. It's possible Loretta Lynn sold a million units earlier than Tammy but, even if not, Patsy Montana almost certainly sold over a million copies of "I Want to Be a Cowboy's Sweetheart" decades prior to Tammy or Loretta recording anything at all. Still, Epic's marketing department saw a branding opportunity and ran with it.) "Stand By Your Man" hit #1 Country, #19 Pop and won most of the awards for which it was eligible, including Tammy's second Grammy. The CMA named her Female Vocalist of the Year for the next three years in a row. To this day "Stand By Your Man" is one of the most recognizable and enduring recordings in the history of popular music. It's been covered by everyone from Tina Turner to Lemmy & Wendy O. Williams to Alvin & The Chipmunks. It's been significantly placed in movies like *Goldeneye*, *My Cousin Vinny*, *The Blues Brothers* and *The Crying Game*. Some of those covers and placements were genuinely reverent. Others were ironic references to the controversy the song has generated and/or become associated with since the day it was released.

The consciously provoked feminist backlash was instant and has proven as everlasting as the song itself. Fans trying to defend the lyrics from criticism usually resort to what-about-ism by pretending to wonder where the difference lies between this and something like "Piece of My Heart," popularized by Janis Joplin's Big Brother & The Holding Company. Why do feminists get so angry about one but not the other? Well, it's because "Piece of My Heart" is a testimonial, in which a narrator shares a personal story, and "Stand By Your Man" is a dogmatic instruction manual. Tammy often claimed to not understand why her song made so many people so upset. Like many of her creative histories, the things she said while defending "Stand By Your Man" had a way of revealing just how much she did understand the reasons everyone was mad. Most of her excuses can be reduced to the notion she only intended to suggest women try being understanding and supportive. She said, "It doesn't say take abuse or anything like that. It just says 'if you love him, you'll forgive him,'" which conservative Christian country singer Jeannie C. Riley found perhaps the most offensive line in the entire song. To her, it very much did imply a woman should take anything her man dishes out while offering only love and forgiveness in return. Loretta Lynn recorded "Stand By Your Man" but also once said, "I think you ought to stand by your man if he's standin' by you. If he ain't standin' by you, why, move over! I think if your man's doin' you right, fantastic. But how many men treat their wives right? Think about it." Over the years, as Tammy collected one divorce after another, she tried to jokingly point to her own personal life as evidence she clearly did not believe a woman should stay with a man through emotional or physical abuse. Then, after she died, one close source after another went on the record to disclose the various abuses Tammy suffered in her final and longest-lasting relationship, with the man she stood by until the end.

If Tammy Wynette truly felt her intentions with "Stand By Your Man" were misinterpreted or misunderstood, then we can only assume she would use her next, say, five singles to clarify her message and make sure everyone knew precisely what Tammy Wynette was all about, right? "Singing My Song" takes her back to "swinging," only this time it's more real than the idle threats made in "Your Good Girl's Gonna Go Bad" and the way the music drops her into the pathetic, broken-spirited delivery of this and only this line informs us an open relationship was definitely not her idea. It's just what she's got to do to keep her man. In "The Ways to Love a Man" she'll do anything and everything to keep him around because if "one little thing goes wrong, then all at once he's gone." In "I'll See Him Through" she waits up all night for a man who no longer even bothers with excuses when he finally comes home but, still, she stays. Same story in "He Loves Me All the Way." Her man stays out all night while she's home "thinking like a woman," worried about him cheating but really it's not so bad because she's never actually seen him cheating, plus it's always great when he does decide to come home and have sex with her for a change. "Run Woman Run" bluntly tells younger women to remain in unhappy relationships because of how hard it is to find a man who meets even the lowest of reasonable standards, so you may as well make yourself believe whatever you've got is true love. Without exception, each of those songs walked back and forth on the line separating Tammy Wynette from the Women's Liberation movement, retreading the same thematic ground until it was worn down to a chin-high trench from which she continued tossing lyrical hand grenades.

There's one post-Y2K Billy Sherrill interview in which he claimed "Stand By Your Man" was written without a single thought of the Women's Liberation movement or how they would respond to it. There's no telling what compelled him to say that—he very well may have been trying to delegitimize someone he viewed as a cultural tourist of a reporter—but anyone who wants to believe such a huge, steaming pile of bullshit has to ignore at least twenty other Billy Sherrill interviews along with an August 1970 issue of *Billboard* in which Epic placed a full-page ad reading, "With apologies to the Women's Liberation movement, we present Tammy Wynette's next number-one single, 'Run Woman Run.'" That prediction was correct, by the way. The only one of those next five singles to not go #1 Country hit #2 and they all succeeded while crystallizing precisely what it was feminists found so infuriating about "Stand By Your Man." If it wasn't already difficult to believe Tammy could ever have been surprised by the backlash, that "Run Woman Run" ad makes it downright impossible for her to've been surprised at any point following the year 1970. As the critics kept coming Tammy grew more comfortable speaking her mind on Women's Liberation, once saying, "Sometimes I think that the ladies makin' the most noise are the least liberated. I didn't have time to go 'round squawkin' about some cause because I was too busy workin'."

Don't get the idea it must have been a bunch of misogynist male fans putting Tammy Wynette records at #1. Sure, guys who appreciated incredible music with lyrics granting them permission to behave like trash bought their fair share of copies. But these records were made for and primarily purchased by other women who felt the same way Tammy did. Everything Billy Sherrill did was strategically manufactured for women because everything he did was informed by market research. If recording "I Don't Wanna Play House" in June 1967 to appeal to the increasing number of American divorcées is any indication, which it likely is, that's probably when Billy received the first of many reports that dictated the rest of his career. One of the market studies he read stated at least half and maybe as many as 65 percent of all country records were purchased by women between the ages of twenty-two and forty-five. It does not matter who conducted this study or what flaws may or may not have been in their methods. If it wasn't true when Billy Sherrill read it, it became true when he started moving millions of units by targeting product at this demographic, millions of whom agreed with country singer and woman Jean Shepard, who once said, "I can't stand for a woman to come up and say, 'I can do anything a man can do.' Maybe mentally she can but I think it's still kind of a man's world and, to be frank, I kind of like it that way. I'd never like to see a woman president, for instance. A woman's too high-strung for that kind of job." Speaking of a woman president, when you're looking for all the reasons why Hillary Clinton lost the 2016 presidential election don't forget to go all the way back to that infamous *60 Minutes* interview in 1992, where the Clintons fielded questions about Bill's affair with Gennifer Flowers until Hillary eventually decided to try saving her husband's career by throwing Tammy Wynette's (mispronounced) name under a bus, saying "I'm not sitting here, some little woman standin' by my man like Tammy [Why-nette.]" Of course, Hillary has since been accused of doing exactly that for the entire duration of her own career. In her memoir *Living History*, Hillary described the "fallout" from criticizing both Tammy Wynette and "Stand By Your Man" as "instant and brutal." Tammy herself responded by releasing an open letter in which she challenged Hillary to a public debate, then condemned Hillary's insult for having "offended every true country music fan and every person who has 'made it on their own' with no one to take them to a White House." Hillary tried to ignore the open letter and ride out the storm but it wouldn't stop and she finally had to go back on national TV to issue a sort of non-apology: "If she feels like I've hurt her feelings, I'm sorry about that."

Hillary Clinton did not invent the invocation of Tammy Wynette's name or songs as shorthand to represent a stereotype of walked-on and cheated-on woman. Such usage has been standard in our vernacular ever since "Stand By Your Man" came out and is evidently never going to go away. The 1970 hit indie film *Five Easy Pieces* starred Jack Nicholson as a womanizing fuckup of a classical pianist, boyfriend to lovestruck dumbass Karen Black, a perfect example of the "Typical Girls" still being mocked by post-punk legends the Slits nearly a decade later with lyrics like "typical girls / stand by their man." In *Five Easy Pieces*, Karen Black's character listens to Tammy Wynette records over and over while wishing Jack Nicholson's character would become worthy of her adoration and forgiveness. He never does but she keeps givin' all the love she can, fightin' to stand by her man right up until the end credits roll. Throughout the film Nicholson's character shows nothing but contempt for Karen's taste in music. His very first line in the movie is a threat to melt her copy of "Stand By Your Man" if she plays it one more time. Later, when he laughs at her for singing a different Tammy Wynette song, she's gullible enough to believe it's a laugh of appreciation.

The song Karen sang in the movie was Merle Kilgore's "When There's a Fire in Your Heart" from Tammy's third LP, *D-I-V-O-R-C-E*. The title track is something of a sequel to "I Don't Wanna Play House," continuing to exploit Tammy's real-life status as a divorced woman. Both of these divorce songs came out prior to "Stand By Your Man" and, predicting that song's sociopolitical message, both songs are 100 percent about commiseration, not redemption. Neither song presents Tammy as a woman strong enough to willfully choose independence over remaining in a bad relationship. Neither song gives her any light at the end of the tunnel. Rather, she internalizes all of the blame for the failed marriages and lets it eat away at her. In "D-I-V-O-R-C-E" she's so broken without a husband, we know she'd take him back in the middle of the song if he walked in the recording studio. After the song opens with a seven-note riff (corresponding to the number of letters in the title), Lloyd Green's pedal steel guitar does a little bit of crying, then Tammy does a whole lot of spelling. It's a great representation of what Emmylou Harris meant when she said Tammy Wynette could "just milk a vowel [. . .] she could give so much melody to just, like, one syllable. But it never sounded contrived." Or, as Roy Blount Jr. once put it, "Lord, can't Tammy sing a letter of the alphabet!"

By this time songwriter Bobby Braddock had given a few minor hits to the Statler Brothers, Little Jimmy Dickens and his old boss Marty Robbins, but "D-I-V-O-R-C-E" was his first #1 record. He originally wrote it as a happy song with a title spelling out the words "I L-O-V-E Y-O-U." By his own admission Bobby Braddock is a pretty weird guy with an unusual sense of humor, so even after he decided to change all of the lyrics and make it a sad song about divorce, he went ahead and kept the original song's happy melody. When that demo didn't get any takers he brought it to fellow Tree writer Curly Putman and asked what was wrong with it, at which point Curly moved the melody in a slightly sadder direction to fall in line with the new words. Billy Sherrill heard this updated version, knew it was Tammy's next #1 hit and they cut it as soon as she returned from the Canadian tour with David Houston and George Jones. The single came out in April 1968 and, sure enough, went #1.

◇   ◇   ◇

The day George Jones dropped by Tammy's house to tell her he was no longer a married man, his pretense for coming over was to hear the latest songs Don Chapel had written. Instead of paying attention to Chapel's songs, though, George kept singing the first line of Tammy's latest hit over and over until she picked up the hint: his D-I-V-O-R-C-E became final that day. Perhaps Don Chapel could have tolerated such attention the same way he'd tolerated his wife riding all over Canada on George's tour bus, so long as he felt his own career stood to benefit. But when George's focus on Tammy actively pulled focus away from Chapel's songs a different picture began to develop in Chapel's mind, and he no longer saw himself in the frame. After George left their house that day Don yelled at Tammy over what had happened.

Tammy always claimed she was totally caught off guard by George suddenly attempting to woo her in front of Don, just as she always claimed that prior to this George "never so much as touched me, except to shake my hand or pat me on the back." According to Don Chapel that's all a load of bullshit. Once everything shook out the way it did, Chapel realized why George's road manager was always asking Chapel to tag along on random errands. It was to give George and Tammy time alone. According to her official biographer, Joan Dew, "Tammy loved George Jones, the singer. She idolized him. He was the epitome of the great country music singer. What would anybody do if they had a chance to have an affair with their idol? I'm real doubtful about whether she loved George Jones, the man." Setting aside her depressing beliefs in the limitations of human fidelity, the implication is clear, Joan was qualified to make it and the way she framed the situation says a lot about the illusions Wynette brought to the relationship. Given her circumstances, beliefs and fantasies, Wynette could not have seen George as anything less than her own personal knight in . . . if not shining armor, then at least fancy armor with a few dings she thought could be buffed out by her love.

In reality Jones was a walking disaster, despite some effort to correct course. It seems his alcoholic father's emergency hospitalization back in 1965 scared George a little bit straight. His parents celebrated their fiftieth anniversary that August and both Jones men stayed sober for the occasion. But the following month George was arrested for a DUI near his home in Vidor, Texas, which may have served as another wake-up call because George then placed Phase II on pause to throw himself into a huge project, perhaps a last-ditch attempt to save his marriage to Shirley Jones. Operating under the assumption his drinking was mostly driven by the anxieties and fears that came with touring, George believed a solution could be to build his own venue near home and make money playing concerts there instead of going back out on the road. He sank thousands of dollars and a lot of his own sweat into constructing an outdoor venue. July 4, 1966, saw the grand opening of the George Jones Rhythm Ranch with a big-ticket lineup featuring himself, Lefty Frizzell and Merle Haggard. They packed in as many thousands of people as could fit on the property, which would've been a huge payday except George didn't charge most of those people to get in. At the end of the night he'd come nowhere near recouping the cost of the land, construction or opening day talent, so he disappeared on a drunk for four days. There was never another show booked at the Rhythm Ranch.

A little over a year later he was on tour in Michigan when he again got a phone call about his father's health. Turns out nobody was making mortgage payments on the house George bought for his parents, so the bank repossessed it. Stressed over losing the home, George's father had a stroke and fell into a coma from which he never awoke. George flew home in time to witness his dad's final day of drawing breath. Several sources claim George responded to seeing the old man lying there comatose by destroying the hospital room but George claimed he wouldn't have done that . . . because it takes "fury" and "hostility" to do something like that. Some say George's father was able to quit drinking before the end. Others say he just got better at hiding it. Sometime after his death they were burning hedges to clear off a bit of land and were surprised by explosions which turned out to be glass bottles full of alcohol. The old man hid booze in the bushes for whenever he wanted to sneak a drink or two.

George cried for days after his dad's funeral, then hit the bottle as hard as ever. That was his state of mind when he came under the spell of Tammy Wynette. Having spent the previous five years woefully fixated upon Melba Montgomery as the magical cure for all his problems, what else could Jones do other than transfer the obsession to Tammy, especially once she demonstrated a willingness to play her role in the fairy-tale love story George so desperately wanted? Simply compare that devastating footage of The King of Broken Hearts singing "Walk Through This World with Me" in early 1967 to the footage of George happily singing the same song about a year and a half later on *The Wilburn Brothers Show*, sporting a handsome new haircut and a "brand-new wife."

In his autobiography, George said he never stole Tammy from behind Don Chapel's back: "That's a lie. I did it in front of his eyes." Whether or not Jones coming to her rescue in Canada had been entirely orchestrated by Tammy, she was clearly pleased by such grand gestures and so they continued, very much in front of Chapel's eyes. On more than one occasion George surprised Tammy and her audience by showing up to concerts where he hadn't been booked and coming out to perform with her. She estimated her first tour bus to be worth fifteen to twenty thousand dollars, though it was difficult to be sure because she bought it from George, who insisted on taking only two thousand dollars for it. (Maybe he knocked off a grand for every bullet hole?) When Chapel painted the side of the bus to read "The Don Chapel and Tammy Wynette Show," her name following his, it served as a daily reminder of the glaring difference between life with her pretentious husband and what she imagined life could be with her magnanimous hero. Tammy's marriage grew resentful. She chose more and more often to ride separately from her husband and band, traveling instead with George.

Before Don Chapel makes a spectacularly ungraceful exit from this story, we should recognize he wasn't only some talentless, opportunistic leech. George Jones did record several of his songs and it wouldn't be right to suggest that was purely compensation for dating the man's wife. None of these events would have taken place the way they did if "From Here to the Door" wasn't a killer song. Chapel's best song is inarguably "When the Grass Grows Over Me," which meticulously predicted the theme of the biggest hit George Jones would ever have a full decade in advance and, at least on paper, is arguably just as masterful a depiction of a love that only death can kill. Tammy later claimed she wrote the song and let Don take the credit but there are several songs she lied about writing and this one has nothing in common with her compositional style. George cut

"When the Grass Grows Over Me" in June of 1968. By the time it was released and hit #2 Country, George and Tammy were publicly referring to each other as husband and wife. They were lying, of course. The divorce George set up for Tammy in Mexico wasn't legal in the States. They had to bring in lawyers to try keeping Chapel from taking everything he could get as compensation for the embarrassment of newspaper headlines reading, "TAMMY WYNETTE LEAVES HUSBAND FOR GEORGE JONES." As the full story emerged over the following years, Don Chapel became the unambiguous villain and his career was forever destroyed.

The night he lost Tammy for good Don was already drunk at home and yelling about George Jones trying to steal his wife when who should show up at the door to join them for dinner but George himself? For the sake of decorum Don tried to dial back his anger but he was too drunk to keep from muttering an occasional sideways comment in Tammy's direction. George either didn't register these comments or chose not to acknowledge them until Don finally called Tammy a "bitch," at which point George went apeshit, flipped over a dining room table probably twice his size and roared at Don that he shouldn't insult Tammy. When Don asked what business it was of his, George confessed he loved Tammy and said he knew she loved him back. Tammy confirmed this was true, so Jones took her and her daughters away from the house. A decade later she wrote in her autobiography, "George and I were to have some rough times, but I never regretted leaving with him that night. It was just fantastic. George got me out of a way of life that was unreal. I couldn't even write how hard it really was. It was rough with Don Chapel. Anything Jones could have done wouldn't have upset me compared to what I had been through with Chapel." A storybook romance come true, she thought. George had purchased a house in Nashville by this time but that first night he put Tammy and her daughters up in a hotel because he knew Don would send police to file a report saying Tammy was at George's house, thus enabling Don to sue George for "alienation of affection," a.k.a. wife-stealing. Sure enough, the cops showed up at George's place, looked around and, after not finding anyone's wives hiding in any closets, they left him alone. The next day George brought Tammy and her kids to stay in his home.

There were very few things in life George Jones enjoyed as much as buying a house and redecorating it, usually in a gaudy, Spanish colonial style. The first night Wynette was in George's home she lay with him on top of the covers of his bed and looked around at all the paintings of bullfighters on the walls of his plush, velvety bedroom while George's favorite movie played on TV. The 1962 film adaptation of Rod Serling's *Requiem for a Heavyweight* stars Anthony Quinn as a boxer who's already had his ticket punched one too many times when Muhammad Ali (then called Cassius Clay) beats the absolute shit out of him in the opening scene. Afterward doctors won't clear him to keep boxing, so he tries to get a job as a kid's camp counselor but his snake of a manager, played

by Jackie Gleason, owes potentially fatal debts to the mob. At one point in the movie Gleason di-
agnoses modern history as a tale about the rich getting richer while the poor get drunk. He pushes
alcohol on the ex-boxer to sabotage the camp counselor job, ruining his client's chances for a better
life and manipulating him into becoming a racist American Indian stereotype of a pro wrestling
character. Wynette was already in love with at least her idea of George Jones, but her heart melted
when she saw him cry at the movie's conclusion, Anthony Quinn sacrificing all dignity to save his
no-good manager by going out to perform as "Big Chief." Wynette spent the night in George's bed
and remembered him being "as gentle and tender and loving" as she'd imagined. The next morning
he took off one of his expensive rings and put it on her hand to formalize their engagement, then
gave her the keys to one of his cars. She thought she must be the luckiest girl in the world.

But she wasn't yet free of Don Chapel, who fell into a breathtaking display of frantic scram-
bling when biographer Jimmy McDonough asked him about trying to blackmail Tammy Wynette
with nude photos. After Chapel first responded by saying Tammy dreamt up the whole thing, he
then said in those days everyone took risqué Polaroids, which was all they were so he couldn't have
been in possession of any film negatives with which to blackmail her, as Tammy claimed. Then
he said Tammy joked about framing one of the nude pictures for display and decided to keep one
of the photos in a secret place with a threat to someday, somehow, blackmail Chapel with a nude
photo of herself. Still not done rambling, Chapel wrapped up his response by saying Tammy wasn't
even pretty and calling her "bowlegged." So, you know, just a calm and rational explanation from a
man who was confident he'd done nothing wrong. In Tammy's version, soon after they were married Chapel began aggressively taking pictures of her whenever she was naked and he remembered
he had a camera. If she was getting in or out of the shower, doing stretches on the floor of their bedroom while nude, whatever, he'd jump in there and grab a shot or two. It made her angry every time
but Chapel wouldn't stop. So she started locking doors before taking off her clothes. A few months
later, a fan at a concert handed an envelope to her. When she opened it in the dressing room while
on a break between sets and found a picture of herself . . . naked . . . in her bathroom . . . in her
home . . . she came unglued on Chapel. He acted like it was no big deal, just him and some other
guys who traded pictures of their wives through classified ads in the back of nudie magazines. With
all the glaring problems in the marriage, this was one thing Tammy couldn't forgive and never
did. Despite Chapel denying any of that happened, George Jones claimed one of his managers
was contacted by Don Chapel, who seemed to think he could get revenge on Tammy by shattering
George's opinion of her with these photos. Instead, the manager bought and destroyed the film
negatives, bringing an end to the whole matter, at least until Tammy told the entire world about it
in her autobiography a decade later. (It's worth pointing out the account George Jones gave in his

autobiography provided additional details not included in Tammy's earlier book. Unlike most of his book, George was not simply repeating or responding to the memories of others when he shared his side of this.) After Tammy's book came out Chapel tried to sue her for somewhere around thirty million dollars, claiming he was harassed and humiliated because of what she wrote . . . and that he took the pictures with Tammy's permission. The lawsuit was quickly dismissed.

Even without the naked pictures scandal, Chapel's career would have been royally screwed as soon as Tammy left him. For all the favors Mr. Tammy Wynette could cash in around Nashville, ex–Mr. Tammy Wynette could barely get his phone calls returned. When Don and Donna Chapel talked to Hubert Long to see what their touring opportunities were without Tammy, they found out there weren't any. Hubert said he could no longer book their tours because Tammy was one of his top clients and he wanted to make sure she stayed happy with him. There are exactly zero significant recordings of any Don Chapel song written after his divorce from Tammy Wynette. Oh, and he didn't even merit a real divorce. One of George's guys discovered an Alabama law stating divorcées must secure permission from the judge on their case if they wanted to get married again within a year. Since Tammy never asked permission from the judge who'd divorced her and Euple Byrd, she was never legally married to Don Chapel in the first place. She let Chapel keep the house anyway.

⬦   ⬦   ⬦

By the time Epic released "Stand By Your Man" in September of 1968, Tammy Wynette and George Jones were already pretending to be married. As the song became a record-breaking shitstorm of a sociopolitical phenomenon, the media zeroed in on Tammy's love life and fed it to the flames of controversy. It would take a whole separate book to unpack the many arguments surrounding the song but, suffice to say, both its defenders and critics somehow believed Tammy's second divorce and remarriage supported their interpretation of the song. No matter which side the women in beauty salons were on, they all read the latest gossip about Tammy's life in the same magazines Wynette used to love and still loved, even though she now knew how glamorous it *didn't* feel to be in those pages: "I guess the loss of privacy goes with the territory of being a celebrity but that doesn't make it any easier to see your personal life splattered all over the papers." In a near-instant response to the sudden presence of the media in their daily lives, Tammy and George moved from Nashville to Florida. By the time George got around to telling his own version of the story his career had been in much better shape than Tammy's for about twenty years, so he acted as if he was the big celebrity who needed to get out of town and away from the media circus. In reality Tammy was quickly becoming one of the most famous women on the planet and it's pretty likely she'd already learned enough about her new fiancé to know he should be kept far away from tabloid reporters.

In the fall of 1968, they took a trip down to Florida for George to show Tammy the vacation home he had kept in his recent divorce. Only, he happened to be renting the house to a married couple he knew and it also happened to be raining very hard when they arrived in Florida. Since George wanted the sun to be out when Tammy saw the house for the first time, they checked into a motel and invited the renters to come meet them in the bar, where everyone but Tammy pretty quickly got drunk. In George's version of the story this alone was enough to provoke Tammy's anger and cause her to start yelling at him. Tammy claimed she had no problem with watching him and his friends get drunk except that it was boring. She said when the friends finally left she took Jones up to the motel room, put him into bed with his clothes still on and was just getting into bed herself when someone began pounding on the door. Apparently the husband of the couple wasn't ready to let the party end and came back to do some more drinking. Fearful of Jones waking up, Tammy quickly jumped out of bed and opened the door to tell the guy to get lost, but she was too late. Jones was already out of bed, half awake, still trashed and extremely pissed off at Tammy for yelling at his friend. He took a swing at her but missed, then shattered a whiskey bottle against the wall, so Tammy decided to make a run for it. She sprinted out of their second-story room, down a set of stairs and off across the parking lot in her bare feet, wearing only a nightgown. Jones tried to give chase but, being drunk and wearing cowboy boots with a pretty tall heel, he tripped near the bottom of the stairs, fell the rest of the way down and landed in a gravel flower bed, breaking his wrist. When Tammy heard him fall she looked back and saw him lying on the ground but kept running until she made it to another motel next door, where she convinced the overnight front desk clerk to give her a room even though she had no money or ID. A couple hours later, dwelling on the fact that Jones hadn't been moving when she looked back and saw him on the ground, she made up her mind to go check and see if he was okay. Since his dead body wasn't lying in the parking lot, she went up to the room and knocked quietly on the door. Right away George called for her to come in and she found him, now fully awake and mostly sober, sitting up in bed with his broken wrist resting on a pillow. After some half-hearted bickering Tammy drove him to a hospital where they put his forearm in a cast. The sun was shining bright the next morning and George was back to being the man who made her feel like the luckiest little lady in the world. They went to see the house, which she loved, and their move to Florida was decided. George's renters still had a few months left on their lease, though, so Tammy and George went back to Nashville until the house was empty.

Despite the decades-old prevailing narrative, this relationship's problems did not begin and end with substance abuse. Among other issues, by the time of this interim period in Nashville, George had already realized Tammy wanted to be around him more often than he wanted to be around anyone. In his words, "There is such a thing as smothering a person." As soon as they began living together his alone time suddenly evaporated. Whether he was going to the store, studio or anywhere in between, Tammy was seemingly incapable of letting him out of her sight. It eventually got to the point where he invented a short-notice out-of-town business trip, then checked himself into a Nashville hotel just to get some solitude for a few days. Tammy wanted to pick up George at the airport when he "got back to town," so he took a cab to the Nashville airport and snuck his way into the terminal in order to approach his waiting bride-to-be from the direction of arriving passengers. He even timed it all out so he'd come walking up soon after "his plane" had landed. The only problem: just a few minutes before George entered the terminal, Tammy heard an announcement about that flight being delayed and was getting settled in for a bit of a wait when there came George, walking up with a big smile on his face long before he was supposed to land. Tammy's curiosity over where he'd been for the past several days did not lead to a mature and honest discussion of their respective needs from a partner.

When George went in the studio for Musicor in November of 1968, Tammy tagged along. She knew how many years George had spent obsessing over his label-mate Melba Montgomery and, well, it's probably not a coincidence that George and Melba's final session together took place in late 1966, a year or so prior to Tammy setting her sights on George. About five months before this late 1968 session George had cut a handful of duets with a new singer named Brenda Carter. When "Milwaukee, Here I Come" nearly went Top 10 with Brenda singing on it, Tammy probably decided to make sure nobody else became George's new recording partner. Even though it went against her contract with Epic, Tammy jumped in George's Musicor session and recorded uncredited background vocals on several songs, including what became the title track of his next LP, *I'll Share My World with You.* Musicor may not have been able to credit her background vocals on the LP jacket but they did make the entire album cover a picture of George and Tammy. By this time George's sessions were regularly led by Owen Bradley understudy Bob Moore, who had by this time also worked with and studied Billy Sherrill for several years. Those keeping track of Sherrill's growing influence on the direction of the Nashville Sound will note the piano on "I'll Share My World with You" has migrated from the Floyd Cramer–esque clusters of notes and the busy honky-tonk style previously heard on George Jones records over to the way Billy Sherrill used piano, sudden and distinct single-note runs, often on the bass half of the keyboard. The single came out in March 1969, hit #2 Country and probably would have gone #1 if it wasn't held down by Tammy's "Stand By Your Man," still sitting on top of the charts.

Along with the rest of his life, Jones had allowed his *Grand Ole Opry* membership to lapse in the early 1960s, so when the *Opry* made Tammy a member in January 1969 they also asked him to rejoin. Around the same time, Hubert Long began booking them as a co-headliner package on tour. Their first engagement was a string of dates in February in Atlanta at the Playroom, the very same venue where Hubert first booked Tammy on her own. In his autobiography Jones reduced the events of this Georgia trip to the shows they performed, the legal marriage they secretly procured and the child Tammy informed him she was carrying. He presented this information in that order, which was the same order this information was presented in Tammy's earlier book. However, Jones did not respond to or even acknowledge the rest of what Tammy alleged happened as a result of his drinking on this trip. What Jones did do, three pages after discussing the Georgia trip, was claim he did not believe he went on "a doozy" of a drunk in 1969 until near the end of the year because he was trying to be well-behaved after breaking his wrist in Florida. This is an indirect refutation of Tammy's Georgia story, which begs the question whether there may be a reason Jones intentionally sidestepped directly refuting her story. Since both accounts cannot be true, the question is whether directly refuting Tammy's story would have called into question the official timeline of circumstances and events both parties claimed led to their marriage, perhaps even to the point of suggesting what they may have really been arguing about several months earlier in that Florida motel room. Did Jones, as Tammy alleged, wait until the second day of their Atlanta gig to disappear for most of a day with the club owner, return drunk enough to accuse her of trying to sleep with members of his band, shove her in the hallway of the tour bus, abandon her onstage one song into the set, then disappear for several days? Not if he was telling the truth about making it almost all the way through 1969 without going on such a bender. To be clear, it's not difficult to believe Jones could and did at some point do all these things while on a weeklong binge. It's just that he said he didn't go on a weeklong binge in the beginning of 1969. If that's true, then it means Tammy did not discover she was pregnant with George's child while he was gone getting drunk for several days, which is what she claimed happened. It means she did not keep the pregnancy to herself when Jones returned to drunkenly say he had decided against ever marrying her, only to wake up the next morning and surprise her out of nowhere by taking her to the courthouse to get married, which is what she claimed happened. So, the question becomes when did these things happen and in what order? Because if Jones was given to saying he didn't want to marry Tammy when he was blackout drunk, then they both agreed he was blackout drunk on the earlier trip to Florida. And it's pretty weird how the friend who started their motel room fight in Tammy's version of the Florida story completely vanished from the rest of the evening. Tammy said this guy pushed his way past her to get all the way inside the motel room before Jones woke up, started swinging, chased her outside, fell down the stairs and broke his wrist. Despite the fact this friend could not have missed any of these events, as soon as he served the narrative purpose of starting the fight, then Tammy's story had no further use for him and he disappeared from her account of the night.

When she looked back while running away, all she saw was Jones lying motionless in the parking lot with a broken wrist. There was no friend calling down from the second-story walkway or crouching over Jones' body to see if he was alright. We're supposed to believe this guy who George knew well enough to rent his vacation home to and invite out for drinks would simply leave him for dead in a Florida parking lot. But if that guy really never came back to the motel to accidentally start a fight between Jones and Tammy, then what might they have been fighting about? While we're asking questions, isn't six months a long time for a couple to pretend to be married—onstage, in interviews, on television—after they've learned there's absolutely nothing standing in the way of them legally getting married? What could have been the hold up? In any case both George Jones and Tammy Wynette always agreed upon the official timeline. First, whatever his reasons, he finally and suddenly took her to a courthouse to get married. Then, a few days later, she told him she was pregnant. Both parties also agreed that George was thrilled to learn about the baby, then heartbroken to hear Tammy miscarried soon after the wedding.

◇　◇　◇

In March, a month after the courthouse wedding and the month "I'll Share My World with You" came out, George and Tammy and her daughters moved into what had previously been his vacation home outside of Lakeland, Florida, a suitably named area with many lakes approximately halfway between Tampa and Orlando. Lakeland in the year 1969 was home to just over forty thousand people, roughly 10 percent the population of Nashville at that time. It was a quiet place and the combined incomes of two country music superstars gave them plenty of time to relax and enjoy it. Even with half of George's songwriting royalties going to his ex-wife, he and Tammy were able to tour less often and still rake in money by earning two headliner-sized checks from every concert while sharing all their expenses, such as the band, vehicles, lodging, etc.

Their new neighbors in Lakeland were Cliff and Maxine Hyder, a married couple who were a bit older than Jones and Tammy, and they all quickly became good friends. They would spend hours playing a board game called Aggravation, a variation on the game most Americans would recognize as Parcheesi, Trouble or Sorry!. It's fitting George Jones met this game under the name Aggravation, though. Not so much because he was competitive but because he couldn't stand to take more than what he believed was his fair share of losing. He'd treat each of his moves as if it were gravely important, deliberating at length before acting, and if that level of concentration wasn't enough to prevent multiple losses in a row, then he'd invariably get angry enough to wait until everyone had left, wait until Tammy had gone to bed, then sneak off and smash the Aggravation board into pieces. They needed to own multiple units of the game at all times to account for such incidents. This was him sober, by the way. Both Tammy and George agreed he rarely ever drank at home the first year in Lakeland. Their lighter touring schedule made it much easier to avoid the problems of his past.

Then they returned to Nashville for the 1969 DJ Convention and the CMA Awards. Like an addict leaving rehab and moving right back into an apartment across the hall from their drug dealer, Jones picked up where he left off as soon as he hit the city. His side of the story was essentially the same as always: he caught up with some old friends and, before he knew it, got drunker than he intended, which was all it took to send Tammy into a rage. According to her, as soon as they checked into the hotel George said he had some errands to run and disappeared. Since Tammy was nominated for Female Vocalist of the Year for the second year in a row she needed to do her hair and makeup instead of staying with George to keep an eye on him. Several hours later the front desk called the hotel room to say a young lady was waiting in a car out front to pick up Mr. George Jones. According to Tammy, that's what made her mad. She ran down to the lobby and out the front door to yell at the woman in the car about how she wasn't taking Mr. George Jones anywhere. A few minutes after she returned to the hotel room Jones came tearing in, saying how dare she tell people where he could and couldn't go or who with, embarrassing him in front of his friends, etc. Tammy said he shoved her, causing her face to hit a wall, and she felt her cheek instantly begin to swell up and bruise as Jones ran out of the room. She tried and failed to cover the physical abuse with makeup, then put on a wig that she pulled down low over her face, hoping it would at least cover some of the swelling.

Jimmy McDonough's 2010 biography of Tammy Wynette does not print a single word about her and George Jones attending the 1969 CMAs, perhaps because this was one of her most egregious and easily disproven fabrications. It's important to understand how much the archival aspect of the Internet has changed our concepts of news media's permanence and, in turn, what events we can and cannot lie about years after the fact. When Tammy published that story in her 1979 autobiography she had no clue a few decades of technological advancement would make it so easy for anyone who cares to find high-res photographs, taken from multiple angles and with differential lighting, of Tammy attending and accepting awards at the 1969 CMAs. It's true she wore a very bad wig, probably because falling into a rage (over her husband's drinking or an attractive young woman trying to take him to an industry party or whatever else) left her real hair too messed up too close to showtime to fix it back up. But the wig was definitely not pulled down low around her face, neither to cover up swelling and bruising nor for any other reason, and no part of her face was swollen or bruised. It's also important to understand that Tammy's autobiography was written while in a physically abusive relationship with a different man, who she had already decided to protect by telling many lies to many people. Being that we know she appropriated other people's stories to tell as if they were her own, we know she consistently portrayed ordinary humans as larger-than-life heroes or villains and she created false timelines to present more flattering sequences of events . . . It is absolutely fair to wonder if Tammy Wynette found a way to open up about George Richey shoving her head into a wall by backdating and attributing the abuse to George Jones. Though Jones' autobiography did not acknowledge or respond to Tammy's allegations of abuse at the 1969 CMAs, elsewhere in the book—after denying several other persistent rumors, like the one where he's supposed to've snapped the heels off 150 pairs of Tammy's shoes so she couldn't walk out on him or the one where he's supposed to've held a gun on her and made her spend a few hours watching him do cocaine, despite the fact he never even tried cocaine until years after they were divorced—Jones said the truth is Tammy was the one who often violently attacked him. He was not the only source to say this. He also claimed he only retaliated once, by slapping her in the face. He didn't specify when that happened but the available evidence would point to an incident at home in Lakeland, Florida. One day Tammy's daughters ran over to Cliff and Maxine Hyder's house for help stopping a fight between Tammy and Jones. By the time the Hyders arrived, Jones was gone and all Tammy would say, over and over, was that she'd hit him first.

◇　◇　◇

In November 1969, the month after the CMAs, Tammy went back in the studio with Jones to record her most blatant uncredited vocal to date on "Never Grow Cold." Husband and wife shared the writing credit for the song but all they did was put new lyrics over the gospel number "Where We'll Never Grow Old," which Jones had recorded several years earlier. Where Tammy's uncredited voice on Jones' recordings was previously blended in with a Nashville-style chorus, here she's much louder in the mix and outright harmonizing with Jones. As there's no mistaking the voice of Tammy Wynette, Pappy Daily avoided a lawsuit by shelving the session for over a year, until after George left Musicor for Epic, possibly with exit terms giving Pappy the right to issue these recordings. Anyone still curious to hear examples of why George Jones was considered The Greatest Country Singer Ever would do well to listen to his cut of "A Wound Time Can't Erase" from these same sessions. On each chorus he turns the word "wound" into a seven second, four syllable word, demonstrating perfect breath and pitch control the whole way through. Tammy also went in the studio on her own while in Nashville for the 1969 award season. That's when she recorded the previously mentioned single "I'll See Him Through," an album filler cover of Jones' hit "I'll Share My World with You" and a song Billy Sherrill wrote in order to avoid being sued . . .

Art Linkletter had recently ended a near-thirty-year run of his wildly popular *Kids Say the Darndest Things* TV and radio segment, in which young children were prompted to give unintentionally hilarious responses to questions and topics they didn't fully understand. Since a similar theme had already proven very successful for Tammy Wynette ("I Don't Wanna Play House," "D-I-V-O-R-C-E," etc.), Billy Sherrill decided to repackage such suitable material into a compilation LP titled *Kids Say the Darndest Things*. Then Epic's lawyers informed him they could be sued if the tracklist didn't contain a song with that title, so Billy and Glenn Sutton wrote one, custom-tailoring lyrics to the Tammy Wynette universe of disappeared daddies and left-behind mommies. Well, Billy brought the tape to Epic's legal department and they must have decided they could still be sued because the recording was shelved until 1973, when someone finally just called Art Linkletter and asked if Epic could release the single and LP. He said he didn't care. The song went to #1 four years after it was recorded, a testament to Billy Sherrill's skill at crafting timeless art like his hero Owen Bradley.

◇　　◇　　◇

Sticking with her go-to narrative device of placing a disastrous argument just before the surprise discovery of a pregnancy, Tammy's autobiography jumps from her account of the 1969 CMA Awards three months ahead to January 1970, when a doctor informed her of another pregnancy. George responded to the news with his own go-to behavior, attempting to straighten up and fly right in the months surrounding the birth of a child. In the year 1970, their home life was mostly stress free and he only backslid into serious binges a couple of times as he occupied himself with various community and business projects in Lakeland. He would soon terminate an eighteen-year professional alliance with Pappy Daily in order to marry his career to Tammy's. Despite such great effort, all of these illusions would fail to hold, as the marriage had started crumbling from the inside out ever since it began as a lie.

FIFTEEN

THRONES

◇ The Protestant Reformation in France ◇ Catherine de Médici Learns to Rule ◇
The Dilemma of the House of Guise ◇ A New Art Form, A Brutal Massacre ◇

Even if we suppose Catherine de Médici was able to resist curiosity and never read *The Prince*—still published today with Machiavelli's dedication to her father, the recipient of the original manuscript—what's a behind-the-scenes political exposé compared to two decades spent beneath the roof of the Valois dynasty in France? It's likely Catherine's father-in-law, King François, could have taught old Machiavelli a thing or two about relentless duplicity. None of the treaties François ever signed with Holy Roman Emperor Charles V meant anything more than, "Okay, you win for a while, and we can take a breather, but this isn't done." François then used each of those intermissions to go around forming new alliances in order to attack Charles again. When it came to politicking with religion François tried everything short of switching sides in the Reformation and declaring France a Protestant kingdom, which he couldn't do without severing his shadowy ties to the Médici popes. It's even possible he'd have gotten around to considering an official national conversion after Pope Clement died, cutting France's ties to Rome, except the following month someone snuck through the royal palace in the middle of the night, undetected (or at least undeterred) by royal guards, and posted a pro-Protestant, anti-Catholic pamphlet on François' bedroom door while the king was asleep inside. Perhaps playing directly into the wishes of whoever planted that pamphlet, François interpreted the stunt as a death threat and ended his previously tolerant acceptance of the Protestant Reformation within France. Thereafter, all Protestants—that's Lutherans, Calvinists and anyone aligned with any other non–Roman Catholic denomination of Christianity—risked imprisonment and perhaps execution as "heretics" should they actively practice their religion on French soil. Outside of France, however, François partnered with Protestant forces willing to join him in attacking Charles V. In fact, after Pope Clement died, François was able to enter a formal alliance that he'd pursued for about a decade with the Ottoman Empire, who were extremely anti-Catholic. For the first time in history Christian and Muslim thrones openly combined strength in opposition against a Christian throne. Naturally, many Catholic and Protestant noble families were horrified by François' pact but the geographical fact remained: Charles V's Holy Roman Empire was now sandwiched between Valois to the west and Ottoman to the east.

About ten years into this new arrangement of the old conflict, François died. The French crown would have then passed to Prince Henri's older brother, also named François, except by this time he was also dead. The likeliest explanation is the younger François never fully shook the tuberculosis he'd contracted while taking his father's place in a Spanish prison cell. However, as with the deaths of many important persons in the era, everyone assumed the young prince had been poisoned. See, he drank an iced beverage just before his health suddenly worsened and, prior to the existence of refrigeration, it was common knowledge that assassins preferred poisoning cold drinks because they'd be consumed quickly, before the precious ice could melt and before the victim realized anything was wrong. The servant who'd brought the drink was tortured until they "admitted" poisoning the heir and, some years later, Henri took the throne as King Henri II of France.

Henri picked up his father's reins, dug in the spurs, and doubled down on the family agenda, taking François' intolerance of the Protestant Reformation within France to its furthest extreme by issuing formal legislation outlawing any Protestant behavior, then mandating a death sentence for all convictions of heresy. Despite such severe policies Henri also maintained his father's military relationships with major Protestant forces located outside of France, the Ottoman Empire and really anyone else he could get to help continue the attacks against Charles V.

In 1555, a new pope was elected who immediately sided with Henri against Charles. Having spent an entire decade fighting his dead archnemesis' son while dealing with every other tiresome problem accumulated during thirty-five years as Holy Roman Emperor and king over approximately half of Western Europe, Charles decided to just quit. He straight up retired, splitting the Habsburg kingdom by ceding the Holy Roman Empire to his brother and leaving Spain to his son, Felipe II. It seems Henri was willing to accept France being bordered by separate branches of the House of Habsburg. He signed more peace treaties with Charles and, to show he really meant it this time, even offered one of his daughters as a wife for Felipe. Because Henri's fatal jousting accident occurred during a tournament held to celebrate his daughter becoming Queen of Spain through this marriage, there's no way to know for certain whether Henri truly intended permanent peace or merely needed another break from external warfare while trying to prevent France being torn apart by civil war.

For all of the same reasons the Protestant Reformation was instantly politicized throughout the rest of Europe, Henri spent the final years of his life learning why it may not have been an excellent idea to draw an immutable line in the dirt of his nation and proclaim anyone who stood on the other side of it an enemy. As citizens and noble families of France took their private and public positions, Henri realized about half of his entire kingdom stood at risk of flipping Protestant, whether motivated by religious true believers or power-hungry houses. Henri calling them heretics wouldn't stop it and neither would dying. He tried both, leaving the national stage perfectly set for an epic fight. Soon after that fight broke out, everyone began to realize what Catherine de Médici had been doing for the previous twenty-five years . . .

◇   ◇   ◇

Given the tragic circumstances of her birth and her horrific experiences during the nine month siege of Florence, most nobles at the Valois court assumed Catherine so meekly tolerated the widespread criticisms of her failures to produce a dowry or a royal child because she was simply grateful to be safe and grateful to be married to a prince, even if Henri was too in love with his weird teacher lady to pay Catherine any more attention than that required by the occasional attempt to make a baby. But the real reason she kept her silence was to watch and learn, waiting for the day when she'd need to fight for the throne. Catherine could not have been surprised when the House of Guise were first to move for France's crown after Henri's death. When Catherine's dowry had disappeared and nobles of the court loudly tried to get her replaced as Henri's bride? That outcry was instigated by the House of Guise, who likely hoped to replace Catherine with a woman of their own blood. When Catherine seemed unable to get pregnant for a period of ten years and nobles of the court continued loudly trying to have her replaced? That outcry, too, had been instigated by the House of Guise. When King François fell ill, knew he was dying and warned Henri which ambitious noble family to never trust and never allow too much power? He named the House of Guise.

Then Henri died, leaving his oldest son to take the throne as François II. Since the new king of France, at the age of fifteen, was already husband to Mary, Queen of Scots, niece of the two brothers at the head of the House of Guise, the Guise brothers swooped in and closed ranks around the boy, figuring they'd kindly kidnap young François and "influence" his reign in order to secure a win for their chosen side in the Reformation, which was Team Catholic. Team Protestant came up with a similar plan to storm the castle and capture the boy king but they botched the entire job, lost more than a thousand lives on their own side and ultimately accomplished nothing other than providing the House of Guise a chance to demonstrate strength. The Guise brothers confidently responded to the plot by arresting the most immediately threatening individual at the head of Team Protestant, a prince from the House of Bourbon in the neighboring kingdom of Navarre.

Up to that point in the conflict Catherine had stayed out of the whole thing. As long as everybody paying attention could see the Guise brothers were in control of the young king's "decisions," nobody placed the blame for those moves upon Catherine or her children, which was her only real concern. Same thing if the House of Guise and House of Bourbon wanted to engage in a power struggle against each other. It wasn't really any skin off Médic—er, Valois backs . . . until the Guise brothers arrested that Bourbon prince and set about trying to orchestrate his execution on trumped-up charges in the name of François II, who by this time had become fatally ill. It was something to do with his inner ear. Doctors weren't really sure, but they did know the boy would soon be dead. Since the House of Guise would lose any claim on the French throne the moment François died without an heir, they were prepared to kick off a full-scale civil war and see if destabilizing the whole country may provide an opportunity for their family to come out of the chaos on top. But the other thing about François dying without an heir was the throne would pass to his younger brother, Charles, then only ten years old and therefore in need of a regent to rule in his stead until he was of age to become king. You know, thirteen years old. So, before the Guise brothers could launch their civil war and ahead of her oldest son's impending death, Catherine made several secret alliances—most importantly with the House of Bourbon—gathering enough support to name herself queen-regent when François II died, which he did shortly thereafter.

As queen-regent, Catherine released the Bourbon prince and invited his house back to the Valois court, then called for peace talks between Catholic and Protestant leaders. When these summits failed to achieve anything meaningful, Catherine just started passing laws to relax the sanctioned intolerance of Protestants within France. In 1562, a couple years into her regency, she legalized Protestants practicing their religion within the privacy of their own homes and/or outside city limits. Pretty soon afterward, the duke of Guise heard about a mostly Protestant town where the residents had converted a barn outside the city walls into a church and held public services under the protection of the queen-regent's new law. So Guise went over there with a crew of his men and slaughtered everyone, which is typically regarded as the beginning of the French Wars of Religion, a thirty-five-year period of episodic violence between Catholics and Protestants that Catherine de Médici persistently tried to bring to an end during the reigns of her sons, King Charles IX and King Henri III.

Though Charles IX technically assumed the throne of France about a year into the Wars of Religion, Catherine remained the true power. The first thing she did when Charles became king was take him and a massive entourage (read: armed guard) on a two-year "grand tour" of France, ostensibly to show her young son his kingdom but more likely intended to keep him away from various treacherous forces at the royal court in Paris. Long after Charles believed he was merely consulting his mother on serious matters the way he consulted other advisors, Catherine used various tactics—including a famous network of beautiful women who gathered and dispersed information by seducing powerful men—to secretly manipulate Charles' council and court into doing Catherine's bidding. It does at least seem she truly was motivated by what she believed to be best for her family. But the same could be said for the House of Guise, who quickly realized doing pretty much whatever they wanted would result in both sides of the Wars of Religion eventually blaming Catherine, since she was known to be the true ruler of France. Her ongoing attempts to coordinate peace were easily made to look as though she refused to pick a side, like the daughter of a Médici playing Machiavellian politics by allowing everyone to remain in a perpetual struggle against each other while she sat above the fray. All the Guise needed to do was casually murder some Protestants every few years, preferably soon after Catherine promised all Protestants some additional measure of tolerance or protection. When Protestants then inevitably retaliated with their own acts of violence against Catholics or even just destruction of Church property, it gave the Guise brothers enough of an excuse to bring in a whole army and "crush the rebellion" with even greater violence, thereby forcing Catherine back to the Catholic fold while weakening her credibility in future attempts to negotiate peace. The Bourbon prince she once rescued eventually tired of this recurring cycle and tried again to kidnap France's young king but failed again. Following another couple years of war, the Bourbon prince was executed for his efforts. Having lost the leader of their movement, the Protestants were forced to return to peace talks while they regrouped, even though they knew any truce would be ignored by the House of Guise, who would undoubtedly continue to murder "heretics" whenever they pleased. This time, however, Catherine had a different plan.

Because the sincerest treaties were sealed with a marriage whenever possible, Catherine decided to marry one of her daughters to the next Bourbon prince, who had been raised Protestant by the Queen of Navarre, a woman who had completely outlawed Roman Catholicism in her country more than a decade earlier. The Queen of Navarre did not trust or even like Catherine de Médici, but this marriage would make it legal for Protestants to hold public office in France, thereby legitimizing the Protestant movement throughout all of France and dissolving Catholicism's sweeping monopoly over affairs of State. So, the Queen of Navarre moved to Paris in spring of 1572 to help plan a royal wedding. By the end of the summer she was dead. Like many others in this era who traveled a significant distance to another country where they may not have developed immunity to local varieties of various illnesses, she probably just got sick and died. But rumors instantly began to spread that the Queen of Navarre was poisoned by Catherine de Médici, whose daughter's fiancé had suddenly become King of Navarre.

◇   ◇   ◇

It's damn near impossible to estimate the percentage of bullshit in any story featuring Catherine de Médici, even if it comes from a seemingly credible history book. She was famous her whole life, her vilification amongst the masses began at the age of ten and every single person in this story had motives to lie, plus an instruction manual for how to do it, plus use of Gutenberg's new printing press to help the lies stick. Thanks to political pamphlets, many people during Catherine's lifetime truly believed she was a Satan worshipper who murdered and ate children. Others believed she was a peace-seeking widow, pushed to the throne by circumstances beyond her control, brought to power not by her own political ambition but by a desire to protect her family.

Probably because her name has been well known for hundreds of years and many interesting developments of early modern history do have a connection to the story of her life, today Catherine de Médici is also falsely credited with introducing all manner of Italian inventions and customs to France, many of them for some reason having to do with dining conventions and cuisine. If a friend of yours ever starts saying something like, "Hey, did you know Catherine de Médici is the reason—" you're probably about to hear a lie, unless that sentence ends with the invention of carousels or ballet.

One of the reasons nobody ever stopped thinking of her as Catherine de Médici even after she married into the Valois dynasty was because Catherine never stopped acting like a Médici. As soon as she became regent the arts and entertainment budget in France went through the roof and stayed there, even after all the royal money was gone and she had to borrow more to keep up appearances. The Médici family always believed in spending big on public and political opinion of the dynasty: extravagant architecture, especially buildings for the Church; patronage of important artists and inventors whose work would similarly stand the test of time, like Michelangelo, Leonardo da Vinci and Bartolomeo Cristofori; huge parties that would still be remembered centuries later. Every noble family did these things to the extent they were able, but the House of Médici came to power by having more money than nearly all of those losers, so the House of Médici did things bigger, much bigger. Where other houses may hold a party over several days, featuring tournaments and plays and dancing, Catherine de Médici literally turned it into an art form.

After her husband Henri's death, when the nobility of France accepted tilting at rings as a suitable replacement for the deadly joust, the already blurry line between chivalry and pageantry disappeared forever. In Catherine's France, tournaments soon evolved from "little wars," heavy on chivalry and bloodshed, to little pageants, retaining some element of contest but much less to do with violence and much more to do with bloodlessly parading around in magnificent costumes. This safer alternative to the tournament was referred to as a *carrousel*, the French take on the Italian word for "little war," later applied to the merry-go-rounds with fake horses commoners could ride to pretend they were in one of Catherine's royal parades. She eventually got the idea to combine versions of all these typical chivalric entertainments into days-long pageants that included a prototype of modern ballet. These massive feats of set design were built to showcase music, dance and stories centered upon the usual chivalric themes of love and war, often complete with epic fake battles. To give some idea of the grand scale, Catherine once staged a ballet on an island, so the audience of nobles needed to be transported to the venue by boats. The show began with actors in one boat fighting off an attack from stagehands operating a huge fake whale.

◇　　◇　　◇

Despite rumors Catherine de Médici had poisoned their recently deceased queen, thousands of Navarrese Protestants who were promised safe passage through France for their king's wedding to Catherine's daughter came to Paris for the celebration. As part of the festivities, Catherine presented a ballet featuring a plot based on the present violent conflict between the individual Catholic and Protestant leaders in attendance, with some of those leaders (like Catherine's son, King Charles IX) playing themselves in the production. A few days later, after nearly all of the thousands of Protestants in Paris for the royal wedding were dragged into the streets and murdered, everyone began to wonder what they've wondered since: whether Catherine's ballet was meant to inspire resolution or aggravation in the Wars of Religion.

It doesn't seem likely she'd want her son Charles to be consumed by guilt over the massacre, fall ill and die. Nor is it likely she'd have welcomed the resulting distrust of her next and final son to rule, Henri III. Catherine couldn't have enjoyed watching the youngest Henri refuse her counsel while only making worse and worse decisions until he was finally assassinated by a monk named Jacques Clément (possible relation to Cowboy Jack unknown). It doesn't seem possible even the House of Guise could have been happy about every single one of Catherine's sons dying without heirs because that's what ended nearly three hundred years of Catholic rule by the House of Valois in France, leaving the throne to none other than the new Protestant King of Navarre from the House of Bourbon. None of these people could have predicted any of these events. Nor could they have known a hundred years later the last Habsburg to rule Spain would also die childless, leaving the Spanish throne to the great-great-grandson of that Bourbon King of Navarre and France. But all of that is what happened and it's only part of the very long story about how a French teenager from the House of Bourbon who didn't even speak Spanish became King Philippe V of Spain.

SIXTEEN

COUNTRY ROYALTY

◇ George and Tammy's Florida Dream Home ◇ The Costs of Recording Duets ◇
Billy Sherrill Sells a Fiction ◇ Lipstick Graffiti ◇ Secret Habits ◇
◇ Somebody Trashes the House ◇ A Fake Divorce, a Real Divorce ◇

In the early 1980s, George Jones shared one of his recent dreams with a reporter. George was driving a car with his ex-wife Tammy Wynette behind the wheel of another car on the road ahead. George understood himself to be chasing after her. But then the road began to flood with water around George's car. Tammy was fast enough to stay just ahead of the water and her car gradually pulled away from him. Even though George kept his gas pedal smashed to the floor, Tammy pulled farther and farther ahead until she was entirely out of sight and George woke up from the dream.

About a decade earlier, near the beginning of the year 1970, Tammy discovered she was pregnant. George reacted to the news by trying to straighten up his behavior and assemble a perfect world for his family ahead of the baby's arrival. He convinced Tammy to let him spend one hundred thousand dollars of their own money on a run-down, sixteen room house upon five acres of land in Florida. This miniature mansion, which they soon took to calling Old Plantation due to its early twentieth-century Colonial Revival design, would become their new home once George fixed it up. He carried out the renovation with a particular sense of urgency, hoping to have the house finished by the time the baby was born so his child's earliest memories would be set in a small palace rather than a construction project. While working on the house George also bought more than thirty-five acres of surrounding property and once again set about building an outdoor country music concert venue. He climbed up on bulldozers and backhoes to level the camping and picnic areas himself, then dug out fishponds and scooped holes to plant rows of trees and shrubbery. With all this manual labor and the additional workload of convincing neighbors and the local government to let him essentially put Permanent Country Music Bonnaroo in their backyards, Jones found very little time or energy for binge drinking, so he didn't. But he also took a page from his father's book and kept bottles of liquor stashed in certain trees and bushes on the property in case he felt the need to sneak a sip or two.

Though their concert schedule remained light compared to the way George had toured in the past, he and Tammy did need to occasionally work in order to fund those two major projects in Florida. Tammy continued to perform through her seventh month of pregnancy. Thanks to the pop crossover success of "Stand By Your Man," their concerts were attended by larger audiences than ever before and fans bore witness to evidence of fertility between the couple they began calling The King and Queen of Country Music. This baby being the child of two country music superstars, there were great expectations. Billy Sherrill said he knew the bloodlines were so good he intended to have a recording contract ready to sign in the delivery room. Two months prior to her due date, Tammy's doctor ordered her to stay home and rest, which meant no more performing and, more crucially, no more ensuring George stayed out of trouble. Sure enough, he never even made it to the first concert without her. Somewhere between Florida and Iowa, he just disappeared. Tammy spent six days in a panic while stalling lawsuits from angry concert promoters by promising makeup dates at no additional cost, even though she couldn't be certain her husband was alive. After nearly a week without news, one of George's sisters called to say he'd been dumped on her porch in Beaumont, Texas, in the middle of the night, mumbling something about how someone must have slipped a drug into one of his drinks. But that was his biggest lapse of 1970 and, like Shirley Jones before her, Tammy Wynette observed a year of mostly sober George following the birth of their child, Tamala Georgette Jones, on October 5. The family moved into Old Plantation later that month and George focused on the launch of his music park.

From the initial purchase of their new house and property through the additional land and renovations for the concert venue, it wound up costing $250,000 to bring this whole scheme from imagination to reality. Part of that cost was a $20,000 marquee at the front entrance to let travelers know they'd arrived at Old Plantation Music Park, "Home of Country Music's George Jones & Tammy Wynette." George placed the covered stage about a half mile from the Old Plantation house so audience members in the concert area could look over during a show to see George and Tammy's home right there. On April 4, 1971, the marquee advertised Conway Twitty as the grand opening's headliner. With Conway a few years into his Owen Bradley–produced run at the top of the Country charts and the certainty of freewheeling performances from both George and Tammy, the park hosted a capacity crowd of more than ten thousand people. Tammy secretly flew in George's old buddy Charley Pride, also several years into a decade-plus run of #1 Country hits, and Charley played his own surprise set. Billy Sherrill and other industry pals flew down from Nashville for the occasion. A great time was had by all. Since George actually charged admission at the front gate this time, the day was also a huge financial success. Unlike the Rhythm Ranch debacle, he managed to create a sustainable operation in Old Plantation Music Park and they continued to book major talent. Sammi Smith, Del Reeves, Bill Anderson, Jack Greene and Jeannie Seely are only a few of the country stars who headlined there. (Strangely, David Houston was booked to headline at Old Plantation despite the fact that a handful of years later Tammy Wynette's autobiography would make the claim Houston and his manager both acted like massive pricks toward her in the 1960s.)

In 1972, prominent segregationist George Wallace survived an assassination attempt that left him unable to walk. Civil rights activist Shirley Chisholm, then the only Black woman serving in Congress, caused a national controversy by visiting Wallace in the hospital. Less surprising: about a month later, Old Plantation Music Park hosted a fundraiser for Wallace's presidential primary campaign. Based on George Jones never really demonstrating much of an interest in politics and Tammy Wynette discussing politics in nearly every interview she ever gave—plus her strong ties to Alabama, where Wallace was governor; plus the fact she once said "this business with the [Black] people has been exaggerated" to defend Wallace and remained friendly with Wallace and his wife for many years—it seems extremely likely the Old Plantation fundraiser for Wallace was her idea. Either way, Wallace lost the election.

◇　◇　◇

When Billy Sherrill attended the music park's grand opening it may have been more than a miniature vacation to support Tammy's new business venture. Two weeks later, Tammy and George traveled to Nashville and, for the first time, recorded together with Billy. This was not quid pro quo, which would've seen Jones defying his contract to record for Epic the way Tammy had previously gone against her own contract to cut tape for Musicor. This was a full transfer of allegiance and it came at great cost. To say Pappy Daily was unhappy to release George from his Musicor contract would be an understatement, since Pappy's very existence in the music industry now depended entirely on his relationship to George Jones. Though it's unclear precisely when George began negotiating the terms of his early departure, the exact details of which are similarly unclear, we do know the eventual deal included George paying somewhere around one hundred thousand dollars and relinquishing future royalties from his Musicor catalog. In other words, he was required to pay Musicor the same amount of money he'd just spent on a small mansion while also forfeiting the future income he otherwise would have received for his previous six years of work as a recording artist. Compared to this financial loss, lighting hundred dollar bills on fire was a joke. As for the rest of the exit terms, we can only make educated guesses based on the evidence. For example, it seems quite likely Epic was obligated to wait until the year 1972 before releasing any George Jones solo recordings because, even though George continued to cut solo material for Musicor (a.k.a. performing unpaid labor) throughout 1971, Epic only recorded him as Tammy Wynette's duet partner until near the end of the year, when this presumed embargo was set to expire. It's also possible Pappy Daily may have negotiated for some kind of control over what material Tammy and George would record together for Epic in 1971. Their first duet single was a new version of "Take Me," a song George wrote with Leon Payne and took to the Country Top 10 several years earlier on Musicor. It went Top 10 again for Tammy and George on Epic, which sent a hefty chunk of money back in Pappy Daily's direction, as did the fact that 50 percent of the songs on Epic's first Tammy and George duet LP were published by Pappy. Despite there being one extremely likely cause for this song selection, when George's biographer Bob Allen cited Peanutt Montgomery's claim that Pappy Daily was allowed to help pick those songs, Billy Sherrill staunchly denied the existence of such a deal, since such a deal would be illegal. The only other possible reason for Billy to record so many of Pappy's songs would be if he picked material George already knew in order to help those first duet sessions go a little easier for everyone involved.

With several years of experience performing duets in concert by this point, one would expect Tammy and George to be pretty good at singing together. One would be wrong. They excelled in showcasing the energy of their relationship's honeymoon phase, allowing audiences the opportunity to watch two newlywed stars adore and/or goof off with each other onstage. As for the actual singing, they were great at taking turns on the microphone while trading verses but, when it came time to sync up their phrasing and harmonize on a chorus, things often went poorly. While George's range and versatility did place him in an entirely separate class of vocalist from Tammy, most of their struggles with performing duets were a result of his tendency to never sing a song the same way twice. The very thing that made him so effective as an artist, his willingness and ability to entirely give himself over to an emotional connection with a song, meant the specific way he may phrase a lyric or lend emphasis to certain words was as unpredictable as any given person's day-to-day changes in mood. Similarly adventurous vocal partners in his past—Johnny PayCheck, Melba Montgomery, Gene Pitney—were only successful because of their ability to jump on George's wavelength and follow him wherever he took a song. Conversely, Tammy Wynette was the kind of vocalist who tried her best to sing a song exactly the same way every time. No matter how often she said their voices blended together as if by "magic" from the very beginning, she was not the kind of singer who could easily harmonize with George Jones on the fly and was regularly frustrated in her attempts to do so. Video clips of their live performances together gain a comedic twist once you learn to recognize how hard they're trying to sync up, taking turns staring at each other's lips and radically lowering the volume of their voices to pull back after small mistakes. Tammy often breaks into a smile whenever she's able to successfully guess what Jones will do and match him. Billy Sherrill clocked this reality right away in their first studio session and, for the rest of his life, consistently spoke of how bad it was for his liver's health to try recording George and Tammy singing together, how it upped his scotch intake and drove all three of 'em nuts. Once you know what to listen for, the problem is evident on every song cut in their first sessions. It's most obvious on "You're Everything" because the married couple accompany each other for the entire song and routinely fail to simultaneously land on consonant sounds. It's in the way they barely miss beginning the word "cold" at the same time in the chorus of "Never Grow Cold." It's in the way their "L" sounds are out of sync all over "Livin' on Easy Street," a flaw you won't find in the recording of George and Melba Montgomery singing the same song in their final session together several years earlier. It's why George and Tammy simply take turns singing separately on several songs, like "After Closing Time." It's why Tammy's voice is barely on "Take Me," the lone single released from their first LP, *We Go Together*.

In addition to the above considerations, the songs on *We Go Together* were all selected to serve the public's perception of this romantic relationship, which was informed by newspaper headlines and concert appearances. Fans believed George and Tammy were true soulmates, two broken halves made whole through a perfect fit, each artist's persona providing the rescue desperately summoned by the persona of the other. The audience of this play thought Tammy Wynette's old-fashioned approach to love had cured whatever was so wrong for so long with George Jones, bringing his heartbroken prodigal son phase to a close and transforming him from The King of Broken Hearts into the man who deserved a love like Tammy's, a husband whose name she could be proud to put hers behind on the side of a tour bus. Billy Sherrill's role in constructing and delivering this fantasy cannot be overstated. Just as much as George or Tammy, Billy performed this fairy tale for this audience, starting with his creation and initial revisions of the Tammy Wynette character.

Back in October of 1967, "I Don't Wanna Play House" had recently gone #1 and Billy knew he wanted to lean into the Divorced Woman thing for Tammy's character . . . but Bobby Braddock had not yet written "D-I-V-O-R-C-E." So, Billy did what he usually did and cracked open a bottle of scotch with Glenn Sutton in order to write a song. For "Good," they pulled from Wynette Byrd's real-life background to make Tammy a barroom waitress. When a lonely customer asks her to dance to a song on the jukebox, Tammy sees an opportunity to get away from the wrong side of town with a man who doesn't know enough about her or her past to suspect she's anything but good. The man does take her away from the honky-tonk life but the end of the song finds her right back in the barroom, waitressing again, presumably because of her cheating ways, because she's *not* good. On the same album, Billy and Glenn wrote "Take Me to Your World," in which Tammy's no-good waitress begs her ex for forgiveness, saying she's ready to try again, ready for him to take her away to his world. This waitress was the kind of woman Billy's final version of the Tammy character would forever be warning us about: the younger or prettier or easier woman who'll take your man if you don't stand by him, swing when and where he wants, love him all the way, etc. On the first album with George, Billy again cast Tammy as a waitress by writing "After Closing Time" with Danny Walls and Norro Wilson. The first three lines are essentially a rewrite of "Good." As before, Tammy begins by telling us she's a honky-tonk waitress who'll dance to the jukebox with male customers but then George pipes up from the corner to let us know none of that matters because everyone knows she's going home with him at the end of the night. The story of "After Closing Time" justifies the waitress from "Good," suggesting her previous relationships failed not due to her own moral weakness but because she believed those men were right to try taking her away from the honky-tonk world rather than join her there the way George does.

When George Jones officially signed a ten-year contract with Epic on October 1, 1971, Billy Sherrill gained full control over the other main character in his Tammy stories. With a small team of songwriters, all skilled at crafting narratives which felt like behind-the-scenes glimpses of their real life, Billy was now able to play out the story across the duets and both artists' solo LPs, exploiting and building upon the George and Tammy narrative created by all the newspaper headlines, interviews, album covers and song lyrics. Billy and Glenn Sutton wrote George's first Epic single, "We Can Make It." Here, the George Jones character sings with metaphysical certainty of love as an unbreakable chain wrapped around himself and the woman we know is Tammy "Stand By Your Man" Wynette. These two are safe from the rough world within each other's arms, where they provide each other shelter from the storm and he no longer needs wine to keep him warm. The record went Top 10.

Billy always claimed the great financial sacrifice George made to prematurely leave Musicor was because of how much George loved Tammy and wanted to record with her, which is precisely the story you'd expect to hear from a man who stood to gain so much by selling it. George eventually decided to claim his early exit from Musicor was in order to escape the greedy villain Pappy Daily. But unnecessarily sacrificing an actual fortune would not be any kind of answer to such a money problem. Plus, there's the fact that in 1975, his memory of then-recent events still fully intact, George told *Country Music* magazine, "Pappy was a fine old man. He really was. But, like everyone else, he has his faults." Based on many sources, including George himself in other interviews, it seems the greatest of Pappy Daily's faults was continuing to stay invested in Melba Montgomery's career after George and Tammy Wynette became romantically involved. Should anyone even say the name of the woman George spent several years pursuing, Tammy was known to begin yelling and cussing up a storm. If anyone ever sent Pappy Daily the memo, he must have ignored it. Not only did he keep Melba signed to Musicor, he continued pushing George to work with her because their duets were far more successful than her solo releases. One day, near the end of George's time with Pappy, Tammy answered the telephone at home to find Melba Montgomery on the line, saying something about a session Pappy scheduled for Melba and George to do overdubs on old recordings so Musicor could release another duet LP. Tammy went ballistic. That overdub session never took place and George soon developed a sudden need to leave Musicor even if it cost him an arm and a leg, which it did.

Melba Montgomery's brother, Peanutt, somehow survived the transition from Musicor to Epic, remaining one of George's best friends, best drinking partners and sometimes rhythm guitarist for the Jones Boys on tour. Peanutt also migrated from Pappy Daily's publishing company over to Billy Sherrill's inner circle of songwriters. While Tammy tolerated all of this, she didn't love it. Whenever Peanutt was around the odds were significantly higher that George may disappear on a weeklong binge. But Tammy either recognized the friendship was too strong to break or felt the risk of occasionally losing her husband to chaos was worth a hit songwriter staying in close enough proximity to create the sort of near-documentary material required by Billy Sherrill's methods. (Early minor hits aside, Peanutt Montgomery began handing in legendary country songs about halfway through George's Musicor period. Bob Dylan once told *Rolling Stone* the George Jones cut of Peanutt's "Small Time Laboring Man" was one of his favorite records of 1968. Also in 1968, George recorded one of Peanutt's masterpieces, "Where Grass Won't Grow." While neither single was a major hit, most fans consider both records to be among Jones' best. Peanutt also wrote George's final Top 10 at Musicor, "Right Won't Touch a Hand," which is phenomenal.) After "We Can Make It" became George's first hit record at Epic, they followed it up with Peanutt's take on the same soulmates-disappear-from-the-world-into-their-love theme, "Loving You Could Never Be Better." It went #2 Country, barely missing the top of the chart, and fit so perfectly into Billy Sherrill's storyline he also had Tammy cut it as filler for a solo LP. From then on most of Billy's albums for Tammy and George, together and separately, featured at least one song written by or with Peanutt, who was better positioned than nearly anyone to create compositions which seemed to provide behind-the-scenes glimpses of what the public believed they knew about this relationship. Another example would be how "The Man Worth Lovin' You" on George's fantastic second album for Epic explains the way Tammy's character redeemed the troubled King of Broken Hearts character who Jones fans knew from concert performances, newspaper articles and gossip.

Perhaps recognizing the inevitability of these two particular country stars' private lives spilling out into the media, Billy told his crew of songwriters to use their personal and professional access to write ahead of where the audience currently was in the George and Tammy story. Among that crew of songwriters was Tammy herself, who Billy had always encouraged to write her own songs. While many of her official writing credits (like those of George Jones) were the product of handshake deals and not her actual pen, some of what she really did put to paper soon after marrying George included heavy foreshadowing. Written with Billy in 1971, Tammy's #2 Country single "We Sure Can Love Each Other" was not the romantic boast suggested by the title. Rather, the lyrics reveal a couple equally talented at hurting each other and the chorus points out how much effort is required to keep their love alive. Tammy wrote the B-side with Carmol Taylor. Today, "Fun" is a rarity, unavailable on major streaming services. But it would probably have been a hit if Billy waited a couple years to release it as an A-side after the public learned more details about the reality of Tammy's marriage to George Jones. Here, Tammy typecasts herself as a housewife who's stuck at home while her husband is off chasing fun. Even though her own idea of fun is having him around and taking care of him, it breaks her heart when he comes home and she can see spending time with her is no fun for him at all. Then there's "A Lovely Place to Cry," which Tammy and Peanutt Montgomery wrote for the second duet LP with George. By the time of this session Tammy had suggested the solution that would be used for the rest of their careers to save everyone the headache of trying to record her and George singing together: he put down his vocal first and alone in order for her to study his part and then overdub hers. As a result of this improvement to their process, they sound more in sync than ever before . . . while singing about how the exterior beauty of their home hides a love that's dead inside.

◇   ◇   ◇

Despite Tammy's misgivings toward the Montgomerys, Peanutt and his wife, Charlene, were semi-regular houseguests at Old Plantation in this period. Tammy would sometimes accuse George of wanting to have sex with Charlene Montgomery, but nobody ever suspected she really meant it and perhaps only thought George would be less likely to fly off into a whirlwind binge if he believed Tammy was already mad at him for something else. One night, early in 1972, the Montgomerys were staying at Old Plantation when Charlene heard George's dogs barking outside after everyone had gone to bed. She walked down the hall, knocked on the door of the main bedroom to tell George and Tammy about the noise, then everyone went outside to look around. After not finding anything out of place, they all turned to go inside when Wynette screamed. Someone had used red lipstick to write the word "PIG" in big letters on a back door. Terrified, Charlene and Wynette ran inside and locked themselves in a bedroom while Jones and Peanutt searched the property again with renewed purpose. They turned up no additional graffiti, no evidence of intruders, no answers.

Later, after Charlene realized Wynette had stopped acting scared once they were away from their husbands and locked in the bedroom, she remembered seeing Tammy deeply invested in a book about the Charles Manson cult in California, who used the blood of victims to write words like "PIG" on the walls of buildings where they committed murders. (That book was probably Ed Sanders' best-selling *The Family*, published in 1971.) Charlene began to suspect Wynette had snuck outside and vandalized her own home with her own lipstick, likely so George would be too worried for Tammy's safety to go chase down some fun.

Another of Tammy's favorite tactics to keep George from drinking was to pretend to get drunk herself. She knew if she seemed to be getting tipsy her husband would set down his own glass to watch out for her, so Tammy would sometimes conspire with a tour manager or band member to keep her in steady supply of vodka cocktails which secretly contained no vodka. She'd drain glass after glass, acting as if each one made her a little more drunk, and this would usually cause George to put the brakes on his own drinking for the night. One reason George may have been so concerned about her hitting the booze could have been the way it interacted with the prescription "diet pill"—Preludin a.k.a. speed—Tammy started taking back when still married to Don Chapel. Assuming several band members and other witnesses were not lying when they recalled Tammy erupting into violent outbursts and trying to beat the shit out of George, it's safe to say the speed contributed more than a little bit to such aggressive behavior and adding alcohol to the mix wouldn't have helped. Of course, another reason George may have been so concerned over Tammy hitting the booze could be the way it interacted with the Valium that she was also prescribed.

In 1977, two years after Tammy was hospitalized for a drug overdose, Joan Dew wrote, "Although they are definitely real, most of [Tammy's] medical problems are brought on by the fact that she never allows herself enough time to recuperate from an illness or operation before heading back to work." By the time Joan walked away from writing Tammy's 1979 autobiography two years later, even if she couldn't put everything in the book, she'd seen enough to know the truth. Yes, there were doctors involved and, yes, Wynette did a much better job than Jones of hiding it, but she was a drug addict who quickly found a new doctor whenever pen stopped being put to prescription pad and/or the word "rehab" came up. Assuming Wynette did not fabricate the stubborn kidney infection she said she suffered while married to Euple Byrd, then her major health problems predated the name Tammy Wynette. She undoubtedly started taking heavy-duty prescription medications before ever getting involved with George Jones. But during the process of giving birth to Georgette in 1970 something went wrong and the doctors gave her an emergency hysterectomy. At that point she was prescribed more and stronger painkillers than ever before. In late 1971, she passed out behind the wheel of a moving car and crashed through two trees near her home in Florida. The official narrative in newspaper articles pinned the accident on blood sugar levels causing her to lose consciousness. In 1973, Wynette was hospitalized nearly a dozen times for various reasons. Joan Dew clearly stated that Tammy would often knowingly exacerbate her own health problems by prematurely resuming a regular tour schedule before incisions from previous surgeries could be allowed to properly heal, thus necessitating return trips to a hospital where Tammy would invariably be given more painkillers. While it's impossible to know how often Tammy intentionally reopened wounds or at what point in her long career as an addict she discovered such tactics to score more drugs, nearly a dozen hospitalizations in one year is a lot. Whether or not she was already actively harming herself, the end result was the same: excessive scar tissue formed on both the outside and inside of her body, which further complicated every medical issue she faced throughout the rest of her life.

Maybe it really was her blood sugar that caused her to pass out while driving a car and run down two palm trees in 1971. Maybe she spent so much of 1973 laid up in hospitals for completely legitimate reasons. Or, maybe the story of how Tammy Wynette's marriage to George Jones turned so wrong in the year 1972 is about more than only his substance abuse. Decades later, Joan Dew would characterize Wynette to biographer Jimmy McDonough as the kind of person who became obsessed with acquiring something (or someone) then lost interest after getting what she wanted. This was one of many examples—and several have already been given—of the fascinating frequency with which friends, family, coworkers and other close sources tried to explain the behavior of Tammy Wynette or George Jones by offering a description of one that could just as easily be applied to the other. Another would be the time Tammy's daughter Jackie said, "I think Mom liked chaos. She liked having things goin' on even if they were bad." This is not to say any of these statements entirely summed up Tammy or George or that they shared identical personalities. For instance, he certainly didn't care as much as she did about staying famous and she shared none of his psychological issues involving money. But where the audience of this story was sold the idea of two characters who came together to form a whole, the actual human beings in the marriage much more closely resembled a mirror image, two broken pieces who couldn't form a whole because the only places they touched was at the points of their jagged edges. For either of these people to rescue the other would be as improbable as one drowning person saving the life of another drowning person.

After George succeeded in assembling a new dream home and sustainable concert venue business for his latest attempt at an ideal life, he was able to relax and enjoy it while drinking less. But "less" for George Jones merely meant it wasn't as often he'd take off on a serious binge. The weight he gained from Tammy's country cooking during these relatively sober years soon led her to put him on the same "diet pills" as her, so adding booze could send Jones roaring out like a tornado that crossed several state lines before it died down a week or more later.

One morning, in 1972, he woke up at home in Florida, got dressed and left in his car to drive less than a mile down to the music park's office building . . . where he never arrived. He just kept driving. Nobody knew where he went or how long he'd be gone. This time he only wound up disappearing for most of a day, but when he returned he was extremely drunk. Tammy claimed she enlisted the help of an employee to get Jones in bed, which they were nearly successful in doing until he violently sprang awake, tried to fight everyone, then misinterpreted Tammy's running away as her trying to leave him for good. So he picked up a gun to stop her for good. She ran out the front door and into the dark night, screaming as she heard the gun fire behind her. She kept running until she made it to a telephone and called a private detective friend, who said not to contact the police unless she wanted to become the next day's news and to just meet him back at the house. Their ex-neighbor, Cliff Hyder, happened to be on the premises, so he and the private eye and Tammy all hid in the bushes outside Old Plantation, listening to what sounded a lot like Jones picking up everything he could lift inside the house and throwing it into everything he couldn't lift—TVs hitting walls, chairs hitting china cabinets, that kind of party. After a while, everyone outside the house decided they really didn't have any other choice but to call the guys in white coats to come take Jones away in a straitjacket, which is what they did. The next morning, Tammy left. She left to do their planned two-week tour of Canada by herself. She left Jones in his padded cell. She left the house destroyed so he could see what he'd done when they let him come home after a week and a half in the psych ward.

In his autobiography George denied ever firing a gun at Tammy and drew attention to the way her account of that night referred to the weapon as both a "30-30 rifle" and as a "shotgun," which are very different, as Tammy would know since she grew up on a farm. That inconsistency may have been the fault of Joan Dew or some editor with a thesaurus but where Tammy's gun story loses significant credibility is with Cliff Hyder. According to Tammy's own version, Cliff witnessed Jones fire a gun at her and he'd have heard from outside the house as Jones destroyed the inside. Cliff presumably would also have seen the damage to the inside of the home that night after Jones was hauled away from the property. Nevertheless, when Tom Carter (co-author of George's autobiography) asked what happened that night, Cliff said nothing about a gun and even substantiated George's claim that he did not destroy the home he'd worked so hard to restore and decorate. When Jones came home from his hospital stay he thought the inside of Old Plantation looked an awful lot like Tammy wrecked the place so the damage would look far worse than whatever Jones had actually done. Cliff Hyder took that theory a step further and suggested Tammy may have enlisted the maids to help her destroy the house, perhaps hoping to shock George with "evidence" of the danger his addiction posed to the whole family, perhaps motivated by the fear he'd be angry about the straightjacket and ten days in a sanatorium if there wasn't sufficient proof he really deserved it. George voiced none of these suspicions at the time, choosing instead to spend the few remaining days before Tammy returned from Canada cleaning up the mess, patching all the holes in the walls and replacing broken items in order to make another try at the good husband routine.

Doctors prescribed Librium, a benzodiazepine used as antianxiety medication and to help ease the symptoms of alcohol withdrawal. George took it, too. Whenever a restless feeling began creeping up he would try to kill it with the Librium, even exceeding the recommended dosage if it didn't seem to be working. Unfortunately, Librium and alcohol have a synergistic effect on each other, each enhancing the power of the other, so the more Librium was in his system the less alcohol it took to put him right back in a blackout. Mixing speed, benzos and booze, George's 66 percent doctor-prescribed binges soon returned to Phase II levels, unseen since the mid-1960s. By 1973, he and Tammy had completely given up on operating the Music Park. Every month or two he'd spin out into the abyss for several weeks at a time, then come back with promises of never doing it again. Then he'd do it again, leaving Tammy to perform concerts on the road without him or sit at home and wonder if he'd turn up dead this time. His face started swelling up so bad when he got drunk that Tammy eventually made him go back to the doctor, who diagnosed cirrhosis. When told his scarred liver would kill him if he continued to drink this way, Jones began drinking even more, as if he was trying to die and to make sure he was drunk when he did it. On several occasions Tammy watched him turn a fifth of liquor bottom up, chug until it made him puke, then put the bottle right back to his lips and force more alcohol down his throat. Tour stops in Nashville were generally the worst, what with all of Jones' old drinking buddies and favorite hangouts in the city. This was the period when he entered the backstage men's room at the *Grand Ole Opry* to find Porter Wagoner standing at a urinal. Aware of a rumor dating back to the 1960s that Porter and Tammy had slept together, Jones decided to show Porter the current score by walking up behind him, grabbing his junk and squeezing with a death grip. Another night after a Nashville show, Jones drunk-drove off in a car, so Tammy sent Peanutt Montgomery after him. Peanutt found Jones a ways down the road, his car pulled onto the shoulder, the driver's-side door hanging wide open and The Greatest Country Singer Ever passed out behind the wheel with vomit everywhere.

In August of 1973, six weeks since Tammy heard any news from or about her husband, she decided to witness no more of his slow suicide. After consulting a doctor and lawyer she came up with a plan to take the children away from Florida to an apartment she and George kept near the Nashville airport, where she waited for him to be served divorce papers. Tammy later swore she never really intended to follow through with this divorce, it was one last shock tactic, meant to scare her sweet George into putting down the bottle for good rather than lose her love forever. But that plan wouldn't work if Jones suspected it was a bluff, therefore the paperwork needed to be legitimately filed, which instantly triggered stories in the local media, then the music media, then the national media: Tammy Wynette was about to stop standing by another man. Jones was still drunk when he heard the news, still drunk when he found Tammy at their apartment by calling every phone number he could remember and still drunk when he arrived in Nashville, swearing he was ready to try to quit booze for good. But Tammy needed him to do more than try. She left him in Nashville and took the kids back to Florida, where she worked on getting used to the idea of her fake divorce becoming real, knowing Jones was doing what he did best back in Nashville. But then he showed up in Florida, sober, claiming he was ready to stay that way. She believed him and withdrew the divorce. A few months later Old Plantation Music Park was again operating at a profit and George, according to Tammy, was "a different man." She claimed he only occasionally sipped wine or beer, which neither he nor Tammy considered really drinking. After a while, they felt it was safe for the family to move back to Nashville together.

It's some story. But the timeline created by Tammy's account of these events is impossible and there is a brazen degree of inconsistency to her story. On page 203 of her autobiography she states the music park's renewed success allowed her and George to return to not touring very much. On page 204, she explains the move away from Florida back to Tennessee by saying they were on tour so much they rarely got home anyway. So, which was it, a little touring or a lot of touring? The fake divorce she filed in August of 1973 is a matter of historical record and therefore cannot possibly have resulted in the family's move back to Nashville "in late 1972," as stated in her book. These and other major discrepancies in the officially presented narrative of her life have no doubt caused stress dreams to anyone seriously trying to pin down what really happened and when. There are two things we do know for a fact. One: aside from gossip, rumors and the lyrics of country songs, the media attention on this near-divorce in August of 1973 gave fans the first concrete evidence all was not well in this fairy-tale romance. Two: that exact plot development was the overt theme of "We're Gonna Hold On," their first duet to go #1 Country, released the same month the fake divorce was filed, August of 1973.

Up to this point, no matter what really went on behind closed doors or was hinted at in some album filler and B-sides, their duet singles stayed squarely on brand, presenting only the newlywed soulmates storyline. After the "Take Me" remake, their second duet record was "The Ceremony," a literal reenactment of wedding vows complete with a priest. When "The Ceremony" came out in June of 1972, an audience with no reason to suspect the fragility of the actual marriage sent the single to

#6 Country. Their next two records were a happy gospel duet, called "Old Fashioned Singing," and another honeymoon anthem, called "Let's Build a World Together." Both bombed, barely entering the Country Top 40. Then, in August of 1973, they flipped the script, giving fans a soundtrack to the divorce Tammy filed two days prior to the release of "We're Gonna Hold On."

They had cut the song about four months earlier, after Peanutt Montgomery and George wrote it on tour. The story goes: Tammy was mad because the two drinking buddies had just come back from being fucked up for a week. She started off yelling at both Peanutt and George but soon turned her focus exclusively to Jones. She began yelling about something to do with money, probably something to do with their most recent duet singles bombing and her fear that it could be a signal of the end of their careers. When George told her it was nothing to worry about and she should trust him because he'd been in the business since before she was a hairdresser, Tammy became even angrier and said she knew they weren't going to make it, to which George replied they would, they just needed to hold on. Well, the bus arrived at their next stop and Peanutt was still annoyed about Tammy yelling at him, so he went down to the hotel bar, drank up a three hundred dollar tab and charged it to her and George's room, just to show her what's what. But the whole time Peanutt was drinking he also kept thinking about what George had said about holding on. The next day Peanutt took a guitar up to his bosses' hotel room. George thought the whole bar tab prank was pretty funny. Tammy didn't. When she started in on Peanutt about it, he started playing what he'd written of "We're Gonna Hold On," and Tammy suddenly wasn't so mad anymore. After George helped finish writing the song, he and Tammy cut it near the end of March 1973. Billy Sherrill slowed Peanutt's tempo way down, then added a whole mess of chords and a key change through which George and Tammy just had to hold on, all the way to the top of the Country charts.

George and Tammy both claimed he was able to stay off the bottle for another year after the fake divorce and their biggest hit record together so far. Again, though, the timeline presented as evidence is impossible. It's not so much we know for a fact Tammy was lying when she backed up the claim by stating that George even made it through his fortieth birthday party without taking a drink. It's that he turned forty two years earlier, in 1971.

After "We're Gonna Hold On" the next single to come out was Bobby Braddock's "(We're Not) the Jet Set," a goofy joke about middle-of-nowhere towns with the same names as fancy vacation spots. Billy Sherrill didn't take a piece of the writing credit but he did come up with what Braddock said was probably the best lyric, about how the Jones and Wynette set "ain't the flamin' Suzette set." For the poor couple in the song who can't afford ritzy destinations, steak or martinis, anywhere they travel together is good enough because of their love for each other. The single did well but the entire concept of the song was the polar opposite of their real lives. Tammy Wynette and George

Jones could afford to go anywhere in the world they wanted. The problem was they'd be there with each other. Their real estate spending spree in this period suggests all was not well. Peanutt Montgomery said, "They'd buy up everything they could get and once they bought it they didn't like it." Whether or not George really did ease off the bottle in 1973, it's almost as if he and Tammy were trying to escape a bigger problem than substance abuse, like they wouldn't have to publicly acknowledge the death of this famous marriage if they somehow discovered a way to leave its ghost haunting a previous residence so their love could be miraculously reborn within a new set of walls. Was that the unhappy truth Tammy's convoluted timelines tried to obscure when explaining how and why they happily returned to Nashville? After first moving back into the Nashville home they had left vacant in the move to Florida, they then split time between a $190,000 French Regency-style house upon a hill seven miles south of the city and a 350-acre farm (which came with a house about the size of Old Plantation) thirty miles to the north of the city. This gave George plenty to do in 1973. Between the farm home and the house on the hill he had two huge residences to refurbish, always a great pleasure to him. Preferring futzing around on a tractor to pretending he was French royalty, he spent more days at the farm than the city house and stocked all their new land with more than 150 beef cattle. But then, instead of settling on either property, in 1974 they sold the farm and moved from the French house on the hill into a thirty-five-room mansion that was only two-and-a-half miles closer to the city. George custom ordered wrought-iron burglar bars to place the musical notation of "Stand By Your Man" across the windows of this new house. By the end of the year, they were legally separated.

Was owning multiple residences within an hour's drive some kind of attempt to give each other space while keeping up the appearance of "holding on" like in the song? Perhaps they thought spending a day or week apart every now and then would be best for both of them, maybe make it easier for George to drink less? Maybe they figured keeping him on a farm a ways out of town would at least put some distance between his drinking and the Nashville reporters who were always sniffing around for a hint of trouble ever since Tammy told the media she only rescinded the divorce because George had sworn off booze. One strong indication he hadn't really quit drinking came in the form of a note his mother left behind when she died in April of 1974, having instructed her other children to give her Bible to George: "I want [George] to have my new Bible and for him to be sure and read it for my sake and his. I love him so much. I made a failure but I hope we all meet in Heaven." If he secretly was still drinking, then it would only take one major fuckup for the media to call Tammy's bluff. Headlines around the world would ask whether Tammy was going to stand by her man or stand up for herself. Tammy and George even wrote a song directly addressing the situation. In 1974, George recorded "Our Private Life." The entire thing drips with his sardonic disdain for tabloid reporters and the readers who "can't wait to read the latest news, all about the big stars and their reckless way of living, who got drunk last week and who got sued." The song came out on George's *The Grand Tour* LP, which further complicated matters because it's the album where Billy Sherrill finally cracked the George Jones code. The title track went all the way to the top of the Country Singles chart, George's first #1 record since "Walk Through This World with Me" in 1967. They followed "The Grand Tour" with "The Door," another #1 single, released in October 1974. Releasing two #1 records in the same year brought a lot of major opportunities and attention to George's career, all of which provided Tammy with a reason to worry about the possibility he'd get drunk in front of a bunch of people and ruin everything.

Worse, after releasing nearly nothing but #1 and #2 solo singles since 1967, the one record Tammy put out in 1974 only went #4. Even worse, in 1974, her sworn-enemy-for-life Melba Montgomery came out of nowhere with a #1 Country hit on Harlan Howard's "No Charge." Worst of all, Tammy felt that specific hit record should have been hers. It was just the kind of conservative mother-as-giving-tree heartstring puller Tammy Wynette had spent half a decade selling. Wynette often boasted to Peanutt and Charlene Montgomery that if their little Melba ever even thought about cutting a hit single, then Tammy would rush right in the studio and cover the song to bury Melba's record. Since Melba Montgomery had never charted a solo single higher than #20, this was nothing more than a bunch of meaningless shit talk . . . until the day Wynette found out Melba just recorded a song everyone said would be a smash hit. After getting someone to bring her a demo of "No Charge," sure enough, Wynette called Billy Sherrill to schedule an emergency recording session. Billy wanted nothing to do with such a mean-spirited ploy and tried to talk her out of it, but Wynette wouldn't back down. Billy eventually caved, cut the song with Tammy and rush-released it as a single the month before Melba's record came out. They even tried to win extra schmaltz points by putting Tammy's young daughter Tina on the track. But it wasn't enough to stop Melba's single. Tammy Wynette attacked with all guns blazing only to watch her own record fail while her greatest nemesis, who had never cut a major hit on her own, walked away with a #1 on the very same song. So, 1974 wasn't a great year for Tammy. She frequently found herself in a state of barely concealed panic, fearing a long walk down from the peak of the mountain while her backslider and oath-breaker of a husband remained on top, along with the woman he used to love.

For most of her adult life Wynette used third-person perspective when discussing the differences between Tammy Wynette and Wynette Pugh. She typically referred to Wynette Pugh in the past tense, as a scared little girl who married too young and made too many mistakes. Wynette Pugh was the person she used to be before becoming Tammy Wynette, the badass country music superstar who went to Nashville, married her idol within two years of getting a record deal and earned more than enough of her own money to support a whole family. Unlike Wynette, Tammy was a woman who not only knew how to solve her own problems but was in a position of power to do so. It's unclear to what degree this was just big talk in interviews or if Tammy truly thought of Wynette Pugh as some previous incarnation, a discarded cocoon. Either way, Wynette was unquestionably still around and there was a lot more of her in Billy Sherrill's Tammy character than it seems she wanted to publicly acknowledge. That one single she released in 1974? The one that only went #4 and caused her so much stress? It was "Woman to Woman." Written solely by Billy Sherrill, the song plainly and directly tells all women that somewhere out there is another woman who is going to take your man: "If you think you got your man / in the palm of your hand, / you better listen" because "She's out there, too, / and she's a whole lot better lookin' than me and you," etc. If we equate "man" with mental well-being and happiness, as Tammy Wynette songs so often do, then read this other "she" as any type of perceived threat to said happiness, these lyrics are probably similar to what it was like for Tammy to live with the voice of Wynette in her head, constantly worried her dream life would turn into a nightmare. Some of Wynette's most obvious appearances were in songs Tammy wrote for herself. There was an interview with *Entertainment Tonight* in which Tammy explained her approach to songwriting as, "Many times I write what I can't talk about. Something that I'm upset about or hurt about, I put down on paper and pretend it happened to somebody else." That was absolutely true. She did pretend certain events, thoughts and feelings happened to another person. That person was Wynette Pugh, who she also pretended was a memory from the distant past rather than an active presence in her daily life.

◇   ◇   ◇

In December of 1974, Tammy and George were in their final recording session of the year when Peanutt and Charlene Montgomery showed up at the studio and Wynette immediately began freaking out. Most of the times in their marriage that Jones had vanished for several days or more, Peanutt was somehow involved. However long Jones really was or wasn't able to keep his drinking in check after returning to Nashville, by this time he was back on his regular schedule of staying straight for a month or two and then tearing off for a week, often going down to Alabama to binge drink with Peanutt. So the moment Peanutt walked into this recording session Wynette started thinking about the upcoming family trip she and George had planned to spend Christmas in Acapulco. If Jones went off to get drunk with the Montgomerys, she probably wouldn't hear anything from him until January, by which time the vacation and Christmas would be ruined. Turns out, there was no need for Wynette to worry. George went over to talk with Peanutt and Charlene for a minute but after that he came back, finished the session, then went home with Tammy. But Wynette had already pressed play on the panic reel and couldn't stop it. As she settled into bed with George for the night, everything came spilling out. For nearly the entire night she kept George awake worrying over their marriage, his drinking and, most of all, her own career. Did her recent #4 record mean she was never going to have another #1 record? What if all her subsequent records continued charting lower and lower until she never had a big hit again? How long could she keep working without major hit records? Would she lose her contract with Epic? The late hours of December 12 turned into the early morning hours of December 13 and, still, Wynette could not stop the flood of anxiety. When George awoke in the morning, unsure how many hours or maybe even minutes of sleep he'd been able to get, he left the house and never showed up to where he was scheduled to be that day. Tammy checked to see if he'd taken his overnight bag and, sure enough, it was gone. Someone who'd been at the house before he left said they overheard George muttering something to himself about how something was just never gonna work. Tammy filed for legal separation that very day, which would be a pretty huge decision to make based solely on some mumbling and the whereabouts of a bag . . .

It's possible Tammy initiated divorce proceedings so quickly because it's what she'd secretly wanted for a while. Eight pages after her autobiography claims she and George booked no concerts for the entire month of December in order to give themselves a period of relaxation before the Acapulco vacation, a new chapter of the book begins with details of the last concert she played that year "in December, right after George left." So what's true and what's a lie? Friend and biographer Joan Dew suspected Tammy Wynette no longer wished to be married to George Jones whether he was sober or not. Wynette craved excitement and crowds of people and whatever else got her adrenaline going. Two of her favorite things to do were ride carnival rides and go to haunted houses, the scarier the better. Conversely, Jones had more haunted houses than anyone could ever enjoy locked away in his mind and he'd much rather have a beer in front of the television than be in the middle of any kind of crowd. Joan Dew believed Wynette was probably bored with the relationship, wanted out and needed George to look like the bad guy. She needed it to be his fault the marriage failed. Though Tammy did shoulder some blame throughout her autobiography for often creating a stressful environment by "nagging" George over his drinking, she insisted the night of December 12, 1974, was the only time she ever unloaded all her worries on him in such a manic episode, which does not gel with the many arguments she and others describe as beginning with her anxiety over various matters. A piano player who worked closely with Wynette Pugh and helped her record some early demos back in the *Country Boy Eddie* TV show days told Jimmy McDonough that Wynette once said she always became afraid before falling asleep, every single night. She didn't know why but some existential fear came over her and she was consumed by dread of where her thoughts might take her in the dark. Considering all the events of 1974, it's difficult to imagine George Jones only spent one night that year listening to Wynette keep him awake in one or another of their big beds, in one or another of their massive homes, giving endless voice to baseless fears it would all soon be torn away from them. It's possible the story about a lone night of panic was yet another instance of Wynette condensing weeks or years of true events into one tidy, little set piece.

Regardless of whatever he was alleged to have said before leaving their home for what turned out to be the last time, George didn't want the marriage to end. He left to go get drunk, yeah, but not for any kind of party. What he did was drive thirty minutes away from home, pick up some liquor, check into a hotel, alone, and drink himself into a stupor for three days. When he called Tammy afterward to say he was coming home, she informed him that he no longer had a home with her and they were done. Following the legal separation in December, she filed for full divorce in January 1975 and the marriage was terminated in March, making August 1974's "We Loved It Away" the final duet single released while they were still married. Two of Billy Sherrill's regular songwriters, George Richey and Carmol Taylor, created this chapter of the reconcilement-after-fake-divorce storyline, in which the "it" George and Tammy love away is the insecurity they each face in the relationship. Where he's been told she treats love like a game and leaves when she's bored, she's been told he's too restless to ever be tied down. But remaining arm-in-arm and hand-in-hand keeps them together through it all. The record became another Top 10 hit. A little over six months after it came out, their real divorce was finalized. Neither Wynette nor Jones handled it well.

Jones moved from Nashville to Florence, Alabama, in order to be close to his drinking partner, Peanutt Montgomery. Florence being only about a two-and-a-half-hour drunk drive from Nashville, this was a trip Jones often made multiple times in a single day, just to drive a few laps around Tammy's circular driveway, just to let her know he still cared. Then he would turn right around and drive all the way back to Florence. Drink and repeat as needed. In the year 1975, Jones didn't merely give up fighting the bottle, he switched to the bottle's side in an all-out war against his own mind and body. He'd go three or four days at a time without eating any solid food, just chugging whiskey until he threw up, then chugging more whiskey.

And 1975 was the year many fans first discovered Tammy Wynette had certain problems of her own. In the early months of the year she played fewer than ten concerts and even that proved too difficult, going out there alone to face audiences who were confused and disappointed by the absence of George Jones. In February, the month before the divorce went through, Tammy played in Tupelo, Mississippi. What should have been a hometown hero show was by all accounts a total disaster. Whatever she took (probably Valium or some other benzo), she took so much of it she could hardly stand. She was so wasted by showtime she needed assistance walking from the bus to the stage, where she sat on a stool with vacant eyes, mumbling something about George Jones between every half-hearted attempt at singing part of a song. That type of concert kept happening. Staying home alone didn't prove any easier. One night, she was taken to a Nashville emergency room to have her stomach pumped of what she later claimed was an accidental overdose. She said she'd gone weeks without a good night's sleep, even while taking the sleeping pills her doctors prescribed, so she decided to double the dosage. When even that didn't knock her out, she threw some Valium into the mix and pretty soon she was too fucked up to remember if she'd actually taken more pills or only thought about taking more pills. Just to be safe, she took some more pills. Next thing she knew, one of Billy Sherrill's songwriters, George Richey, was standing over her and saying everything would be okay while hospital staff piped a tube down her throat. When she later realized how close she came to losing her own life and leaving her children without a mother, Tammy said she swore to "never fool around with pills again." No account of this evening has ever explained how or why she was found by George Richey.

SEVENTEEN

PRIZED BEAUTY

◇ Smiling for Suffrage ◇ Miss America: Another Sincere Fuck You to Feminism ◇
Lenora Slaughter's New and Improved Swimsuit Contest ◇ Pretty Politics ◇

Not many people are paying attention but Miss America is in a pretty bad way. She's got a few different problems but the biggest one is that nearly nobody cares anymore. First televised in the mid-1950s, by the 1960s Miss America's annual broadcast routinely captured roughly 75 percent of the entire national television audience, which was probably when and why the beauty pageant became doomed to fail. Like Bob Dylan said—or was it Abraham Lincoln?—you just can't please all of the people all of the time.

◇ ◇ ◇

One way to view the beginning of Miss America in 1921, only a year after women in the United States started being allowed to vote: a bunch of local business owners in Atlantic City decided to chase tourism dollars by throwing a swimsuit contest and reminding everyone of the role women were supposed to serve in American society. It's no coincidence that one of the ways women had finally gained real support for being allowed to vote after fiftysomething years of suffragist activism was by getting dressed up and made up as if to attend some prestigious ball, then parading their smiling faces through a town's busiest streets to prove their interest in the body politic wouldn't destroy their interest in the body beautiful. They did this because many of the arguments against suffrage were built upon societal fears that becoming involved in politics would lead women to abandon the roles and aesthetics expected of them. Basically, a lot of people worried women who were allowed to start doing things only men were allowed to do would start acting like men across the board, completely disregarding everything from poised and polite behavior to wearing makeup and feminine fashions. So, near the beginning of the twentieth century, smiling suffragists took to the streets serving their finest looks for all to see the nice and pretty ladies who wished to be able to vote, which was made clear by the sashes worn across their bodies reading VOTES FOR WOMEN. These were similar to the sashes worn by women who paraded through the same streets in support of temperance and/or Prohibition. In 1920, the year after federal Prohibition went through, the Nineteenth Amendment was ratified and millions of women were allowed to start voting. Sashes, who knew? In 1921, Atlantic City businessmen responded by throwing those sashes on young women in swimsuits, parading them through the same city streets and declaring one to be the most physically attractive.

Many types of beauty pageant existed for centuries prior to this, and many tamer versions had already generated a great deal of controversy, so the guys who launched this swimsuit contest definitely anticipated haters from day one. But it wasn't women's rights activists who shut down Miss America little more than five years later. It was those same Atlantic City businessmen. What they hadn't anticipated was all the women whose strategy for winning included wearing revealing swimsuits and otherwise provocative fashions. Nearly every contestant in 1927 chose to display a then-scandalous amount of skin in hopes of winning. In 1928, there was no longer a Miss America pageant. The businessmen decided money and publicity couldn't replace their reputations as upstanding citizens of the community and they scrapped the whole affair.

When Miss America returned in the mid-1930s it was with a few modifications to keep history from repeating. Most importantly, they placed a woman named Lenora Slaughter in charge of operations, partly due to her successful track record running other pageants, partly to use a woman as a shield from criticisms of misogyny levied by the increasing number of women's rights activist groups who hated swimsuit contests. Lenora Slaughter added the Talent category which became mandatory from 1938 forward, providing a technically true argument that Miss America was no longer crowned exclusively upon the way she looked in a swimsuit. However, the way a woman looked in a swimsuit could entirely prevent her from even being allowed to enter the pageant because one way Miss America entrants needed to look was white.

As part of Slaughter's plan to keep the pageant "respectable" and all controversy in its past, every contestant was required to be single (meaning never married, divorced or pregnant), "in good health" (meaning no apparent physical or mental disabilities, no visible deviations from the contemporary beauty standards represented in popular movies and magazines) and at least able to pass as white. Though that last requirement was only an official, on-paper rule for a few years, Slaughter ran Miss America with a similar approach for three decades and, as late as 1969, pageant officials were still making statements to the press in defense of their allegiance to "plain American idealism," saying things like, "We are for normalcy. We have no interest in minorities or causes." Of course, the only reason a Miss America representative said such a thing in 1969 was because of all the publicity generated by feminist protests the year before.

Contrary to popular misconceptions, there were no bras burned on the Atlantic City boardwalk outside the 1968 ceremony but there were homemade signs comparing the physical evaluation of women's bodies to a cattle auction. Many widely read articles ran quotes from feminist protestors calling out the overt racism, ableism and misogyny that had been on display throughout the previous fifty years of Miss America. That perspective was not exclusive to the protestors outside the ceremony. Over the previous thirty years many Misses America had pushed back against being viewed almost exclusively as just a person with a physically appealing body. As early as the 1940s some winners resisted making further public appearances in the swimsuit they were required to wear to even be considered for the crown. By the end of that decade *every* winner began changing out of their swimsuit before being crowned. At the beginning of the 1950s one Miss America announced her intention to remain fully clothed for every public appearance in her year under the tiara, to which the pageant's swimsuit sponsor reacted by starting a whole new pageant on the other side of the continent.

Launched in California, Miss USA has always been an unapologetic beauty pageant. Women who enter Miss USA wear a swimsuit to be judged on how they look at the beach. They wear a dress to be judged on how they look at fancy parties. They are interviewed to be judged on how well they speak when spoken to. There is no Talent category. There is also no evidence of the identity crisis suffered by Miss America over the past fifty years, ever since they outright stated a lack of interest in "minorities or causes" only to discover how many contestants and viewers in the TV audience at home cared quite a lot about such matters.

◇　◇　◇

As ratings and profits steadily declined in the wake of declaring an official position at odds with shifting social mores, Miss America set out to once more rehabilitate her image, using the language of female empowerment to combat accusations of patriarchal exploitation. By the end of the 1980s a new Platform category required contestants to speak out on a chosen social "cause," the exact thing rebuked by Miss America officials only two decades prior. Further updates held to this trend, until what began as a beauty pageant morphed into some kind of fake political campaign for a President of Women office that doesn't actually exist. Today, official Miss America messaging refers to contestants as "candidates" and it's no longer a pageant at all but, rather, a "competition." The Platform category has become a "Social Impact Initiative" and, naturally, there is no longer a Swimsuit category at all. Many of these recent changes were made by Gretchen Carlson, Miss America 1989 and ex–Fox News TV personality, who became chairwoman of the pageant's board in 2018, following the scandal caused by her male predecessor's leaked emails.

Sam Haskell may not have been the first executive in the history of the Miss America organization to privately body-shame or slut-shame "candidates" but, post #MeToo, he was the first to be instantly fired and replaced by a woman. As far as human shields go they could hardly have done better than Gretchen Carlson, who many would argue launched the #MeToo age by suing Fox News CEO Roger Ailes for sexual harassment. That background and Carlson's sweeping changes to the pageant format were the stories pushed with every bit of Miss America's public relations might. Well, every bit of it except for Cara Mund, the actual Miss America when Sam Haskell's scandal broke out.

In August of 2018, Cara wrote an open letter stating the Miss America board's "rhetoric about empowering women and openness and transparency is great: however, the reality is quite different." It took her five further pages of text to paint a picture of that reality, in which her own agency, utility and voice as the reigning Miss America were stifled by a team of handlers tasked with ensuring Cara was effectively overshadowed by the narrative of Gretchen Carlson becoming the new face of the pageant, the woman who swooped in to save the day. Whichever media outlets still believed anything that happened at Miss America may be of interest were pushed to interview the chairwoman of the board rather than Cara Mund, the pageant's most recent winner, who claims she was sometimes deceived into missing scheduled appearances in order to lend her the reputation of being "difficult" and unprofessional, thus making it easier to keep her off camera and out of sight. To say the least, if Cara's allegations are true, then this is not the corporate culture one would expect from a "competition" rebranding itself as a place of empowerment for women.

But even without such monumental hypocrisy and cynical insincerity as Cara has alleged, none of these optical maneuvers held much chance of success, considering the entire exercise was a last-ditch gamble that alienating whatever was left of a beauty pageant's ever-diminishing fan base would somehow gain the attention of a larger audience who wanted to see a pretend political campaign for women. The problem is there's no proof such an audience has ever existed. When people pay attention to a beauty pageant it's because they want to watch a beauty pageant. Nobody tunes in to a swimsuit contest because they secretly hope it will transform into a political debate. They tune in to see a swimsuit contest. They tune in to see a cattle auction. They tune in to see a charming and beautiful woman audition for the chance to be crowned royalty, with nothing left to do except wait for a handsome Bachelor to step into frame holding out a rose. And if Miss America won't be that princess on TV, then someone else will.

EIGHTEEN

UNHAPPY HOMES

◇ Tammy Wynette's Lust for Love ◇ Branding George Jones ◇
The One-Dimensional Persona ◇ Tabloids ◇ A Murderous Stalker?
◇ George Richey to the Rescue ◇

"'Til I Get It Right" is something of a decoder ring for the Tammy Wynette character. Unlike most of her love songs, the lyrics make no reference to a man. The song is not about being in love with a man. It's about being in love with the feeling of being in love. It's about how that feeling is the most important thing in life to Tammy Wynette, therefore losing that feeling would be the most terrible thing in life. This one concept succinctly explains the beliefs, actions, fears and tolerance for awful partners throughout all her other songs.

While Tammy the character and Tammy the human were both in love with the feeling of being in love, that resulted in extremely different behaviors from each of them. With very few exceptions, once the Tammy character fixated her love upon one man she was capable of holding it there forever. No matter what that man did or who he did it with, the only way the relationship could end was if he walked away. Even then, the Tammy character would take the man back if he returned before her next chance at being in love came along. This absolutely was not the case with real-life Tammy, the partner who filed for every one of her divorces. Even though it seems there were great reasons to end nearly all of those marriages, almost everyone who intimately knew her described an inability to fixate her love upon one man and hold it there forever. She excelled at the first part, the fun free fall into love, but it was only a matter of time—maybe as little as a year or two—before that initial rush wore off and she began looking around for another dose. Whether they were the one doing the leaving or the one who got left, both Tammys kept falling in love.

According to Larry Henley, one of the writers on "'Til I Get It Right," Tammy and Billy Sherrill were both going to pass on the song, but George Jones happened to be in the room during the pitch and convinced everyone it would be a hit. Tammy cut it in May 1972, about one month after she and George recorded "A Lovely Place to Cry," then the single came out in December, right around the time Tammy and George moved from Florida back to Nashville.

With his biggest artists once more in Music City, Billy Sherrill must have known it wouldn't take long for the troubles he saw in their marriage to spill out of one mansion or another and land in the news. After "'Til I Get It Right" hit #1, Billy dug around in the vault for a record that could play into the rumors of why Tammy and George may have left what was supposed to be their dream home at Old Plantation. The tape he found was "Kids Say the Darndest Things." Though the song was cut three years earlier, the idea of Tammy's children repeating overheard threats of divorce had now taken on a whole new meaning, so Billy released it as a single. A couple months after that record hit #1, Tammy the person filed her bluff divorce from George Jones at the same time Epic put out "We're Gonna Hold On" as a single and Billy Sherrill decided Tammy the character was going to remain unhappily married for a while. Ten out of the eleven songs on her next solo album, *Another Lonely Song*, were about Tammy cheating, being cheated on or sleeping with a new lover to get over the previous one. She and Billy wrote the title track with Norro Wilson after Tammy said she felt like writing "another lonely song." It went #1 as her final single of 1973, then the LP came out in March 1974, the same month Tammy failed to sabotage Melba Montgomery's hit "No Charge." (The B-side of Tammy's "No Charge," a dramatic sort of skit named "The Telephone Call," again recruited daughter Tina for schmaltz points, only this time paired with George Jones, whose attempt at a sweet phone call home to his wife goes wrong thanks to their use of a child as translator.) After "No Charge" failed to become a hit and failed to stop Melba Montgomery from reaching #1, Tammy's next single was "Woman to Woman," the feminist-baiting #4 record she feared may signal the beginning of her end. The following single, "You Make Me Want to Be a Mother," also topped out at #4 despite a title and theme seemingly intent on provoking rabid fury from anyone who had been even mildly annoyed by the philosophy of "Stand By Your Man." Released the month after Tammy filed for divorce from Jones in 1975, "You Make Me Want to Be a Mother" performed no better than "Woman to Woman."

Her first single to come out after the divorce was "I Still Believe in Fairy Tales," written by A-Team guitarist Grady Martin, who worked with Billy Sherrill and Tammy often enough to glimpse how these scripts were created. Grady basically took "'Til I Get It Right" and wrote a new version dressed up as a chivalrous romance. That language was not new to Tammy Wynette records. A year before "'Til I Get It Right" Billy Sherrill and Glenn Sutton had sent out for a bunch of children's books to research "Bedtime Story," a #1 hit about a king being tempted away from his queen. But "Bedtime Story" ended with the king returning to his queen and the two of them living happily ever after. "I Still Believe in Fairy Tales" doesn't give us a happy ending . . . because Grady's song has a dragon in it.

From this side of history George Jones' alcoholism is viewed as integral to his persona and often taken for granted as always having been so. It's true that everyone in the industry and most of his fans saw him drunk off his ass at least once in the 1950s and 1960s. It's true he had a few boozy hits in those decades, like "Just One More" and "White Lightning," and continued to cut drinking songs every now and then, like "Heartaches and Hangovers" on *I'll Share My World with You*. But that song and nearly all others on a similar theme were only used as filler and, in that era of his career, one could purchase several new George Jones albums in a row without hearing any drinking songs at all. His on-record persona was only typecast as an alcoholic following the divorce from Tammy Wynette at the beginning of 1975. Her role in causing alcoholism to become a core trait of the Jones character cannot be overstated. Many years prior to this, Loretta Lynn told her man not to come home drinkin' with lovin' on his mind. Tammy covered that song on her first album, before she and Billy Sherrill landed on the final version of the Tammy character. Once they did, Tammy began wishing and begging for her man to come home for any kind of lovin' no matter how much drinkin' he'd done. Tammy's songs almost always implied the man's drinking was a by-product of him spending time with other women, which was what actually tortured her so much more than the booze. Then, on "I Still Believe in Fairy Tales," a dragon slayed her king.

◇   ◇   ◇

The only reason mainstream entertainment media ever came to know of George's existence was because of his marriage to a much more famous pop crossover artist. For the same reasons Billy Sherrill was able to sell country music in a package that appealed to consumers of pop music, pop culture media became fascinated with the complications and potential for controversy brought by George Jones to the Tammy Wynette narrative. To these journalists the messy end of Tammy's marriage was like blood in the water, and she proved more than willing to dish out sordid details in interviews, concerts and song lyrics.

After George's lawyers responded to her divorce filing with a lawsuit against Tammy and their shared booking agency for somehow conspiring to damage George's career, she immediately reached out to the press and generated headlines with a passive-aggressive statement about George's "illness" and how much "help" he needed. By the end of the year her concerts featured a segment in which she sat on stage with an acoustic guitar and played a miniature set of songs she introduced as being written about the collapse of her marriage to George. Fans paying close attention would have noticed one of these songs was "A Lovely Place to Cry," which dated the beginning of the relationship's end all the way back to Lakeland, Florida, in 1972. One of the newer pieces in that concert segment was "The Bottle," a song Tammy wrote on her own about "a loser" who she hopes sees the face of his now ex-wife and their daughter every time he looks at a bottle. When reporters subsequently asked Jones all the questions one would expect, he never attempted to lie or underplay the role his drinking played in the destruction of the relationship. What was previously left unspoken or addressed only as a problem that could be fixed suddenly became an immutable aspect of the George Jones character.

It was only after Tammy put the spotlight on George's drinking and both artists began openly discussing his alcoholism as the main factor in their divorce that Billy Sherrill and his crew of songwriters decided to play the hand they'd been dealt. The initial post-divorce George Jones singles never mentioned booze at all. First came "These Days I Barely Get By," which was written by Tammy when they were still together and recorded by George two days before he left home with his overnight bag for what turned out to be the last time. Released after the divorce, the single went Top 10 and Tammy said it broke her heart hearing Jones sing it on the radio every day. The first time he went into the studio after the divorce, he recorded "I Just Don't Give a Damn," which he wrote with Jimmy Peppers. Though the lyrics could be read as an explanation of why Jones intends to drink through the night, drinking is never actually mentioned. "I Just Don't Give a Damn" is one of the best country songs in history and is now often placed on greatest hits compilations. However, it was originally released only as a B-side to the downer divorce ballad "Memories of Us" and not, in fact, a hit. Then—two months later, following half a year of press covering this mess—Tammy Wynette's first post-divorce single pointed a finger at "a dragon" and George Jones' on-record persona received a permanent update.

After Tammy released "I Still Believe in Fairy Tales," every George Jones album produced by Billy Sherrill contained at least one drinking song. For George's next album Billy repurposed a forgotten B-side from over a year earlier with lyrics George and Tammy wrote about a man-baby begging a woman to wean him off the bottle with her love. "Wean Me," far too bizarre to ever make it as a single, was placed as an album track on *The Battle*. The title track—written by Norro Wilson, George Richey and Linda Kimball—can only be viewed as a direct response to "I Still Believe in Fairy Tales" because it borrows the same vocabulary of chivalrous romance to depict love as a noble battle. (Coincidences being seldom in any universe controlled by Billy Sherrill, the titles of "The Battle" and "The Bottle" only differing by one letter is significant enough to mention.) The big drinking song on the next George Jones album was "A Drunk Can't Be a Man," written by George and Peanutt Montgomery, and the alcohol songs on all of George's following Epic LPs are just as easy to spot by title. This turn toward alcoholism as a recurring theme plotted a course that would eventually lead to some of George's biggest hits and/or most enduring songs, like "Bartender's

Blues," "If Drinkin' Don't Kill Me (Her Memory Will)," "Still Doin' Time," "Tennessee Whiskey" and many others. This update to his persona proved incredibly marketable through the late '70s and carried his career well into the '80s, in part because it was periodically reinforced by George Jones, the human being, behaving like a total lunatic.

Near the end of the '70s he started doing cocaine like it was his job and, as a result, began acting increasingly self-destructive and insane. But fans in this era already thought of him as a drunk and many had little to no experience with his new (and expensive) drug of choice. So, whenever cocaine happened to be mentioned alongside the booze in headlines or gossip columns, most of his audience assumed it was just some supplemental party favor he casually enjoyed between swigs from a bottle. Besides, Tammy Wynette never sang a song about George Jones doing blow, right? Regardless of his extreme cocaine use in this period, there arose a sick form of synergy whereby every article covering one of his no-shows or other major public fuckups lent more power to every drinking song by or about George Jones, just as every drinking song by or about George Jones lent more power to every article covering one of his no-shows or other major public fuckups. This was when he became country music's heroic drunk, a perpetual underdog. Everybody loves to root for an underdog, even if he's truly only fighting against himself. And it must have been frustrating for Tammy to watch Jones step into this sympathetic persona she'd accidentally helped create for him, since it's the role she thought she was creating for herself.

The fundamental flaw with Tammy's character was she only had one path to sympathy, which was to suffer at the hands of a villain. The men she loved always became the men who left her for the women Tammy always feared would steal her man away, thus making Tammy not a perpetual underdog but an eternal victim. She was cursed to repeat a cycle of giddy happiness at the beginning of a relationship, anxious dread while in the relationship, then guilty loneliness after the relationship's end. Because she only existed in relation to other characters, the plots available to her writers were inherently limited and repetitive, leaving no room for any kind of development without betraying her entire persona. If "Tammy Wynette" had been a major role on a soap opera, viewers would eventually start complaining about the rehashed and worn-out storylines until the show's writers killed her off in a plane crash and brought back the same actress as an evil twin, giving her a much more interesting and unpredictable role as precisely the type of villain who'd inspired such fear in the boring, dead sister. Unfortunately, the cocktail of fact and fiction served by Billy Sherrill and his writers was more delicate than a soap opera and such heavy-handed twists were not an option, regardless of how much the real Tammy behaved like the femme fatales she feared so much in song.

Outside of fiction, if Wynette wanted a man, she'd get him. And it was entirely irrelevant whether he was already in a relationship. There were several instances when it seems a man already being in a relationship only added to her excitement over the romance, perhaps even inspiring her initial attraction. Her own hairdresser claimed Wynette slept with no less than three of the hairdresser's boyfriends, seemingly just to prove she could do it, and would then invent a reason to act angry with the hairdresser in order to avoid expressing any remorse for the transgression. For Tammy's songwriters to introduce such complex real-life behavior to her persona on record would thoroughly unmake the Tammy her fans believed they knew, the Tammy who'd spent years vilifying precisely that type of woman. Her writers had no choice but to stay the course that had been scripted for them, even as fans received glimpses of who Tammy really was as a person, bringing about the same feelings of betrayal as if all her songs suddenly took on the perspective of a man-eating seductress. The more her audience learned about Wynette—someone journalist Alanna Nash once characterized as "a person who needed to cause a lot of chaos in her life, a lot of drama"—the less credible they found Tammy's on-record persona. In the second half of the 1970s, this became an insurmountable problem. Beginning with her increased attempts to engage the press after the divorce from Jones, through several scandals and embarrassing media stunts, then culminating with the publication of several extremely obvious lies in the 1979 autobiography, fans saw much too far behind the curtain and Tammy's solo career never fully recovered.

While George Jones released twelve Top 5 singles during the 1980s, Tammy could only put one record in the Top 10, which was precisely the thing she feared would happen the night(s) she kept George awake wondering if her career may soon be over. And maybe she was right to worry. Maybe this was always going to happen once country music listeners grew tired of the repetitive storylines on her records. Or maybe she manifested her own personal nightmare through clumsy attempts to orchestrate a reality she believed would cause fans to buy into the Tammy persona rather than perceive deceit and begin to doubt her sincerity. Either way, the fear came true.

◇   ◇   ◇

One of the most blatant inconsistencies in Tammy's book was the bit about intentionally not booking any concerts for the whole month of December 1974, immediately followed by an anecdote regarding the final concert she played in the month of December 1974. It's impossible to know exactly which parts of that self-contradictory story are untrue but the reason she told it was to explain how she wound up keeping George Jones' band in the divorce. She assumed the Jones Boys would stay with their original boss when she told them about the end of her marriage and said to contact George after Christmas for information on future gigs. To her surprise, each band member reached out one at a time over the following days to say they'd rather keep working for her. They had enough experience with Jones to know the course his life was probably about to take did not present a stable source of income to anyone who only got paid if their boss fulfilled the terms of a contract. Whatever else one could say about Tammy Wynette, she showed up to work.

At the first concert she played in 1975, someone in the audience yelled out "Where's George?" and Wynette froze onstage, unsure what to say or do. Jones Boy James Hollie stepped up to a microphone and said, "She doesn't know where George is. Even George doesn't know where George is," which defused the situation with laughter. But recycling that line at future concerts and the reliable support of the Jones Boys didn't always work to dissuade hecklers or relieve the anxiety Tammy felt taking the stage each night without George. Then there was the constant fear that selling fewer and fewer records would eventually result in losing her deal with Epic. She self-medicated with pills to the degree she needed to perform several concerts from a stool because she couldn't stand. Then came the "accidental overdose," after which she attempted to correct course through the only method available to her character: publicly vilifying her most recent hero/lover. In June of 1975, Tammy recorded the self-written "Your Memory's Gone to Rest," a song about the night she decided to get her shit together by calling some girlfriends over to the house to help purge all evidence of George once having lived there. Just to prove she could handle hearing him on country radio all the time they listened to a stack of George Jones albums while removing his awards from the walls and his clothes from the closets, putting all of it in boxes. "Your Memory's Gone to Rest" was sequenced next to "The Bottle" on the *I Still Believe in Fairy Tales* LP and placed on the B-side of the title track's single. None of these songs were major hits but all three went in the new, Jones-centric acoustic mini-set of her concerts. As for the other updates to her act, Tammy gave credit (or blame) to Billy Sherrill, who pointed out she could expect hecklers to keep asking where her ex-husband was as long as she continued to tour the exact same package with George the only thing missing. Taking this advice, she rebranded the Jones Boys as Country Gentlemen and fired her longtime opening acts, comedian/banjo player Harold Morrison and singer Patsy Sledd. Since Patsy had also sang backup and harmony vocals during Tammy's set, this position became vacant and Tammy decided to fill it with a full, Nashville Sound–style vocal chorus. News of the opening reached Larry Gatlin, then one of Nashville's newest hitmakers, and he suggested his little brothers and sister for the job. Tammy named her new backup singers Young Country. Soon, much to the dismay of older brother Larry, she began sleeping with Rudy Gatlin.

She said the relationship with Rudy, then around twenty-three years old, made her feel young and came with no expectations because he knew she was also seeing other people. In fact, everyone knew she was seeing other people. The tabloids kept track of newly single Tammy Wynette's nocturnal activities like she was the subject of a nature of documentary about an endangered species released into the wild to find a mate. Readers received so many updates on the various men she was confirmed or suspected to be dating it's a wonder Vegas bookies didn't start taking bets on who she'd choose for her next attempt at monogamy. Since this was roughly three years after the combo of starring in *Deliverance* and posing nude for a centerfold in *Cosmopolitan* made Burt Reynolds one of the biggest movie stars in the world, most gossip rags and fans picked him for the favorite.

Tammy and Burt first met in September 1975, when he came to Nashville to be on an episode of Jerry Reed's TV talk show. Once Burt discovered Tammy was also scheduled as a guest, he asked Jerry to invite her out to dinner with several other friends the night before the taping. She accepted, everyone had a fun time and, after dinner, Tammy and Burt separated from the pack to spend an hour or two on their own, just hanging out and talking. After taping Jerry's show the next day everyone went out for dinner again. Again, Tammy and Burt wound up alone at the end of the night. This time they woke up next to each other in the morning. A couple months later, Tammy used a small gap in some tour dates for a quick trip to Los Angeles to appear on more talk shows. Burt heard she was in town, figured out what hotel she was staying at and phoned to see if she had any time to see him. She told him she was too busy, which may or may not have been true. What definitely was true is one of the talk shows she'd booked was hosted by Dinah Shore, who famously had been in a serious relationship with Burt Reynolds for the previous four years or so. In fact, Tammy wasn't exactly certain whether or not that relationship had actually ended, and the gossip rags had already printed photos of her and Burt at dinner together in Nashville, so she was scared what may happen if Dinah found out she and Burt had slept together. (Whether Dinah ever knew and/or was upset, she never said anything to Tammy about it.) Back in Nashville the following week, Tammy received another call at home from Burt Reynolds, who continued calling every week or two.

Burt being even more famous than Tammy, his "dinner companions" were even more frequently and widely reported than hers, meaning she was constantly reminded of his romantic involvement with other women. Still, she began to develop intense feelings for him, which biographer Joan Dew suspected was the main reason Tammy made at least one of several disastrous choices in the next several years. Either she was trying to sabotage the relationship before Burt wound up breaking her heart or she was trying to make him jealous enough to quit fooling around with other women and commit to monogamy with her. In any case, gossip magazines continued tracking her dating life and she continued providing names worthy of bold type, going out with other glitterati of Nashville society, some famous athletes and . . . George Jones. Or, at least, that's what country music fans were given plenty of reason to believe.

Tammy and George hadn't spoken since the early 1975 divorce when she spotted him at the Nashville DJ Convention near the end of the year. Presumably Jones took a short break from embalming himself in order to show up and rub elbows with power players in the industry, because the person Tammy saw across the room didn't look anything like the "loser" from "The Bottle." He looked like George Jones, The Greatest Country Singer Ever, who'd once committed to a monogamous relationship with her. And they may not have spoken since the divorce but Tammy had seen quite a bit of him. All she needed to do was look out her living room window at the right time to catch Jones driving a few laps in the driveway, just to let her know he hadn't moved on. Was that an unhealthy and manic display of attention? It certainly was. And if Burt Reynolds ever did anything like it, then Tammy Wynette probably would have married him. George's periodic drunk check-ins inspired her to write a song called "I Just Drove By (To See If I Was Really Gone)." Whatever else they discussed at the DJ Convention, she must have told him about this song. Even though it's never been released, Jones recorded it the same month. A month later Tammy joined him onstage at Possum Holler, the Nashville nightclub Jones opened in Printer's Alley the day their divorce went through. The famous exes ran through a performance of their duet act just like the good old days and Tammy told the crowd she was "having a date with Mr. Jones." Only one week prior she'd made a surprise appearance at a George Jones concert in Kentucky, where many audience members witnessed Tammy hop on George's bus after the show for the return trip to Nashville. Both Tammy and George gave quotes to the media explaining they were just friends, trying to figure out how to stay in each other's lives for the sake of their child and so on. However, other "unidentified sources" who claimed to be in the know gave different quotes, saying it was only a matter of time before Tammy and George got back together as they'd done so many times in the past. Fans couldn't be sure which story to believe. Then, in January 1976, Tammy dropped a new single that made just about everyone decide she and Jones must be romantically involved again.

George Richey came up with the title "'Til I Can Make It on My Own" a full year earlier, when Tammy and Jones first split, but Billy Sherrill told him to shelve it for a while and see how the relationship played out. After Tammy and Jones began appearing together in public, Richey called Tammy and Billy over to his house to finish the song. Billy didn't want to be there because he had money riding on a football game, but Richey said they could put the game on TV in another room. Between downs, Billy would come check out whatever Tammy and Richey were doing at the piano, make a few changes, then get back to the TV. Tammy wrote the line everyone agreed was the best one in the song: "'Til I get used to losing you / let me keep on using you." At the beginning of each verse the vocal melody lifts to its highest point as Tammy sings optimistically of future times when she'll no longer have an ex-lover on her mind, when she'll need a friend, when she'll keep trying and when there'll be a brighter day with a morning sun. After each instance of expressed hope, the melody then drops down to match Tammy's sinking spirits in the present, where she's still finding herself back on the phone (and presumably back in bed) with the same ex-lover. Every time she sings that this state of affair is only until she can make it on her own, the melody does not rise to match the optimism of those words, because this is Tammy Wynette and neither she nor anybody else believes she will ever make it on her own. According to Wynette, everybody in the recording studio was silent during playback because they all knew how near these lyrics were to a real-time journal entry for her. When the single came out, feeding into rumors and articles about her apparent reconciliation with George Jones, it became one of her final two #1 records as a solo artist. The other #1 was also written by George Richey with help from Billy Sherrill.

The official narrative claims "You and Me" is about George Richey secretly being in love with Tammy for two years prior to marrying her. However, the official narrative also claims Tammy was shocked to discover Richey and his previous wife were getting a divorce, which is impossible because the sexual affair between Tammy and Richey was a contributing factor in his divorce. According to Joan Dew, Tammy and Richey thought it was hilarious to prank call Richey's wife late at night when she was alone and had no idea where her husband was. If "You and Me" really was about Richey's secret love for Tammy, then it seems she was in on the secret. Billy Sherrill placed musical cues on the record beneath certain lyrics, adding sprinkles of piano to represent rain and a drum to represent the heartbeat of Tammy's lover.

The month "You and Me" came out, Tammy Wynette got married—not to George Richey, George Jones, Burt Reynolds or even Rudy Gatlin—but a man named Michael Tomlin. As usual, it's impossible to know exactly when Tammy and Michael began sleeping together. This time it's because Michael was one of the guys she stole from that hairdresser. Given the way this story is about to unfold it's very likely Michael was not surprised to learn his new girlfriend worked for Tammy Wynette and perhaps the hairdresser was always simply a means to his intended end. Really, it was bound to happen. The more Tammy shared in interviews regarding her desire/need to be married, the more tabloids speculated on who she, a rich and famous serial monogamist, may select for her next husband, the more con men became aware of her as a prime target. If Tammy's hairdresser ever talked about her new boyfriend while at work, Tammy would've heard Michael Tomlin was a rich bachelor who made his money in Nashville real estate and celebrated his wealth in all the stereotypical ways, wearing fancy clothes to drive an expensive car from his fancy office to drink expensive bottles of champagne in fancy nightclubs before returning home to an expensive apartment. After Tammy began sleeping with Michael Tomlin, she was impressed by the way he'd drop everything else going on in his busy life to lease a private jet and come visit her on the road. After she married Michael Tomlin, she received the bill for the jet and paid it with her own money. The marriage lasted a total of about forty days, during which time Tammy learned

Michael's lifestyle was a sham. He wasn't so much a rich bachelor who'd made a fortune skillfully navigating real estate deals as he was a bachelor who spent whatever money he managed to acquire on trying to appear rich. Most of the things he used to signal wealth, right down to the expensive furniture in the fancy office, were rented or placed on various lines of credit.

Nearly everyone in Tammy's life warned her against marrying Michael. The fact she did it anyway is a prime example of the stubbornness Wynette Pugh's mother faced years earlier when trying to make her teenage daughter stop chasing after a married man. Wynette's mom was so alarmed by Michael Tomlin she got in touch with George Jones and asked him to call Tammy to see if he could talk any sense into her. No matter who said it or what they said, Wynette only grew more determined to marry Michael in an extravagant wedding befitting the lifestyle to which they were both accustomed. Tammy paid for it all, of course. When the marriage ended fewer than two months after the wedding, well-informed yet confused tabloid readers began asking what everyone in Tammy's personal life had wondered all along: why on earth did she marry this guy? A few years later, her autobiography offered several different explanations in rapid succession. She was scared of her strong feelings for Burt Reynolds. She was tired of reporters asking if Burt Reynolds would become her next husband. She was worried Michael Tomlin would look like a fool if she called off the wedding right after telling reporters she was in love with Michael. That last one is a particularly strong candidate for the reason she actually went through with saying the words "I do," but it's a certainty she wasn't thinking only of Michael's embarrassment.

According to Tammy, she made the decision to marry Michael approximately forty-eight hours prior to her lawyer finding out the *National Enquirer* was working on a cover story about her relationship with Burt Reynolds. According to Tammy, the *Enquirer* was too close to their print deadline to completely change the cover after she announced her engagement to Michael Tomlin, which was why the magazine pivoted at the last minute from a story about Burt Reynolds dating Tammy Wynette to a story about Burt Reynolds dating Tammy Wynette at the same time he was dating Lucie Arnaz, daughter of Lucille Ball and Desi Arnaz. None of that makes any sense whatsoever, especially when a simple search of the magazine's archives reveals the *National Enquirer* ran that cover three months after Tammy's wedding to Michael Tomlin, by which time they were already divorced. After Tammy told this bizarre tabloid story in her autobiography, Lucie Arnaz publicly admitted to having a fling with Burt Reynolds for a year and a half just prior to the long-term relationship Burt entered into with Sally Field in 1977, the same period of time when he was dating Tammy. As such, it's exceedingly unlikely that cover story was ever supposed to be about Burt Reynolds exclusively dating and possibly marrying Tammy Wynette, meaning the questions Tammy was tired of hearing from reporters were probably not questions about Burt Reynolds exclusively dating and possibly marrying Tammy Wynette. So, did Tammy really decide to marry Michael Tomlin two whole days before reporters showed up asking questions about Burt Reynolds simultaneously dating Tammy Wynette and Lucie Arnaz? Or did she decide to marry Michael Tomlin when she heard herself telling a reporter that's what she was going to do because it was the first thing she thought to say to make them stop asking questions about Burt Reynolds simultaneously dating Tammy Wynette and Lucie Arnaz? If it sounds farfetched to propose Wynette would go through with marrying someone just because she'd lied to a tabloid about being extremely in love with any guy other than Burt Reynolds, consider the fact she told her lawyer, the man who supposedly hipped her to the tabloid article, that exact same lie. She even told the lawyer she was so in love with Michael Tomlin there would be no need for a prenup, no reason to keep their finances separate, because they were going to be together forever. She said this despite—as she later openly admitted in her autobiography—spending her entire wedding day in full cognizance and dread of the horrible mistake she was in the process of making, hating herself the whole time for going through with the ceremony and marrying a guy because she'd lied about being in love with him. Oh, and there's one more explanation she gave for her awful decision-making on this matter. Two months before the wedding, someone tried to burn her house down and she felt like she needed a man around for safety.

◇   ◇   ◇

According to Wynette, the harassment began in the spring of 1975, soon after her divorce from George Jones. It started with some sinister person calling her house late at night to breathe heavily down the phone line, then progressed to death threats received at her concert venues and hotels on tour. Then the death threats started showing up in her mailbox at home. You know the kind, letters cut one by one from a magazine and pasted into a message on a piece of paper so there's no handwriting to recognize or analyze, just like in the movies. Then came the home invasions, almost always including a twist of vandalism, whether it was graffiti left on the walls or a stopped-up sink drain under a running faucet to flood the place with water. Tammy called the cops every time something happened but they never came up with a suspect or even a solid lead, probably eventually concluding what Joan Dew and many other close sources later admitted to believing: Wynette performed most or all of these acts in an attempt to generate attention and sympathy for herself.

Even Tammy's own account of these events comes across like she's begging to be found out, acknowledging the mysterious stalker operated with an almost supernatural awareness of her life and plans. This unknown person somehow seemed aware of everything Tammy was going to do and when she was going to do it. No matter how many times Tammy changed her unlisted phone number, she claimed the prank phone calls kept coming, sometimes only hours after getting a new number.

There was never a break-in or any graffiti left at her home while she was away on tour, only when she was in Nashville. Since the word "PIG" appeared so frequently in all the graffiti left at her home in Nashville, it only makes sense to wonder if these new acts of vandalism were committed by the same person who'd used red lipstick to write the same word on a back door of Old Plantation several years earlier. Charlene and Peanutt Montgomery were convinced only Wynette could have done that. For the three months she hired a private security firm to watch her house, absolutely nothing happened, so she got rid of the surveillance and the break-ins immediately started again. All of this alleged harassment was also evidently carried out by a person without any real interest in killing or even harming Tammy Wynette. Despite over a dozen claimed incidents and many opportunities such a well-informed, homicidal stalker could have used to easily follow through on repeated death threats, they never once actually tried. The details Tammy gave of these events were rarely even halfway plausible. For example, the multiple times she claimed a skylight was left open on her flat, easily accessible roof always coincided with the wires of her security system being severed in the basement of the house. If the intruder entered through the skylight, they'd need to somehow know exactly where her security system was in the basement and be an incredibly fast person to sprint all the way through the house to cut those wires before the alarm was triggered. Alternately, suppose the intruder used a different and undiscovered point of entry, near enough to the basement they could easily locate and cut the security system wires before triggering the alarm. Why would they then choose to leave through a skylight, the furthest of many available exits in the house? Why would the intruder perform this exact combination of actions multiple times solely in order to perform this exact combination of actions toward no other apparent end? These skylight shenanigans were never accompanied by any kind of theft and never resulted in any kind of harm coming to Tammy or even any direct contact with her. It seems the only and entire point of these stealth missions was to leave some wires cut in a basement and a skylight open on a roof. Since there were often cigarette butts left on the roof or in the bushes outside, Tammy deduced the intruder must be a smoker. She was also a smoker at this time but never happened to state whether she and her tormentor enjoyed the same brand.

One night, while Tammy was still dating Rudy Gatlin, Rudy and George Richey took Tammy's daughters roller-skating while she stayed at home with Richey's then wife, Sheila. According to Tammy, she and Sheila were so involved in conversation they hadn't thought to turn on any lights inside the house when the sun went down, so her mysterious stalker probably thought nobody was home and decided to pay a visit. Tammy must have favored the skylight-as-entry theory because she claimed she was talking in the dark with Sheila when all of a sudden they both heard footsteps on the roof of the house. While trying to decide whether they should hide inside or try to run to a car, the phone rang: one of Tammy's daughters, who just so happened to call home from the skating ring. Tammy said to send Rudy and Richey back to the house at once. About ten minutes later the men pulled up to find words like "PIG" and "WHORE" written all over the outside of the house in lipstick or red paint. They checked around for the perpetrator, found nobody, then took the women and children to spend the night at the Richeys' home. When they returned the next day the inside of Tammy's house had also been vandalized with derogatory remarks, including the words "YOU SLUT" on a mirror facing down from the wooden canopy above her bed. Strangely, having already acknowledged the alleged intruder's comprehensive knowledge of the inside of her house, for some reason Tammy couldn't believe they'd found the mirror over her bed.

There's no way Tammy could have faked that entire home invasion on her own, right? George Richey's wife was with her the whole time and the graffiti was seen by both Richey and Rudy Gatlin, right? Well, Tammy's version of what happened that night was significantly different from the account given by Richey in Dolly Carlisle's 1984 biography of George Jones. There, Richey directly stated that Wynette called him at the skating rink to come back to the house. There was no fortunately timed, happenstance phone call from Tammy's daughters checking in at home. Richey also failed to mention seeing any graffiti on the outside or inside of the house when he and Rudy returned from the skating rink. He said, "When we got back, Rudy and I went through every crevice, nook, and cranny in the house. We had no gun. I had a butcher knife and a fireplace poker. Rudy had a fireplace poker. We went through every inch of the house and found nothing." Richey only talked about seeing graffiti the next day when everyone came back to the house. The graffiti he saw was only on the inside of the home, not the outside. Since his ex-wife, Sheila, died of what was ruled a suicide in 1981, she can't clarify exactly what happened when it was just her and Wynette at the house. Sheila can't be asked whether she perhaps dozed off in the darkness of the unlit home only to be awakened by Wynette convincingly terrified over having heard footsteps on the roof. Sheila can't be asked if she heard the footsteps herself. No account of that evening specified whether anyone happened to accompany Wynette when, ostensibly to pack sleeping bags and clothes for her family to spend the night with the Richeys, she went in and out of various rooms where graffiti would only be found the following day. By far the strangest thing about the way Tammy told her footsteps on the roof story is that she tried to sell it as "the most terrifying of the incidents," even though only months later it was followed by a sequence of legitimately terrifying events she could not possibly have staged herself, all much more violent than these early, oblique harassments and some posing great risk of physical harm to both her and her children.

These later assaults were often preceded by Tammy and others inside her house hearing the voices of multiple men speaking to each other outside. At least twice, some unknown person threw large rocks through the windows of her home, sending broken glass flying into rooms where Tammy sat with one or another of her daughters. She could not have done that herself. The night someone tried to burn down her house, she and her family were inside of it. Earlier in the evening Rudy Gatlin had taken Tammy, her Mama Pugh and Aunt Athalene to see *One Flew Over the Cuckoo's Nest* while two of Tammy's daughters had friends over for a slumber party. After returning from the movie, Rudy went home and everyone at Tammy's house had gone to bed when she got a stomachache, went to the kitchen for some antacid and found Aunt Athalene in the kitchen drinking a beer, so Tammy sat down to talk with her. When they heard voices speaking outside, Tammy called Rudy on the phone and asked him to come back with a gun, which he did. Rudy's search of the immediate property turned up no intruders, so he went back inside Tammy's house. A little while later they heard more noises outside and Tammy made up her mind to just go ahead and take the children over to George Richey's house. That's when Rudy smelled smoke, which they soon realized was billowing out from under the closed door to Tammy's office, two rooms down a hall from her bedroom. Someone quickly called the fire department while everybody else ran outside. After the fire trucks showed up and doused the flames without any trouble, the firemen left and the adults inspected the damage to Tammy's office. She was once more preparing to take the children over to George Richey's house when someone again smelled smoke, new smoke, now coming from the room between the burned-out office and her bedroom. Everyone ran outside to look at the house from the lawn and saw it wasn't so much another fire in that room as it was that entire room on fire, flames roaring out of the window and climbing up to the roof, where they spread to further parts of the house. By the time the fire department could be convinced there was a second fire raging at Tammy Wynette's home, not just delayed alerts from the first one they'd already extinguished, nearly half her house was destroyed. The ensuing investigation uncovered obvious evidence of arson and concluded it could only have been performed by someone close to the victim. An inside job, but who?

George Jones, Rudy Gatlin and George Richey are the names most commonly suggested in fan theories as the arsonist. Anyone who suspects George Jones in any of this harassment or the fire is operating from a place of pure fantasy and knows approximately nothing about the man. Even if his alibis on many of those nights didn't include concert appearances several states away in front of thousands of people (which they did), if he had malicious feelings toward Tammy in this period of his life (which he didn't), he'd have simply driven a car into her swimming pool before waging some extended campaign of discreet and sophisticated psychological terror. Considering Tammy's instant response to nearly every one of these harassments was to call either Rudy Gatlin or George Richey on landlines at their own homes, it's safe to say they'd have been physically unable to answer the phone if they were at her house tormenting her. Unfortunately, the police were not so quick to reach that conclusion in Rudy's case. Although he was certainly at his own home when Tammy called for help on the night of the fire, Rudy found himself a primary target in the arson investigation. The local Nashville media even printed his name as a suspect. Once Rudy passed a lie detector test, the police moved on to questioning Tammy's family members, but the stress turned out to be too much for his personal and professional relationship with Tammy. They quit seeing each other shortly after and Young Country quit working for Tammy. As for George Richey, Georgette Jones' 2011 memoir said all of these "incidents" ended as soon as Tammy agreed to marry George Richey, implying his guilt. But the fact is Georgette was a small child when these things happened and the timeline of events she presented was objectively incorrect by a couple of years. Georgette stated the first alleged home invasion took place in 1977 but Tammy said it all started in 1975. When Georgette claimed all of the home invasions, vandalism, death threats and harassment stopped after the night of the arson, she was entirely correct. It's just that there's no disputing the fact Tammy's house was set on fire way earlier, in May 1976, two months before she married Michael Tomlin.

Again, it is not clear precisely when Tammy and Michael began sleeping together or how long he dated Tammy's hairdresser beforehand. If Tammy truly did not stage the earlier and tamer forms of harassment, her full-time hairdresser's boyfriend would certainly have been privy to the information and access needed to pull off many of those stunts. But if Joan Dew and others were right to suspect Wynette of faking those early events, if Michael showed up after the alleged harassment, break-ins and death threats began, how long could it possibly take such a conniving sort of man to work out a way to take advantage of that situation once he realized what was really going on? If this man's biggest goal in life was to attain the kind of wealth he constantly pretended to possess, what might he then decide to do? Pretend we know for a fact Wynette did fake the earlier incidents. Why would she do that? To at least temporarily secure the undivided attention of the men she most often called for help? That would be George Richey, who was married to another woman, and Rudy Gatlin, who was dating other women. A third man in a position to recognize this would also be able to predict that Wynette suddenly becoming a real victim of genuinely violent attacks could only force her to realize how many miles away Richey and Rudy always were when she needed them most. Should that third man want Wynette to feel unsafe and exposed without a husband willing to commit 100 percent of his time to her, it's only a question of how far he'd be willing to go to accomplish his goal. Tammy said Michael Tomlin asked her to marry him on their third or fourth date. At the time she laughed it off because they clearly didn't know each other well enough to be married. Two months after someone set her house on fire, she said "I do."

Michael's whole attitude toward her changed as soon as they were on honeymoon in Hawaii.

He began making offhand insulting comments regarding her previous lovers and took every opportunity to try asserting himself as the dominant partner in the relationship. The only thing that seemed to make him happy was enjoying the luxuries afforded by Tammy's wealth and discussing future plans for how he wished to spend it. The whole week before the honeymoon Tammy was dealing with an excruciating stomachache and it became so bad while in Hawaii she checked into a hospital, where they diagnosed some kind of gallbladder problem, gave her a heavy-duty shot for the pain and said she'd probably require surgery when she returned home. After receiving an operation in Nashville, she was given strict instructions to relax for a week, which she decided to do in a home she owned on the beach in Florida. Michael thought Florida sounded fun and invited some of his friends along for the trip. He and those friends started drinking on the flight. Their first night of partying came to an abrupt end when Michael decided to drunkenly entertain everyone by firing off a pistol on the beach behind Tammy's house. She had to reprimand him like a child to get him to stop. The next day, Michael's friends left and he sulked his way back to Nashville. Tammy had just settled in for her prescribed week of relaxation when the doorbell rang. It was another of Michael's friends who'd been told he could stay at her house for the week. Tammy said "screw it," left her house to the kid and booked the only flight she could find back to Nashville, which coincidentally included a stop in Atlanta, Georgia, where Burt Reynolds just so happened to be filming *Smokey and the Bandit* . . . with Sally Field, the co-star he was rumored to be dating. Tammy never made it onto the second plane due to pain from her unhealed surgery wound, which was now infected after coming open at one end where, according to her, "a stitch had been removed." (If Tammy knew how this stitch managed to come undone or who "removed" it, she didn't say.) For some reason she felt certain Burt Reynolds could recommend a good doctor in the Atlanta area, so Tammy found out where he was staying and checked in to the same hotel. Later that evening Burt visited her room and, just like that, he was all the way back in her life. They spent Thanksgiving through Christmas of 1976 together in Florida with only a few days apart and continued seeing each other, nonexclusively, through the summer of 1977, at which point Tammy said the romance relaxed into "a warm, easy friendship."

Tammy never saw Michael Tomlin again. After they separated, she learned he'd gone to her bank in Nashville while she was hospitalized for the gallbladder surgery and withdrew eight thousand dollars he told the bank was for a hospital bill that turned out to not actually exist. When Tammy tried to have the marriage annulled Michael dug in for a full divorce and a three hundred thousand dollar settlement. Tammy's lawyer, the same one who tried to get her to sign a prenup and avoid all of this, got Michael to agree to go away if allowed to file a joint income tax return with Tammy for the year, giving him 50 percent of her refund check.

Following the failure of Tammy's fourth marriage the media continued snooping around in her private affairs and she gave them plenty to write. In October 1976 the *Enquirer* ran that cover story about Burt Reynolds simultaneously dating her and Lucie Arnaz. In April 1977, *People* magazine ran a cover story on Sally Field that discussed her romance with Burt Reynolds, while *Modern People* magazine ran a cover story about Burt simultaneously dating Tammy, Sally Field and multiple other women. By that time there were rumors Tammy had begun an affair with a married member of her tourmates the Statler Brothers, an affair she later all-but-confirmed was the inspiration for a song she wrote and recorded in July 1977, "That's the Way It Could Have Been." The lyrics find her imagining how beautiful and perfect life would be if only she'd met a certain man before he married someone else. The song wasn't released as a single but it did come out on an album containing one of her final Top 10 hits, so plenty of fans heard it and wondered who she was singing about. Since nowhere near as many people heard the rumors about her dating a Statler Brother as the number of people who saw the various Burt Reynolds articles, Burt once again became a fan favorite speculation. But there was also always George Jones.

◇　　◇　　◇

Billy Sherrill had capitalized on their reunion at the 1975 DJ convention by getting Tammy and Jones back in the studio to record "Golden Ring." Written by Bobby Braddock and Rafe VanHoy, "Golden Ring" could've been a short story or film treatment, but it became one of the best country records of all time. Braddock began work on the song after seeing the 1974 made-for-TV movie *The Gun*, one of those "biopic of an inanimate object" tales (similar to 1993's *Twenty Bucks*), following events which transpire around a .38 special revolver's multiple transfers of ownership. Borrowing heavily from the melody of "Long Black Veil" by Marijohn Wilkin and Danny Dill, the verses of "Golden Ring" track the life of a simple wedding band from a pawnshop purchase by a young couple, through their wedding ceremony, through the marriage falling apart, to the ring landing right back in a pawnshop where another young couple considers buying it. The chorus between each verse stops by to remind us it is love, not a hard rock affixed to a circular piece of metal, which truly keeps a marriage together. Billy Sherrill told drummer Jerry Carrigan to put away his sticks and play the kit with his hands to mimic the warmth of the song's message, leaving Jerry's occasional closing of a hi-hat the only "cold, metallic thing" heard on the record. "Golden Ring" was recorded the month before half of Tammy's house burned down, so that's Rudy Gatlin and his brother, Steve, still around on background vocals. In May 1976, the month the single came out, George Jones gave Tammy a brand-new Ford Thunderbird as a Mother's Day gift. The higher "Golden Ring" climbed the charts, the more nervous it would've made anyone with money riding on Burt Reynolds for Tammy Wynette's next husband. But by the time their comeback record hit #1, Tammy pulled a switcheroo on anyone expecting more than a professional reunion with Jones by entering the blink-and-you-missed-it marriage to Michael Tomlin. After little more than a month, that fell apart, leaving Tammy's adoring/confused audience to wonder if she would now choose Burt Reynolds or George Jones.

After "Golden Ring," Billy Sherrill released the Tammy and George recording of Francis Craig's "Near You," cut in their final session as a married couple. Without the backstory of how the single was made long ago on the night their marriage ended, fans took it as another sign of rekindled love and sent it to the top of the Country chart, making it the final #1 hit by Tammy and George together and the final #1 Country record bearing Tammy Wynette's name. The month "Near You" came out, Tammy was hospitalized for bronchitis while on tour in London and George Jones caught an overseas flight from Nashville to be by her side. On the way to see her, Jones told reporters, "There will never be anyone else for either of us," which was the kind of thing he continued to say in interviews at least as late as June of 1977, when he said "I think we still love each other. I know I love her." The subject matter of their next single together was too on the nose for it to not have been deliberately written into this narrative by Billy Sherrill, George Richey and Roger Bowling. On "Southern California," Jones sounds like he's asking Tammy to stay with him in Tennessee while Tammy explains the pull she feels to explore her options out in Los Angeles. The record hit #5.

Everyone, especially Wynette, knew it would not be long before she walked down the aisle again. Despite whatever grand gestures and statements of devotion George Jones gave to her or the media, she knew he was drinking more than ever. Then, at some point in 1977, he fell more in love with cocaine than he'd ever been with booze. As nice as it may have felt to be courted by Jones again, remarrying him was never a realistic option. Despite Burt Reynolds' occasional, quirky displays of affection (like naming a not-very-flattering character after her in *Smokey and the Bandit*), if he was ready, willing or able to become a one-woman man with Tammy, then it sure seems like he'd at least have made a sincere attempt by this point. One of the things she found most appealing about Burt was the fact he didn't need her money or fame because he possessed more of both on his own. She never had to worry about him secretly being some kind of parasitic social, financial or industry climber. After the Michael Tomlin fiasco she could no longer trust herself to spot such a villain. Tammy also knew Husband #5 needed to last forever or else she'd spend the rest of her life listening to people joke about how Miss Stand By Your Man went through more marriages than could be counted on one hand. Again, how long could it possibly take a conniving sort of man to work out a way to take advantage of this situation once he realized what was really going on? This time the man had been nearby for quite a long while.

◇   ◇   ◇

According to Georgette Jones, George Richey was one of the first people Tammy contacted after realizing the marriage to Michael Tomlin would never work. Shortly afterward, Richey formally left his wife to marry Tammy. They were wed in July 1978 and Tammy spent the rest of her life as Richey's wife, publicly singing his praises and claiming she'd finally found true love with her own personal savior. Tammy's daughters said the secret truth was a totally different story. According to them, it only took about three months after the wedding for George Richey to beat up Tammy and the newlyweds covered up the abuse with a fake kidnapping, followed by decades of lying to police, the media and fans.

By the end of 1978 the marriage entered a period Georgette named the Great Divide, a time when people previously close to Tammy—trusted friends, relatives, employees, those who'd lived and worked with her for years—were gradually pushed out of her life. Although Tammy's children loved their nanny very much, she was soon gone and replaced by someone Richey approved. Tammy's mother and stepfather, Mildred and Foy Lee, who'd practically raised Georgette up to this point, were told they'd be spending less time with their granddaughter, which hurt their feelings so much they moved away from Nashville entirely. Georgette later found out this happened because Richey convinced Tammy her child was being spoiled by the grandparents. Tammy's backing band? The group of guys who were called the Jones Boys until they chose to work for her rather than their original boss who'd given them that name? One by one, they drifted off to get away from Richey, until Charlie Carter, the guitarist so devoted to Tammy everyone assumed he was secretly in love with her, was the only Country Gentleman who remained. Tammy's lawyer? The guy who helped her undo the Michael Tomlin mistake he tried to talk her out of making in the first place? Gone. Joan Dew? Who went out of her way to help obscure severe drug addiction and various embarrassing truths in Tammy's official autobiography? Once the book came out Richey baselessly accused Joan of leaking all that information in the form of gossip around Nashville, then unsuccessfully tried to stiff her on the agreed-upon payment for writing the book.

Because of how much Billy Sherrill and Tammy Wynette trusted and depended upon one another, they each had it written into their separate contracts with Epic that if either ever left the label, for any reason, the two of them could legally continue working together. In 1980, only a couple years after marrying George Richey, Tammy Wynette chose to end her professional relationship with Billy Sherrill.

NINETEEN

SELLING SOAP

◇ A Low Opinion of American Housewives ◇
The Financial and Political Dynamics of Soap Commercials
◇ Peaking in the 1980s ◇ The Death of a Genre? ◇

For most of modern history most soap products have been primarily branded and marketed toward women because, for most of modern history, companies could safely assume most soap was purchased by women, most of whom it could safely be assumed were doing most of the shopping for a household and staying home on weekdays to use various soap products cleaning the house, children, clothing and dishes while men worked outside the home. With the advent of commercial radio stations in the 1920s, all of these very safe assumptions led to daytime programming targeted at the "typical American housewife." Since this hypothetical woman had only recently been given the right to vote, probably did not work outside the home and probably did not have a college degree, she was presumed to have no use for news of politics, economy, academic interests or really anything that didn't directly affect and/or reflect her home, her family or her friends, who were also presumed to be other "typical American housewives." Therefore, most nonmusical programming in the first two decades of daytime radio was educational, based on the premise American housewives were probably a little bit stupid and would (or, perhaps, should) take an interest in bettering their cleaning, cooking, parenting and social skills. In those early days of radio, when every show mentioned its main sponsor so often the brand might as well have been part of the program title (and often was), the advice was sometimes dished out by a brand's fictional spokesperson, like Betty Crocker. Betty had existed as a character in print since the beginning of the 1920s, but the middle of the decade found a human actor's voice bringing her to life on *The Betty Crocker School of Air*, essentially an audio home economics class. Fast forward to the 1940s and *Fortune* declared Betty Crocker (again, not a real person) the second-most famous woman in

America, right after the president's wife. But by the 1940s, Betty was one of only a few voices to survive the most monolithic paradigm shift that ever hit daytime radio: soap opera.

While serialized installments of a continuing narrative were nothing new, the form we recognize as soap opera first hit radio in the 1920s. Its rapid takeover of daytime airwaves began after a station manager at WGN in Chicago decided to center a drama in the home of a fictional Irish-American matriarch. His idea was to attract an audience of housewives who related to either the main character or her daughter, who navigated their social circles within plots which, wouldn't you know it, somehow always found their way around to plugging a sponsor's product. Pitches for the first two iterations of the show were rejected by potential sponsors. Then Irna Phillips, a voice actor looking for more work than she presently had at the radio station, asked for a chance to write a new pilot. Her version was accepted by a sponsor and debuted in 1930 as *Painted Dreams*, generally believed to be the first soap opera on daytime radio. By the end of the decade, nine out of ten shows on daytime radio were soaps.

And how best to differentiate a soap opera from every other form of scripted, serialized drama that is ultimately funded by ad sales? Perhaps it would be instructive to point out the term "soap opera" has always been a sarcastic and implicitly sexist insult. Because who else but a bored, lonely, uncultured, easily manipulated and perhaps even mentally unwell housewife would spend five days a week listening to an extended soap commercial that was barely disguised as melodrama and obviously produced as cheaply as possible in order to consistently deliver new content every weekday? To air a new episode of a scripted radio show every day from Monday thru Friday, it was impossible to hold rehearsals as one would prior to staging a production of a play or filming a movie, impossible for 99 percent of actors to memorize their lines, impossible for anyone involved in any part of the process to do much more than the bare minimum required to quickly churn out some iteration of plot progression 260 times a year. A bunch of actors standing around microphones speaking lines from a script they've only read twice, once or maybe not at all before going live on radio is about as far away as a performance of fiction can get from the grand ole tradition of opera, with its expensive orchestra, expansive sets, virtuoso singers and tightly rehearsed stage directions. The term "soap opera" was never intended as a favorable comparison. (Before "soap opera" took hold, "washboard weeper" was another term regularly used to refer to soaps in the 1930s.) Regardless of such stigma, following the popularity of *Painted Dreams* soap operas became so ubiquitous there was nearly nothing else on major broadcasting networks during the day in the 1940s.

The Guiding Light began as a radio show on NBC in 1937. The sponsor, Procter & Gamble, only learned how massive their audience was when they tried canceling the show a few years into its run and received seventy-five thousand letters from angry fans. *The Guiding Light* was co-created by Irna Phillips, who left WGN after they refused to sell *Painted Dreams* to a national network and

Irna failed to win ownership of the program in a lawsuit. Episodes of *Painted Dreams* had nearly always hinged upon the recurring question of whether the modern-minded daughter would choose to
pursue the career she wanted as a fashion model or, as her traditional-thinking mother encouraged,
settle down with some good man and become a housewife. This was often viewed as a fictionaliza-
tion of Irna Phillips' own real-life internal conflict. Soon after graduating high school she became
pregnant and the young father ran away from his responsibility, leaving Irna on her own to deliver
what turned out to be a stillborn baby. Most folks believed she then spent the rest of her life with
dreams of a good man coming along and walking her down the aisle so she could do the "happily
ever after" thing as a housewife, a dream that never came true, leaving Irna to mine those fantasies
as source material for the stories she told other women across America. However, that tidy little tale
was muddied by conflicting comments Irna gave to the press over the years. Her public statements
on marriage ranged from declarations she would give it all up if the right man came along to openly
mocking that very same notion. Though she never was married, after Irna died in the 1970s details
of her active love life were leaked from a never-published memoir, debunking the idea that she was
some kind of spinster wasting away for want of a man. But it is true that after losing her partner and
the baby, Irna found comfort in listening to the radio broadcasts of a local preacher, who became
the inspiration for the pivotal character in *The Guiding Light*. The title was a reference to the lamp
visible in an office window of the nondenominational minister residents of a Chicago suburb visited
for fatherly advice.

Irna's back-to-back hit shows soon caused imitators to blanket weekday airwaves with soap
operas, most all-but-indistinguishable from each other, thus establishing aspects of the form that
would survive for decades, well beyond the genre's transition from radio to TV. For example, without
any visual information or pages of text to offer omniscient exposition and/or any character's internal
dialogue, radio soaps relied upon a narrator's voice to usher listeners from scene to scene with small
expository segments or recaps of events from previous episodes. Every episode usually ended with
the narrator listing the unresolved predicaments facing each major character, typically underscored
by an intensely dramatic electric organ. If there's one defining characteristic of soap opera, firmly in
place from the beginning and surviving through the entire history of the genre, it's the snail's pace
at which the perpetually open-ended plots proceed. The reason soaps took a 90 percent share of
daytime was because everyone in the radio industry who wasn't contentedly relaxed with already-
successful shows in the other 10 percent of programming scrambled to profit from the discovery of
a consumer demographic more committed and loyal than anybody had ever seen. If whatever minor
twist they came up with on the standard formula managed to break through the competing noise
and gain an audience, that meant they could stop funneling resources into looking for a twist and

start milking the one they'd found for as many years or decades as fans would pay attention. The internal and external conflicts between a show's cast of characters would be aggravated, repressed, compounded and bounced off each other in endless variations but almost never actually resolved. To "fix" any major character's core conflict without putting a more compelling problem in its place would be to essentially unmake the character, erasing all of the questions that kept listeners tuning in to hear what happened next. Since every soap opera's most important goal was to perpetuate itself for as long as possible, any given plot device regarded as especially interesting to fans would be wrung out to the last drop and then some, which inevitably took every successful show to absolutely inane narrative territory. For instance, one early radio soap stretched a character's passage through a revolving door across seventeen episodes as she experienced a series of flashbacks to her past.

◇   ◇   ◇

In 1942, failed pulp novelist turned pop psychiatrist Louis Berg began giving lectures and printing pamphlets on the dangers soap opera posed to women. He claimed soaps were responsible for everything from high blood pressure and vertigo to night terrors and diarrhea. Pop culture media ran with these ludicrous theories and the merit of soap opera as entertainment has been subject to much critical debate ever since. "Studies," polls and market research on soap opera dating back to the 1930s were nearly all tainted by the previously mentioned contemptuous assumptions about the genre's audience. Not until the 1970s did proper research finally begin to overturn the stereotype of soap opera fans addicted to events in a fictional universe they were dumb enough to confuse for some kind of documentary about real people living real lives. By that point, soaps had taken over daytime television the same as radio, complete with a couple decades of hand-wringing over the apocalyptic damage these TV shows were sure to wreak on American society. Housewives in the 1930s could listen to their trashy radio shows while doing all the cleaning and cooking, but if they needed to sit and look at a screen to keep up with these stupid stories, then the next thing you know men would be coming home from work to dirty houses, unbathed children and empty dinner tables, etc.

The moral panic over bringing soaps to TV meant as little to sponsors and creators as all previous mockery of radio soaps. Their problem with the transition to TV was they doubted it could even be accomplished. Adding a visual dimension to the genre would bring an exponential increase to the shoestring production budgets that made these shows so profitable. With the costs of cameras, sets, lighting, costumes, makeup and the additional staff required for all these new departments, you could say goodbye to your hefty profit margin. Some clumsy attempts to move radio soaps over to TV tried to entirely ignore these new concerns. In 1946, Procter & Gamble aired *Big Sister* on CBS by simply aiming one camera at the radio actors as they stood around a microphone speaking lines from a script, basically broadcasting a behind-the-scenes livestream which fans of the pre-existing radio show had not requested and did not want. But Procter & Gamble kept experimenting with production techniques, CBS kept making room in their daytime schedule for the genre and this was the partnership that eventually broke soaps on television. By the mid-1950s, CBS was referring to themselves in industry trades as The Network That Invented Daytime and Procter & Gamble was spending more money on TV than any other sponsor in the medium. Procter & Gamble had long been aware of serialized narrative's power as a vehicle for advertising, ever since the marketing agency handling their Ivory soap account came up with the idea of launching a comic strip in the Sunday paper about a family who exclusively used Ivory soap. The great results from that campaign influenced their decision to invest so heavily in sponsoring soaps on radio and again through the challenging transition to television. One of their first big hits on TV was Irna Phillips' *Guiding Light*, approximately fifteen years into a nearly uninterrupted run on radio when licensed to Proctor & Gamble buddies, CBS.

Though TV soaps did eventually accept the inevitable and add budgets for things like costuming actors and building a set or two, the industry philosophy of working as fast and dirty as possible didn't change at all. Heavy use of electric organ still reinforced the emotional tone of a scene for viewers and unrehearsed actors. The all-knowing narrators were still around to provide verbal exposition, especially when it could save an episode from needing additional scenes or sets. As production teams discovered various techniques to disguise their minimal budget, several new tropes of the form were established, like filling the screen with lingering close-ups on the faces and upper bodies of actors to keep viewers from focusing on sparse and cheaply built sets. For all these reasons TV soaps carried on the long tradition of being mocked by the intelligentsia. The second half of the twentieth century provides countless examples of successful soap writers, actors, producers, networks and sponsors attempting to distance themselves from the genre, often outright claiming their biggest soaps were not actually soaps at all. Soon after the transition to TV, the term "soap opera" was essentially banned within the industry. One could be fired for using it to refer to a program on set or in an interview. The euphemism most commonly used in its place was "daytime drama."

The one person most often credited with turning the soap opera into daytime drama is Agnes Nixon, who created *All My Children* and *One Life to Live* near the end of the 1960s. A few decades earlier, Agnes' first job in soap opera was as an apprentice working under Irna Phillips at radio, where she learned to write soap and became familiar with all the criticisms highbrow detractors threw at the field. Since most attacks focused on the soap-opera-as-vehicle-for-shameless-advertising angle, Agnes helped introduce a little subtlety to that necessity, such as the way a

January 1963 episode of Irna Phillips' *As the World Turns* opened on two women washing dishes at a kitchen sink. Neither woman mentions the brand of soap in use but, seeing as how this scene was immediately preceded by a commercial for the main sponsor's soap, we don't really need a character to come right out and say it, do we? Because soaps were so often criticized for milking every drop of interest from a plot point through slow-motion story progression, Agnes Nixon established a way to remix the genre's trademark pacing while remaining true to the same old philosophy of self-perpetuation. Rather than episodes comprising a series of scenes shown from beginning to end, each reaching a conclusion in sequential order, Agnes scripted episodes to cycle through the scenes piecemeal, bringing all the threads to a climax and/or cliff-hanger near the same time at the end of each installment. For example, say a new episode opens on a Plot Development (probably a return to whatever happened at end of the previous episode), then cuts to the beginning of Conversation 1 (probably some characters talking about the Plot Development), then cuts to the beginning of Conversation 2 (probably a different set of characters talking about the Plot Development), then cuts to commercial. We would return from commercial by checking in on how the Plot Development has escalated, then how Conversation 1 has escalated, then Conversation 2, then more commercials, rinse and repeat until each strand of the episode reaches maximum lather . . . just in time to tell viewers they need to come back tomorrow if they want to find out what happens next. Agnes Nixon took over as head writer on the TV version of *Guiding Light* by the beginning of the 1960s and by the end of the decade TV soaps either structured episodes with her new method or got crushed by all the shows that did. The themes she introduced to storylines of her shows were similarly influential.

As one would expect from programming owned and/or sponsored by companies beneath the umbrellas of various conglomerates with so much to gain by upholding the status quo, soaps up to and through the 1950s largely celebrated traditional—one could even say conservative— perspectives on marriage, "family values," gender dynamics and so on. Characters who disregarded social norms or even expressed a desire to do so were unambiguously depicted as misguided, confused, downright mentally unwell or maybe just plain wicked, a roadblock in the way of good and upright characters pursuing their American dreams. In the event any of these insane deviants ever visited a psychiatrist to discuss qualms over, say, being a housewife who believes she'd rather enter the workforce, she'd likely be told the key to happiness lay in forgetting such foolishness, staying home and accepting the role expected of her gender. Characters who couldn't or wouldn't happily perform stereotypical gender roles were often introduced only to depict someone failing in attempts to take an unconventional path. Such characters who were not then written off a show typically stopped resisting and found happiness by conforming to society. The genre's most influential early voice, Irna Phillips, does seem to have actually subscribed to this ideology and rejected the Women's Liberation movement that rose to prominence around the time soaps transitioned from radio to TV. But it was soon Agnes Nixon's turn to run things and she had a newer way of thinking.

Though she's largely credited with elevating the form to daytime drama, Agnes preferred the euphemism "realistic drama" when discussing her soaps. She's believed to be the first writer to sympathetically portray main characters dealing with health scares and physical illness, rather than using either as mere devices to punish progressive-minded characters or to bring minor characters in and out of a story. She routinely included characters who represented conservative perspectives but did so while allowing positive (or at least tolerant) portrayals of liberal stances on hot-button issues, like feminism, abortion, anti-war protest and so on. Another Irna Phillips protege, William J. Bell, spent the second half of the 1960s doing away with the genre's reliance on chaste, chivalric courting and innuendo toward off-screen romance, then replaced all of that with undisguised vocal and physical expressions of feminine sexuality. The women on his shows possessed libidos and made no secret of it. Between Agnes, William and their imitators, characters who'd have been punished on the soaps of previous decades for not adhering to gendered stereo- types were now allowed more complexity, introducing the so-called "scheming villainess" and "tor- tured hero" stereotypes so prevalent in late '60s/early '70s daytime TV. These were crafty women who tried using their minds and/or bodies for personal gain and to destroy the lives of enemies; beastly men whose rough and rude exteriors hid some secret pain, usually only able to be reached by the love of a good (or bad) and beautiful woman. In 1966, ABC began airing the supernatural soap *Dark Shadows*, which introduced daytime to a male vampire and male werewolf, both of whom were openly lusted after by the show's women characters and the show's audience. From there the writers of *Dark Shadows* did pretty much anything they could think of to create thrilling and surprising narratives, like kill off main characters then travel through time or to an alternate universe so the starring actors could remain on the show, with no regard for what Agnes Nixon called "realistic drama," the approach favored by most soaps through the '60s and into the '70s.

Unfortunately, the Civil Rights and Women's Liberation movements so heavily represented throughout and largely responsible for the genre's newfound realism did not bring many signifi- cant roles for non-white or non-straight characters. Due to soap opera's reliance on family and romance as the matrix connecting any given show's cast, it was often explained that making a non- white or non-straight person a major part of that world would've practically demanded featuring an interracial or non-hetero relationship on daytime television. While it's true the move from radio to TV brought several changes to the back end of the industry—most notably the number of pro- grams owned by writers, production companies or television networks rather than a sponsor—if all the companies buying commercials on your block of programming cancel their account, then you no longer have a block of programming. So, the companies writing the biggest checks still held the power to define where a line was and make sure a program never crossed it. Irna Phillips spoke of wanting to "integrate" her soaps as far back as the 1960s, but Procter & Gamble would only allow her to place Black characters in background roles, which she felt was offensive, therefore she chose to use no Black characters at all. In 1964, when Irna wanted a main character on *Another World* to receive an illegal abortion, show owners Procter & Gamble refused to allow it until Irna clarified the woman would get an infection during the operation and lose the ability to have more children, at which point Proctor & Gamble agreed to this "negative" depiction of abortion.

Aside from needing the money men to approve controversial decisions, head writers on TV soaps had near-universal creative control over their stories. The genre's viewers being so forthcoming with fan mail, audience desires were perhaps sometimes taken into consideration but the only way a soap was able to churn and burn five new episodes of scripted television a week was by allowing nearly nobody other than a head writer to have an opinion. Most people on the set of any given soap rarely even met the head writer. They were deliberately kept apart in order to prevent personal relationships from causing difficulties. What if an actor's contract came up for renegotiation right around the time they began feeling like the biggest star on the show and they decided to ask for a much larger salary? If the actor was good friends with the head writer that could make it quite difficult to get them written off the show. Because it was the head writer who, usually alone but sometimes with a partner or assistant, locked themselves away to create an outline of what would happen to all the characters on a show over, say, the next six months. That outline was then segmented into individual episodes which were assigned to various associate writers, who fleshed out the story with dialogue and stage directions faithful to what the audience knew about each character. These associate writers, too, were typically kept away from the actors even though they had no power to decide major plot points. At every stage of production after the head writer's outline, everyone else—the other writers, the actors, the directors, everyone—was just unquestioningly following a plan which may as well have been set in stone.

By the 1960s this process was working so well for daytime TV that ABC decided to try scheduling a soap opera in the evening, a.k.a. prime time, when millions of working-class people were at home, creating an exponentially larger audience with higher ad rates to match. Of course, they never called it a soap opera. The executive producer of *Peyton Place* insisted, even though they hired Irna Phillips as a consultant, the program was a "high-class anthology drama." *Peyton Place* was a huge hit at prime time, creating instant stars of Ryan O'Neal and Mia Farrow; though it only ran for five seasons because ratings dropped when Mia Farrow left the show to be "a serious actor."

She wanted to make cinema, not soap opera. Regardless of such ongoing dismissive attitudes, more soaps followed on prime time and the genre entered the 1970s more popular and profitable than ever. In the second half of the decade, home videotape technology became affordable to the working class. With the ability to set a timer on a VHS or Betamax recorder, soap fans with day jobs could keep up with TV shows on their own schedules, no matter the time of airing. Daytime drama surged toward its commercial (and many would say creative) peak.

In 1978, CBS premiered the big-budget, prime-time soap *Dallas*, still one of the most-referenced TV shows ever, thanks to the third season ending on a cliff-hanger where the main villain was shot by an unseen assassin, leaving viewers to spend eight months wondering "Who shot J.R.?" while watching the brand-new *Dallas* spin-off soap, *Knots Landing* . . . which also became a hit and stayed on the air for fifteen years. In 1981, ABC launched *Dynasty* in prime time. *Dallas*, *Knots Landing* and *Dynasty* all centered around families who struck it rich in the oil business, reflective of a new trend in soaps to largely ignore real-world political and social issues, focusing instead on one type of fantasy or another. That trend persisted through the end of the decade. When *The Bold and the Beautiful* launched in 1987, it featured a family who struck it rich in the fashion industry and lived and dressed accordingly. For most of the genre's working-class audience, such wealth was itself a fantasy and, naturally, soap creators ran through endless modern reiterations of centuries-old fables based on romance between a rich character and a poor character. But this new penchant for fantasy went far beyond tales of marrying into high society, adding further elements of such nonrealistic genres as action/adventure and even science fiction on soaps that had never previously ventured in those directions. For instance, in the beginning of the 1980s, a villain on *General Hospital* tried to send an entire city back to the ice age using a weather-control device. The suspension of reality necessary for such storylines to work was perhaps assisted by another trend: the extended daydream sequence. Any given soap's "real-world" plotline may have seemed a bit more believable when placed alongside the things audiences saw by following characters into their imaginations, where love or lust for another character could be acted out with comically inflated dream logic, sometimes straight up reenacting classic fairy tales or famous movie scenes. These late '70s/early '80s trends all coincided with an increased focus on kissing, both in daydreams and the "real world," to such a degree it almost seemed like soaps were trying to prove two people making out could be a form of pornography. Many critics, journalists and historians have suggested the genre's escape into horny make-believe, still acted out nearly exclusively by heterosexual Caucasians, wasn't so much a backlash against the previous decades' focus on various social inequalities as it was a result of naively assuming those issues, having been acknowledged, were now resolved. Whatever the case, these were the tropes carried into the genre's commercial golden age.

Without question, the single most-watched event in soap opera history was the 1981 wedding of Luke and Laura, the so-called supercouple of *General Hospital*. 1981 was also the year Rick Springfield, fairly certain his fifth solo album would sell as poorly as his previous few and looking for a steady paycheck, took the role of Dr. Noah Drake on *General Hospital*. When that album's first single "Jessie's Girl" went #1 Pop, Rick Springfield simultaneously became a rock star and a soap star, continuing to play Dr. Noah Drake for another two years. In the year 1984, soaps brought in nearly $1.25 billion in ad sales, a figure the industry had never reached before and never would again. In 1986, her recording career in shambles, Tammy Wynette took a role on the soap opera *Capitol*, which aired on CBS, under the same corporate umbrella as Columbia subsidiary Epic Records. Surprising nobody, the part Tammy played was that of a hairstylist who decided to become a barroom singer and, one night at closing time, invited a customer back to her place. It was only after the sparks flew that she discovered the guy was a prominent judge and congressman, whose children would become quite suspicious Tammy was just some social climber looking to improve her financial circumstances. The role didn't last very long but neither did the show, as it was canceled about a year after her character appeared.

◇   ◇   ◇

Soap opera's slide into irrelevance was not sudden but consistent and observable. By the 1990s, every soap's creators were obviously well aware of the genre's diminishing returns. One can tell merely by looking at all the desperate attempts to correct course. Placing hot-button political issues back in the spotlight? They tried it. Allowing non-white, non-straight characters to play significant parts in main storylines? They tried it. Having an evil witch bring a children's doll to life? They tried it. That last one happened on *Passions*, the late '90s/early '00s soap at least partially intended as a deadpan spoof of the genre . . . created by the same writer responsible for a character on *Days of Our Lives* much more seriously becoming possessed by Satan a full five years earlier. Within a four-year period around 2010, *All My Children*, *One Life to Live*, *As the World Turns* and *Guiding Light* were all canceled. With only two brief hiatuses since beginning on radio in 1937, the seventy-plus-year span of *Guiding Light* makes it the longest-running serialized performance of narrative fiction in history.

Nowadays, anyone who tunes in to network TV in the morning or afternoon is likely to find content somewhat similar to the daytime programming which preceded the rise of soaps on radio: variations on a talk show or roundtable discussion, presented as educational or at least informational, only now with more focus on the state of culture outside a viewer's home, though perhaps with the occasional easy and delicious recipe still thrown in the mix. There are four legacy soaps that remain on the air: *General Hospital, The Bold and the Beautiful, The Young and the Restless* and *Days of Our Live*s. It's probably not a coincidence all four are scheduled to run during the lunch hour, giving fans something to watch while on their break from work. Other than these holdouts, the genre's extinction seems inevitable.

Those still paying attention have many theories to explain how this happened. For one thing, the longest-running shows all came with decades of backstory a person would need to catch up on in order to have the full context for events in new episodes and, for nearly the first thirty years of the genre's existence on radio and TV, programs were broadcast live, never recorded. The best a potential new viewer of a long-running soap in the 1990s could hope to find would have been a fan website with recaps of major storylines. However, this theory fails to account for all the new soaps launched in the 1980s and 1990s that never found an audience. There's a more plausible conspiracy theory among fans: even though making soap opera has always been cheap, it is nowhere near as inexpensive as producing a talk show, where you can use the same exact set every single day and do not need to hire nearly as many people to net the same amount of viewers as a fully scripted series. This theory supposes networks and production companies avoided the backlash of suddenly ending beloved soaps for the sake of profit margins by knowingly hiring writers who either had no experience in the genre or were known to despise it, then leaving them to sabotage legacy soaps with storylines that repelled longtime fans, thereby justifying cancellation.

The truth is soap opera hasn't died and probably never will. It's only gotten better at disguising itself. Increased production values, slightly quicker pacing and maybe cutting back the release of new episodes to one a week so actors can take the time to rehearse has allowed several soaps to hide in plain sight. The most obvious characteristics of the genre—like lingering shots of the facial expression on each character before the scene cuts to commercial—may have been toned down a little, updated or done away with entirely but a strong soap influence was undeniably there in long-running shows like *Beverly Hills 90210*, *ER*, even *Supernatural*. One could say the same thing about several of the longest-running shows currently more than a decade into airing during prime time . . . but none of the creators would ever admit to making a soap opera.

TWENTY

DIVORCE/DEATH

◇ The Best Country Song of All Time ◇
Billy Sherrill vs. George Jones and Cocaine ◇ The Divorce/Death Trilogy ◇

According to endless lists published in the last fifty years, "He Stopped Loving Her Today" is The Best and/or Saddest Country Song of All Time. Millions of people believe the George Jones recording of that song was the peak of an entire musical genre and any suggestion otherwise would be tantamount to heresy. But anyone able to discard such inherited beliefs and nostalgic attachment in order to listen objectively should be able to hear the strain in a singer's voice caused by several years of attacking his nasal cavity and vocal cords with cocaine. It's nowhere near the best George Jones vocal performance, so how can it be his best recording, let alone the peak of a whole genre? Billy Sherrill denied the record was anything like a masterpiece of production, saying he was much prouder of his own work on Charlie Rich's "The Most Beautiful Girl." He said all he did on "He Stopped Loving Her Today" was use a bunch of tricks to emotionally manipulate the audience.

Really, "He Stopped Loving Her Today" isn't even the best song on 1980's *I Am What I Am* LP. Simply allow the turntable needle to drag through to the following track, "I've Aged Twenty Years in Five." It's true Jones spent much of the year prior to that recording session living in a car parked in a Nashville alleyway, saturating his body with poisons and arguing about a hallucinated reality with multiple personalities in his mind until a friend finally committed him to a mental institution. It's true a time-lapse video of the visible aging to his face from the years 1975 to 1980 would look like something from a horror film. But you don't need to know any of the backstory to hear and believe the trauma in his haunted delivery of the lyrics "I've seen the dark side of life." That line appears only once in the song, during the bridge, never allowing its impact to become diminished through repetition, leaving us to wonder if Jones couldn't face the thought of saying those words twice. To be clear, this is also not The Best and/or Saddest Country Song of All Time. It's merely one very good reason "He Stopped Loving Her Today" doesn't deserve that title.

Mass consensus on the peak of an entire art form is never good for that art form. It's in everyone's best interest to agree there is no such thing. But forget about The Best Country Song part for a minute. If any song does deserve to be called The Saddest Country Song, then it surely could never have been a hit single. Truly devastating music is much too dangerous to hit #1. What #1 record could possibly be sadder than some writer pouring pain and grief into a song that never becomes commercially successful because it leaves everyone who hears it so emotionally wrecked they never buy a copy? "He Stopped Loving Her Today" wasn't even written as a sad song, which becomes blatantly apparent once you disregard the record and look only at the lyrics. In 1980—the year the single came out and was almost instantly labeled The Saddest Country Song Ever—one of the writers, Curly Putman, told the *Montgomery Alabama Journal*: ". . . saying that somebody loved somebody that much and the day he died is the day he stopped loving her is positive." The other writer, Bobby Braddock, said he and Curly originally set out to write the song as comedy, not tragedy.

Braddock was accustomed to having his songs land differently than intended. It's the kind of thing that can happen when you try to make jokes out of things many people take very seriously. His original version of "D-I-V-O-R-C-E" was written to be as ironic as a Monty Python sketch until Curly Putman adjusted the melody, making it possible for Tammy Wynette to break hearts all the way to #1. Conversely, Braddock was being dead serious when he wrote the song "Her Name Is" about his longing for the day he wouldn't need to sneak around with the married woman he was covertly dating at the time. Then, right after Braddock's "Golden Ring" went #1 for George Jones and Tammy Wynette in 1976, Billy Sherrill ran what sounds like a clavinet through pedal steel guitarist Pete Drake's famous talkbox device and turned "Her Name Is" into a cutesy joke, which fans interpreted as Jones stopping just short of publicly announcing a secretly rekindled romance between himself and ex-wife Tammy Wynette. The single hit #3 and stayed in Jones' set lists for the rest of his career. For live performances, at the point where the lyrics dropped out on the record, he routinely subbed in the words "her name is Tammy," playing into the long-held fan theory that he remained in love with Tammy until the day he died. So, it shouldn't come as a surprise to learn Braddock believed he was writing a hilarious song when he began work on "He Stopped Loving Her Today" in 1977, nor that he still thought it was hilarious after Curly came in to help finish it.

The shade of comedy is admittedly quite dark but it's certainly there. The original comedic intent would be plain as day were the song performed in the style of an artist like Johnny Russell, who actually did get to the song before George Jones and recorded two versions of it, but neither was ever released. The joke is told using the same bleak tone as an alcoholic who swears he's quit drinking . . . except on holidays, special occasions and days that end in "y." The punch line is in that "oh, I get it" moment when the lyrics reveal the narrator's father just died. The only things that cause this moment and the rest of the song to play as sincere tragedy on the George Jones record are his vocal delivery and the arrangement Billy Sherrill placed behind him. Billy's deliberate reversal of the original intent required multiple rewrites to make the trick possible before he even attempted to record it. The biggest problem to overcome was how soon the lyrics reached the punch line. Following the principles of a decent knock-knock joke, Braddock and Putman initially wrote their way to the comedic payoff as quickly as possible. The title and first line of the finished song remain as artifacts of that design. If we know the title is "He Stopped Loving Her Today" and the first words we hear after pressing play are "He said 'I'll love you 'til I die,'" there's really only one direction the story could be headed and the original lyrics wasted no time getting there. But Billy Sherrill wanted drama, which requires heightened suspense. For his audience to experience tragedy instead of comedy, they needed enough time to dread the inevitable, enough time to realize they were dreading the inevitable. That's why the final version gives us two entire verses before a chorus fulfills the promise made by the title and first lyrics. When the old man's death is eventually confirmed, a bridge recitation prolongs the cathartic moment by including the sound of the woman he loved crying at his funeral, then one last chorus brings the whole thing home. It took a long time, probably more than a year, to land on that verse-verse-chorus-bridge-chorus song structure. Billy claimed to've carried around a one-inch-thick notebook full of nothing but ideas, changes and rewrites for this one song.

The challenges didn't begin and end on paper. As George Jones' physical and mental health rapidly deteriorated due to his cocaine addiction in the second half of the 1970s, Billy Sherrill had no choice but to find ways of working around his artist. When Jones failed to show up for a session, Billy would record the musicians playing their parts without a lead vocal, creating backing tracks for Jones to later overdub his part. It wasn't an ideal way to work, but it got the job done and the results were preferable to what came out of sessions where Jones showed up unable or unwilling to sing well, which was often. His singing was so quickly and severely hampered by cocaine in the late '70s, Billy told Jones that if he was going to be a drug addict, then he should at least shoot heroin like Ray Charles instead of snorting a drug that destroys the vocal cords. On many occasions musicians and studio techs were paid to endure take after take of the same song while Billy tried to keep track of which lyrics still needed a decent delivery from Jones in order to later Dr. Frankenstein an acceptable record together from all the tape. There were other times in this period when Jones showed up with seemingly no other agenda than to be a giant pain in the ass. Such was the case with "He Stopped Loving Her Today."

One of Billy Sherrill's favorite things to say was if he couldn't get a song on tape in thirty minutes, then he'd scrap it and move on because he wasn't going to get it at all. While that may have been true in most cases, he and George Jones spent a year battling each other over "He Stopped Loving Her Today." The record's final session took place in February 1980 but they first tried cutting it all the way back in early 1979. Despite various parties attempting to revise history it's a well-documented fact Jones hated the song from the first time he heard it through to his last day working on the record. He didn't like the lyrics because he thought they were too gloomy. He didn't like the melody because he thought it was too close to Kris Kristofferson's "Help Me Make It Through the Night." Just to be an asshole, he sang the lyrics of "He Stopped Loving Her Today" to Kristofferson's melody so many times it stuck in his head that way and, even after deciding to sincerely sing the song and get it over with, he accidentally continued slipping into the wrong melody. Billy consistently claimed the finished product was a cut-and-splice job with some pieces of tape dating all the way back to the early 1979 sessions. Bobby Braddock doubted this was true because he and Curly Putman only wrote the bridge recitation the day before Jones' final session for the song. However, that recitation was written upon Billy's request. It's possible he always knew he wanted a recitation and made a place for it when he began recording the backing tracks without Jones. It's also possible he originally recorded that bridge section without planning for a recitation, instead intending it to feature Millie Kirkham's background vocal alone to represent the woman sobbing at the funeral, only later deciding Jones should explain this plot development through narration. Ultimately, these technical details are trivial and have no bearing on what happened when the record came out, which is what's been happening ever since.

◇   ◇   ◇

This may not be a story about The Best and/or Saddest Country Song of All Time but it is a story about the biggest comeback in country music history. Now that so many superlatives have been heaped upon "He Stopped Loving Her Today" for so long and George Jones is so widely considered The Greatest Country Singer Ever, it can be difficult to remember how long he was regarded as an outsider and, at one time, beginning to be written off as a has-been. This record brought him back from the living dead.

After winning just about every notable country music award for "She Thinks I Still Care" in the early 1960s, Jones fell off the planet until the year 1980, at least as far as the award voting committees were concerned. Other than a few awards from *Cash Box* for duets with Tammy Wynette, in those two decades Jones received zero recognition from the industry, no matter how many other legendary country singers said he was the best and no matter how many hit records he sold. The suits had their reasons, just as obvious then as they are now. For one thing, Jones' recurring wars against sobriety posed serious threat of embarrassment to any award ceremony that asked him to attend. More consequentially, though, his records largely held no crossover potential and, other than "She Thinks I Still Care," did not inspire many contemporary covers. While ambassadorial reach outside of the genre and memetic spread within it were not the only priorities of country establishment voters, the songs and artists they did choose to award speak for themselves. This is true of all the major committees but the easiest example to use is the CMA, who began giving out awards in 1967. In the final years of the '60s, George Jones released several major hits, like "Walk Through This World with Me," "A Good Year for the Roses," "I'll Share My World with You" and "When the Grass Grows Over Me." In those years the CMA awarded Song and Single of the Year to "There Goes My Everything," "Harper Valley P.T.A.," "A Boy Named Sue," "Okie from Muskogee," "Sunday Mornin' Comin Down," "The Carroll County Accident" and Bobby Russell's "Honey." Setting aside any subjective arguments regarding the relative quality of any of these songs, it's an objective fact that every one of the awarded records crossed over to the Pop charts and/or inspired a wildfire-like spread of country covers and/or found itself at the center of some pop culture media narrative with an audience larger than that of the entire country music genre. Despite the fact that nearly everyone (including Tammy herself) said Tammy Wynette was technically not a great vocalist, her crossover success and incomparable presence in pop culture media helped her take home Female Vocalist of the Year in 1968, 1969 and 1970.

These awards have never truly been important as anything other than a gauge of the establishment's self-perception. But the longer such voting committees ignored George Jones, the more country music audiences understood the difference between artistic priorities of fans and commercial priorities of industry. Jones' uninterrupted exclusion from any type of winners' circle between the years 1963 and 1980 became its own kind of anti-award, a badge of integrity worn by the people's champion, the greatest vocalist who was too wild for the Nashville industry to celebrate and never got the credit he deserved. When we read about country-rock artist Gram Parsons (of the Byrds, the Flying Burrito Brothers and the International Submarine Band) mentioning George Jones as his hero in interviews, covering Jones songs live, singing Jones songs with Emmylou Harris and crying to Jones songs in front of Pamela Des Barres, it's important to remember that Gram Parsons died in 1973. He never heard "He Stopped Loving Her Today" and never had any reason to believe George Jones would ever be recognized as The Greatest Country Singer Ever outside the community of hardcore country fans, let alone have that recognition spread beyond country music to take root and become dogma in pop culture. Gram's fan worship of Jones was based almost entirely upon the Musicor era and earlier. Jones only began working with Billy Sherrill during the final two years of Gram's life. It's even possible Gram may have been among the many fans who were nervous about Jones making the move to Epic to work with Billy.

Just as their children and grandchildren in the punk and indie music scenes would later do, hardcore country fans had come to internalize the outsider status of their favorite artist as an aspect of their own identities. Being a George Jones fan put you in the corner of a guy who was too country for the Pop charts, too talented to be imitated outside almost-novelty tributes and too drunk to be allowed near the microphone at stiff, tuxedo-filled award shows. By 1971, the year Jones moved to Epic, everyone knew Billy Sherrill stood in diametric opposition to all those things. His slick productions regularly crossed over to the Pop charts because they were consciously designed to do that very thing, blatantly packaged to appeal to the much larger market of music consumers who purchased genres other than country. As these were priorities Billy shared with industry voting committees, he, his artists and his songwriters typically wound up giving acceptance speeches on the microphone at all those stiff, tuxedo-filled award shows. Fans knew it was possible that working with Billy would finally bring George Jones the recognition he'd long deserved from the establishment, but the fearful question in their minds and hearts was what Jones would need to do to get it. One standout example of the type of thing they dreaded would be the George Jones and Tammy Wynette cut of "The World Needs a Melody" from early 1973. A lot of country fans would tell you there should never have been a string section on the song at all but many more would say the strings should absolutely not be doing whatever you'd call the travesty that takes place during the "Old Time Religion" portion of the song. Was George Jones selling out his love of real country music to make this watered-down nonsense with his pop crossover wife? Opinions were as varied and the debate has proven as never-ending as any other instance of this topic coming up in the career of any other artist. To some fans and critics, Billy Sherrill took Jones unforgivably deep into pop country territory for the next twenty years. To others, George Jones records continued to serve as definitive time capsules of the ever-evolving genre that is country music.

A 1976 profile of Billy Sherrill in the *Chicago Tribune* jumped into the debate by questioning whether Billy really was such a genius or merely lucky to have worked with a few talented artists who'd have been successful with any producer. They mentioned his failure to give either Barbara Mandrell or Jody Miller any major hits. After calling attention to George Jones' supposedly low sales figures at Epic, they wondered if Billy's style could ever work for Jones or Jones' fans. But this could be seen as either an attempted hit piece or an incompetent analysis because, by the time of that article, Billy and Jones had released more than a dozen Top 10 singles, including #1 records on "The Grand Tour," "The Door" and (with Tammy) "We're Gonna Hold On." Even if those songs were somehow such big hits despite "disappointing" sales figures, they were much bigger hits than anything Jones released on Musicor and certainly sold many more copies.

As for George's own opinion on whether he was selling out, whenever provided with an opportunity he directly attacked pop country as harshly as he'd bad-mouthed rock music in the past. In 1977, discussing country music with the *Pensacola News Journal*, he said, "They're trying to bring it too far uptown to the big city . . . Trying to modernize it too much, especially the sound. Production-wise, it's overdone too much. Everybody is money hungry. Ninety percent of what you hear on the radio isn't really country music." He goes on to acknowledge the difficulty in defining what constitutes "good" and "bad" country music but, to give an example of what he hears in "bad" country, he references the inclusion of "acres of violins." That's very interesting language because it's exactly the way detractors characterized the records Jones made with Billy Sherrill. In fact, the phrase "acres of violins" almost certainly entered the lexicon of Jones and music critics by way of it being one of Billy's favorite terms, one he often used in the studio and in interviews to describe his own production process. So, either George Jones was oblivious to the fact he literally quoted the negative reviews of his own records to bad-mouth everyone else's records . . . or he'd figured out the audacious politician's trick of projecting his own crimes onto everyone other than himself.

Three years prior to that interview the CMA awarded Female Vocalist of the Year to Olivia Newton-John (for all the reasons detailed above) and Jones responded by forming the Association of Country Entertainers, a group intended to protest outside influences on the Nashville country music establishment and to give a platform to country artists who stayed "true" to the genre. This happened when he was still married to Tammy, so they hosted the first ACE meeting at their house and sent invitations to Jimmy C. Newman, Hank Snow, Jean Shepard, Bill Anderson, George Morgan, Barbara Mandrell, Billy Walker, Conway Twitty, Porter Wagoner and Dolly Parton. After failing to come up with an actual game plan it only took a few more meetings before all these singers realized nobody could define "outside influence" or "pop country" in a way that wouldn't indict every last one of them for failing to remain true to "real country," which they also couldn't define. ACE disbanded without ever settling on the changes or policies they'd have liked to see implemented in the Nashville industry. But Jones' rhetoric against pop country only grew stronger. Much the same way his own records, like "White Lightning," were apparently excluded from his disdain for rock-tainted country music in previous decades, he spent the rest of his career trashing pop country as if a gun trained on his head couldn't force him to commit such an abomination, despite the fact that every second of tape he cut in Texas would be considered pop country to previous generations of country fans and his music began to meet contemporary notions of pop country the moment his autopilot recording sessions moved to Nashville.

The truth is George Jones could have remained on Musicor until his dying day and the records he released from the late 1960s forward would still bear Billy Sherrill's influence, to the same degree and for the same reasons his previous work with the Nashville A-Team owed such a profound debt to Owen Bradley despite never working with the man. The first step Jones took from Owen's sound over to Billy's sound was all the way back in 1966 on the first Jones recording of "Almost Persuaded." Bob Moore, who played bass on the original David Houston cut, served as uncredited producer for Jones and provided approximations of Billy Sherrill's exaggerated dynamics. From there, Owen Bradley's signature on George Jones records gradually received more and more Sherrill-esque flourishes. The piano was more often given to single note runs on the bass end of the instrument. There was liable to be at least one key change or strange chord. Drummers were allowed to get much fancier and the dynamics were pushed further, then further still. A similar evolution can be heard in the sessions of most artists recording on Music Row, regardless of whether they ever even met Billy Sherrill. Billy's influence began creeping into Charlie Louvin's work near the end of 1967, on the fantastic original recording of "Will You Visit Me on Sundays." It's in the subtle-yet-busy drums and the way that low-end piano intro riff gets moved to various positions throughout the song. By 1969, when Bob Moore produced the George Jones cut of the same song, the drums and piano had become twice as busy with a more varied and dramatic attack . . . plus there were strings. The last Jones LP released on Musicor while he was still with the label is the ultimate case-in-point. Even though Pappy Daily was credited as producer on the back of the album and actual producer Bob Moore finally received label credit on the biggest hit single, "A Good Year for the Roses," many Jones fans mistakenly believe 1971's *With Love* was his first LP produced by Billy Sherrill. There's a very good reason for that. Most of the album comes off like a tribute to Billy's production style. This was not some attempt to compete with the sound Musicor knew would be on the albums Jones made at Epic because several of the most emblematic tracks were cut nearly two full years earlier, before anyone could have suspected Jones would leave Musicor for any reason. The oldest and arguably most dynamic recording on the album is "I Know," written by Jones and Tammy Wynette, then given a downright startling string and piano intro riff by Bob Moore. On "Loving You Makes You Mine," Bob's lethargic bass briefly and briskly jumps alive beneath a few hopeful lyrics, just the way he'd have been asked to play the part if Billy Sherrill was running the session. Then there's "Try," surely the most optimistic thing George Jones ever recorded, which features a glistening string arrangement. Those three songs were all recorded in 1969, before anyone involved had any clue Jones would someday work with Billy Sherrill.

In 1970, Bob Moore produced what many would call his crowning achievement, "A Good Year for the Roses." Written by Jerry Chesnut, this is one of those Opposite Day premises. In real life everything was actually going pretty great for Jerry, except he'd planted a bunch of fancy rosebushes along the walkway to his new house only to watch the buds fall off before they ever bloomed. When he called the flower shop to ask what mistakes he made, they told him the weather was all wrong and it just wasn't a good year for the roses. Well, Jerry got to thinking about how it really wasn't so bad because things could've gone the other way around. He could've been looking at a beautiful walkway of rosebushes leading to the entrance of a house where everything inside had gone to shit. That's the song he wrote. The George Jones record opens with a rhythm section panned to the right and, in the left channel, a mysterious low-end swell, like a heavy dirigible lifting into flight, almost certainly provided by a pedal steel player running their signal through a Jordan Boss Tone unit and a tape delay to mimic a cello. Then Jones enters as the world's saddest archivist, surveying the last things his soon-to-be-ex-wife's lips have touched on her way out the door: the multiple cigarettes she needed to smoke while packing her things, the cup of coffee she realized didn't need to be finished before she left, *not* his own lips. Then the instruments soar together with Jones into the chorus as he finds one thing going well: the roses outside sure look great. But sometimes the only thing worse than having nothing is watching one stupid and inconsequential thing go right while everything else goes wrong, so the song drops back into apathy. The single hit #2 in 1970 and from there George Jones' musical arrangements were on a one-way street to Billy Sherrill's neighborhood, no matter who became his producer. The strings on his Musicor sessions only grew more prominent and grandiose, right up to the end of his time with the label. One of the last things he cut there was "High on the Thought of You," written by Charlene Montgomery and arranged by Bob Moore like he'd spent a week taking peyote while listening to Nancy Sinatra and Lee Hazlewood records. Comparing Jones' final Musicor sessions to his first recordings for Epic, it's absolutely fair to say Billy Sherrill dialed everything back a few notches to show everyone the value of restraint, the difference between being produced in the style of Billy and actually being produced by Billy. It may not have been enough to impress the *Chicago Tribune*, but Billy and Jones began making Top 5 records immediately and only took a couple years to figure out how to hit #1 together.

Whenever asked how he changed the style of George Jones records, Billy usually said something to the effect that all he did was make Jones start working harder for a living. He once said, "Jones used to never record anything with over two chords in it. I think if you do something a little more complicated, it sounds like the style changes, but it's really not. Some songs require singing and some songs don't. You can take a song like some of his old stuff, like 'Why Baby Why,' and that don't require any singing. But you take something like 'He Stopped Loving Her Today' and that requires singing. You can't just mouth through it and expect it to be good."

◇　　◇　　◇

Here's another quote from Billy on working with Jones: "I don't even remember the first time I met George. I saw him sporadically with Tammy from time to time before the signing. We just met to say 'hi' a few times. Then, when he signed with Epic Records, we were standing there looking at each other. Both of us were kind of nervous, wondering if we could get along in a studio together. Then, later, about ten minutes into our session, after he found out I wasn't an ogre, we had a good time. We've had good times ever since." Billy said this in the early '80s, so even though they surely did have some good times together, by that point he had been through some pretty fucking terrible times with George Jones. He's also on record about there being moments in the studio when they wanted to kill each other.

Jones and Billy first worked together right after the opening of Old Plantation Music Park, when Jones and Tammy were the closest they ever got to really being the infinitely happy honeymooners they playacted as on the early Epic LPs. Occasional binges aside, Jones' health was fairly solid his first two years or so on Epic. He then began the downhill slide into the 1975 divorce, which was soon followed by a tumble off a cliff made of cocaine. His physical, mental and financial wasting away in this period are all well-documented, partly because 1974 was the year Columbia Records finally hired a dedicated PR staff for Epic's Nashville office. When Jones and Tammy split the following year, they left Epic in the awkward position of a friend who isn't sure which side to pick in a divorce. Jones made the choice a little easier by mostly ignoring his career in order to focus on drinking, so Epic's new PR team got behind Tammy and pushed her to do as much press as possible. One of the new PR hires, Mary Ann McCready, said, "We were very concerned. Their duet career had been so strong and their ability to draw [crowds] had been so strong that everyone was concerned that neither one alone would have the strength of the two of them together. We started a major campaign on Tammy. We got the cover of *Family Weekly* and covers of other magazines. Then we arranged for her to perform at the White House. We promoted her as 'The First Lady of Country Music performs for The First Lady of the Country.'"

In the beginning, the plan seemed to work well enough. But then something they hadn't planned started to happen. As Tammy put more of herself out there in interviews, songs and concert banter, the harder she tried to force real-life events to gel with her one-dimensional persona, the more it forwarded everyone's attention right along to George Jones, whom she'd unintentionally given a more interesting role in her narrative. All he needed to do in order to capitalize on this was change exactly nothing about his lifestyle. Punishing his body with extreme alcohol abuse and running away from his celebrity played out in print like the tragicomic "just don't give a damn" antihero this audience wanted.

Strangely, these events happened to coincide with a resurgence of rockabilly in the mid-to-late

1970s. When bands like Rockpile and Stray Cats, along with the TV show *Happy Days* and the movie *American Graffiti*, brought a retro cool factor to 1950s rock and fashion, Jones got pulled into the wave of hype and his early '50s rock-tinged Starday records became collector's items, which only added to his fame and legend.

Also in the mid-1970s, music journalist and country fan Chet Flippo was an editor in *Rolling Stone*'s New York City office, where he wrote about country artists whenever he could get away with it. (His coverage of Waylon Jennings in this period is mandatory reading on the outlaw country movement.) In 1976, Flippo and his wife entertained some guests from Nashville, including Mary Ann McCready from Epic's new PR department. Over dinner they talked about how country music was still largely regarded as a joke in New York City. That Madison Square Garden spectacular with George Jones and Buck Owens had taken place more than a decade earlier and all it really meant was there were enough people in the city who'd buy tickets if all of the biggest artists in the genre appeared at one concert together. The Garden show didn't result in country music becoming popular all across New York City or anything like that. In 1973, Hilly Kristal had opened a new music venue in Manhattan called CBGB, which stood for Country, Bluegrass and Blues, the styles of live music Hilly intended to feature. But there still wasn't enough of a crowd for those types of bands to keep even a small club alive and, by the time of this dinner at Flippo's house, CBGB had become ground zero for New York City's hippest punk, rock, and catchall counterculture crowd. So Flippo knew he could spend the rest of his life publishing articles about country music but it wasn't likely to inspire many readers to begin taking the genre seriously. His own coworkers at *Rolling Stone* still cracked jokes about Flippo liking country and they heard him talk about it all the time. Then somebody at the table suggested seeing one good George Jones concert ought to cure just about anyone of such foolishness and the comment landed with more weight than the rest of the idle conversation. Because, seriously, what might it accomplish for all of country music if Jones came to New York City and played a full set, not only for ticket-buying fans but a room purposefully stocked with the nation's media elite? Flippo and his dinner guests decided this needed to happen. It was going to happen. After nearly a year of planning, it happened.

If you traveled back in time to September 6 and 7 of 1977, to a trendy, 400-cap theater in Manhattan called the Bottom Line, you'd find journalists from the *New York Times*, *Newsweek*, *Time*, most of *Saturday Night Live*'s cast, Walter Cronkite, Dan Rather and many other celebrities, influencers and entertainment industry power players, all gathered for intimate showcase performances from George Jones. You would not, however, find George Jones. He completely ghosted on both nights. He didn't even get on the plane to New York. All the big shots in the audience took it as a "fuck you" from a country boy who didn't care how important these city people were supposed to be. This was perhaps informed by some comments Jones had recently made to the media. Two months earlier, he told a reporter the record business was motivated only by maximizing profits and they were trying to modernize country music too much, saying, "They used to make fun of us, call us hillbillies, wouldn't have a thing to do with us. Now some of the biggest businessmen in the world out of New York and the West Coast have taken over Nashville. It's nothing but a syndicated rat race now. Not a thing like when I first came to Nashville." Naturally, the crowd of New Yorkers he stood up at the Bottom Line interpreted his failure to show up as a premeditated act of hostility. But they weren't offended. They loved him for it. They thought it made him the real deal, a bona fide living legend who only did what he wanted when he wanted, which was the story several journalists went home and wrote. It didn't matter that Jones wasn't taking any kind of stand or making any kind of statement. It didn't matter that he failed to show because he was terrified. The pressure of going to New York City to sing for such an important audience under such circumstances would've been enough to send him running at any point in his career. The fact he started doing large amounts of cocaine about six months earlier definitely didn't help his paranoia, either. But the media had their story and they ran with it. In 1977, the year *Rolling Stone* moved their main headquarters from San Francisco to New York City, their critics' poll hailed George Jones as Country Artist of the Year.

A month after pulling the biggest no-show of his life to date, Jones met the pop culture media halfway by going in the studio and covering an artist they already understood. The first time an executive at Columbia played the James Taylor B-side "Bartender's Blues" for Jones, it was mostly as a joke. The song and performance, which Taylor called a tribute to George Jones, were so blatantly derivative some folks at the label just wanted to see how Jones would react if he heard the record without being forewarned. It took about forty-five seconds for him to say something like "Hey, wait a minute, that guy's trying to do me!" and everyone laughed while listening to the rest of it, pointing out each time Taylor laid into a particularly Jones-ish bit. When Billy Sherrill said they obviously had to cut the song, Jones agreed. He also evidently felt the need to prove his George Jones impersonation was better than anyone's because, within the first fifteen seconds of the record, he put down a vocal run nobody else on the planet would've dreamt to try and it's not even the most impressive part of his performance. Years later, both Billy and Jones confessed they didn't much care for the record because Jones was really just showing off. He probably wanted to make sure James Taylor could hear the way it was done when they sent the tape for Taylor to cut background vocals. The single came out in January 1978 and hit the Top 10 a couple months later, by which time Jones' cocaine use had become terrifying.

◇   ◇   ◇

To fully understand the impact of "He Stopped Loving Her Today" upon release, it's necessary to understand not only what fans believed about George Jones' career in the immediately preceding years but also what they believed to be true about his chaotic personal life due to the fragments they picked up from the media. He spent thousands and thousands of dollars to pack his nose with blow while buying, trading, gifting, flushing and torching his way into massive debt. He took out huge loans from banks and borrowed cash from other country artists but, rather than put that money toward his debts, he just used it to keep doing all the same things, digging himself even deeper into the hole. The more debt he incurred, the less motivated he was to make any attempt toward solvency because whatever money he made from a concert, hit single or any other type of deal wouldn't come anywhere near putting a dent in the total he owed, so why bother? In 1978, he's supposed to have missed more than fifty concerts. In August of that year, after Tammy Wynette married George Richey, she sued Jones over Georgette's unpaid child support. In September, after working himself up into a particularly deranged mood over the fact Peanutt Montgomery had dedicated his life to Christ and would no longer drink or disappear with him on days-long binges, Jones tried to murder Peanutt with a .38 special revolver. In November, a Nashville bank sued Jones for not making payments on more than fifty thousand dollars of loans. In December, Jones filed for bankruptcy, claiming $1.5 million of debt. He no longer owned a house in Tennessee and the hotels all stopped giving him rooms on credit, so anyone looking for George Jones in Nashville in the year 1979 stood a pretty decent chance of finding him living out of a car parked in Printer's Alley, consuming more cocaine and alcohol than solid food or water, talking to a life-size cardboard standup of Hank Williams and hallucinating zombies who tried to attack him from the shadows. Such was the state of Jones' life and mind when Billy Sherrill first began trying to record "He Stopped Loving Her Today" in early 1979. By the end of 1979, Peanutt Montgomery had Jones committed to a mental institution. According to the doctors there, Jones was "suffering from an acute paranoid state with suicidal and homicidal potential to a high degree." They also mentioned "chronic and acute heavy intake of alcohol" and "the suspicion of chronic use of cocaine."

Since newspapers and gossip magazines weren't able or aiming to communicate the full details or horrific reality of the situation, even these events continued playing into Jones' image as a heartbroken party animal. Much of his audience tracked the media coverage of this behavior as nothing but a more intense version of the way they'd seen him act when hopelessly in love with Melba Montgomery. Many believed (and still do) that George Jones simply dove further into a bottle over Tammy Wynette because that's how much more he loved Tammy and couldn't find a way to stop loving her. This notion was originally inspired by the flirty comments and public appearances they made circa their professional reunion in 1976 on "Golden Ring" and "Near You," the 1-2 hit record combo with lyrics that further reinforced the theory they were still in love. Then, after Tammy's divorce from the two-month marriage to Michael Tomlin nobody seemed able to understand or explain, there was Jones offering a tidy solution by unambiguously telling the media neither he nor Tammy would ever be happy with anyone but each other. It's possible if not probable he even meant those things when he said them. Immediately after the divorce he certainly fixated on Tammy's absence as his motive for falling deep into the bottle, then the baggie. But if he were approached in 1978 with the proposition of making a choice between Tammy Wynette or a giant sack of blow, it's difficult to imagine he'd take her over the drug he now relied upon to such a degree it caused him to try murdering his best friend. Nevertheless, nearly every article on his financial problems, missed concerts, even the attempted shooting of Peanutt and subsequent trip to an asylum at least implied it could all be blamed on Jones' heartache over the split from Tammy Wynette and, now, her for-real marriage to George Richey, the man who Tammy said was finally The One. These stories often contained quotes attributed to anonymous sources supposedly close to the situation, who knowingly stated Jones' undying love for his ex-wife was the root of all his problems.

After years of the media and fans running with that narrative, when the first single Jones put out after his much-discussed stay in a mental hospital was "He Stopped Loving Her Today," millions of people heard it as third-person perspective on the coming day when death would finally free him of the torturous love he still held for Tammy Wynette. Released in April 1980, the record hit #1 in July. Having never given George Jones a single award, the Academy of Country Music voted him Male Vocalist of the Year. Having never given George Jones a single award, the Country Music Association voted him Male Vocalist of the Year. The CMA also named "He Stopped Loving Her Today" Best Single of the Year and Best Song of the Year. The record won George Jones his first Grammy Award. When the song was placed on the *I Am What I Am* LP, it became his first album to go platinum. In 1981, the CMA again awarded Best Song of the Year to "He Stopped Loving Her Today" and Male Vocalist of the Year to George Jones. The record had not inspired a wildfire-like spread of covers (or even a notable one) within the genre. The record had not crossed over to the Pop charts. But it had found itself at the center of a media narrative larger than the entire genre of country music. Or, more accurately, it was placed there by Billy Sherrill, like a crown jewel on top of a stack of articles about The Greatest Country Singer Ever destroying himself over the woman who broke his heart forever. Never mind that it wasn't the truth, it played. Judging by the results, it may have played better than any producer has played the game before or since.

⋄　　⋄　　⋄

Bobby Braddock has often tried to find polite ways of saying he knows for a fact "He Stopped Loving Her Today" isn't the best of the more than one thousand songs that bear his name as a writer, let alone The Best Country Song of All Time. He's called it an "okay" song on paper and admitted he still hears things in it he would change if offered the chance to go back in time. He believes most people who give the song such high praise are really talking about the record, i.e., the vocal performance by George Jones and production by Billy Sherrill. In an interview with Napster.com, Braddock called it "a perfect country record" and said his favorite part was the string section building and building in the chorus. To him, the sound of those violins represented the old man's soul ascending to heaven. Not such a sad thought at all but, again, Braddock never set out to write a sad song and was accustomed to having the intention of his compositions reversed, especially when Billy Sherrill was involved.

Billy removed Braddock's humor from this song with such surgical precision, George Jones is supposed to've said something along the lines of "ain't nobody gonna buy that morbid sumbitch" right before walking out of his final vocal session for the record. If Jones really said that, he obviously underestimated the satisfying tragedies Billy was able to create from the right combination of suspense, release and semantic ambiguity. Relocating the original joke's "punch line" to the song's second half delayed that moment of clarification long enough for the music and vocals to set a somber mood, giving the audience time to attach their own personal memories to the mood and the accompanying lyrics. As nearly everyone believes the plot of "He Stopped Loving Her Today" to be direct and apparent, it may come as a surprise to learn how many different interpretations of the lyrics there are. A lot of people who've heard and enjoyed the song dozens of times do not perceive it to involve death in anyway. It only takes mishearing or inferring another meaning from the one line about a wreath on a door to interpret this as a song about the old man's friends deciding they aren't going to let his lovesick bullshit ruin another Christmas, so they come over to his house with some holiday decorations, make him get dressed up and drag him to a party where he gets so drunk he has to be carried home. But he does get over the woman and just smiles in her face when she finally tries to come back to him. Alternately, there are many listeners who believe the woman died first, prior to the events of the song. Because who could walk away from a man capable of such devotion? And what kind of man in his right mind would spend twenty years obsessed with a woman who chose not to be with him? No, the song isn't about the aftermath of a divorce. That woman died while they were still together, maybe holding his hand while bleeding out on the side of the road after a car crash or lying in a hospital bed with some disease eating the life from her body. She told him it would be alright, he'd eventually find love again, but he could never get over her death. In fact, he couldn't even accept that she was gone. It broke his mind and he spent every day of the rest of his life waiting for her to walk back in the room. When we hear the woman during the bridge, she's not crying at the man's funeral. It's her spirit come to escort his to the afterlife.

Such varied interpretations are not an accidental by-product of vague songwriting. They are deliberately provoked by professionals who reach into our minds with intentionally semi-specific language. Like psychics performing a cold read, if songwriters do their half of the job correctly, then we complete the task for them. When Bobby Braddock told SongwriterUniverse.com George Jones and Billy Sherrill turned his and Curly Putman's "okay" song into a great record, the reporter asked what made a song great. Braddock replied, "I think it's subjective really. It can be the simplest thing in the world and if somebody thinks it's great, then to them, it is great. It's in the ear of the beholder. I guess the thing to do is figure out what you can do to get the greatest number of people to think something is great." He was talking about the cold read, a semi-specific language used by songwriters to pull an audience's sympathetic memories into a story, thereby invoking happiness, sadness or whatever other desired mood far more effectively than relying on empathy to bridge the gap between listener and a set of hyper-specific circumstances. For example, say a writer composes a song inspired by the death of their very own father. Is the song more or less likely to be selected by a producer for Tammy Wynette's next recording session if the writer gets as specific as possible with real-life details, down to using their father's real first name and the name of the place where he lived? Or should the writer use more general terms, like "daddy" and "hometown"? If the goal is to record a hit song, "daddy" and "hometown" should be used because of how many more potential listeners have lost a father figure who stayed in their hometown than have lost a "Richard" or "Jerry" who lived in "Broussard" or "Muncie" or any other proper noun one could choose.

◇   ◇   ◇

Lyrics about divorce and death are not inherently sad. Those themes are approached in country music just as often and as easily from a comedic perspective. Lyrics about divorce and death are only sad to whatever degree the vocal performance and music effectively call forth the listener's own sad experiences with divorce and death. Further, when it comes to these two particular topics, a writer adept in semantic ambiguity may craft a song which can be interpreted by various listeners as being about death, divorce or both, prompting a potent response from a much larger audience who can project their own experiences with any of those matters into the song. This is precisely what happens when we listen to the George Jones songs "He Stopped Loving Her Today," "The Grand Tour" and "A Good Year for the Roses." Similar to the Moonshine Trilogy earlier in his career, these songs could be thought of as a Divorce/Death Trilogy. All three provide examples of the way our own interpretations can feel so certain and self-evident until we discover others have drawn from different lived experiences to reach a different understanding, sometimes revealing a deeper tragedy than we could ever have imagined.

It seems the vast majority of listeners interpret the first installment of the trilogy, "A Good Year for the Roses," as a song strictly about divorce. However, there is an alternate read on the lyrics that presents a little death and not only in the way all divorce can be called the death of a marriage. Jerry Chesnut said in interviews he started writing this as one of those songs about the wife leaving, the baby crying and the dog dying. But he was only talking about the way he started writing what he wanted to be a very sad song. Since he knew putting a dead dog in the song would've turned it into a joke, the kind made by people who don't listen to country music and want to insult it, Jerry didn't write a dog into the lyrics at all. The whole story opens up once you notice George Jones does not sing "when you turned and walked away" in the past tense, as most lyric websites incorrectly transcribe. He clearly sings "when you turn to walk away," which places the main action of the song in present tense. We're not alone with the narrator as he reminisces about what happened when his ex-wife left him. We're with him and the soon-to-be-ex-wife as she finishes packing and walks out the door. We're with him as the door behind her "closes," present tense. So, if this isn't a song about a man sitting in silence after his wife has left him and taken their infant child with her, then the reason he mentions the absence of the sound of a crying baby is because that baby's no longer alive. In fact, the absence of the sound of that crying baby is why the wife is leaving. They aren't talking as she packs because, however the baby died, instead of turning to one another to cope with the tragedy, the parents turned on each other, said too many terrible things and caused their love to die as well. If it's been a good year for the roses, then it hasn't been raining much (since young rose plants do not thrive in heavy rain, as Jerry Chesnut would have learned when he called the flower shop about his own roses), so the narrator's observation that the lawn needs to be mowed means he's been incapacitated for many dry-weathered days, not just since that morning. This isn't the first day the wife has failed to make the bed simply because she decided that morning to leave. It's because she's been trying to process her grief and keep their normal routine going but the husband was irreparably damaged by the loss and cannot heal, so she's now giving up on him the way he's given up on everything.

The middle song in the Divorce/Death Trilogy is the most ambiguous and, as a result, arguably the saddest. There is very little information available on the writing of "The Grand Tour." The initial idea for a song with that title came to George Richey as a result of how many country stars in Nashville were opening museums or their own homes to public tours. Richey then brought in Carmol Taylor and Norro Wilson to help finish it. It seems plausible Richey noticed how few people ever picked up on the baby's death in "A Good Year for the Roses" and decided he could probably get a hit on a song that was unmistakably about both a dead baby and a dead wife, which is when Carmol and/or Norro may have explained that's not the way it works and offered to help obscure the original, singular meaning. Even then, this song still barely stops short of saying the quiet part out loud. For decades, the most popular interpretation of "The Grand Tour" has been the same as "A Good Year for the Roses," that it's strictly about a divorce. But every lyric assumed to be about divorce could just as easily be a reference to death and there are at least five additional clues pointing beyond divorce. For starters, if a stranger told you the story of their divorce would "chill you to the bone," you would laugh in their face. It is death, not divorce, which chills bystanders to the bone. Not just any death—only a tragic death, too horrible to name outright— would send shivers down the spine of a total stranger. After beginning his story this way, the narrator recalls happier times, like when his wife would bring the newspaper to him and sit on his lap to say she loved him or all the times they lay in bed in love with each other. He shows us a photo of the wife but not one of the baby, and we have to wonder if there may be a reason he doesn't have a photo of the baby, like maybe it was never born. He says the wife's picture only serves as a reminder she cannot touch him—not "will not" touch him, is unable touch him. It is death, not divorce or lack of desire, which removes the very possibility of physical touch. Unlike "A Good Year for the Roses," there are no lyrics to suggest his wife was anything less than perfectly content in the relationship and there are no lyrics to suggest the narrator of "The Grand Tour" was anything less than a perfect husband. He shares no memories of unhappy times. He also shares no memories of the baby, crying or otherwise. In fact, there are no lyrics to suggest there was ever a baby in the nursery, only that the loving and expecting parents made one in the home. It is death, not divorce, which brings the narrator certainty his wife is gone from his life forever, as would nearly never be the case in a divorce involving a small child who hasn't died. The wife did not leave her ring behind. She left all of her rings behind, along with every article of clothing she owned. In fact, she took none of her possessions—only the baby and his heart— because we have to leave this world the same way we enter it: with nothing but our body. And some people happen to leave while another body is growing inside of them.

Since this is all very upsetting to think about, it's not exactly a surprise how many George Jones fans refuse to acknowledge "The Grand Tour" could be about more than a divorce. These fans invariably resist the death interpretation by clinging to two instances of the narrator saying the words "she left." There's the line about how "her clothes are in the closet like she left them when she tore my world apart" and "she left me without mercy." Of course, everyone leaves their clothes behind when they die and "she left me without mercy" doesn't have to mean the wife leaving him was a merciless act which she consciously undertook. Taken literally, it's a straightforward description of the state in which he's been left, one without mercy. (Too, some people name their daughters Mercy.) The narrator's world was torn apart when "she left" him in the exact same way we're supposed to see a character's world has been torn apart when they scream "don't leave me" at a dead or dying person in a death scene of a movie. Still, some fans so badly need this song to be about anything but two tragic deaths, one popular theory casts the narrator as an abusive liar, a manipulative monster who tells his saddest sob story and leaves out every trace of the part where his wife was so afraid of him she took the first chance she got to leave everything and run for her life and that of her baby. Believe whatever you like but there is just as much evidence in the lyrics, which is none whatsoever, that the guy's wife left him because she fell in love with Bigfoot. If anything, the narrator saying "I have nothing here to sell you" at the very start of the story seems to preclude the It's All a Lie theories, almost as if the same knowledge of craft which enabled these writers to hide nightmarish epiphanies between the lines of country songs came with an awareness of the lengths some listeners would go to try explaining it away, to make it not real, to pretend they'd never glimpsed the possibility of such a terrible curse.

TWENTY-ONE

DANGEROUS THREADS

◇ Stunting on the Poors ◇ Fashion as Caste-Based Sorting System ◇
The War on Drag ◇ Masquerade Balls and Authenticity Fetishes
◇ Crystal LaBeija and the Invention of Modern Ballroom ◇ Realness ◇

One of the biggest reasons noble families in Europe spent their medieval fortunes on extravagant architecture and other ostentatious displays of wealth was to reinforce popular notions of why they were the ruling class: their ancient bloodlines and God made them rich, everyone else poor, and that's the way it would always be because that's the way it was supposed to be. It's certainly the reason Catherine de Médici ramped up the arts and entertainment budget as soon as she rose to power in France, then kept spending at that rate even after doing so required borrowing the money. She rode aristocratic elites around in *carrousel* parades not simply because it was fun to dress up in lavish couture and sit on a horse but in order to stun the lower classes with unattainable splendor and centuries-old eminence, sort of like a military parade's demonstration of power, only demonstrating social superiority instead.

Throughout history a primary purpose served by fashion has been to rank people by class with a form of visual identification nearly as blatant and immediate as the uniform decorations which rank military personnel. Just as it is currently illegal in the United States for someone to falsely claim they received certain military decorations in order to qualify for money, property or other tangible benefit, there have been various forms of legislation—collectively falling into the category known as sumptuary laws—established in various places and times to prevent ordinary citizens from dressing above their social station. In some cases, a person could be put to death for even assisting someone else in pretending to belong to a higher caste. But the punishment for breaking a sumptuary law was more often some kind of fine for not adhering to a rule that technically stood for everyone, thereby providing the appearance of equality while actually assigning a dress code to the poor. For example, say it's illegal for any man of any standing to wear whatever is determined to be an excessive amount of jewelry or expensive fabric or certain color dye in their clothing. If the punishment is nothing more than a fine, then this is a sumptuary law that functions much more like a fashion tax, easily paid by the wealthiest members of society while a prohibitive expense to the poor, who would likely also rack up some additional punishment if unable to actually pay the fine when caught breaking the law. This is not any kind of modern radical perspective mapped onto history, by the way. Many sumptuary laws were written in plain, contemporary language to explicitly prohibit citizens from dressing as if they possessed more money or status than they really did. The shogunate system of government in feudal Japan involved a detailed and complicated dress code dictated entirely by a citizen's social rank. In the colonial United States it was illegal for any person who didn't have a certain level of wealth to wear any clothing with silver thread, golden thread, lace or embroidery. That mindset was inherited directly from England, where the House of Tudor allowed only the royal family to wear silk fabric, gold jewelry or the color purple. The Tudors allowed anyone to wear fur but only nobles titled at the level of earldom or higher were allowed to wear the fur of sables.

Even without such legislation there are unwritten sumptuary laws woven into the fabric of modern society. Clumsy attempts to dress above one's station will likely be met with mockery from one's peers or even strangers. A guy who shows up to a nightclub in an expensive yet ill-fitting suit will often find his friends making fun of him for trying to front. A pretty girl who wears a T-shirt for a rock or metal or punk band will often find some dickhead in a record store wants to give her a pop quiz to see if she's a poser. Any deviation from what is perceived to be the defining visual codes for any given category of person will at least be noted in the minds of observers, if not commented upon or legislated.

Of course, those funded and favored by high society have often been granted exemption. The wealthy will allow certain members of the lower ranks to wear the costumes of wealth. One need only fight a bull as well as Costillares or provide some other entertainment with world-class skill, such as playing the piano as well as Beethoven, whose notorious ill temper and bad manners gave cause for Phillipe V's great-grandson to issue a royal decree stating typical rules of court etiquette did not apply to Beethoven. Otherwise the famed musician of common birth may have suffered jail time or worse as the lawful consequence for mouthing off to someone of noble blood.

The most important thing to understand about all sumptuary laws—written or unwritten—is there are only consequences for those who get caught. A poor person walking down the street dressed like a rich person will only be questioned if they present the appearance of a poor person dressed like a rich person. Anyone who presents the appearance of a rich person walking down the street dressed like a rich person will be viewed and treated as exactly that.

◇   ◇   ◇

So let's say there were sumptuary laws in place throughout the United States near the beginning of the nineteenth century, which there were, intended to prevent citizens from dressing in drag, meaning "men" made up like "women" and vice versa. Let's also say there were exemptions to those laws, which there were, allowing citizens to dress in drag as long as it was to attend a masquerade ball, the way the ruling class had by this point done for centuries to flaunt their above-the-law existence, easily paying fines or arranging exemptions to throw such balls. (It's impossible to know what percentage of these elites actually identified as bi, gay or trans, just as it's impossible to know whether the documented prevalence of drag and homosexuality among working-class men in remote logging towns and mining camps of the American West was a result of not many cis women being around or the product of gay men and trans women deliberately seeking out such an environment on the outskirts of civilization.) What do you think happened in the middle of the nineteenth century, when previously underground LGBTQ communities began taking advantage of masquerade ball exemptions to gather in large numbers in public places, dressed in the clothes of whatever gender they liked? The answer is a legal crackdown, repurposing outdated laws originally written to deter roadside bandits from dressing in disguise and creating new laws that banned all masquerades, then selectively applying this legislation to target and harass lower-class individuals for participating in behavior which continued largely unchecked in upper-class communities. Again, this is all simply a matter of historical record, not any kind of conspiracy theory. For instance, near the beginning of the twentieth century in New York City, citizens with the financial means to do so purchased licenses from local government in order to throw masquerade balls, some including or even blatantly themed around attendees wearing drag. The largest of these parties were attended by hundreds of people and city cops were often hired to work security. Meanwhile, on the other side of town, police stopped lower-class citizens who appeared to be violating whatever dress code they were assigned at birth and made them submit to genital inspections.

Then federal Prohibition went into effect at the beginning of the 1920s. Customs and laws that previously prevented men and women from integrating en masse in saloons were laughed off within the devil-may-care culture of illegal speakeasies. It suddenly became easier for any given individual to blend in with a crowd of drunk people, whether dressed as a man or a woman. When mob outfits paid bribes for police to not bother bar patrons, they meant *all* of their patrons. If an LGBTQ person had a good time in a certain joint, they were liable to return with friends. A greater number of U.S. citizens than ever before were exposed to members of previously underground communities only to learn someone they'd been taught was insane or perverted or evil was really just as normal as any other person they'd ever met, breaking merely one or two more laws beyond those presently being broken by everyone in the room.

While this was not the permanent end of homophobia or transphobia in the United States, the Prohibition era did coincide with a window of increased tolerance in mainstream society. It became almost de rigueur for speakeasies with primarily straight clientele to feature at least one drag queen or king on a bandstand lineup, where they pantomimed or parodied popular songs, told dirty jokes and roasted audience members in an act peppered throughout with reminders the entertainer was in drag, this being the pivotal concept of the entire subversive performance. That surge in drag shows led to a backlash of moral panic from all the usual suspects, many of whom had campaigned to unknowingly enable this culture in the first place. Approximately six months after the Eighteenth Amendment was eventually repealed and the barroom economy again became dependent upon receiving liquor permits from local governments, the same attitudes that withheld permits from bars known to serve "deviants" cemented what's known as the Hays Code in Hollywood, preventing nearly every major studio film from depicting "any inference of sex perversion" until the 1960s. Since everyone knew what these words, laws and attitudes really meant, the LGBTQ community returned underground and the rise of drag was momentarily halted.

◇   ◇   ◇

One of the romantic notions rich folks always held about the masquerade ball was that it supposedly rendered all attendants equal and classless through the anonymity of masks. How could a woman know whether she was dancing with a prince or a pauper when she couldn't see his face? Never mind the fact paupers don't have much money to spend on elaborate new costumes every time there's a trendy ball. The aristocracy's penchant for such fantasies is probably what helped them also develop an obsession with "authenticity," which they've evidently always believed can simply be purchased. By the end of the nineteenth century, one of the most popular themes for costume balls, with or without masks, was for attendees to dress as near as possible to famous historical figures. The quality, volume and price of silver- and golden-threaded embroidery at these parties was entirely off the charts. The perceived "authenticity" of one's costume often came down to how much of a fortune was spent on it, usually in order to acquire and incorporate some kind of actual antique. In 1883, Alva Vanderbilt threw a ball in New York City which she attended wearing pearls that once belonged to Catherine the Great. In 1897, to attend another New York City ball, Cornelia Bradley-Martin spent what would be nearly ten million dollar in modern currency (more than 10 percent of that entire party's budget) for her Mary, Queen of Scots costume to appear "authentic." This was literally the class of party thrown by elites who could afford to buy government licenses and skirt anti-masquerade laws, with or without drag involved. Many balls centered upon drag in this period were a few rungs lower on the social ladder and most balls thrown by actual LGBTQ communities were hosted secretly, without permits. But all who wished to participate in this ritual aspired to the same aesthetic ideals. Whether licensed or underground, ruling elite or working class, nearly every costume ball would at some point in the evening have a contest. Entrants paraded their looks in front of each other and a judge or panel of judges designated the best, sometimes awarding titles for multiple categories, like Best Military Leader, Best King . . . or Best Queen.

Then federal Prohibition went into effect at the beginning of the 1920s. The illegal speakeasy culture which saw a surge in drag shows on bandstands and emboldened more people to appear in public dressed however they felt comfortable outside the context of masquerade balls also coincided with a surge in drag balls. As drag shows and drag masquerades became more and more common in mainstream society, even the previously underground drag balls became a little less clandestine. There was a major difference between drag stage shows and the drag masquerades, though. Where the drag show drew ironic attention to the offstage identity of an artist subversively adopting an onstage persona, contestants won the prize at authenticity-obsessed drag balls by being the most adept at making their identity disappear inside a convincing embodiment of the category. When Prohibition ended and the LGBTQ community took their drag masquerades back underground, it was with these aesthetic ideals, which were largely upheld for several decades.

Once the format of competition for secret drag balls became influenced by mainstream beauty pageants, like Miss America, entrants could expect to be judged on the way they walked and talked, the way they looked in a gown or swimsuit and the way they did their hair and makeup. Even though secret balls were likely to be racially integrated to some degree there were still blatant biases equating only pale skin with glamor and eminence, as the noble families of Europe had done for centuries and as Miss America continued to do. Well into the 1960s, even after the Hays Code fell out of favor and drag returned to greater visibility in hit movies like 1959's *Some Like It Hot*, queens with dark skin tones had little hope of winning a ball unless they used powder and makeup to lighten their skin, which many did try to do. But the panel of judges was still likely to be all or mostly white and still likely to crown a winner they could tell was "authentically" white. So the non-white ballroom crowd eventually began throwing their own parties in order to be judged on the assignment, not the color of their skin.

◇　　◇　　◇

Though histories of truly oppressed groups are often difficult to piece together, it's generally agreed that modern ballroom came into existence as a result of the race-based discrimination Crystal LaBeija experienced in mainstream drag pageants. The fact she—a Black queen who still lightened her skin with makeup—needed to first win Miss Manhattan at a predominately white drag ball in order to qualify for competition in New York City's Miss All-American Camp Beauty Pageant in 1967 was all the information she needed to know exactly how robbed to feel when a panel of celebrity judges (including Andy Warhol and Terry Southern) dismissed her with fourth place. Crystal's explosive reaction was captured on film and released in the 1968 documentary *The Queen*. You can hear a man respond to Crystal's rant by telling her she was showing her "color." Five years after the infamous snub one of Crystal's drag queen friends, named Lottie, asked for help creating a new ball. Crystal agreed under one condition: it must be thrown in honor of Crystal LaBeija. 1972's inaugural House of LaBeija Ball debuted and established the structure of ballroom which exists to this day.

Thrown out of their homes by intolerant families, vulnerable to all manner of violent hate crimes and discriminated against by a healthcare system that officially regarded their identities as a form of mental illness, LGBTQ people have always been forced by a society hostile to their very existence to live in tight-knit groups whenever they're able to find one. Looking out for each other is a matter of survival, not to mention a source of acceptance and familial love. Members of the community in a position to offer guidance, housing and support often do, creating what are essentially orphanages for teenagers and young adults with nowhere else to go. However, Crystal LaBeija was the first to formally proclaim herself mother of a "house" in ballroom. Within three years of her debuting the House of LaBeija in 1972, several other houses were formed, like the House of Dupree, House of Dior, House of Corey and House of Wong. Crystal intentionally chose the word "house" as a reference to the elite fashion houses of early twentieth-century Europe, like the House of Worth, House of Chanel and House of Balenciaga, whose in-"house" designers provided elegant pieces of clothing to the world's wealthiest socialites. Ballroom houses have traditionally created most of their own looks, too. After others followed Crystal's lead and established their own houses, though, they began to function much more like the noble family houses of Europe. For one thing, members typically adopted the name of the house as a surname. (After Lottie co-founded the House of LaBeija, she became known as Lottie LaBeija and so on.) But also, one of the primary goals of each house was to battle with other houses for coveted trophies and crowns at drag balls, which quickly drove the intensity and quality of ballroom competition to unprecedented territory.

By the end of the 1970s there were maybe a dozen houses recognized in New York City ballroom (Omni, Ebony, Plenty, Pendavis, Chanel, Christian, etc.), each taking turns hosting a monthly ball. This proliferation of houses coincided with an explosion in the variety of competition categories. Prior to this point the categories were as basic as any beauty pageant divided into gendered looks. Entrants in masculine drag competed in the butch categories and entrants in feminine drag competed in femme categories. But, here in the '70s, when so many contestants lived in drag part- or full-time (and some were even in various stages of transitioning), their safety in the outside world sometimes depended on the ability to code switch, legitimately passing as either butch or femme whenever necessary. So, some individuals were able to successfully compete in both butch and femme categories, which helped the relatively quaint, no-risk and outdated notions of "authenticity" handed down from high-class masquerades evolve into "realness." If "authenticity" meant spending millions of dollars trying to dress like Mary, Queen of Scots, "realness" means working with a shoestring budget to convince a room full of people you motherfucking *are* Mary, Queen of Scots. Where categories were previously as simple as Best Butch Face or Best Evening Gown, this new era introduced complex categories like Executive Butch Realness and Runway Femme Realness. Can you sell a room on the idea you are not only a straight man but a C-level executive who bosses other straight men around? Can you sell a room on being not just a woman but an actual supermodel? Some fashion-oriented categories—like Bizarre Couture or, simply, Opulence—have been less focused on gendered variants of "realness." But the same level of confidence necessary to win realness categories has always been an unspoken prerequisite for any category and any tie in the judges' scoring began to be settled by contestants hitting a runway simultaneously in a head-to-head presentation. At some point in the 1980s this combative display of aesthetic beauty evolved into what we now call voguing.

Like other aspects of this history, the origins of vogue are hazy but runways in modern ballroom are set to the beat of club music, so it likely began as something like a ballroom version of a breakdance battle. The physical tropes of the original ("Old Way") form include a fluid sort of glitching through a series of briefly held static postures, almost as if a camera shutter was set to snap every so many beats and the dancers' goal was to get into a new pose in time, freeze for each picture, then get into a new pose and repeat, as if participating in the most efficient fashion photo shoot possible. In fact, one of the most common and plausible origin stories for vogue features legendary queen Paris Dupree in a dance battle when she allegedly pulled out an issue of *Vogue*, opened it to a random page and held up the magazine while pulling the same pose as the model on that page, then flipped to another random page to repeat the act with the next model's pose, again and again, proving she could effortlessly assimilate not one supermodel but all supermodels.

Most of the world found out about voguing through the Madonna song "Vogue," which seems to be a fairly straightforward rip-off of Malcolm McLaren's earlier "Deep in Vogue." McLaren's track featured vocals from ballroom legend Willi Ninja and name-checked several houses of ballroom instead of doing what Madonna did and listing a bunch of famous white people who had nothing to do with vogue or ballroom. Neither "Vogue" nor "Deep in Vogue" would exist without those musical artists being introduced to ballroom by the maker of *Paris Is Burning*, a (controversial) hit 1991 documentary named after Paris Dupree, one of several drag queens who mistakenly believed she would become rich and famous when the movie came out and/or Madonna's song was such a huge hit. Several queens and the ballroom scene in general certainly did become more well-known but the money did not follow, at least not for their generation.

With hit TV shows like *RuPaul's Drag Race*, *We're Here*, *Pose* (now canceled), and *Legendary* (now canceled), ballroom and drag are more visible than ever, perhaps beginning to finally receive more credit for all the innovations lifted by pop culture. In recent years some members of the ballroom scene have criticized Realness categories for reinforcing the various gender stereotypes contestants are asked to present. Other members of the community claim these criticisms miss the entire point of a Realness category, which is that it only presents something to marvel at when you're in a room full of people who know they're looking at a performance. If you took that same degree of realness out on to the street, nobody would question what they were seeing for a second.

TWENTY-TWO

PULLING STRINGS

◇ FAME ◇ Experimenting in Nashville ◇ Recording Women, Redeeming Men ◇
Communist Pop Country Outlaw Nazi ◇ Checking Out ◇

Billy Sherrill was one of the most controversial figures in the history of country music, not only because of his personal politics, which he consistently injected into the records of one of his most famous artists, Tammy Wynette. Billy was the most successful and most imitated producer in country music for a period of roughly twenty years, during which time he did things exclusively the way he wanted, using only a small group of Nashville artists, songwriters and musicians that was nearly impossible for outsiders to join. That fostered jealousy and resentment from those outside the circle, which was nearly everyone else in the industry.

The closest he ever came to caring how a single other person felt about his approach was the time he flew to New York City to meet with Clive Davis, then the president of Columbia Records, the parent company of Epic, where Billy worked. Billy said he was aware of other Columbia-associated producers from all over the nation who complained they weren't allowed to record songs they'd written or co-written in order to make extra money on royalties while Billy Sherrill was down in Nashville putting several of his own songs on all his artists' albums. But all he wanted to know was did Clive Davis have a problem with that? Telling the story to MixOnline.com in 2002, Billy remembered Clive responding with another question, "Who am I?" Billy answered that Clive was the president of Columbia Records. Clive asked, "Can I fire you?" Billy answered that he could. Clive asked, "Do you want to get in trouble with me?" Billy said he did not. Then Clive told him, "So go back down to Nashville and keep doing what you're doing and making hit records," which is exactly what Billy Sherrill did, much to the annoyance of others in the industry who didn't directly reap the profits of his process.

Tammy Wynette said an unnamed Nashville songwriter once told her there was no point in pitching new songs to her because she only recorded stuff written by her producer, to which she responded she would cut whatever that songwriter came up with the day he brought in something better than a Billy Sherrill song. Hit songwriter Bobby Braddock always said Billy was one of the few producers in Nashville who could change a line or two in one of Bobby's songs and it would almost always be an improvement to the original lyrics. Braddock also once said, "I think Billy is an American original who made his mark on country music like no other producer, with the possible exception of Owen Bradley."

In Robert Altman's *Nashville*, when the Haven Hamilton character throws a fit during a recording session and demands the piano player be replaced with Pig, it's a reference to Pig Robbins. That's because the first thing Altman would have learned while researching the Music Row studio system in 1975 is nearly everyone tried to copy whatever Billy Sherrill did. Almost any major label artists who couldn't be produced by Billy would at least want to use the same musicians Billy used, the players who knew the most about the way Billy worked and could bring that knowledge to a session. In the same MixOnline.com article quoted above, Billy's engineer Lou Bradley said, "A lot of people tried to copy what Billy did. And they'd hire that studio, they'd hire the same engineer. And they'd hire the same musicians and background singers. But they wouldn't get it because they were listening to the end result. And the end result was what you heard after you walked the path to get there." Here's the path Billy Sherrill walked to get there.

◇　　◇　　◇

He was born in 1936, about thirty miles south of the Florence-Muscle Shoals region in Alabama. His father was a preacher, so when Billy began playing piano around the age of six years old he was soon put to work playing during services. For the rest of his life Billy said he learned everything he knew about making music from gospel composers like Virgil O. Stamps. However, he was given to making such sweeping statements, often tailored toward whatever he believed would most intrigue or confound the particular journalist interviewing him. If pressed to clarify or speaking to a different journalist, Billy was just as likely to gush at length over Johan Strauss II and other composers of Viennese waltzes. He also enjoyed more popular forms of music, as evidenced by one of his favorite stories, about the time he decided to play a hymnal arrangement of "That's Where My Money Goes" ("She has a pair of hips just like two battleships / who cares? that's where my money goes . . .") while the collection plate was passed in his father's church. His father caught on to the joke and whipped Billy's ass when they got home. He took his first paying gig a little more seriously, earning ten dollars to play piano at a funeral.

After his interest in music spread from piano to other instruments, Billy spent his teenage years playing guitar in bands at square dances, which in the early 1950s were more popular than ever and eventually led to the swell of interest in folk music that spilled out into mainstream culture near the end of the decade with the Kingston Trio. But Billy didn't really care about folk or country music and only took those gigs for the money, so he could buy B. B. King records like "Woke Up This Morning (My Baby She Was Gone)." By the time he moved into his own apartment around the age of eighteen he'd learned to play saxophone and would assemble various R&B bands to play gigs on the side of his usual thirty to forty dollars a week square dance business. That's when he met Rick Hall, not in one of the various R&B bands (as is often incorrectly reported) but as members of Carmol Taylor & His Country Pals, a country band formed to play square dances in approximately 1954, when Carmol and Billy were still teenagers and Rick Hall was in his early twenties. Rick had just returned to Alabama from serving in the U.S. Army during the Korean War and sincerely loved country music. The Carmol Taylor band was just another paying gig for Billy, until 1955, the year he was one of very few people to hear the George Jones single "Seasons of My Heart" on the radio before its flip side became a big hit. Even after George Jones converted him to a fan of country music, Billy persisted in trying to make it with an R&B band and recruited Rick Hall to the side mission.

Rick later described Billy as someone who never partied like the other guys in bands. Billy was such a shy and conservative boy it made Rick consciously try to avoid using swear words around him. According to Rick, Billy was more than a loner. He was straight-up isolated from the world around him and the condition only grew more severe after Billy's mother died in 1955, then again when Billy's father passed away in 1957. Since Rick Hall's young wife had also died in 1955 in a car accident and his father died only two months later in a tractor accident, he was the only person Billy knew could relate to the pain of such immense loss. The two became as close as brothers, sticking together through the ups and downs of trying to make their musical dreams come true. In one especially rough period they lived out of an old two-door Mercury coupe someone abandoned beneath a bridge. The big turnaround came from starting to write songs for other artists.

In 1956, Kelso Herston and James Joiner launched an indie record label in Florence and put out word they were looking for songs. In late '57 or early '58, Rick and Billy drove over to the label's office with a bunch of songs they'd written. Or, really, Rick talked Billy into at least riding over there with him and waiting in the car because Billy was too scared to go inside. Rick went in alone with the songs, some they'd written together and some apart. Kelso Herston took an interest in the entire lot but was most impressed by "Your Sweet Love," one of Billy's. Rick said the songwriter was sitting in a car outside, so Kelso went out to meet him. Billy could only stick his hand out the window for a handshake, too shy to even look up and make eye contact. Kelso Herston was probably the first person other than Rick Hall to see this stack of sincere love songs Billy wrote. In 2010, when journalist Barry Mazor asked a seventy-three-year-old Billy Sherrill what he hoped his legacy would be, Billy's eyes teared up as he said, "Let's see . . . Somewhere there might be a boy and a girl . . . And he's too shy to tell her that he loves her and she's too shy to tell him . . . So, I tell them. All they have to do is play my record. That's it."

Kelso Herston's label had a deal with Tree Music's Buddy Killen where they'd forward along their best songs to Buddy in Nashville and then split the publishing on anything that got covered. A couple months after Rick and Billy met Kelso, a guy named Bobby Denton cut the Hall-Sherrill composition "Sweet and Innocent." Though few people remember Bobby Denton's name anymore, he was the first artist to record "A Fallen Star" prior to Jimmy C. Newman running away with the hit cover. Bobby's regional career was still pretty hot when "Sweet and Innocent" came out on the B-side of a record. Two months later, Chet Atkins placed a cover of it on the B-side of one of Roy Orbison's two failed singles at RCA. (It wouldn't do Rick or Bill any good until close to twenty years later but, in 1971, a reworked version of "Sweet and Innocent" sold over a million copies as Donnie Osmond's first solo single.) When another local guy took out a newspaper ad saying he needed songwriters to launch a publishing company, Rick Hall and Billy Sherrill showed up with these recent minor successes. In 1959, they all partnered in founding Florence Alabama Music Enterprise, a.k.a. FAME.

They built what passed for a recording studio above a drugstore in Florence and, since many of the musicians in their circle were broke and homeless, several people often just slept in the studio at night after working all day. That's where Dan Penn, a writer on "Do Right Woman—Do Right Man" and "The Dark End of the Street," got his start in the music business. After becoming the singer in one of Billy Sherrill's R&B bands, the Fairlanes, Dan was told to bring some original songs by the new studio, where he found Billy, Rick, Peanutt Montgomery and Hurshel Wiginton (later of vocal group the Nashville Edition) all still asleep, having spent the night in the studio. Pretty soon the Fairlanes recorded their first single, Billy Sherrill's "Comin' After You." It wasn't any kind of hit and by the time it came out, Billy already had his sights set on relocating to Nashville, thanks to Owen Bradley cutting "Your Sweet Love" with Bob Beckham. "Your Sweet Love" wasn't any kind of hit, either, but it did land on the B-side of Beckham's "Just as Much as Ever," which hit the Pop Top 40. The four thousand dollar check Billy received in the mail was all the incentive he needed to make the move to Music City.

Upon arriving in Nashville with two other Muscle Shoals guys, Billy created a studio out of a gigantic room on the third floor of the old 7th Avenue Masonic Lodge building, where the Tree, Sure-Fire and Sam Phillips publishing companies all had offices. Decades later Billy would say this first Nashville studio, called Sonico, was only fit to record demos, but he was making a joke to downplay his past. Two *Billboard* articles from June 1960 announced Sonico's opening as "the fourth major studio" in Nashville and pointed out it was also the biggest, the live room being larger than those at the Quonset Hut, RCA and Starday. Sonico was also the only studio in the city at that time with a 4-track stereo recording unit. Unfortunately, Sonico was only open for a few months when Billy realized they weren't getting enough business to afford the rent in Nashville. Since Kelso Herston had by this point come up from Florence to work in the same building at Sam Phillips' publishing company, Billy asked if Sun Records might want to own a studio in Nashville. Turns out they did. Sam Phillips bought Sonico, renamed it Phillips International and kept Billy on staff at one hundred dollars a week to engineer sessions for artists on Sun.

When the second of those *Billboard* articles about Sonico mentioned Billy Sherrill signing an artist contract with Mercury Records, what they meant was Mercury would begin releasing the late-night creations of one man with the power to break Musician's Union rules by overdubbing multiple instruments himself. These recordings can be hard to find but they are extremely interesting. Forget the throwaway lyrics of 1960's "Like Makin' Love" and focus instead on the unique sound of a sped-up tape recording of a piano. Not being a drummer, one of the ways Billy faked percussion parts was by taking a silent section of some vinyl LP or acetate and scratching logarithmic grooves of varying depth into the surface. He'd then "play" this disc on a turntable and record the sound of the needle popping in rhythm over those scratches, essentially creating an analog click track, which he then treated with radical EQ and reverb until it sounded something like a drum kit when looped. "Like Makin' Love" wound up being the only Billy Sherrill single Mercury actually released, which is a shame, because he was certainly already on to something great, as evidenced by the B-side, "Rules of the Game." Again performing all the instruments and vocal parts himself, Billy pieced together a haunting, broken-hearted performance that simply must be heard to be believed.

Billy's move to Nashville did not end his relationship with Rick Hall or break up the Fairlanes. They released a couple more singles and Billy would drive to Alabama or the band would pick him up on the way to Kentucky for concert gigs. But nothing big ever came together for the group. In the end Billy said he left the Fairlanes and sold his shares in FAME because he grew tired of how overbearing Rick became in the studio. Billy was not the only person who ever made that complaint. Rick's aggressive attempts to dominate recording sessions and leave his own mark upon the work can perhaps be partially explained by the many comments he made in several interviews regarding how greatly he disliked his reputation as the guy who rode Billy Sherrill's coattails to success. Rick did eventually leave his own mark on an enormous swath of American music but only after parting ways with Billy and getting out from under his shadow. Without a band to take him out of town every so often, Billy focused entirely on learning everything he could in recording sessions during the day, then teaching himself to use the studio as an instrument at night.

In 1960, Tommy Roe released the song "Sheila" as a single and pretty much nobody cared except for producer Felton Jarvis, who couldn't understand why nobody seemed to like what he believed to be a sure thing hit record. In 1962, he brought the tape to Billy Sherrill and Billy overdubbed a simple tom drum part across the entire recording, which was evidently the only difference between a song bombing in 1960 and becoming a Pop #1 in 1962. The following year ABC Records released the second and final of Billy's one-man studio creations to see the light of day. The A-side "Tipsy" brought back the sped-up, woodpecker piano from "Like Makin' Love" and this time Billy chose to hit a real cymbal on top of the fake drum kit trickery. Aside from some fantastic "drink pour" foley, his growing skills as a composer and arranger are the real star of the record. Billy's fake drum technique can best be identified on the B-side, "Drag Race." His instrumental counterfeit is impressive, achieved by manipulating the EQ of each click on a slowed-down tape recording and then ramping it up to speed, but the trick is revealed by how perfectly metronomic the results sound. No human plays drums like that.

1963 was also the year Jerry Kennedy left his job as Shelby Singleton's sidekick at Mercury Records because Columbia needed someone to run the new Nashville office for their Epic imprint. When Mercury offered way more money for Jerry Kennedy to come back, he agreed to return, leaving Columbia with a recommendation to hire Billy Sherrill instead. At that time the hotshot producer working at Epic was Bob Morgan, the guy who took Bobby Vinton from being an artist nobody cared about to having #1 Pop hits, like "Roses Are Red (My Love)." Bob Morgan was the person Jerry Kennedy told to hire Billy. Bob tried several times to interview Billy for the position but each time they met for dinner in Printer's Alley they wound up just getting drunk and hanging out instead of talking about the job. When it came time to make the decision, Bob figured, What the hell? The guy Columbia hired before said Billy was the best guy for the job and Bob had a great time with him, so, in 1964, Billy was offered control of Epic's Nashville office. With a chance to become a full-time producer, Billy asked Sam Phillips for permission to go to Epic. Sam gave his blessing and spent the rest of his life praising Billy Sherrill's innovations and extravagance, calling him one of the best things to happen to the music industry.

However, it did take a little while before Billy did anything that would inspire journalists to go ask Sam Phillips to provide quotes about his career. His first couple years at Epic he was paid a little less than two hundred dollars a week to produce artists none of the label's other producers wanted to risk being associated with in case they were dropped from their deals. Billy later summed up this era of his career by saying, "I was low man on the totem pole. They sent artists down to my office that no one else could do anything with. They didn't want to drop them, so they figured, give the new guy a shot. In terms of production, I was stealing from everyone—Chet [Atkins], Owen [Bradley], Phil Spector. If you asked me who was the greatest producer around, I would say there was Owen Bradley, and then there was everyone else. He cut stuff fifty years ago that sounds like it was recorded yesterday." A couple years before hiring Billy, Columbia had purchased the 804 16th Avenue compound. From the beginning Billy's Epic sessions were held in studios built by Owen Bradley and Billy's production style quickly veered in the same direction as the work of the man who built those rooms.

As for the artists "no one else could do anything with," most were country and R&B acts. Country singer Charlie Walker had about a decade of records and only a handful of hits behind him when he got handed off to Billy. Info on these sessions is scarce, but it sounds like Pig Robbins playing tack piano (a piano with a thumbtack pressed in to each hammer so it strikes the string with a cheap and metallic sound) on "Close All the Honky Tonks." That first single with Billy only made it halfway up the Top 40 Country records, but their third single together, the Carmol Taylor song "Wild as a Wildcat," hit the Top 10. Another country act Billy produced from 1964 until the end of the decade was bluegrass brothers Jim & Jesse. It took a few years, but they eventually created the biggest record the duo ever had, a sort of truckin' song called "Diesel on My Tail." Lois Johnson's records never broke through until the mid-1970s, long after she left Epic, but 1965's "The Whole World Is Turning (Just for Us)" is a clear example of how quickly Billy Sherrill was learning to mimic Owen Bradley while working with Owen's A-Team musicians. Listen to the way the dobro, piano and pedal steel keep handing off the melody to each other underneath the lead vocal. Columbia put their subsidiary label Okeh on some of the R&B records Billy produced in this period, like Ted Taylor's biggest hit ever, "Stay Away from My Baby." Surprisingly, though, many of the soul singers Billy worked with were released on Epic proper. Obrey Wilson never found a hit song but Billy placed a great arrangement behind him on "Love Will Be Right There." It took signing with Stax in the 1970s for the Staple Singers to finally break through to the mainstream, but Billy produced their sessions the first four years they were on Epic, including the Civil Rights anthem title track of *Freedom Highway*, a live album recorded in a church in Chicago. The B-side of that single was a phenomenal rendition of Hank Williams' Luke the Drifter piece "The Funeral." Billy also worked with a few pop acts, like Cliff Richard of the Shadows, a superstar pretty much everywhere in the world except the United States. Cliff's "Wind Me Up (Let Me Go)" and "The Minute You're Gone" were both giant hits in Europe but did nothing stateside. Billy co-produced these singles with Bob Morgan, who also brought Billy to some Bobby Vinton sessions in this period, including the session for "What Color (Is a Man)."

There was not an outsized number of Billy Sherrill compositions in any of these early sessions. When he first came to Nashville he signed to write exclusively for Tree, where he and Buddy Killen co-wrote a near-instrumental called "Sugar Lips," which eventually hit the Pop Top 40 when recorded by Al Hirt on RCA. By the time that contract with Tree expired, Billy was in a position to not need to agree to write exclusively for anyone.

◇   ◇   ◇

Al Gallico came to Nashville as a result of working for the Painted Desert publishing company. One of their writers was Merle Kilgore, who spent nine weeks at #1 Country with Claude King's recording of "Wolverton Mountain," a song that crossed over to the Pop Top 10 in 1962. When Gallico saw the size of those "Wolverton Mountain" checks, he decided to quit Painted Desert and form his own publishing company, Al Gallico Music, established in 1963. He leased an office a few doors down from the Quonset Hut, in the 812 16th Avenue building where Johnny Cash, Screen Gems, SESAC and a couple of booking agencies all had offices. The following year, Epic leased some additional office space in the same building. Billy Sherrill had already filed a few songs with Gallico but, now that they were neighbors passing each other in the hall all the time, that relationship grew stronger and Billy started getting friendlier with some of Gallico's writers, especially a guy named Glenn Sutton, who Gallico had poached away from Starday to come join the big boys on Music Row. Soon after Glenn and Billy met they began going to lunch together, playing pinball after work, talking a lot about songwriting and writing songs. Their first notable cut was "Kiss Away," recorded by Ronnie Dove on the small Diamond Records label in 1965. Ray Stevens deserves a ton of credit for arranging the fantastic cello intro but everything that follows was baked into the composition by Glenn and Billy, including the Strauss-ian crescendo before the refrain, a dynamic device Billy would return to a few years later on Tammy Wynette's "Stand By Your Man." "Kiss Away" made it about halfway up the Pop Top 40, as did the next notable song by Billy and Glenn . . . only the next one was a little more impressive because it also happened to be a country song.

Like most well-informed folks Billy always shied away from defining exactly how country music "should" sound but he was never afraid to talk about who and what it was for: "Country music is adult music, adult entertainment. Everybody that's interested in a story with a beginning and an ending will like it. It's sheer entertainment." Billy learned to appreciate listening to country songs from hearing George Jones, how to produce country songs from working with the Nashville A-Team and he learned everything he knew about writing country songs from Glenn Sutton. In the beginning Glenn handled most of the lyrics and left the catchy melodies to Billy. They put in equal amounts of work on the bottle of scotch typically taken down over the course of a writing session. When Al Gallico found out Glenn and Billy were writing songs together he asked if they'd mind him sitting in on the process some time. They told Gallico he could hang out and watch them come up with something for Billy's next Charlie Walker session. After quickly landing on a plot and writing all the verses, Glenn and Billy found themselves staring at the blank space where a chorus should be. With the added pressure of Gallico being there to watch they were soon pretty seriously stuck. Billy had stopped going to church a long time before this because he said he couldn't find one teaching a literal enough interpretation of the Bible. But he never stopped loving gospel music and always kept books of hymns around, so he grabbed an old hymnal and started thumbing through it to look for ideas. The song that caught his eye was from the late 1800s and inspired by Acts 26, where Paul speaks of his conversion on the road to Damascus and "almost persuadest" Agrippa to become a Christian. After hearing a sermon on that story, a guy named Philip Bliss wrote the hymn "Almost Persuaded," which is about how almost becoming saved is to still remain damned. (The Louvin Brothers recorded a particularly compelling version.) Well, Billy saw that title and decided to subvert it in service of the song he and Glenn were writing about a man who was almost persuaded . . . to commit adultery with a beautiful woman in a bar. He even took a little bit of the hymn's chorus but changed the melody enough to perhaps prevent his father from rolling over in the grave. Charlie Walker's bad luck put him out on tour and the recording session this song was written for too many days away for Billy to wait on cutting what he knew was a great song. Since he had a David Houston session scheduled for the next day, that's where it went, put to tape within hours of being written.

"Almost Persuaded" was not David Houston's first hit record, though it's difficult to gauge how much of his success was real, given manager Tillman Franks' self-admitted fondness for using payola tactics to boost David's chart rankings. Prior to working with David, Tillman Franks was something of a Pappy Daily–like figure in the country music scene of Shreveport, Louisiana. He didn't own a record label, but becoming Johnny Horton's manager in the mid-1950s and helping turn Horton into a star gave Tillman a certain amount of clout, which he then used to help launch the careers of other artists, like Jerry Kennedy and David Houston. Houston was just a teenager when he first came to Tillman for guitar lessons in the early 1950s and Tillman started letting the kid sing on his Saturday morning radio show. Fast forward to 1963, Tillman had a recording of David singing a song called "Mountain of Love," which he and David both believed could be a hit. Houston had already been signed and dropped by various labels who released his early singles only to watch them all flop, so Tillman just needed another label to give David a new contract and release "Mountain of Love." He went up to Nashville, where both RCA and Decca said they liked the song but neither would drop everything else in order to release the single at once like Tillman requested. He talked to Jerry Kennedy at Epic, but it was right as Jerry was heading from Columbia back to Mercury, not a good time for Jerry to make fast-and-loose moves at either label. Then Tillman talked to Al Gallico, who said he could absolutely get the record pressed on Epic at once so long as the song was filed with his publishing company, which Tillman agreed to arrange. When the record was released, it quickly became David Houston's first hit. Listening to it, though, one must wonder whether Tillman's urgent need for the song to come out right away may have been due to him already somehow securing a high chart placement for Houston's next single in an upcoming issue of a certain industry trade magazine, provided the single was released in time to appear in that issue. The song and performance are totally fine but the quality of the recording sounds cheaper than anything ever cut for Starday in Jack Starnes' living room. Nevertheless, "Mountain of Love" charted at #2 Country and David Houston's first hit made him one of Billy Sherrill's early major artists. It took a few sessions for Billy to figure out how David's records should sound but, once he did, they created several more hits, like the cheating song "One If for Him, Two If for Me," which barely missed the Top 10. It's frustrating that David's version of "Cowpoke" was never released as a single. It's one of the greatest vocal performances in the history of country music and Billy's production, particularly the layered vocal tracks, explains why Marty Robbins later became obsessed with trying to get Billy to produce his sessions in the 1970s.

When Epic released "Almost Persuaded" three days after it was written, they actually put the song on the B-side of an entirely forgettable single, called "We Got Love." Then Mac Curtis, a DJ in Atlanta, played the flip side exactly once and his radio station received about one hundred phone calls from listeners wanting to know who the artist was and where they could buy it. Curtis did Epic the favor of getting in touch to say they were pushing the wrong side of David Houston's new record. According to Billy Sherrill, selling twenty-five thousand units of a single was enough to hit #1 Country in those days, so when Epic's Atlanta distributor called in an order for ten thousand copies of "Almost Persuaded" he assumed it was some kind of mistake. A few hours later, the Atlanta distributor called back to say they'd better make it twenty thousand copies. After Epic switched "Almost Persuaded" to the A-side on future pressings, the publisher of the original A-side "We Got Love" called to give Billy grief over their song being demoted to the back of the record. Billy said Epic would be happy to put a completely different song on the B-side of a guaranteed smash hit if that's what they preferred and the publisher stopped complaining. "Almost Persuaded" stayed at #1 Country for more than two months, hit #25 Pop, and won three Grammy Awards. The song was cut by pretty much everyone with a record deal at the time: the Statler Brothers, Louis Armstrong, Jim Nabors, Conway Twitty, Patti Page, George Jones, Etta James. In the late 1960s when he was still on Little Darlin', Johnny PayCheck recorded both versions of "Almost Persuaded," the original hymn and Billy's appropriation of the title, within about a year of each other. After such unbeliev-able success, Billy was no longer shy about bringing his own songs to recording sessions. Nearly every artist he ever had under contract cut a version of "Almost Persuaded." When he discovered Tammy Wynette, the song went straight on her first album. A couple years later he brought "Kiss Away" to the sessions for her *D-I-V-O-R-C-E* LP.

◇　◇　◇

Though he continued to write specifically for other artists, most of Billy's writing sessions over the next fifteen years were with Tammy Wynette in mind. It's clear from counting credits on album jackets he felt more comfortable writing for her voice than any other. Perhaps it was his fondness for the Tammy character they created. Perhaps it was his appreciation for her unquestioning faith in him. Tammy often told reporters she was so confident in Billy Sherrill's genius that if he walked in the studio and said they were cutting "Yankee Doodle" her only question would be in what key.

　　Around the time "I Don't Wanna Play House" became the second Sherrill/Sutton composition to start winning Grammy Awards, Billy hired Glenn Sutton as a staff producer at Epic in order to keep his main writing partner close, with plenty of incentive to keep creating great songs. The next Sherrill/Sutton composition to come out as a Tammy Wynette single was the product of a writing session intended for one of Glenn's own artists, Beverly Byrd. Glenn even got as far as recording "Take Me to Your World" with Beverly but when he gave the tape to Billy to overdub strings on it, Billy heard the finished product and said it needed to go to Tammy. Her cut went #1 and the reason nobody's ever heard of Beverly Byrd is because Epic dropped her soon after that, probably because her best chances at recording hit songs continued being viewed as better chances for Tammy Wyn-ette to record bigger hits.

　　Around the same time, Glenn Sutton married country singer Lynn Anderson and became her producer. Though they remained married for nearly ten years, Lynn later disclosed how frustrating it was for Glenn to come home from writing sessions with Billy Sherrill and tell her about these incredible songs they'd written . . . only to then say Lynn couldn't record any of the best ones because they were going to Tammy Wynette. Lynn understood that was part of Glenn's job description at Epic and the professional relationship with Billy predated his relationship with her by several years. But that didn't make it any easier to have a husband working so hard for an artist Lynn regarded as (quoting her) "direct competition," especially when only a few women were allowed to even attempt maintaining major label recording careers at any given time. Lynn's husband did write her a few hits, like "Keep Me in Mind" and "You're My Man," but nowhere near as many as he wrote for Tammy. Lynn had to go find her biggest record entirely on her own. In fact, Glenn tried on multiple occasions to talk her out of cutting Joe South's "Rose

Garden" because he thought the song only worked from a man's perspective. Lynn just kept bringing it into the studio and one day they had twenty minutes left at the tail end of a session, so Glenn finally let her record it. When Billy Sherrill said he had a string section booked for a couple of Tammy's songs and asked if anyone else needed strings while they were there, Glenn gave him "Rose Garden." Cam Mullins threw together an arrangement and everyone agreed it was Good Enough for album filler. But Clive Davis happened to be in town and dropped by the studio right as they were listening back to the tape. When Clive heard it, he told them to cancel whatever plans they had for Lynn Anderson's next single because they were listening to it right now. "Rose Garden" became one of the biggest country records of all time.

Billy Sherrill continued to sign other women after hitting with Tammy but rarely with such great results. One night in the late '60s, he was hanging around Printer's Alley and caught a set from the Mandrell Sisters. Billy asked if they ever thought about making a record and Barbara Mandrell came to see him at his office the next day. He gave her a record deal and became her producer for the next five years, writing and producing her first Country Top 40, "Playin' Around with Love." All of Barbara's singles produced by Billy were minor hits and some even made it into the Top 10, like 1973's "The Midnight Oil." Billy wanted a mandolin on the song, but his regular mandolin player was out on tour, so he turned to an old trick, went in the studio late at night himself to overdub tack piano onto a slowed-down tape, then brought it up to playback speed, which raised the pitch somewhere near the register of a mandolin. Despite all their minor hits together, Barbara and Billy never created a smash. Same thing with Jody Miller. Without much of a career to show for the couple of minor records she charted at Capitol in the 1960s, Jody contacted Billy. He was already a fan and signed her to Epic, then produced her sessions for the next six years. Billy didn't consider Jody's voice to be very "country" but decided to treat this as an asset rather than a hindrance by placing country arrangements behind old pop hits. Her versions of "Baby, I'm Yours" and "He's So Fine" were back-to-back Top 5 records. In 1972, Glenn Sutton and Billy Sherrill wrote "There's a Party Goin' On" for Jody Miller. When that went Top 5 as well, Lynn Anderson got mad at her husband. She understood Tammy Wynette was a higher priority than any other women on Epic, but she'd be damned if Glenn was gonna write hits for Billy's new girl over her. Fortunately for Glenn's marriage, Jody Miller's run near the top of the Country charts didn't last much longer . . . but that was also around the time Billy found another girl singer: a thirteen-year-old Tanya Tucker, whose first single came out in 1972.

Nearly every journalist who ever visited Billy's office wrote about the stacks and stacks of tapes he listened to every day at work. Almost all those tapes were songs people wanted Billy to consider recording with one of his major artists but some of the tapes were from singers trying to become one of his artists. One day he put in a tape and heard demo recordings of "Put Your Hand in the Hand" and "For the Good Times," songs Billy knew were already major hits, so he understood this was one of the tapes where he was supposed to be paying attention to the voice. He liked the voice. Then he found out it belonged to a girl who was barely a teenager and he liked the voice even more. Upon bringing Tanya Tucker to Nashville, Billy learned he had not just discovered the girl who would cut the country hit on Donna Fargo's "The Happiest Girl in the Whole U.S.A." In some versions of the story, Billy asked her to record that song for her debut single. In his version of the story, he point-blank told her the song was going to be her debut single. In every version, Tanya didn't like the song and told Nashville's most successful producer it was not going to be her debut single, no matter what. Billy liked to say Tanya Tucker was a diamond in the rough and the rough never wore off. He also said she was the only person he ever recorded who had no fear and was entirely confident in the studio. During one of their first sessions together Billy was trying to tell the musicians what he wanted on a song but Tanya was having a loud and distracting conversation in another part of the room, so he turned and yelled at her to shut up. Everyone in the room became very quiet . . . until she yelled back, "YOU shut up!" So, after a thirteen-year-old girl shot down his idea for her debut single, Billy began looking around for something she might like a little better.

One night he was watching Johnny Carson and saw Bette Midler do a song called "Delta Dawn," which he then found out Midler hadn't recorded yet, so Billy got Tanya to cut it the very next day. If it sounds like there are a lot of singers on the record, that's because Billy booked two separate vocal groups, the Jordanaires and the Nashville Edition, to sing together on the session. When the single went Top 10 and the label needed an album quickly thrown together around it, Billy found it necessary to tell every publishing company in town to stop sending over children's songs because Tanya was "young, but not a kid." Her second single, "Love's the Answer" by Emily Mitchell and Norro Wilson, hit the Top 5. She then released an amazing three-song run of singles that all went #1: "What's Your Mama's Name?" by Dallas Frazier and Peanutt Montgomery, "Blood Red and Goin' Down" by Curly Putman and "Would You Lay with Me (in a Field of Stone)" by David Allan Coe. Billy did get Tanya to cover "The Happiest Girl in the Whole U.S.A." on her first LP, by the way, but it was never released as a single. Neither was "Soul Song," with a chorus written by George Richey and verses by Billy and Norro Wilson, though it did become Joe Stampley's first #1 a few months later.

Several years passed and everyone in Nashville who laughed behind Billy's back about him making the age-old mistake of signing some cute kid whose voice was gonna change, they heard Tanya Tucker's voice change for the better and they heard it all over the radio because she continued releasing hit after hit. By 1975, the laughter turned to talk of how Billy Sherrill had done it again, he'd discovered one more voice to sculpt hit records around, one more artist who trusted and depended on him the way Tammy Wynette did. Whenever his name came up in an interview, Tanya talked about how much she loved working with Billy Sherrill, how he listened to her and treated her with the same respect he'd give an adult artist. When he found out there were people on her team, including a manager, who wanted Tanya to take choreography lessons and wanted to sexualize her image like some child beauty pageant Lolita, even though Tanya herself wanted no part of it, Billy ensured the whole plan was shut down. So, everyone was shocked when her initial three-year contract came up for renewal and Tanya left Epic to sign with MCA. Turns out, one of those managers, who was later dropped by Tanya because of this, completely botched the contract renegotiation with Columbia's New York City office and insulted Tanya's parents in the process. By the time Billy found out about the problem it was too late for anything to be done. Afterward, he said, "We had a short, beautiful relationship and then dark, dismal, lurking, corporate powers took over and we separated. I still like her, and she still likes me." Regardless of the fact that he and Tanya both hated it, she was gone. According to some close sources, losing Tanya crushed Billy. But he still had Tammy Wynette and, by the mid-1970s, the bet he'd placed on Charlie Rich years earlier was finally paying off.

◇   ◇   ◇

After "Mohair Sam" climbed halfway up the Pop Top 40 for Charlie Rich in 1965, his subsequent singles all tanked and Smash Records dropped him. Billy signed Charlie to Epic in 1968 with the intention of recording him as a country artist. Though it took close to five years before the general public noticed, their work together was amazing right from the start. *Rolling Stone* called Charlie's third Epic single as good as anything he'd ever done, which was correct. Unfortunately, the magazine was incorrect when they proposed it could be a hit on pop, R&B, easy listening and country radio all at once. Though it's now regarded as one of Charlie's greatest recordings, "Life's Little Ups and Downs" didn't even crack the Top 40 Country singles upon release in 1969. But Charlie and Billy continued making great music together, mostly for the pleasure of doing so, until the early 1970s, when they hit with two Kenny O'Dell songs back-to-back. First, "I Take It on Home," which was pretty much the same concept as "Almost Persuaded" except Charlie Rich was more of a stud than David Houston, so he needed to turn down a lady pretty much every time he went to a bar. After that went Top 10 Country it was followed by O'Dell's "Behind Closed Doors." (Billy did change a couple of the lyrics but took none of the writing credit.) This was the first of seven #1 Country records in a row for Charlie Rich, five of which crossed over to the Pop Top 40. The single he released after "Behind Closed Doors" went all the way to #1 Pop. Both songs were recorded on the same day but the second one had been written much earlier. Well, kind of.

Norro Wilson first got into the business as a singer for various vocal groups, including the

Omegas, who were produced by Owen Bradley on singles like the punny "Failing in Love." None of those vocal groups ever worked out, so Norro took a job as a song plugger at Screen Gems while waiting for another recording contract to come along. When Screen Gems fired him, Norro went across the hall and became a song plugger for Al Gallico's publishing company. Around the same time Charlie Rich signed to Epic, Norro signed to Smash and asked one of the label's promotion guys, Rory Bourke, to help him write a hit single. Bourke came up with the idea of a song about a guy who regretted ending his relationship with a beautiful girl and was searching for her to apologize and get back together. Norro figured this guy would describe the girl when asking if people had seen her, so they began coming up with physical attributes for a beautiful girl, then realized calling her tall, short, blonde, brunette or any other single thing would limit the commercial appeal of the song because every person is attracted to a different type of girl. Since they were trying to write a hit that would be appreciated by as many folks as possible, they decided to leave the girl's beauty undefined and Norro cut the song as "Hey Mister." Nobody cared. Norro tried several times to get Billy Sherrill interested in the song for any of his artists on Epic but Billy wanted nothing to do with it. Norro's next single for Smash was called "Mama McCluskie," about basically the same exact thing as "Hey Mister" except this time Norro gave the girl a last name and went straight to her mother to express his regret. Nobody cared about this record, either, but when Billy was pitched this one he said they might be on to something if they took the best parts of both songs and turned them into a different song, which is what Billy did to create "The Most Beautiful Girl" for Charlie Rich.

Released in fall of 1973, it took little more than a year for "The Most Beautiful Girl" to sell over two million copies. Charlie won Entertainer of the Year and Album of the Year at the 1974 CMAs and probably would have taken home even more awards had "Behind Closed Doors" not already won four CMAs the previous year. Charlie became tied with Eddy Arnold for the artist to release the most #1 records in a single calendar year, each having five. Two of Charlie's #1's during that streak were just some old recordings RCA issued as "new" singles due to his massive success at Epic. There was one week when three different Charlie Rich records held the top three positions on the Country chart. After hitting with "The Most Beautiful Girl," Norro Wilson and Billy Sherrill began writing songs together specifically for Charlie, including "I Love My Friend" and "A Very Special Love Song," which both went #1. These were all profoundly influential records. You won't find many artists with a years-long streak of such market dominance who were not then immediately imitated by the rest of their industry. Prior to Charlie Rich, nearly every artist who recorded in the Quonset Hut stood on the thirteenth tile from the wall to sing, as this was believed to be the room's sweet spot for vocals. But Charlie liked to cut vocal tracks while standing by Pig Robbins at the piano, so he could better hear and see the piano parts he'd need to play while performing the songs on tour. After Charlie spent a couple years releasing nothing but #1 singles standing over by the piano, other artists stopped standing on tile thirteen and started standing by the piano.

◇　　◇　　◇

Just as Owen Bradley's many imitators previously pulled him and his Nashville Sound into the debate over what constitutes pop, country or pop country music, so did Owen's greatest imitator find himself and his records at the center of the same debate. The only real difference was that everyone started calling Billy Sherrill's version of the Nashville Sound "countrypolitan," which is a ridiculous word for several reasons but mostly because it was initially coined by country radio stations in Southern metropolises to describe their listener demographics in industry trade ads. These radio stations were not calling the music they played "countrypolitan." They were telling potential sponsors the airwaves reached a "countrypolitan" audience of listeners near enough to a major city to pick up its radio stations but rural enough to work in booming industries like agriculture, which meant those listeners had a lot of money to spend. If that sounds like a direct result of the Country Music Association forming two decades earlier at the beginning of the Nashville Sound era in order to educate radio stations on the subject of how much money country music fans could spend on advertised products, it's because that's exactly what it was. The actual music Billy Sherrill was making in Nashville during this so-called countrypolitan era was nothing more than the Nashville Sound recorded with newer and better instruments and equipment, resulting in a cleaner sound with more space in the mix and a wider dynamic range. As such, lazy usage of "countrypolitan" leads right back to the same confusing issues found in discussions of the Nashville Sound, where production and arrangement techniques become a misguided argument over genre.

The first thing everyone did in a Billy Sherrill session was make sure the piano sounded good because that's the first thing everyone did in an Owen Bradley session, because Owen's Nashville Sound was built around piano. Remember how much Billy loved listening to Johan Strauss? It's not a coincidence that Owen Bradley cut an entire album's worth of Strauss waltzes for Coral Records in the early 1950s. The only exercise one really needs to perform to realize Billy Sherrill was simply a continuation of Owen Bradley's Nashville Sound is to take a listen to the records Owen Bradley made in the 1970s, like basically anything from Loretta Lynn or Conway Twitty. They sound very similar to Billy Sherrill records, not because Owen all of the sudden wanted to start sounding like Billy but because Billy was always trying to make the records Owen would have made in the 1950s and 1960s if somehow able to use the newer and better equipment available to Billy. If Billy was forced to use Owen's gear from the '50s and '60s on everything he produced for Epic, it would all sound virtually indistinguishable from Owen's Nashville Sound because it was the same people doing the same stuff in the same rooms for the same reasons. Nashville

Sound–era utility man Charlie McCoy also played on thousands of Music Row sessions in the so-called countrypolitan era. When he accepted an award for Instrumentalist of the Year at the 1972 CMAs, long after the word "countrypolitan" started being thrown around, Charlie referred to the records then being made by the A-Team as the Nashville Sound. So should we.

It's important to make these distinctions because the pop country debate in the 1970s was more widespread and heated than ever before, thanks to Willie Nelson and Waylon Jennings bringing unprecedented numbers of rock music fans to form their first opinions on country music via the "outlaw" movement. Many of those opinions cast Billy Sherrill in the role of Country Music's Biggest Enemy, previously played by Owen Bradley and Chet Atkins. Just like blaming Chet Atkins' production work on Owen Bradley or believing Owen Bradley's Brenda Lee records somehow negate his work with Loretta Lynn or Warner Mack, that is completely ignorant.

Anyone whose definition of outlaw country doesn't include Johnny PayCheck automatically has no idea what they're talking about. Billy probably saved PayCheck's life by signing him to Epic in 1970, two years before Waylon Jennings released the *Ladies Love Outlaws* LP and three years before Wille Nelson released *Shotgun Willie*. PayCheck had put out a few minor hits at Little Darlin' in the 1960s but, by the end of the decade, he and producer Aubrey Mayhew wanted nothing to do with each other. In 1970, Johnny was out in L.A. trying to drink and drug his way over feeling burned by the industry when Billy called to say he should come back to Nashville for one more try at Epic. Their first single together was a version of Swamp Dogg's "She's All I Got" that became a #2 Country hit, the biggest of PayCheck's career at that point. They followed it up with "Someone to Give My Love To," a #4 record for Johnny. For the next several years his Epic singles stayed dialed in to that love song theme and most were successful, including several more major hits, like "Mr. Lovemaker." Then outlaw country broke through to mainstream pop culture, PayCheck grew a beard to go with his mustache and began cutting songs that could have been pulled from the pages of his life story, like the Mack Vickery, Wayne Kemp and Bobby Borchers song, "I'm the Only Hell (Mama Ever Raised)." After that went Top 10 Country, Paycheck sent the David Allan Coe song "Take This Job and Shove It" all the way to #1 as the title track of a platinum-selling LP produced by Billy.

Another thing many thousands of outlaw country fans get wrong is the role Billy Sherrill supposedly played in trying to keep Columbia from releasing Willie Nelson's crossover hit album, *Red Headed Stranger*. The most important fact to understand is Willie Nelson's business dealings with Columbia went through the New York City office, not Billy Sherrill's Epic office in Nashville. The story about Waylon Jennings flying in the *Red Headed Stranger* tapes to play them for Columbia is a story about him taking the tapes to Bruce Lundvall in New York City, not Billy Sherrill in

Nashville. Bruce Lundvall was the person who made Waylon angry by saying they should have Billy Sherrill overdub strings on the album and Lundvall said that to Waylon before Billy had even heard those tapes. When Billy Sherrill did hear the tapes, he did say they sounded like demo recordings . . . because by contemporary standards they sounded exactly like demo recordings. That cannot be misconstrued as some Nashville executive failing to understand country music. Anyone in the known universe who believes they are "more country" than Charlie Louvin is dead wrong and Charlie said he thought *Red Headed Stranger* sounded worse than a demo. Even after the album became wildly popular, Charlie never understood why anyone liked it. In 1975, the year *Red Headed Stranger* came out and made a bunch of Columbia executives in New York City look like fools who then tried to forward their embarrassment along to Billy Sherrill in Nashville, Willie Nelson wrote in an issue of *Picking Up the Tempo* that he and Billy Sherrill never had anything but fond words for each other. Willie said it was "other people" who tried to portray him and Billy as being against each other when they really never were.

Billy inspired a great deal of jealousy throughout the music industry. His dedication to creating hit records with little regard for anything else, especially social niceties, rubbed many executives, artists and fans the wrong way. Glenn Sutton said he believed artists were intimidated by Billy because you could never tell if he was happy or not. Tammy Wynette stated as much in her autobiography and said for the first six months she was around Billy she thought he was the strangest man she'd ever met. If there were five or six people hanging out in his office, Billy would get up and leave without saying a word to anyone, then not return. Tammy later realized it was because being around groups of people anywhere but in a recording studio gave Billy anxiety, which was probably the same reason he spent the first ten minutes of nearly every interview he ever did cracking jokes in response to each question before giving a real answer and probably the same reason why everyone, save for a select few, always found it very difficult to secure a meeting with him. The story goes that Wynette was only able to see him the first time because Billy was temporarily without a secretary and/or Wynette waited outside his office for several hours until he had no choice but to talk with her if he wanted to go home at the end of the day. A lot of people misread his intense social anxiety as the aloofness of a man who believed his own press when someone called him a genius. It was an easy mistake to make, given his talent for saying outrageous things combined with the unshakeable confidence and control he assumed in the studio, the one place where he felt comfortable.

Billy was once explaining to journalist Walter Campbell how easy it is for an artist and producer to get burned out on working together when Walter asked what about the studio musicians? Billy admired the Nashville A-Team so much that at first he didn't even understand the question.

As Walter began to clarify what he meant by pointing out Billy worked with the same studio musicians far more than he worked with any given artist, Billy interrupted to firmly state, "No. They're all great." In a different interview he said, "I knew what I wanted to hear, and [the musicians] knew what they wanted to play. Sometimes, it happened to be the same thing. But there was always a mutual respect." Pedal steel guitarist Lloyd Green said he always believed Billy to be the best producer in Nashville because "he literally choreographed the entire song, every song he did." Like Owen Bradley before him, Billy would sometimes ask musicians for opinions or suggestions, but anytime he gave a direct instruction it was not to be doubted or second-guessed. If he told you exactly what he wanted, it's because he knew exactly what he wanted and that's what he was going to get. If he happened to be incorrect about something, everyone found out together when the record was released because nobody stood in the way of Billy Sherrill and the sound he heard in his head. Such certainty came without much patience for artists who failed to understand these decisions were based upon knowing what made each particular artist unique and hoping to spotlight that for the rest of the world. David Houston once tried to suggest they do something differently than Billy instructed, so Billy said he was going to go take a piss, then didn't come back for two hours, at which point they made the record Billy's way. Billy was Lefty Frizzell's producer at Epic for a little while, right up until the day Lefty said he didn't want to cut Mel Street's "Borrowed Angel." Billy just walked out of the studio after calling in Glenn Sutton to take over the session, which wound up being Lefty's last, since he was dropped from the label soon after. These are the type of stories that give life to persistent rumors Billy Sherrill was secretly a Nazi.

Some folks believe Billy said, "What would Hitler do?" or stamped a swastika on someone's hand not to be outrageous because he was bored in a record label meeting he didn't want to attend . . . but because he was secretly a Nazi. He'd put *Triumph of the Will* on his TV not to let everyone know a party was over and it was time to get out of his fucking house . . . but because he was secretly a Nazi. To be clear, he knew these things were offensive when he said and did them. Like so many ignorant kids in the 1970s UK punk scene who were not actually Nazis, that was the entire reason he said and did them. But he was no more serious in these or other references to the Third Reich than he was the time a journalist asked what was left to accomplish in his career and Billy responded, "Faith healing." When George Jones biographer Bob Allen point-blank asked if Billy was supportive of Adolf Hitler or Nazis or fascism—in the same conversation that he asked Billy to confirm he was not a communist, if that offers any indication of how impossible it could be to get a read on the guy—Billy wholesale denied a sincere fondness for the Third Reich and said he was no more interested in World War II than he was interested in the history of Ancient Greece and Rome. To be clear, Billy was deeply interested in the history of Ancient Greece, Rome and World War II. There's no question of his fascination with

Hitler's ability to manipulate the minds of millions of people. That's the same thing Billy was trying to do to the hearts of millions of people. It's what Orson Welles and George Lucas were trying to do to millions of eyeballs, which is why they studied and took influence from *Triumph of the Will*. Lucas went so far as to call Leni Riefenstahl "the most modern filmmaker." Unlike David Bowie, Billy's interests never led him to call Hitler a "rock 'n' roll star" or publicly praise Hitler's stage presence and ability to work a crowd. Unlike Lemmy Kilmister, Billy was never photographed wearing Nazi military garb from a collection of World War II paraphernalia. But Billy Sherrill was a country music producer from Alabama with Southern Baptist religious beliefs and unapologetically conservative politics. Where all those other artists get a pass, he gets accused of being an actual Nazi rather than one more student and practitioner of emotional manipulation, taking lessons from unconventional places on how to convince an audience of an alternate reality, even if only for the running length of a song.

There's simply no way to know for certain where Billy would land on today's political spectrum. He held politically conservative stances for most of his adult life but his statements on several issues, like social tolerance toward non-heterosexual people, seemed to drift toward the center with age. There's no telling exactly how serious he was when he said he stopped going to church because he couldn't find one teaching a literal enough interpretation of the Bible but there was also no single topic that ever made him angrier than that of megachurch evangelists. Billy Sherrill offered nothing but undisguised scorn for what he referred to as the "electric church" and the prosperity doctrine so beloved by today's far right.

Convenient sensational narratives aside, he was not the heartless, fascist dictator of country music. There are too many examples of his actual behavior conflicting with the provocative things he said and did to intentionally cultivate such an intimidating persona. Emily Mitchell, a former secretary at Epic who was eventually promoted to the executive level, said Billy always claimed to hate cats but then she noticed that any time a stray cat began hanging around the street near the office Billy couldn't stop worrying about its safety until someone managed to find it a home. When he saw a homeless person near Music Row, he always made sure someone sent food over to them. If anything, it seems he felt too much, too strongly and saying controversial things was one of several shields he tried to place between himself and the rest of the world.

◇　◇　◇

When Tammy Wynette quit working with him early in 1980, it wounded Billy more deeply than any other event in his career. Possibly to save face, he claimed this split was partly the result of him "checking out" and becoming bored with the job. Though he never gave consistent answers for exactly when that supposedly happened, there are several bits of evidence to suggest it could only have been after Tammy left him, if at all. Johnny PayCheck lost his record deal with Epic after pleading no contest to charges of misdemeanor sexual assault against a minor. That's a long, complicated story and has nothing to do with Billy but it did happen in 1982, so Billy must have checked out prior to then, since he sometimes didn't even come down to the studio for PayCheck's final Epic sessions, choosing instead to have an audio line run up to a monitor in his office so he could call down with any instructions. It doesn't seem Billy was checked out four years earlier, when Charlie Rich left Epic in 1978, almost certainly negotiating a better deal at United Artists on the strength of his #1 record the year before, "Rollin' with the Flow," which Billy hunted down on the B-side of a T. G. Sheppard single. Then there's the fact that smack in the middle of those two mile markers, at the beginning of the 1980s, Billy's output as a songwriter suddenly plummeted, as if he lost the desire to write songs the moment he no longer had Tammy Wynette's voice to sing them. Since writing was the thing he used to do to make up for not finding any good material in the piles of tapes heaped on his desk, he spent most of the rest of his career listening to those tapes and hating 99 percent of everything he heard.

Still, Billy continued churning out hit records for most of his artists and, whether or not he ever really did check out, it's easy to hear which ones were the favorites who kept him interested in doing the job, like George Jones, Lacy J. Dalton and David Allan Coe. DAC was first signed to Columbia in 1974 but his albums were produced by Ron Bledsoe until 1978. Really, it was only a matter of time before Billy took over. Just listen to the dramatic blend of gospel and heartache across the entire B-side of *Human Emotions*, the first album they made together, virtually guaranteed against success at commercial radio because of the way every song transitions seamlessly into the next. This is most effectively employed in the jump from the title track to "(She's Finally Crossed Over) Love's Cheatin' Line." That type of magic is not something that happens with a checked-out producer in the control room. Billy and DAC would have their biggest hits together years later, on mid-1980s songs like "The Ride" and "Mona Lisa Lost Her Smile." Most relevant to this topic, there's what sounds like a rare and uncredited background vocal from Billy high in the mix on 1985's "I'm Gonna Hurt Her on the Radio." Billy signed Lacy J. Dalton in 1979, just prior to Tammy leaving him, and clearly gave much of himself to Lacy's sessions, as evidenced by his lifting an old favorite Virgil O. Stamps hymn "Beyond the Clouds" for the intro of "16th Avenue" in 1982. Sadly, none of these records ever made the impact of his work with Tammy Wynette or Tanya Tucker and, through to the end of his career, George Jones was the only artist whose returns were equal to what Billy invested in the sessions. However, it was also Billy's work with George Jones that resulted in not only his greatest professional embarrassment but Elvis Costello's as well.

Almost Blue by Elvis Costello is probably the favorite album of everyone who thinks it would be great if they asked their mailman to pretend to be a country music singer. Costello's previous albums were released through Columbia in the United States and everything he put out at the time sold at least half a million copies, so it wasn't difficult to get Billy Sherrill's attention when Costello for some reason decided to make a country album and asked Billy produce it. While this request was apparently rooted in Costello being a huge fan of the George Jones records Billy produced, every cover of a Jones song on the resulting album was from prior to George's time on Epic. (It's possible Costello was one of many people who mistakenly believed Jones and Billy began working together on "A Good Year for the Roses," one of the songs on *Almost Blue*.) Whatever logic did or didn't go into planning the project, the catastrophic results were well documented because they had a video crew there to film the sessions. This documentary is not easy to find for reasons that are about to become obvious but anyone who manages to find and watch it will see Billy Sherrill trying and failing to understand why Elvis Costello has a recording career while hating every second spent in the studio until he can finally escape and take his boat out on the lake. In interviews prior to the album's release, Billy did a decent job of talking up the collaboration, hitting the usual talking points about it being an opportunity to "try something new," and how surprised Billy was to learn this Elvis Costello guy was such a big country music fan, etc. But his disdain for Costello's voice and band butchering a bunch of classic country songs could not be disguised at all on camera and, in the end, neither could Billy's financial motivation for taking the gig. Within a few years he and Costello were regularly talking shit on each other in the press, Costello calling Billy "a hack" who didn't have an ounce of feeling left in him and Billy calling Costello the worst singer he'd ever heard.

◇   ◇   ◇

One of Billy's last great thrills in the business was getting to work with Ray Charles. Ray's two *Modern Sounds in Country and Western Music* albums may have been very popular but a more accurate title for both would have been *Country and Western Songs in Modern Sounds*, as these and his other recordings of country material all repurposed them into big band jazz and R&B arrangements until he signed with Columbia in 1982 and began making actual country music. Ray self-produced most of these sessions, including his first minor country hit on Columbia, "Born to Love Me." But Ray didn't get into the Country Top 10 until he put Billy Sherrill in the control room, first on the comical George Jones duet "We Didn't See a Thing," then the Willie Nelson duet "Seven Spanish Angels."

Whenever he later reminisced on his time spent in the studio with Ray, Billy spoke like the excited teenager he'd been when he first started obsessing over Ray Charles records, saying things like "Ray Charles, man, he's it!" After getting the gig with Ray, Billy dove headfirst into finding songs that were good enough to record. When he heard "Seven Spanish Angels," he first wanted

Ray to cut it with Ronnie Milsap but Ronnie wasn't into the song. Since Troy Seals and Eddie Setser wrote it as a "what would Willie Nelson's version of Marty Robbins' 'El Paso' sound like?" type of thing, they'd also sent a demo to Willie. Once Billy found out Willie liked the song and wanted to record it, he suggested singing it with Ray and everyone loved the idea. Billy did his session with Ray in Nashville, shipped the tape down to Texas for Willie to overdub his part, then back to Nashville for Billy to overdub strings and background vocals. Listening to the finished tape, Billy decided he didn't like the way the song ended by going into a whole different melody to wrap up the plot with a tidy explanation, so he just added a fade out before the record reached that part, leaving the story's end open to interpretation.

Few things in life ever gave Billy Sherrill as much satisfaction as knowing he'd helped make Ray Charles' only #1 Country record. One of the other things was the time Johnny Cash, then signed to Columbia, happened to stop by one of the Ray Charles sessions and accepted Billy Sherrill's impromptu offer to sing on the song "Crazy Old Soldier." Billy said when he got in bed that night all he could do was lay awake for hours thinking about how the day had really happened. He'd really just come home from running a session for Ray Charles and Johnny Cash. How could he fall asleep if he was already living some kind of dream?

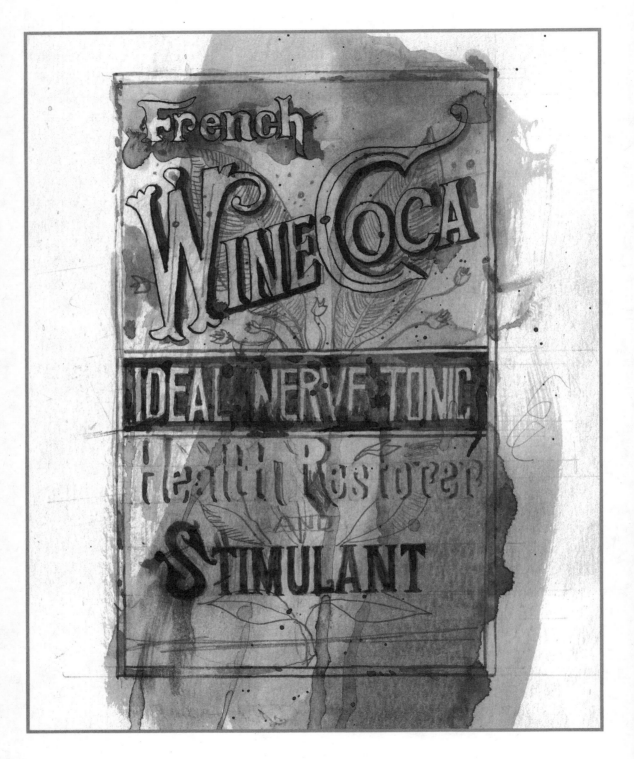

TWENTY-THREE

COCAINE BLUES

◇ Coca Leaves of the Incan Empire ◇ Sigmund Freud Ruins the World ◇
When America Loved Cocaine, Then Didn't ◇

Everyone knows about how the recipe for Coca-Cola once contained a little bit of cocaine—9 mg per serving, to be exact. What usually goes unmentioned with this piece of trivia is that Coca-Cola was created in a time when anyone with 25¢ could walk into an American pharmacy and walk out with 1 gram of powdered cocaine. And we all assume we know what we're talking about when we use the word "cocaine" but the vast majority of blow on the streets of the United States has been diluted with all kinds of cutting agents. It rarely contains more than 65 percent of actual cocaine. Usually, it's more like 40 percent and often much less. These days, the experience most Americans believe they've had with cocaine is actually experience with the stimulating effects of snorting powdered caffeine or sugar, combined with the numbing effects of some cheap anesthetic, plus the bitter taste of quinine and—somewhere in there—maybe half the weight of illegal narcotics that was paid for. Then there are all of the Americans no longer having any kind of experiences at all because they accidentally died from an overdose of the fentanyl being used to cut a great deal of modern cocaine. But it wasn't always like this . . .

◇　　◇　　◇

When we refer to the Incan Empire, we're really talking about the dozens of peoples conquered by the Inca, nearly everyone living on or close to the Andes Mountains in what is now called South America. The Aymara? Conquered by the Inca. The Chimu? Conquered by the Inca. The Uru? Conquered by the Inca. The list of cultures subjugated by the Inca is long and, for thousands of years, many of these groups chewed leaves from the coca bushes native to the region. Out of more than 150 species of coca, several contain the alkaloid now called "cocaine." Without this alkaloid, it's unlikely the people of the Andes would have believed coca to be a gift from their gods. In addition to use for religious rites, coca leaves have long been regarded as suitable for casual use in daily life. Wrapped in a small bundle with an alkaline substance—such as the ash from burning another plant or quicklime—then stuffed between the gums and inner cheek or lip like chewing tobacco, the chemical solution produces a slight numbness or tingling sensation as saliva transmits cocaine into the body. The ensuing effects are often compared to a particularly strong cup of coffee. The user feels more alert and is able to work or walk or think for a long time without becoming as tired, hungry or thirsty as they otherwise would. Same thing if consumed in the form of hot tea. One cup of coca tea is typically made from about a gram of leaves, which only contains 4 mg or so of the cocaine alkaloid, nowhere near the amount of powder you'd need to offer to someone at a party if you didn't want to be mocked. It's also not enough to induce anything like the modes of consciousness we tend to associate with cocaine.

As the Inca rose to power in the middle of the fifteenth century they restricted access to the divine coca among their conquered subjects. The leaves were still used in religious ceremonies but practical daily use was limited to Incan royalty and those to whom they granted exemptions, like government officials, military personnel, physical laborers on important projects, couriers delivering state messages over a great distance on foot, etc. A couple decades into the sixteenth century, civil war broke out between two Incan princes who each hoped to rule over the entire empire. Their infighting weakened existing power structures and common people regained access to coca for casual daily use. This was around the time Spanish conquistadors showed up on the continent. When the conquistadors noticed a relationship between use of coca leaves and increased productivity in the fields and mines, they pushed slaves and other workers to consume more and more coca to please the Spanish crown with greater harvesting of wealth from this "new world." By the time the last Incan emperor was executed in the 1570s, bringing an end to their empire, Spain's throne was sat upon by Felipe II, Holy Roman Emperor Charles V's Habsburg son, who was married to the daughter of Henri II and Catherine de Médici. In service of his plan to replace all indigenous religions with Christianity, Felipe decided to ban this coca leaf he'd heard was so important in Andean rituals. That is, until his conquistadors reported the withdrawal had instantly hamstrung laborers, who became tired, depressed and virtually unable to work. So, Felipe re-legalized coca, only now with a hefty 10 percent tax placed on the leaves.

Coca leaves were sent back to Spain on some of the first ships to make the return voyage after a conquistador tried the drug. There are records dating coca's first appearance in Europe to the sixteenth century. But the plant's active ingredient couldn't withstand the conditions and duration of such distant sea travel at the time, so nobody in Europe really understood what all the fuss was about for another few hundred years. It took until 1855 for the cocaine alkaloid to be successfully isolated and extracted from coca leaves. In 1859, a better extraction process was discovered, yielding more and purer cocaine from each batch of leaves. Both extraction processes were discovered in Germany and it didn't take their medical or scientific communities long to begin experimenting with this new drug. In 1860, the German pharmaceutical company still doing business today as Merck began producing and selling cocaine as an energy supplement and a treatment for "sinus difficulties."

Early trials found cocaine to bring users a sense of physical, mental and emotional well-being, even pleasure or ecstasy. It seemed cocaine caused a person to feel more focused and energetic, happier and more excited about the idea of socializing with other humans . . . for roughly an hour or so, at which point the user needed to take more cocaine to keep feeling this way. While the user was having such a great time for that first hour, their body was busy increasing its tolerance to the drug, so producing another hour of the same effects would require consuming more cocaine than they took the first time, until the person who kept taking more cocaine to keep feeling as good as the last time found themselves in a pretty terrible state: angry, unable to sleep, heart beating so fast they felt like they were going to die, especially due to a growing sense of paranoia, full-on hallucinations and maybe the belief that bugs were crawling around underneath their skin. Addicts such as this would usually lash out at friends, family or anyone else who cared enough to try keeping them from continuing to do cocaine. Should the addict actually decide to stop, though, they would find it quite difficult, considering their brain had grown accustomed to receiving far more dopamine than it was capable of manufacturing on its own and would try to get the dopamine by causing the addict to feel depressed, agitated, confused and inconsolable until they either did more cocaine or successfully kicked the addiction, however many weeks or months that required. Tragically, it took doctors and scientists a while to discover all of that stuff except the very first part, the part where it sounded like cocaine was awesome and everyone should do it.

One famous early advocate was the young neurologist Sigmund Freud. In his eagerness to make an important contribution to science and land himself a spot in medical history, Freud spent much of the 1880s destroying who knows how many lives by writing articles and essays recommending the new wonder drug to basically any adult who wanted to feel good about being alive. Among other exciting-yet-baseless claims, Freud suggested cocaine was a safe and nonaddictive method to wean addicts off much more dangerous substances, like opium. However, when he actually put that theory to the test it only resulted in opium addicts also becoming addicted to cocaine. Freud wrote that the alkaloid which caused slight numbness where it touched human membrane in plant form seemed to render the same membrane totally numb when a higher concentration of cocaine extract was used. Another doctor in his social circle grasped the implications of this, began experimenting and—long story short—the reason the name of every local anesthetic ends in the suffix "-caine" is because they were all created to mimic the targeted numbing effect of cocaine, which literally established modern concepts of local anesthesia. So, there's one for the plus column. For the most part, Freud's cheerleading of cocaine brought about disastrous results.

◇   ◇   ◇

In 1884, the United States Hay Fever Association named cocaine the official remedy for hay fever. By 1885, Americans could go to a pharmacy and buy powdered cocaine in packages that advertised the contents would "supply the place of food, make the coward brave, the silent eloquent and render the sufferer insensitive to pain." By the time the U.S. Surgeon General recommended cocaine for treatment of depression in 1887, many thousands of American citizens were way ahead of him. One popular delivery method of the era was cocaine-laced cigarettes, sold in packaging which listed the ten reasons why "cocarettes should be smoked by all smokers," including that "coca is the finest nerve tonic and exhilarator ever discovered" and "the coca neutralizes the depressing effects of the nicotine in the tobacco" and "cocarettes can be freely used by persons in delicate health without injury and with positively beneficial results." As with most medicinal advertising of the age, that language was imprecise and misleading so it's important to again draw a distinction between actual cocaine—a pure and potent alkaloid extract—and the coca leaf, which at equivalent volume contains barely 1/100th the amount of said alkaloid. These are entirely different creatures. Much of Europe was regularly consuming coca leaves with relatively little problem for twenty years before anyone ever heard of Sigmund Freud.

In the early 1860s a French chemist found that placing coca leaves in liquid containing a significant percentage of ethanol alcohol, like wine, would pull the cocaine alkaloid out of the leaves and into the liquid. In 1863, he put his own last name on the concoction and began selling it as Vin Mariani. Containing about 6 mg of cocaine per ounce, Vin Mariani was an instant hit in France and quickly spread beyond. Mariani was something of a marketing genius for his time and leaned heavily on celebrity endorsements to promote his product, taking out ads that boasted Vin Mariani was enjoyed by no less an esteemed customer than the pope. It was true, too. The current pope enjoyed coca wine so much, he sent a gold medal as a token of gratitude to its inventor. Other known enthusiasts included Jules Verne, H. G. Wells, Thomas Edison and U.S. Presidents William McKinley and Ulysses S. Grant. Stateside, there was a doctor in Columbus, Georgia, named John Pemberton, who found himself saddled with a nasty morphine addiction after treating an injury sustained while fighting for the Confederacy in the Civil War. When Pemberton heard all the fuss about coca wine (including early rumors it could help wean someone off morphine), he decided to check it out and liked what he found. Knowing there were thousands more ex-soldiers with addictions like his (and that Mariani must be raking in money hand over fist with this stuff), Pemberton decided to launch a competing version. Like many others attempting to piggyback off Mariani's success, Pemberton hoped to entice users over to a new brand by advertising a higher percentage of cocaine in his recipe, Pemberton's French Wine Coca. Soon after he hit the market, in the mid-1880s, Fulton County passed local Prohibition laws. Pemberton quickly removed the alcohol from his formula, kept the 9 mg of cocaine (and caffeine from kola nuts), then rebranded as the temperance-approved beverage Coca-Cola.

By this time many within the medical community were aware of the cocaine alkaloid's highly addictive nature and the extremely negative effects of regularly using high concentrations of cocaine extract. But the damage had already been done. Even if every esteemed authority who heaped praise on the drug only a few years earlier was willing to come out, say they were wrong and let their professional reputations take the hit (which they weren't), hundreds of thousands of people around the world had acted on those initial rave reviews. By 1902, there were roughly two hundred thousand Americans addicted to cocaine. Hardly anyone using cocaine on a daily basis wanted to admit there was anything wrong, lest it complicate their ability to continue easily acquiring the drug they now couldn't imagine living without. It was regularly used in blue-collar jobs, often handed out by managers and business owners to keep workers awake and active on overtime or overnight shifts. There are many documented instances of cocaine being pushed on Black laborers, as it was believed to produce harder, faster and better work from their race.

With such widespread use, everyone not addicted to cocaine could readily observe what it was doing to everyone else, regardless of how safe it had ever been deemed by any doctor or scientist. As the drug became more closely associated with the lower classes than the medical elite, an inevitable backlash finally arose, complete with all the classist and racist rhetoric puritans always use whenever they want to ban something: "fill-in-the-blank turns the dregs of society (especially the Black ones) into murderous and sex-crazed lunatics," etc. Only then did the government step in with regulation. In 1902, the state of Georgia banned all sales of cocaine and Coca-Cola removed it from the recipe. (Yes, they did and do still use coca leaves—without the cocaine alkaloid—as a flavoring agent.) In 1906, the federal government started down a road that eventually led to establishing the Food and Drug Administration by introducing the Food and Drug Act. Among other things, this legislation required manufacturers to list cocaine or opium on the label if either was included in foods, beverages, supplements, elixirs, tinctures, tonics, liniments, etc. Then, in 1914, came the Harrison Narcotics Tax Act, which brought opium and cocaine under government control through a system of granting and denying licenses to manufacturers and requiring a doctor's prescription to legally buy cocaine or opium from a pharmacy, as would also be done with alcohol a handful of years later. The Jones-Miller Act of 1922 essentially ended nearly all legal access to cocaine, banning any form of recreational consumption and placing tight restrictions on medicinal use. By the end of the decade, the drug had gone underground.

Largely replaced as anesthesia by amylocaine and procaine, soon to be replaced as a stimulant by amphetamines, cocaine stopped being manufactured at industrial volume for public consumption. As rare and expensive contraband, it was used in large amounts only by those with sufficient financial means to pursue the habit. Supposedly, actress Tallulah Bankhead once said something like she knew cocaine wasn't habit-forming because she'd been using it for years. In her autobiography, she tried to play off the unshakeable quote as a recurring joke she came up with after being prescribed cocaine cough drops. But other versions of the story depict her angrily yelling that line down a phone at whoever was on the other end trying to explain the government had made it very difficult for the actress to keep buying cocaine. And if such a rich and famous person could no longer easily powder her nose, you can imagine the situation for everyone else. Cocaine quickly drifted into obscurity within the United States. Even the puritanical moral panic moved on, as evidenced by 1936's *Reefer Madness*, a movie that would perhaps make some kind of sense if it were a propaganda film about the dangers of cocaine. Instead, it's a propaganda film created by people who apparently believed smoking whatever ditch weed was around in the 1930s would lead users down the same psychotic and horrific roads as the worst cocaine addiction.

◇   ◇   ◇

Reefer Madness was just another typical attempt to demonize something by pretending it is disproportionately popular with and inspires particular evils within poor and/or Black communities, especially those where musicians can be found playing any variety of raucous music, like jazz, blues or country. While these types of musicians have historically been only too happy to freak out the squares, it's interesting to note the pronounced difference between the way cocaine and cannabis were treated in songs of those genres between the 1920s and 1940s, almost as if musicians were willing to stand up and sing about enjoying illegal substances . . . unless they believed the government had a good point.

In 1936, Stuff Smith recorded and had a hit with "You'se a Viper." The song is a fairly undisguised and unrepentant ode to smoking weed, in the decade-or-so-long tradition of jazz records about the very same thing, all of which made Harry Anslinger furious. For those unfamiliar with the name, Anslinger was the first head of the Federal Bureau of Narcotics and the guy who said he believed federal Prohibition of alcohol would have been a success if the penalties for breaking the law were harsher. He was also the guy who said the best reason to outlaw cannabis was its effect on "the degenerate races," the guy who called jazz music "Satanic" and the guy who said cannabis was bad because it made Black men think they're as good as white men. (That's not an exact quote and your day will not be improved by looking up the exact quote.) In 1937, the year after "You'se a Viper" hit, Anslinger was successful in campaigning to effectively outlaw recreational use of cannabis. But that didn't stop songs in unmitigated praise of pot, both coded and indiscreet, from continuing to be recorded. In fact, Fats Waller recorded a cover of "You'se a Viper" in 1943, with the even more aggressive title "Reefer Song" and a spoken word intro stating that he intended to keep smoking weed no matter how many cops Anslinger sent to his door. That is not the attitude or message you'll find in most jazz, blues and country records about cocaine during the same period.

Take Victoria Spivey's 1927 recording of "Dope Head Blues" with Lonnie Johnson on guitar. Sure, she sounds like she's having a great time and keeps talking about how much more cocaine she wants to do but give it a closer listen before hearing that as an endorsement from a trustworthy source. It doesn't seem like a very good thing that she thinks she's feeling better than ever despite having "double pneumonia" and one bite from her mouth being enough to turn forty dogs rabid. "Tell It to Me," an older song of unknown origin, first recorded by the Grant Brothers in 1928, advocates for drinking corn liquor instead of doing cocaine because cocaine has already killed the singer's girlfriend. The more time passed after the government's ban of cocaine, the more it became relegated to the status of Other; something for Other people, from an Other place, in an Other time, and an Other experience the listener was absolutely not recommended to seek out for themselves. Even songs where the narrator was still using cocaine and acknowledged the temporary pleasure of doing so increasingly skewed toward the tone of cautionary tales. By the time Ethel Merman sang Cole Porter's "I Get a Kick out of You" in the 1934 musical *Anything Goes*, the reference to cocaine from an admittedly inexperienced source was just some vague allusion toward something she's heard some people do somewhere else.

Lead Belly's early 1930s version of "Take a Whiff on Me" is the first known recording of a much older song whose author and origin remain unknown. Here, again, at first it sounds like Lead Belly's attending a swell party and one he doesn't intend to leave. But, again, a close read of the lyrics reveals he's begging for money to buy more cocaine because he's "gotta keep on whiffin' until I die," regardless of the fact that "doctor said it kill ya, but he don't say when." Lead Belly finishes the song by outright stating men shouldn't do cocaine. We know the song "Take a Whiff on Me" predates Lead Belly's version because he said so but also because there are earlier recordings of other songs that borrow elements of it. Luke Jordan took some of the lyrics (and some lyrics from another song called "Furniture Man") to create "Cocaine Blues," first recorded in 1927. Both Luke Jordan's version and the folkier Dick Justice version feature lyrics about the narrator being so broke his furniture gets repossessed and his girlfriend needs to steal from her job in order for them to be able to eat. These money problems are aggravated by the amount of cocaine they both need in order to feed their addictions, which a doctor says will kill them both sooner or later and the girlfriend will probably have a nonfunctional nose by the time she checks out.

However old "Take a Whiff on Me" truly is, it was around long enough for Lead Belly's recording to be preceded by versions from other artists who changed the lyrics from being about cocaine, nearly impossible to acquire after the early 1920s, and turned it into a song about alcohol, like Charlie Poole's 1927 recording under the title "Take a Drink on Me." It's pretty likely Charlie and others updated the lyrics to resonate with crowds in the illegal speakeasies where they performed during Prohibition. If patrons of those bars could find blow, Charlie wouldn't have had any reason to change the song. But if everyone was there to drink alcohol and wish they still knew where to get some blow, then doing a song about cocaine was liable to make half the audience think this country musician must know where to score and try hitting him up between sets. Whatever the case, we know it wasn't simply a matter of Charlie being too timid to sing a song about illicit substances. For one thing, despite alcohol's illegality, his lyrics for "Take a Drink on Me" did not warn listeners away from it. But also, the most famous Charlie Poole story is about the time a speakeasy was raided while his band was playing on stage. Rather than run or submit to arrest for being in a bar, Charlie smashed his banjo over the head of a police officer.

TWENTY-FOUR

THE DARK

◇ George Jones Goes Broke ◇ The Old Man and DeeDoodle ◇ Attempted Murder ◇
1,000 Lawsuits ◇ Very Bad Music ◇ Rehab, Relapse, Repeat ◇ Working with Tammy Again ◇

George Jones was in terrible shape, easily the worst condition of his life to that point, when he met Shug Baggott. There's really no reason to assume or even suspect Jones' life may have gone in any other direction if he never met Shug Baggott. But Shug does happen to be the reason George Jones was first given cocaine. The two first met in early 1975. Shug came from the night-club industry, not the country music industry, so he didn't really have a clue which famous country singer would make a suitable face for the country nightclub he wanted to open in Printer's Alley in Nashville. When he asked a friend for a list of suggestions, George Jones was mentioned. Not yet divorced but already separated from Tammy Wynette, Jones spent most nights at one or another of his regular drinking spots. Everyone on Music Row knew they could get in touch with Jones or at least leave a message for him at the bar of places like the Hall of Fame Motor Inn or Spence Manor Hotel. One night Shug found Jones in some hotel lounge, introduced himself and, over many drinks, made the pitch. Because Jones stayed so drunk in this period, Shug had to find him again and pitch him again close to ten times before Jones even remembered they'd met before, but he did eventually agree to the proposal while halfway sober. After all, he'd put his name on the sign of a Nashville nightclub before and it almost went very well.

Possum Holler had opened in 1967 on the same block as Tootsie's Orchid Lounge, sharing the same back alley as Ryman Auditorium. Country fans who came to town for the *Opry* or any other reason quickly found out the stage at Possum Holler hosted George Jones and/or other living legends joining the house band for informal and unannounced concerts nearly every night, never for any additional cost over the five dollar cover at the door. Almost immediately Jones was drawing larger crowds than Tootsie Bess. But his place got shut down in less than a year. The space he leased was on the second floor of a building owned by Roy Acuff. Roy had no problem with the nightclub. He often hung out there and got up on stage to sing. The problem was the first floor of the building housed the Roy Acuff Museum & Gift Shop and every time the Possum Holler bathrooms flooded, which was often, it rained piss and shit down into Acuff's museum exhibits. No more Possum Holler.

Jones was still married to Shirley at that time, so even though he regularly got out of hand hanging out in his own club night after night, on some level he knew there'd be hell to pay if he did anything that made it too difficult for her to keep their money in order at home. Eight years later, when Shug Baggott presented an opportunity to get back in the Nashville nightclub business, Jones was entirely off leash. The second Possum Holler opened the day his divorce from Tammy went through in 1975 and Jones took the opportunity to continue digging himself into a financial hole so deep it seemed he'd never escape. The main factor was how much he still hated touring. One reason his old band chose to go with Tammy in the divorce was Jones had already announced his intention to tour as little as possible. That proved to be a smart decision for the Jones Boys. The new band members their ex-boss hired in the following years routinely went months without ever receiving a paycheck. His stage fright had only grown worse with time, as each show felt like it brought more pressure than the last to go out onstage and be The Greatest Country Singer Ever for a room full of strangers. Whenever he dealt with that anxiety by getting too drunk to perform well, he usually fled the concert and landed himself in a lawsuit. The times he didn't run, though, someone typically handed him thousands in dollars in cash at the end of the night. Jones' ability to treat money like it didn't matter depended entirely upon receiving those injections of cash several times a week. His only other form of income was the periodic arrival of royalty checks in the mail. Once Jones decided to stop touring in 1975 and quickly burned through all his cash (sometimes literally), he got more money by taking out multiple six figure loans against the next round of expected royalty checks, then burned through all of that cash before it was even his to spend.

When Shug Baggott showed up to propose opening a second Possum Holler, Jones initially responded as though he could front 50 percent of the capital. After speaking with the accountants, Shug learned the truth. George Jones was as good as broke. Tammy was about to make one uncontested divorce too many, taking all their shared assets except for one of the houses and one vehicle, leaving Jones to drunkenly spend, trade, borrow, gift and destroy his way into poverty. Shug took out loans and moved forward without giving Jones a percentage of ownership, instead merely negotiating a fee to pay for use of the country star's name. Jones would later claim he never received these payments but there's little chance he could be certain of that and impossible to know how much cash he personally borrowed from Shug in this period, especially after the banks quit giving Jones additional loans.

Even if he didn't spend all his royalties long before they were actually sent, those checks would have only grown smaller and smaller the longer Jones resisted touring. It's simple Music Business 101. New singles and new albums receive less airplay and sell fewer units when artists don't travel to promote their latest product through concerts and media appearances. This was one reason why very few George Jones singles charted in the Top 10 during the second half of the 1970s. The hits he did have in that period, without exception, all benefitted from some alternate form of publicity. "These Days I Barely Get By," "The Battle" and "Her Name Is" all played into the George-and-Tammy-will-love-each-other-forever tabloid narrative. "Bartender's Blues" capitalized on his New York City no-show by appealing to rock media's preexisting love for James Taylor. The cover of Chuck Berry's "Maybelline" performed as a duet with Johnny PayCheck came out a few months after PayCheck went #1 and sold over two million units with "Take This Job and Shove It." Those records aside, Jones rarely charted higher than the Top 20 in the late '70s, which demonstrates how his inability/unwillingness to tour spiraled out into diminishing returns from every branch of his career.

Jones recognized the issue. Possum Holler was supposed to be the fix, a new revenue stream that allowed him to keep making public appearances while avoiding the stress and substance abuse he associated with life on the road. When spending most nights in a club with his name on the sign proved just as much of a threat to his liver and fiscal responsibilities, he did try to take corrective action. The nightclub hadn't thrown Shug into debt and Shug was always able to lend some cash when Jones needed it, so Shug is who he asked to become his new manager and help him get out of the hole. After Shug agreed, the first thing he did was go to the accountants again and find out exactly how much debt Jones was dealing with, which was around three hundred thousand dollars. The logical fix, obvious to anyone with any kind of sense, would have been to turn on the cash flow Jones shut off at the beginning of the year and get him back on tour. And Shug could have done that. He could've signed Jones to a booking agency, maybe even the best one in Nashville, and they'd have sent him out on the road, thousands of miles at a time, grinding his way out of debt one concert after another. Instead, Shug conjured a business deal that was nothing less than a work of art, a solution that should and would have provided a path to financial freedom for just about anyone not named George Jones.

By searching for an answer outside of typical music industry circles, Shug turned up a millionaire named Bob Green. This was the guy who founded the successful Executive Inn chain of hotels in Kentucky and Indiana. Several of those hotels were attached to theaters, Las Vegas–type showrooms with dinner tables and booths, much more upscale than the honky-tonk bars and fair-grounds on the regular country tour circuit. For $750,000, Shug's deal sold Bob Green the ex-clusive right to book live appearances by George Jones for one year. Green subcontracted out the actual booking of dates to a real agency, who did book concerts in other venues when big money was on the table, but the main idea was to keep Jones performing in the showrooms of Executive Inns. If fans needed to travel to see him in one of those theaters, they were likely to make a night or weekend of it by also booking hotel rooms onsite, thereby upping Green's profits far beyond those of a typical concert promoter who only made money by selling tickets and alcohol. Aside from a giant paycheck, the main incentive for Jones to take the deal was every Executive Inn loca-tion being roughly three to five hours away from the two places he spent the most time: Nashville, Tennessee, and Florence, Alabama. Here was a way to receive touring income again without need-ing to do much touring at all. Not only that, Green agreed to hand over a $150,000 advance at the contract signing. In theory, Jones could have used that one check to instantly knock out half of his $300,000 debt and the rest of the $750,000 would have put his entire life in the black within a year. In practice, he paid off only a few of the most pressing loans, spent $65,000 on a new tour bus, quickly pissed away the rest of the cash and immediately went back to Bob Green asking for another $100,000 advance. Flashing neon warning sign be damned, Green forked over the addi-tional money, which meant Jones failing to uphold his end of this deal would put him $250,000 in debt to Green on top of the original $300,000 deficit.

There's a story from this era that may communicate something about the frame of mind of a person who could be so reckless and irresponsible. Jones was riding on that new tour bus to or from some show with Billy Wilhite, a friend for nearly twenty years at this point, now acting as a road manager. Since Jones was drinking heavily, he decided Wilhite ought to drink, too, but Wilhite didn't feel like getting drunk and declined the bottle. Jones responded by taking out a loaded revolver and firing a round . . . not at Wilhite, but in his general direction, putting a hole in the wall of the new tour bus and securing the undivided attention of everyone inside. Unsure what to do, the bus driver kept rolling down the road while the rest of the band and crew locked eyes on their boss. Jones re-turned eye contact one person at a time, staring, as he slowly and deliberately squeezed the trigger again . . . and again . . . and again. Everyone else was counting rounds in their heads, so the moment Jones put his last bullet through the side of the bus they all jumped him at once, stuffed him inside one of the bunk beds and forced him to stay there until he stopped behaving like a maniac.

◇   ◇   ◇

At this time, Jones was not living alone but with Linda Welborn, Peanutt Montgomery's sister-in-law, who Jones began dating right after the divorce from Tammy. Well, sort of. Though Jones and

Linda held some kind of fondness for each other, this was arguably the saddest of all his romantic relationships, a stopgap that lasted years longer than it should have. Biographers typically characterize Linda as a simple person of little sophistication and low ambition. Jones himself "affectionately" referred to her as his "little, dumb woman" or just "Dumb Linda." Speaking after the fact, Linda guessed it was loneliness, not love, that brought and kept them together. She'd recently been through her own divorce and Jones presented at least the illusion of companionship while expecting little from her. In return, she gave him free rein to do pretty much whatever he wanted, even and especially destroy himself, without having to hear any criticism from her. While they technically lived together into the early 1980s, what that really meant was Linda lived in his house while he was gone for weeks and months at a time. In October of 1975, Jones used part of his second advance from Bob Green to buy a house in Florence, Alabama, along with a piece of property where he built a larger house in 1976. During the year and a half or so that Jones privately and publicly courted ex-wife Tammy Wynette in earnest, Linda Welborn was waiting at home for him in Alabama. Even when he did go back to Florence, it wasn't necessarily to Linda. They enjoyed bowling and fishing together, but Jones was just as likely to get drunk and invite a bunch of random strangers over to the house for a few days of partying or suddenly leave again just to drive the few hours to Nashville and make a couple laps around Tammy's driveway to let her know he still cared.

Perhaps in order to avoid returning home to such a melancholy relationship, Jones mostly fulfilled the terms of his contract with Bob Green for approximately the same year and a half. That lighter version of touring, bouncing around between the same small handful of stages within a few hours' drive, made it physically and psychologically easier to get his body where it was supposed to be at showtime, even if he was rarely sober. But the longer he worked for money he'd spent long before stepping foot onstage, the harder it became to see the point in even trying to pay off all those debts and the easier it was to just open another bottle instead. Whenever he did manage to get one of the banks or another creditor caught up, Jones often celebrated by turning around and asking for another loan, then disappeared to drink until he ran out of cash again. Each time he returned from a binge having blown through the same amount of money he'd just paid off, plus invariably racking up even more debt and lawsuits by missing more concerts, he found himself deeper in the hole than ever and suffering a hangover like few will ever know.

In March of 1977, he arrived at an Executive Inn after a particularly intense blowout, knowing he would never be able to sing. The only reason he even showed up was so Shug Baggott and Bob Green could see his present state of exhaustion and hopefully agree to let him recuperate before going back to work. Next thing he knew, he was out onstage feeling better than he'd felt in years—maybe decades, maybe ever—thrilled to be performing for his fans and suffering no fatigue whatsoever. It was all made possible by a doctor who happened to be in the house that night. This doctor overheard Shug talking about how wiped out Jones was, how he'd never be able to sing, and the doctor told Shug there was an easy solution. He said if Shug could get Jones dressed in his stage clothes, then there was no reason for the show to not take place as scheduled. Shug did as he was told and called in the doctor, who took out a syringe and gave Jones some kind of injection that instantly provided enough of an energy boost for him to perform. He went on to do a whole week of concerts with each night's show preceded by another "energy shot" from the same doctor. About three months later, Jones had settled back into his regular no-show routine, so Shug got in touch with that doctor to ask what was in those shots. Turns out, it was liquified cocaine. And they didn't need a doctor to get cocaine. Once Jones learned what had been in those syringes, he began buying whatever blow he could scrounge up in barrooms, the stepped-on stuff street dealers cut with quinine, baking soda and who knows what else. That is, until Shug realized what kind of trash was going up the nose of The Greatest Country Singer Ever and, perhaps more importantly, how much money Jones was paying for it. Shug decided to become the wholesale supplier for his artist's new drug habit and went through nightclub connections until he found a guy willing to bring up kilos of fishscale from Miami. Since that powder was so pure and Jones so freely shared it with his entire social circle, Shug Baggott quickly became the main plug for most of Nashville's celebrity skiers.

To simply say George Jones became a cocaine addict would be an understatement on the level of saying LeBron James plays basketball or Pablo Picasso painted pictures. Very few people in their entire lives will meet a single person who even has a frame of reference for how much of this drug Jones consumed. For example, Waylon Jennings was someone who famously did more blow than one human should be able to survive, a habit he estimated at its peak cost him somewhere around $1,500 a day. (That would be a little over $4,000 a day in modern U.S. dollars.) When Waylon was arrested by the DEA it was in connection to an entire ounce of cocaine someone tried to send him through the mail as a special gift. Comparatively, George Jones kept an ounce of cocaine in his pants pocket at all times just for personal use. He kept another little baggie in his shirtfront pocket with a plastic straw sticking out to ensure all he needed to do was tilt his head down to the side whenever he wanted a toot. One day Jones and Waylon were riding around Nashville in a car and they hit a red light, so Jones pulled out a vial of coke to have a snort while they waited for the light to change. Waylon thought Jones was out of his mind, sure to get them arrested with such public use of an illegal narcotic. Jones thought nothing of it and continued behaving in such a manner for approximately seven years. As with his drinking, if you think that sounds like a big party, know that it wasn't.

◇　◇　◇

By this point it's possible his alcoholism and stage fright had escalated to the degree where a schizophrenic break from reality was inevitable even if he never began doing cocaine. In 1976, before he ever tried blow, Epic Records got him booked on Willie Nelson's Fourth of July Picnic down in Texas. They wanted to see how George Jones went over with the audience of longhairs and weirdos in the outlaw country scene. That was the year 140 people were arrested, four people were stabbed, four others were kidnapped and one person drowned at Willie's Picnic. When Jones got down there, heard about all that trouble and saw what looked to him like thousands of psycho freaks waiting to rip his well-dressed Nashville ass a new one, he was ready to make a run for it. Mary Ann McCready (of Epic's PR department) recognized the telltale signs of Jones prepping to make an unannounced exit and went for help from Jones' friend and label-mate, David Allan Coe. DAC went over and pointed out that his own overgrown hair and prison tattoos put him in the same crowd of people Jones was so worried about, then swore there wasn't a bigger George Jones fan on the property. He offered to walk Jones to the stage and stand off to the side during his entire set to ensure nobody caused any problems. After Jones did his show, that crowd of psycho freaks demanded he return for an encore. Most reviews of the festival, including those in noncountry media outlets, called Jones a highlight of the entire weekend. A little more than a year later, after he'd been introduced to cocaine, there were no longhaired ex-convicts to escort him on the plane to New York City and *Rolling Stone* rewarded Jones for standing them up at the Bottom Line by naming him 1977's Country Artist of the Year.

By 1978, cocaine had helped kick open a door in his mind that allowed two additional personalities to walk in, take up full-time residence and occasionally use his mouth as their own. The Old Man spoke in a nasally, serious and usually disapproving tone, often compared to Walter Brennan, only if Brennan was cast in the role of a news anchor providing real-time narration for the fearful thoughts and shameful actions of George Jones. Then there was DeeDoodle, a raving mad court jester who alternated between casual wisecracks and furious rebuke, all voiced in a piss-poor imitation of Donald Duck. Forget about fictional representations of multiple personality disorder in TV shows and movies. George Jones did not black out or otherwise lose consciousness while DeeDoodle and the Old Man took his body for a joyride. Nor was he some kind of silenced passenger forced to bear witness to their actions. Jones became one of three participants engaged in an active struggle over what his mouth was going to say. When he won control, he used it to apologize to whomever was in earshot as the Old Man disgustedly pointed out how terrible George Jones should feel for letting anyone call him The Greatest Country Singer Ever or to the whole concert hall full of Canadians who heard DeeDoodle scream at them to go fuck the Queen of England. (These are not hypothetical situations. Both of those things happened.)

Jones grew extremely paranoid as a result of these developments. If he couldn't trust his own mouth or mind, then how could he trust any other person? He soon adopted a safety-in-numbers approach to security, keeping a crowd of people around whenever possible, even if they were mostly strangers. He did this on tour, in the studio and at home with Linda Welborn. Sure, he couldn't trust any of these people individually but perhaps having multiple witnesses in the room would prevent anyone with truly malicious intentions from attacking him. He was also rarely without one or more firearms in this period, so if he ever got a really bad feeling about someone, then he'd just fire a few warning shots into the walls or ceiling. According to Linda, Jones would pretend to be asleep so he could hear if any of that day's hangers-on said bad things about him. (This behavior was one of the retroactive explanations sometimes given for his nickname, Possum, even though he was first called that decades earlier.) On lonely nights when he scared away the entourage with gunplay or never assembled one in the first place, the key to feeling secure was as much light and sound as could be created at once. Wherever Jones was, he'd turn on every light, every radio and every television, then make late-night calls to anyone who'd pick up the phone and talk to him. Maybe he hoped the sensory overload would confuse DeeDoodle and the Old Man into silence or at least prove they weren't the only ones who could fill his head with pandemonium.

While both split personalities meet horror movie standards for demonic entities and a couple witnesses said the Old Man was the scarier of the two, it must have been deeply unsettling to hear what sounded like a psychotic duck speaking through George Jones' mouth. The dour, off-character things the Old Man said could've easily been mistaken for confusion or depression and his voice explained away as Jones having a cold. On the other hand, DeeDoodle was unmistakably Not George Jones. This was not a voice that could be explained away. Worse, DeeDoodle seemed to believe it was his job to scream things Jones didn't even want to say aloud. If they were in the recording studio and Jones kind of wanted Billy Sherrill to do something but decided it wasn't important enough to speak up, here came DeeDoodle to impatiently scream the demand. On one occasion Shug Baggott could only watch in stunned silence as what began with him receiving a vicious cursing from DeeDoodle, periodically interrupted by apologies from Jones, devolved into Jones and the Duck using Jones' mouth to have a full-blown argument with each other in front of Shug. Most detrimental to his career, whenever Jones forgot the lyrics to songs during concerts, it wasn't the Old Man but DeeDoodle who came to the rescue, quacking out absurd and terrible renditions of everyone's favorite George Jones classics.

At some point in 1978, Jones and DeeDoodle and the Old Man began making lists of the people they wanted to kill. Peanutt Montgomery's name made its way on to one list for no apparent reason other than his conversion to Christianity about a year prior. Peanutt would no longer drink or go off on wild adventures and he was now given to the occasional lecture about eternal damnation but Jones was still allowed over as a houseguest. When he did visit, Jones would often question Peanutt's faith, asking if his friend really believed all that Jesus stuff and how come there were so many things wrong with the world if God existed? It seems Jones felt in some way abandoned by Peanutt's conversion, perhaps even abandoned by God, left on his own to be tormented by the Old Man and DeeDoodle. One day he asked Peanutt to meet in a remote location and, after Peanutt pulled up in a car with the window rolled down to talk, Jones screamed something about finding out if God could save Peanutt from a bullet and then fired a pistol at him. In a photo the media ran of Peanutt standing by the car he was driving, it looks like the bullet lodged in the car door maybe two or three inches beneath the open window. Jones was arrested but Peanutt dropped all the charges after learning Jones would face a criminal trial for attempted manslaughter. Peanutt instead took out a restraining order, which Jones regularly ignored without consequence.

◇ ◇ ◇

Whatever reputation George Jones may have earned for getting his act together while married to Tammy Wynette, whatever functional purpose he initially believed cocaine served to help him meet professional obligations, every bit of that was history, flushed down the toilet like so many hundred dollar bills. Following the Bottom Line no-show, he and Shug Baggott entered a breakup/makeup routine which lasted the next several years, during which time Jones bounced between managers and agents all over Nashville. He agreed to whatever partnerships or concert bookings came with any kind of advance, then typically tried to disappear with the money and without holding up his end of the deal. Since he was quickly earning a reputation in the Nashville industry for doing that very thing, making his escape often entailed giving the slip to whatever babysitters and handlers were hired to keep him from running away. There are dozens of stories about Jones climbing through a bathroom window or out a roof hatch on a tour bus in order to make off with a sack full of money, sometimes only going as far as the nearest bar, other times paying a taxicab driver to take him somewhere several hundred miles away. If he needed money badly enough, though, he could be equally determined to keep an engagement. Once he was in the middle of a binge and had already been awake for a couple of days near home in Florence when presented with a short-notice opportunity to earn some serious cash. He hopped in a car, sped off to the airport, parked on the sidewalk in front of the main terminal entrance, then left the car there with its engine running and the keys locked inside. When airport security investigated the situation, they found a note on the windshield reading, "Please, to whom it may concern. I was in quite a hurry, this flight was very important. My name is George Jones with the *Grand Ole Opry* and I'll be back tomorrow evening."

The car idled on the sidewalk in front of the main airport entrance for close to two days before one of his friends got the dealership to cut new keys so they could drive it back to his house.

One of the most remarkable things about this period of George Jones' career is that he burned nearly every professional bridge it was possible to burn but did it at such a great scale and incurred such massive debts many of his ex-associates felt they had no choice but to agree when he came back asking for another chance, just in case he actually held up his end of the bargain this time and earned some of their money back. It became impossible to keep track of who officially represented his various business interests at any given time. At one point Billy Sherrill sincerely requested he stop being introduced to new managers and agents because of how many times he called someone with an opportunity for Jones only to learn the representative had been fired or quit. In January of 1978, following a makeup with Shug, Jones sent a telegram to Billy reading, "There has been some confusion to whom is to manage my affairs which has caused more confusion in my life. I apologize for what it's caused in your life. This is to confirm to anyone whom may be concerned that Shug Baggott is my manager and acting in my behalf to represent me. I would appreciate your coopera-tion in this matter to help me straighten out so many problems." Within a year of Jones sending that telegram, Shug booked a redemption concert at Nashville's Exit/In and convinced as many people in the industry as he could to come see how much better George Jones was doing now that he was back with Shug. Jones actually showed up for the gig, too. Then he forgot the words to the first song and DeeDoodle took over to sing the rest of the set while Jones openly wept, watching the most impor-tant audience of his life lose hope and trickle out of the room, some of them also crying as they left.

In the second half of 1978 most of Jones' creditors finally gave up and hit him with a relentless onslaught of lawsuits. Within a matter of months he was sued by a bank, a furniture store, Tammy Wynette, the IRS and almost every major concert promoter in the business. According to one of his attorneys, George Jones was sued more than a thousand times in his career. That number is well within reason. According to Jones himself, he missed more of his scheduled appearances than he kept that year. However, according to one of his booking agents in this period, Shorty Lav-ender, a lot of the blame for that should go to Shug Baggott, who refused to let a small thing like being fired stop him from continuing to book concerts and take deposits for events on dates when Shorty had Jones booked elsewhere, hundreds of miles away. When Shorty Lavender sued Shug for pretending to represent one of Shorty's clients, Shug's defense hinged upon the claim he had a signed contract that allowed Shug to book concerts for Jones. That very well may have been true but, since it's physically impossible to be in two places at the same time, even when Jones tried to do what he was supposed to do and showed up to perform a concert Shorty booked, he was liable to be earning another lawsuit by failing to perform another concert Shug booked somewhere else on the same night. Faced with a staggering volume of legal action, in December of 1978 Jones filed for bankruptcy . . . and was promptly denied by the court because his life was in such a state of disrepair he couldn't even provide accurate documentation of all the money he owed. Believe it or not, he somehow failed to keep a paper record of every instance he did something like trade a custom, one-of-a-kind pair of Nudie cowboy boots for a pair of sneakers worn by a stranger or sell a forty thousand dollar boat for five hundred dollars on a day when he needed five hundred dollars in his pocket more than he needed to own a forty thousand dollar boat. A couple months later, a new team of lawyers was able to submit enough evidence for the bankruptcy to be granted and a payment plan approved to settle approximately 20 percent of his debt. In other words, if George Jones owed you one dollar, then he was now legally obligated to pay you twenty cents. That sounds like a pretty good deal (and it was) but his total debt at the time amounted to somewhere around $1.5 million, 20 percent of which put him right back in the hole for three hundred thousand dollars, the same position he was in when he first asked Shug Baggott to become his manager in 1975.

Because of the way Jones had lived his life since then, this three hundred thousand dollars was going to be exponentially more difficult to scrounge up. His total assets—a mobile home, some furniture, stage clothes, jewelry, guitars, plots of land in Florida and Alabama—were valued at little more than sixty thousand dollars. No kind of touring revenue was on the table. Even if his fans wanted to watch DeeDoodle the Duck in concert, most of this debt was the result of how many concert promoters had been repeatedly burned by Jones and/or Shug Baggott. Waylon Jennings and Johnny Cash gave Jones about sixty-five thousand dollars to make a first payment to the court as evidence he was sincerely making an effort but, soon after that, the judge on the case saw no way forward other than seizing Jones' only steady source of income: royalty checks. The only reason George Jones survived the following years was the charity of friends, like Cash and Waylon, who continued giving him five figure sums of money with no expectation of ever getting it back.

◇　◇　◇

In February 1979, the same month his bankruptcy was granted, Jones recorded his next single, "Someday My Day Will Come." The Greatest Country Singer Ever failing to meet his full potential is still quite amazing but there's a previously unheard fragility in his voice and a trace of doubt in his pitch control. This is most noticeable in the verses, where Billy Sherrill largely leaves Jones to sing by himself until he's joined on the chorus by background singers, lending much more support than usual beneath the shaky lead vocal.

The only George Jones LP released in the year 1979 was *My Very Special Guests*, a collection of collaborations with major country and rock artists, like Waylon Jennings, Johnny PayCheck, Linda Ronstadt and Elvis Costello. The concept for *My Very Special Guests* originated over two years earlier with Columbia's vice president of marketing, Rick Blackburn. Along with Billy Sher-rill, Blackburn led the fight to uphold Jones' recording contract in 1977, when other executives at the label were ready to drop Jones as a lost cause after he began doing cocaine and racking up debt. In an effort to salvage the career of a legend, Blackburn began calling in all kinds of favors, gathering significant guest artists who all agreed to waive the payment they'd normally receive for appearing on a George Jones album in order for the money to instead go to Jones. *My Very Special Guests* took more than two years to record because of how rarely they could get Jones to show up for a session at all, let alone prevent DeeDoodle from taking over whenever his real voice faltered. By the time it came out in December of '79, the bankruptcy lien sent all proceeds toward his debt, which wound up not making much difference because the album sold poorly for several reasons.

Mostly it was just a bad album, arguably the worst in Jones' massive discography. Some of the blame for that goes to the selection of songs and guest artists. The audience of people listening to George Jones in the 1970s had not asked for and did not want Elvis Costello anywhere near one of Jones' recording sessions. It sure sounds like Jones and Johnny PayCheck were having a blast in the studio together but not many people were wondering what their version of "Proud Mary" would sound like. (The same recording of "Proud Mary" was also included on the full-length LP Jones and PayCheck made together in this period. Released in 1980, *Double Trouble* suffers from some of the same problems as *My Very Special Guests*, namely an overly coked-out George Jones and a lot of unfitting 1950s rock material, probably selected in hopes of playing to Jones' newfound cachet with the late '70s retro-rockabilly crowd. That being said, *Double Trouble* does have its moments, like the opening track "When You're Ugly Like Us [You Just Naturally Got to Be Cool]," and the whole album features some vicious playing from A-Team musicians.) The sad reality is George Jones was mostly to blame for how much these recordings miss the mark. Even though his guest artists were essentially performing an act of charity, they all sound fully committed to their parts. It's possible Jones' contributions sounded acceptable to fans of the famous guest artists who were unfamiliar with his work. But George Jones fans recognized when their favorite singer was phoning in an impersonation of himself, trying to approximate what he thought people expected from him rather than sincerely connecting to the performance. If that wasn't enough to doom *My Very Special Guests* to failure, Jones "promoted" the album's release by openly telling the media he found it unlistenable, for all the same reasons you don't enjoy seeing video or hearing audio of yourself that was recorded while you were blackout drunk. Since none of the tracks were worth releasing to country radio as singles, none were. In a strategic attempt to drive up sales for what they knew was a bunk product, Epic decided James Taylor's background vocals on "Bartender's Blues" made it eligible for inclusion on the album . . . except it had already been released two years earlier as a Top 10 single and the title track of a different LP, so that didn't work, either.

The month *My Very Special Guests* came out, Peanutt Montgomery finally had George Jones committed. If he didn't, it's unlikely Jones would've lived much longer. His weight had dropped to below a hundred pounds, from eating nothing more than half a sandwich every three or four days while pouring entire cases of whiskey on top of who-knows-how-much of whatever-kind-of-cocaine he began buying after Shug Baggott got arrested in August 1979 for trying to sell more than two pounds of blow to an undercover police officer. Jones spent most of '79 living in a car with DeeDoodle and the Old Man. They didn't have the money or credit to get hotel rooms and obviously couldn't go stay with Linda Welborn after becoming convinced she and Shug were conspiring to drive all three people in Jones' head crazy. They discovered Shug had taken out some kind of life insurance policy on Jones, so that probably meant he was planning to have Jones murdered, right? Linda refused to take a lie detector test and refused to admit she didn't believe in God, even when Jones put a gun to her head and said he'd kill her if she didn't say it. (Jones faked a heart attack to spare himself the embarrassment of not shooting her like he said he would.) Then there were the hallucinations. Anytime Jones went inside a building there was a pretty good chance the window curtains would turn into ghosts and start laughing at him, which was one reason why staying in a car felt safer, even though there were still horror movie monsters stumbling around outside and trying to attack him through the windshield. After about a year of all this, Peanutt was able to convince an Alabama judge it couldn't possibly be much longer before Jones seriously injured himself or someone else.

Jones was placed in a psych ward, where doctors decided it would be best to drop him into a medically induced coma rather than leave him conscious for what they estimated could be five days of extreme physical withdrawal symptoms. That estimation was inaccurate. When they brought Jones out of the coma after five days, his withdrawal symptoms were still so severe he needed to be given pentobarbital, a powerful sedative, before anyone could have a rational conversation with him. Only then were the doctors able to learn that the "patient blames all of his problems on the fact that all of the income is tied up to pay his debts. The patient states that he has felt that everyone is against him. The patient's history further indicated that he feels he is unable to perform. He is a top star in his field, and his inability to function in this capacity has been extremely depressing also to him." From the psych ward Jones transferred to a rehab center where, for the first time in his life, an addiction specialist told him the way he'd been taught to think about alcoholism was incorrect. It was not a result of moral failure, weakness or evil. Jones wrote in his autobiography, "They explained the theory of self-hatred to me: Many men who had been beaten by their fathers hated themselves. My young mind felt I was worthless as a human being and therefore deserving of the beatings my dad had given me. When Dad was no longer around to beat me, I strove to beat myself through various forms of abuse. They said I felt unworthy of anything good, that I had recklessly wasted money, even flushed it down the toilet at times, because I subconsciously felt unworthy to have it. They said I lashed out against women who loved me because I felt unworthy to be loved. Some of their teaching made a lot of sense to me. I wish it had taken." It didn't take. He checked out of rehab in January of 1980, feeling so great and well-rested the first thing he decided to do was celebrate by picking up some beer and tossing all his favorite hiding places until he found an old baggie of cocaine.

◇   ◇   ◇

Tammy Wynette's new brother-in-law, a guy named Paul Richey, happened to also be an addict in recovery. As soon as he heard about Jones being committed, Paul went down to Alabama to keep an eye on things and began making calls around Nashville to raise funds for the hospital bills. It's possible Shug Baggott would've done something similar if he wasn't serving a three-year prison sentence. With Shug on ice and Paul Richey already going so far out of his way to involve himself, after Jones came out of the coma he asked Paul to become his new manager. Curiously enough, Paul taking the job seems to have automatically triggered a professional reunion in the studio and on tour between George Jones and Tammy Wynette. Tammy was repped by the Jim Halsey Agency, one of the biggest agencies in country music at the time, and Halsey immediately signed Jones to his own contract. Less than a month after checking out of rehab, Jones held a press conference with Tammy, George Richey and Paul Richey to announce all of this wonderful news. The main statement Jones gave to the media was that he intended to only work as little as necessary to meet his financial obligations. He was still worried about how much touring negatively affected his state of mind and wanted to focus on making sure he stayed well-rested to avoid history repeating itself. His new management either wasn't listening or they stopped caring what Jones wanted the moment his first record back with Tammy became a bigger hit than anything she'd done in years.

Tammy claimed she wrote "Two Story House" on her own but had to give Glenn Douglas Tubb and Dave Lindsey each 25 percent of the credit because they came up with the title. The version of the story hunted down by Jimmy McDonough rings closer to true: Glenn and Dave wrote the whole song, Tammy and Jones rearranged a few of the lyrics, then asked for 25 percent each. In the end Glenn and Dave split 50 percent of the writing credit, Jones got nothing and Tammy walked away with the other 50 percent all to herself. As for the publisher's share, "Two Story House" was filed with Tammy's publishing company, the one operated by her brother-in-law and Jones' new manager, Paul Richey. Whoever really got screwed on the deal, "Two Story House" hit #2 and was quickly followed by the release of "He Stopped Loving Her Today," at which point Jones was booked solid through the foreseeable future, both as a solo act and with Tammy.

In March of 1980 they both guested on the celebrity panel for Country & Western Week on *Hollywood Squares*. Jones, sporting a ridiculously ill-advised perm hairdo, was very serious about playing the game and later said he had a good time. Their spot as musical guests on *The Tonight Show* did not go as smoothly. In the middle of performing "Two Story House," Jones forgot the lyrics, froze and—not realizing they were on live television—asked if they could do another take, at which point the show's producers cut to commercial. Mere months after leaving rehab Jones began an interview with Alanna Nash by saying he felt like he'd already been "overdoing it" and touring much more than he'd prefer. He restated his desire to get off the road but said he did feel his oft-disappointed fans were owed one more tour. He wanted another chance to actually show up and perform but, after holding up his end, he'd like to go home and stay home. That is not what happened.

Between the unbelievable success of "He Stopped Loving Her Today" and the boost the re-union singles brought to Tammy's career, the Richey brothers saw no reason to let Jones slow down. Rather than taking a farewell victory lap and retiring from the road, as he clearly stated he wished to do, Jones found himself working harder than ever and playing higher-profile, anxiety-inducing gigs to boot. In August of 1980, he was dragged to New York City where he finally played a showcase at the Bottom Line for an audience of prestigious media elite. Earlier that day, in the middle of an interview with the *New York Daily News*, Jones began to cry while admitting he was terrified his sore, hoarse and overworked throat would prevent him singing well enough to impress all of those important people, which is precisely what happened. The Manhattan audience was presented with a visibly frightened George Jones, who sang off-pitch at a barely audible murmur. But they didn't seem to mind at all. "He Stopped Loving Her Today" had gone #1 the week prior and everyone in attendance knew it was a miracle he'd survived the previous couple years of his life. Here was their underdog, back from the dead, and they were in his corner to cheer him on through a difficult concert, no matter what. After taking a break, Jones returned for a second set. Though his voice was still hoarse and shaky, now that he knew the crowd would not turn against him he sang with a little more confidence, especially once Linda Ronstadt and Bonnie Raitt came onstage to perform backup vocals.

Less than a year after the New York show, Jones split with Paul Richey and told the press he was just as much of a thief as Shug Baggott. He explained, "I made more money last year than I have made in my whole life, and I don't know where the funds are. I haven't seen no receipts. I haven't seen nothin' regarding my last eighteen months with Paul Richey." It's true, his career was hotter than a branding iron. "He Stopped Loving Her Today" won nearly every award possible in 1980 and his recording of Tom T. Hall's "I'm Not Ready Yet" hit #2 as the follow-up single. In another interview, Jones said, "For a man who's won all the awards I'm supposed to've won and achieved all the things I'm supposed to've achieved, I have nothing to my name." Though he spent the rest of his life calling Shug Baggott and Paul Richey the two worst managers he ever had, there are reasons to wonder how much credence should be lent to those statements.

The official narrative given to media in this period, that rehab had more or less "fixed" Jones and made it possible for him to enjoy a casual drink or two without losing control, was entirely untrue. All of the CMA Awards he won in 1980 were accepted on his behalf by Loretta Lynn and Barbara Mandrell because nobody wanted to risk Jones appearing on a live television broadcast. Years later, those award statuettes began to turn up in garage sales around Nashville. Jones had either sold, traded, gifted or thrown them away. Nobody knows because he doesn't remember. When he eventually told the true story of this period, everyone learned his substance abuse only became worse after rehab, since he believed he'd discovered a genius approach to everything. He'd just go as hard as he could for as long as he could, working and drinking and snorting until it all got too exhausting or DeeDoodle started showing up too much, then he'd check into another rehab for a month of assisted recuperation before starting the cycle all over again. It was kind of like a routine juice cleanse or detox protocol, except with a fuckload of cocaine, guns and IV drips. One of the rehab centers he visited several times ultimately decided he was incurable and stopped admitting him, but Jones didn't care. As far as he was concerned he'd found the way to keep his career and addictions running at the same time without having to sacrifice one for the other, so that's what he continued to do for nearly another five years, long after parting ways with Paul Richey. Sure, his gross revenue may have been higher in 1980 than any other single year of his career to date but there's very little chance Jones knew one way or another if it was enough to pay off his old debts and all the new ones accrued from continuing to do all of the insane things that put him in debt in the first place, like pulling no shows or behaving recklessly with money and assets. It's possible his accusations of theft stemmed from nothing more than frustration over Paul Richey placing him on a strict allowance of one thousand dollars per week, an amount deliberately chosen because it was insufficient to fund Jones' self-destructive lifestyle. Not that it stopped him from trying. After blowing through the allowance, he often needed to borrow money from his own band members to buy food when he got hungry on tour.

Then again, maybe there's some truth to Jones' side of this story. He claimed he finished one of the reunion tours with nothing to show for it except less than three hundred dollars in a bank account and bruises from the physical beatings he received for having the audacity to ask Paul and

George Richey where the rest of the money was. According to a member of the Jones Boys who was on that tour, George Richey once said the only thing Jones understood was being treated like a dog. For these and many other reasons, it's an indisputable fact that George Jones hated working with Tammy Wynette in the 1980s. Oh, he put on a good show for the journalists and fans who still bought into the eternal soulmates storyline, waiting to see if the script would ever reward Jones' undying devotion to Tammy by writing The King and Queen of Country Music back together. From here until the end of his career, he played to the cheap seats by continuing to slip Tammy's name into the lyrics for live performances of fan favorites, like "If Drinking Don't Kill Me (Her Memory Will)," a Top 10 solo single from Jones, released at the beginning of 1981, right in the middle of the reunion tours. In concert he'd typically sing the last iteration of the chorus as "if drinking don't kill me, Tammy's memory will," the implication being he wasn't over her and never would be, despite the fact that couldn't be further from reality. (When Tammy's autobiography was adapted into a made-for-TV movie later in 1981, taking her nonsensical version of history at face value, then reducing real human beings to such ridiculous caricatures they may as well have animated it as a cartoon, Jones often sang the line as "if drinking don't kill me, Tammy's movie will.")

Despite the unshakeable persistence of fan theories, the professional reunion between George and Tammy was not motivated by lingering romance or even a desire to sing with her again. It happened because Jones naively gave up control of his career to the same family that was in control of Tammy Wynette's career, which had been in steady decline for years. She hadn't released a solo #1 record since 1976, hadn't hit the Top 5 since 1978 and the buzz generated by her fib-filled autobiography in 1979 wasn't the good kind or any other kind that translated to record sales. Tammy's co-author on the book, Joan Dew, was only one of many insiders who said the reunion with Jones could be entirely attributed to Tammy not releasing "a real hit" in years. The whole time Jones was onstage working his recurring bits—referring to George Richey as his new "husband-in-law," calling Tammy his "favorite ex-wife," singing about how her memory would always haunt him—what he truly felt was exploited, used by a bunch of leeches with selfish motives for pretending to help him. Decades later, his daughter Georgette revealed another reason Jones felt that way.

Though one would assume her parents collaborating again might mean her father was around more often, Georgette still spent very little time with Jones and even when they were together he behaved awkwardly, like being around her made him uncomfortable. Later in life she discovered that George Richey had used Wynette's custody of Georgette as a bargaining chip. If Jones stopped touring with Tammy, then he wouldn't get to see his daughter. Jones agreed, then found spending time with Georgette only served as a reminder of all the ways he was being manipulated. Throughout most of her childhood Georgette was told her father never paid child support. That was true during the late '70s, when his debts were at their worst. But he started making payments again shortly after beginning to get his life back in order during the '80s. When Georgette found out several years later, she asked Tammy why nobody ever said her father started paying again. Turns out Tammy didn't know either because Richey handled all their finances and never said anything. Tammy asked Richey about it and he responded, "What difference does it make?" Richey's extortion and manipulation of this father-daughter relationship adds a whole new dimension of tragedy to "Daddy Come Home," a duet Jones recorded with his then ten-year-old daughter, which she remembered believing would send Richey away and bring her parents back together if only she sang it well enough. In April 1981, HBO taped a George Jones concert special with a similar concept and featuring many of the same artists as *My Very Special Guests*. Twice during his and Georgette's performance of "Daddy Come Home," the camera cuts to Tammy crying as she watches from the side of the stage. Soon after the taping, Jones blew up the reunion tour.

The last night of the tour began with Jones going to George Richey to say he was too drunk to put on a good show and wasn't going onstage, to which Richey responded not only would Jones get his ass out there, tonight he was opening for Tammy instead of the other way around. So, Jones decided Tammy and Richey would be staying up past their bedtime. He was supposed to play a forty-five-minute set before clearing the stage for Tammy. Instead, he went out and played every song he could remember. Two and a half hours into Jones' set, Richey tried to make him stop by having the sound system shut off, but Jones just picked up an acoustic guitar and kept going without amplification, knowing that no matter how long he stayed out there Tammy would still have to play her whole show or else she and Richey would be sued for breach of contract. The King and Queen of Country Music didn't work together again for nearly fifteen years.

Jones' first attempts to escape the Richey brothers nearly led to him signing with Billy Bob Barnett, owner of Billy Bob's, "The World's Largest Honky Tonk," in Fort Worth, Texas. But Billy Bob came on way too strong. Jones still wanted exactly the same thing he declared in the post-rehab press conference, to work the bare minimum necessary to cover expenses and make payments on his debts. More than anything he wanted to stay off the road and not be reminded he was any kind of famous. So, when Barnett celebrated their imminent partnership by throwing huge parties with VIP guest lists and lots of media, it was exactly the wrong move. Jones got spooked, ghosted on the deal and went back to signing with whatever managers and agents would temporarily tolerate his new strategy of drinking whiskey and snorting cocaine until DeeDoodle shot up a party and it was time to check into another rehab. Columbia executive Rick Blackburn recalled visiting Jones during one of the trips to rehab in this period. He said Jones started crying while talking about how all he wanted was to be able to afford a house where he could live quietly like a normal person.

◇　　◇　　◇

By the end of 1981, everyone paying attention to country music in any capacity knew George Jones was full of shit when he said the whiskey and cocaine were under control because—that October, unlike the previous year—Jones attended and performed at the CMA Awards. Prior to the telecast Ralph Emery privately gave him one of the diamond-encrusted wristwatches WSM had custom-made for *Opry* members. As soon as Ralph walked away, Jones threw the watch in a nearby trash can. He'd already drunk close to a fifth of whiskey. He was so embarrassed over having brought Linda Welborn that he made her sit alone in the balcony instead of with him. He was so petrified about singing on a live national telecast that it took multiple handlers to keep him from running away. The first CMA award he ever accepted in person was for Male Vocalist of the Year. Unmistakably blacked out at the podium, he slurred his way through a twelve-second acceptance speech, which was sort of successful in that it convinced the show's producers to let him out of performing "He Stopped Loving Her Today." But there was also the matter of emcee Barbara Mandrell's #1 record, "I Was Country When Country Wasn't Cool."

Jones had sung two lines on the hit single and everyone knew he was in the building, so he was expected to be a part of Barbara's performance. Evidently nobody thought he could be too fucked up to sing two lines during someone else's song. They were wrong. Several accounts of this story, including versions published in multiple books (like *Ragged But Right* and Jones' own autobiography) are completely untrue. Barbara Mandrell typically receives blame for the whole disaster by erroneously claiming she walked a microphone into the audience and put it in Jones' face even though she'd been told to leave him out of the number. Video of the performance reveals that is not at all what happened. First, it's very unlikely Barbara was told to leave Jones out of the performance because he's holding his own wireless microphone while seated in the audience. The instant Barbara says his name from the stage, Jones starts singing his part in the wrong place of the song until his voice gives out. It's only at that point Barbara comes offstage to lend support . . . and when the television audience at home must have realized she could never fix whatever was wrong with George Jones. Anyone could see his nerves eating him alive as he stands with Barbara right in front of a camera. He tries to sing again but neither his timing nor pitch are in the same solar system as the song and he knows it, so he tries to just pretend he's having a good time with a series of ad-lib interjections, fake smiles and no less than three quick henpeck kisses to Barbara's lips (one of his go-to moves with both women and men when anxious on TV during the cocaine years). As soon as the cameras cut away, he bolted through a side exit and raged into the night.

TWENTY-FIVE

LIVING LEGENDS

◇ Lewis & Clark Serve New Looks ◇ Bill Cody Gets Famous ◇
Enough Truth to Sell a Lie ◇ Buffalo Bill's *Wild West* ◇

In the early nineteenth century anyone referring to "The West" of North America meant everything west of the Mississippi River. During the previous century Spain and France took turns pretending to own roughly 40 percent of that land, then a massive territory known as Louisiana, which was never truly controlled by Spain or France in any meaningful way. Other than a few cities, like New Orleans, Biloxi and St. Louis, the vast majority of Louisiana was unchecked wilderness, mainly inhabited by American Indians. In fact, that's why it was called The West, because it was west of anywhere most U.S. citizens ever planned or hoped to be. Then, in 1803, Napoleon Bonaparte sold the whole thing to the United States in the Louisiana Purchase and President Thomas Jefferson decided to get some idea of exactly what was out there.

Most importantly, he wanted to know if it was possible to travel by boat from the Mississippi River all the way to the Pacific Ocean, which would open up a new east-west trade route spanning the entirety of North America from coast to coast. That's a whole different story . . . but when officers Lewis and Clark and several dozen soldiers shipped out of St. Louis in 1804 to map as much of the Missouri River as they could and hopefully reach the shores of the Pacific, they were dressed in clean, new U.S. military uniforms woven from wool or linen, wearing Hessian or Wellington boots on their feet. When the expedition returned in 1806, two years spent in nature had mostly destroyed those uniforms and they were dressed more like hunters and fur trappers: shirts, pants and moccasins made of elk leather; otter furs stitched together and wrapped around whatever body parts needed warmth or padding.

Though migration and massacres over the next several decades would soon change what and where everyone thought of when referring to the West, the way the Lewis and Clark expedition was dressed upon their return constituted the earliest definition of "Western wear." Even as popular definitions of the West moved farther and farther west—then a short while later became heavily focused on the ranching culture of Texas and the Southwest—western wear never abandoned these earliest influences and continued to draw from the clothing of frontiersmen and American Indians in the Midwest, Great Plains and Pacific Northwest.

◇   ◇   ◇

The long fringe hanging off seams on shoulder yokes and sleeves of buckskin jackets has often been explained as a practical means to help the leather dry faster should the wearer be caught in a rainstorm, with capillary action wicking moisture away from the body via each strand of leather. That's not what would really happen in said situation. You'd just be wearing more wet leather. However, hundreds of years ago there were endless reasons a person who may not see modern civilization for another month could use long, thin pieces of scrap leather to tie something up, off or back together. If a person did have such a need, they wouldn't want to spend that month wishing they'd never cut off and discarded the excess pieces of leather when making their jacket. And so, jacket fringe. It's also an unappetizing fact that leather can be and was eaten in the absence of proper food on long journeys. But it's unlikely many members of the Chicago audience considered all the potential practical applications of Buffalo Bill Cody's jacket fringe as they watched it swishing around during the debut of his first play in 1872.

Chicago theater critics hated *The Scouts of the Prairie* because Buffalo Bill couldn't act to save his skin. Chicago theater critics were also the only people in the room under the impression they were there to watch some good acting. Everyone else showed up to see Buffalo Bill tell stories from the highlight reel of his thrilling life, which they'd read all about a few years prior in a series of front-page newspaper articles written by the author of this play, Ned Buntline. That wasn't the guy's real name, of course. By this point Buntline's past held a long string of failed newspapers, failed novels, various debts, leave-town-in-the-middle-of-the-night class fuckups, several instigations of political violence, more than one imprisonment and the distinction of nearly being hung by a lynch mob. Despite being a heavy drinker in private, Buntline's regular racket at the time he met Buffalo Bill was to visit various towns and give public speeches in favor of temperance. He was the epitome of the kind of guy who at a certain point just needed to completely scrap his given name and start using a different one.

The western William who Buntline originally set out to meet was Bill Hickok, then gaining fame as a Kansas lawman who'd just as soon kill a criminal as arrest one. The night Buntline found Hickok in a Kansas saloon he launched right into a pitch about interviewing Wild Bill and writing a novel based on his life, to which Hickok replied Buntline had precisely twenty-four hours to get out of town before being added to the list of People Shot and Killed by Wild Bill Hickok. So Buntline moved down the ranks of Wild Bill's entourage until he found someone far more receptive to becoming a larger-than-life legend. About ten years younger than Hickok, Bill Cody was quite eager to make a name for himself. While it's impossible to ascertain at what age Cody began exaggerating or outright fabricating the details of his past in order to captivate and impress whoever would listen, it's not like his backstory needed much help. He either earned the nickname Buffalo Bill by winning an eight-hour buffalo hunting contest or because he was so good at hunting buffalo the U.S. Army sent him when the Kansas Pacific Railway asked for a hunter to supply workers with meat as they built a line through Kansas. Whichever story is true (and either or both of them could be), all of that buffalo killing was done with a hunting rifle Cody named "Lucretia Borgia" after seeing an opera based on a Victor Hugo play, itself based on centuries-old conspiracy theories that Lucretia—sister of Cesare Borgia—was equally talented at treachery and a wickedly successful assassin. Not exactly a modest, down-home pedigree for the name of weapon. Talking to Buffalo Bill, Ned Buntline immediately recognized he was the perfect star for a set of frontier tales and the two of them began nailing down the major selling points of his life story.

Nobody will ever know how much of the resulting tall tale that made it into print was fabricated by Buntline, a lie told to Buntline by Cody or a collaboration of two men "improving" the facts. Whatever the case, by the time the story made it to readers of the *Chicago Tribune* and *New York Weekly* (then, later, Buntline's wildly popular line of Buffalo Bill dime-store novels and Cody's own autobiography); his father's nonfatal stabbing for publicly speaking out against slavery in Kansas had become a preteen Bill riding thirty frantic miles on horseback to warn his father of a white supremacist assassination plot; his teenage job of carrying messages from an office of the Pony Express' parent company down to a telegraph station three miles away had become hundreds and thousands of dangerous miles ridden through treacherous wilderness as a messenger for the Pony Express; his trying to enlist with the Union Army in the Civil War but getting turned away for not being old enough had become the years he spent as a spy for the Union, etc.

Cody really did enlist in the U.S. Army, but only after the Civil War ended, which is when he learned to become a scout. That's someone who knows or can quickly learn the local land in order to survive, hunt, track another party, plan or evade attack and so on. He was capable enough at all those things that when Buntline printed the tall-tale version of Buffalo Bill in a series of articles for readers back east, the city slickers who began showing up in Kansas to hire Cody for buffalo hunts and other western adventures were satisfied by their skillful guide. Photos of Buffalo Bill from this period present a long-haired, mustached man with a wide-brimmed hat cocked back on his head, holding Lucretia Borgia the Rifle while wearing a fur-trimmed leather overcoat with long fringe hanging from the sleeves—exactly the type of figure all his new fans would expect from the stories. If any of those fans came across a photo of Cody from only five years earlier, they'd have seen a clean-shaven young man around the age of twenty with short, neat hair, dressed in an immaculate military uniform buttoned all the way to the neck.

◇   ◇   ◇

In 1872, Cody accepted Ned Buntline's invitation to travel up to New York City and attend a different writer's live adaptation of the first Buffalo Bill novel. By the end of the year, Cody was in Chicago to star in Buntline's *The Scouts of the Prairie*. Buntline gave himself an onstage role in the play and his attempt at dressing the part of long-haired frontiersman involved stuffing what looks like a Stetson "Boss of the Plains" hat onto a woman's wig of thick, curly ringlets. He also wore what seems to be a fake leather jacket, maybe made of khaki fabric or burlap, with pieces of a high-pile rug stitched on the cuffs and lapels to simulate fur trim, then perhaps long strips of paper confetti glued down the seams of the sleeves to simulate leather fringe. In other words, the man looked ridiculous. But there is no record of whether Chicago audiences even noticed a difference between Buntline's sham garb and the western clothing worn by Cody, nor how many in attendance realized the Sioux and Cheyenne villains were white people wearing red body paint.

Regardless of critics panning the play, it was popular and successful enough that Cody and a co-star—another actual scout named Texas Jack—were able to convince Wild Bill Hickok he should join the troupe and spend a few seasons touring out east in a different play, *Scouts of the Plains*. Hickok had already tried and failed to launch a western-themed circus in upstate New York a few years earlier, so it's not like he was entirely averse to the idea of show business, but he only lasted a few months in the play. Maybe he didn't realize there's a significant difference between speaking in public and acting in public. Hickok discovered he so loathed the latter that he usually tried to deliver his lines while partially hidden behind various pieces of the stage set. One time Hickok reacted to a spotlight engineer trying to put some light on him by drawing a pistol and shooting out the spotlight bulb. After Hickok left the play, Buffalo Bill and Texas Jack continued touring it to great acclaim for another two years, then split off to each start their own shows.

Prior to the existence of indoor air conditioning most theater houses completely shut down in the summer because it was too hot to pack a room full of people. So Cody spent about a decade acting in various Buffalo Bill plays out east during theater season, then heading back west to work as a scout in the summer. All the while Ned Buntline (and now other authors) continued to churn out Buffalo Bill novels, adding to Cody's fame by fabricating further legendary exploits. Since the time he actually served in the U.S. Army coincided with the Army's primary task being the eradication, subjugation or relocation of American Indians, many of those tall tales revolved around the notion of Buffalo Bill as sworn enemy and consummate slayer of Indians. That was the character he pretended to be in this period, including in his own autobiography, despite admitting in private correspondence the Buffalo Bill of print killed more Indians in one story than Cody had killed in his entire life.

Cody was not a delusional man. He knew the product he spent a decade selling in plays all over the nation was not The Truth. Rather, it was The Bare Minimum of Truth Necessary in Order to Sell a Lie. At a certain point in his career, he began wondering how audiences would react if these ratios were flipped. Instead of touring a couple of actual scouts who recreated just enough of their actual jobs to get away with telling fake stories on fake sets wearing fake clothes next to fake animals and fake Indians for an audience of people who probably couldn't even begin to tell the difference . . . What if there was a way to build a show around as many elements of the actual West as possible? It's unclear exactly when he began asking himself this but there's no chance he ever missed which parts of the plays received the biggest response from city crowds. Instead of shooting at a few immobile targets to convince a room full of folks who'd never seen a live buffalo how many he had to kill in a day to get the nickname Buffalo Bill, what if he could stampede an actual herd of buffalo before their eyes? Instead of having Texas Jack perform a few tricks with a lasso to communicate some idea of the things it was possible to do with a rope, what if Cody could bring an actual rodeo to major cities? Instead of pretending a half dozen white people in red body paint were some kind of fearsome enemy, what if Cody put his audience in a room with actual Lakota warriors?

However much time he spent pondering these things, Buffalo Bill was finally given the opportunity to try out some ideas in 1882, when a town in Nebraska hired him to throw the biggest Fourth of July shindig ever. The Old Glory Blowout began with a parade through town, Buffalo Bill's Cowboy Band supplying a lively march while spectators marveled at the long line of rodeo riders, scouts, sharpshooters, bad guys with bandanas covering their faces, good guys wearing white hats or military uniforms and—in traditional clothing, including feather headdresses for the warriors, as though headed into battle—members of the Lakota nation, whom Cody had leveraged his celebrity and reputation with the U.S. government to hire away from forced confinement on reservations. The parade ended at an outdoor venue, where the audience took in scene after scene straight from the pages of Buffalo Bill novels: stunt riders and rodeo events; displays of marksmanship with pistols, rifles, bow and arrow; a mock buffalo hunt with real bison; reenactments of famous battles from the American Indian Wars, especially those Cody could plausibly lay claim to being in, even if his involvement was as exaggerated as the sensationalist and exploitative performances the Lakota warriors were encouraged to give. In 1883, Cody presented an even bigger version of this event (including a stagecoach robbery, thwarted by Bill, of course) as Buffalo Bill's *Wild West*, the three-to-four hour extravaganza he'd spend almost thirty-five years touring around North America and Europe, entertaining millions of people, inspiring many copycat shows and branding modern society's collective consciousness with images of a mythological Old West, which to this day are commonly perceived as historical fact.

TWENTY-SIX

LIVING LIES

◇ A Fake Kidnapping ◇ From Pills to Needles ◇ The Big Makeover ◇
Rehab, Almost ◇ "Justified and Ancient" ◇ Happily Never After ◇

In the epilogue of Tammy Wynette's autobiography she breathlessly shared the wonderful news of her recent marriage to George Richey. Dated one month after their July 1978 wedding, this piece of writing tells of how they were platonic friends for so long that it shocked her to realize they'd fallen in love with each other. She explains how freeing it was to give Richey control over her home and business affairs, allowing Tammy to focus solely on music. Gone are the fears of anonymous harassment, break-ins and threatened violence, which readers would expect given how often Richey came to her rescue during such nastiness in previous pages. Though it's impossible to know how involved Richey may have been in helping Tammy stage any of those incidents, two months after that epilogue was written—before the book was even published—many credible sources claim Richey and Wynette faked a violent abduction in order to provide an explanation for visible evidence that Richey hit her in the face. Despite such abuse, Tammy remained married to Richey. Her public statements about the relationship never wavered from the happily-ever-after, Richey-as-heroic-genius narrative until . . . well, until the end of her life, no matter how unhappy that life became behind closed doors.

Aside from a few employees and coworkers, some of whom probably felt obligated to stick to Tammy's official story in order to avoid insinuating she was a liar, there were never very many people with nice things to say about George Richey. When Tammy's biographer Jimmy McDonough asked Merle Haggard, Billy Sherrill and George Jones what they thought of Richey, since all three men had been around Richey quite a bit, Haggard pleaded the Fifth Amendment, Billy said he couldn't even describe how "weird" Richey was and Jones responded, "I believe a lot of things went on that shouldn't have went on." Joan Dew, co-author of Tammy's autobiography, said Richey was "very two-faced and hypocritical." After George Richey was assigned to be his producer at Capitol Records, Charlie Louvin entirely walked out on his association with the label he'd been on for more than fifteen years, both as a solo artist and member of the Louvin Brothers. Charlie claimed he told Ken Nelson it was either quit or go to prison for murdering Richey. Nearly twenty years later, when Charlie and Tammy Wynette recorded a version of "If I Could Only Hear My Mother Pray Again," Richey was told to wait in a car outside the studio while the session took place. This sure is a lot of smoke for there to not be some kind of fire here.

While pretending she herself was not a factor in the dissolution of Richey's previous marriage, Tammy claimed to have been best friends with his wife, Sheila. Most definitions of "best friend" probably wouldn't include sleeping with a woman's husband, then prank calling her late at night when she was home alone with no idea of said husband's whereabouts, as Joan Dew claimed Wynette did. But Tammy probably did spend enough time with Sheila to've heard about the time Richey celebrated their first wedding anniversary by kicking Sheila out of the house in the middle of the night, leaving her no choice but to walk to a neighbor's house for shelter while wearing nothing but underwear. Soon after that incident Sheila filed for divorce from Richey on the grounds of "cruel and inhuman treatment." For some unknown reason Sheila withdrew that petition, remained married to Richey for several more years, then filed another divorce in October 1977 after learning her husband was having an affair with Tammy Wynette. Perhaps Tammy believed Sheila must have exaggerated Richey's capacity for abuse. Or maybe she thought something about the nature of her own relationship with Richey would prevent him from treating her the same way.

Tammy's daughter Georgette characterized the marriage to Richey as "unromantic," essentially the business arrangement Tammy herself described in the autobiography's epilogue except without the true love part. If that's accurate, one could view Tammy's marriage to Richey as yet another PR strategy, this time intended to clean up the whole Burt Reynolds/Michael Tomlin tabloid mess by ensuring Husband #5 appeared to be The One, finally affording Tammy Wynette the reputation of being able to stand by her man, even if the secret truth was she simply married her business manager. Richey's few defenders pointed out he was already wealthy from operating and then selling a publishing company, which meant he didn't need Tammy's money and wouldn't have been financially motivated to take the "job" of being her husband, spending the next twenty years keeping up appearances by waiting on her hand and foot. That's true and Tammy raised the same point in her autobiography as a reason she felt she could trust Richey. But money can't buy everything, and Tammy possessed something else Richey did not have, something he couldn't get on his own and knew he'd be able to share if he accepted the role of her husband: she was incredibly famous.

In fact, she was quickly drifting in the always-undesirable direction of being more famous than rich. Having spent years discovering the media's obsession with her dating life did not translate to record sales, here was a one-stop solution in Richey, giving tabloids the husband they demanded while placing a sound business mind in charge of her career.

If the marriage truly was an act of sacrificing passion and romance in order to save her career, then it could explain why Tammy felt the need to get bombed on Demerol before the wedding ceremony. It's also possible she already had good reason to suspect she'd picked the wrong guy for the job. But it was too late for a rewrite of the story she spent the previous year selling to Joan Dew; a story about Tammy Wynette marrying the man she said was perfect for her; a story that would completely unravel only weeks later if anyone found out the bruises on Tammy's face came from Richey instead of an unknown assailant who abducted her at gunpoint from a shopping mall parking lot; a story that only grew less credible and more bizarre the longer Tammy tried to stick to it.

◇   ◇   ◇

Because of an extraordinary effort to cover up the truth it is impossible to know precisely what happened to Tammy Wynette on October 4, 1978. George Richey's alibi required him to be in Nashville to react with shock when given the distressing news that his wife had been kidnapped and assaulted, so it's safe to presume Wynette drove herself halfway to the Tennessee-Alabama border and parked in a field, where she tightly tied a pair of pantyhose around her own throat, then stumbled toward the nearest house for "help." She asked the family inside to please call Richey, which they did. She also asked them to not call the police but they did it anyway. When Wynette arrived at the hospital she was met by an agent from the Tennessee Bureau of Investigation, who noted the only visible evidence of her being injured was limited to one small abrasion on one of her cheeks. The second time that same TBI agent saw Wynette he concluded the entire event must have been some kind of publicity stunt. This was in Tammy Wynette's home, where she was giving television interviews to Walter Cronkite and other major media figures while sporting an enormous and unmistakably fake bruise that she or someone else had applied with makeup over the small abrasion the agent previously noticed on her cheek, plus a smaller fake bruise on the side of her lower jaw. Photographs of her face taken over the following days show the size, shape and location of both bruises shifting with reapplication of the makeup. Tammy told the world her cheekbone had been broken.

On October 6, two days after she wandered out of a field claiming an abductor broke her cheekbone and forcefully strangled her with a pair of pantyhose, Tammy Wynette sang a full-length concert in Columbia, South Carolina. There were fifty newly hired bodyguards standing between her and the audience when Tammy said into a microphone, "[the abductor] could possibly be here,

I just don't know." Evidently fans were supposed to believe the villain was actually there at the concert because someone backstage "found" a note that read, "I'm still around, I'll get you." Evidently fans were supposed to believe Tammy's would-be murderer chose to follow her more than four hundred miles away to that concert venue and sneak undetected through a security force half a hundred strong solely in order to leave a threatening note instead of dispatching her with ease two days earlier while she was unguarded and defenseless in the middle of a field.

When the CMA Awards were held three days later without Tammy being so much as nominated in any category, the rumor mill kicked into high gear. Her clearly fabricated story was widely viewed as a desperate bid for attention from an industry she feared was beginning to forget about her. Given her consistent presence in national tabloids, there was no chance the CMA merely forgot about Tammy Wynette in the year 1978. Since the CMA was founded on the mission of rehabilitating country music's image with the general public, it's far more likely the CMA deliberately avoided nominating Tammy in an attempt to distance the genre from her increasingly embarrassing actions. Of course, they wouldn't have been able to ignore Tammy if her music was still selling at the same rate and volume as before, but it wasn't, probably because country fans were similarly turned off by the Tammy Wynette they read about in magazines. There's really no other satisfying explanation for how her biggest single of 1978 and final Top 5 record as a solo artist was neither a #1 hit nor nominated in any category of the CMAs in a year when Single of the Year was awarded to an objectively worse song that also hit #1 on a similarly sexual theme, made far creepier by the fact it came from the Kendalls, who were a father-daughter duo. "Heaven's Just a Sin Away" is a sleazy cheating song, written as vaguely and poorly as any quickly tossed off, first-generation rock & roll record, complete with more "whoa oh's" than anyone would ever need or want in a two-and-a-half-minute single. Compared to that, Bobby Braddock's "Womanhood" is a work of genius about a young woman trying to lose her virginity without displeasing God. Between Tammy Wynette's delivery and Billy Sherrill's dynamic arrangement, the record was a timeless classic, released at a very unfortunate moment in an overly-complicated life and career. Same thing with her next single, Bobby Braddock's "They Call It Makin' Love," which looked at a spectrum of sad sex from one-night stands to married couples barely going through the motions. Released in January 1979, "They Call It Makin' Love" performed even worse than "Womanhood," possibly a result of Wynette's ongoing attempts to hard-sell her ludicrous kidnapping story.

She'd given a press conference about the abduction in November 1978 and was still taking bodyguards everywhere she went so everyone would know how much danger she faced just by leaving home. In February of 1979, she did an episode of *Donahue*, fielding questions from Phil and his Chicago audience for more than forty-five minutes on everything from what it's like to be a rich and famous country music star, to what it's like being hated by so many feminists, to what her diet was like and whether or not she had a weight problem. Phil himself seemed particularly interested in talking about all of Tammy's divorces but he may have been trying to piss off George Richey. There's no telling what kind of interactions Donahue and Richey had earlier in the day but, during the episode, after grilling Tammy for maybe twenty minutes on all her previous husbands, Donahue introduces Richey in the audience and calls him a "dreamboat." Whether Donahue was being sarcastic or not (and he probably was, because Richey was dressed like a complete asshole, as if being married to Tammy Wynette automatically made him a pop star, too), Richey definitely didn't take kindly to the comment. When the camera pans over to him, he does that thing where you pretend to scratch your face with a middle finger in order to covertly tell someone to fuck off . . . directly at Phil Donahue on national television.

Tammy revisited a lot of the same territory in a 1980 interview with Alanna Nash, then took things much further. Speaking with almost alarming verbosity—as if she was just glad to be talking to someone . . . talking to someone . . . still talking to someone—she rambled about developments in the kidnapping case. Apparently deciding to merge the violent abductor storyline with the anonymous intruder storyline from years earlier, Tammy tells Alanna how this bad guy has again broken into her home, gone into the basement to cut the burglar alarm wires, tapped her phone and then cut her phone lines, without seeming to realize there would be no kind of sense in anyone tapping a phone if they were also going to cut the line and render the phone unusable. In this interview and for the next several years, Tammy expressed surprise the police and FBI hadn't made any arrests when she and Richey were able to independently discover that the kidnapping was part of a conspiracy and multiple people knew Tammy was going to be abducted before it happened.

At one point she began telling the media about some prisoner who said his cellmate confessed to the crime. In a 1982 TV interview on *Miller & Company*—while displaying many indicators of a person struggling to remember their own previously stated version of events—Tammy recounted the night of the kidnapping, including the various things she could remember the kidnapper saying to her, which directly contradicts the account she gave on camera days after the event when she was adamant the kidnapper only repeated the word "drive," over and over, saying absolutely nothing else. For all but the most die-hard or dense fans, it was simply too much bullshit to stomach. The longer Tammy pretended to be the victim of this obviously nonexistent nefarious plot, the more her recording career suffered. The whole thing had already become a punch line by 1980, when San Francisco punk band the Maggots released a single titled "(Let's Get, Let's Get) Tammy Wynette," with a sleeve featuring one of the photos of Tammy looking miserable while wearing fake bruises. Yet she continued the charade for several more years.

◇   ◇   ◇

Meanwhile, Richey remained engaged in what Georgette labeled the Great Divide, doggedly separating Tammy from longtime friends, family, employees and peers in order to entirely surround her with his own sycophants, many of whom shared his last name. Richey's brother, Paul, was placed in charge of Tammy's publishing company. Paul's wife ran Tammy's office, placing eyes on any piece of paper that came through the door and keeping both Richey men informed of everything. Since Tammy's income determined everyone's income and that income was steadily declining, George Richey put Tammy on a five hundred dollar per week allowance. If she wanted to buy a washing machine or similarly expensive gift for one of her daughters, it was sure to at least be an argument and one she may not win. Meanwhile, Richey's kids were allegedly tooling around town in fancy cars. Whenever she decided to make some big credit card purchase as a "fuck you" to Richey, Paul's wife saw the statement at the office and ratted Tammy out. Tammy's daughters recalled their mother defying Richey more often during the early years of the marriage. Every now and then, they'd get in some huge argument and she'd even threaten divorce. But each reiteration of the threat only weakened its potency, suggesting Wynette would never actually follow through. And the Great Divide grew wider.

Many witnesses accused Richey of exacerbating and manipulating Wynette's preexisting drug addiction in order to foster an us-versus-the-world environment where he and his crew of loyalists became the only voices who told her she didn't have a drug problem, which was what she wanted to hear, wanted to believe. By this time no member of Wynette's inner circle could have remained oblivious to her constant dependence on painkillers or attributed it to proper use of a prescribed medication, no matter how many doctors and surgical procedures were involved. Though her relationship with Demerol began in pill form, Richey soon learned to administer higher doses of the wildly addictive opiate through intravenous injection, thereby becoming her own private and unlicensed nurse. Tammy spent the two days prior to that 1980 Alanna Nash interview laid up in bed because she allegedly fell down some stairs. During the actual interview she pulled down her shirt to show Alanna all her newest bruises while sharing her recent medical history, an alarmingly long list of major and minor operations, all followed by a premature return to work before she could properly heal, inevitably resulting in further trips right back to a hospital for more treatment, surgeries and industrial-strength painkillers. According to Georgette, after Wynette's daughters reached adult age and moved away from home, whenever Tammy wound up back in a hospital Richey would sit by her bed and talk about how surprised he was that none of the children had come to visit or called on the phone, all the while knowing damn well they hadn't been informed of Wynette's hospitalization. So, Georgette was surprised when Richey came to her and said it was time to stage an intervention for her mother. He said everyone needed to finally admit Wynette did have a drug problem and help her get the proper treatment. Georgette agreed and got her sisters together. When Wynette and Richey walked in the room, Richey pretended to know nothing about the intervention and acted outraged toward Wynette's daughters for suggesting their mother was "a junkie."

There were many nights on tour when Tammy's bus took a detour to the nearest hospital to try to score drugs. According to the Jimmy McDonough biography, Jan Smith (Tammy's hairdresser, who always rode on that bus with the backup singers and Richey) said Tammy once waited until she and Jan were alone to ask if there were people in the Nashville music industry who called her a drug addict. When Jan said there were, Tammy only wanted to know if Billy Sherrill was likely to have heard such talk. This conversation must have taken place somewhere near the beginning of 1980 because, when Jan said Billy did know about the drugs, Tammy started making plans to go to rehab. When Richey found out, he told Tammy she wasn't a drug addict and canceled her plans for rehab. Come spring of 1980, Billy Sherrill was no longer her producer.

◇   ◇   ◇

The only explanation Tammy ever came up with for how she could bring herself to walk away from Billy Sherrill, the one person she always credited with giving her a career, was essentially that he became too busy to find or write good songs for her. Whether she thought of that line herself or Richey told her to say it, there's no chance she sincerely believed it. The lie is revealed by the list of artists she'd offer as examples of the people supposedly taking up all of Billy's time. For one thing, the lists were always very short, but they also usually included Charlie Rich, who left Epic two years before Tammy stopped working with Billy, and Tanya Tucker, whose split with Billy caused a huge stir within the industry . . . all the way back in 1974. Out of respect for Tammy, Billy tried his best to go along with her story, invariably suggesting he was probably just so burnt out on the job that it must have stopped being fun, so he and Tammy decided she should try a different producer.

But if Billy was checked out of the whole business in 1980, then someone forgot to tell his work with George Jones, then at the peak of its critical and commercial success. Anyone can verify Billy never started phoning in Tammy's records just by listening to them. After Emmylou Harris had a hit on the Louvin Brothers' "If I Could Only Win Your Love," Billy got Tammy to cut the song as an album track and that's his uncredited vocal accompanying her throughout. If he ever recorded a lead harmony with George Jones, it's never been released. Billy and Steve Davis wrote "No One Else in the World," a one-night-stand-turns-instant-soulmate anthem released as the follow-up single to "They Call It Makin' Love," and it is as great as any song David Lynch has ever used on a soundtrack. The fact it wasn't as successful as Tammy's earlier records probably had a lot less to do with Billy's work than it had to do with Tammy's off-putting dedication to telling absurd lies on national television. Even then, the record still went Top 10 in 1979. Billy didn't write any of the songs on *Only Lonely Sometimes*, the last album he made with Tammy, not because he was too burned out to write anything but because only two of the songs came from outside Tammy's publishing company, the one entirely under Richey control. The album's first single, "Starting Over," barely made it into the Top 20, perhaps because it's an overly serious rendition of a Bob McDill song that, whether intentionally or not, could have been delivered just as well as a comedy. Before taking that as evidence Billy was paying little enough attention to miss the mark, consider this comedy-as-tragedy formula was exactly what he used the very same year to give George Jones the biggest hit of his entire career. There's every reason to assume Billy wanted the same accolades for Tammy and worked just as hard to bring them to her.

Many close sources said Tammy's decision to end this partnership was not influenced by any sort of mutual dissatisfaction. They said her choosing to leave bothered Billy much more deeply than he ever publicly admitted. Again, it speaks volumes that his name appears as a writer on more songs originally cut by Tammy Wynette than any other artist he produced. Hers was the voice he had in mind when writing most of the songs he ever wrote and one only needs to listen to the records to hear that. Though Billy was credited on five of the eleven songs on 1970's *The Ways to Love a Man*, the only one he wrote by himself was "Still Around." He never recorded it with another of his artists because that would diminish the impact of Tammy Wynette being the only person to ever sing such a lonely song, with the circular chord progression and fadeout implying she'll be singing it, alone, forever.

Neither Tammy nor Billy named George Richey as the cause of their professional split but Georgette said she could never imagine it happening without Richey's involvement. Indeed, the sequence of events spells things out pretty clearly. Tammy quit working with Billy almost immediately after Paul Richey became George Jones' manager, when the first post-rehab George and Tammy single came out. They didn't even wait for the release of the full reunion LP, rush-recorded the same month Tammy made her final album with Billy. If George Richey had been waiting for a now-or-never moment to wedge Billy and Tammy apart, he couldn't do any better than her seemingly charitable reunion with Jones, which for once put the right kind of media attention on Tammy and was secretly controlled on both sides by the Richey brothers. By the time Jones and Tammy hit #2 with "Two Story House," Billy Sherrill was no longer her producer and no longer around to accept credit for the expected revival of Tammy's career. It's very unlikely Billy had anything to do with selecting "A Pair of Old Sneakers" as the follow-up duet single or that he intended it to be anything more than album filler. With a collection of legitimately moronic shoe-based puns by Glenn Sutton and Larry Kingston, the funny lyrics/serious delivery trick failed again. The record barely entered the Top 20. There were no more George and Tammy singles released for another fifteen years.

While the Richey brothers may not have been able to get Jones back in the studio with Tammy, they could and did extort him into remaining on the reunion tour, which pulled down more money than either artist could earn in royalties. (A greater percentage of every purchased concert ticket goes toward the artist than the percentage of profits they receive from sale of a single or LP.) The nearest thing to a compliment George Richey regularly received from industry peers was acknowledgment of his relentless tenacity securing the maximum amount of money for Tammy Wynette in any kind of business deal. Richey knew any promoter, sponsor or other corporate entity capable of sending Tammy a big check could almost always afford to send a bigger check and he rarely agreed to any deal without first bumping up Tammy's end at least a little bit. Of course, Richey controlling Tammy's money and keeping her on an allowance meant her income was literally his income, so it's not like his motives were altruistic. Other behind-the-scenes sources pointed out Richey's grueling tour schedules certainly contributed to Tammy's near-constant state of physical infirmity and her dependence upon drugs. It's true Tammy wouldn't spend much time idling at home before asking when they'd be back on the road. Being on tour meant performing for crowds of adoring fans who gave her applause and asked for autographs. It also meant occasionally being away from Richey while he was off handling business, which by all accounts put Wynette in a good mood. When Richey wasn't around she was more likely to socialize with her band and crew, laughing and telling war stories about the good old days with Jones. But being on the road also gave her plenty of excuses to justify acquiring and injecting more drugs, more often. And the definition of "enablement" is helping a person do the self-destructive things they want to do. For the rest of her life, touring remained Tammy Wynette's primary source of income, even after George Jones bailed on the reunion, even after ticket sales started to slow, even as her recording career continued to fizzle out.

◇　◇　◇

Following the departure from Billy Sherrill, Richey first took Tammy to Chips Moman, the Memphis producer behind Elvis Presley's "Suspicious Minds." Chips either never spent much time listening to Tammy Wynette or mistakenly believed it could be a good idea to try taking her in a new musical direction. Both singles released from *You Brought Me Back*, the only Tammy LP produced by Chips, betray a comprehensive ignorance of what Tammy Wynette fans enjoy about her music. "Cowboys Don't Shoot Straight (Like They Used To)," co-written by Chips, crammed in far too many lyrics for a torch singer like Tammy to sound anything but clumsy attempting to spit out all those syllables. Then, on her version of the Everly Brothers' hit "Crying in the Rain," Chips had Tammy do the exact opposite of belting out a huge chorus like those found on so many of her biggest records.

Each time the song reaches the title lyrics, Tammy bypasses her vocal cords to produce a hoarse wheeze, which sounds less like the emotional affectation Chips presumably intended and more like Tammy was just losing her voice.

Surprising nobody, George Richey then took over Tammy's sessions and produced her next three albums, doing his best impersonation of Billy Sherrill the entire time. Initially, it seemed to do the trick. Bringing back a Sherrill-esque arrangement and allowing Tammy to actually sing on "Another Chance," her first single with Richey at the helm, resulted in a rare up-tempo hit and her first Top 10 record in three years. But it also turned out to be her last-ever Top 10 Country record and the other rare thing about it is that it was a good song, unlike nearly everything else Richey brought to the studio.

Considering he was credited as a writer on some of her final major hits, it's worth asking why Richey never wrote another big song for Tammy after the split with Billy. Had his contributions to those earlier hits been exaggerated? Did he lose interest in writing? Almost everything Tammy recorded in this period came from her publishing company's catalog, which seemed to be the only criterion Richey considered when selecting material. He certainly didn't seem to care if the songs were good or not because Tammy's next three singles were all terrible and each one charted worse than the last. Could he have truly believed "I Just Heard a Heart Break (And I'm So Afraid It's Mine)" was good enough to even listen to after reading that title on the demo tape, let alone worthy of being released as a Tammy Wynette single? Whatever his opinion of the song, the record charting at #46 let him know everyone else hated it.

Despite his many other faults, George Richey was not a delusional man. He recognized the necessity of some kind of change if they were going to rescue Tammy's recording career. In April 1983, he hired Stan Moress to manage Tammy, thereby freeing up enough of Richey's time to go looking outside their in-house publishing company for at least the singles to Tammy's next album. The first song he settled on was "Unwed Fathers" with lyrics by Bobby Braddock and John Prine speaking to an issue Tammy raised in her autobiography and often brought up in interviews: society's practice of dumping the responsibility of pregnancy solely on young women. Everything about the record was right. They started with a great song, then gave it a great vocal performance and the style of production Tammy's fans wanted. The message of the lyrics even achieved the impressive feat of aligning with Tammy's established persona while simultaneously ceding some ground to her feminist critics. So, it must have been a shock when the single came out in June of 1983 and performed worse than any regularly released record of her entire career to date. Then the follow-up single did even worse. Her team reached the only logical conclusion: record buyers were finished with the Tammy Wynette they'd gotten to know through the media in the previous five years. Booking her on bigger TV shows and pitching more magazine interviews wasn't going to help if the audience disliked the person they saw, fumbling to remember what was supposed to be her own account of wildly implausible events, struggling to add new details to the various conspiracies against her. Richey still refused to send her to rehab but he, Stan Moress and Epic's vice president of marketing all agreed Tammy's image was undeniably and immediately in need of an overhaul.

Just like Wynette and Jones had done years earlier when they needed to place some distance between his alcoholism and the Nashville media, she and Richey moved to Florida while setting the new plan into motion. First, they got rid of all the wigs she'd been wearing ever since her very first album and gave her a new close-cropped hairstyle. Then her entire wardrobe was updated to more modern fashions; relaxed-fit pantsuits, businesslike skirt and jacket combos, sparkling Bob Mackie dresses, etc. Most surprisingly, given her decades-long reputation for standing stock-still while producing one of the loudest voices in country music, they brought in a choreographer for six weeks of dance lessons. In the beginning she was apprehensive of such sweeping changes but gained confidence through the process of making them. One of her daughters claimed Wynette even started talking more often in this period about divorcing Richey. At one point Tammy recruited her daughters (except Georgette) for a secret mission to discover why Richey had recently started going around to different banks and setting up multiple lines of credit. Richey carried this briefcase nobody else was allowed to look inside and Wynette wanted to know what he kept in there. She and her daughters came up with a plan to get Richey out of the house, giving the girls a window of time to make it look like criminals had broken in and forced open the briefcase during an attempted robbery. Then Wynette chickened out at the last minute, confessed the whole plan to Richey and he flew into a rage, banishing her daughters from the house.

Tammy 2.0 made her debut at a Las Vegas concert in May of 1984. The makeover was a hit with her ticket-buying audience and her next single was released the same month. Produced by Jerry Crutchfield, who'd done all of Tanya Tucker's biggest hits after she left Billy Sherrill, "Lonely Heart" matched Tammy's updated image with an updated version of the Nashville Sound, which is to say it very much resembled the records Billy Sherrill was making at the time, incorporating new instruments to his old sound. Enough fans bought "Lonely Heart" to send it to #40 but that wasn't enough for Epic. The way the label saw it, Tammy had fewer fans than ever and wasn't likely to gain more. They decided it wasn't worth releasing a full-length album and shelved all plans to do so. This proved to be the beginning of Tammy's sunset era, the final fifteen years of her life, during which she shifted focus almost exclusively to near-constant touring. Epic kept her signed for another ten years but it was ten years of directionless sprawling, trying anything and everything to generate sales.

The label would've probably dropped her contract much earlier if not for a few events that inspired hopes of a resurgence. In November of 1984, Tammy recorded "Sometimes When We Touch" as a duet with Mark Gray of Exile. Because Tammy Wynette is still a well-known name and Mark Gray is not, modern sources tend to refer to this as a Tammy Wynette single with a guest appearance from Mark Gray. However, Exile kicked off a five-year streak of releasing nearly nothing but #1 hits in 1983. Mark Gray was far more successful than Tammy Wynette at the time and "Sometimes When We Touch" was from his second solo album. Anyone who happened to see her name on the label of the single and expect a Tammy Wynette record had those expectations corrected the moment they pressed play. It sounded nothing like anything she'd ever done before. After Mark Gray helped get Tammy Wynette back in the Top 10 . . . George Richey fired Stan Moress and became Tammy's manager, again placing himself in a position to receive credit for what he believed was the beginning of a comeback, precisely the way he took over the moment it seemed her career may be saved by the reunion with George Jones. Tammy enjoyed working with producer Steve Buckingham on the Mark Gray single (and Buckingham had already made several hits with Mark), so Epic hired Buckingham to run the sessions for her next LP. Since the Tammy 2.0 image still hadn't appeared on an album cover, there was a lot of pressure on this LP to at least generate the impression that Tammy's big makeover brought about some increased measure of popularity for her. Toward that end they threw the Mark Gray duet on the tracklist and named the album *Sometimes When We Touch*, which was enough to significantly outsell the previous two Richey-produced LPs. But that's not saying much. The album's only single, "You Can Lead a Heart to Love (But You Can't Make It Fall)," tanked even worse than her previous solo record, probably because the title of the song is awful, it gets repeated three times in every chorus and the production sounds as flimsy as a karaoke backing track.

When everyone went back to the drawing board and retraced their steps to the last time they were consistently happy with Tammy's sales figures, they landed on Billy Sherrill, who had not missed the Top 10 with a solo single from George Jones since "He Stopped Loving Her Today" five years earlier. Once the idea of reuniting with Billy got floated, suddenly Tammy and Richey no longer seemed to believe he was such an albatross. But by this point the interviews Billy gave to entertainment journalists were full of complaints about how difficult it had become to source hit songs in Nashville. There were too many financial relationships at work within the Music Row studio system for the best material in town at any given time to not already be promised elsewhere, often before it was even written. All you could really hope to find were songs with hacky lyrics like "if I could, I'd take a gun, aim it at the past and shoot to kill," which does come close to derailing "Alive and Well," the reunion single with Tammy. But Billy's production—as lush and dynamic as ever—keeps the record on track, reminding us why he and Tammy were made to work together in the studio, why there was never an acceptable substitute for either half of this partnership, even on subpar material they wouldn't have cut as filler ten years before. Released in July 1986, "Alive and Well" flopped. Tammy Wynette and Billy Sherrill never worked together again.

◇   ◇   ◇

A few months after the failure of her reunion with Billy, Tammy finally checked into rehab. She still wouldn't admit her drug use was a problem but she must have known it. Too many friends, employees and family members over the years had tried to intervene, only for George Richey to act appalled that they could insult Tammy by suggesting she was "a junkie" rather than a very sick woman receiving legitimate medical treatment. Wynette did spend much of her adult life in some kind of serious pain. From the 1970s forward, she had more operations performed on her body than would be reasonable to assume anyone has ever been able to accurately number, perhaps a dozen on her stomach alone by the early '80s, with all the accompanying external and internal scarring to show for it. But how many of those surgeries were the result of returning to work before properly healing? How often was she motivated to do that by the prospect of having more reasons to acquire more pain medication? No matter the spin she or Richey put on it, Tammy was indisputably a drug addict and it wasn't much of a secret. A 1984 article in the *Tennessean* detailed an episode from several years earlier, when Tammy needed to be airlifted to a hospital because she was experiencing such great pain . . . right up until the moment a doctor refused to give her pain meds, which is when she stood up and walked out, unassisted. A spokesman for the hospital said, "Sometimes a patient comes in for severe stomach pains and wants something for the pain. Maybe a doctor has administered a certain pain-killer before, but most doctors would not administer pain medication until they know what's wrong."

Also in 1984, when asked to describe the relationship between Tammy and Richey, Joan Dew said, "Look, the only reason Tammy stayed with Richey this long is the drugs." Some took that to mean Richey, like a garden variety pimp, kept Wynette hooked on drugs so she'd feel the need to stay with him, her easiest avenue to the next fix. Others speculated Richey always performed this role at Wynette's behest. They said he was so intent on facilitating her drug addiction because that was part of his job description from day one. If he ever became unwilling to help her use, then she'd fire him, bringing his whole "famous rockstar" ride to an end. Either way, by the mid-1980s her drug use was itself a threat to Richey's fame trip because of what it was doing to Tammy's career, especially after she started taking Butalbital with the Valium and Demerol.

She could survive poor record sales as long as there was a sizable audience willing to buy tickets to her concerts. However, there were not very many people who wanted to watch Tammy Wynette forget lyrics and mumble incoherently while hallucinating and falling asleep on a stool. Whenever she got that bad the band and crew (privately, amongst themselves) called her "Virginia," as in their real boss, Virginia Wynette Pugh, had gotten too fucked up to perform the role of Tammy Wynette. If fans were sitting in the crowd waiting for a Tammy Wynette concert to begin and someone in the crew walked out to put a stool on the stage, that audience was probably about to witness a performance from Virginia. And nobody ever knowingly bought a ticket to watch Virginia Wynette Pugh sit on a stool. By October of 1986, Virginia's stool shows were taking place at a rate Tammy's career could not survive and she checked into the Betty Ford Center in California.

The following day, she checked herself out, claiming she could kick Valium on her own. This is perhaps telling, perhaps an indication Wynette regarded only her Valium use as problematic and was maybe under the mistaken impression professionals at Betty Ford could help her selectively drop one but not all of her favorite narcotics. A couple weeks later, after Tammy's inability to kick Valium on her own led to more of Virginia's stool shows, she checked back into Betty Ford. Newspapers reported the cancellation of all her concerts for the rest of the year and the headlines told everyone why. On the second attempt she was able to stay in rehab for a few weeks prior to leaving, but not because she completed the program. One day a bowel obstruction caused her to physically collapse and she was transferred to a medical hospital, where they gave her another major stomach surgery and then put her in a bed for two months with some of her favorite painkillers on an IV drip. Although Tammy spent the rest of her life praising the Betty Ford Center as if they'd fixed her right up, the truth was she never checked back into the program and never successfully kicked narcotics. She and Richey merely got better at hiding her drug use from the public, for a while.

Probably hoping the George Jones playbook would work for Tammy Wynette, as soon as she was discharged from the hospital Epic put her back in the studio with Steve Buckingham. They recorded all her vocals for an LP in only two days. Also from the Jones playbook, Tammy was paired with a notable guest artist on every song of *Higher Ground*. Released in July 1987, the back cover prominently advertised all the famous guests. Vince Gill, Emmylou Harris, Rodney Crowell, Gene Watson, the Gatlin Brothers, Dennis Wilson and others performed background vocals. "Some Things Will Never Change" was a duet with Vern Gosdin. The first single, "Your Love," hit #12 Country with Ricky Skaggs singing harmony. "Talkin' to Myself Again" hit #16 with the O'Kanes on background vocals. Emmylou Harris helped Tammy take "Beneath a Painted Sky" to #25. Though the album's gimmick worked to give Tammy her final Top 40 Country singles, it didn't bring her sales figures back to where the label wanted them. Still, she assumed Steve Buckingham would remain her producer and was surprised when he declined the position, saying he didn't have any idea what else to try. In order to make up for poor sales and the lost concert revenue during her rehab/hospital stay, Tammy hit the road harder than ever.

Then it turned out all of Richey's frequent bank visits in Florida probably had something to with some stupendously bad business investments. In the process of defaulting on a $750,000 loan, they were forced to sell their Florida home and borrow $50,000 from Burt Reynolds to move back to the Nashville house, which was then repossessed by federal marshals in September of 1988 after Tammy filed for bankruptcy. Evidently she thought bankruptcy meant she and Richey were entirely broke and he did nothing to correct that misunderstanding, allowing her to believe nonstop touring was the only way to keep them out of poverty. In 1989, Richey landed a huge deal, securing General Motors Truck Company as the underwriter of an eighteen-month tour. That meant GMC covered nearly all of the tour's expenses and paid a mid-six figure sponsorship fee to Tammy on top of her regular guarantee for each concert. All in all, it was probably at least twice as much money as she'd ever made on the road—millions of dollars over the course of the tour—and she only needed to perform a thirty-five-minute set each night because her role was to essentially play host to a different headlining act on each leg of the tour. The headliners were younger and more popular artists, like Randy Travis, Clint Black, Shenandoah and the Judds. Wynonna Judd bonded with Tammy on this tour, often going to Tammy's tour bus or dressing room to hide out after arguing with her mother, Naomi. When Wynonna later got a little pet pig, she named it Tammy Swine-ette, as a pun on the popular mispronunciation of Tammy's last name.

Although the GMC tour made for great publicity and a big payday, it did not translate to record sales. *Next to You*, the album Tammy released in conjunction with the tour, was another flop. Norro Wilson's production sounded only slightly better than demo recordings and neither of the singles were ever significant in any way. The album's best track was the non-single "If You Let Him Drive You Crazy (He Will)," written by Curly Putman, Don Cook and Max Barnes. The plodding rhythm guitar, bass and drums in the arrangement are a shame because Tammy's voice still sounds great on this "he'll love you then leave" song that Billy Sherrill would have turned into a classic. Tammy's next notable recording session was a duet with Randy Travis for his 1990 *Heroes & Friends* LP, a reversal of the trope where an aged legend collaborates with younger stars. Both singles released from the album were hits. The first, a duet with George Jones, went Top 10 and the title track went Top 5 without a guest vocalist. Even though Tammy only appeared on an album cut, Epic must have believed there was some chance it may generate some buzz because they released her final solo LP the month after *Heroes & Friends* came out. If anyone in Nashville still believed giving their best songs to Tammy Wynette made any kind of financial sense, then Bob Montgomery's wonderful production would undoubtedly make *Heart Over Mind* the best of her post-Sherrill LPs. Unfortunately, the material just wasn't there and the entire album fell through the cracks. Tammy must have been physically exhausted the day they recorded the album's best song, "What Goes with Blue," because her voice came out sounding more than a little like Tanya Tucker, which is never a bad thing, especially on lyrics about a not-exactly-young-anymore woman who's heartbroken and nervous about dating again after a failed marriage. It wound up being Tammy Wynette's final regularly released single as a solo artist.

◇　　◇　　◇

When her mother died in 1991, most of Wynette's inner circle said she seemed to take it as an opportunity to give up trying to curb her drug use. Photos taken of Tammy over the next several years reflect this, depicting unnatural aging and weight loss similar to that of George Jones at the worst of his cocaine addiction. The year 1991 was also when the TNN Music City News Awards (now known as the CMT Music Awards) made Tammy the ninth person to receive their Living Legend honor. It's clear from the telecast Tammy didn't have a clue she was about to hear the previous year's winner, Merle Haggard, announce her as 1991's recipient. It's also clear she was ecstatic to receive the recognition. But "living legend" awards are usually not an indication of a thriving career. (The following year's Living Legend was an eighty-one-year-old Roy Rogers and George Jones only charted one Top 10 hit after receiving the same award in 1987.) Perhaps inspired by the accolade, Epic released a new Tammy Wynette greatest hits compilation in 1991. They added Tammy's recent duet with Randy Travis to the tracklist and even released it as a single, but it did the same amount of nothing everyone by now had come to expect. It's frustrating, too, because everything's there. The song, "We're Strangers Again," written by Merle Haggard with Leona Williams, is truly amazing. Tammy and Randy both sound great on vocals. Kyle Lehning's production, which owed a heavy debt to Billy Sherrill, was perfect, both here and on close to ten #1 singles he'd produced for Randy Travis by this point. One has to wonder what more anyone could have done to prolong Tammy Wynette's career?

The answer, obviously, was hire her to sing on a Jimi Hendrix–infused club remix of a song about the Justified Ancients of Mu Mu by the KLF, a bizarro act from the U.K. (Or, as seems to be more accurate to this author, perhaps ripped straight from the pages of one of the funniest books ever written, *The Illuminatus Trilogy*, by Robert Anton Wilson and Robert Shea.) In pursuit of their mission to either save pop music or mock it to death or possibly both, the KLF decided to put Tammy on a remix of "Justified and Ancient" because it was the thing that made the least amount of sense to do and/or because they suspected it would become a #1 Pop song in multiple countries, which it did. One half of the KLF, Bill Drummond, flew to Nashville to record Tammy's vocal. According to Drummond, the session was not easy. Tammy couldn't find the beat in this style of music that was completely alien to her and, consequently, didn't know where or how to sing. Being a devoted fan, Drummond was crushed to not secure a usable take. But when he got back to London, the other half of the KLF (Jimmy Cauty) saved the tape by applying early rate stretch and pitch correction technology to bring Tammy in line with the song. (This is probably why the first two syllables of Tammy singing the word "justified" for the second time in the song sound a little bit like a tape being fast-forwarded.) The single came out in November of 1991 and was at or near the top of Pop charts around the planet by the end of the year. It hit #11 Pop in the United States. With nearly a one million dollar budget at their disposal, the KLF flew Tammy to London and shot an epic-scale music video, which also became an international hit. Her appearances in the video were accompanied by scrolling on-screen text, reading:

> Miss Tammy Wynette. 25 years in the business. 11 consecutive #1 albums. 20 #1 singles. 5 times voted CMA Vocalist of the Year. 'Stand By Your Man' still the biggest-selling country song of all time. 2 Grammy awards, 5 marriages, 3 children. First lady in the world to sell more than 1 million copies of one album. June 10th 1991, presented with the most coveted Living Legend award sponsored by *TNN* and *Music City News*. Miss Tammy Wynette is the most successful female country singer ever. Miss Tammy Wynette IS the First Lady of Country.

Some of that fan worship may have been wildly inaccurate—she had four children, for example—but this was the crash course in Tammy Wynette history broadcast around the globe in the early '90s. It's pretty likely the ubiquity of the song and video was why Hillary Clinton even thought to reference Tammy during that infamous *60 Minutes* interview in January 1992 and unquestionably one reason so many people rushed so aggressively to Tammy's defense. Such pervasive and positive exposure surely brought some sort of surge in sales of at least her various greatest hits compilations. However big such a boost may have been, Epic didn't feel it was significant enough to warrant recording or releasing another solo LP and they never did. What the KLF collaboration did do was open up several new geographical markets around the world to Tammy's booking agents and drive up her asking price everywhere she toured.

In 1992, Tammy (or, really, George Richey) was able to purchase the Nashville home that Hank Williams bought for his wife, Audrey, who then spent who-knows-how-much money renovating and expanding it into the extravagant house Richey became adamant about buying. This even though Wynette, still cautious from the recent bankruptcy, didn't want to live in a big house again. After someone incorrectly informed her that Audrey died in the main bedroom of the house,

Tammy began sleeping on a couch whenever she was home, which wasn't often, due to her grueling tour schedule.

A 1992 tour of Australia was prematurely cut short because Tammy's failing health led to several collapses and hospitalizations. Epic waited for her to recuperate and then got her back in the recording studio in February 1993. Still regarded as unsellable on her own but a potentially high-value "participant," the label decided to group Tammy with Loretta Lynn, another legend whose career was then in an even worse state, and Dolly Parton, who was still capable of releasing the occasional #1 single and clearly the main draw of the project. Dolly was by that time co-producing her own albums with Steve Buckingham, so the two of them ran the sessions for *Honky Tonk Angels*. All the songs were genre standards or significant titles pulled from the back catalog of each artist. They invited Kitty Wells to the studio so the album could open where its title (and history) demanded, with an update of "It Wasn't God Who Made Honky Tonk Angels." There was another interesting throwback later on the LP, where the Patsy Cline recording of "Lovesick Blues" produced by Owen Bradley had new background vocals overdubbed by Dolly, Loretta and Tammy. (Note that Floyd Cramer was still alive when Dolly cracked that joke about his age during the piano solo.) Released in November 1993, *Honky Tonk Angels* sold well enough to enter the Top 10 Country albums and Top 50 albums in any genre, all without radio support for the only single, "Silver Threads and Golden Needles," which only reached #68 Country.

By the time *Honky Tonk Angels* came out, Tammy had already begun another project but sessions went on hold when she was hospitalized two days after Christmas, suffering from breathing problems and a new type of pain that she said made it impossible to sleep through the night. Shortly after checking into the hospital, her blood pressure plummeted and she dropped into a coma. Though doctors feared it may be too late to save her life, they performed emergency surgery on what they discovered was an infected bile duct and Wynette pulled through. Two weeks later, even though she had to wheel around a portable IV everywhere she went, Richey put her back to work. In April 1994, she performed at Carnegie Hall. Later in the year, TNN launched a new talk show, *The Legends of Country Music*, with Tammy hosting the first six episodes before Willie Nelson took over to finish the season. During her time on the show, Tammy brought out longtime friends, like Loretta Lynn, and recent collaborators, like Randy Travis, for casual chats on working in the music business, stories about touring and singing together, all the typical country music talk show stuff. What would otherwise be pleasant viewing was given a depressing edge by Tammy visibly struggling to breathe while doing nothing more than sitting and talking.

In October, Epic took advantage of her new national television platform by releasing another album, *Without Walls*. They let Tammy sing lead vocals by herself for two songs but all the others have special guest artists, this time pulled from outside country music, like Sting, Elton John, Smokey Robinson and Cliff Richard. Elton gave Tammy an autographed picture of himself with the inscription, "To the Queen of Country Music. From the Queen of Pop," and was fond enough of their duet together to put it on his own album of special guest collaborations. But Epic chose not to release "A Woman's Needs" as a single. The track with Joe Diffie probably would have made the most sense to spotlight, both because Diffie was at the peak of his popularity and because it's one of the few high points on the album. But Epic chose not to release "Glass Houses" as a single. Instead, the label picked the Wynonna Judd track, "Girl Thang," the sassy, girl power sort of number the Judds dominated country radio with in the '80s and Shania Twain was about to use to become the best-selling woman artist in all of twentieth-century country music. However, Tammy Wynette was not the Judds and she was not Shania Twain. The single would almost certainly have bombed no matter what because it wasn't Tammy's style, but her shaky live performances made matters much worse. During a *Late Night with David Letterman* appearance, she lost the rhythm several times, which precluded any hope of delivering the lyrics with the level of confidence required to sell the sassy energy. After the taping, Richey yelled at her for messing up the song and they spent most of the night arguing in a hotel room. The next day they had to get up early for Tammy to do morning television. Right before she walked out to do an interview—knowing she was nervous and embarrassed and tired because of what happened on *Letterman* and the late-night hotel argument—Richey told Tammy she looked like shit and, according to Georgette, said the orange outfit she was wearing made her look like "a carrot with boobs."

The marriage had grown more toxic than ever. At some point in 1993, Wynette was showing off a bunch of surgery scars to a couple of friends when she revealed bruises on her ass and upper thighs that she said were given to her by Richey. She then seemed to become scared of what Richey would do if he knew she'd told anyone about the bruises and swore her friends to secrecy. This was around the same time she confessed to one of her daughters the kidnapping stunt in the late '70s was staged to cover up a beating she received from Richey. One day Georgette found her mother crying in the kitchen and asked what was wrong. Wynette said she'd been arguing with Richey and he yelled that their entire marriage had been nothing but a waste of his time, which hurt her feelings. When Georgette asked why she didn't just leave him, Wynette said she couldn't. Richey told her if she ever left him, then he'd write a book and make sure the entire world knew she was "a fucking druggie and a whore."

◇　　◇　　◇

Tammy Wynette and George Jones released their final album together in June 1995. The groundwork for this last reunion was laid during Tammy's near-death close call in December of '93 when, after the surgeons saved her life, Jones came to visit her in the hospital. Tammy then sang on one of Jones' "special guests" albums in '94 and soon their teams were both talking about how another reunion album and tour could be great for everyone involved. Despite the statements they gave in interviews and other media appearances to promote the album and tour, this had less to do with any creative or nostalgic desire to work together again and more to do with how much financial sense it made, since Jones recently found himself beginning to receive as little airplay from country radio as Tammy was long accustomed to receiving: nearly none.

The title track and only single from *One* is easily the worst song of the project. The word "one" is repeated in every line, sometimes multiple times, to the point where it starts to sound like the lyrics were written on a calculator. There are examples of better writing (and passable versions of some genre classics) across the rest of the album but it's really just not fair for anyone to expect any kind of fireworks here. Even if *One* had been an album Jones and Tammy made solely because they were motivated by the thrilling opportunity to sing together again, the sessions took place soon after Jones underwent heart surgery and Tammy's body was so wracked by drugs and malady that musician Harold Bradley didn't even recognize her when she walked up to say hello the first day in the studio. Despite the poor quality of the product, their long-awaited reunion spawned enough publicity to sell enough copies that they just missed the Top 10 Country Albums, coming in at #12.

On the subsequent tour Tammy's failing health and debilitating addiction caused many of the same concert delays and cancellations that Jones' addictions had caused decades earlier. They were supposed to appear on *The Tonight Show* to promote the album release but Tammy was forced to cancel. Two months later she also pulled out of the makeup date at the last minute, leaving Jones to perform on *The Tonight Show* by himself. On days she was feeling good, Tammy did enjoy singing with Jones, still her favorite country singer. And, of course, Jones couldn't resist pulling her leg from time to time. At the very first concert of the tour, he dropped the last song from his solo set and told the band to start playing the first duet with Tammy, knowing she'd be caught off-guard and need to rush to the stage. However, the sheen quickly wore off and gave way to the bickering and ego clashes of their previous reunion tours, leaving both artists' teams to try corralling the whole thing forward so everyone could cash in as much money as possible. The *One* tour rolled through Nashville in October of 1995. During a hometown show at the Grand Ole Opry House, Tammy made sure to give special thanks to Epic Records, her label for the past thirty years. She didn't know they'd made the decision a week earlier to drop her.

◇　　◇　　◇

On April 6, 1998, at the age of fifty-five, Tammy Wynette died on a couch in her kitchen. For the previous several years this couch was where she spent her days and nights while at home, watching TV whenever she wasn't asleep.

She once told a friend she'd rather die singing than laid up in a bed somewhere and the way she spent the final years of her life ceaselessly touring through all manner of health concerns may seem to back up that statement. Yet Jerry Taylor, one of the songwriters signed to Tammy's publishing company for many years, outright stated it was Richey who worked her to death. He said, "She was married to and managed by one of the greediest people ever in this business." Georgette knew Richey kept Wynette on a tight allowance and made her account for every purchase. She'd seen her mother squirreling away any money she could—stashing ten, twenty and fifty dollar bills in various hiding spots—just in case she needed to help out one of her daughters with some cash, a kindness Richey rarely allowed. There were several other sources who said no amount of money Tammy could ever earn would have been enough to satisfy Richey. In a 1987 interview for a BBC documentary, Tammy said she'd like to do "five or six more years of steady work" before she'd probably enjoy slowing down on her touring schedule. The following year was when she and Richey were forced to file for bankruptcy. Whether she'd have ultimately chosen to slow down her tour schedule or sing until it killed her, the freedom to make that decision was taken away from her.

Booking agent Tony Conway remembered talking to Tammy before a performance at a state fair. She told him she was worn out, just plain exhausted to the point of insecurity over whether she could even put on a good show. Many years earlier Tammy developed hand signals to flash the band behind her back when she needed to speed through the rest of a song, cut it short entirely or when she wasn't even going to attempt reaching a particular note so the backup singers should help her out. As her health deteriorated over the years, someone came up with the idea of putting a segment in the middle of the show where various backup singers and band members would take turns singing some songs while Tammy left the stage to take a break and catch her breath during a costume change. By the mid-'90s, she required such long breaks they started letting the bus driver take the mic for a song, anything to fill the contractually obligated time. One night Tammy prepared for bed the same way she did every night, removing the rings from her fingers and massaging her sore knuckles one at a time as she slowly drifted off to sleep. The only problem is she was still onstage, heavily medicated, halfway to unconsciousness and entirely oblivious to the audience in front of her. Tony Conway eventually quit his job as Tammy's booking agent, saying he couldn't keep his conscience clear helping Richey to work her so hard while she was in such bad shape. Tammy played her final concert in March of 1998.

She spent the last month of her life much the same way she killed downtime on tour, watching TV with her husband. Back when they only had a VCR on the bus, it used to be a lot of the same movies over and over. Wynette loved Westerns—cowboys, good guys, bad guys, damsels in distress—whereas one of Richey's favorites was *Reversal of Fortune*, based on the true story of Claus von Bülow, who was convicted but then acquitted of attempting to murder his wife by administering an insulin overdose. Once they got a satellite dish on the bus Tammy became obsessed with true crime television, following the OJ Simpson, Menendez brothers and JonBenet Ramsey cases as closely as her favorite soap operas. When they were home Tammy and Richey merely traded the couches of the tour bus for two couches in the kitchen, the only room in Audrey Williams' large house Tammy found much use for in her final years. Toward the end there was a lot of religious programming in Tammy's television diet and usually a Bible somewhere in close proximity, as well as a yellow legal tablet on which she inventoried personal items and assets, each entry annotated with who should inherit it upon her passing.

◇   ◇   ◇

Georgette was working a shift as a hospital nurse when she found out her mother died. Nobody called her. Some coworkers who saw the news on television asked if she was alright and Georgette didn't have a clue what they were talking about. Tammy's other daughters had been contacted sometime after seven p.m. that evening, nearly two hours later than members of Richey's inner circle recall being told the news. It would take another two hours, around nine p.m., before anyone called 911 to report Tammy's death. When her daughter Jackie showed up around nine-thirty, Tammy's kitchen was full of Richey's friends, who were hanging out and talking and drinking coffee and smoking cigarettes like Tammy Wynette's dead body wasn't on a couch in the room with them. The skin of Wynette's face had begun to crack from the swelling of a few hours' death. By the time two police detectives arrived Richey was screaming about how there would be no autopsy. According to Georgette, Richey appeared "drugged up" and seemed to be putting on some kind of performance depending on who was in the room. One minute he'd be wailing, as if overtaken by grief, the next he'd be handling business on the phone, talking excitedly about how he wanted to ensure Tammy's memorial was an even bigger media event than Princess Diana's funeral. Though only family and close friends were supposed to be at the house on that first night, Richey called all sorts of celebrities and invited them over to socialize in a kitchen with Tammy Wynette's corpse on the other side of the room.

Despite a police report stating the body was discovered by Richey and a housekeeper, the version Richey told for the rest of his life stated the housekeeper had left to run some errands when Richey returned to the kitchen from a trip to the bathroom and realized his wife was no longer breathing. Whatever really happened that day, the housekeeper from the police report never spoke of it on the record again. Instead of calling 911, Richey's first call was to a Dr. Marsh in Pennsylvania. According to Richey, this Dr. Marsh said to not even bother calling 911, he'd get on a plane to Nashville and sign the death certificate himself. Marsh determined the cause of death to be a pulmonary embolism (a diagnosis that is impossible to confirm without autopsy), then sent the body to a mortuary, where it was embalmed, thus precluding the possibility of anyone ever being able to secure an accurate toxicology report. Dr. Marsh told police Tammy was only on four anti-biotics and a blood thinner at the time of her death. A Tennessee medical examiner named Bruce Levy accepted Dr. Marsh's word as fact.

Most of Tammy's friends and employees described the scene at the house in the days after her death as being a little different than what one would expect. That is, unless what one would expect was Richey's family and friends hanging out to party for a while before grabbing some kind of dead celebrity keepsake on their way out the door. One person who came for a private viewing swore they saw one of Richey's relatives walk up to Wynette's body, remove a diamond necklace from around her neck and leave with it.

Naturally, the public memorial at the Ryman was always going to be a massive deal, regardless of whether Richey wanted that or not. Everyone who was anyone in country music was there. Dolly Parton spoke and performed a song she'd newly written, called "Shine On." Merle Haggard sent in his eulogy on video, along with an acoustic performance of "If I Could Only Fly," though he was too emotionally distraught to play his guitar and practically apologized afterward, saying, "That's the best I could do and it's not very good but . . . Goodbye, Tammy." Richey's displays of grief at the memorial were again called into question by many witnesses. Off-camera, in private, all he could talk about was how many viewers he'd heard were watching the live coverage on CNN and the BBC overseas. But if a famous person or a camera crew came through the room, then he'd suddenly erupt with an emotional outburst or drop into the broken-by-despair routine he presented onstage during the service.

When Richey got on the microphone, speaking in a strange, halting sort of whine, he began by thanking Billy Sherrill for discovering Tammy, then spoke of the constant care she required from Richey over the previous five years. After that—for some reason, perhaps in an attempt to make sure millions of people heard his version of events before they heard any other—Richey started talking about what happened on the day Tammy died. As soon as he said the two of them were alone on the couch when she died, potentially about to discredit both the story he told in the police report *and* the story he told about finding Tammy's body upon returning from the bathroom, a nearby Lorrie Morgan began reaching for Richey's microphone as others approached from behind to try to get him to stop talking and leave the stage. More than one of Tammy's friends remembered thinking Richey was about to confess to her murder right there in front of the whole world. But all he did was ramble off a few more thanks, beginning with George Jones, another person, like Billy Sherrill, who Richey would want to appear friendly toward in public in case they ever decided to reveal some unpleasant history.

After the memorial Richey returned home, went in his office and started making the necessary phone calls to exploit Tammy's legacy for "millions." Among his plans were a collectible Tammy Wynette figurine he sold in TV infomercials. There was also a tribute album plagued by completely senseless arrangements of Tammy's major hits, like a version of "Apartment #9" from Melissa Etheridge featuring the kind of brushed snare you usually only hear over slow-motion footage of the underdog runner breaking through victor's tape to win a gold medal at the end of a movie.

Richey, his brother and their sister were named the executors of Tammy Wynette's estate. Since the yellow legal pad upon which Tammy carefully detailed how her assets should be divided was never seen again after her death, each daughter (except Tina, who refused the insult) was given $5,000 and each grandchild was given $10,000. A life insurance policy her daughters had been told would pay out to them instead went toward "debts on the estate." A few weeks after Tammy died, George Richey bought a new BMW.

Many friends stopped visiting the house because they were disturbed by the regular presence of women thirty years younger than Richey hanging out in skimpy swimsuits. These were possibly acquaintances or old coworkers of Richey's new girlfriend, Sheila Slaughter, who used to be a cheerleader for the Dallas Cowboys. Richey and Sheila denied being romantically involved prior to Tammy's death but Sheila did start coming around a lot in the last year or so of Tammy's life, to the degree Wynette told at least one friend there was something weird about it. There was also something weird about the fact that one of Tammy's credit cards was used to purchase women's clothing in the days preceding her death, the day of her death . . . and three days after her death. Within weeks of the memorial Sheila Slaughter was allegedly seen driving around in Tammy's Rolls-Royce, wearing Tammy's clothing and wearing Tammy's jewelry.

◇   ◇   ◇

SEPTEMBER 1998: Tammy Wynette is inducted to the Country Music Hall of Fame the same month tabloids report her daughters have hired a private investigator to look into the death of their mother.

◇   ◇   ◇

OCTOBER 1998: Tammy's daughter Tina gets kicked out of a Tammy Wynette tribute concert for accusing George Richey and Sheila Slaughter to their faces of pretending to be heartbroken while freely spending Tammy's money on fancy clothing, cars and throwing parties in Tammy's house.

◇   ◇   ◇

DECEMBER 1998: Tammy's daughters Tina, Jackie and Georgette officially request an autopsy of their mother's body. The request is denied.

◇   ◇   ◇

FEBRUARY 1999: The daughters are able to meet with Bruce Levy, the medical examiner assigned to Tammy's death, and convince him to contact Dr. Marsh in Pennsylvania. Dr. Marsh finally admits Tammy died with painkillers in her system, a fact he had not previously disclosed.

◇ ◇ ◇

APRIL 1999: The daughters file a fifty million dollar million wrongful death lawsuit against George Richey and Dr. Marsh after local reporter Jennifer Kraus discovers among the shipments of prescription painkillers Tammy received at home was Versed, a powerful drug that should only be administered in a hospital or in an ambulance because of the risk of respiratory depression and/or cardiac arrest. Tammy's old booking agent, Tony Conway, convinces Richey to allow an autopsy by saying Richey has nothing to fear if he didn't do anything wrong. Richey announces the upcoming autopsy during a press conference that he also uses to shame Tammy's daughters for being "willing to work so hard to discredit their mother." Though the cause of death remains undetermined, the autopsy reveals no evidence in Wynette's body of the previously pronounced embolism.

◇ ◇ ◇

MAY 1999: Bruce Levy reports his suspicion there was an attempt to provide the authorities with minimal information at the time of Wynette's death. It comes out that, in addition to revealing Tammy's usage of strong painkillers, Dr. Marsh also confessed he'd been contacted the day prior to Tammy's death because she felt unwell with symptoms he suspected were caused by a potentially fatal blood clot. Though Dr. Marsh had strongly suggested Tammy immediately be taken to a hospital, she was not. Richey claims it was Wynette who said she didn't want to go to the hospital because she started to feel better. Richey is removed from the daughters' wrongful death lawsuit. Dr. Marsh is still named in the lawsuit but continues to deny any wrongdoing. According to *Billboard*, CMT, *The Tennessean*, and Jimmy McDonough (who claims to've seen the documents), the lawsuit between Tammy's daughters and Dr. Marsh eventually ended in a confidential out-of-court settlement with no admission of wrongdoing from Dr. Marsh.

◇ ◇ ◇

In the year 2000, Jackie became the first of Tammy's daughters to write a book revealing her side of the story, which was mostly backed up by Georgette about ten years later in her own book. Both daughters shared previously undisclosed and damaging things Wynette said about George Richey, several abusive things Richey said or did to Wynette and details of the lies told to cover it all up. Richey instantly responded to the allegations in Jackie's book by going to the media and campaigning his own innocence. He and Sheila Slaughter appeared together on *20/20* to deny they were romantically involved at any point prior to Tammy's death. Richey denied having anything to do with Tammy's death and said Dr. Marsh never told him Versed was such a dangerous drug. Richey claimed he had "absolutely" no plans to marry Sheila Slaughter. About a year later, he married Sheila Slaughter. George Jones sent a letter to talk radio personality Don Imus, wondering why Richey was never arrested for practicing medicine without a license when "enough Versed went through [Tammy's] home to kill a bull," which is a really great question.

Near the end of the 2000s George Richey and his new wife, Sheila, decided to forego a typical family Christmas card in lieu of mailing out homemade DVDs featuring interviews with Tammy's daughters which had been edited out of context in an attempt to undermine their allegations against Richey. These clips were combined with various pieces of footage of Tammy Wynette throughout the years, talking about George Richey as her knight in shining armor, exactly the way he'd been written into the script. Richey then turned the official Tammy Wynette website into a tool to further the narrative that he was the best thing to ever happen to Tammy. At least one user who posted comments criticizing Richey was doxxed through the website and Tammy Wynette fans were encouraged through the website to harass that person.

◇　　◇　　◇

When George Richey, a longtime cigarette smoker, died of lung disease in July of 2010, the news was kept private for nearly a month. He had requested to be buried without a public memorial service, before the public could be notified of his death.

TWENTY-SEVEN

STONED SINGERS

◇ Buffalo Bill Introduces the Lakota Nation ◇
First-Wave Silver Screen Cowboys ◇ Tom Mix and Edward Bohlin Glam It Up
◇ Wearable Folk Art: Rodeo Ben and Nathan Turk ◇ The Nudie Suit ◇

There's a saying children often hear from a parent or teacher: anything worth doing is worth doing well. A common humorous twist on the adage, frequently attributed to such varied twentieth-century quotable figures as Mick Jagger, David Letterman and Robert A. Heinlein but, really, dating back to well before the nineteenth century: anything worth doing is worth overdoing.

◇　　◇　　◇

In 1911, near the end of a three decade run for Buffalo Bill's *Wild West*, the Society of American Indians became the first national organization to start advocating for the unification, rights and interests of all American Indians, collectively, not solely on a tribal basis. One early stance taken by the Society was against any tribe appearing in movies, vaudeville programs or Wild West shows which perpetuated the kind of demeaning and dehumanizing stereotypes that helped make Buffalo Bill Cody perhaps the most famous American of his time, stereotypes Cody never really abandoned at any point in his entertainment career.

While it's true he did fight against and kill American Indians in battles and skirmishes, that was not out of any personal hatred, sworn enmity or ambitions toward genocide. Exponentially more of his interactions were diplomatic than militant and it was precisely because of his experiences in combat that Cody knew for a fact American Indians were no more "savage" than white men. In private, candid conversation, Bill Cody said every so-called "Indian uprising" he'd ever seen was a product of the U.S. government breaking promises and going back on treaties. Where most postwar American attitudes regarded Native ways of life as inferior and endeavored to keep such societies confined to reservations until Indians learned to live like white people, Cody believed the Lakota hired for his show were equal to all the other talent and treated them accordingly. They were paid the same amount of money as other employees and Cody tolerated no degree of discrimination against the group of people he eventually took to addressing as, simply, Americans.

Many Lakota actors credited Cody with helping to preserve certain aspects of their culture. In his Wild West show they were paid to perform ceremonial dances which were banned on the reservations. Cody did not only hire men and take them away from their families but urged them to bring their wives and children off the reservations to travel with the tour. Upon arriving in a new town Lakota families pitched tipi villages where local townsfolk were encouraged to visit, interacting with perhaps the only American Indians they'd ever see in real life, speaking with them face to face, meeting their families, learning things about their culture. Cody supplied Lakota men and women with materials at cost in order for them to make moccasins, satchels and other crafts to sell as souvenirs, keeping the profits for themselves. By the end of Buffalo Bill's life in 1917, American Indian beadwork, leatherwork, patchwork, turquoise jewelry and various other items including such imagery as arrowheads and thunderbirds were all integrated with contemporary concepts of western wear.

◇   ◇   ◇

Within a few years of getting into the entertainment business and becoming rich, Buffalo Bill began dressing for his new role as a showman. His personal taste in western wear ran toward the flashiest directions then available: bright red shirts; fringed leather riding gloves with a large five-pointed star inlaid on the back of each hand; all types of velvety fabrics that shone in the sun or spotlight; golden chains strung through the belt loops of his military-style pants; a diamond-covered buffalo head pin gifted to him by a Russian grand duke; custom saddles accented with liberal amounts of silverwork and a full-body portrait of himself tooled into the leather fender on each side; shirts, vests, jackets, even felt cowboy hats absolutely saturated with floral embroidery.

When Hollywood began making Western movies near the start of the twentieth century, they went in the opposite direction, forsaking the showbiz look in hopes of presenting a more realistic vibe by dressing actors in clothes that working cowboys actually wore. One of the first Western stars of the silent film era was William S. Hart. There are only a couple of movies where he wore anything flashier than a dented ranger or cowboy hat, bandana tied around his neck, gingham shirt, leather arm cuffs, a gun belt, work pants, plain cowboy boots and dirty spurs. In one movie, the snazziest thing he wore was a sombrero that does appear gaudy in contrast to the rest of his clothes, but it was really only a traditional sombrero with all the accompanying embellishments. In another movie, the only change to his regular outfit was the gingham shirt being replaced by one with a louder pattern of circles and squares. That was about as wild as the first-wave Hollywood cowboys got with their fashion choices onscreen. Then a bunch of European immigrants and a guy named Tom Mix came to Tinseltown.

Tom Mix was only a little kid when he decided he would grow up and join the circus, which was pretty much what he eventually did. By the time Tom turned thirty, around the year 1910, he was working as a hand on Oklahoma's 101 Ranch and skilled enough at shooting, riding and roping to have won multiple national rodeo contests. To the people who live that lifestyle, taking first place at major rodeos has always been a very big deal, so most anyone who could do it usually started dressing like they were a very big deal. See: Prairie Rose Henderson, who began winning rodeo championships in the 1890s, then started designing and making her own extraordinary costumes, like a riding suit with billowing pants and maybe a twelve inch band of fur around the knees, a shirt bearing a massive embroidered rose across most of the chest, etc. It's pretty likely Tom Mix had already developed a taste for fashion that would've made even Buffalo Bill blush by the time he was cast in a nationally touring Wild West show launched by the 101 Ranch. But when Tom was selected to star in a short documentary about the life of a ranch hand in 1910, they wanted him to appear on camera dressed in everyday work clothing, not as a rodeo star. When the documentary was a hit, opening the door for Tom to begin playing bit parts in silent Westerns, he continued to dress like an ordinary cowboy, as did all other actors in Hollywood cowboy movies at the time.

Unlike nearly everyone else in Hollywood cowboy movies at the time, Tom Mix was able to perform all of his own stunts and did. It only took a few years for close-up shots of his roping, riding and shooting skills to turn him into a movie star and only a few more before he started dressing like a movie star in the movies themselves. For 1916's *$5,000 Reward*, the only item in Tom's outfit you'd be surprised to see on William S. Hart years earlier was a button-up shirt with smile pockets and simple white piping along the shoulder yoke. By 1918's *Fame and Fortune*, he'd added the comically large cowboy hat which would remain synonymous with his image forever. In 1920's *The Untamed*, the uppers of his dark cowboy boots were covered in white stitching that by 1922's *Do and Dare* was replaced with dozens of white flowers and green grass inlays. The reason for such a colorful upgrade in 1922 was that Tom had met a man who would help him revolutionize the way cowboys were portrayed on the silver screen.

Edward Bohlin was born in Sweden and came to the United States in 1910 when he was only fifteen years old. As soon as he was able Edward headed west where he found work on ranches in Montana and Wyoming, eventually landing in Cody, the Wyoming town named after its co-founder Buffalo Bill, who spent his final years living there on a ranch. Bohlin got a job at that ranch and, perhaps inspired by pieces which once belonged to Buffalo Bill, began to learn the craft of leatherwork. Fast forward to the beginning of the 1920s and Bohlin was on tour doing lasso tricks and shooting off revolvers in a Wild West show that made a stop in Los Angeles, where Tom Mix attended a performance. After seeing Bohlin's leather coat and alligator boots, Mix approached him after the show to demand Bohlin sell him those items on the spot and tell him where to get more clothes from the person who made them. When Bohlin said he made them himself, Mix insisted he move to Los Angeles and start making custom clothing worthy of a Western movie star. In 1922 Bohlin opened the Hollywood Novelty Leather Shop.

While modern scholars tend to associate Bohlin's name with his legendary horse saddles, which incorporated more intricate leatherwork and metalwork than anyone in ranching, rodeo or Westerns had ever seen, Bohlin took the same approach to all his pieces and his influence touched nearly everything made from leather. For example, his professional relationship with Tom Mix was largely responsible for popularizing both leather belts and flashy belt buckles in western culture. Pants were not even mass produced with belt loops until Levi's blue jeans added them at this point in the 1920s because, in the nineteenth century and early twentieth century, nearly all American men wore suspenders. The exception to that were military men, ex-military men or others posturing toward the military look. Make no mistake, even for the military, belts were always more about the look than anything else. Sure, men who carried a sword needed a scabbard and it only made sense to hang something like that from a belt but that's the same reason gun belts existed. In every picture of Wild Bill Hickok wearing a gun belt, if he's also wearing a waistcoat, then you can bet money there were suspenders under his jacket. Nineteenth-century military personnel in America and Europe wore belts as another visual indicator of rank—indicated via the cloth belt's color, the buckle's grade of metal or both—and to enforce good posture while causing a man's waist to appear slimmer than his chest, giving him a more muscular and intimidating look. That is the same reason many military officers wore corsets under their clothing. (It's also why early professional baseball players wore belts.) Tom Mix served four years in the U.S. Army during the Spanish-American War. Being an ex-military man and playing one so often on-screen, he did typically wear belts, though they were basic and unadorned prior to meeting Ed Bohlin. After he saw the art Bohlin could create from leather and metal, Tom lost his taste for plain leather and requested ornately tooled pieces with silver and gold accents, plus inlays of diamonds, rubies or U.S. currency. The buckles on Bohlin's early belts were frame-style horseshoes in silver or gold but he quickly became interested in the medium of plate-style buckles, which he treated as something of a blank canvas. Previously a plain rectangular or oval field for some basic emblem or logo, the plate buckle soon became a centerpiece of western wear. The coveted grand prize at several major rodeos in the 1920s was a custom Bohlin belt buckle, which helped establish the tradition of buckles-as-rodeo-trophies that still stands today. Bohlin's shop also offered cloth fashions but, in the clothing department, Tom Mix was afforded the luxury of a range of specialists.

Bernard Lichtenstein was born in Poland and apprenticed with a tailor as a young boy before coming to the United States when he was only fourteen years old, somewhere around the year 1907. Upon reaching adulthood Bernard (or Ben, as he came to be known) found work in America as a traveling fabric salesman based out of Philadelphia. One day a local tailor called looking for fabrics in the loudest combination of colors anyone had ever requested—bright purples, blues and greens— so Ben became curious what it was for. After being told a Wild West show had just arrived in town and the performers wanted these materials to make their own costumes, Ben said he could get the colors but would love a chance to make the costumes himself. When the performers and everyone else saw the outfits, they were so thrilled it resulted in Ben receiving enough orders from other Wild West shows, rodeo riders and Hollywood cowboys that everyone began calling him "Rodeo Ben." In 1930, he opened a storefront in Philadelphia, known as "The East's Most Western Store." The following year, he started using basic metal snaps meant for women's gloves in place of buttons on the shirts he made for cowboys, then upgraded to ivory and mother-of-pearl snaps to match the extravagant piping and floral chain-stitch embroidery on many of his pieces, thereby giving the modern western shirt one of its foundational elements. Though Rodeo Ben stayed in Philadelphia his whole career, he served thousands of clients around the world, including movie stars in Hollywood. When asked why he didn't open a location in Texas or L.A., Ben replied, "As long as I make the right stuff in the East, they'll buy it in the West." One of Ben's first famous clients was Tom Mix. He went on to make outfits for Gene Autry, Roy Rogers and Dale Evans. Such big-name customers placing orders from the other side of the continent was a testament to Rodeo Ben's craft, as there wasn't any shortage of magnificent rodeo tailors in Hollywood.

Nathan Turk was also born in Poland and apprenticed with a tailor as a young boy before emigrating with his parents to the United States as a teenager. In 1923, he opened a dry cleaning business that could also do clothing alterations in an area of L.A. which happened to be near several of the ranches where Western movies were regularly filmed. Actors, stuntmen and rodeo riders were not Turk's only clients but the clothes they brought in were his favorite to work on and there was enough of those jobs to eventually pivot completely out of the dry-cleaning business to start designing and fabricating high-end western wear. What Ed Bohlin did for leatherwork in the same era, Turk's shop did for immaculate embroidery, which he produced at a previously unseen level. His wife perfected symmetrical smile pockets with arrows stitched around the openings. Turk made outfits for Gene Autry and Roy Rogers but he was also responsible for the most surreal costumes worn by the Maddox Brothers and Rose in the 1940s, including the stage clothes they wore for their only appearance on the *Grand Ole Opry* in 1949. (Do yourself a favor and run an image search.)

Nuta Kotlyarenko was born in Kiev in 1902. The son of a bootmaker, he apprenticed with a tailor as a young boy before his parents sent him to the United States at the age of eleven. He claimed to have been given the name "Nudie" as a child, when an immigration officer at Ellis Island misheard his real first name, but there are a lot of reasons to question whether that's true. For one thing, despite the long life of that particular cultural myth, nearly no immigrants had their names changed by officers at Ellis Island. The other thing is that Nudie Cohn was the kind of guy who, after becoming the most famous western wear tailor in history, would drive around in poor neighborhoods passing out cash with photos of his own face pasted atop those of the U.S. presidents on the bills. So, either an immigration officer gave a flamboyant self-marketer the most prophetic of all the very rare new names to ever come out of Ellis Island . . . or Nuta later earned the nickname by employing his skills as a tailor to make costumes for performers in burlesque shows.

By the time Nudie started doing that—between the late 1920s and early 1930s, the tail-end of illegal speakeasy culture during federal Prohibition—the striptease or "nudie" portion of burlesque shows had become the main attraction. Performers and venue owners like New York City's Minsky brothers stood out from the competition by pushing against the boundaries of social limitations and laws that dictated how much of a woman's body could be revealed in a show. Believe it or not, in the mid-1920s in New York, it was actually legal for a woman to appear topless on stage as long as she stood still, no dancing or other titillating, dynamic movements. So, the dance portion of a show was limited to the first, say, 90 percent of a performance, the part where women artfully removed pieces of their outfits in a gradual buildup to the grand finale: a static presentation of naked breasts. Toward the end of showing as much skin as legally possible, this art form gave rise to the G-string, usually the last article of clothing still worn by a showgirl as she stood topless at the end of a routine. By the time Nudie Cohn opened a Manhattan storefront, Nudie's for the Ladies, in 1934, he knew there was an opportunity for the G-string to place just as much of an exclamation mark on the end of a performance as the reveal of a nearly naked woman. However, toward the end of showing as much skin as legally possible, there really wasn't much fabric for Nudie to work with on such a skimpy garment. So he did what eventually made him famous— the absolute most extra thing possible—and covered as much of the fabric as he could in rhinestones, which are essentially fake diamonds made of glass that strongly reflect beams of light from every facet. The effect of basically strapping a disco ball over the vagina of an otherwise-naked and spotlit woman turned out to be quite a crowd-pleaser. Nudie devoted attention to the rest of each client's outfit but the rhinestone G-string was always the star of the show and the thing that brought him great business . . . right up until New York City outlawed burlesque. See, Mayor Fiorello La Guardia was never a fan. He called burlesque shows "a corrupting moral influence" and began raiding striptease venues in 1936, about five years prior to his ban on pinball. In 1937, after a stripper at Abe Minsky's place in Harlem decided to spruce up the end of her act by not wearing a G-string or anything else, burlesque was immediately banned in New York City. Nudie Cohn, having lost all of his clients, left town.

After a few years spent wandering, Nudie popped back up in Los Angeles during the early 1940s. But the reputation he'd made for himself in New York City meant approximately nothing on the other coast and, frankly, his skills as a tailor could not produce anything comparable to the finest work of the already-successful Nathan Turk or Rodeo Ben. What Nudie could do was pump out approximations of their most basic outfits and that's what he did as an apprentice in Turk's shop. One of the first friends Nudie made in California was Tex Williams. In 1947, Tex had recently left a star-making role as the singer of Spade Cooley's Western Swing Band and was looking to start booking gigs as a solo artist, just as soon as someone made a dozen or so stage outfits for him and his band. Nudie said he could make the clothes if he only had the right sewing machine, so Tex sold a horse to buy the machine and Nudie was in business. They carried out the measuring session for the costumes in a celebratory manner. Everyone being drunk, the arm and leg measurements accidentally got switched around and Nudie wound up making all the suits with the arms as long as the legs should have been and vice versa. He had to go back to the fabric guy who'd given him all the fabric on credit and demand to be given more fabric on credit or else he wouldn't be able to fix the suits, Tex wouldn't be able to play the shows and Nudie wouldn't get the money he needed to pay the fabric guy. By the end of the decade Nudie opened a storefront in L.A.—first called Nudie's of Hollywood, then Nudie's Rodeo Tailors—with the tags on all his garments featuring a topless cowgirl, a tribute to his past in burlesque.

◇   ◇   ◇

The mental image nearly everyone gets from the term "Nudie suit" does not reflect Nudie's actual tailoring skills. His was not the precisely symmetrical abstract embroidery of Nathan Turk, borrowed from Slavic folk art. His were not the brightly colored embroidered flowers of Rodeo Ben, borrowed from Polish folk art. One of the first things Nudie fell in love with about American culture was Western movies. He never understood why the actors playing cowboys in the starring roles didn't wear more dazzling outfits to visually set themselves apart from the rest of the cast, like the way matadors dressed to stand out from their team of bullfighters. But Nudie could never have made a *traje de luces*, a primary visual and teleological influence on every showbiz rodeo tailor.

In 1951, flush with cash from a #1 hit on "If You've Got the Money I've Got the Time," Lefty Frizzell came to Nudie for some new stage outfits. The suits Nudie made for him look like what Buffalo Billy Cody would have worn if he was a comic book superhero in the 1930s. One of Lefty's suits seems like someone took Rodeo Ben's most basic template of a western suit, attached a dense curtain of fringe around the entire shoulder yoke (and, for some reason, beneath the front pants pockets), then put Lefty's initials on the front and back of the shirt in crude leather patches bordered by a sloppy frame of rhinestones. There's a green one from a couple years later with a less outrageous amount of fringe, more crude leather patches (like a wagon wheel on the chest and a horse on each pant leg), plus maybe four times as many rhinestones, again bordering the leather patches but also covering the entire shirt collar, tagging along the piping on the shirt cuffs and belt loops and formed into sloppy horseshoes beneath sloppy smile pockets. Each time Lefty came back for more suits he asked Nudie to use more rhinestones and these original Nudie suits became a massive hit with country singers and their audiences. After seeing Lefty's suits, Little Jimmy Dickens became another of Nudie's early customers. Little Jimmy was supposedly the first person to wear a rhinestone suit on the *Grand Ole Opry*. His earliest Nudie pieces also looked like first-generation superhero couture. Again starting with the most basic template of a western suit, Nudie added a triangular bib front to a shirt, lined the inside of the bib with rhinestones and stitched Jimmy's initials inside a large circle taking up most of his chest. He looked like Hillbilly Superman. Though it's a fact mostly lost to history, Nudie never became a tailor who was capable of stitching the famous suits now synonymous with his name, featuring embroidered imagery as photorealistic as an oil painting. He just found people who were already doing that kind of work and hired them to do it in the backroom of his shop.

The two people who deserve most of the credit for the pieces of art which eventually began coming out of Nudie's Rodeo Tailors were Viola Grae and Manuel Cuevas. Manuel was born and raised in Mexico and learned to sew from his older brother. By the time he was a teenager he'd become so good that all the girls in his town wanted their prom dresses to be made by Manuel. Around the age of nineteen, he came to L.A. and took whatever tailoring work he could find, quickly landing a job with Sy Devore, suit maker to the Rat Pack. With such wealthy clients Manuel could probably have stayed in that job for decades and even spun it into making a name for himself . . . but then someone took him to see the Rose Parade in Pasadena. After one look at all those horse saddles designed by Ed Bohlin, all the pieces of western wear designed by Nathan Turk, Manuel knew what he wanted to do for the rest of his life. Upon visiting Turk's store and discovering it was Viola Grae who'd performed the most intricate embroidery in the parade and Viola Grae who Nudie Cohn hired whenever a customer asked for such embroidery, Manuel arranged to become her apprentice.

The practice of adorning western wear with symbols of import to the owner dates back at least to the first custom-ordered cowboy boots and moved over to fabric long before Prairie Rose

Henderson started embroidering roses on her rodeo clothes. But the tradition of country singers wearing outfits covered in masterfully embroidered images that referred to their own hit songs, their own name or some other pertinent theme, that mostly comes from Viola Grae. Though Nathan Turk was very good at embroidery, the style of his work was abstract, featuring patterns that looked like a dozen sets of deer antlers jumbled up into a symmetrical design. When someone like Rose Maddox came around asking for the most realistic roses anyone in the shop could embroider on an outfit, Nathan knew that was a job for Viola Grae. Unfortunately, not much is known about Viola's background, only that she came to L.A. from Minnesota. But Nathan Turk, Nudie Cohn and Manuel Cuevas would all tell you she was simply the best of her time.

For these reasons, it's very easy to tell who did the actual work on pieces that came out of Nudie's shop. If it looks like someone patched on a piece of clip art from some other material or haphazardly tacked on a bunch of gemstones, Nudie did that. If you can take a magnifying glass to it and see the detailed work of someone who spent years honing a craft 99 percent of people could never master in a lifetime—like Webb Pierce's "In the Jailhouse Now" suit, Gram Parsons' "Drugs and Jesus" suit, the myriad illustrated rhinestone suits of Hank Snow and Porter Wagoner—that was done by someone Nudie hired, someone like Viola or Manuel, who was promoted to head tailor and lead designer at Nudie's by the early 1960s.

What landed Nudie in the history books was not being a competent tailor of basic designs, which he surely was, but discovering gimmicks, branding a business and promoting himself as the face of that business while leaving the creation of art to the true artists. Around the same time Nudie invented rhinestone suits, he and Manuel also began customizing the longest convertibles they could find into vehicles worthy of cowboy superstars. They replaced the entire interiors with hand-tooled and -painted leather, affixed bandoliers and holsters all over the place (stocked with bullets and guns, of course), threw a set of giant bull horns on every grill, a horse saddle in the place of every console and silver dollars pretty much any free spot where a coin could be embedded. Driving these cars around town and claiming some of the gaudiest suits to come from the back room of the shop for his own personal wardrobe, everywhere Nudie went was inherently a sales pitch for both his business and his own status as a celebrity. He was also very good at targeting famous clients who he knew would bring in more business by wearing his products.

The Porter Wagoner Show first aired on TV in 1960. In footage of Porter performing the song "Misery Loves Company" in 1961, he's wearing such a basic suit and tie it looks like he's going to work a shift as a bank teller after the taping. In footage of Porter and Grandpa Jones performing the moonshine anthem "Good Ol' Mountain Dew" barely a year later in 1962, Porter's jacket looks like it must weigh about fifteen pounds due to an uninterrupted sheet of rhinestones covering every inch of the fabric. That's because Nudie offered the host of one of television's most popular country music programs a free rhinestone suit, thereby gaining one of his most loyal customers ever—a decades-long living billboard for the Nudie brand—as well as an excuse to pump out dozens of iterations of the old wagon wheel motif from those early Lefty Frizzell suits.

Nudie was happy to go along with the publicity stunts of others, too. The gold lamé suit Elvis Presley wore on the cover of *50,000,000 Elvis Fans Can't Be Wrong* in 1957, when his singles were still topping the Country charts prior to the formation of the CMA? Colonel Tom Parker famously claimed to have paid Nudie ten thousand dollars for it, which made for a great story but Nudie revealed some years later he hadn't charged anywhere near that amount.

◇　　◇　　◇

Like virtually anything else about country music, rhinestone suits are a point of contention among fans. Were they an iconic contribution to American fashion or a dated trend? Another example of country artists blazing their own trail or another example of country artists catering to a pop audience? You can probably start an argument about it with someone in your local honky-tonk tonight, if you want. If they say something like they only listen to country music from back before artists started dressing up in cowboy drag, make sure to ask them when that was. The answer is sure to be entertaining. Sometimes they'll complain about the Wranglers and Stetsons that seemed to become mandatory for every male country artist in the 1990s. More often, though, it'll be a derogatory rant on rhinestone suits from some tough guy who probably wouldn't be happy with the result of running an image search to see what Merle Haggard looks like trying one on in Nudie's store. If you bring up the fondness for cowboy hats displayed in the 1940s and 1950s by Hank Williams, Ernest Tubb, Lefty Frizzell and pretty much any country artist who came from or rose to fame anywhere near Texas (not to mention any artist even tangentially related to western swing), you'll likely see the goalposts move east of the Mississippi . . . because now you're suddenly talking to someone who just doesn't understand why Appalachian artists began dressing up like cowboys in, well, whatever decade they believe that happened. Maybe in the 1930s, when Bill Monroe wore jodhpurs and western-style hats? Or perhaps it was the 1920s, when Stanley Hicks, the Possum Hunters, the Gully Jumpers, the Dixie Clodhoppers and maybe half the regular lineup of the *Grand Ole Opry* wore the gingham shirts and/or cowboy hats and/or cowboy boots then being worn by actors in Western movies?

The next time you see some pop or rock music journalist with a college degree talking about how "authenticity" matters so much more to country music fans, make sure to ask how many sharecroppers they've seen hoe a row or pick cotton while wearing their initials across the chest of a rhinestoned shirt the way Lefty Frizzell and Little Jimmy Dickens began appearing onstage about a decade after young Gene Autry fans were able to buy little cowboy costumes with Gene's name similarly plastered all over them. As for the reason someone like country artist Hank Thompson would want to walk out of Nudie's shop with rhinestoned fringe shirts and jackets nearly identical to those already being worn in Westerns by Rex Allen and Roy Rogers? That's easy. Anything worth doing is worth overdoing.

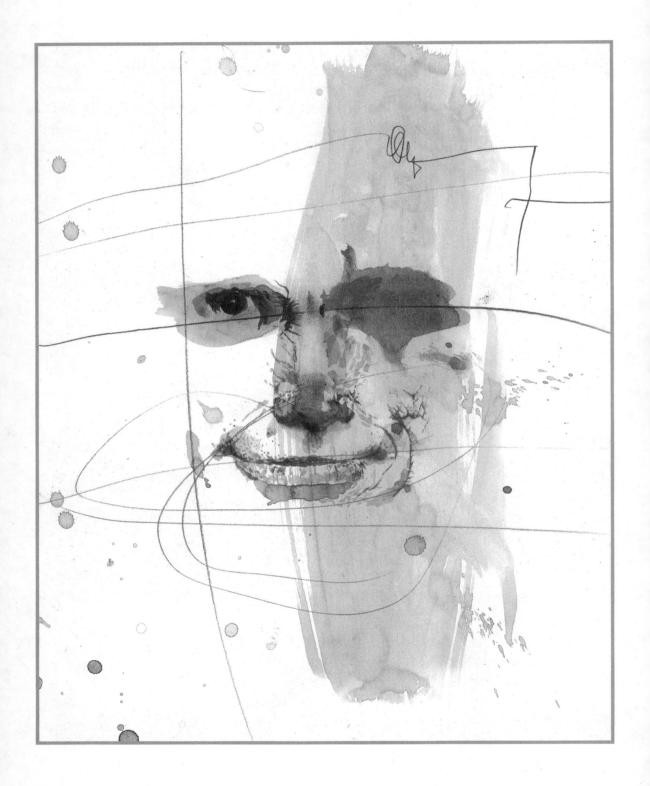

TWENTY-EIGHT

BACK TO LIFE

◇ George Jones Gets His Voice Back ◇ Meet Nancy ◇
A Cocaine Conspiracy in Florence ◇ Searching for Rock Bottom
◇ Billy Sherrill vs. Country Radio ◇ Jones Plays the Clown ◇ One Last Relapse ◇ The End ◇

Early in the year 1982, Columbia executive Rick Blackburn said, "It would not surprise me to get a phone call any day saying that George [Jones] had been found dead or had had a fatal car accident." After Jones' trainwreck of a performance on the CMA Awards telecast only a few months prior, it's fair to assume nobody would've been shocked to receive such a phone call. Despite claims his stay in rehab put Jones back on track, everyone could see the truth. His records released in this period made no attempt to disguise it, doubling down on the sentiment of "If Drinkin' Don't Kill Me (Her Memory Will)" with follow-up single "Still Doin' Time," about being trapped in the honky-tonk lifestyle like it was a type of prison. Released in September of 1981, the record went all the way to #1, his second single to do so in as many years.

In November, one month after the CMA Awards fiasco, Epic renewed his contract with a ten-albums-in-five-years deal, giving Jones a 20 percent royalty rate on sales and the option to draw up to a three hundred thousand dollar advance on each LP. If any fans were anxious about quality control with Jones releasing two albums a year in his fraught psychological condition, those worries were assuaged right away in 1982 with a full-length collaboration LP featuring Merle Haggard and a double-album greatest hits compilation. The compilation featured no previously unreleased material, but it was the first real greatest hits collection gathered from Jones' first decade on Epic, so it sold very well. The title track of the album with Merle Haggard was a version of the Willie Nelson song "Yesterday's Wine," which became the next single bearing George Jones' name to hit #1. Haggard being perhaps the second-most popular nominee for Greatest Country Singer Ever, many country fans were thrilled with the pairing, even if those hoping to settle the debate were dismayed to hear Jones had not yet won his voice back from cocaine. But again, that couldn't have come as much of a surprise.

A few months prior to the release of *A Taste of Yesterday's Wine*, Jones was pulled over just south of Nashville for swerving all over the interstate in a car with "POSSUM 3" scribbled on a piece of cardboard where the license plate should have been. When a local news crew showed up to film the roadside arrest Jones became angry and fought against the police officer in an attempt to kick a cameraman, which was enough to tack a resisting arrest charge on top of the DUI while simultaneously giving the media some footage worth broadcasting far and wide, which is what they did. Two months prior to that roadside arrest, Jones had been arrested in Mississippi for possession of cocaine. To many fans, knowledge of these events actually lent credibility to his subpar performances on the album with Merle, especially since most of the songs were about getting fucked up and staying fucked up no matter who had any kind of problem with it.

While it wasn't anywhere near as bad as his work on *My Very Special Guests* or the *Double Trouble* LP with Johnny PayCheck, on *Yesterday's Wine* Jones' voice sounds thinner and frequently misses correct pitch in ways it never would when he was at his best. However, *Yesterday's Wine* succeeds in two departments where those other albums missed: the selection and arrangements of the songs. Everything on the Haggard album serves the function of capturing two of the most country voices ever, even if only one of them was operating at 100 percent. There are no attempts to reach outside the frame by cutting rock standards or borrowing arrangements from genres unfamiliar to either artist. Haggard pulled from his deep Dixieland jazz influences to write the second single, "C.C. Waterback," a tale about partying at Jones' house that went #10. On top of the hit singles, several of the album cuts are at least as good and have proven at least as enduring with fans, a trend that continues through the remaining collaborations between Jones and Billy Sherrill. Written by Max Barnes and Vern Gosdin, "Must've Been Drunk" is a microcosmic encapsulation of the entire LP's swaggering and unapologetic party animal aesthetic. Glenn Martin helped Jones write "No Show Jones," taking what would otherwise have remained a disparaging nickname and (again, unapologetically) turning it into something of a theme song that Jones performed at most of his concerts for the rest of his life.

By the following year, he'd mostly stopped doing cocaine and finally recovered his voice. The title track and lead single of his next solo LP, "Shine On," hit #3 Country, despite being the worst song on what was otherwise one of the best albums in his discography. The second single, "I Always Get Lucky with You," flaunted the return of his voice so dramatically Epic's marketing department decided to promote it as the first time George Jones ever slipped all the way into falsetto on a record. Billy Sherrill later dismissed that as hype, saying Jones was just spreading it on a little

BACK TO LIFE ◇ 431

thick in the session. Since Jones cut the song in December of '82, weeks earlier than the rest of the album, he likely felt confident and adventurous in the studio, hearing his voice on its way back to full form for the first time in a long time. Falsetto or no, it's an impressive performance. That proved to be his final #1 record but Jones was unmistakably back. His next single, "Tennessee Whiskey" by Dean Dillon and Linda Hargrove, reached #2 Country, the third major hit from *Shine On*. Here, again, Jones and Billy did not save all the good stuff for the singles. The rest of the album provided many opportunities for Jones to remind everyone of what he could do on a microphone, from Bobby Braddock's "She Hung the Moon," to a vital rerecording of "Almost Persuaded," to a self-referential cover of O. B. McClinton's "Ol' George Stopped Drinkin' Today." Chuck Howard's "The Show's Almost Over" introduced a "love me while I'm here 'cuz I won't be for long" theme that Jones would successfully revisit time and again in the following decades. It's unclear whether Billy Sherrill chose to record a cover of Eddy Raven's #13 hit "I Should've Called" as an homage to Eddy's fantastic record or a potshot toward producer Jimmy Bowen's evolution of the Nashville Sound. Either way, the Jones version is wonderful.

The three hits from *Shine On* kept Jones on the radio through the end of 1983, so there were no singles released from his other new full-length of the year, the equally great *Jones Country*. Since "Radio Lover" opened the album and Epic backtracked to release it as a single about six years later, they probably had it pegged as the obvious hit. Given the engaging plot and surprise ending of this story about a DJ, there's virtually no chance the record would have bombed if sent to radio in the early 1980s. John Anderson's "Girl at the End of the Bar" seems the likeliest candidate for a follow-up single, since there's nobody better equipped than George Jones to sing about the title character with such empathy. The other reason Epic released no singles from *Jones Country* was Jones' appearance on a Ray Charles special guests LP, which also become a hit at country radio in 1983. Written by Gary Gentry, "We Didn't See a Thing" plays on Ray Charles' blindness—a thing Ray often did—for a story about two up-to-no-good pals who are always willing to provide each other with an alibi. The next Jones solo single was possibly another Billy Sherrill dig at Jimmy Bowen, the producer on Dean Martin's original, late '60s hit recording of "You've Still Got a Place in My Heart." Billy's arrangement on the Jones version is almost certainly what he'd have put behind the best singer in the Rat Pack. Where Bowen chose to center a shrill organ on the Dean Martin record in the '60s, Billy Sherrill brought Jones an inviting piano and string section, then relaxed the tempo to give his star vocalist some room to stretch out. Released in March 1984, "You've Still Got a Place in My Heart" went #3 and was followed in August by another #2 hit, "She's My Rock," the only song Jones sang by himself on *Ladies' Choice*. This second special guests LP paired Jones only with women artists. The album's other two singles, one featuring Brenda Lee and the other featuring Lacy J. Dalton, were minor hits . . . but also his first records since "He Stopped Loving Her Today" to not reach the Top 10.

The closing track of *Ladies' Choice* was "Best Friends," a duet with Leona Williams, who wrote the song with Hank Cochran and gave it to Jones for the same reason "She's My Rock," originally recorded by Stoney Edwards over a decade earlier, opens the album: to make sure fans understood that George Jones wasn't actually available to any of these ladies. For everyone who didn't know about his marriage to Nancy Sepulvado the previous year, on the first verse of "Best Friends," Leona sang "but you're on your way to recovery and you're not alone / 'cuz Nancy sure loves you and she's gonna take care of ol' Jones." The exact same sentiment is implied by Jones singing the line "she took me in and made me everything I am today" on the chorus of "She's My Rock," which means *Ladies' Choice* is literally bookended by summarized versions of what instantly became part of the George Jones mythology. The notion that Nancy saved his life was essentially just a reboot of the storyline from his previous marriage. This time it was an unknown rather than another country star, but George Jones fans were once more told a woman rescued him with her love. That narrative was strongly reinforced by the audible return of his singing ability and more or less supported by the first biographies of Jones, *Ragged but Right* by Dolly Carlisle and *George Jones: The Life and Times of a Honky Tonk Legend* by Bob Allen, both published in 1984, the same year *Ladies' Choice* came out. To a certain extent, this time it was the truth. If he hadn't met Nancy Sepulvado, then Jones probably would have died in the early 1980s. However, the succinct "all he needed was someone to love him" explanation offered by these songs does not begin to convey the reality of his personal life during these years. Fans who looked beyond the albums to the biographies and continued following the story as more facts were revealed over the following years found a more complicated truth, one that includes the most horrific events and despicable behavior in George Jones' entire life.

◇   ◇   ◇

George and Nancy first met through a road manager's girlfriend, who was asked to bring a friend for Jones when she flew from Shreveport, Louisiana, to meet the tour in New York City. At the time, Nancy was a single mother who worked on the assembly line of a telephone factory. There were not very many exciting things going on down in Shreveport and Nancy's daughters happened to be visiting their father when a friend asked if she'd like to see New York City in the style of a country music star, so Nancy said yes to the brief trip. According to George's autobiography, this was in November of 1981, the month after his disastrous appearance at the CMAs. But Nancy hadn't seen or heard about the show and didn't really know much about George Jones. She didn't know this was a man who'd tried to murder one of his best friends after spending a few months arguing with multiple personalities in his mind. She also didn't see any evidence of his self-destructive behavior during the trip to New York City. The two of them just talked through the night, watched the sun come up over the city together, then went their separate ways. After that, though, Jones couldn't stop thinking about her. He fixated upon how nice she was, her determined optimism and strong work ethic, the way spending time with her made everything seem like it could turn out alright. Pretty soon he showed up in Shreveport to spend more time with her. Nancy didn't know Jones was bailing on scheduled concerts, leaving himself open to lawsuits and costing many people many thousands of dollars in order to take her out to dinners and movies. It just felt like they were in their own private world, where his career didn't even matter. But then the road manager figured out where Jones was and convinced him to come back to the tour.

In his autobiography, Jones claimed Linda Welborn was still living in his Alabama home but that they were no longer a couple when he became romantically involved with Nancy. Whether or not the separation between relationships really was so clean—and there are several other sources plus what seem to be deliberately confusing chronological jumps in that section of Jones' book to suggest it was not—it is true he practically lived on the road and was barely ever home in late 1981/ early 1982. That winter hadn't yet turned to spring when he called Nancy to ask her to quit her job in Shreveport and come join him on the road. She decided to go for it. Leaving her youngest daughter with the ex-husband, Nancy brought her fourteen-year-old, Adina, and moved into the RV Jones had purchased for them to travel separately from his band and crew. It was only then she realized the extent of his alcoholism, learned what cocaine was and met Jones' split personalities. Nancy soon became convinced Jones was possessed by what she called "a devil" and made up her mind to drive that devil away. Before long, he started hitting her.

Jones admitted to slapping Tammy Wynette once, perhaps in response to her hitting him. Linda Welborn once had an arrest warrant taken out against him for assault but dropped the charge and later said, "George never beat me, though it seemed to come out that way in the papers later. Oh . . . He did bite my lip once and it bled real, real bad. And he did slap my face a few times, too. But who didn't do that when they're married or living together and get themselves into an argument?" By anyone's definition and without any type of provocation, he beat Nancy. He was blacked out, never remembered doing it, appalled in disbelief to later learn of his actions—all the things we always hear from abusive addicts—but he beat her. And she stayed. When later asked why she stayed, Nancy always gave the same explanation, which was she needed to find a way to get Jones sober so they could spend the rest of their lives together, because when he was sober he was the best man she'd ever known. It seems she also believed Jones when he told her there were other sinister forces at play. According to the official story, Jones and Nancy were pitted against a full-fledged conspiracy involving drug dealers, gangsters and local law enforcement, all working together to keep George Jones hooked on cocaine against his will.

Nothing about the way Jones presents this alleged conspiracy in his autobiography makes any kind of sense but there's also no reason to expect accuracy in whatever memories he had or believed he had from the year 1982. To say he was confused, delusional, drunk or high would all be gigantic understatements. "George Jones" was still the drug-induced collective of multiple personalities who spent much of 1979 hallucinating Romero monster movies onto reality, made lists of the people they wanted to kill and went so far as attempting to follow through on one entry. He was still ingesting the same substances at the same volume that fueled such deranged thinking and behavior. In this new conspiracy, those movie monsters were joined by malevolent human gangsters, which may seem like at least a less scary thing to hallucinate but, in fact, it only became more difficult for Jones to tell which beings were really there or not. Instead of living this nightmare alone in a parked car, he was now living with a woman and her teenage daughter.

Since his drinking and cocaine use were always worse on tour, Jones and Nancy and Adina didn't live in the RV for very long before deciding to get off the road and try getting him off drugs. He bought a house in Muscle Shoals, across the river from Florence, Alabama, where Nancy did her damndest to keep Jones sober . . . only to become furious after learning the man who ran a popular rec center in town, where they and their friends were always hanging out, was secretly Jones' cocaine dealer. She gave the guy hell, told him to stay away, then did everything in her power to keep them apart. That's when Jones said the drug dealer put spies on him—apparently 24/7—because it seemed like anytime Nancy left the house to run an errand, the dealer or someone from his crew would show up, take Jones away and make him do cocaine. Nancy believed she somehow flipped a person on the inside of this drug operation and made them her own personal informant but the tips she received only gave her enough time to rush in a little too late, finding Jones (quoting him) "helpless" and being "forced" to do cocaine. So, Nancy got wise and taught Adina to drive before she was legally of age, then sent her daughter to run errands while Nancy stayed home to watch Jones. Once the dealer and his crew understood they weren't going to catch Jones alone anymore, several men at a time would force entry to the home, then allow Nancy to scream at everyone while one guy snuck off, found Jones and forced him to do more cocaine. Any single instance of blow entering Jones' body was worse than a simple relapse, it held the potential to send him off on a binge with DeeDoodle and the Old Man for a couple weeks or longer. Even worse, it could lead to all three of them hanging around at home for a couple of weeks, forcing Nancy and Adina to stay inside because of the "platoons of criminals" Jones imagined were holding the house under siege.

Near the end of March 1982, Jones agreed to let Nancy and Adina drive him to see one of his sisters in Texas before checking into another rehab. He brought a sack of cocaine for the trip down and was using in the car but, a few hours into the drive, Nancy talked him into tossing the drugs out of the window. They were somewhere around Jackson, Mississippi, and Nancy was behind the wheel when Jones, upset because he wanted to go back for his bag of blow, slammed his foot down over Nancy's on the gas pedal and kept it floored, leaving her no choice but to try using only the steering wheel to stay on the road as they sped over 90 mph with her daughter in the backseat. Fortunately, when a cop pulled behind them and threw on a siren, Jones took his foot off the gas and allowed the car to be stopped. The police brought in a K9 unit and the dog found enough spilled cocaine in the vehicle to arrest Jones for possession on top of other reckless endangerment charges. After being booked, he spent a few hours in jail, then spent the night getting drunk in a motel room. The next morning Jones had the car keys, so they headed back in the direction of home . . . until a few hours into the trip, when Jones decided Nancy had somehow set him up to be arrested the previous day. He pulled over, kicked Nancy and Adina out of the car, then sped away. A few miles down the road, he wrecked at high speed, flipping the car several times and earning himself a visit to the hospital. While Jones was laid up Nancy arranged for his family to have him committed again and he was transferred to a mental institution, where he got kicked out a couple of weeks later after testing positive for the cocaine he was having smuggled inside. That DUI arrest captured on camera by a Nashville news crew happened about a month later.

Meanwhile, back in Florence, Nancy started hearing rumors the nefarious drug dealer and his gangster friends wanted her out of the picture for good and were planning to do something about it. One night she and Adina were driving across the bridge between Florence and Muscle Shoals when a car sped up from behind and repeatedly rammed into their vehicle, trying to run the car off the bridge and, presumably, cause them to drown in the river below. The only way Nancy got herself and her terrified daughter across the bridge was by veering in and out of oncoming traffic. There was another incident when Adina was supposedly kidnapped from school but then Nancy's "informant" arranged to have her returned almost instantly.

Naturally, Jones and Nancy thought about moving far away from the area where these awful events took place. They even tried to leave several times but these criminal masterminds were always one step ahead. After several escape attempts were thwarted, Jones and Nancy decided to try sneaking out of town in the middle of the night. As they drove away, some crooked cops pulled them over for no reason, arrested them, then locked Nancy in a jail cell so they could take Jones over to the dealer's place and force cocaine on him. Toward the end of 1982, George rented a house in Lafayette, Louisiana, and they packed all their belongings to make another run for it. This time the wicked villains waited until just before George and Nancy pulled out of the driveway before swarming on to the property and blocking their exit. Seeing how much it upset Nancy to know they'd been stopped from leaving yet again, Jones valiantly told her not to worry and selflessly volunteered to leave with the gangsters so Nancy and Adina could make the trip to Louisiana. Upon arriving in Lafayette, Nancy sent a friend who was able to locate Jones and extract him from Florence, which was how they finally got away from Alabama for good.

Now, that whole story has at least as many plot holes in it as the grandest of Tammy Wynette's fictions. Similar to many of Tammy's stories, the entire "conspiracy" to keep George Jones trapped in Florence and addicted to cocaine really only makes sense if the person claiming to be the victim was at or near the head of the scheme. His own account of the situation does everything except fill in the blanks. By his own telling, Jones was literally not of one mind when it came to kicking cocaine. One side of him did agree to go to rehab and did allow Nancy to talk him into throwing a bag of cocaine out a car window. But at least one of his other sides, whichever one(s) nearly killed everybody in the car because they wanted to go back for the drugs, definitely *didn't* want to quit doing cocaine. So, the question becomes which side was in control more often and how far would they go to defend their way of life against a perceived threat? At the beginning of this saga Jones admitted he would routinely go to the rec center under false pretenses in order to willingly score drugs behind Nancy's back. Why would he stop going behind her back to score drugs just because she caught on to the first method he came up with for deceiving her? What's more plausible, a drug dealer placing a full-time surveillance crew on Jones in order to repeatedly kidnap him whenever he was left alone? Or one of that drug dealer's most dedicated clients simply waiting for Nancy to leave before calling the dealer to bring more cocaine over to the house? Jones claimed the drug gang forced a steady supply of cocaine on him to keep him addicted even when they knew he was financially broke. But, why? Toward what end? Where's the return on investment for all the resources necessary to maintain that 24/7 stakeout? It only makes sense if they expected to get more cash from him at some point down the road and the easiest way for George Jones to get more cash was by going on tour, which would require the gang allowing him to leave Florence. If Jones wanted to get away from Florence so badly, why not leave town under the pretense of doing some concerts and then just never return? Ah, but what if he secretly did *not* wish to leave? It wouldn't require a criminal mastermind to make another phone call and keep those dealers informed of the escape plans Jones was pretending to go along with until, oh no, here are those "gang members" again, showing up at the last minute and forcing him to stay. We're already being asked to believe local police were corrupt enough to arrest George and Nancy on their way out of town in order to make him do drugs. How would it be any less believable for that arrest to have been arranged in advance by a phone call from Jones? It is disturbing to wonder if he was in any way involved with a car trying to run Nancy and Adina off a bridge to their deaths. It's also disturbing to know for a fact that this man and his split personalities tried to murder his best friend only a few years earlier. The time Adina was "kidnapped" from school? When Nancy got home from retrieving her daughter she found the drug dealers had stopped by to see Jones. According to Jones' own account of the day, his response was to do just a little bit of cocaine on his own because he wanted it . . . but then those dealers began "mercilessly" cramming more up his nose.

Nancy tried to leave him once in this period because dealing with all these events had her so confused she felt she might be headed toward her own nervous breakdown. And she probably was, trying to make sense of life with this man who hadn't changed much at all since a doctor a few years earlier diagnosed him as "suffering from an acute paranoid state with suicidal and homicidal potential to a high degree." Many years later Jones admitted some of the things he did to try driving Nancy away, the times he kicked her off a tour bus at night in the middle of nowhere or told the pilot of a private plane to leave without her. What he didn't talk about was the time he kicked Nancy out of the house in Alabama in order to move Linda Welborn back in for a couple weeks. Evidently, at least one side of him thought staying in the Florence area with a woman who let him do whatever he wanted would be preferable to moving away from town with a woman who was trying to get him off drugs. However, Linda's time back in the house was short-lived. Nancy called with a fake anonymous tip about how the Mafia were on their way down from Nashville intent on killing everyone inside George Jones' house, so Linda got scared and left. By the time Linda returned Nancy was back in the house and told her to take a hike. A few days later, Jones and Nancy were driving somewhere when he hit her, left her on the side of a road, then had one of his lawyers draft a letter telling Nancy to stay away from him.

Between DeeDoodle, the Old Man and all his other hallucinations, this was a man who spent years not knowing who or what was real. He did not magically get better the moment he left Alabama. After moving to Louisiana in late 1982, Jones booked a few tour dates and those Alabama gangsters showed up in one town. On this particular occasion Jones was already in the middle of a relapse, already doing blow on his own and looking to score some more. So, despite every supposed instance of these drug dealers having already tried to ruin his life, perhaps even trying to murder his girlfriend and her daughter, Jones was happy to see them, which again begs the question of whether these criminals took it upon themselves to track him down or Jones merely called in a cocaine order for delivery. However they got there, Jones invited the dealers into his hotel room, kicked Nancy out, locked the door behind her, bailed on that night's concert and vanished.

Two weeks later, he called Nancy to say he was ready to quit drinking and ready to quit doing cocaine for good. She told him to come on home. He listened. But DeeDoodle and the Old Man came with him. Jones was still trashed and, for some reason, insisted everyone leave the house to go check into a hotel. Adina got her own room, next door to the adults. According to Nancy, once she and Jones were in their room, he began addressing her by the names of the Alabama gangsters he'd been hanging out with the last time she saw him. When Nancy insisted she wasn't one of those people because she was Nancy, he became angry with her for pretending to be Nancy. He knew who she really was. She was one of those bastards who was always showing up and forcing him to do cocaine, keeping him from being able to live a happy life with Nancy, the woman he loved. That's what he yelled about as he started to hit her, ripped her clothes off and kept hitting her while Adina hammered her fists against the locked door between their rooms, screaming to try to stop what she could hear happening to her mother. The next day, even though Nancy's bruised face and body presented undeniable evidence she'd been beaten, and she told him he was the person who did it, Jones could not and would not believe it. That was not the last time he did cocaine.

Nancy stayed. Or, she tried to stay. After the hotel beating, Jones pushed her away again and Nancy became inconsolable. Convinced he was sure to be dead soon, she tried sending messages to reassure him that she cared nothing about his fame or talent or money. She just wanted a life with him. She wanted him to choose life by choosing to be with her. But it didn't seem like he was going to do that. According to a friend, Nancy somehow became convinced that taking her own life was the only way to prove to Jones she really loved him. If there was a chance her suicide could provide the wake up call he needed, she felt it was worth it. She overdosed on some pills but was found in time for her stomach to be pumped. Upon being released from the hospital, she immediately made another attempt to the same outcome, pumped stomach, still alive. Though it's unclear whether Nancy's suicide attempts were in any way responsible, Jones did ultimately decide she must really be in love with him, and they got back together for good.

◇   ◇   ◇

In early 1983 they moved to east Texas. It was a little farther away from Florence but, more importantly, much closer to Jones' family. For the first time Nancy had more help than her young daughter could give to keep George away from drugs. Unlike George Richey's attempts to damage the relationships between Tammy Wynette and her daughters, Nancy encouraged Jones to speak with his children and spend time with them. He did relapse a few more times but by that point Nancy was thoroughly self-educated on the latest approaches to treating addiction and able to quickly help Jones back on course to recovery. As he reentered a normal plane of reality and found a way to stay there, it inspired a desire to put his whole life back together, which manifested the same way it had so many times in the past: the planning and construction of an outdoor concert venue. He again bought up property piecemeal and climbed onto heavy machinery to landscape his vision into existence. Whenever funds ran out he called some honky-tonk promoter, set up a short-notice gig or two, then phoned country radio stations to plug shows in the area during brief on-air interviews. He pocketed several grand at each show and returned home to work on the venue he'd begun calling Jones Country.

In March 1983, at a small and private ceremony in the living room of George's sister's house, he and Nancy were married. After the wedding they went out to eat at Burger King, then returned to work on Jones Country. They spent their wedding night in the trailer home on the property where they lived during construction. That September, one month before the *Jones Country* LP came out, George celebrated his birthday a couple weeks early and gave the park a trial run by playing a Labor Day show for more than ten thousand people. The following April, Johnny Cash came down from Nashville to play the official grand opening. *Ladies' Choice* was released in May and George Jones fans were told specifically who to thank for the sudden return of his voice on record, as well as his recent success rate of actually showing up to perform at concerts, usually not falling-down drunk. Then the first single from his next album posed a question George probably spent the rest of his career wishing he'd left unasked.

✧   ✧   ✧

A couple years later—after country radio stopped playing his records—Jones started complaining about it at nearly every opportunity and continued complaining about it until the end of his life, which is probably why so many fans these days hear "Who's Gonna Fill Their Shoes?" as a question criticizing the mainstream country music industry. But songwriters Troy Seals and Max Barnes did not receive a vision and try to warn everyone of the genre's baby-faced, pop crossover future. That is not what the song was ever meant to be or why it exists. The intent was not to bemoan the death of a genre but to suggest its future lay in a younger generation of artists who would be influenced by its greatest legends, several of whom (like Waylon Jennings, Merle Haggard, Willie Nelson and Conway Twitty) were still regularly charting Top 10 and even #1 Country singles. That's why the music video, the first one George Jones ever made, ends on a car full of kids with guitars pulling into a gas station as George's tour bus pulls out. It's obvious the old man at the gas station who just showed Jones his collection of country music memorabilia is going to tell the kids with guitars that George Jones was just in there, then show them the same collection of country music memorabilia. The explicit point was that, someday, somebody would fill the shoes of these legends. Released as a single in the summer of 1985, "Who's Gonna

Fill Their Shoes?" hit #3, George's eleventh Top 10 solo record in a row. The music video won Video of the Year at the CMAs.

His next two singles also went Top 10. Featuring the cleanest baritone Jones ever hit in a studio, Gary Gentry's "The One I Loved Back Then" stars another one of those gas station old-timers who seems to be complimenting Jones' car, until it becomes clear he's actually complimenting the woman in the passenger seat. "Somebody Wants Me Out of the Way" casts Jones as a barfly whose tab keeps getting picked up by an unknown benefactor because they want him to stay at the bar instead of going home. These records hit #3 and #9, respectively. The latter was by writing partners "Doodle" Owens and Dennis Knutson, who also wrote his following two singles, giving them three Top 10 George Jones hits in a row. Released in the fall of 1986, the title track from his next LP, *Wine Colored Roses*, is about a woman who wants to come to Jones but writes to ask if he's still too deep in a bottle to give their love another chance. Unable to face telephoning or writing, he sends a bouquet of wine-colored roses as a coded message that he still cares but not enough to quit drinking. It hit #10. Released in January 1987, "The Right Left Hand" has a title that could cause someone to expect the kind of song people mock when they make fun of country music, something with rapid-fire dumbass comedy lyrics or one of those hacky pun-filled things a writer turns in because they think a semantic gimmick is more clever than it really is. But this song is an example of the mark all those writers are trying to hit when they miss, an example of why they take aim in the first place. Here, "The Right Left Hand" is a reference to at last marrying the perfect person after failing in marriage several times. Wisely, the lyrics never attempt to get any more clever than that, supporting the title line with what would be a great love song by any other name. It hit #8 and became Jones' fifteenth Top 10 record in a row. There was no reason to believe his shoes would need filling any time soon.

Then he broke the streak, missing the Top 10 and the Top 20 in April 1987 with "I Turn to You." There's nothing necessarily wrong with the song, certainly not to the degree it should only have charted at #26. It does get off to a bit of a rocky start, repeating the word "turn" several times more than it probably should. But just when it begins to feel like one of those hacky gimmick things the lyrics change approach. It's not a bad song. The song wasn't the problem. The problem was commercial country radio decided to answer the question George Jones had asked approximately two years earlier, "Who's gonna fill their shoes?" All of the sudden, artists anywhere near the age of forty and above found their records programmed less often, then not at all. Billy Sherrill saw what was happening and tried his best to make radio keep playing Jones. After the DJs and programmers didn't go for "I Turn to You," Billy responded with the single "The Bird," which interrupted a long string of ballads with an up-tempo and defiant pun allowing Jones to sneak a middle finger at an ex onto the airwaves. That is, it would have if radio played it, which they didn't. "The Bird" charted as poorly as his previous single, so Epic pulled out the big guns.

Everything about "I'm a Survivor" sounds like Billy Sherrill walked in the studio, declared someone would be winning a Grammy Award for the work they did that day and he didn't care who it was so everybody better try their best. They started with one of Billy's favorite things, a great song full of direct references to the recent media narrative surrounding his artist. Jones had already recorded several love songs to reference marrying Nancy but "I'm a Survivor," written by Keith Stegall and Jim McBride, was the first single to acknowledge and respond to the rest of what those 1984 biographies uncovered about George Jones' violent childhood, chaotic private life and toxic relationship with fame. Between the content, Billy's production and Jones' perfor- mance, the only universe where this record wasn't a hit is the one where country radio stations didn't play it because George was too old to fit the hip new image those stations had decided upon for themselves. It charted at #52, his worst showing in more than twenty-five years, bad enough to warrant rush-releasing another single two months later, which landed even worse.

Billy Sherrill must have known "I'm a Survivor" bombing was the beginning of an irreversible end and it's unlikely he sent "The Old Man No One Loves" to country radio because he believed the maudlin song stood any chance of receiving airplay. He probably just wanted to put that title on the label of a 45 to confront country DJs and radio programmers with the fact that they were treat- ing The Greatest Country Singer Ever like an old man no one loved anymore. Epic didn't release another George Jones solo record for six months. But they did give him a guest spot on the debut single of nineteen-year-old Shelby Lynne.

After an appearance on *Nashville Now* convinced everyone Shelby was the next big thing, Epic had beat out three other record labels in a bidding war to sign her. As with "I'm a Survivor," everything about "If I Could Bottle This Up" sounds like a swing for the fences. Even at nineteen years old, Shelby was one of the few vocalists who could hold her own with Jones in his prime. Hit songwriters Dean Dillon and Paul Overstreet handed over a song with as much commercial poten- tial as anything else Jones ever sang with the word "bottle" in the title. Billy Sherrill was signed on to produce half of Shelby Lynne's forthcoming debut LP, so there's a reason his production work sounds like he had skin in the game. Released in fall of 1988, "If I Could Bottle This Up" failed to make even the Top 40.

When the label did put out another solo George Jones record they already knew it was a hit because Johnny Horton took it to #7 in the 1950s. Maybe Billy Sherrill's relentless "shame the DJ" campaign inspired some radio folks to play the song for nostalgic reasons or perhaps Dwight Yoakam helped clear a path by taking a different Johnny Horton cover, "Honky Tonk Man," to Top 5

Country a couple of years earlier. Whatever the reason, even though there's nothing especially remarkable about Jones' cut of "One Woman Man" compared to his other singles ignored by radio in this period, they let it on the playlists and it hit #5, becoming his final Top 10. Epic reacted by packaging "One Woman Man" as the title track of a sort of clearance compilation LP. They did cut a few new songs but, to minimize recording costs for an artist with diminishing sales, they also got Jones to just lay down new vocals over the backing tracks of old, unreleased tapes, then padded out the tracklist with some previously released yet under-promoted material. Other than the title track, two singles from *One Woman Man* did break into the Country Top 40, which was about the best Jones could hope for from that point forward. First, Roger Ferris' "Ya Ba Da Ba Do (So Are You)," another one that on paper looks like one of the most unhinged concepts in the genre. When Jones' lady leaves, she takes everything except the things she doesn't want: him, his collectible Elvis Presley statuette whiskey bottle, an old Flintstones jelly jar and a table piled high with some other random bullshit. Jones clears some room on the table, cracks open the Elvis bottle and starts pouring whiskey four fingers at a time into the Flintstones jar, until he gets drunk enough to start talking to Fred Flintstone and Elvis Presley. By playing it straight the whole way through, Jones took what could have been a goofy novelty number and made it a honky-tonk classic. (The reason most fans know the song as "The King Is Gone [So Are You]" is because the title was changed soon after release when Hanna-Barbera threatened a lawsuit, possibly intentionally instigated by Billy Sherrill and/or Epic just to drum up some kind of controversial publicity in lieu of airplay. Considering how careful Epic was about releasing Tammy Wynette's "Kids Say the Darndest Things" fifteen years earlier, they must have known what they were doing when they originally issued this George Jones 45 in a picture sleeve with Fred Flintstone's face in a TV set on one side and his trademarked phrase in a Bedrock font on the other.) The next single went in a weepier direction. In "The Writing on the Wall," a man who's walked out on his family can't shake a memory of the message his small children scribbled on the wall just before he left. He returns home to find the message still there but his family long gone. The final single released from *One Woman Man* was the unchanged recording of "Radio Lover" from six years earlier, probably chosen in hopes of the DJ-centric plot generating some attention from radio, which it did not do.

As Tammy Wynette was forced to do a decade earlier when her sales began to drop, Jones shifted the focus of his career away from records and toward touring. Nancy effectively became his manager around the time they were married in 1983 but she was also tasked with overseeing nearly every aspect of the Jones Country operation. There were about five steady years when the park booked impressive concert lineups. In 1987 alone: Memorial Day weekend found Jones' venue hosting Vern Gosdin, Leon Everette, Conway Twitty, Jack Ripley, Kitty Wells, Johnny Wright and Loretta Lynn; on the Fourth of July weekend, they brought in Johnny Russell, Jimmy C. Newman, Mel McDaniel and Randy Travis; then Labor Day weekend had Little Jimmy Dickens, Becky Hobbs and Merle Haggard. Within a couple years, though, Jones needed to get back on the road to earn real money. In the autobiography he tried to claim that busier tour schedule was a result of his recording career getting "hot" again but the hits he cited to justify the claim were all from years earlier. His tour schedule did not ramp up as a result of thriving record sales. It was a way to make up for lackluster sales. However, since kicking cocaine and getting his voice back he'd begun to regain the trust of concert promoters and fans by showing up to perform well. So, Nancy was able to keep him steadily booked in bigger and better venues than ever, pulling in anywhere from twenty to fifty thousand dollars a night. The only problem was Nancy couldn't run Jones Country from the road and George couldn't be sent to tour heavily on his own. His stage fright never went away and all the other old stressors were still there. On his own, he'd end up back in a bottle, or worse. In 1989, George and Nancy listed Jones Country for sale and moved to Nashville.

◇   ◇   ◇

Jones claimed the move was partially motivated by a desire to be near his record label but he must have already been aware Billy Sherrill planned to retire after making one last George Jones album. It's possible Jones meant he wanted to be near his next record label, knowing whichever country division he signed with after Epic would have offices in Nashville.

The last album George made with Billy Sherrill is yet another strong argument against Billy's claims that he retired because he was burned out and bored with the whole process of making records. Maybe he thought that excuse sounded better than the truth, which was country radio stations had won and Epic would no longer waste money or resources trying to promote a hopeless product, even though Billy knew it was great work. Because if *You Oughta Be Here with Me* wasn't Billy trying his hardest to create a masterpiece to close out his professional relationship with George Jones, then he did it on autopilot while burned out and bored. Everybody knew the singles stood no chance of commercial success, so this isn't the usual collection of a few likely hits padded out with other material. It's a great album, front-to-back, no hits, no filler. Sequencing the track which under normal circumstances would have the most commercial potential at the close of the album seems like another middle finger from Billy to country radio, signing off with such an undeniably awesome song that nobody could fail to notice George Jones was being prematurely put out to pasture in order for younger artists to succeed without facing any competition from The Greatest Country Singer Ever. When "Ol' Red" was covered by Blake Shelton twelve years later, it nearly hit the Top 10 and became something of a signature song for him, despite sounded like a cartoonish joke compared to the swampy and sinister original by Jones, who sang this fantastic legend of a prison break aided by a horny hound dog as if he wanted you to hear the story more than he wanted you to believe he sounded cool and sexy enough to be on modern country radio. Without receiving major airplay or significant promotion from the label, *You Oughta Be Here with Me* came out in August of 1990 and barely registered in the Top 40 Country Albums of the summer.

In 1991, Epic released another special guests compilation, *Friends in High Places*, gathering duets from as far back as an Emmylou Harris collaboration in 1984 packaged with more recent one-offs like the Shelby Lynne single and the guest spot on Randy Travis' "A Few Ole Country Boys." By the time *Friends in High Places* came out, Jones was already headed from Epic over to MCA to continue working with Randy Travis' producer, Kyle Lehning. First, they tried to play it straight, as if all they needed to do was go in a studio and make a George Jones album, then ship the singles to radio, who would suddenly change their minds and start playing his records again. *Along Came Jones* was in no way inferior to anything else on country radio in 1991, but stations did not suddenly change their minds and start playing his records again. The crickets in response to their promotion of the first single, "You Couldn't Get the Picture," taught MCA what Epic already knew. It wasn't enough for Jones to prove, at sixty years old, his voice showed no sign of weakening and he could still outsing anyone in the business. The second single, "She Loved a Lot in Her Time," received even less attention, despite its exploitation of what should have been the bankable theme of a mother trying to deal with her son's alcoholism.

From there, MCA picked up the gimmicks Epic already tried and carried them even further. The first single from *Walls Can Fall*, produced by Emory Gordy, Jr., was "I Don't Need Your Rockin' Chair," which the label on the record listed as being by George Jones (with Special Guests: Vince Gill, Mark Chesnutt, Garth Brooks, Travis Tritt, Joe Diffie, Alan Jackson, Pam Tillis, T. Graham Brown, Patty Loveless and Clint Black). Yes, all of those people were on this one song and the lyrics made it clear why, point-blank addressing Jones' struggle against ageism while stopping just short of antagonizing the programmers and DJs Jones hoped would play the record. But stations hadn't stopped playing him because they were under the delusion he felt ready for the junkyard. They made that decision for him and they really didn't give a shit how many cool, younger friends he had. Though every one of his guest artists had records all over modern country radio, them appearing together en masse on one George Jones record received little airplay. Even without radio support, "I Don't Need Your Rockin' Chair" won a CMA award for Vocal Event of the Year and *Walls Can Fall* sold a half million copies or so, enough to go gold. Fans who picked up a copy discovered some great deep cuts, like "There's the Door," in which Jones comes home drunk for what his wife has decided will be the last time.

In 1992, he was inducted into the Country Music Hall of Fame and used his acceptance speech to criticize country radio for no longer playing his music. All it did was piss off the programmers, who played his records even less. Only one year prior, they were happy to send Alan Jackson's "Don't Rock the Jukebox" to #1 with George Jones' name in the chorus like a statue in a museum. When it came to treating Jones like a living artist who was still creating some of his best work, forget it, especially after he took them to task during such a prestigious moment at the Hall of Fame. Jones and MCA kept trying various strategies to break through the barrier but the results were often quite embarrassing. Though the rest of the decade brought some great musical moments from him, they were fewer and further between. A couple of high points were "The Love in Your Eyes," which demonstrated the viability of taking Billy Sherrill's approach to arrangement and updating the instrumentation to sounds modern country fans were accustomed to hearing. "I Must Have Done Something Bad" is every bit as good as the version Merle Haggard cut twenty years earlier. But the closest thing Jones had to a hit in the immediate wake of the Hall of Fame acceptance speech was "High-Tech Redneck," one of the dumbest songs ever written and one that probably helped set a course for the "listing my possessions and interests makes me country" hellscape where the genre would soon land.

While making a clown of himself still wasn't enough for country radio to let go of the idea they were too young and sexy to play George Jones records, an old man acting goofy worked differently on country music television. The sales that drove "High-Tech Redneck" to #24 were mostly a product of the music video, featuring Jones singing the song in front of giant walls of TV screens intercut with footage of some moron in a recliner having his mind blown by all types of gadgetry, "hot babes" using computers, and what seems to be a dream sequence of Jones dressed all in leather as some sort of reference to *Terminator 2*. Following the commercial failure of every subsequent attempt to make everyone take him seriously again, this foolish version of Jones was invariably trucked back out for the cameras.

The Bradley Barn Sessions were meant to reimagine his biggest hits by pairing him with major rock and country artists at Owen Bradley's studio outside town. It may have been a creative success, too, if Owen himself came out of retirement to prevent every song from being given a radically different and often senseless arrangement. Throughout work on the project Jones hated the daily mixes played for him, but the record label thought he was just too used to the way Billy Sherrill tracked most of a song live, not catching up quickly enough to the modern practice of piecing everything together with overdubs. MCA did manage to choose the best track for the only single, even if that version of "A Good Year for the Roses" with Alan Jackson was about as artistically compelling as a Frisbee compared to the original record. Alan Jackson only missed the Top 10 exactly once as a solo artist in all of the 1990s but country radio wouldn't play him when paired with George Jones. Soon after that record tanked Jones started supplementing his income by licensing his name and image to a line of dog food. In the remaining years of his life he would also hawk lines of bottled water and breakfast sausage.

The year 1995 brought the half-hearted Tammy Wynette reunion album, *One*, co-produced by Norro Wilson and Tony Brown. Tony later said *One* "wasn't a great record" and he believed neither Tammy nor Jones had as much fun making the album as he did getting to work with two legends. Norro called it a "tough project" and said they found the best results from recording Jones and Tammy separately. Norro was likely not talking about the production practice Tammy and Jones started using in the '70s to record their vocals separately but rather the fact that there was friction whenever both artists were in the same room. Tony Brown, who called George Richey "a flashy guy" and "the opposite kind of person" to George Jones, remembered having problems whenever Richey and Jones were in the studio at the same time.

The reunion was followed by the always-blatant marketing tactic of releasing an autobiography in tandem with a new album bearing the same title, *I Lived to Tell It All*. The lead single, "Honky Tonk Song," served up a sanitized rewrite of the one Drunk George Jones story everyone who's ever heard of George Jones knows, then played it for laughs by putting him on a riding lawnmower in the music video. "Honky Tonk Song" was yet another flop, probably because Vince Gill's "One More Last Chance" already hit #1 just a few years earlier with a blatant reference to the exact same Drunk George Jones story in the lyrics. Vince even got Jones to do a cameo on a riding mower in the music video. By the time Jones tried to exploit his story for himself everyone had already seen it.

At that point it seems MCA concluded the same thing as Epic: spending time and resources to promote George Jones records was a futile waste. None of his following three solo singles entered the charts at all. By the time Patty Loveless released her cut of Jim Lauderdale's "You Don't Seem to Miss Me" as a single in 1997, vinyl 45s had been replaced by compact discs, which gave her record label more space to print her name in large script and hide "with special guest George Jones" in a tiny font underneath. His "appearance" in the music video was limited to a brief shot of a George Jones concert poster when his voice is first heard. With Jones only singing harmony, the song slipped through a crack in the brick wall separating him from country radio. The single hit #14 and won a CMA award for Vocal Event of the Year.

In 1998, Jones released his final album for MCA, *It Don't Get Any Better Than This*. His voice was still holding up very well but most of the album sounds like neither he nor anyone involved cared enough to do more than go through the motions to create what they knew would be another bomb. Producer Norro Wilson claimed to be able to tell when Jones didn't like a song by the way he'd suck on his teeth, which was the same thing Tammy Wynette said Jones would do when he felt like going off and getting drunk. There was undoubtedly a lot of teeth sucking in these sessions. The first three tracks may have been written by Bobby Braddock, but they are easily three of his worst songs and the writing rarely gets better at any point on the LP. The album's high point is the title track, on which Jones sounds like he's at least managing to have a little fun in the studio with guests Waylon Jennings, Merle Haggard, Willie Nelson, Bobby Bare and Johnny Counterfit (a Johnny Cash impersonator). MCA didn't bother shipping it as a single but "It Don't Get Any Better Than This" was used as the theme song for Jones' country music talk show, which also began airing on TV in 1998.

Both Jones and Tammy Wynette used fake living room sets for their talk shows. But where Tammy took a more typical approach, interviewing guests one at a time between musical performances with everything done before a studio audience, Jones' stage fright required a closed set with no audience at all and the guests all hanging out together at once for a more freewheeling conversation, interspersed with impromptu singalongs and group commentary when video clips were shown of each guest. Promotional musical performances were then filmed separately in front of a crowd and edited in later. The whole thing came off as intended, like a series of casual hangout sessions with George Jones and his famous friends. It was successful enough to get picked up for a second season, proving Jones was still a hit with audiences if given a chance to be in front of one.

◇　◇　◇

When Tammy Wynette died in 1998, Jones and Nancy helped with the funeral plans in every way they were allowed. By all accounts Tammy's death hit Jones hard. After sitting through Richey's horrific play-acting at the Ryman memorial, Jones got on a rented tour bus with Nancy and asked the driver to chauffeur them around aimlessly for hours, like those dark all-night rides he used to take alone, minus the pills and whiskey and guns, but still trying to escape . . . something.

Almost exactly a year after Tammy died, Jones accidentally drove his Lexus SUV into a concrete bridge abutment at highway speed, totaling the vehicle, puncturing a lung and tearing his liver. He wasn't wearing a seat belt when he crashed and it took two hours to extract his body from the wreck. Initial reports stated alcohol was not a factor in the accident but, five days later, investigators disclosed they had found a half-empty pint of vodka in the car. Turns out, Jones was drunk-driving at approximately one-thirty in the afternoon, trying to talk on his cell phone while listening to rough mixes from his latest recording sessions on the way home. He plea-bargained his way to a $550 fine and a mandatory alcohol treatment program. When Jones claimed in his autobiography a few years earlier that he was able to casually enjoy wine or beer without drinking to excess, many people took him at his word. Then news broke of this drunk-driving accident and everybody realized they'd perhaps been right to wonder if George Jones was slurring his words a little more than usual in concert, on record, during TV appearances or in dog food commercials over the past fifteen years or so. Two months after the wreck, he released his next single.

"Choices," written by Billy Yates and Mike Curtis, was one of the songs Jones had on the tape in his SUV that day and the final song to become synonymous with his name while he was alive. The lyrics have him recognize it is ultimately he who would need to take responsibility for all the wrong done in his life, all of the bad decisions made in spite of all the good people who tried to guide him toward a better path. Released in the summer of '99, immediately after the DUI accident, country radio stations were flooded with phone calls from listeners requesting "Choices." Many still refused because George Jones was too old, but some stations did relent and play the record, allowing it to become his first in over five years to break into the Top 40 Country singles. The CMAs nominated "Choices" for Single of the Year. George was supposed to perform it on the award show telecast but the producers asked if he could do an abbreviated version to take up less time. Feeling disrespected, Jones refused to play or attend the awards at all. On the live broadcast, in the middle of Alan Jackson's scheduled performance of "Pop a Top," instead of coming back into the song after a lead break, he and his band finished with a chorus of "Choices." Many in the audience knew what Alan had done and why and gave him a standing ovation. Rather than smile and wave for the applause, Alan turned around and walked off the stage with his guitar as soon as he was done singing. Speaking later about the award show's treatment of George Jones, Ricky Skaggs said, "Country music doesn't honor its elders." "Choices" didn't win that CMA award but, five months later, it did win a Grammy for Best Male Country Vocal Performance and eventually sold enough copies to go gold as the biggest single from *Cold Hard Truth*, Jones' only studio LP for Asylum Records.

Asylum was the first Nashville label run by women: Evelyn Shriver, once Randy Travis' publicist, and Susan Nadler, once Tammy Wynette's publicist. These two, along with Alan Jackson's producer, Keith Stegall, comprised the team that got George excited again about going in the studio to make great country music for its own sake, radio stations be damned. *Cold Hard Truth* was his best album in years. You can hear in his voice how emotionally and creatively invested he was in the performance of every song. Even the up-tempo numbers, such as "Ain't Love a Lot Like That," are all much better than the novelty territory he'd recently explored. The arrangement on torch song "This Wanting You" reaches way back to the old-school with Pig Robbins' piano weaving throughout the first half of a verse, then giving way to Stuart Duncan's fiddle. No other single broke through the way "Choices" did, but that one hit and all the surrounding publicity drove the album to chart at #5, his first Top 10 LP since 1986.

After spending nearly two decades pretending his alcoholism lay entirely in the past, the very wreck that revealed the lie was also what made it easier to believe George when he swore he'd finally been scared straight, no longer taking even sips of beer or wine. Still, his image and persona could never be separated from how much of his life was spent in a bottle. When video screen backdrops at concerts became the hot new thing, nobody ever doubted Jones' slideshow scrapbook would include his roadside DUI arrest footage from 1982, which it did, along with references to many other famous Drunk George Jones stories.

Since no good deed in the music industry goes unpunished, Asylum folded soon after the success of *Cold Hard Truth*. Evelyn and Susan formed Bandit Records and took Jones over there, where he stayed for the rest of his life. From the title track of the first Bandit LP, *The Rock: Stone Cold Country 2001*, you'd never know this seventy-year-old man had punctured a lung in a car accident two years prior. Here, again, the strength of the project is Jones' renewed interest in the process from being given the freedom to record whatever he wanted, like "I Am," without major label pressure to cater to radio or fit into any other kind of new mold.

Within a couple years of moving from Asylum to Bandit, his voice began to give out. Or, really, it was his lungs. In the remaining years of his life, George canceled concerts and entire tours with increased frequency as a result of upper respiratory problems and chronic emphysema. Though Jones was never very politically aware, let alone politically active (other than the brief George Wallace association in the 1970s, which, again, was almost certainly orchestrated by Tammy Wynette), it seems he underwent some kind of transformation in that area toward the end. In 2004, he recorded a campaign ad endorsing Democrat Wesley Clark, saying, "Wes Clark knows what it means to put his life and career on the line for this country and he'll put the nation's interests first—not the Washington special interests." Similar to Tammy upon recognizing death was drawing near, George also returned to God. According to witnesses, the first thing he did when he woke up in the hospital three days after the SUV accident was start singing gospel songs. In 2002, Nancy convinced Billy Sherrill to come out of retirement and produce a double CD of gospel music for George. Released in 2003, *The Gospel Collection* presented the first studio evidence of him losing his voice for good. Despite that, listening to such an accomplished sinner put every ounce of his weakening voice into "Amazing Grace" is still enough to inspire goose bumps. From here to the end, most of what he recorded is heartbreaking to listen to, not because it's bad but because he no longer possessed the range, strength, laser-specific pitch control or velvety tone nobody could ever forget they heard come from that mouth.

On 2005's *Hits I Missed . . . And One I Didn't*, a pointless rerecording of his most famous hit ever ("He Stopped Loving Her Today") was packaged with newly recorded versions of songs he was pitched and didn't cut only to watch them become megahits for the artists who did, like when Alan Jackson took "Here in the Real World" after Jones passed on it. In 2006, Jones and Merle Haggard reunited for *Kickin' Out the Footlights . . . Again*, on which each singer did a few of the other's hits along with some duets. Haggard's voice was still at least 90 percent intact and it's awesome to hear his take on some of the Jones classics, like "Things Have Gone to Pieces." George's solo tracks are poignant for entirely different reasons. On "Sing Me Back Home" it truly sounds as if he doesn't have very far left to go in life. George's final single, recorded the same month as the Haggard project, was one last duet with his daughter Georgette. "You and Me and Time" is about the renewed connection between a now-grown child and their celebrity musician parent who was always gone. The song came out on a collection of unreleased duet recordings pulled from as far back as the '70s, packaged and released in 2008. It was his final LP to be released while he was alive.

◇   ◇   ◇

Most of George's friends were gone. Waylon Jennings died in 2002. When Johnny PayCheck died in 2003, his financial situation wasn't great, so George helped with the cost of the funeral and even donated a spot for PayCheck to be buried right next to George. You can find them near each other in Woodlawn Memorial Park in Nashville. June Carter Cash died three months after PayCheck and was followed by Johnny Cash another four months later. When Don Pierce of Starday Records died in 2005, George served as a pallbearer at the funeral. Buck Owens died in 2006. George sang at Porter Wagoner's Ryman memorial in 2007. There were some old-timers still around, so he wasn't exactly the last man standing but he knew he was one of the last.

As far back as *The Bradley Barn Sessions* in 1994, George talked about how he'd sing until he died as long as people still wanted to listen to him. True to his word, he toured right up until the end. The fans kept buying tickets long after his voice became a phantom of what it once was, because he was a living legend, because he still went out there to do the best he could every night the doctors would let him. In March of 2012, George was forced to cancel all his scheduled dates due to an upper respiratory tract infection. In May, he checked into a hospital for further breathing problems and was only released under the condition he stop mowing the lawn himself, since his lungs could no longer handle what had always been one of his favorite pastimes. August brought the announcement of the Final Grand Tour, his big farewell and the last opportunity for fans to come see him in concert. George struggled to get through most of the tour and several dates were canceled. On April 6, 2013, he walked offstage, knowing the difficult performance he'd just given would be his last. He went home to spend time with Nancy.

Fewer than two weeks later, trying to draw breath into his lungs caused George so much pain that Nancy called an ambulance to take them to the hospital, where George asked if he was dying.

When the doctors said he was, he requested pain meds and a preacher. George told Nancy there wasn't any need for her to cry because he'd lived eighty-one years, paid for all the years he'd messed up and was now going to heaven. He fell into a coma. Nancy wasn't sure if he'd wake up again but wanted to be there in case he did, so she stayed by his side. Days later, she heard him say something like "Hiya. I've been looking for you. I'm George Jones." Then, he died.

TWENTY-NINE

FOR THE ROSES

O Rose thou art sick,
The invisible worm,
That flies in the night
In the howling storm:

Has found out thy bed
Of crimson joy:
And his dark secret love
Does thy life destroy.
                                        —William Blake

"The Sick Rose," from William Blake's *Songs of Innocence* collection in 1789, is deceptively simple and, thus, open to infinite interpretations. Many who've studied Blake tend to view it as a piece about the futility of projecting imaginary ideals onto life in the natural world. Any individual "rose" we choose to fixate upon as a perfect example of beauty in the physical world can only serve that symbolic function for so long before time and entropy reveal the true state of things. It's nearly certain Blake did intend to draw attention to that idea, since each stanza of the poem contains the same number of words in its corresponding lines—five, three, five, four—but the pattern of syllables in each line is not mirrored between stanzas, creating asymmetrical, lopsided verses only revealed by close inspection. It's also fairly certain Blake knew most readers would believe this poem was about a rose becoming diseased and destroyed by a worm. But William Blake did not write this poem for most readers. He wrote it for those who could grasp the mystic theology running through his entire body of work, where ideals are more important than the material world and the concept of a rose, unlike any individual rose, lives forever.

In Blake's theology what is commonly called the human imagination is literally Christ within. He once wrote, "All Things are comprehended in their Eternal Forms in the divine body of the

Saviour, the True Vine of Eternity, The Human Imagination." With that in mind, revisit the title of "The Sick Rose." It could just as easily be a statement about The Sick becoming healed and rising again. If "rose" is a verb and not a noun, then this is a poem about resurrection, not death. Some versions of Blake's accompanying illustration for the poem depict part of a caterpillar, no ordinary worm, burrowing into a rose blossom that, though hanging from a weak-looking plant, appears lovely and in full bloom, not sick at all. There are tiny humanoid figures upon the sickly green stalks, and they do seem similarly frail, but there's a woman emerging from the vibrant rose blossom who looks ecstatic, happy as a butterfly. So, does the worm's dark secret destroy the life of the rose? Or does the rose's life destroy the dark secret of the worm?

◇   ◇   ◇

All deciduous perennial flowers are suitable for allegories of beauty and life commingling with pain or death, but very few have been used for such purposes so often as the rose.

◇   ◇   ◇

A common alternate title for the murder ballad "Down in the Willow Garden" is "Rose Conley," after the murder victim in the song. Though not directly stated, the lyrics imply Rose has become pregnant with the narrator's child, which would be a great reason for him to make good on past promises to marry her, except his father has already voiced displeasure toward the relationship. In fact, the father has gone so far as to suggest the narrator would be better off to kill Rose and rely on the family's wealth to keep him out of serious trouble. It's therefore reasonable to assume Rose does not come from a similarly wealthy background, which is probably what the father doesn't like about her. All things considered, despite his love for her, the narrator decides to please his father by poisoning Rose, stabbing her, then throwing her in a river to drown. Only, it turns out his father was wrong to trust the family's money as a shield. The song ends with the narrator being caught and hung from the gallows.

◇   ◇   ◇

In one version of a story from Greek mythology, the beautiful Adonis was attacked by a wild boar, secretly the war god, Ares, in disguise, jealous over how much time Adonis spent with Ares' lover Aphrodite. As Adonis lay dying, white roses sprung from the ground touched by his blood. When Aphrodite learned of the attack she ran to the scene, paying no mind to the cuts received on her bare feet and lower legs while rushing through untamed thicket. But she arrived too late and all she could do was weep over Adonis' body, the blood from her feet and legs falling onto the white rose blossoms and turning them red, which is how red roses came to exist.

On the island of Rhodes they minted coin money with the head of sun god Helios upon one side and, upon the other, a rose, the symbol of Helios' lover Rhode, who was the island's patron nymph, sometimes said to be the daughter of Aphrodite by Poseidon. The story goes Helios witnessed Aphrodite being unfaithful to Poseidon and announced his attention to tell everyone, at which point Aphrodite cursed Helios, causing him to fall in love with a human woman and forget about poor Rhode, who hadn't done anything wrong.

In *The Iliad*, Homer wrote of Aphrodite washing the slain Hector's corpse with rose oil to prepare him for embalming. Ancient Greeks really did use rose oil and rosewater for such purposes but, distillation not yet being discovered, they made these solutions by steeping rose petals in oil or water. Since this process required a massive volume of rose blossoms to produce liquid with a potent fragrance, only the wealthiest members of any given Greek city-state could afford such infusions. Still, those who were able gladly paid the price because the mere scent of roses was believed to ward off disease. The "dog rose" is so named because Greeks believed its roots could be used to cure the symptoms of a bite from a rabid dog. Red roses were used in so many different medicinal concoctions they comprised an entire category of medicine, called "diarrhodon."

◇　◇　◇

Romans became obsessed with emulating the Greeks right around the time Alexander the Great established the second-largest empire that had ever existed by conquering most of the largest, the First Persian Empire. Though Alexander then died young and his Macedonian Empire was split through civil wars between the generals of his army, the next several centuries of history in this corner of the world are known as the Hellenistic period because of how strongly the culture of Ancient Greeks (or Hellenes) influenced other Mediterranean peoples. That influence has often been portrayed as some innate superiority of Greek culture over inferior ways of life but this is an extremely naive interpretation of events. For at least a few hundred years prior to the age of Alexander, Greeks had been in contact with and influenced by Egyptian society. Setting aside the architectural achievements of the pyramids, Egyptians spent thousands of years planting sophisticated gardens to grow plants for food, medicine, religious rites and aesthetic beauty before the Greeks came along with relatively primitive orchards. It's not possible to argue Greek society was so influential because it was simply superior. What happened was Greek currencies, bloodlines and social connections became more highly valued in regions where Alexander the Great established Greeks as the ruling class.

Near the end of the fourth century BC, after Alexander's death, one of his old generals, named Ptolemy, defeated rivals to become pharaoh of Egypt. Since Egyptian locals had always resisted Persian rule, they regarded both Alexander and Ptolemy as saviors. Neither Greek warrior wished to undermine that love, so they never attempted to eradicate and replace local customs or religions. Alexander was known to adopt local fashions and participate in religious rites of the lands he conquered in order to ingratiate himself to ordinary citizens, which is what he did in Egypt. As pharaoh, Ptolemy followed suit, going so far as to push his heirs to adopt the Egyptian custom of marrying their siblings. Thus, it went for nearly 250 years until the last of the Ptolemaic pharaohs, Cleopatra, who was the only ruler of the dynasty in those hundreds of years who ever even bothered to learn the local language rather than continue to speak Greek. Says a lot about who the ruling class believed should be included in the conversation during the Hellenistic period, no? The priorities of non-Greeks hoping to climb the social ladder in territories conquered by Alexander adjusted accordingly.

In the third and second centuries BC, a conservative senator in the Roman Republic named Cato the Elder railed against what he perceived as Rome's best citizens abandoning their own cultural identity in order to try to live as though they were Greek elites. To Cato, it seemed like as soon as Romans of any means and status learned about some custom of wealthy Greeks, they not only replicated the custom but engaged in its furthest extreme. Take the fascination with roses. Because the Greeks had long used roses in medicine and perfume, wealthy citizens of Rome all strove to keep private rose gardens in their homes. Those who couldn't keep a garden for whatever reason spent small fortunes to stay in steady supply of fresh roses. It was to the point where Roman women used roses like some kind of currency. You couldn't go to a dinner at someone's house without being served some dish containing rosewater, rose petals or rose hips. The thing that bothered Cato the most, though, was the wreaths. He had no issue with the way Greeks fashioned the branches of olive or laurel trees into wreaths for crowning champions of prestigious athletic events or monumentally important battles, nor the way they used the same wreaths to commend great artists or philosophers. The problem was every Roman man hoping to look like a big shot now viewed the wreath ceremony as the achievement itself rather than a recognition of extraordinary achievement. Worse, Cato's peers freely granted unremarkable men permission to wear the wreaths, adorned with roses even, probably hoping to have one bestowed upon themselves in the near future. Cato attempted to do away with such self-indulgence by petitioning to reduce the number of knights and senators in Rome, then campaigned for sumptuary laws to limit the number of people in attendance at any given party, to limit the amount of wealth that could be accumulated by women, to limit the various extravagant fashions worn by all Roman citizens. He probably would have lost his mind if he lived through the turn of the millennium to witness Rome become an empire and the Rosalia become one of its most popular types of festival.

A Rosalia was not necessarily the drunken Bacchanalia influenced by Greek Dionysian orgies, but it was also typically not a sober affair. Rosalias were usually held in honor of various gods, military leaders, important figures, dead family members or any person rich enough to establish a fund for the sole purpose of ensuring a Rosalia was thrown in their memory once a year. Most of the budget for a Rosalia went toward the wine and the roses consumed and worn by guests.

In the first century, Roman emperor Nero began suspending thousands and thousands of rose petals from the ceiling of his banquet hall in order to then shower them down upon guests at the beginning of a feast, establishing a tradition which persisted for hundreds of years. In the third century, teenage emperor Elagabalus supposedly dropped three times an ordinary amount of rose petals from his banquet hall's ceiling and accidentally suffocated many attendees of a feast. Raining roses down upon these parties was obviously intended as a display of unrepentant decadence but that's not all it was. Centuries earlier, when Greeks ruled Egypt without caring to learn its language, they misunderstood depictions of the child form of sun god Horus to be holding his finger over closed lips in the gesture Greeks (but not Egyptians) thought of as the signal we still use for covertly telling another person to be quiet. For that reason, Greeks adopted Horus as their own god of silence and secrecy, though they called him "Harpocrates" because that's what it sounded like the Egyptians said when discussing the child form of Horus. From there, Harpocrates was plugged into existing Greek mythology. In one version of one story, Aphrodite gave a beautiful rose to Eros, her son with Ares. When Harpocrates later witnessed Aphrodite sleeping with someone other than Ares, young Eros gave the rose to Harpocrates as a bribe to stay silent on his mother's affair. Centuries later, when roses were dropped from (or painted or sculpted on) the ceilings of Roman banquet halls, it was a reminder the party took place *sub rosa*, that is "beneath the rose." Nothing said or done beneath the rose should be shared later with anyone who wasn't present.

◊   ◊   ◊

Umberto Eco's first novel, *The Name of the Rose*, is a postmodern mystery which rejects the genre cliché of tidily wrapping up the plot by revealing the hidden logical forces behind initially confusing events. He once said he chose the title because "the rose is a symbolic figure so rich in meaning that by now it hardly has any meaning left." Being a professor of semiotics, Eco's view of the rose was likely colored by study of floriography, the so-called secret language of flowers, which became one of the biggest fads of the nineteenth century in Europe and the United States.

When socialites in Romantic-era England found out about the popularity of recently published "flower language" dictionaries in France, they rushed to local bookshops in order to learn what type, color and number of flowers should be sent to communicate fun coded messages to friends, family, lovers, etc. The trend quickly spread to the rest of the Western world and book publishers couldn't print floriography dictionaries fast enough. They flooded the market with books on the subject and, whether from trying to create products that were different than all the rest or trying to skip over researching actual history in order to quickly throw together some nonsense as a cash grab, there became a library of floriography books which ascribed many conflicting meanings to the same flowers. This fad persisted until nearly the 1900s, during which time "flower talkers" needed to be sure they were using the exact same floriography dictionaries as whoever was on the other end of a conversation or there'd be no hope of understanding one another, due to the varied definitions from book to book. That is one reason why trying to research the symbolic importance of, say, a white rose now turns up just about any imaginable interpretation, the situation Umberto Eco was describing when he said the rose has too many meanings to mean much of anything at all.

But if the influence of a brief floriography craze could somehow be erased from history, we'd be left with the core ideas surrounding roses, ideas which have lasted for thousands of years, only receiving minor alterations/additions when incorporated to a newly dominant culture. Ancient Greeks wore rose oil as perfume and threw rose petals at victorious athletes and great performers. Rose oil is still one of the most common scents in perfumery, prominent in some of the most popular perfumes of all time, including Chanel No. 5. The winning horse and rider of the Kentucky Derby are still draped in a blanket of hundreds of rose blossoms when they enter the Winner's Circle. Matadors who give an especially crowd-pleasing performance still have roses thrown to them in the bullring.

◇　　◇　　◇

The Latin word used to refer to a rose garden in the home of a wealthy Roman was *rosarium*, the source word for the collection of prayers which came to be called the Rosary in Roman Catholicism. Some early Christians objected to that word being used in reference to these prayers (and, later, the associated string of beads) because they felt "Rosary" called to mind the Rosalias thrown in honor of various Roman gods. Such objections were ignored and Christianity inherited the symbol of the rose, much the same as Romans previously inherited it from the Greeks. The roses carved into the wood of many Catholic confessional booths are a reference to the Roman *sub rosa* policy of secrecy. The five-petaled rose in Christian art is often a representation of the wounds Christ received in crucifixion, prior to the resurrection, when he "rose" again. The Luther rose was developed by Martin Luther for use by him and his followers as a symbol of Lutheran theology. He specified the insignia should contain a black cross at the center to represent pain and suffering; placed inside a red heart to represent salvation through faith in the Crucified; placed inside a rose which should be white because white is the color of the spirits and angels that bring us joy, comfort and peace not found in the material world; placed inside a field of blue to represent a heavenly tomorrow; placed inside a golden ring to represent eternity.

Valentine's Day began as a Roman Catholic holiday, a feast thrown in honor of one or two third century Christian martyrs named Valentine. It had nothing to do with flowers as displays of love and affection until that association was fabricated wholesale during the New Age of Chivalry in the fourteenth and fifteenth centuries. Perhaps the most popular chivalric text of the fourteenth century was titled *The Romance of the Rose*, an allegoric (and vulgar) commentary on dating in the era of courtly love. It's important to recognize the word "romance" in this title was not in any way a reference to love. At the time it came out, everyone would have understood *The Romance of the Rose* to mean "A Story of the Rose, Written in a Language Descended from That of the Romans." That's what the word "romance" originally meant, until fantastic stories of knights and magic and chivalric love became the only thing most people wanted to read in that language for two or three centuries, which is what led to modern usage of the term "romantic" when describing such passionate themes.

While the association of roses with love and tragedy dates back at least as far as Aphrodite, no single storyteller ever used this device to greater impact than William Shakespeare. Just the word "flower" appears more than one hundred times throughout his body of work. There are several instances of his characters explicitly stating the symbolic importance of various flowers used or referenced in a scene, like in *Hamlet*, when a grieving Ophelia finally loses her mind and breaks into song while handing out flowers with explanations of their meaning. Shakespeare must have regarded the rose as especially significant because it alone is mentioned more than seventy times throughout his work, from his early comedy and history plays to the great tragedies that came later. Perhaps the most famous lines in the history of theater, aside from *Hamlet*'s "to be, or not to be" monologue, are *Romeo & Juliet*'s "What's in a name? That which we call a 'rose' by any other word would smell as sweet." And it's only fitting because a theater named the Rose was probably the first to stage a production of any William Shakespeare play, which was probably part of his *Henry VI* trilogy. These days, most people describe *Henry VI* (along with Shakespeare's *Richard III*) as an epic series about the Wars of the Roses. But nobody would have described these plays that way when they came out. The Wars of the Roses were not called that at the end of the sixteenth century.

When the real Henry VI, of England's House of Lancaster, became regarded as a weak-minded and weak-willed king, it led to thirty years of civil war over his throne, fought primarily against an ambitious rival branch of the Lancaster family, the House of York. In the end every legitimate male heir of both houses died, leaving Henry Tudor with a claim that his mother being descended from a Lancaster born out of wedlock meant England's crown was his by right, so long as he killed Richard III in battle, which he then promptly did. As Henry VII, Tudor married his third cousin, a princess from the House of York, which made her the Queen of England and their male children heirs to Henry's newly founded House of Tudor. To symbolize this union between two houses previously at war, Henry created the Tudor Rose by placing the white rose used as an emblem of the House of York atop the red rose used as an emblem of the House of Lancaster. It's a historical fact the Lancasters had truly almost never used a rose in their heraldry and when they did the rose was usually gold, not red. But Henry knew what he was doing, creating a memorable and meaningful symbol for the new House of Tudor. His own claim to the throne hinged upon the notion he was born a Lancaster, so Henry VII did not actually use the new Tudor Rose during his reign. He instead sealed letters and rode under the banner of the red rose he needed everyone to believe Lancasters had used for centuries, so when his son took the throne as Henry VIII and started using the Tudor Rose it told a symbolic story to the people of England.

William Shakespeare was happy to carry on the storytelling tradition. For *Henry VI* he fabricated a scene where noblemen in a church rosarium revealed their allegiance to either House York or House Lancaster in a coming war by selecting a white or red rose, respectively. We know this was the specific scene Sir Walter Scott had in mind when he referred to "the wars of the White and Red Roses," soon shortened through subsequent popular usage to the "Wars of the Roses," because the title page of that 1829 installment of Scott's *Waverley* novels included a quote from Shakespeare's *Henry VI*. Though he attracted hordes of theatergoers in London and was extremely popular with commoners, Shakespeare was not widely regarded by the highbrow critics of his time as a creative genius or even particularly influential. The critical reevaluation of Shakespeare's work only began in the eighteenth century. By the time Sir Walter Scott was quoting him on title pages, consensus had formed that Shakespeare was the greatest playwright in the history of the English language. His rampant use of flowers as symbols helped set the stage for the popularity of floriography during the nineteenth century, which muddied the "language of flowers" forever.

◇   ◇   ◇

But perhaps the rose is still as sick as it ever was. In the mid-1960s Tom Stoppard's *Rosencrantz and Guildenstern Are Dead* debuted in London. Stoppard's play positioned two minor roles from *Hamlet* as main characters. We see what they might have gotten up to while offstage in Shakespeare's tragedy, which it turns out is much hilarious argument and confusion over the events of *Hamlet*, an inability to remember anything prior to Act I (or, indeed, which of them is Rosencrantz and which is Guildenstern), plus all around failing to recognize the mounting evidence they are, in fact, fictional characters in a play. Especially as performed by Gary Oldman in the film adaptation, Stoppard's Rosencrantz (whose name means "rose wreath") was particularly childlike, confounded whenever Hamlet said things such as "there is nothing either good or bad, but thinking makes it so." Rosencrantz was curious enough about the world to often nearly discover some law of physics or an absurdly impossible instance of his reality failing to obey such laws. Still, he somehow never seems to fully understand much of anything, which makes it a bit more heartbreaking when he joins the more violent and angry Guildenstern in fulfilling the promise of the play's title.

As the plot of *Rosemary's Baby* is fundamentally an inverse of the Immaculate Conception— what's the worst thing that could happen to a woman who wasn't born without sin?—the name of Ira Levin's title character was probably not a reference to the herb rosemary but rather a combination of the names Rose and Mary. Years before becoming the recipient of Rosary prayers, the Virgin Mary had long been associated with roses in Roman Catholic imagery and writings. This was yet another remnant of the Rosalia, since many of those Roman festivals allowed only women who were virgins to wear rose wreaths. Like everything else about Roman Polanski's film adaptation of *Rosemary's Baby*, all of these associations only became more disturbing through several conversational and visual references to roses, including a nightmare-inducing scene that features a rose print on a bare mattress.

◇　◇　◇

One of the folk tales collected by the Grimm Brothers at the beginning of the nineteenth century was published as *The Rose*. In this tale a poor woman lives by the woods with her two children. It's the youngest child's job to go out into the forest every day and bring back wood for use in the family's fire. One day, the young child needs to go much farther than usual to find enough wood and dreads the thought of walking all the way home carrying such weight when another kid mysteriously shows up out of nowhere offering to help. The first child isn't sure what to do until the stranger offers the gift of a single rose, still so young it hasn't bloomed. The stranger says to take the rose home, put it in water and when the bud opens into full bloom then the stranger will come visit again. The child accepts the rose and the stranger's help in carrying the wood back home. After easily making the return trip together, the child turns to thank the stranger and is surprised to find nobody there. Upon being told this story, the mother believes the mysterious stranger is a figment of her child's imagination, even after the child presents the rose as evidence. But the mother still places the rose in some water as requested. A few days later, when her child doesn't get out of bed at the usual time, the mother checks and finds her youngest is dead. The rose on the table by the child's bed is in full bloom.

◇　◇　◇

O, Rose, thou art sick . . .

THIRTY

BABY BOY

◇ The Jones Family's Great Depression ◇ A New Guitar in the City ◇
From Church to the Barroom ◇ Hero Worship ◇ Jail Time ◇ A Singing Marine ◇

The following events took place in an area of east Texas known as the Big Thicket, a region covering the spectrum of ecosystems from swampland shared with Louisiana on the state's eastern border through densely wooded forests and, eventually, as one travels farther west, some prairie lands. However, for most of human history, the Big Thicket wasn't an area anyone did much traveling through at all. Most often, people chose to go around it because of both the difficult terrain and the castoffs of society who had no choice but to call such an unwelcoming place their home. The Thicket was where bandits and murderers hid from consequences. The Thicket was where the poorest of folk were driven by dire economic circumstances to perform dangerous work and scratch out whatever life they could from the land.

As is sometimes the case with such impoverished places, folklorists and faux historians invented their own versions of the Big Thicket, describing the area and its culture with all manner of lie and legend, usually combining garden variety classism with a fetish for outlaws. Thus, many people who lived outside the Thicket came to think of its residents as a bunch of uneducated deviants living by some backwards but locally codified sense of thieving trickster's honor, similar to the Court of Miracles in Victor Hugo's *The Hunchback of Notre Dame*. In truth, the only lives and people to be found in the Big Thicket were hard and made harder by hard times.

◇   ◇   ◇

The Jones family first came to Texas from Alabama in the early 1800s. Nearly a hundred years later, George Washington Jones' mother was only fourteen years old and knew she was pregnant when she decided to leave her husband. After the baby was born in 1895, she gave him to her own parents to raise and resumed her dedication to drinking. From his first job at the age of eleven, working as the water boy in a sawmill, all George ever knew was getting by however he could. As he grew older, that often meant hard labor in the logging trade. He developed into an ox of a man with a lumberjack's muscles stacked over six feet tall. When George wasn't working he drank and danced his worries away. His own musical abilities were limited to hammering out a few chords on guitar and blowing a little harmonica. By all accounts his singing voice was no smoother than sandpaper.

The Patterson family came to Texas by way of Mississippi. Clara Patterson's father, a deeply religious man, built a small country church where he served as deacon. All his children were taught to worship the Lord through song. He was devastated when, in 1915, his twenty-year-old daughter Clara eloped with George Washington Jones, a hard-partying, no-account hand at a local sawmill. It's unclear whether marrying Clara was enough to inspire a change in George's lifestyle or if that change came three years later, as a result of the birth of their first child, a girl named Ethel. Either way, George reined in his drinking and stepped up to become the father of a family that continued to grow one or two children at a time over the next fifteen years.

Most of the honest (and dishonest) labor in the Big Thicket came from the timber and oil industries. Anyone who didn't work near a saw or an oil rig probably provided some kind of service to (or stole from) the people who did. George supported his family by taking any job he could find, often at least two at a time, supplemented with various random gigs on the side. He could work on cars, so he was sometimes paid to do that. He built all his own family's furniture by hand, so other families sometimes paid him to build theirs. Life in the Thicket had taught him enough about patching up a human body that the local doctor sometimes called when he needed assistance with a patient. Clara fashioned their children's clothing from used flour sacks. She used to play piano in her father's church and, like all Pattersons, sang in a voice the neighbors found pleasant, some would even say beautiful. Clara sang to all her children until they began singing back and George loved to listen to his family sing. In the Thicket music was free entertainment, so long as you could make it yourself. Nothing else came as easily but the family got by alright.

Then, in 1926, the Jones family's five children began passing around malaria between themselves. The eldest, Ethel, was eight years old when she caught the fever and died. All the family loved Ethel dearly and everyone old enough to understand death was traumatized by hers, but George never came close to recovering from the loss of his first child. He was soon drinking again and not like before, when he drank for fun. This was drinking to forget, drinking to place a layer of insulation between his consciousness and his memories. Since the rest of the family's survival depended on him, George still worked through the week, only now with white knuckles. Every payday Clara needed to meet George at the village store to take enough of his money that she could pay off enough of their tab for the family to be given more groceries on credit to survive the next week. If Clara didn't get the money before George made it to the local saloon, there wouldn't be any money left when he came home drunk, however many days later that was. And George never came home happy again. During the workweek, he'd walk in sober and a little sad but still treat his family with kindness. When he came home on the weekend, which he'd sometimes turn into a four-day thing, he'd be drunk, easily angered and physically abusive. George threw things, broke things, hit Clara, hit their children. The kids often wished their mother would just be quiet instead of criticizing and shaming George for coming in drunk because that only seemed to make him angrier. It's unclear whether Clara simply couldn't keep herself from yelling at her husband or she did it to make sure he focused his wrath on her before there was a chance to become upset with one of the kids. Sometimes George's rage was so explosively violent that Clara became too scared to stay in the house and took at least the youngest children to stay with the nearest neighbors.

When the Great Depression hit in the late 1920s, George lost his primary job delivering huge bricks of ice from a local icehouse to customers in the area, nearly all of whom instantly disappeared, along with most of the honest work. He soon resorted to sneaking on to land owned by timber companies, sawing down trees in the middle of the night and dragging them back home in the dark to turn a profit selling whatever furniture or useful goods could be made from the poached lumber. George was also known to own a working still, should anyone need to buy or make some moonshine liquor.

◇　◇　◇

In 1931, George and Clara had their last child, George Glenn Jones. The baby weighed a whopping twelve pounds at birth, which all his family agreed must have contributed to the arm bone fracture he suffered during delivery, though some say the break happened when the backwoods doctor tried pulling the huge infant out of Clara and others say the surprising weight made the doctor drop the baby on the floor. Either way, he entered this world the already-broken youngest son of George and Clara Jones. With two Georges now in the house, everyone took to calling the baby George Glenn or, more often, just Glenn.

The other kids adored their baby brother and helped take care of him, but nobody doted on Glenn like Clara, who favored the infant as though she already knew—after birthing eight children, including two sets of twins—this would be her last, forever the baby of the family. She sang to Glenn all the time. The first song Clara got the sense her baby enjoyed was a folk ballad called "Billy Boy," in which a young man responds to questions of where he's been lately by listing attributes of the girl he's courting, then regretfully admitting she's too young to marry. In a comedic twist at the end of the song, the woman is revealed to be much older than Billy, thus insinuating the entire song is a result of him foolishly believing her absurd excuses for not wanting to get married. Several sources suggest "Billy Boy" was a sanitized rewrite of a much older murder ballad, known by the titles "Lord Randall" or "Henry, My Son," in which we also glean from the young protagonist's responses that the woman he's trying to marry has mortally poisoned him. Another of little Glenn's early favorites was "Give Me the Roses While I Live," written in the 1920s by James Rowe and R. H. Cornelius, then recorded first by the Carter Family in 1933, when Glenn was barely two years old.

Many children during the Great Depression who grew up in poor communities were surrounded by extreme starvation, disease and death, all while knowing other people elsewhere in the world possessed far more than was necessary to survive. These children developed a strong distrust, sometimes even hatred, toward the wealthy of the world. Young Glenn certainly noted the effects of a lifetime of poverty upon his own father. Later in life he said, "You never would see my dad smile or laugh about anything. You could tell a joke and he'd be just as solemn."

In 1938, nearing the end of the Depression, George's job opportunities began to pick back up and the Jones family was able to buy their first radio set. While living in Saratoga the radio piped in Cajun music from KVOL in Lafayette, Louisiana, plus hillbilly and *norteño* music from XERA, a high-power station in Mexico that also broadcast many supernatural-themed talk programs with astrologers, fortune-tellers and numerologists. On Saturday nights George was likely to still be drunk or passed out on the ground somewhere far away from home and unlikely to return until at least the next day, so the rest of the family felt free to relax and enjoy the *Grand Ole Opry* on their local NBC affiliate. Bill Monroe and His Blue Grass Boys made their *Opry* debut in 1939 with a performance of Jimmie Rodgers' "Mule Skinner Blues." Though Bill Monroe quickly became one of young Glenn's favorites, he knew he was liable to get comfortable and fall asleep during the broadcast, so he gave his mother strict instructions to ensure he was awake whenever Monroe came on. The other artist Clara received such instructions for was Roy Acuff. From the time he was eight years old on, Glenn remained a fan of both artists but Roy Acuff was something bigger, a hero, an icon. Before it shut down, the George Jones Museum in Nashville held his personal collection of Roy Acuff memorabilia on proud display. It's unclear when George Washington Jones first returned home drunk, woke up his children and made them stand in a line to sing for his entertainment under threat of a beating to any child who stopped or didn't sing well enough. But one of the songs Glenn remembered singing on those occasions, which he later recorded, was Roy Acuff's gospel song "The Precious Jewel."

◇   ◇   ◇

Near the end of 1941, the family moved a little deeper into the Big Thicket, to a town named Kountze, where George worked a legitimate job in the timber industry. Clara found a new church there, the

First Gospel Tabernacle, led by a Pentecostal minister everyone called Brother Burl. Burl's wife, Sister Annie, taught the Sunday school for children Glenn's age. Glenn's favorite part of Sunday school was when Sister Annie took out her guitar to lead sing-alongs. He'd often hang around after the other children left to ask questions about music and have Annie show him how to play things on the guitar. But then his family suddenly moved away.

When Japan bombed Pearl Harbor and the United States entered World War II, it created all manner of work in the Port Arthur shipyards near Beaumont, so the Jones family moved there in early 1942. They lived in a small apartment unit in one of the Beaumont housing projects rapidly built after the war brought so many new jobs and new people to the area. As a pipe fitter in the shipyards, George made decent money, enough to buy an officially licensed Gene Autry acoustic guitar built to 3/4 scale, a manageable size for its recipient, his youngest son. Glenn at once became inseparable from the instrument. In nearly every picture of him as a young child he's holding either this or another guitar.

The year George received the Gene Autry guitar, Autry's version of "(I've Got Spurs That) Jingle Jangle Jingle" was a #12 Pop hit and sold more than a million copies. The following year Ernest Tubb joined the *Grand Ole Opry* and brought a new honky-tonk sound with him. These were still the days when many people who owned radio sets reacted to the start of a country music program by changing the station to see if anything else was on, so for everyone who missed Ernest Tubb's "Walking the Floor Over You" when it was a minor Pop hit in 1941, Al Dexter's "Pistol Packin' Mama" became the first honky-tonk country song they ever heard. "Pistol Packin' Mama" charted at #1 Country and #1 Pop in 1943 and was one of the most ubiquitous records of World War II. These jazz-inspired, backbeat-heavy songs were what country music sounded like on the radio and what Glenn tried to reproduce with his voice and Gene Autry guitar.

The family's life in Beaumont was very different from what their life had been in the Big Thicket. Not that Clara ever made her baby boy do chores, but with only a two-room apartment to keep clean, no garden or farm animals to tend, nor any need to bring up water from a well, there just weren't many chores for anyone to do. Glenn was mostly left on his own to entertain himself however he wanted. Since all he wanted to do was play guitar and sing, that's all he ever really did. Many days he even entirely blew off school to find some remote place where he could practice.

He was somewhere around eleven years old the first time he performed in public. There are different explanations for how this came to happen. According to Glenn, he was hanging around with his guitar outside an arcade, playing songs purely for his own amusement, when he looked up and saw a crowd had gathered to watch and listen, so he quit playing. When some people tossed money to him and told him to keep playing, he kept playing. Each time he finished another song and stopped for a minute, more people threw more money, so Glenn ran through every song he knew multiple times and then quit to see how much money he had. Back then, twenty-four dollars was roughly equivalent to several hundred dollars in modern money. Glenn went in the arcade and blew it all on games and candy. Telling the story many years later, he said, "I gave those pinball machines hell that day." (It would be another ten years before they ever met but it's exceedingly likely those pin games were installed in that arcade by Pappy Daily.) The only real difference between this version of the story and others is it's sometimes said George pushed his son to perform on the street that day in order to take most of the money and go get drunk. Since the whole reason the Jones family moved to Beaumont and Glenn got a guitar was because George found a better-paying job in the area, those versions are almost certainly untrue and likely a product of backdating stories from later years when George really would come around to hit up his youngest son for some drinking money. Whatever happened the first time, Glenn repeated the act and, one way or the other, the cash never made it back home to his family.

Once Glenn discovered that magic trick to pull money from the pockets of strangers he cared even less about school and his already poor track record of attendance became even worse. After repeating seventh grade, he completely dropped out. Pretty soon he was using his guitar in place of bus fare, performing songs for the driver and passengers while in transit to and from Kountze to visit Sister Annie for more guitar lessons. He'd ask her how to play different chords and, as an aspiring lead player, was also interested to know more about scales. Sister Annie remembered Glenn would come back a couple weeks later, not only playing and singing while incorporating the latest things she'd shown him but pushing beyond her most recent lesson to demonstrate additional things he'd worked out on his own. Before long Sister Annie and Brother Burl invited Glenn to sing and play lead guitar with them during church service and at special events, sometimes just posting up near a restaurant or public park to play gospel music for whoever was around.

Between the moral education he picked up on those trips to the Kountze church and the way his saintly mother always reacted to his father coming home drunk, Glenn eventually got the idea George must not be a very good person. He decided there was some type of wrong and wicked thing the old man could only keep hidden inside by not drinking. Nobody knew when that wrong and wicked thing would come crashing through the front door with a bottle in its hand, ready to terrorize the whole family. Once Glenn started to get good at playing guitar, he received most of the wrong and wicked thing's attention. Whenever George came home drunk and made the kids get out of bed to sing, he'd sit down in a chair to listen. Eventually, he would begin to pass out but the children knew they needed to keep singing because George was liable to come back awake already throwing punches if the music stopped or he heard any other unexpected noises. The only way to make a clean escape was for one kid to sneak off from the group at a time, usually by climbing out the apartment's window, since that was quieter than using the door. But little Glenn was the only one with an instrument. The lone guitar dropping out of a song would be more noticeable than one of several voices drifting off into the night. So Glenn had to stay and keep the rhythm going until he was the last kid left, then try to get out of the window without waking up the monster. There were many times he didn't make it. After years of such physical and psychological abuse, some kind of altercation between father and son caused Glenn to leave home in 1947, when he was around fifteen years old.

◇   ◇   ◇

He probably assumed money wouldn't be a problem so long as he had a guitar and a piece of sidewalk to stand on while playing it. He may even have been right about that, if he understood the first thing about how to manage money. Later in life, he said he wasn't thinking about money at all, "When I started out I had no thoughts of being a star. I didn't even have thoughts about making a decent living. I didn't care if I made a dollar. I never thought where my next meal was coming from. I was at my peak when I had my guitar in my hand and I was singing, whether I was by myself, at my house, in a club, or wherever. I was really more concerned with my own pleasure than whether or not [anyone] enjoyed my singing." For a while he lived as a vagabond, moving around between the homes of older siblings who'd already married and moved out, sleeping on whatever other couches, floors or shared mattresses his friends could provide. When he was feeling flush he'd sometimes splurge on renting a room somewhere but that went very wrong one time when a bill came due just after he'd blown all his cash. The landlord locked up Glenn's possessions as collateral and kicked him out into the street. Another aspiring teenage musician, Dalton Henderson, found out the kid who played on sidewalks in Beaumont was in a bad way and asked his parents if Glenn could come stay with them. Dalton's parents agreed and even handed over some money to get Glenn's stuff released from lockup.

Moving in with the Hendersons took Glenn right back up into the Big Thicket, near the town Jasper. Dalton had a semi-regular gig singing on morning radio and, whenever Glenn was around, he'd often guest on the show, using the airtime to plug whatever stages or street corners he had lined up for performances later in the day. This whole time he treated the Hendersons' house more like a hotel than a home, stopping by for a few days of steady meals and a place to sleep before heading out to find more pickup gigs. Not yet old enough to legally enter the roadhouses, old barns and decommissioned icehouses turned into dance halls and honky-tonks where country bands played, Glenn began sneaking in. Once inside, he'd wait for that night's band to take an intermission then he'd try to get the crowd to pay attention to him and his guitar. Sometimes they did, sometimes they didn't.

This was also the point in time when Hank Williams hit country radio harder than anyone ever had. As a voracious fan of the genre and a kid trying to make it his business to know every popular country song a local audience member may request, Glenn probably jumped on the Hank Williams bandwagon at "Move It On Over," a Top 5 Country hit in 1947. But the B-side of that record, "(Last Night) I Heard You Crying in Your Sleep," is a better example of the sound Hank introduced to popular country music by blending Ernest Tubb's brand of honky-tonk with Roy Acuff's emotional vocal delivery. Glenn couldn't afford to buy a record player or records, but he did usually have enough coins to drop in a jukebox and play a new song the few times it took him to learn it. Once his voice started to drop with puberty, he found replicating the high, lonesome sounds of Roy Acuff and Bill Monroe played hell on his throat, especially in smoke-filled honky-tonks. Hank Williams records became his instruction manual for how to bring that high, lonesome emotion down into his new natural range. By the time Hank joined the lineup of the *Louisiana Hayride* in 1948, he was Glenn's favorite singer.

When he started playing secular music in raucous, sin-filled barrooms, Glenn stopped playing gospel music with Sister Annie and Brother Burl. Almost a decade later he decided it was okay to mix the secular with the sacred and got back in touch with Brother Burl to write some of the most powerful gospel music ever recorded, like "Cup of Loneliness." But at the beginning of his career he didn't believe it was right to play before a congregation on Sunday morning after spending all of Saturday night playing in a bar. So, Glenn walked away from the church and over to the wild side of life. The first time he got drunk he was riding around in a car with Dalton Henderson and some other boys, one of whom had a bottle. After drinking too much cheap whiskey Glenn requested the vehicle be pulled over so he could throw up, which he did, while stumbling around in a cow pasture and falling down. When the highway patrol pulled up Glenn was taken to jail, drunk, covered in vomit and cow shit. But he continued to drink.

Sometimes when he drank, his personality changed so much it scared his friends. According to Dalton Henderson, if Glenn got enough alcohol in him, he was liable to try fighting anyone at the drop of a hat and it didn't matter that he was usually the smallest person in any bar. Whenever Glenn found a problem with someone, whoever it was, he'd lower his head and charge like a blind bull, the ineffective approach to combat he kept using for the rest of his life, much to the detriment of his win/loss record. Of course, alcohol cannot put such violence and rage into a person. It's got to already be there, waiting somewhere under the surface. Sober, Glenn was the kind of kid who enjoyed a good joke, whether that be winding up his friends, playing a prank or saying something just to get a rise out of someone. One time, while he was staying with the Hendersons, Dalton's father told Glenn to stop his good-natured teasing of an elderly relative and it caused Glenn to run out of the room. Seeing the boy was upset, Mrs. Henderson waited a few minutes before going to check on him in the bedroom where Glenn stayed. When she got there the lights were off, so she flicked the switch and found Glenn slamming his hands and face into a mattress, trying to get rid of his anger without losing a safe place to sleep for the night.

At some point in 1948, Glenn and a few friends were hanging around a hamburger drive-in, watching a local husband and wife country music duo who played shows under the name Eddie & Pearl. He was too shy to do it himself but a friend went up and asked Eddie & Pearl to let Glenn join them on lead guitar for a couple tunes, saying he knew every Hank Williams and Ernest Tubb song they'd already played and probably knew the next two as well. Eddie & Pearl let him come up and it must have gone well because they continued inviting him onstage whenever they saw him at shows. One day they let him take the mic to sing lead on a song, heard what he could do with his throat and asked Glenn to join the act full-time. He was about sixteen years old when they moved him into their house and began paying him $17.50 to perform on the radio five days a week, then play various burger joints and honky-tonks in the evenings. Where Glenn's father was a binge drinker, one who stayed sober through the workweek and then dropped a hammer on his consciousness over the weekend, Eddie was more of a chronic alcoholic, one who never let the fact he was at work stop him from continuing to drink. One night, after overserving himself during a show, Eddie climbed behind the wheel of their car to drive everyone home and wound up steering halfway into a small river before passing out. Pearl left Glenn to make sure Eddie didn't drown while she walked back to the bar and got someone who could tow out the car, then she drove everyone home. Just another night on the job with Eddie & Pearl.

Since the crowd response to Glenn's voice was always so strong, Eddie & Pearl gave him a segment in the show where he took over singing lead for a while. Pretty soon there were audience members reaching onstage to stuff tips directly into Glenn's pocket instead of the tip jug he shared with Eddie & Pearl. At all the drive-in burger spots, anyone who wanted to drink while listening to the band ordered sodas which they then spiked with their own alcohol brought from home. One day the owner at one of these places realized, for whatever reason, customers ordered more sodas while the teenage kid was playing his segment of Eddie & Pearl's show, so he offered Glenn a solo gig on the side and Glenn took it. In this period, he also teamed up for some shows with future Sons of the Pioneers member, Luther Nallie, who was very impressed by the depth of Glenn's country music knowledge. The kid was a walking jukebox of all the latest records from Hank Williams, Bill Monroe, Roy Acuff and Ernest Tubb, plus he seemed to know everything from before that, dating all the way back to the first hit records in the genre by Jimmie Rodgers, the Carter Family, Vernon Dalhart, you name 'em. If anyone requested it, he could even pull out pre-twentieth-century gospel and folk ballads dating back to the Old World. According to Luther, Glenn's performance style in those days was high energy. He hopped all over the stage while playing and singing. Glenn was also sure to look back with a scowl anytime Luther threw a fancy jazz chord into a country song. Even while working all these side gigs, for as long as he lived in their house, Eddie & Pearl remained Glenn's main job, which was how he came to meet his favorite singer of all time.

The first Hank Williams single of 1949 was also Hank's first #1 record, "Lovesick Blues," which came out that February and, according to play count mechanisms on jukeboxes, turned out to be the twenty-fourth most-played song of that year in any genre, not just country music. The record was so popular its B-side saw enough action to hit #6 Country, even though it was just a reissue of Hank's little-heard debut single, "Never Again (Will I Knock on Your Door)," recorded in 1946 during his first session at Castle's WSM operation in Nashville. So now Glenn's favorite country singer was everyone else's favorite country singer, too, which was great news for Glenn's barroom career because of how well he could sing like Hank. The follow-up single to "Lovesick Blues" was "Wedding Bells," recorded in 1949 at Castle's Tulane Hotel studio during Hank's first session with Dale Potter on fiddle. The record came out in May and hit #2, another huge single. That string of hits kept Hank on tour long enough to eventually bring him straight through Glenn's little corner of Texas. In fact, the radio station where Hank booked an appearance to promote his show in the area happened to be the very station Glenn played five days a week with Eddie & Pearl. After Glenn realized how easy it would be for him to meet his idol, he realized there was an opportunity to do something so much more than that. He wasn't just going to meet Hank Williams. He was going to play a song with Hank Williams. Sure enough, the offer Eddie & Pearl put in to back up Hank when he played his new single on the radio was approved. The day of the concert arrived and so did Hank, pulling into the radio station parking lot with little time to spare before his scheduled promo spot, much less than however much time Glenn would have needed to spend with Hank to realize he was just a guy, not some superhuman entity. Hank rushed inside, chatted on-air with the DJ about the latest events in his career, plugged that night's concert and then it was time to play his new single with Eddie & Pearl . . . but not Glenn. Oh, Glenn was supposed to play on it. He was right there in the room with his guitar on and everything. It's just that he thought he was supposed to kick off the song by playing the fiddle intro from the record on his guitar but Hank launched into the thing on his own and Glenn's hands froze. In what may have been his first ever attack of stage fright, all Glenn could do was stand and stare at Hank Williams' back as his hero sang "Wedding Bells."

After they were off-air Hank killed some time hanging around the station and Glenn was able to talk with him enough for the nervousness to wear off. He even got up the courage to demonstrate his Hank Williams impersonation, which amused the country star. But Hank also must have been at least a little impressed by the musical ability in the kid standing before him, because he shared a piece of wisdom which would alter the course of country music history when Glenn applied it in a recording studio some five years later. Hank admitted that all he ever wanted to do when he first started out was sing like Roy Acuff. He even got good enough at singing like Acuff to gather crowds of people to listen, good enough to launch a performing career. But when it came time to launch a recording career Hank learned the record business already had one Roy Acuff and not much use for another. Hank told Glenn the record business wasn't ever likely to need another Hank Williams, so he better start looking for his own voice. At the concert that night, Hank dedicated "Wedding Bells" to his #1 fan in the audience, Glenn Jones, who it's safe to say would've taken a bullet for Hank Williams at any point in life from that moment forward.

It's impossible to exaggerate how far beyond the typical fan/artist relationship his adoration reached, the personal pride Glenn must have felt when his favorite singer joined the *Grand Ole Opry* that June, the urgency with which he rushed to absorb Hank's newest records as soon as they were released. Glenn continued absorbing those Hank records even as a near-metaphysical darkness crept in from the edges on songs like "I'm So Lonesome I Could Cry," "They'll Never Take Her Love from Me" and "Lost Highway." Glenn copped every lick and nuance from every Hank Williams single, adding it all to the bag of tricks honky-tonk crowds loved to hear. But he also began exploring his own voice the way he'd previously explored guitar, taking apart the things he picked up from others and putting the pieces back together into something different, something new. He broke down every part of his vocal pathway and experimented with each, learning how to load his lungs, then restrict and direct airflow into somersaults of notes, how to smoothly move the sound between the resonating chambers of his chest and throat and skull, how to bite down on certain syllables to half-hum a lyric into clenched teeth.

By the end of 1949 he was no longer playing with Eddie & Pearl. The cash was simply better when he didn't have to split it, so Glenn struck out on his own. He was soon able to put a down payment on his first car. But he still had no clue how to manage money. After he missed a few payments on the car, a repo man showed up to take it back from one of Glenn's regular gigs, a place called Lola & Shorty's. Instead of handing over the car Glenn tried to fight the guy and wound up getting his stomach sliced open with a knife, which required a trip to the hospital where they stitched him up and saved his life. That's the kind of thing that happened at Lola & Shorty's and many other honky-tonks where Glenn played. Another of his regular spots in Beaumont was Neva's, which was almost certainly where Jack Starnes first heard Glenn sing.

That was also around the time Glenn discovered his second-favorite country singer. Considering Lefty Frizzell was born only a couple hundred miles away and his pre-fame touring circuit regularly brought him to the same stages Glenn played, it's pretty likely the two crossed paths before Lefty ever made a record. If not, he certainly came on Glenn's radar the moment he did release a record, because nearly nobody in any genre of music has ever come out of the gate with the stylistic confidence of Lefty Frizzell on "If You've Got the Money I've Got the Time." The single spent over twenty weeks on the Country chart and three of those weeks were at #1. But it was Lefty's second record, also a #1 hit, that sparked a revolution in country music vocal techniques. Without "I Love You a Thousand Ways" and the singing style it introduced, there would be no George Jones, no Merle Haggard, no Keith Whitley, no Randy Travis, nor any of a hundred other legendary voices in country music. Most fans bought Lefty's records to enjoy listening to them but every country singer in the world, even those who never actively tried to incorporate Lefty's style, studied those records to try and at least understand what the guy was doing to create that sound. Every second of his relaxed and subdued virtuosity made a statement about the things he wasn't doing but could if he wanted. The emotional power Hank Williams generated by channeling the energy of his entire being into his throat, Lefty Frizzell produced while making it sound like he was barely trying. Whenever Glenn first heard Lefty sing, he instantly got to work adding that voice to his bag of tricks, until Lefty became another collection of pieces Glenn could take apart and put back together as something new, like a freshly painted hot rod rolling out the door of a chop shop. The size of the crowds at Glenn's shows grew with his evolving skill. It's pretty likely the earliest recordings of his voice would have been taped during this period had he not enlisted in the Marines near the end of 1951.

◇   ◇   ◇

He surely wouldn't have enlisted in the Marines if he never met a young woman named Dorothy Bonvillian. The two may have met as early as 1949, when Glenn was seventeen and just starting to build a local following. Dorothy and her parents saw him play, thought he was great and watched him for a while before coming up to introduce themselves at an all-ages outdoor venue called Playground Park. Dorothy's father owned a commercial painting service, so the Bonvillians were fairly well off. The family's wealth may not have been the main thing that attracted Glenn, but he sure didn't mind driving Dorothy around in her father's fancy car or the new guitar, amplifier and small PA system the Bonvillians bought for him. Glenn was only eighteen when he and Dorothy got married in June of 1950 with Brother Burl officiating the ceremony. In a photograph taken on their wedding day, Dorothy and her mother look happy, as if they've gotten something they wanted. Glenn and his mother do not. According to one of Glenn's sisters, he said Dorothy and he liked each other alright and everything but they probably never would've been married, and certainly not so quickly, except Dorothy's parents were always pushing them to be together.

After the wedding the Bonvillians continued to support Glenn's attempts to break into the music business. According to a steel guitar player named Jerry Fox, Mr. Bonvillian even paid for Glenn to make some recordings with 4 Star but the marriage fell apart before anyone could figure out what to do with the tapes. If that session did happen, the tapes have never surfaced. (It's possible Jerry Fox was confusing that alleged Bonvillian-funded session for another 4 Star session that definitely took place in March 1951, when Slim Watts cut "I Lost My Little Darling," at least partially written by Glenn Jones, the first composition Glenn ever published. He was surely thrilled when Gene Autry recorded the song in 1949. A few years later, Glenn recorded it himself for Starday Records, under the title "My Sweet Imogene.") Glenn and Dorothy were husband and wife for approximately eleven months, during which time it became clear that she, coming from an affluent background, had no intention of doing any cooking or cleaning in their apartment and wouldn't even know where to start if she did. Glenn once asked her to perform some basic cleaning task and she responded by telling her father, who yelled something at Glenn about how "no daughter of his" was going to be treated like a maid, etc. Another time, Dorothy insulted one of Glenn's sisters, so he slapped Dorothy in the face. Whenever they argued in any way, Dorothy would go stay with her parents for a little while but she came back each time.

Then Dorothy got pregnant and everything changed. Or, really, everyone else decided everything about Glenn needed to change. Now that he was going to be the father of their grandchild, Dorothy's parents felt Glenn should stop spending so much time in the awful, smoke-filled honky-tonks where he played. Maybe it was even time to entirely give up on those dreams of being a country singer. Maybe it was time to get a real job. They suggested he go into the family business and work at Mr. Bonvillian's painting company. Glenn did try to make them happy. He went out with a crew a few times to paint hospitals and houses, but it made him depressed enough to want to day drink, so he started doing that, too. Whenever anyone noticed the alcohol affecting his behavior, Glenn said the paint fumes were making him feel loopy. Even after giving up on the painting gig, Glenn kept trying to find what Dorothy's parents called "a real job." He drove a 7-Up delivery truck for a while but couldn't stick with it. He worked in a funeral home for however many days it took until someone asked him to undress a dead body and that was the end of that job. Nothing he tried ever lasted more than a few weeks and he eventually decided he was either going to make it in life as a country singer or he wasn't going to make it in life at all.

In July 1951, Dorothy filed for divorce on the grounds he was "a man of violent temper," "addicted to the drinking of alcoholic beverages" who had "threatened [her] with physical violence and harm." Glenn was ordered by the court to pay thirty-five dollars a week in child support and, because the baby wasn't yet born when the divorce went through, another five hundred dollars toward the eventual medical expense of the delivery. With barroom gigs his sole source of income, he just couldn't make those payments. When one of Glenn's sisters found out he was forced to pawn his first guitar, the little Gene Autry acoustic that was a gift from their father, she went and bought it from the pawnshop to keep it safe for him. One month after the divorce, Glenn was thrown in jail for not making his full child support payment. The next month, he was thrown in jail again for the same thing. Eventually a judge told him this was obviously going to keep happening, so Glenn may as well join the military and put the government in charge of sending child support home for him. Since there were waiting periods to enlist in the Army and the Navy, Glenn Jones became a Marine in November of 1951.

After basic training he was stationed near San Jose in California, where he stayed for two years. Upon arriving in the area he scouted out the roadhouses and honky-tonks with country bands who may let him talk his way onstage to sing a song or two. Knowing the latest hit records and being able to sing them better than anyone else in town, Glenn quickly built a local following and everyone started calling him The Singing Marine. Cliffie Stone brought him on KXLA's *Hometown Jamboree* and there were a few other DJs who also let him guest on their shows, which helped him get booked in the area as "Little Georgie Jones." (Perhaps being so far away from home where nobody was at all likely to have met his father inspired Glenn to start going by his given first name.) Some of those steady gigs in San Jose required sneaking off base and risking AWOL charges but the money was too good to pass up. Even better, any cash the Marine Corps didn't know about was cash the Marine Corps couldn't send home to his ex-wife. So Little Georgie Jones did often choose to go AWOL, then sneak back on base in the early morning hours, hopefully undetected.

One morning, while just getting back to his bunk after a show, a Marine in the next bunk whispered over to him. Everyone knew Hank Williams was Glenn's favorite singer, so the Marine knew he'd want to hear about the radio announcing that Hank Williams was dead at the age of twenty-nine. Glenn was probably aware of Hank's famous struggles with alcoholism, even if he didn't know how much Hank's self-medication was an attempt to deal with physical pain from being born with spina bifida occulta. But there's no question Glenn was familiar with Hank's latest single, "I'll Never Get Out of This World Alive." Since it had already been out for nearly two whole months, Glenn probably sang it during his set earlier in the night. Thinking about the death of his hero, George Jones lay in his bunk and cried until the sun rose.

ACKNOWLEDGMENTS

The list of family, friends and complete strangers I have to thank for where I currently am in life would take another few hundred pages, so I will try to keep this limited to those who directly contributed to this individual work. My gratitude to:

All fans of the podcast, especially those who chose to offer financial support through Patreon during the much-longer-than-expected gap between the first and second season. The amount of faith it took for you to do that is still shocking to me and I sincerely hope you feel the wait was worth it.

Everyone involved in creating all of the music discussed in these pages. There would have been no reason to write the book without those singers, songwriters, studio musicians, producers, engineers, etc.

The historians, journalists and biographers who documented these subjects before me and all of the custodians of the genre at the Country Music Hall of Fame and Museum. In particular, I must thank Kathleen Campbell for inviting me to research in the archives and putting up with me when I did, as well as Peter Cooper for routinely taking time out of his day to listen to first drafts of theories put forth in this book.

Mark Mosley, Brett Martin and Geoff Edgers. It meant a lot to know you guys were fully aware of all the risks I intended to take and still stayed in my corner the whole time.

Stephen Bedford and Johanna Li at Simon & Schuster, thank you for helping me put this thing together. Marc Gerald, I'm certain you're the best literary agent I could ever have found. Lara M. Robbins, I have a great deal of appreciation for your attention to detail. Stuart Roberts, you started this.

Wayne White, you tapped directly into the universe of this book and brought back so many pieces of it for us all to see.

Mark Z. Danielewski and David Lynch, without *House of Leaves* and *Twin Peaks: The Return* (along with Melville's *Moby-Dick*) it's very unlikely I'd have known the way this story needed to be told.

Jody Benham, for everything.

A NOTE ON SOURCES

Thorough information on this book's primary sources can be found online at http://cocaineand rhinestones.com/book-sources

INDEX

"A-11," 53
ABC (network), 291, 292
ABC Records, 332
abortion, 292
Academy of Country Music, 310
"Aching, Breaking Heart," 52, 126, 127
Ackerman, Willie, 22
"Act Naturally," 143
Acuff, Roy
   Acuff-Rose founded by, 59
   on *Grand Ole Opry*, 59
   as Jones' hero, 466
   Jones influenced by, 11, 48
   and Melba Montgomery, 132
   "Night Train to Memphis," 60
   and Possum Holler nightclubs, 362
   Hank Williams' admiration for, 473
Acuff-Rose, 59, 64
Adonis, 454
"After Closing Time," 239, 240
Ailes, Roger, 260
"Ain't Love a Lot Like That," 448
Akeman, Stringbean, 22
"Alabama," 160
"Alcan Run, The," 27
alcohol abuse/alcoholism, 36, 37
   of Jones, 99–108, 130–132,
      135–136, 140, 141, 155–156, 214,
      221–223, 245–249, 251, 253,
      265–267, 301, 306, 309, 361,
      365, 367, 373, 376, 378, 379,
      434, 435, 447–449, 470
   of Jones' father, 464–466, 468–
      469
   of Hank Williams, 476
   of Wynette, 243
alcoholic beverages, 31–41
   see also Prohibition
Alexander the Great, 455–456

Alexander VI, Pope, 202
Al Gallico Music, 334, 341
"Alive and Well," 400–401
"All Around the World," 45
Allen, Bob, 238, 345, 432
Allen, Rex, 427
All My Children, 289, 294
All Things Must Pass, 137
Almost Blue, 347–348
"Almost Persuaded," 193, 304, 335–
   337, 431
Along Came Jones, 444
Along the Navajo Trail, 68
Altman, Robert, 328
Alvin & the Chipmunks, 209
"Amazing Grace," 449
American Indians
   advocating for, 417–418
   Buffalo Bill as enemy of, 385, 417
   clothing of, 382
   entertainment stereotypes of, 217,
      417–418
   in the West, 381
amphetamines, *see* speed
Anderson, Bill, 143, 237, 303
Anderson, John, 431
Anderson, Lynn, 337–338
animal cruelty, in bullfighting, 94–
   95, 116–117, 120
Anita Kerr Singers, 71, 77, 79, 83,
   125, 126
"Another Chance," 398
Another Lonely Song, 264
Another World, 292
Anslinger, Harry, 356–357
Anthony, Susan B., 37
Anti-Nashville Sound, 19, 20, 22
Anti-Saloon League (ASL), 37, 38
"Any Old Time," 70
"Apartment #9," 188–191, 193, 412

Aphrodite, 454, 455, 457
Ares, 454, 457
Armstrong, Louis, 336
Arnaz, Lucie, 273, 280
Arnold, Eddy, 49, 84–86, 130, 341
Arnold, J.C., 139
ASL (Anti-Saloon League), 37, 38
Association of Country Entertainers,
   303
As the World Turns, 290, 294
Asylum Records, 449
A-Team, *see* Nashville A-Team
   musicians
Atkins, Chet
   as country music's enemy, 343
   and Nashville Sound, 47, 65, 66,
      81, 84, 86–87
   and pop crossover, 192
   as Presley's session leader, 83
   as producer, 20, 75, 77–79, 330
Austin, Bobby, 188, 190
authenticity, 320–321, 323, 426–427
Autry, Gene, 68, 69, 421, 427, 467

"Baby, Ain't That Fine," 138
"Baby, I'm Yours," 338
backbeat, 73–76
"Back to the Country," 9
Baffle Ball, 3
Baggott, Shug, 361–366, 368–371,
   373, 374
Bailey, DeFord, 61
Bakersfield Sound, 47
ballads, 109, 124, 129–130
balls
   drag, 321–324
   masquerade, 319–321
Bally, 3, 4
Ballyhoo, 3
Bandit Records, 449

banjos, 23, 60
Bankhead, Tallulah, 356
Barber, Glenn, 16, 17, 21
Bare, Bobby, 84, 447
Barnes, Benny, 17, 123
Barnes, Max, 403, 430, 439
Barnett, Billy Bob, 378
"Bartender's Blues," 266–267, 308, 363, 372–373
Bashful Brother Oswald, 23
bass (instrument), 73, 74, 76–77, 80
Battle, The, 266
"Battle, The," 363
"Battle of New Orleans, The," 80
Beach Boys, 77
Bear Family Records, 103
Beatles, 137
beat (rhythm), 73–76, 78
beauty pageants, 257–260, 321
Beckham, Bob, 330
"Bedtime Story," 264–265
Beethoven, Ludwig van, 318
"Behind Closed Doors," 340, 341
"Being Together," 138–139
Belew, Carl, 158
Bell, William J., 291
Belmonte, Juan, 115–121
belt buckles, 420
belts (clothing), 420
"Beneath a Painted Sky," 402
Berg, Louis, 288
Berry, Chuck, 363
Best and/or Saddest Country Song of All Time, 297–300, 311–312
"Best Friends," 432
Betty Crocker, 285–286
Betty Ford Center, 402
Beverly Hills 90210, 295
"Beyond the Clouds," 347
big band jazz, 59–60, 68, 348
Big Bopper, 44–46, 103
Big Brother & The Holding Company, 210
Big Sister, 288–289
Big Thicket, the, 463, 464, 466
Billboard magazine
  ad buys in, 194
  chart data for, 4
  country singles lists in, 13
  on Daily at United Artists, 128
  Daily's interview in, 104
  Duff ad in, 7
  Epic's anti-feminist ad in, 211
  Jones as Male Vocalist of the Year in, 130
  on Jones' new deal with United Artists, 127

launch of, 4
on lawsuit of Wynette's daughters, 413
most-played songs tracked by, 4
Don Pierce as man of the year, 24
renamed charts of, 68–69
songs on charts of, 86, 108
on Sonico, 331
Starday mention in, 6
on Wynette's debut, 190
Bill Clifton and His Dixie Mountain Boys, 23
Bill Monroe and His Blue Grass Boys, 466
"Billy Boy," 465–466
"Bird, The," 440–441
Black, Clint, 403, 444
Black, Karen, 212
Blackburn, Rick, 102, 372, 378, 429
Blackie Crawford & The Western Cherokees, 6
"Black Land Farmer," 21–22
"Black Smoke," 23
Blake, William, 453–454
Bliss, Philip, 335
"Blood Red and Goin' Down," 339
Blount, Roy, Jr., 213
Bluebird, 158
"Blue Christmas," 126
bluegrass, 22–24, 307, 333
Blue Grass Boys, 85, 144
blues, 307, 357
Blue Sky Boys, 22
BMI awards, 27
Bohlin, Edward, 419–420, 424
Bolan, Marc, 70
Bold and the Beautiful, The, 293, 294
Bond, Johnny, 22, 25, 27
Bono, Sonny, 130
Bonvillian, Dorothy, 474
Bonvillian family, 474–475
bootleggers, 33, 39, 41
boots, 148–149
Borchers, Bobby, 343
Borgia, Cesare, 202
Borgia, Lucretia, 383
"Born in the USA," 207
"Born to Love Me," 348
"Borrowed Angel," 345
"Bottle, The," 266, 269
Bourke, Rory, 341
Bowen, Jimmy, 431
Bowie, David, 346
Bowling, Roger, 281
"Boy Named Sue, A," 301
Brad Brady and His Tennesseans, 61

Braddock, Bobby
  on great songs, 312
  on "He Stopped Loving Her Today," 310–312
  on Sherrill, 328
  songwriting by, 213, 248, 280, 298–300, 392, 398, 431, 447
Bradley, Harold, 67, 80, 82, 408
Bradley, Lou, 328
Bradley, Owen, 58–71
  as country music's enemy, 343
  and dynamic sound, 73, 74, 126–127
  imitators of, 342
  Jones' sound influenced by, 304
  and Nashville Sound, 47, 77, 79–80, 84–87, 342–343
  and old-timey instruments, 20
  as producer, 47, 78, 80–82, 84–87, 330
  and Sherrill, 189, 333, 342
  studios of, 9, 47, 50, 445
Bradley Barn Sessions, The, 445
Bradley's Barn, 86, 87
British Invasion, 25, 53, 137
Britt, Elton, 61
Brooks, Garth, 444
Brower, Cecil, 82
Brown, T. Graham, 444
Brown, Tony, 446
Bryant, Boudleaux, 75
Buckingham, Steve, 400, 402–403, 406
Buck Owens & The Buckaroos, 144
Buffalo Bill's *Wild West*, 386, 417, 418
Bugs Bunny, 89
Bullet label, 61
bullfighting, 89–96, 115–121, 458
Buntline, Ned, 382–383, 384
Burgess, Wilma, 86
burlesque shows, 422–423
Burns, Sonny, 9, 11, 104–105
Busby, Buzz, 23
Bush, Johnny, 69–70
Byrd, Beverly, 337
Byrd, D.C., 179, 183, 192
Byrd, Euple, 179–184, 190, 218
Byrd, Gwendolyn Lee, 179, 180
Byrd, Jacquelyn Fay, 180, 181, 244, 410, 412, 413
Byrd, Tina, 182, 250, 264, 412, 413

Campbell, Archie, 22
Campbell, Glen, 25–26
Campbell, Walter, 344–345
cannabis, 356–357
Capitol, 294

Capitol Records, 390
Capitol Studios, 188, 190
Capone, Al, 39
Cargill, Henson, 161
Carlisle, Dolly, 276, 432
Carlson, Gretchen, 259, 260
Carmol Taylor & His Country Pals, 329
carousels, 172–173, 232–233
Carrigan, Jerry, 280
"Carroll County Accident, The," 301
Carson, Joe, 47–48
Carson, Martha, 186
Carter, Brenda, 220
Carter, Charlie, 282
Carter, Tom, 245
Carter Family, 466
Carter Sister, 66
Cash, Johnny
    death of, 450
    hit songs of, 12, 13
    Jones as favorite of, 48
    at Jones Country, 439
    Jones given money by, 371
    and Jones' hits, 129, 130
    Jones' tours with, 107, 131
    on Louisiana Hayride, 105
    and rockabilly sound, 47
    on song with Ray Charles, 349
Cash, June Carter, 450
Cash Box
    Jones' awards from, 130, 300
    Melba Montgomery as Second-
        Most Promising Country &
        Western Female Artist in, 135
    songs on charts of, 108
Cassiday, George, 40–41
Castle Recording Laboratories/
    Castle Studios
    Owen Bradley's sessions at, 61–62, 71
    Harman at, 75
    and Nashville Sound, 72
    new location for, 65
    origin of, 61
    Webb Pierce's session at, 80
    Hank Williams' sessions at, 472
Catholic church, see Roman
    Catholicism
"Cathy's Clown," 75
Cato the Elder, 456
Cauty, Jimmy, 405
CBGB, 307
CB radio, 28
CBS, 288, 289, 293, 294
"C.C. Waterback," 430

Cedarwood Publishing, 64
celebrity/fame
    for athletes, 118
    for Jones, 130–131 (see also
        Greatest Country Singer Ever)
    loss of privacy with, 218
    for matadors, 118–121
"Ceremony, The," 247–248
Cervantes, Miguel de, 168
"Chantilly Lace," 44
Chapel, Don, 186–187, 192–194, 196, 213, 215–218
Chapel, Donna, 193, 196, 218
Chapel, Jean, 186
Chapman, Gary, 48
chaps (clothing), 147
Charles, King of Spain, 202–203
Charles, Ray, 299, 348–349, 431
Charles IX, King of France, 230–231, 233
Charles V, Holy Roman Emperor, 203–204, 227, 228
Chart records, 26
"Chattanoogie Shoeshine Boy," 66
Cher, 130
Chesnut, Jerry, 160, 304–305, 313
Chesnutt, Mark, 444
Chisholm, Shirley, 237
chivalry, 167–169, 172, 232–233, 458–459
Choates, Harry, 22
"Choices," 448
Christianity, 92–93, 199–204, 227–230, 458
Chuck Guillory and His Rhythm
    Boys, 109
"City Lights," 17
City Slickers, 89–90
Civil Rights movement, 291
Clancy Brothers with Tommy
    Makem, The, 23
Clark, Wesley, 449
Clement, Jack (Cowboy), 129, 159, 160
Clément, Jacques, 233
Clement VII, Pope, 203, 204
Cleopatra, 456
Cline, Patsy
    Owen Bradley's production of, 73, 74, 77, 80, 81, 85, 86, 406
    hits of, 25, 73
Clinton, Bill, 212
Clinton, Hillary, 212, 405
"Close All the Honky Tonks," 333
clothing, see fashion
CMA, see Country Music Association
CMA awards, see Country Music
    Association awards

"Coal Miner's Daughter," 82
Coca-Cola, 351, 355
cocaine, 351–358
    Jennings' use of, 366
    Jones' use of, 100, 267, 281, 299, 306, 308–310, 361, 365–367, 373, 430, 434–436, 438
"Cocaine Blues," 358
Cochran, Hank, 85, 140, 432
Code of the Mountains, 23
Cody, Buffalo Bill, 382–385, 417–419
Coe, David Allan (DAC), 339, 343, 347, 367
Cohen, Leonard, 123–124
Cohen, Paul, 62–65, 71, 186
Cohn, Nudie, 111, 422–427
Cold Hard Truth, 448
"Color of the Blues," 49, 50, 130
Columbia Records
    and "Bartender's Blues," 308
    Owen Bradley's studios sold/
        rented to, 86
    Elvis Costello at, 348
    Jones at, 372
    Grady Martin at, 80
    and Willie Nelson, 343–344
    and PR staff for Epic, 306
    Sherrill at, 327, 332, 333
"Comin' After You," 330
Como, Perry, 21
Complete Starday and Mercury
    Recordings, The, 103
Coniff, Ray, 60
"Convoy," 28
Conway, Tony, 409, 413
Cook, Don, 403
"Cool Water," 68
Coral Records, 342
Cornelius, R. H., 466
corruption
    during Prohibition, 39–41
    by rock & roll, 44
    in Roman Catholic Church, 199–202
Costello, Elvis, 271, 347–348, 372
Costello, Frank, 2
cost of recording, 110, 157
Counterfit, Johnny, 447
Country Boy Eddie Show, The, 184
Country Gentlemen, 269, 282
country music
    pop music vs., 71, 81, 83, 85, 87
    and rock & roll, 16–17, 44, 47, 70–71
    see also specific types, artists, and
        songs

Country Music Association (CMA)
Don Pierce on board of, 24
purpose of, 47
Country Music Association (CMA)
awards
avoidance of awarding Wynette
at, 392
and "Choices," 448
and formation of Association of
Country Entertainers, 303
for "Heaven's Just a Sin Away," 392
for "He Stopped Loving Her
Today," 310
for "I Don't Need Your Rockin'
Chair," 444
for Jones, 310, 376, 379, 444
Jones' attendance and
performance at, 379, 429, 440
for the Kendalls, 392
for Charlie McCoy, 343
mission of, 392
for "Most Beautiful Girl," 341
for Newton-John, 303
pop culture's influence on, 301
for Charlie Rich, 341
for Bobby Russell, 301
for "Who's Gonna Fill Their
Shoes?," 440
for Wynette, 301, 405
Wynette's 1969 attendance at,
223
for "You Don't Seem to Miss Me,"
446
Country Music Hall of Fame, 445
Country Music USA (Malone), 65
"countrypolitan" music, 342
country radio
and "Choices," 448
Hometown Jamboree, 104–105,
476
Houston Hometown Jamboree, 9
Jones' music ignored by, 441–442,
444–446
Jones' self-promotion on, 439
Louisiana Hayride, 5, 13, 105,
109, 470
"Nashville Sound" coined by, 342
number of stations, 24
pop country on, 47
promoting "White Lightning" to,
44
public's reaction to, 467
WSM and Grand Ole Opry, 58–59
(see also Grand Ole Opry)
Country Song Hits, 15
country & western, 68, 72
Coursey, Farris, 85

cover songs, 12–14
see also individual songs/artists
cowboy apparel, see western wear
Cowboy Copas, 22
"Cowboys Don't Shoot Straight (Like
They Used To)," 397
"Cowpoke," 336
Craig, Francis, 61, 281
Cramer, Floyd
career of, 81
music of, 44, 74, 77, 79, 81–82,
85, 125
Parton's joke about, 406
Pig Robbins' impersonation of, 126
"Crazy," 74
"Crazy Arms," 17, 76, 107
"Crazy Old Soldier," 349
Cristofori, Bartolomeo, 72
Crosby, Bing, 7–8, 68
Crowell, Rodney, 402
Crutchfield, Jerry, 399
"Cry, Cry Darlin'," 109
"Crying in the Rain," 397–398
Crystal, Billy, 89–90
Crystals, the, 136
Cuevas, Manuel, 424, 425
"Cup of Loneliness," 470
Curtis, Mac, 336
Curtis, Mike, 448
custom record press operations,
20–21, 26–27

DAC, see Coe, David Allan
"Daddy Come Home," 378
Daily, Harold (Pappy), 4–6
and Big Bopper's music, 44–45
character of, 154–155
and country radio, 44
and D Records, 44
as effectively Jones' manager, 128
filler content produced by, 125,
157–159, 162
and 4 Star, 5, 7, 21
on gatekeepers, 104
and Jones at Musicor, 137, 139,
240–241
and Jones' early career, 9–12
and Jones' Mercury contract, 128
Jones' relationship with, 154–155
on Jones' songwriting, 123
Jones' split from, 105, 154
and Jones-Wynette duets, 238
and Mercury merger, 18, 19
Roger Miller's soundalikes for,
108–109
and Melba Montgomery, 52–53,
135

and Musicor, 137
and "Never Grow Cold," 224
and Webb Pierce, 12–13
as producer, 63–64, 159–160
ruthlessness with songwriters,
160–162
songs per session wanted by,
155–156
at Starday, 6–7, 10
successes of, 103
and "Treasure of Love," 46–47
at United Artists, 128
and "Walk Through This World
with Me," 141
Dallas, 293
Dalton, Lacy J., 347, 432
Dangerous Summer, The, 91
"Dark as the Night, Blue as the Day,"
85
"Dark End of the Street, The," 330
Dark Shadows, 291
Davis, Clive, 327, 338
Davis, Skeeter, 77–79, 143
Davis, Steve, 395
Day, Jimmy, 110
Days of Our Lives, 294, 295
Death in the Afternoon
(Hemingway), 90
Decca Records
Owen Bradley at, 62, 64, 65, 77
Burgess at, 86
Paul Cohen at, 71
Goldie and Tommy Hill at, 21
Bill Monroe at, 84, 85
Webb Pierce at, 12, 13
sounds of music produced at, 69
Twitty at, 87
"Deep in Vogue," 323–324
"Delta Dawn," 339
Denny, Jim, 64
Denton, Bobby, 330
Devore, Sy, 424
Dew, Joan, 182
on George Richey, 390
on Wynette and Jones, 214, 252,
377
on Wynette and Reynolds, 270
on Wynette and George Richey,
272, 401
on Wynette's distortions of reality,
176, 274
on Wynette's medical problems,
243, 244
Dexter, Al, 467
Diamond Records, 334
Dickens, Little Jimmy, 213, 424, 426,
443

"Did I Ever Tell You," 127
"Diesel on My Tail," 333
"Diesel Smoke, Dangerous Curves," 27
Diffie, Joe, 407, 444
Dill, Danny, 280
Dillon, Dean, 431, 441
disc jockeys, 104, 105
distilled liquors, 31–35, 40
D-I-V-O-R-C-E, 212–213, 337
"D-I-V-O-R-C-E," 213, 298
Divorce/Death Trilogy, 312–315
divorces, 211
   of Jones, 196–197, 213, 246–247,
      252–253, 264–266, 306, 362,
      475–476
   of George Richey, 272, 390
   of Wynette, 192, 193, 210,
      212–213, 216, 218, 246–247,
      252–253, 263–266, 273, 279,
      306, 362, 393
Dixie Clodhoppers, 426
Dixie Records, 14
Do and Dare, 419
Dominguín, Luis Miguel, 90–91
Donahue, Phil, 392–393
Don Quixote (Cervantes), 168
"Don't Be Cruel," 17, 83–84
Don't Fence Me In, 68
"Don't Fence Me In," 68
"Don't Keep Me Lonely Too Long,"
   141
"Don't Let the Stars Get in Your
   Eyes," 21, 75
"Don't Rock the Jukebox," 445
"Don't Stop the Jukebox," 110
"Don't Stop the Music," 110, 123,
   129–130
"Don't Touch Me," 85, 86
"Door, The," 250, 302–303
"Dope Head Blues," 357
"Do Right Woman–Do Right Man,"
   330
Double Trouble, 372
Douglass, Frederick, 37
Dove, Ronnie, 334
"Down in the Willow Garden,"
   454
drag (fashion), 319–324
"Drag Race," 332
Drake, Pete, 22, 137, 189, 209
D Records, 44
"Drugs and Jesus," 425
drug use
   cannabis, 356–357
   cocaine, 351–358 (*see also* cocaine)
   by Jennings, 366

   by Jones, 100, 140, 144–145, 245,
      246, 267, 281, 299–300, 306,
      308–310, 361, 365–366, 373,
      376, 378, 379, 434–436, 438
   by Wynette, 243–244, 253–254,
      269, 394–395, 397, 401–404
   speed (amphetamines), 100, 144,
      243, 246
Drummond, Bill, 404–405
drums, 72–76
"Drunk Can't Be a Man, A," 266
Dudley, Bill, 103
Dudley, Dave, 27, 135
Duff, Arlie, 6–9
Duffy, Steve, 129
Duncan, Stuart, 448
Dupree, Paris, 323, 324
Dylan, Bob, 23–24, 241
dynamic range, 72
dynamic sound, 72–73, 77, 126, 304,
   305
Dynasty, 293

Eco, Umberto, 457, 458
Eddie & Pearl, 471–473
Eddings, Eddie, 145
Edison, Thomas, 354
Edwards, Darrell, 11, 12, 140, 156,
   162
Edwards, Stoney, 432
Egypt, ancient, 455–457
Eighteenth Amendment, 36, 38, 320
Elagabalus, 457
El Gallo, 119, 121
"El Paso," 60, 80
Emery, Ralph, 144, 162, 379
Emmons, Buddy, 22, 86, 110, 132
"End of the World, The," 77–79
Endsley, Melvin, 25
"Engine Engine No. 9," 25
England, 204, 318
   see also individual royals
Epic Records
   Don Chapel at, 196
   Frizzell at, 345
   David Houston at, 336
   Jones at, 237, 238, 240, 241, 302,
      304–306, 429, 431, 441–444
   PayCheck at, 343, 347
   PR staff for, 306
   Charlie Rich at, 340, 347
   Sherrill at, 187–189, 193, 196, 225,
      282, 332–334
   Sutton at, 337, 338
   Wynette at, 193, 209, 211, 225,
      238, 282, 306, 399–400, 402,
      405–408

EPs, 14–15
ER, 295
Eros, 457
Etheridge, Melissa, 412
Evans, Dale, 421
Everette, Leon, 442
Everly, Don, 75
Everly Brothers, 17, 75, 397
Executive Inns, 364, 365
Exile, 400

"Failing in Love," 341
Fairlanes, 330, 331
fake percussion parts, 331, 332
"Fallen Star, A," 64, 330
Fame and Fortune, 419
FAME Studios, 127, 330, 331
Fargo, Donna, 339
Farrow, Mia, 292–293
fashion, 320–321
   in bullfighting, 115–118
   as class identification, 317–318, 320
   in cowboy automobiles, 425
   dressing in drag, 319–324
   houses of, 322–323
   military clothing, 420
   rhinestone suits, 423–427
   western wear, 147–150, 381–385,
      418–427
   and women's voting rights, 257–258
Felipe II, King of Spain, 352
feminism, 207–212
Ferris, Roger, 442
"Few Ole Country Boys, A," 444
fiddles, 70–71, 73
Field, Sally, 273, 279, 280
*50,000,000 Elvis Fans Can't Be
   Wrong*, 426
filler content, 125, 157–160, 162
Fisher, Sonny, 17
Five Easy Pieces, 212
Flatt & Scruggs, 23
Flippo, Chet, 307
Florence, 170–171, 204
Florence Alabama Music Enterprise
   (FAME), 127, 330, 331
floriography, 457–458, 460
Flowers, Gennifer, 212
Foley, Fern, 188
Foley, Red, 10, 61, 62, 66, 83
folk music, 329
Food and Drug Act, 355
Ford, Tennessee Ernie, 13
Forest Ranger, The, 68
"For Sale or For Lease," 8
"For the Good Times," 339
Foster, Fred, 80, 85

4 Star, 5–7, 21, 475
"Four Walls," 64, 65
Fox, Jerry, 475
France, 170–172, 203, 204, 227–233
    see also individual royals
France, Bill, Sr., 41
Francis, Connie, 130
François, King of France, 203, 204,
    227–228
François II, King of France, 229, 230
Franks, Tillman, 193, 194, 335
Frascuelo, 118
Frazier, Dallas, 138–139, 162, 339
Freedom Highway, 333
Freud, Sigmund, 353–354
Friends in High Places, 444
Frizzell, Lefty
    covers of, 127
    cowboy hats of, 426
    at George Jones Rhythm Ranch,
        214
    Jones' admiration of, 8, 473–474
    Jones' impersonation of, 9
    musical style of, 473–474
    rhinestone clothing of, 423–424,
        426
    and Sherrill, 345
    stage outfits for, 423–424, 426
    and Starnes, 5–6, 8, 11
"From Here to the Door," 187, 215
"Fun," 242
"Funeral, The," 333
"Furniture Man," 358

Gaillard, Slim, 56
Gallico, Al, 190, 334–336
gambling games, 1–4
Gannaway, Al, 67
Garland, Hank, 22, 44–45, 80, 110,
    111, 125
gatekeepers, in music business, 104
Gatlin, Larry, 269, 277–278
Gatlin, Rudy, 269, 275, 276, 278, 280
Gatlin, Steve, 280
Gatlin Brothers, 402
gender
    and masquerade balls, 319, 320
    stereotypical, 290–291, 324
General Hospital, 293, 294
General Motors Truck Company, 403
genre, 87
    see also specific genres
Gentry, Gary, 431, 440
George and Gene, 138
George Jones (Allen), 432
George Jones Chuck Wagon
    restaurant, 112

George Jones Museum, 466
George Jones Rhythm Ranch, 214
"Ghost Riders in the Sky," 68
Gibson, Don, 84, 186
"Giddyup Go," 28
Gill, Vince, 402, 444, 446
Gilley, Mickey, 129
"Girl I Used to Know, A," 159
"Girl Thang," 407
"Give Me Forty Acres (To Turn This
    Rig Around)," 27
"Give Me the Roses While I Live,"
    466
Glad Music, 135
"Glad to Let Her Go," 51, 124
Glaser, Tompall, 2–3
"Glass Houses," 406–407
Gleason, Jackie, 217
Glenn Patterson (alias), 162
"God Bless Her ('Cause She's My
    Mother)," 160
"Golden Ring," 280, 298, 309–310
Gold Star Studios, 9, 11, 110, 111, 133
Gómez Ortega, Joselito, 121
Gómez Ortega, Rafael (El Gallo),
    119, 121
"Gone," 64, 126
"Good," 239–239
"Good Ol' Mountain Dew," 425–426
"Good Year for the Roses, A," 160,
    301, 304–305, 312, 313, 348,
    445
Gordy, Emory, Jr., 444
Gosdin, Vern, 402, 430, 442
Gospel Collection, The, 449
gospel music
    Atkins' production of, 83
    by Jones, 103, 110, 449, 470
    of Jordanaires, 83
    Sherrill's interest in, 335
Goya, 117
Grae, Viola, 424, 425
Grammy Awards
    for "Almost Persuaded," 336
    for Glen Campbell, 25–26
    for "Choices," 336
    for "I Don't Wanna Play House,"
        337
    for Jones, 310
    for Wynette, 193, 209
Grand Ole Opry
    artists on, 5, 59, 66, 83, 109, 321,
        466
    honky-tonk sound on, 467
    Jones on, 107, 110, 220
    music played on, 60, 64, 75, 131
    origin of, 58

    package tours of, 9, 13
    western wear on, 408, 424, 426
    Hank Williams on, 473
    Wynette on, 220
Grand Ole Opry's New Star, 133
"Grand Tour, The," 250, 302–303,
    312–315
Grant, Ulysses S., 354
Grant Brothers, 357
Gray, Mark, 400
Grayson and Whitter, 22
"Great Balls of Fire," 43–44
Greatest Country Singer Ever, 47–50,
    100, 130–131, 300, 301
Greeks, ancient, 454–455, 457, 458
Green, Bob, 363–363, 365
Green, Lloyd, 111, 212–213, 345
"Green, Green Grass of Home," 194
Greene, Jack, 237
Grimm Brothers, 461
G-strings (clothing), 422–423
Guiding Light, The, 286–290, 294
Guillory, Chuck, 109
guitar, 60, 74, 76, 80
Gulf Coast Recording, 129
Gully Jumpers, 426
Gusto, 26, 28
Guthrie, Woody, 23

Habsburgs, 203–204, 227–230, 233
Haggard, Merle, 25
    early career of, 188
    at George Jones Rhythm Ranch,
        214
    impersonations by, 48
    on Jones, 48–49
    at Jones Country, 443
    on Jones' LPs, 447
    Jones' songs with, 429–430, 450
    as legend, 439
    popularity of, 429–430
    on George Richey, 389
    singing style of, 474
    on Wynette, 187
    and Wynette's award, 404
    and Wynette's memorial, 411
Hall, Bill, 129
Hall, Rick, 127, 329–332
Hall, Tom T., 48, 376
Hamilton, Alexander, 34–35
Hamlet (Shakespeare), 459, 460
Hank Smith (alias), 16
"Happiest Girl in the Whole U.S.A.,
    The," 339
Hargrove, Linda, 431
Harman, Buddy, 74–79, 85, 126
"Harper Valley P.T.A.," 301

Harpocrates, 457
harpsichord, 72
Harris, Emmylou, 48, 158, 213, 301, 395, 402
Harrison Narcotics Tax Act, 355–356
Hart, William S., 418
Haskell, Sam, 260
hats, western, 147, 384, 426
"Have Mercy on Me," 156
"Have You Seen (My Boogie Woogie Baby)," 75
Hayes, "Big Red," 10
Haynes, Walter, 126
Hays Code, 320, 321
"Heartaches, by the Number," 25
Heartaches and Tears, 143
"Heartbreak Hotel," 15, 16, 81, 83, 106
"Heartbroken Me," 9
"Heart in Hand," 77, 78
Heart Over Mind, 404
"Heaven's Just a Sin Away," 392
Helios, 454, 455
Hellenistic period, 455–456
"Hello Mary Lou," 136
Helms, Bobby, 71
"He Loves Me All the Way," 210
"Help Me Make It Through the Night," 85, 300
Hemingway, Ernest, 89–91, 115, 119
Hemphill, Paul, 65–66
Henderson, Dalton, 469, 470
Henderson, Prairie Rose, 424–425
Henley, Larry, 263
Henri II, King of France, 170–172, 204, 228–229
Henri III, King of France, 230, 233
Henry VI, King of England, 459
Henry VII, King of England, 459–460
Henry VIII, King of England, 204, 460
Henry VI (Shakespeare), 460
Henry VI trilogy (Shakespeare), 459
"Here in the Real World," 450
"Her Name Is," 298, 363
Heroes & Friends, 403
Herston, Kelso, 159, 187, 329–331
"He's a Rebel," 136
"He's So Fine," 338
"He Stopped Loving Her Today," 297–301, 305, 309–312, 375, 376, 432
"He Thinks I Still Care," 130
"Hey Mister," 341
Hickok, Wild Bill, 382–384, 420
Hickory Records, 186

Hicks, Jeanette, 133–134
Hicks, Stanley, 426
Higher Ground, 402
"High on the Thought of You," 305
"High-Tech Redneck," 445
Hill, Goldie, 21
Hill, Tommy, 21, 26
Hirt, Al, 334
Hits I Missed . . . And One I Didn't, 449–450
hit songs
life cycle of, 156–157
see also specific songs
Hobbs, Becky, 443
Hollie, James, 269
Holly, Buddy, 46
Hollywood Canteen, 68
Holy Roman Empire, 202–204
holy wars, 92–93
Homer, 455
Hometown Jamboree, 104–105, 476
home videotape technology, 293
"Honey," 301
Honky Tonk Angels, 406
"Honky Tonk Man," 441–442
honky-tonk music
"Any Old Time," 70
"Black Land Farmer," 21–22
and Jones' alcoholism, 99, 106
and Jones as greatest singer, 106
in Jones' career, 104, 439
"Just a Little Lonesome," 71
Mullican's piano for, 62
at Neva's, 5
perceived as disreputable, 58–59
"Pistol Packin' Mama," 467
"Play It Cool Man—Play It Cool" as, 8–9
rock vs., 16–17
style of, 73, 75, 76, 220, 467, 473
"Treasure of Love," 45
in Wynette's early career, 180, 182
"Ya Ba Da Ba Do (So are You)," 442
"Honky Tonk Song," 71, 73, 446
Horton, Johnny, 80, 102, 105, 335, 441–442
Horus, 457
"Hound Dog," 82
House of Bourbon, 229–231, 233
House of Guise, 229–231, 233
House of LaBeija, 322
House of Lancaster, 459–460
House of Tudor, 318, 459, 460
House of York, 459
Houston, David, 193–196, 237, 304, 335–336, 345

Houston Hometown Jamboree, 9
Howard, Chuck, 431
Howard, Harlan, 25, 87, 250
Howard, Jan, 187
How Nashville Became Music City USA (Kosser), 63
Human Emotions, 347
"Hurtin' Time," 196
Huskey, Junior, 22, 63
Husky, Ferlin, 64, 103, 126, 130
Hyder, Cliff, 222–224, 245–246
Hyder, Maxine, 222–224

"I Always Get Lucky with You," 430–431
"I Am," 449
I Am What I Am, 297, 310
Iberian Peninsula, 92–93, 95, 157
"I Can't Get Used to Being Lonely," 140–141
"I Can't Help It (If I'm Still in Love with You)," 125
ice cream, 55–58
ice trade, 56–57
"Ice Water," 16–17
"I Don't Need Your Rockin' Chair," 444
"I Don't Wanna Play House," 193, 211, 239, 337
"I Fall to Pieces," 73, 74, 85
"If Drinkin' Don't Kill Me (Her Memory Will)," 267, 377, 429
"If I Could Bottle This Up," 441
"If I Could Only Fly," 411
"If I Could Only Hear My Mother Pray Again," 390
"If I Could Only Win Your Love," 395
"If I Didn't Care," 69
"If I Don't Love You (Grits Ain't Groceries)," 45
"If You Believe," 156
"If You Don't Believe I Love You, Just Ask Me," 160–161
"If You Let Him Drive You Crazy (He Will)," 403
"If You've Got the Money, I've Got the Time," 5, 9, 474
"If You Were Mine," 8
"I Get a Kick Out of You," 357
"I Guess I Had It Coming," 50
"I Just Don't Give a Damn," 266
"I Just Drove By (To See If I Was Really Gone)," 271
"I Just Heard a Heart Break (And I'm So Afraid It's Mine)," 398
"I Know," 304
"I Let the Stars Get in My Eyes," 21

Iliad, The (Homer), 455
I Lived to Tell It All, 446
"I'll Never Get Out of This World Alive," 476
"Ill Never Smile Again," 60
"I'll See Him Through," 210, 224
I'll Share My World with You, 220
"I'll Share My World with You," 301
Illuminatus Trilogy, The (Wilson and Shea), 404
"I Lost My Little Darling," 475
"I Love My Friend," 341
"I Love to Boogie," 70
"I Love You a Thousand Ways," 474
"I'm a Survivor," 441
"I'm Gonna Hurt Her on the Radio," 347
"Imitation of Love," 158
"I'm Not Ready Yet," 376
"I'm Saving My Love," 79
"I'm So Lonesome I Could Cry," 473
"I'm Sorry," 77, 78
"I'm the Only Hell (Mama Ever Raised)," 343
"I Must Have Done Something Bad," 445
Incan Empire, 351–352
Ink Spots, 69
instruments, 70–76, 81
    see also individual instruments; individual songs
"In the Jailhouse Now," 425
Irving, Lonnie, 26–27
"I Saw Me," 159
"I See the Want To in Your Eyes," 87
"I Should've Called," 431
Islam, 92–93
I Still Believe in Fairy Tales, 269
"I Still Believe in Fairy Tales," 264–266
"I Take It on Home," 340
It Don't Get Any Better Than This, 446–447
"It Don't Get Any Better Than This," 447
"It's Alright," 48
"It's Been a Long, Long Time for Me," 50
"It's My Way," 190
"I Turn to You," 440
"It Wasn't God Who Made Honky Tonk Angels," 21, 61–62, 406
"I've Aged Twenty Years in Five," 297–298
"I've Got a New Heartache," 76, 138
"I've Got Five Dollars and It's Saturday Night," 138

"(I've Got Spurs That) Jingle Jangle Jingle," 68, 467
Ives, Burl, 27, 61, 85
"I Want to Be a Cowboy's Sweetheart," 209
"I Want to Be Wanted," 77
"I Want You, I Need You, I Love You," 83
"I Was Country When Country Wasn't Cool," 379
I Was There When It Happened (Franks), 194, 195

jackets, western, 382, 384
"Jack o' Diamonds," 27
Jackson, Alan, 108, 444–446, 449, 450
Jackson, Shot, 22, 132, 135
Jackson, Stonewall, 107, 108, 143
Jackson, Tommy, 47, 70, 82, 110, 125, 126
James, Etta, 336
James, Sonny, 64
Japanese dress code, 318
Jarrett, Keith, 72–73
Jarvis, Felton, 332
jazz, 59–60, 72, 73, 356, 357
Jean, Norma, 184–185
jeans, 148
Jefferson, Thomas, 381
Jennings, Waylon
    and Akins, 84
    cocaine use by, 366
    death of, 450
    as gambling addict, 2–3
    Jones' collaboration with, 271
    Jones given money by, 371
    on Jones LPs, 447
    as legend, 439
    and outlaw country, 307, 343
    and *Red Headed Stranger* tapes, 343–344
    songwriting by, 48
"Jessie's Girl," 294
Jim Halsey Agency, 374
Jim & Jesse, 333
"Jingle Bell Rock," 71
John, Elton, 407
John, Little Willie, 45
Johnson, Junior, 41
Johnson, Lois, 333
Johnson, Lonnie, 357
Joiner, James, 329
Jones, Chuck, 89
Jones, Clara, 464–467
Jones, Dorothy, 474–475

Jones, George Glenn
    alcohol abuse by, 99–108, 130–132, 135–136, 140, 141, 143–145, 155–156, 214, 221–223, 245–249, 251, 253, 265–267, 301, 306, 309, 361, 365, 373, 376, 378, 379, 434, 435, 447–449, 470
    and "Almost Persuaded," 336
    at Asylum Records, 448–449
    autobiography of, 194
    awards for, 130, 300–301, 308, 310, 376, 379, 404, 444
    ballads by, 109–110, 124, 129–130
    at Bandit Records, 449
    band of, 132 (*see also* Jones Boys)
    bankruptcy of, 309, 371, 372
    and Best and/or Saddest Country Song of All Time, 297–300, 311–312
    charity to others by, 153–154
    choice of songs by, 159–162
    at Columbia, 372
    comebacks of, 300–310, 374–376, 429–432, 439–441
    and Elvis Costello, 348
    in Country Music Hall of Fame, 445
    country radio's avoidance of, 439, 441–442, 444–446, 448
    and covers of songs, 129–130
    Daily's relationship with, 128, 154–155, 169–170
    death of, 450–451
    and death of friends, 450
    Divorce/Death Trilogy of, 312–315
    as DJ, 103
    drug use by, 100, 140, 245, 246, 267, 281, 299–300, 306, 308–310, 361, 365–367, 373, 376, 378, 379, 430, 434–436, 438
    drums used by, 75
    early career of, 8–16, 101–112, 476
    early music interest of, 466–469
    at end of career, 449–450
    at Epic, 237, 238, 240, 241, 302, 304–306, 429, 431, 441–444
    on expressing feelings, 112
    on fame and being a star, 153
    family background of, 463–469
    and father's death, 214–215
    fighting by, 107–108, 131, 470
    and fire at Wynette's house, 277
    first LP of, 15, 17
    first paying jobs of, 469–471
    first #1 record of, 43–47
    following divorce from Wynette, 298, 309–310

follow-up rewrites of hits by, 159
as Frizzell fan, 473–474
George Jones Rhythm Ranch, 214
as Greatest Country Singer Ever, 47–50, 100, 130–131, 300, 301
health of, 299–300, 306, 449, 450
with Henderson family, 469–471
impersonations by, 8–11, 103, 125, 158–159, 470, 472–473
influences on songs of, 125, 127, 139, 304–305
Jones Country venue of, 438, 442–443
label jumps by, 157–158
love-scarred persona of, 142–143, 266–267
and Madison Square Garden shows, 143–144, 307–308
managers of, 129
in the Marines, 474, 476
marriage to and child with Dorothy, 474–475
marriage to and family with Shirley, 103, 105–106, 112, 124, 128, 139–140, 196–197, 214, 362
marriage to and family with Tammy, 154, 221–225, 242–253, 264–266, 306, 362
marriage to and relationship with Nancy, 432–439, 442, 443
at MCA, 444–447
mental health of, 101, 102, 145, 245–246, 297–300, 309, 367–370, 372–374, 376, 378, 434, 436, 437
at Mercury, 19, 126–128
at Mercury-Starday, 107, 127
money problems of, 102, 134–135, 237, 244, 248, 309, 362–364, 369–373, 376, 378, 469, 473
and Melba Montgomery, 52, 132, 134–135, 139, 141, 220
at Musicor, 137–142, 220, 237, 240–241, 304, 305
in music videos, 439–440, 445, 446
near-impersonations of, 130
at Willie Nelson's Picnic, 367
non-music businesses of, 112
and Old Plantation Music Park, 236–237
Old Plantation of, 235–236
and Buck Owens, 143–144
on package tours, 104
PayCheck's rumored influence on, 49–52

performance style of, 105–106, 471–472
and Pitney, 52–53, 137–138
on pop country, 303
and Possum Hollers, 361–363
on processing his emotions, 139
public perception of Wynette and, 239–242
and quality of Nashville studios, 110–111
in regional markets, 13–14
rerecordings by, 157–159
on George Richey, 389–390
Paul Richey as manager for, 374–375, 396
on rock & roll, 15
sad sons of, 140–143
as Sherrill favorite, 347
Sherrill influenced by, 329
Sherrill's influence on songs of, 304
1980s hits of, 268
singing on television by, 124, 135, 142, 375, 379, 447
singing style of, 473, 474
songwriting by, 123–124, 266, 475
soundalikes by, 16
and sound quality of recordings, 110–111
split from Daily by, 105, 154
stage fright of, 100, 131, 144, 362, 367, 443, 447, 472
at Starday, 8–12, 99, 102–105
Starday's soundalikes of, 125–126
talk show of, 447
tests of friendship by, 154
and "Til I Get It Right," 263–264
touring harmony singer for, 124–125
troubling behaviors of, 99–108, 130–132, 134–135, 140, 143–145, 236, 267, 309, 362, 364, 368–370, 429, 430, 433, 435
at United Artists, 128, 136
waning career of, 441–444
and Welborn, 364–365, 373, 379, 433
as Hank Williams fan, 472–473, 476
Wynette and David Houston's tour with, 194
and Wynette following divorce, 270–272, 280–281
and Wynette's death, 414, 447
Wynette's duets with, 196, 238–239, 242, 271, 300, 302, 374–375, 396, 397, 403, 407–408, 446 (see also individual songs)

Wynette's first meeting with, 186–187, 190–191
Wynette's love for music of, 180
Wynette's relationship with, 154, 162, 196–197, 213–222, 269, 377
Jones, George Washington, 463–467
Jones, Jack, 136
Jones, Nancy, 439, 442, 447, 449–451
Jones, Shirley
    divorce from George, 196–197
    on George's stage behaviors, 105–106
    marriage to and family with George, 103, 105, 112, 124, 128, 139–140, 214
Jones, Tamala Georgette
    birth of, 236
    book by, 413
    Jones' last duet with, 450
    and mother's death, 410, 412
    and George Richey, 278, 282, 377–378, 390, 394–395, 407, 409
Jones Boys, 132, 241, 268–269, 282, 362, 377
Jones Country, 439, 442–443
Jones Country, 431
Jones-Miller Act of 1922, 356
Joplin, Janis, 210
Jordan, Luke, 357–358
Jordanaires, the, 70, 71, 82, 83, 126, 339
jousts, 169–170, 172, 228
Joy of Cooking, The (Rombauer), 56
Judd, Naomi, 403
Judd, Wynonna, 403, 407
jukeboxes, 3–7, 22, 104, 470, 472
"Juke Box Man," 67
"Just a Little Lonesome," 71
"Just as Much as Ever," 330
Justice, Dick, 358
"Justified and Ancient," 404–405
"Just One More," 17, 49, 109–110, 123, 129

"Keep Me in Mind," 337
Kemp, Wayne, 141, 343
Kendalls, 392
Kennedy, Jerry, 126, 190, 209, 332, 335, 336
"Kentucky Waltz," 71, 84–85
Kerr, Anita, 79
Kickin' Out the Footlights, 450
Kids Say the Darndest Things, 224, 225
"Kids Say the Darndest Things," 264

Kilgore, Merle, 212, 334
Killen, Buddy, 43, 45, 47, 48, 330, 334
Kilmister, Lemmy, 346
Kimball, Linda, 266
King, B. B., 329
King, Ben E., 209
King, Claude, 334
King, Pee Wee, 22, 26
"King Is Gone (So Are You), The," 442
King of Broken Hearts, 143
Kingston, Larry, 397
Kingston Trio, 22, 23, 329
Kirkham, Millie, 126, 300
"Kiss Away," 334, 337
KKK (Ku Klux Klan), 38
KLF, 404–405
knights, 165–170, 172, 456, 459
Knots Landing, 293
Knutson, Dennis, 440
Köln Concert, 72–73
Kosser, Michael, 63
Kotlyarendko, Nuta (Nudie), 421–423
Kraus, Jennifer, 413
Kristal, Hilly, 307
Kristofferson, Kris, 85, 300
KTRM, 103
Ku Klux Klan (KKK), 38
Kyser, Kay, 68

LaBeija, Crystal, 321–322
LaBostrie, Dorothy, 55–56
Ladies' Choice, 431–432, 439
Ladies Love Outlaws, 343
La Guardia, Fiorello, 2, 422–423
Lakeland, Florida, 222
Lakota people, 417–418
"Last Date," 82
"(Last Night) I Heard You Crying in Your Sleep," 470
"Last Town I Painted, The," 51
Lauderdale, Jim, 446
Lavender, Shorty, 370
Law, Don, 67, 69, 70, 80
Lead Belly, 357, 358
"Least of All," 141
Lee, Brenda, 77, 78, 81, 82, 431
Lee, Dickey, 129
Lee, Foy, 177–178, 193, 282
Lee, Mildred, 177–180, 182, 183, 193, 273, 282
Legendary, 324
Legends of Country Music, The, 406
Lehning, Kyle, 404, 444
"Le Me Be the One," 66
Leo X, Pope, 200, 202, 203

"Let Me Be Your Salty Dog," 9
"Let's Build a World Together," 248
"(Let's Get, Let's Get) Tammy Wynette," 393
Levin, Ira, 461
Levy, Bruce, 411, 413
Lewis, Jerry Lee, 17, 43–44, 47
Lewis and Clark expedition, 381–382
LGBTQ persons, 319–323
Lichtenstein, Bernard (Rodeo Ben), 420–421, 423
"Life's Little Ups and Downs," 340
"Life to Go," 108, 123
"Like Makin' Love," 331
"Likes of You, The," 161
Lindsey, Dave, 374
Linkletter, Art, 224, 225
Little Darlin', 26, 343
Little Richard, 55–56
Living History (Clinton), 212
"Livin' on Easy Street," 239
Locklin, Hank, 5, 66, 81, 82, 84
Loesser, Frank, 68
Lola & Shorty's, 473
"Lonely Heart," 399
"Lonely Street," 158
"Lonesome Wind," 23
Long, Hubert, 190, 194, 218, 220–221
"Long Black Veil," 280
Lonzo & Oscar, 22
"Lost Highway," 473
Louisiana Hayride, 5, 13, 105, 109, 470
Louvin, Charlie, 304, 344, 390
Louvin Brothers, 160, 335, 390, 395
"Love Bug," 141
"Lovebug Itch, The," 62
"Love in Your Eyes, The," 445
Loveless, Patty, 444, 446
"Lovely Place to Cry, A," 242, 264, 266
"Lovesick Blues," 406, 472
"Love's the Answer," 339
"Love Will Be Right There," 333
"Loving You Could Never Be Better," 241
"Loving You Makes You Mine," 304
LPs, 14–15, 25, 156, 157
  see also individual LPs
Lucas, George, 346
Lundvall, Bruce, 343–344
Luther, Martin, 199–201, 202, 458
Lynch, David, 395
Lynn, Loretta, 25
  Owen Bradley's production of, 82
  on fiddles vs. violins, 73

hard country approach of, 47
Jones' CMA awards accepted by, 376
at Jones Country, 443
on Legends of Country Music, 406
sales by, 209
on "Stand by Your Man," 210
on Wynette, 190
with Wynette and Parton, 406
Wynette's cover of, 265
Lynne, Shelby, 441, 444

Machiavelli, Niccolò, 201–202, 227
Maddox, Rose, 421, 425
Maddox Brothers, 421
Madison Square Garden, 143–144, 307–308
Madonna, 323, 324
Maggots, The, 393
Makem, Tommy, 23
Malone, Bill C., 65
"Mama McCluskie," 341
management contracts, 370
  for Frizzell, 5–6
  for Horton, 335
  for David Houston, 237, 335
  for Jones, 128, 129, 154–162, 217, 363, 369–371, 374–376, 378, 396, 442
  for Tucker, 340
  for Wynette, 193–195, 398, 400, 409
Mandrell, Barbara, 195, 302, 303, 338, 376, 379
Mandrell Sisters, 338
"Man Who Shot Liberty Valance, The," 53, 136
"Man Worth Lovin' You, The," 241
Marsh, Dr., 411, 413
Martin, Dean, 431
Martin, George, 64
Martin, Glenn, 430
Martin, Grady, 44, 80, 110, 125, 264
Martin, Jimmy, 23
masquerade balls, 319–321
"Maybe Little Baby," 44, 45
Maybelle, Mother, 66
"Maybelline," 363
Mayhew, Aubrey, 343
Mazor, Barry, 330
MCA, 340, 444–447
McBride, Jim, 441
McCall, Bill, 7
McCall, C.W., 28
McCall, Darrell, 160–161
McClinton, O. B., 431
McCoy, Charlie, 85, 343

McCready, Mary Ann, 306, 307, 367
McDaniel, Mel, 443
McDill, Bob, 396
McDonough, Jimmy
  on documents of Wynette's death, 413
  Wynette's biography by, 177, 183, 217, 223, 252, 374, 395
McKinley, William, 354
McLaren, Malcolm, 323
Mèdici, Catherine de, 170–172, 204, 227, 229–233, 317
Mèdici, Giovanni de, 202
Mèdici family, 170–171, 203, 204, 227, 232
medieval tournaments, 165–170, 172, 228, 232–233
Meek, Joe, 64
"Memories of Us," 266
Merck, 353
Mercury Records, 13
  Jones at, 44, 126, 127
  merger with Starday, 18–19
  repackaging by, 143
  Sherrill at, 331
  and "Treasure of Love," 46–47
  Donny Young at, 52
Mercury-Starday
  flagship single of, 110
  and Jeanette Hicks, 134
  Jones at, 44, 107, 128
  Jones sent back to Gold Star by, 110, 111
  Roger Miller at, 108
  origin and termination of, 18–19
Merman, Ethel, 357
#MeToo, 260
Mexico, 147
MGM Records, 5
Midler, Bette, 339
"Midnight Oil, The," 338
Miller, Frankie, 21–22
Miller, Jody, 302, 338
Miller, Roger, 50, 108–109, 111, 127, 141, 162
Milsap, Ronnie, 349
"Milwaukee, Here I Come," 220
"Minute You're Gone, The," 333
"Misery Loves Company," 425–426
Miss America, 257–260, 321
Miss USA, 259
"Misty Blue," 86
Mitchell, Emily, 339, 346
Mitchell, Guy, 25, 70
Mix, Tom, 418–421
MixOnline.com, 327, 328
Modern People magazine, 280

Modern Sounds in Country and Western Music, 348
Moeller Talent, 190
"Mohair Sam," 340
Moman, Chips, 397–398
"Mona Lisa Lost Her Smile," 347
Monroe, Bill, 23
  at Castle's hotel studio, 61
  clothing style of, 426
  at Decca, 84–85
  on Grand Ole Opry, 466
  at Madison Square Garden, 143, 144
Monroe, Charlie, 23
Monroe, Vaughn, 68
Montana, Patsy, 209
Montes Reina, Francisco (Paquiro), 117–118
Montgomery, Bob, 403–404
Montgomery, Carl, 135, 137–140
Montgomery, Charlene, 242–243, 251, 305
Montgomery, Earl (Peanutt)
  on Daily, 238
  at FAME, 330
  Jones' attempted murder of, 310, 368–369
  as Jones' best friend, 241
  Jones committed by, 373
  and Jones' drinking, 251
  and Jones' drunk driving, 246
  songwriting by, 135, 138, 140, 160, 162, 241, 248, 266, 339
  and threats against Wynette, 242–243
Montgomery, Melba
  career of, 135
  Cash Box award for, 135
  on Daily, 155
  Daily's investment in, 240–241
  Jones influenced by, 52, 53
  Jones' songs with, 134, 160, 220, 238
  at Musicor, 241
  at New River Ranch, 132
  songwriting by, 140, 141, 162
  and Wynette, 250
Mooney, Ralph, 188
moonshine, 31–36, 39, 41
Moonshine Trilogy, 51, 159
Moore, Bob
  as A-team musician, 47, 63, 74, 80
  on Daily, 156
  on "End of the World," 77
  Jones' work with, 126–127, 139, 304–306

  on Bill Porter, 66–67
  tic-tac bass of, 82
  as uncredited producer, 80, 126, 220
Moress, Stan, 398–400
Morgan, Bob, 332–334
Morgan, George, 303
Morgan, Lorrie, 411
Morricone, Ennio, 69
Morrison, Harold, 269
"Most Beautiful Girl, The," 297, 341
"Mountain of Love," 335–336
"Move It On Over," 74, 470
movies
  Hays Code for, 320, 321
  in 1980s, 3
  in 1940s and 1950s, 56
  songs from, 68, 69
  westerns, 217, 418, 419, 423
  see also individual movies
Mr. Country and Western Music, 140
"Mr. Fool," 50
"Mr. Lovemaker," 343
"Much Too Young to Die," 75–76
"Mule Skinner Blues," 466
Mullican, Moon, 22, 62, 75
Mullins, Cam, 338
Mund, Cara, 260
Muscle Shoals, 63
Music Man, 48
Musicor
  founding of, 136
  Gusto's acquisition of, 26
  Jones at, 137–142, 237, 241, 304, 305
  Jones' split from, 237, 240
  Melba Montgomery at, 241
  Pitney at, 136–139
  and Wynette, 187, 220
Music Row, 65
Muslims, 228
"Must've Been Drunk," 430
"My Elusive Dreams," 194
"My Heart Cries for You," 25
"My Shoes Keep Walking Back to You," 17, 76
"My Special Angel," 71
"My Sweet Imogene," 475
My Very Special Guests, 371–373

Nabors, Jim, 336
Nadler, Susan, 449
Nallie, Luther, 471–472
Name of the Rose, The (Eco), 457
NASCAR, 41
Nash, Alanna, 268, 375, 393, 394

Nashville
    A-Team musicians in (see Nashville
        A-Team musicians)
    as capital of country music, 24,
        58–59
    Jones' difficulty staying sober in,
        223, 246–247, 251, 297
    George and Nancy Jones' move
        to, 443
    Jones' objections to country
        music establishment in, 303,
        308
    Mildred and Foy Lee's moves to
        and away from, 193, 282
    making country music in, 22,
        60 (see also Nashville Sound;
        individual producers and
        musicians)
    Music Business issue on, 55
    PayCheck's and Jones' burials in,
        450
    Presley's refusal to return to, 83
    recording studios in, 49, 58, 61–67,
        70, 110–111 (see also specific
        studios)
    record labels in, 61, 79 (see also
        individual labels)
    sourcing hit songs in, 400–401
    stars' museums and public home
        tours in, 313–314
    Wynette's and Jones' move from
        Lakeland to, 247, 249, 264
    Wynette's and Jones' move to
        Lakeland from, 218–220,
        222–224
    see also specific places in Nashville
Nashville (Altman), 328
Nashville A-Team musicians
    and Akins, 66
    in Owen Bradley's sessions,
        79–80
    on Double Trouble, 372
    in Connie Francis' session, 130
    in Jones' sessions, 125
    and Nashville Sound, 139, 343
    Sherrill on, 344–345
    training of, 74
    versatility of, 86
Nashville Edition, 339
Nashville Sound, 64–87
    and Anti-Nashville Sound, 19, 22
    Jimmy Bowen's evolution of, 431
    of Owen Bradley, 342
    definitions for, 47, 64–87
    glory days of, 47
    on Jones' records, 125, 127, 139
    Nashville A-Team records as, 343

and pop country music, 67–68,
        70, 71
    and pop music, 84
    in Ray Price's songs, 17
    Sherrill's version of, 342
Nashville Sound, The (Hemphill),
    65–66
Nation, Carrie, 37
National Enquirer, 273
Navarre, King of, 231, 233
Navarre, Queen of, 231
"Near You," 61, 281, 309–310
Nelson, Ken, 64, 390, 439, 472
Nelson, Ricky, 136
Nelson, Willie
    Fourth of July Picnic of, 367
    Jones' music with, 348, 447
    on Legends of Country Music, 406
    and Sherrill, 344, 349
    at Starday, 20
    and styles of country music,
        343–344
    "Yesterday's Wine," 429
Nero, 457
Ness, Eliot, 39–40
Neva's, 5, 6, 473
"Never Again (Will I Knock at Your
    Door)," 61
"Never Grow Cold," 224, 239
New Favorites of George Jones, The,
    158
Newman, Jimmy C.
    "Fallen Star," 64, 330
    and first ACE meeting, 303
    on Grand Ole Opry, 109
    hits of, 109–110
    at Jones Country, 443
    on Louisiana Hayride, 105
    "Seasons of My Heart," 12
New River Ranch, 131–132
Newton-John, Olivia, 303
Next to You, 403
Nicholson, Jack, 212
Night Life, 158
"Night Train to Memphis," 60
Nineteenth Amendment, 258
95 Theses (Luther), 199–201
Ninja, Willi, 323
Nixon, Agnes, 289–291
Noack, Eddie, 140, 162
"No Charge," 250, 264
"No Fault of Mine," 123
"No Money in This Deal," 9
"No One Else in the World," 395
"No One Will Ever Know," 180
"No Place for Me," 20
"No Show Jones," 430

"Not What I Had in Mind," 159
Nugget, 132

O'Dell, Doye, 27
O'Dell, Kenny, 340
"Oh, Lonesome Me," 84
"Oil on My Land," 21
O'Kanes, 402
Okeh, 333
"Okie from Muskogee," 301
"Old Fashioned Singing," 248
Oldman, Gary, 460
"Old Man No One Loves, The," 441
Old Plantation Music Park, 236–237,
    246, 247
"Ol' George Stopped Drinkin' Today,"
    431
"Ol' Red," 443–444
Omegas, 341
"Once Again," 123
One, 408, 446
O'Neal, Ryan, 292
O'Neal, Tom, 27
"One Day a Week," 52
"One If for Him, Two If for Me," 336
"One I Loved Back Then, The," 440
One Life to Live, 289, 294
"One More Last Chance," 446
"One Step Nearer to You," 18
One Woman Man, 442
"One Woman Man," 442
"Only Love Can Break a Heart," 53,
    136
"Open Pit Mine," 158
Orbison, Roy, 80–81, 330
Ordóñez, Antonio, 90–91
organized crime, 39
    cocaine conspiracy, 434–438
    slot machines, 2
Osmond, Donnie, 330
"Our Private Life," 249–250
outlaw country, 343, 367
"Out of Control," 51
Overstreet, Paul, 441
Owen, Fuzzy, 188
Owens, Buck, 47, 48, 87, 125–126,
    143–144, 450
Owens, "Doodle," 440

Page, Patti, 336
"Painless Heart," 11
Painted Dreams, 286, 287
"Pair of Old Sneakers, A," 396–397
Paquiro, 117–118
Paris Is Burning, 324
Parker, Tom, 426
Parsons, Gram, 301–302, 425

Parton, Dolly, 48, 190, 303, 406, 411
Passions, 294
Patterson, Clara, 464
Patterson, Ethel, 464
PayCheck, Johnny
   "Almost Persuaded," 336–337
   "Apartment #9," 188
   Hank Cochran's hits for, 85
   death of, 450
   at Epic, 343, 347
   introduction of Jones as Hank
      Williams by, 101–102
   and Jones, 48–53, 238, 271, 363,
      372
   name of, 50
   and outlaw country, 343
   "Waltz of the Angels," 127
Payne, Leon, 140, 162, 238
payola, 25, 194–196, 335
Pearl, Minnie, 22, 62
pedal steel, 78, 106, 126, 129, 305,
   333
Pemberton, John, 354–355
Penn, Dan, 330
Penniman, Richard, 55–56
Pennington, Ray, 196
Pensacola News Journal, 303
People magazine, 280
Peppers, Jimmy, 266
Pete Seeger & The Weavers, 23
Pet Sounds, 86
Peyton Place, 292–293
"Phantom 309," 28
Philippe V, King of Spain, 93–95,
   233
Phillips, Irna, 286–292
Phillips, Sam, 332
Phillips International, 331
piano, 71–74, 78, 81–82, 333, 342
Picking Up the Tempo, 344
"Piece of My Heart," 210
Pierce, Don
   and Anti-Nashville Sound, 22
   and bluegrass, 23
   and Glen Campbell's recordings,
      26
   and custom press program, 20–21
   on Daily, 159
   death of, 450
   at 4 Star, 7
   and Tommy Hill, 21
   influence of, 24–25
   and Jones' drinking, 102
   and King Records purchase, 26
   and "Maybe Little Baby," 44
   on melody, 27–28
   and Mercury merger, 18

   and Frankie Miller, 21–22
   Roger Miller's songs for, 108
   and repackaging music, 24, 125
   retirement of, 24, 28
   on rockabilly music, 17
   at Starday, 7, 10, 14, 15, 19–20, 45
   successes of, 103
   and truckin' songs, 27
   on "Why Baby Why," 11–12
Pierce, Webb
   Owen Bradley's production of, 66
   at Castle's hotel studio, 61
   Cedarwood Publishing launched
      by, 64
   clothing of, 425
   Cramer in sessions of, 81
   Jimmy Day in sessions of, 110
   experiments with rock and country
      by, 70, 71
   at 4 Star, 5
   "Honky Tonk Song," 73
   at Madison Square Garden, 143
   Martin and Garland in sessions
      of, 80
   and Nashville Sound, 71
   "Slowly," 21
   "Why Baby Why," 12–13
pinball, forms of, 1–4
"Pin Ball Boogie," 2
"Pinball Machine," 26–27
pinball machines, 1–4
"Pinball Millionaire," 2
"Pink and Black," 17
pipe organ, 72
"Pistol Packin' Mama," 467
Pitney, Gene, 52–53, 136–140, 238
"Playin' Around with Love," 338
"Play It Cool Man—Play It Cool," 8–9
"Please Help Me, I'm Falling," 82, 84
Poitiers, Diane de, 171–172
Polanski, Roman, 461
Poole, Charlie, 358
"Poor Little Rich Boy," 158
"Poor Man's Riches," 17
Poovey, Joe, 140
pop country music, 72–76
   and Owen Bradley's work, 77, 84
   on country radio, 47
   debate over, 87, 343
   drums in, 43, 75
   instruments in, 138
   Jones' attacks on, 303
   Nashville Sound as, 67–68, 70, 71
   piano in, 81
   "Strange Little Girl," 72
   "White Lightning," 43–44
   "Zeb's Mountain Boogie," 61

pop crossover
   and Owen Bradley's work, 77
   by Jones, 301, 302
   and Jones-Wynette marriage, 265
   from movie Westerns, 68, 69
   by Sherrill and Atkins, 192
   "Singing the Blues," 70
   "White Lightning," 43, 44
   by Wynette, 301
pop-folk music, 22–23
pop music
   Atkins' attempts at, 192
   "Chantilly Lace," 44
   by Hank Cochran, 85
   country music vs., 71, 81, 83, 85, 87
   and covers of Jones' songs, 130,
      136
   disco tropes in, 87
   "Don't Touch Me," 86
   "End of the World," 78
   "I'm Saving My Love," 79
   "I'm Sorry," 78
   influences on, 73
   and Jones-Wynette marriage, 265
   from movie Westerns, 68, 69
   and Nashville Sound, 84
   "Near You," 61
   negative influence on country by,
      74–75
   "Never Again (Will I Knock at
      Your Door)," 61
   of Pitney, 52–53, 136–138
   rhythm in, 74
   "Singing the Blues," 70
   slip-note piano in, 82
   "Tutti-Frutti," 56
   vocal chorus in, 84
   "White Sport Coat (And a Pink
      Carnation), A," 60
Porter, Bill, 66–67, 75
Porter, Cole, 68, 357
Porter Wagoner Show, The, 425–426
Pose, 324
Poseidon, 455
Possum Holler, 361–361
Possum Hunters, 426
"Possum" (nickname), 103
Potter, Dale, 45, 70, 472
"Precious Jewel, The," 466
Presley, Elvis
   backup singers for, 82–84
   on Country charts, 15, 17, 47
   Kirkham on record of, 126
   on *Louisiana Hayride*, 105
   Moman's production of, 397
   pinball playing by, 3
   at RCA, 81

Presley, Elvis (*cont.*)
   soundalikes of, 16
   Stoker on, 63
   suits of, 426
Price, Ray
   at Castle's hotel studio, 61
   Hank Cochran's hits for, 85
   Jimmy Day on hits by, 110
   drums in music of, 75–76
   and "Heartaches by the Number,"
      25
   and Jones as best country singer,
      48
   at Madison Square Garden, 143
   Night Life LP, 158
   songwriting by, 107
   sounds of, 17
   tours of, 9, 13, 107
Pride, Charley, 84, 145, 236–237
Prince, The (Machiavelli), 201–202,
   227
Prine, John, 398
"Prisoner's Song, The," 85
Procter & Gamble, 286, 288–289, 292
Prohibition, 38–41, 319–321
Protestant Reformation, 227–230,
   233
Protestants, 201, 227–231
Ptolemy, 455, 456
Pugh, Mildred, 175–176
Pugh, Virginia Wynette (Nettiebelle),
   175–179, 250–251, 402
   see also Wynette, Tammy
Pugh, William, 175–178
Pugh family, 182–184
Putman, Curly
   on saddest country song, 298
   songwriting by, 194, 213, 300, 312,
      339, 403
Putnam, Norbert, 63
"Put Your Hand in the Hand," 339

Queen, The, 321–322
Quinn, Anthony, 216, 217
Quinn, Bill, 9
Quonset Hut, The
   Owen Bradley's sessions at, 67, 86
   establishment of, 67
   Connie Francis' session at, 130
   Jones' sessions at, 111, 130
   Bill Monroe's sessions at, 85
   Charlie Rich's session at, 341–342
   Wynette's initial session at, 189

"Race Is On, The," 135–136, 141, 160
racial discrimination, 321–322
racial integration, 291–292, 321

radio
   country stations (*see* country
      radio)
   daytime, 284–289
"Radio Lover," 431, 442
Ragged but Right (Carlisle), 432
"Rain, Rain," 44–45
Raitt, Bonnie, 375
Raney, Wayne, 20
"Rank Stranger," 23
Raven, Eddy, 431
Ray, Johnnie, 17
R&B, *see* rhythm & blues
RCA Records, 65–67, 75, 78, 79, 81,
   83–85
realness, 323, 325
recording studios
   of Owen Bradley, 9, 47, 50, 58, 70,
      445
   cost of recording at, 110–111, 157
   filler sessions at, 125, 157–158
   home studios, 8
   in Nashville, 61–67, 70 (*see also*
      specific studios)
   quality of recordings, 110–111,
      155–157
   songs per session in, 156–157
record labels
   Jones' changes of, 157–158
   in Nashville, 61, 79
   new artists' songs covered by, 12
   in regional markets, 13–14
   soundalikes of, 14
   Wynette's lies about, 186
   see also individual labels
records, LP and EP, 14–15
Red Headed Stranger, 343, 344
Reed, Jerry, 270
Reefer Madness, 356
"Reefer song," 357
Reeves, Del, 237
Reeves, Jim, 47, 64, 65
refrigeration, 56–57
repackaging music, 24, 125, 157
Requiem for a Heavyweight, 216–217
"Revenooer Man," 51, 159
Reynolds, Burt, 270, 273, 274,
   279–281
Reynolds, Debbie, 189
rhinestones
   on clothing, 111, 423–427
   on G-strings, 422–423
Rhodes (island), 454–455
Rhodes, Jack, 127
rhythm (beat), 73–76, 78
rhythm & blues (R&B), 74, 329, 333,
   348

Rich, Charlie, 297, 340–342, 347,
   395
Richard, Cliff, 333, 407
Richard III, King of England, 459
Richardson, J. P. (the Big Bopper),
   44–46, 103
Richey, George, 254
   after Wynette's death, 412–414
   Tony Brown on, 446
   character and reputation of,
      389–390
   death of, 414
   divorces of, 272, 390
   and Phil Donahue, 393
   and Jones, 374, 375, 377, 378
   marriage to Wynette, 224, 282,
      310, 389–391, 393–395, 399,
      407, 409–410
   songwriting by, 253, 266, 271, 281,
      313, 339
   Hank Williams' house bought by,
      405–406
   Wynette controlled by, 377, 378,
      397–401, 403, 406, 409
   and Wynette's death/memorial,
      410–411
   and Wynette-Sherrill split, 396
   and Wynette's threatening
      incidents, 275–278
Richey, Paul, 374–377, 394, 396,
   397
Richey, Sheila, 275, 276, 390
Riddle, George, 124–125, 131, 132,
   153
"Ride, The," 347
Riders in the Sky, 68
Riefenstahl, Leni, 346
"Right Left Hand, The," 440
"Right Won't Touch a Hand," 241
Riley, Jeannie C., 210
Ripley, Jack, 442
Robbins, Marty, 9, 25, 69–71, 80,
   213, 336
Robbins, Pig
   on Daily, 155
   on Jones' drinking, 99–100
   piano playing by, 43, 46, 126, 341,
      448
   and Charlie Rich, 341
   and Sherrill's sound, 328
   tack piano by, 333
Robertson, Don, 81–82
Robinson, Floyd, 43
Robinson, Smokey, 407
Rock, The, 449
rockabilly music, 17, 110,
   306–307

rock & roll
  and country, 16–17, 44, 47
  influences on, 73
  and Nashville Sound, 70–71
  paradigm shift caused by, 15–16
Rodeo Ben, 148
Rodgers, Jimmie, 466
Rodríguez Costillares, Joaquín, 96,
    115–117
Roe, Tommy, 332
Rogers, Roy, 68, 404, 421, 427
Rolling Stone
  Atkins' apology in, 84
  Dylan on Jones in, 241
  Flippo at, 307
  headquarters location for, 308
  Jones as Country Artists of the
    Year in, 367
  Jones' eulogy in, 48
  on Charlie Rich's single, 340
Rollins, Don, 136
"Rollin' with the Flow," 347
Roman Catholicism, 199–204, 227–
    231, 458–459, 461
romance
  and chivalry, 167–169, 459
  in soap operas, 291, 293 (*see also*
    soap operas)
Romance of the Rose, The, 459
Romans, ancient, 455–457
Rombauer, Irma, 56
Romeo & Juliet (Shakespeare), 459
Romero, Francisco, 95, 96, 117
Romero, Pedro, 117
Ronstadt, Linda, 271, 375
"Root Beer," 159
Rosalias, 456–457, 461
Rosaries, 458
Rose, The (Grimm Brothers), 461
"Rose Conley," 454
"Rose Garden," 337–338
Rosemary's Baby, 461
Rosenberg, Neil, 23–24
*Rosencrantz and Guildenstern Are
    Dead* (Stoppard), 460
roses, 453–461
"Roses Are Red (My Love)," 332
"Roving Kind, The," 25
Rowe, James, 466
Roy Acuff Museum & Gift Shop,
    362
royalties, 327
  for custom press clients, 20
  for Jones, 125, 197, 222, 237, 362,
    363, 371, 429
  for Don Pierce, 19
  for Schroeder, 136

  for Sovine, 13
  for Wynette, 192, 193, 268–269
"Rubber Ball," 136–137
Ruby, Texas, 22
"Rules of the Game," 331
running of the bulls, 89–90, 92
"Running Scared," 80–81
"Run Woman Run," 210–211
RuPaul's Drag Race, 324
Rush, Benjamin, 36
Russell, Bobby, 301
Russell, Johnny, 298–299, 443
"Rye Whiskey," 27

Saddest Country Song Ever, 297, 298
Sam Phillips, 330, 332
"Satisfied," 186
"Satisfied Mind, A," 10, 19, 45, 127
Schroeder, Aaron, 136, 137
Scott, Sir Walter, 460
Scott, Wendell, 41
Scouts of the Prairie, The, 382,
    384–385
Screen Gems, 341
Seals, Troy, 349, 439
"Seasons of My Heart," 12, 105, 109,
    329
Seeger, Pete, 23
Seely, Jeannie, 85, 86, 237
Selzer, Eddie, 89
"Send Me No Roses," 190
Sepulvado, Adina, 433–438, 443
Sepulvado, Nancy, 432–439
  see also Jones, Nancy
Serling, Rod, 216
Setser, Eddie, 349
"Seven Spanish Angels," 348–349
"Shadow My Baby," 17
Shakespeare, William, 459, 460
"Shakin' the Blues," 51, 123
Shea, Robert, 404
"She Didn't Color Daddy," 188, 189
"She Hung the Moon," 431
"Sheila," 332
"She Loved a Lot in Her Time," 444
Shelton, Blake, 443
Shenandoah, 403
"She Once Lived Here," 158
Shepard, Jean, 10, 211–212, 303
Sheppard, T. G., 347
Sherrill, Billy
  artists' sounds influenced by, 304,
    305
  on "Bartender's Blues," 308
  career of, 328–349
  and Don Chapel, 196
  on country music, 334

  Daily's songs recorded by, 238
  and "D-I-V-O-R-C-E," 213
  following Jones-Wynette divorce,
    271, 272, 281
  and "He Stopped Loving Her
    Today," 297–300, 309–312
  on hit songs in Nashville, 400–401
  influence of, 327–328
  and Jones' addictive behaviors,
    299–300
  Jones' collaborations with, 250,
    302–303, 305, 430, 431
  and Jones' drinking songs,
    265–267
  and Jones' gospel music CD, 449
  Jones supported by, 372
  on Jones' voice quality, 430–431
  and Jones-Wynette duets, 239
  marketing to women by, 211
  Peanutt Montgomery with, 241
  Bob Moore's work with, 220
  and Nashville Sound, 127
  at Old Plantation Music Park, 237
  political views of, 345–346
  pop crossovers of, 302
  as producer, 392, 440–441
  and public perception of Jones and
    Wynette, 239–242
  retirement of, 443
  and George Richey, 389, 411
  songwriting by, 191–192, 224, 225,
    239, 240, 264, 329–330, 334,
    341, 347 (*see also specific songs*)
  split with Wynette, 395–397
  and "Stand By Your Man," 207–
    209
  and "(We're Not) the Jet Set," 248
  and Wynette-Jones marriage, 263
  Wynette's contract with, 282,
    346–347
  and Wynette's early music,
    188–194
  on Wynette's hecklers, 269
  Wynette's persona created by, 192,
    193
  on Wynette's pregnancy, 236
  and Wynette's song characters,
    239–240, 251, 264, 265, 267,
    337
  and Wynette's sound, 187–188
"She's All I Got," 343
"(She's Finally Crossed Over) Love's
    Cheatin' Line," 347
"She's Got You," 74, 85
"She's My Rock," 431
"She Thinks I Still Care," 129, 130,
    155, 158–160, 300, 301

Shine On, 431
"Shine On," 411, 430
shirts, western, 148, 149
Sholes, Steve, 83
Shore, Dinah, 270
Shotgun Willie, 343
"Show's Almost Over, The," 431
Shriver, Evelyn, 448, 449
"Sick Rose, The" (Blake), 453, 454
"Silver Threads and Golden Needles,"
    406
Simpson, Jimmy, 27
Sinatra, Frank, 60
"Singing My Song," 210
"Singing the Blues," 25, 69, 70
Singleton, Margie, 18, 127, 134
Singleton, Shelby, 18, 19, 52, 126, 127
"Sing Me Back Home," 450
"Six Days on the Road," 27, 135
"Sixteen Tons," 13
Skaggs, Ricky, 402, 448
Skinner, Jimmie, 18, 22
"Skip a Rope," 161
Slaughter, Lenora, 258
Slaughter, Sheila, 412–414
    see also Richey, Sheila
Sledd, Patsy, 269
"Sleeper Cab Blues," 27
slip-note piano, 82
slot machines, 2
"Slowly," 21, 66
"Small Time Laboring Man," 241
Smash Records, 340, 341
Smith, Carl, 13, 107
Smith, Jan, 395
Smith, Sammi, 237
Smith, Stuff, 356
Smokey and the Bandit, 28
Smokey Mountain Boys, 22, 59, 132
Snow, Hank, 75, 303, 425
Snyder, Tom, 48
soap operas, 285–295
soap products, 285, 286
social classes, 317–318, 320
social injustice
    in bullfighting, 94–95
    during Prohibition, 40–41
Society of American Indians, 417
Solomon, Jack, 141
"Somebody Wants Me Out of the
    Way," 440
"Someday My Day Will Come," 371
Some Like It Hot, 321
"Someone to Give My Love To," 343
"Some Things Will Never Change,"
    402
Sometimes When We Touch, 400

"Sometimes When We Touch," 400
"Sometimes You Just Can't Win,"
    158–159
SongwriterUniverse.com, 312
Sonico, 331
Sons of the Pioneers, 27, 68, 69
"Soul Song," 339
soundalikes, 14, 16, 109, 125
South, Joe, 337
South Coast Amusement Company, 4
"Southern California," 281
Sovine, Red, 12, 13, 22, 28
Spain
    bullfighting in, 89–96, 115–121, 157
    kings of, 93–95, 202–203, 233
speakeasies, 39–41, 319–321, 358
Spears, Billie Jo, 187
Spector, Phil, 64
speed (amphetamines), 100, 144,
    243, 246
Spivey, Victoria, 357
split-publishing, 110
Springfield, Rick, 294
Springsteen, Bruce, 207
Stampley, Joe, 339
Stamps, Virgil O., 328, 347
"Stand By Me," 209, 334
"Stand By Your Man," 154, 207–212,
    218, 220, 249
Stanley Brothers, The, 18, 22, 23,
    61, 129
Staple Singers, 333
Starday-King, 26
Starday Records, 5–8
    album jackets of, 19–20
    bluegrass catalog of, 23
    Johnny Bond at, 25
    Sonny Burns at, 104–105
    business strategies of, 15
    custom press operation of, 20–21,
        26–27
    Dixie Records, 14
    Duff at, 6–8
    early "studio" of, 8
    first LP release of, 17
    Tommy Hill at, 21
    Jones at, 8–12, 99, 102–105
    Jones catalog at, 125
    legacy act artists from, 22
    legacy pop acts at, 25
    major label castoffs at, 22
    merger with Mercury, 13, 18–19
        (see also Mercury-Starday)
    and Frankie Miller's songs, 21–22
    new studio for, 22
    repackaging by, 24, 125
    rock & roll from, 17

soundalikes of, 14, 16, 125–126
    Starnes' split from, 10
    and truckin' songs, 27–28
Starnes, Bill, 8, 10
Starnes, Jack, 5–8
Starnes, Neva, 5–7
"Starting Over," 396
Statler Brothers, 213, 336
"Stay Away from My Baby," 333
"Stay on Board," 161
steel guitar, 70–71, 73
Stegall, Keith, 441, 448
Stevens, Ray, 334
Steward, Wynn, 188
Stewart, Slam, 56
Stewart, Wynn, 127, 158
"Still Around," 396
"Still Doin' Time," 267, 429
Sting, 407
stock car racing, 41
Stoker, Gordon, 63, 83
Stone, Cliffie, 476
Stoppard, Tom, 460
Story, Carl, 18, 22
Strait, George, 49
"Strange Little Girl," 71, 72
Strauss, Johan, 342
Street, Mel, 345
string sections, 68, 72, 76–79, 305
Strzelecki, Henry, 76
substance abuse
    and fame/success, 104
    see also alcohol abuse; drug use
"Success," 82
"Sugar Beet," 75
"Sugar Lips," 334
sumptuary laws, 317–319
Sun Also Rises, The (Hemingway),
    90–91, 115, 119
"Sunday Mornin' Comin Down," 301
Sun Records, 331
Supernatural, 295
Sure-Fire Music, 135
"Suspicious Minds," 397
Sutton, Bill, 193, 264
Sutton, Glenn
    marriage of, 337
    as producer, 337–338
    on Sherrill, 344
    songwriting by, 161, 190, 192,
        193, 225, 239, 240, 334–335,
        396–397
Sutton, Popcorn, 31, 32, 41
Swamp Dogg, 343
"Sweet and Innocent," 330
Sykes, Bobby, 27
syncopation, 73–74

"Take a Drink on Me," 358
"Take a Whiff on Me," 357, 358
"Take Me," 238, 239, 247
"Take Me to Your World," 240, 337
"Take the Devil Out of Me," 110
"Take This Job and Shove It," 343, 363
"Talkin' to Myself Again," 402
"Tall, Tall Trees," 108, 111
Tally, 188, 190
Tally Ho!, 23
Talmadge, Art, 18, 107, 128, 136, 137
Tammy and the Bachelor, 189
Tammy Wynette (McDonough), 177
Taste of Yesterday's Wine, A, 429, 430
Taylor, Carmol, 242, 253, 313, 329, 333
Taylor, James, 308, 363, 372
Taylor, Jerry, 409
Taylor, Ted, 333
"Teddy," 18
"Teddy Bear," 28
"Teenage Boogie," 70
telecommunications technology, 14
    see also specific technologies
"Telephone Call, The," 264
television, 14
    beauty pageants on, 257, 259
    Black characters on, 292
    country music TV, 445
    drag on, 324
    gender roles in, 290–291
    Jones on, 124, 131, 135, 142, 375, 379, 447
    in 1980s, 3
    in 1940s and 1950s, 56
    soap operas on, 287–295
    Wagoner on, 184, 185, 425
    Wynette on, 180, 184, 185, 270, 393
"Tell It to Me," 357
temperance movement, 36–38
"Tender Years," 52, 126
"Ten Little Bottles," 25
Tennessean, 401
"Tennessee Whiskey," 267, 431
Texas Jack, 384, 385
"That's All You Gotta Do," 77
"That's the Way I Feel," 108, 111
"That's the Way It Could Have Been," 280
"That's Where My Money Goes," 328
"There Goes My Everything," 301
"There'll Be No Teardrops Tonight," 125
"There's a Party Goin' On," 338
"There's Gonna Be One," 161

"There Stands the Glass," 66
"There's the Door," 444
"These Days I Barely Get By," 266, 363
"They Call It Makin' Love," 392
"They'll Never Take Her Love from Me," 473
Thibodeaux, Rufus, 110
"Things Have Gone to Pieces," 140, 450
"This Wanting You," 448
Thomas, Dick, 68
Thompson, Hank, 21, 427
Thumper Jones (alias), 16, 44, 125
tic-tac bass, 76–77, 82
"Til I Can Make It on My Own," 271–272
"Til I Get It Right," 263–264
Tillis, Mel, 67
Tillis, Pam, 444
Tillman, Floyd, 22, 194–196, 335–336
"Tipsy," 332
TNN Music City News Awards, 404
"Together Again," 87
"Together Forever," 87
"Tom Dooley," 22
Tomlin, Michael, 272–274, 278–279, 281, 310
Tommy Dorsey and His Orchestra, 60
"Too Much Water," 111, 125
"Town Without Pity," 53
"Traveling Shoes," 25
Travis, Merle, 13, 444
Travis, Randy, 403, 404, 406, 443, 474
"Treasure of Love," 45–47, 50
Tree Music, 193–194, 330, 334
T-Rex, 70
Tritt, Travis, 444
Triumph of the Will, 345, 346
truckin' songs, 27–28, 333
"Try," 304
Tubb, Ernest
    at Castle, 61, 62
    cowboy hats of, 426
    drums used by, 75
    gospel music of, 83
    on *Grand Ole Opry*, 467
    Jones influenced by, 11, 49
    at Madison Square Garden, 143
    record shop of, 59
    strings and vocal chorus used by, 68, 71
Tubb, Glenn Douglas, 161, 374
Tubb, Justin, 22

Tucker, Tanya, 338–340, 395, 399
Tudor, Frederic, 57
Tudor, Henry, 459
Tumbling Tumbleweeds, 69
"Tumbling Tumbleweeds," 69
Turk, Nathan, 421, 423–425
Turner, Scotty, 188
Turner, Tina, 209
Turner, Titus, 45
Turner, Zeb, 61
"Tutti-Frutti," 55–56
Twain, Shania, 407
"twang," 81, 82
"24 Hours from Tulsa," 53, 136
Twitty, Conway, 87, 236, 303, 336, 439, 442
"Two Story House," 374–375, 396
Tyler, T. Texas, 22

United Artists Records, 127, 128, 133, 136, 143, 158
Untamed, The, 419
Untouchables, 39–40
"Unwanted Babies," 162
"Unwed Fathers," 398

Valens, Ritchie, 46
Valentine's Day, 458–459
Valois-Habsburg conflict, 203–204, 227–230, 233
Vanderbilt, Alva, 320
VanHoy, Rafe, 280
Vee, Bobby, 136
Verne, Jules, 354
"Very Special Love Song, A," 341
Vickery, Mack, 343
Vinton, Bobby, 332, 334
violins, 73, 77, 303
vocal chorus, 82–84, 269
"Vogue," 323–324
voguing, 323–324
Volstead Act, 38–39
voting rights, 37–38, 257–258

"Wabash Cannonball," 59
Wagoner, Porter
    and Atkins, 84
    death of, 450
    and first ACE meeting, 303
    hard country approach of, 47
    Jones' bathroom encounter with, 246
    at Madison Square Garden, 143
    on *Ozark Jubilee*, 10
    rhinestone suits of, 425–426
    on television, 184, 185, 425–426
    and Wynette, 184–185

Walker, Billy, 303
Walker, Charlie, 333, 335
Walker, Wayne, 140
"Walkin' After Midnight," 73, 74, 77
"Walking the Floor Over You," 467
"Walk Through This World with Me,"
    53, 141–142, 194, 215, 301
Wallace, George, 237
Waller, Fats, 357
Walls, Danny, 240
Walls Can Fall, 444
"Waltz of the Angels, The," 127
"Wandering Soul," 103
Warhol, Terry Southern, 321–322
Warren, Ray, 188
wars
    in fifth century, 165
    religious, 201, 202
    tournaments in place of, 165–170,
        172, 232–233
    Valois-Habsburg conflict, 203–
        204
Wars of Religion, 230, 231
Wars of the Roses, 459, 460
Washington, George, 35, 36
Watson, Gene, 402
Watts, Slim, 475
Waverly novels (Scott), 460
"Wave to Me, My Lady," 61
Ways to Love a Man, The, 396
"Ways to Love a Man, The," 210
"Way Up on Clinch Mountain," 27
"Wean Me," 266
Webb, June, 132
"We Can Make It," 240
"Wedding Bells," 472, 473
"We Didn't See a Thing," 348, 431
"We Got Love," 336
We Go Together, 239
Welborn, Linda, 364–365, 368, 373,
    379, 433
Welles, Orson, 89, 346
"We'll Find a Way," 70
Wells, H. G., 354
Wells, Kitty, 21, 61–62, 127, 406, 442
"We Loved It Away," 253
"We Must Have Been Out of Our
    Minds," 52, 133, 135
"We Need a Whole Lot More of Jesus
    (And a Lot Less Rock and Roll),"
    20
"We're Gonna Hold On," 247–249,
    264, 302–303
We're Here, 324
"(We're Not) the Jet Set," 248
"We're Strangers Again," 404
West, Dottie, 143

West, Speedy, 27
West (US region), 381–386
western music, 68, 69
Westerns (movies), 217, 418, 419,
    423
western wear, 147–150, 381–385,
    418–427
"We Sure Can Love Each Other," 242
"What Am I Worth," 11, 13–14, 106
"What Color (Is a Man)," 334
"What Goes with Blue," 404
"What's Wrong with You," 11
"What's Your Mama's Name?," 339
Wheeler, Wayne, 36–41
"When It's Springtime in Alaska (It's
    Forty Below)," 80
"When the Grass Grows Over Me,"
    216, 301
"When There's a Fire in Your Heart,"
    212
"When Two Worlds Collide," 127
"When You're Ugly Like Us (You Just
    Naturally Got to Be Cool)," 372
"Where Grass Won't Grow," 241
"Where We'll Never Grow Old,"
    224
Whiskey Rebellion, 35–36
whiskey tax, 34–35
"White Lightning," 43–47, 50, 111,
    136, 303
"White Sport Coat (And a Pink
    Carnation), A," 60
Whitley, Keith, 474
"Whole Lotta Shakin' Goin' On," 44
"Whole World Is Turning (Just for
    Us), The," 333
"Who's Gonna Fill Their Shoes?,"
    439–440
"Who Shot Sam," 51, 159
"Why Baby Why," 11–13, 17, 19, 49,
    101, 105, 109, 305
Wiginton, Hurshel, 330
Wilburn Brothers, 130
"Wild as a Wildcat," 333
"Wild Side of Life, The," 21
Wilhite, Billy, 364
Wilkin, Marijohn, 280
Willet, Slim, 21
Williams, Audrey, 405
Williams, Hank
    artists influenced by, 49, 50
    at Castle, 61, 62
    cowboy hats of, 426
    Jimmy Day on hits by, 110
    death of, 476
    and honky-tonk, 11
    house bought by, 405

impersonations of, 8–9, 21, 103,
    125, 470, 472–473
Jones influenced by, 101, 472–473,
    476
Jones' introduction as, 101–102
and rhythm, 74, 75
soundalikes of, 157–158
tours of, 5
unreleased recordings of, 180
Williams, Lemmy & Wendy O., 209
Williams, Leona, 404, 432
Williams, Tex, 423
Willis Brothers, 27
Wills, Bob, 74
"Will You Visit Me on Sundays," 304
Wilson, Brian, 77, 86
Wilson, Dennis, 402
Wilson, Norro
    career of, 340–341
    and "Good Year for the Roses," 313
    on Jones, 446–447
    on *One*, 446
    songwriting by, 240, 264, 266,
        313, 339, 341
Wilson, Obrey, 333
Wilson, Robert Anton, 404
Wilson, Woodrow, 38–39
"Wind Me Up (Let Me Go)," 333
"Window Up Above," 49, 51, 123–
    126, 129, 155
Wine Colored Roses, 440
With Love, 304
Without Walls, 406–407
"Woke Up This Morning (My Baby
    She Was Gone)," 329
"Wolverton Mountain," 334
"Womanhood," 392
"Woman's Needs, A," 407
"Woman to Woman," 251, 264
women
    and beauty pageants, 258–260
    branding and marketing toward,
        284–285, 292
    dangers of soap operas for,
        288–289
    and laws on nudity, 422
    stereotypical gender roles for,
        290–291
    voting rights for, 37–38, 257–258
Women's Liberation movement,
    207–208, 211, 291
"World Needs a Melody, The," 302
World War II, 4, 58, 59, 345, 346,
    467
"Worst of Luck," 140
"Would You Lay with Me (in a Field
    of Stone)," 339

"Wound Time Can't Erase, A," 224
Wrangler, 148
wreath ceremonies, 456
Wright, Johnny, 442
"Writing on the Wall, The," 442
WSM radio, 58–61, 64–65
Wynette, Tammy
    alcohol use by, 243
    and anti-feminism, 207
    awards for, 193, 209, 223–224, 301, 404
    backup singers for, 269
    bankruptcy of, 403
    biography of, 177
    on *Capitol*, 294
    and Don Chapel, 186–187, 196
    daughters' allegations about death of, 413, 414
    death and memorial of, 408–414, 447
    declining hits by, 268, 269
    distortions of reality by, 176, 177, 247, 252, 268, 393
    drug use by, 243–244, 253–254, 269, 394–395, 397, 401–404
    early career of, 154, 181, 184–197
    early life of, 175–183
    ECT treatments of, 182, 183
    end of Sherrill's relationship with, 282, 346–347
    at Epic, 238, 306, 399–400, 402, 405–408
    fake abduction of, 389, 391–393
    and feminism, 207–212
    as First Lady of Country Music, 209, 306
    fundamental persona flaws of, 267–268
    harassment and assaults on, 274–278
    on her songwriting, 251
    and David Houston, 194
    infidelity of, 183
    and Jones' child support, 309, 378
    Jones' duets with, 238–239, 242, 271, 300, 302, 374–375, 396, 397, 403, 407–408, 446 (*see also individual songs*)
    and Jones following divorce, 270–272, 280–281
    Jones' relationship with, 154, 162, 197, 213–222, 269, 298, 309–310, 377
    Jones sued by, 309
    legacy of, 412
    love for music, 180
    makeover for, 399
    marriage to Byrd, 179–184, 192, 218
    marriage to Don Chapel, 192–193, 214–218
    marriage to Jones, 235, 236, 242–253, 264–266, 306, 362
    marriage to George Richey, 224, 282, 310, 389–391, 393–395, 399, 407, 409–410
    marriage to Tomlin, 272–274, 278–279, 281, 310
    and Melba Montgomery, 241, 250
    and the Montgomerys, 242–243
    music video of, 405
    nude photos of, 217–218
    and Old Plantation Music Park, 236–237
    in pop culture media, 301
    public perception of Jones and, 239–242
    and Burt Reynolds, 270, 273–274, 279–281
    George Richey's control over, 397–401, 403, 406, 409
    severe health problems of, 243–244, 279, 401, 406, 408, 409
    on Sherrill, 344
    and Sherrill songs, 327, 328, 337, 400–401
    song characters portrayed by, 239–240, 263, 267–268
    split with Sherrill by, 395–397
    talk show of, 447
    voice quality/style of, 187–188
    waning career of, 391, 392, 397–399, 404–407
    and Wynette Pugh vs. Tammy Wynette, 250–251

"Ya Ba Da Ba Do (So are You)," 442
"Y'all Come," 7–8, 19
Yates, Billy, 448
"Yearning," 133, 145
"Yellow Rose of Texas, The," 75
"Yesterday's Wine," 429
Yoakam, Dwight, 441–442
"You All Come," 6–7
"You and Me," 272
"You and Me and Time," 450
You Brought Me Back, 397
"You Can Lead a Heart to Love (But You Can't Make It Fall)," 400
"You Couldn't Get the Picture," 444
"You Done Me Wrong," 107
"You Don't Seem to Miss Me," 446
"You Gotta Be My Baby," 106–107, 123
"You Make Me Want to Be a Mother," 264
Young, Donny, 50–52, 109, 123
Young, Faron, 107–108, 130, 138–139
Young and the Restless, The, 294–295
Young Country, 269
"Young Love," 64
You Oughta Be Here with Me, 443–444
"You're Everything," 239
"You're in My Heart," 9
"You're My Man," 337
"You're Still on My Mind," 51
"Your Good Girl's Gonna Go Bad," 191, 192
"Your Love," 402
"Your Memory's Gone to Rest," 269
"Your Picture (Keeps Smiling Back at Me)," 132
"Your Sweet Love," 329, 330
"You'se a Viper," 356
"You've Still Got a Place in My Heart," 431

"Zeb's Mountain Boogie," 61